D1561175

Dictionary of Literary Biography

Dictionary of Literary Biography Documentary Series

Dictionary of Literary Biography Yearbooks

Concise Series

Concise Dictionary of American Literary Biography, 7 volumes (1988–1999): *The New Consciousness, 1941–1968; Colonization to the American Renaissance, 1640–1865; Realism, Naturalism, and Local Color, 1865–1917; The Twenties, 1917–1929; The Age of Maturity, 1929–1941; Broadening Views, 1968–1988; Supplement: Modern Writers, 1900–1998.*

Concise Dictionary of British Literary Biography, 8 volumes (1991–1992): *Writers of the Middle Ages and Renaissance Before 1660; Writers of the Restoration and Eighteenth Century, 1660–1789; Writers of the Romantic Period, 1789–1832; Victorian Writers, 1832–1890; Late-Victorian and Edwardian Writers, 1890–1914; Modern Writers, 1914–1945; Writers After World War II, 1945–1960; Contemporary Writers, 1960 to Present.*

Concise Dictionary of World Literary Biography, 4 volumes (1999–2000): *Ancient Greek and Roman Writers; German Writers; African, Caribbean, and Latin American Writers; South Slavic and Eastern European Writers.*

Dictionary of Literary Biography® • Volume Three Hundred Fifteen

Langston Hughes:
A Documentary Volume

Dictionary of Literary Biography® • Volume Three Hundred Fifteen

Langston Hughes:
A Documentary Volume

Edited by
Christopher C. De Santis
Illinois State University

A Bruccoli Clark Layman Book

THOMSON

GALE

Detroit • New York • San Francisco • San Diego • New Haven, Conn. • Waterville, Maine • London • Munich

Dictionary of Literary Biography
Volume 315: Langston Hughes
A Documentary Volume
Christopher C. De Santis

Editorial Directors
Matthew J. Bruccoli and Richard Layman

LIBRARY OF CONGRESS CATALOGING-IN-PUBLICATION DATA

Langston Hughes : a documentary volume / edited by Christopher C. De Santis.
    p. cm. — (Dictionary of literary biography ; v. 315)
"A Bruccoli Clark Layman book."
Includes bibliographical references and index.
ISBN 0-7876-8133-4 (hardcover : alk. paper)
1.   Hughes, Langston, 1902–1967. 2. Poets, American—20th century—Biography. 3. African American poets—Biography. I. De Santis, Christopher C., 1966– II. Series.
    PS3515.U274Z6694 2005
    818'.5209--dc22
                                  2005005553

Printed in the United States of America
10 9 8 7 6 5 4 3 2 1

To Arnold Rampersad, for his work in Hughes studies

Contents

    Living with Mary Langston–from Hughes, *The Big Sea: An Autobiography*

    New Arrangements–from *The Big Sea*

    Hughes on Central High School–from *The Big Sea*

    Facsimile: First page of Hughes's short story in the Central High School *Monthly*

    I've Known Rivers–from *The Big Sea*

    Facsimile: A copy of "The Negro Speaks of Rivers"

    Facsimile: Hughes letter to James Nathaniel Hughes Jr., 19 December 1921

    Facsimile: Hughes letter to R. J. M. Danley, 14 May 1922

    A Letter from Africa–Hughes letter to Carrie Clark, 21 July 1923

    Remembering a Paris Romance–from Anne Marie Coussey letter to Hughes, 3 June 1926

    Our Wonderful Society: Washington–Hughes, *Opportunity,* August 1927

    An Award-Winning Poem–Hughes, "The Weary Blues"

    Hughes letter to Carl Van Vechten, 17 May 1925

    Facsimile: Blanche Knopf letter to Hughes, 18 May 1925

    Facsimile: Hughes letter to Claude McKay, 25 July 1925

    Facsimile: W. E. B. Du Bois letter to Hughes, 6 August 1925

    On Being Discovered–from *The Big Sea*

    Introducing Langston Hughes to the Reader–Van Vechten, preface for *The Weary Blues*

    Poet on Poet: Review of *The Weary Blues*–Countee Cullen, *Opportunity,* February 1926

    Euterpe Learns the Charleston: Review of *The Weary Blues*–Theophilus Lewis, *The Messenger,* March 1926

Plan of the Series

. . . Almost the most prodigious asset of a country, and perhaps its most precious possession, is its native literary product—when that product is fine and noble and enduring.

Mark Twain*

The advisory board, the editors, and the publisher of the *Dictionary of Literary Biography* are joined in endorsing Mark Twain's declaration. The literature of a nation provides an inexhaustible resource of permanent worth. Our purpose is to make literature and its creators better understood and more accessible to students and the reading public, while satisfying the needs of teachers and researchers.

To meet these requirements, *literary biography* has been construed in terms of the author's achievement. The most important thing about a writer is his writing. Accordingly, the entries in *DLB* are career biographies, tracing the development of the author's canon and the evolution of his reputation.

The purpose of *DLB* is not only to provide reliable information in a usable format but also to place the figures in the larger perspective of literary history and to offer appraisals of their accomplishments by qualified scholars.

The publication plan for *DLB* resulted from two years of preparation. The project was proposed to Bruccoli Clark by Frederick G. Ruffner, president of the Gale Research Company, in November 1975. After specimen entries were prepared and typeset, an advisory board was formed to refine the entry format and develop the series rationale. In meetings held during 1976, the publisher, series editors, and advisory board approved the scheme for a comprehensive biographical dictionary of persons who contributed to literature. Editorial work on the first volume began in January 1977, and it was published in 1978. In order to make *DLB* more than a dictionary and to compile volumes that individually have claim to status as literary history, it was decided to organize volumes by topic, period, or

From an unpublished section of Mark Twain's autobiography, copyright by the Mark Twain Company

genre. Each of these freestanding volumes provides a biographical-bibliographical guide and overview for a particular area of literature. We are convinced that this organization—as opposed to a single alphabet method—constitutes a valuable innovation in the presentation of reference material. The volume plan necessarily requires many decisions for the placement and treatment of authors. Certain figures will be included in separate volumes, but with different entries emphasizing the aspect of his career appropriate to each volume. Ernest Hemingway, for example, is represented in *American Writers in Paris, 1920–1939* by an entry focusing on his expatriate apprenticeship; he is also in *American Novelists, 1910–1945* with an entry surveying his entire career, as well as in *American Short-Story Writers, 1910–1945, Second Series* with an entry concentrating on his short fiction. Each volume includes a cumulative index of the subject authors and articles.

Between 1981 and 2002 the series was augmented and updated by the *DLB Yearbooks*. There have also been nineteen *DLB Documentary Series* volumes, which provide illustrations, facsimiles, and biographical and critical source materials for figures, works, or groups judged to have particular interest for students. In 1999 the *Documentary Series* was incorporated into the *DLB* volume numbering system beginning with *DLB 210: Ernest Hemingway.*

We define literature as the *intellectual commerce of a nation:* not merely as belles lettres but as that ample and complex process by which ideas are generated, shaped, and transmitted. *DLB* entries are not limited to "creative writers" but extend to other figures who in their time and in their way influenced the mind of a people. Thus the series encompasses historians, journalists, publishers, book collectors, and screenwriters. By this means readers of *DLB* may be aided to perceive literature not as cult scripture in the keeping of intellectual high priests but firmly positioned at the center of a nation's life.

DLB includes the major writers appropriate to each volume and those standing in the ranks behind them. Scholarly and critical counsel has been sought in deciding which minor figures to include and how full their entries should be. Wherever possible, useful references are made to figures who do not warrant separate entries.

Each *DLB* volume has an expert volume editor responsible for planning the volume, selecting the figures for inclusion, and assigning the entries. Volume editors are also responsible for preparing, where appropriate, appendices surveying the major periodicals and literary and intellectual movements for their volumes, as well as lists of further readings. Work on the series as a whole is coordinated at the Bruccoli Clark Layman editorial center in Columbia, South Carolina, where the editorial staff is responsible for accuracy and utility of the published volumes.

One feature that distinguishes *DLB* is the illustration policy–its concern with the iconography of literature. Just as an author is influenced by his surroundings, so is the reader's understanding of the author enhanced by a knowledge of his environment. Therefore *DLB*

volumes include not only drawings, paintings, and photographs of authors, often depicting them at various stages in their careers, but also illustrations of their families and places where they lived. Title pages are regularly reproduced in facsimile along with dust jackets for modern authors. The dust jackets are a special feature of *DLB* because they often document better than anything else the way in which an author's work was perceived in its own time. Specimens of the writers' manuscripts and letters are included when feasible.

Samuel Johnson rightly decreed that "The chief glory of every people arises from its authors." The purpose of the *Dictionary of Literary Biography* is to compile literary history in the surest way available to us–by accurate and comprehensive treatment of the lives and work of those who contributed to it.

The *DLB* Advisory Board

Introduction

Langston Hughes was one of the most influential, prolific, and popular writers to emerge from the Harlem Renaissance, a cultural movement that generated an unprecedented bounty of African American art, literature, and music. Over the course of a professional writing career that spanned nearly five decades, Hughes gained international acclaim in nearly every genre of writing, including poetry, the short story, the essay, drama, the novel, history, autobiography, journalistic prose, children's and adolescent literature, the libretto, and song lyrics. He was also a popular speaker, reading his poetry and sharing his ideas, particularly about the role and duty of black artists, to audiences around the world. Hughes's subjects were as varied as his genres. Keenly aware of his own milieu as well as issues affecting people worldwide, Hughes wrote as powerfully—and with as much personal conviction—about jazz, the blues, and the African American working and middle classes as he did about the U.S. occupation of Haiti, the effects of revolutionary socialism on Soviet Central Asia, and the Fascist threat in Spain. Whatever his subject or genre, Hughes wrote with passion, clarity, and humanity, blending a critical awareness of the ideologies and institutions of oppression with a subtle, ironic, and blues-toned sense of humor, finding the comic in the tragic and celebrating the healing powers of laughter.

Although Hughes's aesthetic sensibilities and thematic commitments were not fully evident in his writing until he reached maturity in the 1920s, their seeds were planted when he was still a boy. His memories of childhood were peopled with heroes and heroines of the long struggle for racial equality in the United States. His grandfather, Charles Langston, had been tried in 1858 for protecting a fugitive slave; another relative died with John Brown at Harpers Ferry. Hughes's grandmother, Mary Langston, ensured that the boy was well versed on the lives and exploits of civil rights pioneers such as Nat Turner, Frederick Douglass, Ida B. Wells Barnett, Mary White Ovington, and W. E. B. Du Bois. Equally vivid in Hughes's memories were the painful incidents of racial discrimination that made him, even as a child, all too aware of the subordinate status of black people in the United States. Recalling in *Fight for Freedom* (1962) the Fourth of July speeches that celebrated "liberty and justice, freedom and democracy" that he heard as a boy, Hughes "knew they did not apply to me because I could not even buy an ice cream soda at the corner drug store where my mother bought the family soap. I could not go to the movies in Lawrence, Kansas, because there was a sign up: COLORED NOT ADMITTED." Perhaps as influential to his growth as an artist—and his development of specific aesthetic and thematic interests—was his own father's contempt for poor people and African Americans. "My father hated Negroes," Hughes recalled in *The Big Sea* (1940). "I think he hated himself, too, for being a Negro."

Rejecting his father's prejudices and challenging literary aesthetics that he perceived as elitist, Hughes immersed himself in the culture of ordinary black men and women and embraced as worthy literary subjects people who were "workers, roustabouts, and singers, and job hunters on Lenox Avenue in New York, or Seventh Street in Washington or South State in Chicago—people up today and down tomorrow, working this week and fired the next, beaten and baffled, but determined not to be wholly beaten, buying furniture on the installment plan, filling the house with roomers to help pay the rent, hoping to get a new suit for Easter—and pawning that suit before the Fourth of July" (*The Big Sea*). In *The Weary Blues* (1926) and *Fine Clothes to the Jew* (1927), his earliest volumes of poetry, Hughes showed his fascination with the actions, music, and patterns of speech of black people living their lives and created an aesthetic that many critics recognized as entirely new in American literature. While Hughes certainly owed a debt to poets such as Walt Whitman, Paul Laurence Dunbar, and Carl Sandburg, all of whom he read and admired, he was yet doing something never before attempted in poetry—convincingly representing the rhythms, tone, and emotive qualities of jazz and the blues on the page. His early poems captured the sheer excitement and energy that characterized Harlem during the 1920s, proclaiming to the world a poet who loved African American culture and was unafraid to represent all its aspects—good and bad—in his writings.

Such a perspective was by no means without controversy in black America during the 1920s. Keenly aware of the challenges attending black life in the twentieth century and convinced of the power of art to effect social change, Du Bois urged black writers to represent through propagandistic techniques and themes the most positive aspects of African American culture. The journalist George S. Schuyler, by contrast, challenged the very premise that a black culture existed apart from a white culture in the United States. In his essay "The Negro-Art Hokum" (*The Nation,* 16 June 1926), Schuyler questioned whether art produced in the United States was in any way influenced by race. In the midst of the excitement surrounding the publication of Alain Locke's anthology *The New Negro* (1925), which heralded a rebirth in African American visual arts, literature, music, and scholarship, Schuyler registered strong and bitingly sarcastic skepticism that the movement known as the Harlem Renaissance was anything more than racial propaganda and the self-promotion of an elite few. Central to Schuyler's argument was the idea that "race" is a cultural construct, a product of social class, caste, and physical environment rather than a biological determinant. Schuyler pointed out in his essay that the concept of fundamental differences among the races was historically used in the United States to erect a white-supremacist ideology that cast African Americans as inherently inferior to white Americans, and insisted that celebrations of a distinct African American art—which might be translated by whites as a "peculiar art"—could only serve to legitimize such an ideology.

Hughes understood the merits of Schuyler's argument concerning "fundamental differences" among races, but he was incensed by Schuyler's suggestion that African Americans were merely "lampblacked" Anglo-Saxons. In a letter to the editor of *The Nation* (18 August 1926) that appeared shortly after Schuyler's essay was published, Hughes made his own position clear:

> . . . For Mr. Schuyler to say that "the Negro masses . . . are no different from the white masses" in America seems to me obviously absurd. Fundamentally, perhaps, all peoples are the same. But as long as the Negro remains a segregated group in this country he must reflect certain racial and environmental differences which are his own.

Hughes had enumerated these differences two months prior to this letter in "The Negro Artist and the Racial Mountain" (*The Nation,* 23 June 1926), his finest essay and a virtual declaration of independence for the younger artists and writers of the Harlem Renaissance. Troubled by what he perceived to be a reliance on dominant white standards of art and culture among the African American middle classes and intelligentsia,

Hughes challenged black artists and writers to embrace a racial aesthetic and a source of creativity generated from within the black communities in the United States rather than from without. In creating a truly racial art, the black artist could not be swayed by critiques of his or her subject matter or techniques, nor could fears of revealing aspects of black life that dominant standard-bearers of propriety frowned upon stand in the way of artistic inspiration. "An artist must be free to choose what he does," Hughes insisted in the essay, "but he must also never be afraid to do what he might choose." In this respect, Hughes believed that a vast storehouse of largely untapped artistic material resided within the culture of the African American working masses. Jazz, the spirituals, and the blues offered the artist a wealth of resources for the creation of a distinct black aesthetic, and the often conflicted relations between black and white people in the United States furnished "an inexhaustible supply of themes" for the writer and dramatist. In utilizing these resources, the black artist could—indeed, *must*—begin to challenge and overturn dominant white standards of beauty that limited the representation of blackness to minstrel-show stereotypes. Hughes dismissed Schuyler's argument that environment and economics had transformed African Americans into darker Anglo-Saxons, issuing in its place a code of responsibility to the artists of his generation: " . . . It is the duty of the younger Negro artist, if he accepts any duties at all from outsiders, to change through the force of his art that old whispering 'I want to be white,' hidden in the aspirations of his people, to 'Why should I want to be white? I am a Negro—and beautiful!'"

Hughes attempted to live up to his convictions about artistic duty both in his own writing and in his advocacy of other writers who were challenging dominant attitudes about art. He believed that many African American writers were being held back by timeworn attitudes and openly criticized those members of the black bourgeoisie who rejected the work of writers such as Jean Toomer and Rudolph Fisher on the basis of their representations of conflict, violence, and sexuality within African American communities. Hughes extended his advocacy to white writers whom he perceived to be attempting realistic representations of African American life. He took a controversial stand, for example, in favor of Carl Van Vechten's sensationalistic novel *Nigger Heaven* (1926), which had caused a firestorm of criticism among many black readers and intellectuals for what were perceived as its stereotypical depictions of Harlem society and nightlife. A combination of his friendship with Van Vechten and a desire to shock the black bourgeoisie—and perhaps a sincere conviction that he was correct—compelled Hughes to pronounce the novel "true to the life it pictures." Relating the reception of Van Vechten's novel to charges by critics that his own writing was mired in the lives of the lowest classes of black America, Hughes countered, "Is life among the better classes any cleaner or any more worthy of a poet's consideration?" (*Pittsburgh Courier,* 16 April 1927).

Hughes's implicit response to this question, particularly as the nation headed toward economic collapse in the late 1920s, was a resounding "no." The Great Depression brought to an abrupt halt the growing sense of joy and hope in African American art he had proclaimed in "The Negro Artist and the Racial Mountain." The gaiety of the Harlem Renaissance gave way to the stark reality of economic crisis, and Hughes responded by revising his aesthetic to more powerfully critique the racist and classist attitudes that he believed were increasing in the United States. The Scottsboro Case—in which nine black youths were wrongfully accused of raping two white women in 1931 and sentenced to death by all-white juries—especially reinforced in Hughes's mind the connections between race and class. Further, the case convinced him that conservative thinking among blacks and whites alike was leading the nation, and particularly its millions of black citizens, toward disaster. Concerned that the Scottsboro boys would perish by actual or legal lynchings, Hughes wrote poems, essays, and even a play that dramatized the vagaries of a racist Southern justice system.

Hughes's critique of black leadership, including many who remained silent about the Scottsboro trials, is clear in poems such as "To Certain Negro Leaders"—"'Be meek and humble, / All you niggers, / And do not cry / Too loud'" (*New Masses,* 1931)—and extended in essays such as "Cowards from the Colleges" (*Crisis,* 1934), a scathingly ironic piece in which Hughes took black college administrators to task for bowing down to the demands of white philanthropists. Hughes's personal experiences with white patronage during the Harlem Renaissance certainly contributed to the honest conviction with which he criticized such philanthropy in the 1930s. He had been well supported by a wealthy white woman while writing his first novel, thoroughly enjoying the opportunity to focus on his art without having to worry about where his next paycheck would come from. The moment his work took on a radical edge of social critique, however, his patron withdrew her support.

The kind of hypocrisy that often festered behind philanthropic fronts troubled Hughes long after the end of the Harlem Renaissance and the largesse of wealthy patrons who supported it. In a statement prepared for the first American Writers' Congress (1935), Hughes called on African American writers to reveal through their art

the lovely grinning face of philanthropy—which gives a million dollars to a Jim Crow school, but not one job to a graduate of that school; which builds a Negro hospital with second-rate equipment, then commands black patients and student-doctors to go there whether they will or no; or which, out of the kindness of its heart, erects yet another separate, segregated, shut-off, Jim Crow Y.M.C.A.

In what is arguably his most radical statement Hughes championed the transformative powers of the written word and urged writers to use their art to effect social change. Black writers *must* use their talents, Hughes argued, to overturn minstrel stereotypes and establish racial unity "on the *solid* ground of the daily working-class struggle to wipe out . . . all the old inequalities of the past." They *must* reveal, he continued, "the sick-sweet smile of organized religion" and the false leaders within black communities who fear speaking out against injustice.

Although he was deeply involved with issues affecting black communities in the United States, Hughes was not a racial or national provincial. His trip to Haiti in 1931, for example, confirmed for him the extent to which the military intervention of the United States in that country, purportedly on humanitarian grounds after a violent 1915 coup d'état, had cast an ugly net of racism and economic exploitation over a once proud people and had stripped the Haitian government of all vestiges of independence. Hughes's love of foreign travel was fed in part by his desire to temporarily escape the racial prejudice and discrimination of the United States. The discovery that soldiers of the American occupation enforced Jim Crow customs in Haiti was thus a painful blow to the young writer, as also was the reality of the color line drawn between the mulattoes and the blacks and the fact that the Haitian ruling class segregated itself from the workers. Moving away from the themes and techniques that characterized his early writings, Hughes documented his Haitian experiences in essays and poems that were increasingly polemical.

A trip to the Soviet Union in 1932 gave Hughes a sense of renewed optimism about the possibility of an egalitarian society. The contrast between the Soviet Union and the American South, where Hughes had spent more than four months on a speaking tour, could not have been more pronounced. Warmly greeted at a Moscow train station, Hughes was whisked across Red Square in a luxury sedan to the Grand Hotel, where he found courteous attendants and a clean, comfortable room. "Everything that a hotel for white folks at home would have," Hughes remarked in "Moscow and Me" (*International Literature,* 1933), "except that, quite truthfully, there was no toilet paper. And no Jim Crow." In essays and poems written during this trip (and later, when he lived in Madrid as a correspondent during the Spanish Civil War), Hughes embraced revolutionary socialism as a viable alternative to the class and race antagonism that characterized life in the United States. "Put one more s in the U.S.A. / To make it Soviet," he boldly suggested in a poem published in the *Daily Worker* (1934). Such sentiments–and the techniques through which he expressed them–were characteristic of Hughes's writings of the 1930s. Discontented with the policies and practices of his own nation, Hughes turned to the global community to seek the ideals of democracy that he believed had been lost or compromised in the United States. Although Hughes was frequently hailed as the "Poet Laureate of Harlem," he was in fact an international man of letters, a spokesperson for oppressed people around the world.

While his radical zeal waned in the latter part of his career for many reasons–chief among them his being persistently hounded by fundamentalists and the political Right; his disillusionment with the Soviet Union because of the Nazi-Soviet Nonaggression Pact of 1939; and later his coming under investigation by the FBI and being subpoenaed to testify during the McCarthy hearings–Hughes remained committed to his vision of art as a vehicle for social change. Hughes continued to articulate what he perceived to be the social responsibilities of black writers, though his views differed markedly from his insistence on artistic freedom during the Harlem Renaissance. In "The Need for Heroes" (*Crisis,* 1941) he emphasized a moral responsibility among black writers to chronicle the strongest individuals and best achievements of the past and present rather than the faults and defeats of black America:

> It is the social duty of Negro writers to reveal to the people the deep reservoirs of heroism within the race. It is one of the duties of our literature to combat–by example, not by diatribe–the caricatures of Hollywood, the Lazy Bones of the popular songs, the endless defeats of play after play and novel after novel–for we are not endlessly funny, nor always lazy, nor forever quaint, nor eternally defeated.

In making this statement, Hughes may have had in mind some of his own earlier writings–such as the violent play *Mulatto* (1935)–and Richard Wright's *Native Son* (1940), a novel that shocked many readers with its brutal representations of a black man's crimes.

Hughes grew increasingly uncomfortable with some of the literature being produced by a younger generation of African American writers. In "The Task of the Negro Writer as an Artist" (*Negro Digest,* 1965), he argued that "pride, nobility, sacrifice, and decency are qualities strangely lacking in some of the most talented outpourings by or about Negroes these days." Thinking of the recent victories of the Civil Rights Movement, Hughes reminded black writers that "there is today no lack within the Negro people of beauty, strength and power–world-shaking power. If I were a young writer, I would try to put some of these qualities on paper and on stage." It is fitting that Hughes chose to conclude his last published statement about art with the words, "Ours is a social as well as a literary responsibility." Though he expressed this belief differently at various stages of his career, he always remained committed–both in his actions and in his writings–to its basic premise.

DLB 315: Langston Hughes documents Hughes's career as a writer through his statements about his own work as well as the works of other writers; representative samples of his creative writings; reviews of his work; letters; facsimiles of his works in progress; and photographs that illustrate his sociocultural milieu. The volumes of the *Dictionary of Literary Biography Documentary Series* are conceived as portable research and reference resources that provide access to material usually available only in the archives of large research universities. Such access is particularly important in the case of Hughes, who was named by the Academy of American Poets as one of the nation's most significant literary figures. Simply put, there is no existing book that documents the life and work of Hughes in the manner of this volume of the *DLB*. The outstanding *Collected Works of Langston Hughes,* which was published in sixteen volumes by the University of Missouri Press, addressed the need for reliable, definitive volumes of Hughes's published writings. However, the vast majority of the manuscripts, photographs, journal entries, and other documents that can provide a deeper and more comprehensive understanding of Hughes's life and works are available only at Yale University's Beinecke Rare Book and Manuscript Library, the Schomburg Center for Research in Black Culture, and a select few other libraries. *DLB 315: Langston Hughes* provides all readers with access to some of these important materials. This book thus contributes to the larger, ongoing project among African Americanists to recover, understand, and celebrate works by black American writers that have been historically slighted in the American literary canon.

–Christopher C. De Santis

Acknowledgments

This book was produced by Bruccoli Clark Layman, Inc. George Parker Anderson was the in-house editor.

Production manager is Philip B. Dematteis.

Administrative support was provided by Carol A. Cheschi and Lesia C. Radford.

Accountant is Ann-Marie Holland.

Copyediting supervisor is Sally R. Evans. The copyediting staff includes Phyllis A. Avant, Caryl Brown, Melissa D. Hinton, Philip I. Jones, Rebecca Mayo, Nadirah Rahimah Shabazz, and Nancy E. Smith.

Pipeline manager is James F. Tidd Jr.

Editorial associates are Jessica R. Goudeau, Joshua Shaw, and Timothy C. Simmons.

In-house vetter is Catherine M. Polit.

Permissions editor is Amber L. Coker.

Layout and graphics supervisor is Janet E. Hill. The graphics staff includes Zoe R. Cook and Sydney E. Hammock.

Office manager is Kathy Lawler Merlette.

Photography editors are Anthony J. Scotti Jr. and Mark J. McEwan. Photography assistant is Dickson Monk.

Systems manager is Donald Kevin Starling.

Typesetting supervisor is Kathleen M. Flanagan. The typesetting staff includes Patricia Marie Flanagan and Pamela D. Norton.

Library research was facilitated by the following librarians at the Thomas Cooper Library of the University of South Carolina: Elizabeth Suddeth and the rare-book department; Jo Cottingham, interlibrary loan department; circulation department head Tucker Taylor; reference department head Virginia W. Weathers; reference department staff Laurel Baker, Marilee Birchfield, Kate Boyd, Paul Cammarata, Joshua Garris, Gary Geer, Tom Marcil, Rose Marshall, and Sharon Verba; interlibrary loan department head Marna Hostetler; and interlibrary loan staff Bill Fetty, Nelson Rivera, and Cedric Rose.

The editor thanks the helpful staffs at Milner Library, Illinois State University; Spencer Research Library, the University of Kansas; the Beinecke Rare Book and Manuscript Library, Yale University; the Schomburg Center for Research in Black Culture, New York Public Library; and the University of Illinois libraries. Additionally, the editor warmly thanks Illinois State University for granting him sabbatical leave to pursue this project; George Anderson of Bruccoli Clark Layman for his generous and expert assistance in preparing this volume; Arnold Rampersad of Stanford University, to whom this volume is dedicated, for providing a wonderful model of Hughes scholarship and for responding to queries in the early stages of the project; and Christine De Santis for the many ways in which she helped see this volume through to completion.

Permissions

Afro-American Newspapers

Illustration on p. 231.

Hughes, "Hughes Bombed in Spain," *Afro-American* [Baltimore], 23 October 1937. Reprinted with the permission of *Afro-American Newspapers* Archives and Research Center.

AP/Wide World Photo

Illustration on p. 217, AP Photo (APA6305642).

The Association for the Study of African American Life and History

Carter G. Woodson, "Fearlessly Presenting His Case: A Review of Jim Crow's *Last Stand*," *Journal of Negro History,* October 1943.

John W. Parker, "A Brilliant and Shockingly Accurate Exposé: Review of *Simple Speaks His Mind,*" *Journal of Negro History,* January 1951.

Arthur P. Davis, "A Sensitive and Fascinating Work: Review of *Montage of a Dream Deferred,*" *Journal of Negro History,* April 1951.

Articles from *Journal of Negro History* reprinted with permission of The Association for the Study of African American Life and History.

James Baldwin Estate

James Baldwin, "Sermons and Blues: Review of *Selected Poems of Langston Hughes,*" *New York Times Book Review, 29 March 1959.* Published by The New York Times, Co. Reprinted by arrangement with the James Baldwin Estate.

Bourne Music Publishers

Lyric excerpts from *Simply Heavenly,* Langston Hughes and David Martin (New York: Dramatic Play Services, Inc., 1958), pp. 7–13. Used by permission of Bourne Music Publishers.

Pearl S. Buck Estate/A. P. Watt Ltd.

Illustration on p. 197, used with permission from A. P. Watt Ltd. on behalf of Pearl S. Buck Estate.

Chicago Defender

Dewey R. Jones, "Songs of the Lowly," *Chicago Defender,* 5 February 1927.

Hughes, "Negro Writers and the War," article for the *Chicago Defender,* 24 August 1942.

Hughes, "Why and Wherefore," *Chicago Defender,* 21 November 1942.

Hughes, "Conversation at Midnight," *Chicago Defender,* 13 February 1943.

John Henrik Clarke, review of *Selected Poems of Langston Hughes, Chicago Defender,* 4 July 1959.

Reprinted with permission.

College Language Association Journal

W. Edward Farrison, "Review of *Simple's Uncle Sam,*" *College Language Association Journal,* 9 (March 1966): 296–300.

Farrison, "Review of *The Panther and the Lash,*" *College Language Association Journal,* 11 (March 1968): 259–261.

Theodore R. Hudson, "Langston Hughes's Last Volume of Verse," *College Language Association Journal,* 11 (June 1968): 345–348.

Reprinted with permission.

Contrast

Richard Rive, "Taos in Harlem: An Interview with Langston Hughes," *Contrast,* 14 (1967): 33–39.

Roy DeCarava Archives

Illustration on p. 279, © Roy DeCarava.

Estate of Duke Ellington / CMG Worldwide

Illustration on p. 270, TM/© 2005 Estate of Mercer K. Ellington by CMG Worldwide. www.CMGWorldwide.com.

Farrar, Straus and Giroux

Hughes, *The Big Sea: An Autobiography* (New York: Knopf, 1940), pp. 16–17, 23–24, 29–30, 51–56, 212, 311–324, 324–326.

Hughes, *I Wonder as I Wander: An Autobiographical Journey* (New York: Rinehart, 1956), p. 41.

Hughes, *Laughing to Keep from Crying* (New York: Holt, 1952), pp. 97–105.

Hughes, "Foreword: Who Is Simple?," in *The Best of Simple* (New York: Farrar, Straus & Giroux, 1961), pp. vii–viii.

Reprinted with permission of Farrar, Straus and Giroux.

Henry Louis Gates Jr.

Henry Louis Gates Jr., "A Tragedy of Negro Life," in Langston Hughes and Zora Neale Hurston, *Mule Bone: A Comedy of Negro Life,* edited by Gates and George Houston Bass (New York: HarperCollins, 1991), pp. 5–24.

Getty Images

Illustrations on pp. 185 (Images #50869526 and #50484746), 188 (Images #50481427 and #50485365), 201 (Image #50524794), 215 (Image #50393367), and 220 (Image #50410206).

Harvard Crimson, Inc.

Jonathan Beecher, "Hughes' *I Wonder as I Wander:* Reveries of an Itinerant Poet," *Harvard Crimson,* 13 December 1956. Copyright 2003. The Harvard Crimson, Inc. All rights reserved. Reprinted with permission.

Don Hunstein Photography

Illustration on p. 213, photograph by Don Hunstein and used with permission.

Indiana University Press

Hughes, "Foreword," in *Poems from Black Africa,* edited by Hughes (Bloomington: Indiana University Press, 1963), pp. 11–15.

Webster Smalley, "Introduction," in *Five Plays by Langston Hughes* (Bloomington: Indiana University Press, 1963), pp. vii–xvii.

James Weldon Johnson Estate

Illustration on p. 76, used with the permission of Dr. Sondra Wilson on behalf of the James Weldon Johnson Estate.

William Kirtz

William Kirtz, "Mr. Hughes' Shadings," *Quincy* (Mass.) *Patriot Ledger,* 17 April 1963, p. 32. Reprinted with permission of William Kirtz.

Langston Hughes Review

Richard Barksdale, "A Chat With Langston Hughes," *Langston Hughes Review,* 2 (Fall 1983): 25–26.

"Amiri Baraka on Langston Hughes," *Langston Hughes Review,* 15 (Winter 1997): 30–38.

"James Baldwin on Langston Hughes," *Langston Hughes Review,* 15 (Winter 1997): 125–137.

Maurice A. Lubin, "Langston Hughes and Haiti," *Langston Hughes Review,* 6 (Spring 1987): 4–7.

Michel Fabre, "Hughes's Literary Reputation in France," *Langston Hughes Review,* 6 (Spring 1987): 20–27.

Jerry W. Ward Jr., "Langston/Blues Griot," *Langston Hughes Review,* 12 (Fall 1993): 27.

Copyright © Langston Hughes Review. Reprinted with permission.

Little, Brown and Company, Inc.

"Introduction," by Langston Hughes, *The Best Short Stories by Negro Writers: An Anthology from 1899 to the Present,* edited by Langston Hughes (Boston: Little, Brown, 1967), pp. ix–xiii. Copyright © 1967 by Little, Brown and Company. By permission of Little, Brown and Company, Inc.

Massachusetts Review

Doris E. Abramson, "'It'll Be Me': The Voice of Langston Hughes," *Massachusetts Review,* 5 (Autumn 1963): 168–176. Reprinted with permission of the *Massachusetts Review.*

The Nation

George S. Schuyler, "The Negro-Art Hokum," *The Nation,* 16 June 1926.

Hughes, "The Negro Artist and the Racial Mountain," *The Nation,* 23 June 1926.

Hughes, letter to the editor, "American Art or Negro Art?" *The Nation,* 18 August 1926.

Keneth Kinnamon, "The Man Who Created 'Simple,'" *The Nation,* 205 (4 December 1967): 599–601.

Reprinted with permission from *The Nation.* For subscription information, call 1–800–333–8536. Portions of each week's *Nation* magazine can be accessed at http://www.thenation.com.

National Urban League

Hughes, "Our Wonderful Society: Washington," *Opportunity,* August 1927.

Countee Cullen, "Poet on Poet," *Opportunity,* February 1926.

Margaret Larkin, "A Poet for the People," *Opportunity,* March 1927.

Sterling Brown, "The Simplicity of Great Art: A Review of *Not Without Laughter,*" *Opportunity,* September 1930.

Hughes, "Brown America in Jail: Kilby," *Opportunity,* June 1932.

Reprinted with permission of The National Urban League.

New York Amsterdam News

William M. Kelley, "Langston Hughes: The Sewer Dweller," *New York Amsterdam News,* 9 February 1927. Reprinted with permission of *New York Amsterdam News.*

New York Post

Wallace Thurman, "An Enviable First Performance: A Review of *Not Without Laughter,*" *New York Evening Post,* 28 July 1930.

Horace Gregory, "Sandburg of Negro Verse," *New York Evening Post,* 2 August 1932.

Herschel Brickell, "Langston Hughes Produces a Remarkably Fine Book of Short Stories," *New York Post,* 28 June 1934.

Martha MacGregor, "Simple is Back," *New York Post,* 15 September 1957.

Joseph Mancini, "Langston Hughes Dies: The Poet of Harlem," *New York Post,* 23 May 1967, p. 2.

Ted Poston, "The Legacy of Langston Hughes," *New York Post Magazine,* 27 May 1967, p. 5.

Copyright © 1934, 1957, 1967 *New York Post.* Reprinted with permission of *The New York Post.*

New York Public Library / Schomberg Center for Research in Black Culture

Illustrations on pp. 77, 116–117, 223, 263, 298, and 307. Langston Hughes Collection, Manuscripts, Archives and Rare Books Division, Schomburg Center for Research in Black Culture, The New York Public Library, Astor, Lenox and Tilden Foundations. Reprinted with permission.

New York Times Company

Jo Thomas, "Gathering Up Every Word of the Prolific Langston Hughes," *New York Times,* 31 July 2001, pp. B1–B2.

Copyright © 2001 New York Times Company. Reprinted with permission.

Harold Ober Associates/Langston Hughes Estate

Illustrations on pp. 23, 24, 26, 28–29, 30, 37, 54–55, 71, 90–91, 100, 102, 110–111, 119, 121, 130, 138, 152, 158, 160, 163, 166–167, 179, 194–195, 204, 208, 230, 261, 276, 283, and 322.

Hughes, *The Weary Blues* (New York: Knopf, 1926), pp. 23–24, 25.

Hughes, *Not Without Laughter* (New York: Knopf, 1930), p. ix–xiii, 50–61.

Hughes and Arna Bontemps, *Popo and Fifina: Children of Haiti* (New York: Macmillan, 1932), pp. 26–32.

Hughes, "Swords Over Asia," *Fight against War and Fascism,* 1 (June 1934): 3.

Hughes, *The Ways of White Folks* (New York: Knopf, 1934), pp. 121–128.

Hughes, "To Negro Writers," in *American Writers' Congress,* edited by Henry Holt (New York: International Publishers, 1935).

Hughes, "Writers, Words and the World", speech by Hughes, 25 July 1938, Paris, France.

Hughes, *The Big Sea: An Autobiography* (New York: Knopf, 1940), pp. 16–17, 23–24, 29–30, 51–56, 212, 311–324, 324–326.

Hughes, "Concerning 'Goodbye, Christ,'" Hughes statement, January 1941.

Hughes, "Democracy, Negroes, and Writers," Hughes statement, 13 May 1941.

Hughes, "My America," in *What the Negro Wants,* edited by Rayford W. Logan (Chapel Hill: University of North Carolina Press, 1944), pp. 299–307.

Hughes, preface, in *I Hear the People Singing: Selected Poems of Walt Whitman* (New York: International Publishers, 1946), pp. 7–10.

Hughes, *Laughing to Keep from Crying* (New York: Holt, 1952), pp. 97–105.

Hughes, introduction, in *Uncle Tom's Cabin* (New York: Dodd, Mead, 1952).

Hughes, *I Wonder as I Wander: An Autobiographical Journey* (New York: Rinehart, 1956), p. 41.

Hughes and David Martin, *Simply Heavenly* (New York: Dramatists Play Service, 1958), pp. 7–13.

Hughes, introduction, in *Pudd'nhead Wilson* (New York: Bantam, 1959), pp. vii–xiii.

Hughes, "Remarks by Langston Hughes in Acceptance of 45th Spingarn Medal," 26 June 1960.

Hughes, foreword, in *The Best of Simple* (New York: Farrar, Straus & Giroux, 1961), pp. vii–viii.

Hughes, introduction, in *The Best Short Stories by Negro Writers: An Anthology from 1899 to the Present,* edited by Hughes (Boston: Little, Brown, 1967), pp. ix–xiii.

Hughes, "From Harlem to Paris," *New York Times Book Review,* 26 February 1956.

Hughes letters to Carrie Clark, 21 July 1923; Carl Van Vechten, 17 May 1925; W. E. B. Du Bois, 11 February 1928; Claude McKay, 5 March 1928; McKay, 13 September 1928; Wallace Thurman, n.d.; Thurman, 29 July 1929; Van Vechten, 4 February 1931; Amy Spingarn, 14 May 1931; James Weldon Johnson, 14 August 1931; Mary McLeod Bethune, 15 February 1932; Spingarn, 20 March 1933; Clark, 14 December 1934; Richard Wright, 15 February 1941; Malcolm Cowley, 2 January 1941; Countee Cullen, 23 July 1943; Edward H. Dodd Jr., 28 June 1952; and Pearl Bailey, 6 December 1959.

Copyright © 2005 by Arnold Rampersad and Ramona Bass Kolobe, Administrators cta of the Estate of Langston Hughes.

Hughes, Introduction, in *Selected Poems of Gabriela Mistral* (Bloomington: Indiana University Press, 1957), pp. 9-12.

Copyright © 1957 by Langston Hughes. Copyright renewed 1985 by George Houston Bass, Executor of Langston Hughes.

Hughes letter to Arna Bontemps, 2 May 1946, Hughes letter to Arna Bontemps, 18 February 1953, published in *Arna Bontemps–Langston Hughes Letters 1925-1967* (Dodd, Mead, 1980).

Copyright © 1980 by George Houston Bass, Executor and Trustee u/w Langston Hughes.

Oxford University Press

Hughes and Arna Bontemps, *Popo and Fifina: Children of Haiti* (New York: Macmillan Company, 1932), pp. 26–32. Reprinted with permission of Oxford University Press.

Phylon

Owen Dodson, "Shakespeare in Harlem," *Phylon,* 1942.

Hughes, "My Adventures as a Social Poet," *Phylon,* 1947.

Hughes interview, "Some Practical Observations: A Colloquy," *Phylon,* Winter 1950.

John W. Parker, "Poetry of Harlem in Transition," *Phylon,* Second Quarter 1951.

Nick Aaron Ford, "Odyssey of a Literary Man," *Phylon,* 1957.

Parker, "Another Revealing Facet of the Harlem Scene," *Phylon,* Spring 1959.

Reprinted with permission.

Pittsburgh Courier

Hughes, "These Bad New Negroes: A Critique on Critics," *Pittsburgh Courier,* 16 April 1927. Reprinted with permission of *The New Pittsburgh Courier.*

Random House, Inc.

Illustrations on pp. 36 and 94.

Hughes, *The Weary Blues* (New York: Knopf, 1926), pp. 23–24, 25. Excerpts from *The Weary Blues* by Langston Hughes, copyright 1926 by Random House, Inc. Used by permission of Knopf, a division of Random House, Inc.

Hughes, *Not Without Laughter* (New York: Knopf, 1930), pp. ix–xiii, 50–61. Excerpts from *Not Without Laugh-*

ter by Langston Hughes, copyright 1930 by Random House, Inc. Used by permission of Knopf, a division of Random House, Inc.

Hughes, *The Ways of White Folks* (New York: Knopf, 1934), pp. 121–128. Excerpts from *The Ways of White Folks* by Langston Hughes, copyright 1934 by Random House, Inc. Used by permission of Knopf, a division of Random House, Inc.

Hughes letter to Carl Van Vechten, 17 May 1925. Excerpts from *Remember Me to Harlem: The Letters of Langston Hughes and Carl Van Vechten, 1925–1964,* edited by Emily Bernard, copyright 2002 by Random House, Inc. Used by permission of Knopf, a division of Random House, Inc.

Hughes, introduction, in *Pudd'nhead Wilson* (New York: Bantam, 1959), pp. vii–xiii. "Introduction" by Langston Hughes, copyright 1959 by Random House, Inc. from *Pudd'nhead Wilson* by Mark Twain. Used by permission of Bantam, a division of Random House, Inc.

Simon & Schuster

Illustration on p. 273, used by permission of Simon & Schuster.

University of Kansas

Illustration on p. 364, photograph by Aaron Paden, KU University Relations, University of Kansas.

University of Southern California

Illustration on p. 171, courtesy of the University of Southern California, on behalf of the USC Specialized Libraries and Archival Collections.

Carl Van Vechten Trust

Illustrations on pp. 34, 41, 42, 44, 49, 58, 59, 65, 73, 97, 112, 165, 232, and 247.

Carl Van Vechten, "Introducing Langston Hughes to the Reader," in *The Weary Blues,* pp. 9–13.

Photographs and text by Van Vechten, permission granted by Carl Van Vechten Trust.

The Wichita Eagle

"4 Churches Hit Poet's WSU Visit," *Wichita Eagle,* 26 April 1965. Reprinted with permission of *The Wichita Eagle.*

Langston Hughes:
A Documentary Volume

Dictionary of Literary Biography

Works by Langston Hughes

See also the Hughes entries in *DLB 4: American Writers in Paris, 1920–1939; DLB 7: Twentieth-Century American Dramatists; DLB 48: American Poets, 1880–1945, Second Series; DLB 51: Afro-American Writers from the Harlem Renaissance to 1940; DLB 86: American Short-Story Writers, 1910–1945, First Series; DLB 228: Twentieth-Century American Dramatists, Second Series;* and *DLB Documentary Series 15: American Expatriate Writers: Paris in the Twenties.*

BOOKS: *The Weary Blues* (New York: Knopf, 1926; London: Knopf, 1926);

Fine Clothes to the Jew (New York: Knopf, 1927; London: Knopf, 1927);

Not Without Laughter (New York & London: Knopf, 1930; London: Allen & Unwin, 1930);

The Negro Mother and Other Dramatic Recitations (New York: Golden Stair Press, 1931);

Dear Lovely Death (Amenia, N.Y.: Privately printed at Troutbeck Press, 1931);

Scottsboro Limited: Four Poems and a Play in Verse (New York: Golden Stair Press, 1932);

The Dream Keeper and Other Poems (New York: Knopf, 1932);

Popo and Fifina: Children of Haiti, by Hughes and Arna Bontemps (New York: Macmillan, 1932);

The Ways of White Folks (New York: Knopf, 1934; London: Allen & Unwin, 1934);

A New Song (New York: International Workers Order, 1938);

The Big Sea: An Autobiography (New York: Knopf, 1940; London: Hutchinson, 1940);

Shakespeare in Harlem (New York: Knopf, 1942);

Freedom's Plow (New York: Musette, 1943);

Jim Crow's Last Stand (New York: Negro Publication Society of America, 1943);

Lament for Dark Peoples and Other Poems ([Amsterdam: Van Krimpen], 1944);

Fields of Wonder (New York: Knopf, 1947);

One-Way Ticket (New York: Knopf, 1949);

Troubled Island, libretto by Hughes, music by William Grant Still (New York: Leeds Music, 1949);

Simple Speaks His Mind (New York: Simon & Schuster, 1950; London: Gollancz, 1951);

Montage of a Dream Deferred (New York: Holt, 1951);

Laughing to Keep from Crying (New York: Holt, 1952);

The First Book of Negroes (New York: Franklin Watts, 1952; London: Bailey & Swinfen, 1956);

Simple Takes a Wife (New York: Simon & Schuster, 1953; London: Gollancz, 1954);

The Glory Round His Head, libretto by Hughes, music by Jan Meyerowitz (New York: Broude Brothers, 1953);

The First Book of Rhythms (New York: Franklin Watts, 1954; London: Bailey & Swinfen, 1956);

Famous American Negroes (New York: Dodd, Mead, 1954);

Famous Negro Music Makers (New York: Dodd, Mead, 1955);

The First Book of Jazz (New York: Franklin Watts, 1955; London: Bailey & Swinfen, 1957);

The Sweet Flypaper of Life, text by Hughes, photographs by Roy De Carava (New York: Simon & Schuster, 1955);

The First Book of the West Indies (New York: Franklin Watts, 1956; London: Bailey & Swinfen, 1956); republished as *The First Book of the Caribbean* (London: Edmund Ward, 1965);

I Wonder as I Wander: An Autobiographical Journey (New York & Toronto: Rinehart, 1956);

A Pictorial History of the Negro in America, by Hughes and Milton Meltzer (New York: Crown, 1956; revised, 1963; revised again, 1968); revised again as *A Pictorial History of Black Americans,* by Hughes, Meltzer, and C. Eric Lincoln (New York: Crown, 1973; revised, 1983); revised again as *A Pictorial History of African Americans,* by Hughes, Meltzer, Lincoln, and Jon Michael Spencer (New York: Crown, 1995);

Simple Stakes a Claim (New York & Toronto: Rinehart, 1957; London: Gollancz, 1958);

The Langston Hughes Reader (New York: George Braziller, 1958);

Famous Negro Heroes of America (New York: Dodd, Mead, 1958);

Tambourines to Glory, A Novel (New York: John Day, 1958; London: Gollancz, 1959);

Selected Poems of Langston Hughes (New York: Knopf, 1959);

Simply Heavenly, book and lyrics by Hughes, music by David Martin (New York: Dramatists Play Service, 1959);

The First Book of Africa (New York: Franklin Watts, 1960; London: Mayflower, 1961; revised, New York: Franklin Watts, 1964);

Ask Your Mama: 12 Moods for Jazz (New York: Knopf, 1961);

The Best of Simple (New York: Hill & Wang, 1961);

The Ballad of the Brown King, libretto by Hughes, music by Margaret Bonds (New York: Sam Fox, 1961);

Fight for Freedom: The Story of the NAACP (New York: Norton, 1962);

The Gospel Glory: A Passion Play (New York: The Author, 1962);

Black Nativity (London: Wyndham Theatres, 1962; Woodstock, Ill.: Dramatic Publications, 1992);

Something in Common and Other Stories (New York: Hill & Wang, 1963);

Five Plays by Langston Hughes, edited by Webster Smalley (Bloomington: Indiana University Press, 1963)—comprises *Mulatto, Little Ham, Soul Gone Home, Simply Heavenly,* and *Tambourines to Glory;*

Simple's Uncle Sam (New York: Hill & Wang, 1965);

The Backlash Blues (Detroit: Broadside Press, 1967);

The Panther and the Lash: Poems of Our Times (New York: Knopf, 1967);

Black Magic: A Pictorial History of the Negro in American Entertainment, by Hughes and Meltzer (Englewood Cliffs, N.J.: Prentice-Hall, 1967); republished as *Black Magic: A Pictorial History of Black Entertainers in America* (New York: Bonanza, 1967); republished again as *Black Magic: A Pictorial History of the African-American in the Performing Arts,* with a foreword by Ossie Davis (New York: Da Capo Press, 1990);

Black Misery (New York: Paul Eriksson, 1969);

Good Morning, Revolution: Uncollected Social Protest Writings, edited by Faith Berry (New York & Westport, Conn.: Lawrence Hill, 1973);

Langston Hughes in the Hispanic World and Haiti, edited by Edward J. Mullen (Hamden, Conn.: Archon Books, 1977);

African American History: Four Centuries of Black Life, by Hughes and Meltzer (New York: Scholastic, 1990);

Mule Bone: A Comedy of Negro Life, by Hughes and Zora Neale Hurston, edited by George Houston Bass and Henry Louis Gates Jr. (New York: HarperPerennial, 1991);

The Collected Poems of Langston Hughes, edited by Arnold Rampersad and David Roessel (New York: Knopf, 1994);

The Return of Simple, edited by Akiba Sullivan Harper (New York: Hill & Wang, 1994);

Langston Hughes and the Chicago Defender: Essays on Race, Politics, and Culture, 1942–62, edited by Christopher C. De Santis (Urbana: University of Illinois Press, 1995);

Short Stories of Langston Hughes, edited by Harper (New York: Hill & Wang, 1996);

The Pasteboard Bandit, by Hughes and Arna Bontemps (New York: Oxford University Press, 1997);

The Political Plays of Langston Hughes, edited by Susan Duffy (Carbondale: Southern Illinois University Press, 2000);

The Collected Works of Langston Hughes, 16 volumes (Columbia: University of Missouri Press, 2001–2004)—comprises volume 1, *The Poems: 1921–1940,* edited by Arnold Rampersad (2001); volume 2, *The Poems: 1941–1950,* edited by Rampersad (2001); volume 3, *The Poems: 1951–1967,* edited by Rampersad (2001); volume 4, *The Novels:* Not Without Laughter *and* Tambourines to Glory, edited by Dolan Hubbard (2001); volume 5, *The Plays to 1942:* Mulatto *to* The Sun Do Move, edited by Leslie Catherine Sanders and Nancy Johnston (2002); volume 6,

Gospel Plays, Operas, and Later Dramatic Works, edited by Sanders (2004); volume 7, *The Early Simple Stories,* edited by Donna Akiba Sullivan Harper (2002); volume 8, *The Later Simple Stories,* edited by Harper (2002); volume 9, *Essays on Art, Race, Politics, and World Affairs,* edited by De Santis (2002); volume 10, Fight for Freedom *and Other Writings on Civil Rights,* edited by De Santis (2001); volume 11, *Works for Children and Young Adults: Poetry, Fiction and Other Writing,* edited by Dianne Johnson (2003); volume 12, *Works for Children and Young Adults: Biographies,* edited by Steven C. Tracy (2001); volume 13, *Autobiography:* The Big Sea, edited by Joseph McLaren (2002); volume 14, *Autobiography:* I Wonder As I Wander, edited by McLaren (2003); volume 15, *The Short Stories,* edited by R. Baxter Miller (2002); and volume 16, *The Translations: Federico García Lorca, Nicolás Guillén, and Jacques Roumain,* edited by Dellita Martin-Ogunsola (2002).

Editions and Collections: *Don't You Turn Back: Poems,* edited by Lee Bennett Hopkins (New York: Knopf, 1969);

The Simple Omnibus (Mattituck, N.Y.: Aeonian Press, 1978);

Laughing to Keep From Crying and *25 Jesse Semple Stories* (Franklin Center, Pa.: Franklin Library, 1981);

The Block: Poems, illustrated by Romare Bearden (New York: Viking Children's Books, 1995);

Carol of the Brown King: Nativity Poems, illustrated by Ashley Bryan (New York: Atheneum, 1998).

PLAY PRODUCTIONS: *Scottsboro Limited,* Los Angeles, 8 May 1932;

Mulatto, revised version, New York, Vanderbilt Theatre, 24 October 1935; original version, Cleveland, Karamu House, 1939;

Little Ham, Cleveland, Karamu House, 24 March 1936;

When the Jack Hollers, by Hughes and Arna Bontemps, Cleveland, Karamu House, 28 April 1936;

Troubled Island, Cleveland, Karamu House, 18 November 1936; opera version, libretto by Hughes, music by William Grant Still, New York, New York City Center, 31 March 1949;

Joy to My Soul, Cleveland, Karamu House, 1 April 1937;

Soul Gone Home, Cleveland, Cleveland Federal Theatre, 1937;

Don't You Want To Be Free? New York, Harlem I.W.O. Community Center, 24 April 1938;

Front Porch, Cleveland, Karamu House, 16 November 1938;

The Organizer, libretto by Hughes, music by James P. Johnson, New York, Harlem Suitcase Theatre, March 1939;

Cavalcade of the Negro Theater, by Hughes and Bontemps, Chicago, American Negro Exposition, 4 July 1940;

Tropics after Dark, Chicago, American Negro Exposition, 4 July 1940;

That Eagle, New York, Stage Door Canteen, 1942;

The Sun Do Move, Chicago, Good Shepherd Community Center, 30 April 1942;

For This We Fight, New York, Madison Square Garden, 7 June 1943;

Street Scene, by Elmer Rice, music by Kurt Weill, lyrics by Hughes, New York, Adelphi Theatre, 9 January 1947;

The Barrier, libretto by Hughes, music by Jan Meyerowitz, New York, Columbia University, January 1950; New York, Broadhurst Theatre, 2 November 1950;

Just Around the Corner, by Amy Mann and Bernard Drew, lyrics by Hughes, Ogunquit, Maine, Ogunquit Playhouse, Summer 1951;

Esther, libretto by Hughes, music by Meyerowitz, Urbana, University of Illinois, March 1957;

Simply Heavenly, New York, Eighty-fifth Street Playhouse, 21 May 1957; New York, Playhouse Theatre, 20 August 1957 (transferred 8 November 1957 to Renata Theatre);

The Ballad of the Brown King, libretto by Hughes, music by Margaret Bonds, New York, Clark Auditorium, New York City YMCA, 11 December 1960;

Black Nativity, New York, Forty-first Street Theatre, 11 December 1961;

Gospel Glow, Brooklyn, New York, Washington Temple, October 1962;

Tambourines to Glory, music by Jobe Huntley, New York, Little Theatre, 2 November 1963;

Let Us Remember Him, libretto by Hughes, music by David Amram, San Francisco, War Memorial Opera House, 15 November 1963;

Jerico-Jim Crow, New York, The Sanctuary (Greenwich Mews), 12 January 1964;

The Prodigal Son, New York, Greenwich Mews Theatre, 20 May 1965;

Mule Bone, by Hughes and Zora Neale Hurston, music by Taj Mahal, New York, Lincoln Center, Ethel Barrymore Theater, February 1991.

WORKS EDITED: *The Poetry of the Negro, 1746–1970,* edited by Hughes and Arna Bontemps (Garden City, N.Y.: Doubleday, 1949);

The Book of Negro Folklore, edited by Hughes and Bontemps (New York: Dodd, Mead, 1958);

An African Treasury: Articles, Essays, Stories, and Poems by Black Africans (New York: Crown, 1960; London: Gollancz, 1961);

Poems from Black Africa: Ethiopia, South Rhodesia, Sierra Leone, Madagascar, Ivory Coast, Nigeria, Kenya, Gabon, Senegal, Nyasaland, Mozambique, South Africa, Congo, Ghana, Liberia (Bloomington: Indiana University Press, 1963);

New Negro Poets U.S.A. (Bloomington: Indiana University Press, 1964);

The Book of Negro Humor (New York: Dodd, Mead, 1966);

The Best Short Stories by Negro Writers: An Anthology from 1899 to the Present (Boston: Little, Brown, 1967).

TRANSLATIONS: *Masters of the Dew,* by Jacques Roumain, translated by Hughes and Mercer Cook (New York: Reynal & Hitchcock, 1947);

Cuba Libre, Poems, by Nicolás Guillén, translated by Hughes and Ben Frederic Carruthers (Los Angeles: Anderson & Ritchie, 1948);

Selected Poems of Gabriela Mistral, edited and translated by Hughes (Bloomington: Indiana University Press, 1957);

La Poesie negro-americaine, edited and translated by Hughes (Paris: Seghers, 1966);

Blood Wedding; and, Yerma, by Federico García Lorca, translated by Hughes and W. S. Merwin (New York: Theatre Communications Group, 1994).

LETTERS: *Arna Bontemps–Langston Hughes Letters, 1925–1967,* edited by Charles H. Nichols (New York: Dodd, Mead, 1980);

Remember Me to Harlem: The Letters of Langston Hughes and Carl Van Vechten, 1925–1964, edited by Emily Bernard (New York: Knopf, 2001).

Chronology

1902

1 February   James Langston Hughes is born in Joplin, Missouri, to Carrie Mercer Langston Hughes and James Nathaniel Hughes. Soon after his birth he is referred to simply as Langston Hughes.

1903

October   Hughes's father begins work in Mexico and decides to remain there indefinitely. Carrie and Langston Hughes remain in the United States; Langston lives mainly with his maternal grandmother, Mary Langston, in Lawrence, Kansas, while his mother pursues employment in other states.

1907

April   Hughes and his mother travel to Mexico, where Carrie and James Hughes attempt a reconciliation. Their efforts fail, and Carrie and her son return to Lawrence, Kansas.

1908

Late Summer   Hughes is denied admission to Harrison Street School in Topeka, Kansas, because of his skin color. His mother successfully appeals to the school board, and Hughes enters the first grade class at Harrison.

1909

April   Hughes returns to Lawrence to live with his grandmother and attend school.

1915

8 April   Hughes's grandmother dies.

Late Summer   Hughes moves to Lincoln, Illinois, to live with his mother, her second husband, Homer Clark, and Clark's son from a previous marriage, Gwyn "Kit" Clark.

1916

Spring   Hughes is elected class poet at Central School in Lincoln, Illinois, where he was one of only two African Americans in the eighth grade class.

Fall   Hughes moves to Cleveland, Ohio, where he enters Central High School.

1918

February   Hughes publishes his first poems in the *Monthly,* the Central High School literary magazine.

| December | Hughes publishes his first short story, "Those Who Have No Turkey," in the *Monthly*. |

1919

| June | James Hughes arrives in Cleveland. Hughes accompanies his father back to Toluca, Mexico, where he lives for the summer. |

1920

| June | Hughes graduates from high school. |
| July | Hughes returns to Toluca to live with his father. |

1921

June	Hughes publishes the poem "The Negro Speaks of Rivers" in the *Crisis,* the official magazine of the National Association for the Advancement of Colored People (NAACP).
September	Hughes enrolls at Columbia University in New York.
Fall	Hughes meets Jessie Redmon Fauset, W. E. B. Du Bois, and Countee Cullen.

1922

| Late Spring | After completing most of his final examinations, Hughes drops out of Columbia University. He begins working at a truck farm on Staten Island and continues to write poetry and prose. |

1923

June	Hughes joins the crew of the *West Hesseltine,* a freighter bound for Africa. On 3 July the ship lands at Dakar, Senegal. Hughes remains in Africa for three months.
October	Hughes returns to New York.
December	Hughes publishes the essay "Ships, Sea and Africa: Random Impressions of a Sailor on His First Trip Down the West Coast of the Motherland" in *Crisis*. He boards the freighter *McKeesport* as a messboy and sails to Europe.

1924

| February | Hughes jumps ship in Holland and goes to France, where he works for several months as a cook's helper in a Paris nightclub. |
| Fall | Hughes moves to Washington, D.C., to live with his mother. |

1925

| March | Hughes gets a job as personal assistant to Dr. Carter G. Woodson, the founder of the Association for the Study of Negro Life and History. |
| May | Hughes wins first prize in a contest sponsored by *Opportunity* magazine for his poem "The Weary Blues." At the awards banquet he makes important connections with rising stars of the Harlem Renaissance, including Countee Cullen and Zora Neale Hurston. Carl Van Vechten facilitates a contract with the publisher Knopf for Hughes's first book of poems. |

| November | While busing tables at the Wardman Park Hotel in Washington, Hughes meets poet Vachel Lindsay, who at a later reading to a large audience announces his "discovery" of a Negro poet. |

1926

January	*The Weary Blues,* Hughes's first book of poems, is published by Knopf, the company that will publish most of his major poetic, fictional, and autobiographical works.
February	Hughes enrolls at Lincoln University in Pennsylvania.
23 June	Hughes publishes his manifesto of the Harlem Renaissance, "The Negro Artist and the Racial Mountain," in the *Nation.*

1927

January	Hughes's second book of poems, *Fine Clothes to the Jew,* is published by Knopf to mixed reviews. Some critics are offended by Hughes's language and subjects, while others praise him for his blues aesthetic.
February	Hughes meets Charlotte van der Veer Quick Mason, a wealthy philanthropist who provides financial support to Hughes and other writers and artists of the Harlem Renaissance.
9 April	Hughes defends himself against harsh criticism of *Fine Clothes to the Jew* in "These Bad New Negroes: A Critique on Critics," published in the *Pittsburgh Courier.*

1928

| 16 August | Hughes completes the first draft of *Not Without Laughter.* |

1929

| June | Hughes graduates from Lincoln University, Pennsylvania. |
| October | The United States stock market crashes, signaling a downturn in the philanthropical support enjoyed by Hughes and other artists of the Harlem Renaissance. |

1930

February	Hughes sails to Cuba, where he meets the poet Nicolás Guillén.
Spring	Hughes collaborates with Zora Neale Hurston on *Mule Bone.*
May	Charlotte Mason ends her friendship with and financial support of Hughes because he is unwilling to submit to her artistic vision. The break leads to further conflicts between Hughes, Alain Locke, and Zora Neale Hurston, all of whom benefited from Mason's patronage.
July	*Not Without Laughter,* Hughes's first novel, is published by Knopf.

1931

April	Hughes travels with artist Zell Ingram to Cuba and Haiti, gathering material for prose and poetry that he will publish in *Crisis* and the communist magazine *New Masses.*
Spring	Hughes meets poet Jacques Roumain in Port-au-Prince, Haiti.
July	Hughes returns to the United States and visits Mary McLeod Bethune, who encourages him to make a reading tour through the South.

September	Hughes is awarded a Rosenwald Fund grant for his Southern reading tour.
October	*The Negro Mother and Other Dramatic Recitations* is published by The Golden Stair Press, which Hughes and Prentiss Taylor, an artist and theater designer, co-founded in 1931 with the financial support of Carl Van Vechten. *Dear Lovely Death,* a collection of poems, is privately printed in an edition of one hundred copies at Amy Spingarn's Troutbeck Press. Spingarn, the wife of NAACP executive Joel Elias Spingarn, is a wealthy patron of Hughes and other black artists.
3 November	Hughes begins a long reading tour through the South, Midwest, and West at the Downingtown Industrial and Agricultural School for Boys in Pennsylvania. The tour ends on 14 May 1932 at Berkeley High School in California.

1932

January	Hughes visits the Scottsboro Boys at the Kilby State Penitentiary in Montgomery, Alabama.
Spring	*Scottsboro Limited: Four Poems and a Play in Verse* is published by Golden Stair Press. The book shows Hughes's increasingly far-left political commitments.
8 May	Hughes's first produced play, *Scottsboro Limited,* is performed in Los Angeles.
June	Hughes sails to the Soviet Union with a group of African Americans to make *Black and White,* a movie about U.S. race relations that is never completed. He remains in the Soviet Union for a year and writes about Soviet Central Asia after the Revolution.
Summer	*The Dream Keeper and Other Poems,* Hughes's first book for children, is published by Knopf.
Fall	*Popo and Fifina,* a children's novel that Hughes co-authors with Arna Bontemps, is published by Macmillan.
December	*The Negro Worker* publishes Hughes's controversial poem "Goodbye Christ."

1933

Spring–Summer	Hughes leaves the Soviet Union and visits Korea, Japan, and China. In August he returns to the United States and takes up temporary residence at Noel Sullivan's home in Carmel-by-the-Sea, California.

1934

Spring	*The Ways of White Folks,* Hughes's first collection of short stories, is published by Knopf.
Summer	Hughes attends meetings of the John Reed Club in support of the International Longshoremen's Association strike.
July	Hughes, who has received threats because of his support for workers in California labor disputes, leaves Carmel.
22 October	Hughes's father dies.
Winter	Hughes travels to Mexico to attend to his father's estate.

1935

Spring	Hughes receives news that he has been awarded a Guggenheim Fellowship to work on a new novel.
September	Hughes returns to New York for the Broadway opening of his play *Mulatto,* which premieres at the Vanderbilt Theatre on 24 October.

1936

Spring

Hughes travels to Cleveland for the 24 March premiere of *Little Ham* at the Karamu Theatre, home to the predominantly black Gilpin Players theatrical troupe.

July

The Spanish Civil War begins after the military revolts against the republican Popular Front government. Hughes's sympathy with the battle against fascism leads him to travel to Spain the following year.

18 November

Troubled Island, Hughes's play about Haiti, opens at the Karamu Theatre.

1937

1 April

Joy to My Soul opens at the Karamu Theatre.

Summer

Hughes travels to France, and in July he makes a speech against fascism at the Second International Writers' Congress in Paris.

July

Hughes travels to Spain to report on the civil war for the Baltimore *Afro-American* newspaper.

1938

Winter

Hughes works with Louise Thompson to launch the radical Harlem Suitcase Theatre in New York.

Spring

A New Song is published by the International Workers Order. The booklet of poems is issued in an inexpensive edition of ten thousand copies.

21 April

Don't You Want to Be Free? premieres at the Harlem Suitcase Theatre.

3 June

Hughes's mother dies.

July

Hughes travels to France to deliver a speech at the Paris meeting of the International Writers Association for the Defense of Culture.

16 November

Front Porch premieres at the Karamu Theater in Cleveland.

1939

18 July

Hughes attends the Los Angeles premiere of *Way Down South,* a motion picture on which he collaborated with Clarence Muse.

1940

August

The Big Sea: An Autobiography is published by Knopf. Van Vechten and Bontemps had encouraged Hughes to write his life story.

November

At a promotional luncheon for *The Big Sea* in Pasadena, California, Hughes is picketed by followers of evangelist Aimee Semple McPherson for his poem "Goodbye Christ." The FBI begins assembling a file on Hughes.

1941

January

Hughes sends a statement to friends and publishers in which he repudiates radical writings such as "Goodbye Christ."

Winter

Hughes travels to Chicago and founds the Skyloft Players, a small theatrical company.

7 December	The United States enters World War II when Japan attacks Pearl Harbor. Hughes writes frequently about fascism and segregation in the armed forces during the war years.
16 December	Hughes moves back to New York.

1942

2 February	Hughes joins the editorial board of *Common Ground,* a magazine sponsored by the Common Council for American Unity.
16 February	*Shakespeare in Harlem* is published by Knopf. Hughes had protested to the publisher that the illustrations by the white artist E. McKnight Kauffer stereotyped blacks.
24 April	*The Sun Do Move* is performed by the Skyloft Players in New York.
August	Hughes accepts an invitation to take up residence at the Yaddo artists' colony, where he meets the novelists Carson McCullers and Katherine Anne Porter.
29 October	Hughes accepts an offer to become a regular columnist for the *Chicago Defender.*
21 November	Hughes's inaugural column for the *Chicago Defender* is published, beginning a twenty-year relationship with the newspaper during which he writes hundreds of topical pieces.

1943

13 February	Hughes introduces the fictional character Jesse B. Semple ("Simple") to his *Chicago Defender* column.
18 May	Hughes receives an honorary doctorate of letters from Lincoln University, Pennsylvania.

1944

October	Hughes is denounced as a Communist by the House of Representatives's Special Committee on Un-American Activities.

1945

Summer	Hughes collaborates with Mercer Cook on a translation of Haitian writer Jacques Roumain's novel *Masters of the Dew.*
September	Hughes begins working with Elmer Rice and Kurt Weill on *Street Scene,* an opera based on Rice's 1929 play of the same title.

1946

6 January	Hughes launches a long reading tour through the West and Midwest in Los Angeles.

1947

9 January	*Street Scene* opens on Broadway at the Adelphi Theatre.
February	Hughes begins work as a visiting professor of creative writing at Atlanta University.
Spring	*Fields of Wonder,* a book of lyrical poems, is published by Knopf to negative reviews from radical critics who accuse Hughes of abandoning his political commitments.

1948

July	Hughes makes Harlem his permanent place of residence when he buys his first home, a brownstone row house at 20 East 127th Street.

September	Hughes completes a draft of his experimental, book-length poem, *Montage of a Dream Deferred.*
Winter	*Cuba Libre: Poems by Nicolás Guillén,* which Hughes cotranslated with Ben Frederic Carruthers, is published by Anderson and Ritchie. Hughes and Guillén had traveled together in Spain during the Spanish Civil War.

1949

January	*One-Way Ticket,* which introduced Hughes's humorous poetic persona Madam Alberta K. Johnson, is published by Knopf. *The Poetry of the Negro, 1746–1949,* which Hughes co-edited with Bontemps to garner black poets a broader audience, is published by Doubleday.
1 March	Hughes begins work as a teacher at the Laboratory School at the University of Chicago, a three-month position.
30 March	Hughes and William Grant Still's opera *Troubled Island* premieres in New York.
November	Blanche Knopf declines the manuscript of "Montage of a Dream Deferred," temporarily ending the long-term relationship of the publishing house with Hughes.

1950

18 January	Hughes and Jan Meyerowitz's opera *The Barrier* opens at Columbia University.
14 April	*Simple Speaks His Mind,* the first book made up from Hughes's *Chicago Defender* columns, is published by Simon and Schuster. It has better initial sales than any of Hughes's previous books.

1951

February	*Montage of a Dream Deferred* is published by Henry Holt, the company that accepted the book after it had been declined by Blanche Knopf.
Fall	Hughes's translations of Federico García Lorca's *Gypsy Ballads* are featured in the first *Beloit Poetry Chapbook.*

1952

January	*Laughing to Keep from Crying,* Hughes's first book of short fiction in nearly twenty years, is published by Henry Holt.
Winter	*The First Book of Negroes* is published by Franklin Watts, a New York firm specializing in books for children and adolescents. Hughes writes five more volumes in the *First Book* series.

1953

26 March	Hughes testifies before Senator Joseph McCarthy's Senate Permanent Sub-Committee on Investigations and is grilled about his radical affiliations and publications.

1954

Winter	*The First Book of Rhythms* is published by Franklin Watts, and *Famous American Negroes* is published by Dodd, Mead. Both nonfictional books are part of Hughes's commitment to provide children with a deeper appreciation of the rich history and culture of black people.
17 July	Hughes begins writing his second autobiography, *I Wonder as I Wander.*

1955

November | *The Sweet Flypaper of Life,* in which Roy DeCarava's black-and-white photos of Harlem life are juxtaposed with Hughes's fictional narrative, is published by Simon and Schuster.

1956

November | *I Wonder as I Wander* is published by Rinehart, which had offered Hughes a large advance, and *A Pictorial History of the Negro in America,* co-authored with Milton Meltzer, is published by Crown.

1957

21 May | *Simply Heavenly* premieres in New York.

1958

Spring | *The Langston Hughes Reader* is published by George Braziller, a small, independent publishing house. Hughes selected and arranged the contents, revising some of the pieces. *Famous Negro Heroes of America* is published by Dodd, Mead.

Winter | *Tambourines to Glory,* Hughes's second novel, is published by John Day after having been rejected by Rinehart and Simon and Schuster. *The Book of Negro Folklore,* co-edited with Bontemps, is published by Dodd, Mead.

1959

March | *Selected Poems,* in which Hughes selected and often revised his poems, is published by Knopf.

1960

Spring | Hughes brings two books of African history and culture to press with *The First Book of Africa,* published by Franklin Watts, and an edited collection, *An African Treasury: Articles, Essays, Stories, Poems by Black Africans,* published by Crown.

26 June | In St. Paul, Minnesota, Hughes delivers a speech and accepts the NAACP's Spingarn Medal, awarded for distinguished achievement by a black American.

1961

24 May | Hughes is inducted into the National Institute of Arts and Letters at a ceremony in New York.

Fall | *Ask Your Mama,* a long experimental poem, is published by Knopf, and *The Best of Simple* is published by Hill and Wang.

3 November | Hughes attends a luncheon at the White House in honor of Léopold Sédar Senghor, president of Senegal.

11 December | *Black Nativity* premieres in New York.

13 December | Hughes travels to Africa to participate in an African American and African arts festival in Lagos, Nigeria.

1962

Spring | Hughes becomes a regular columnist for the *New York Post.* His weekly column features his opinions on topical events as well as the philosophical musings of his fictional character Jesse B. Semple.

Summer	Hughes speaks at a writers' conference in Kampala, Uganda, and then travels to Egypt and Italy, where his musical *Black Nativity* is featured at a festival in Spoleto.
Fall	*Fight for Freedom: The Story of the NAACP* is published by Norton. Hughes wrote this official history at the request of the civil rights organization and is gratified by the praise it receives from leaders such as Thurgood Marshall.

1963

March	*Something in Common and Other Stories,* Hughes's last volume of short fiction, is published by Hill and Wang.
April	*Five Plays by Langston Hughes,* edited by Webster Smalley, is published by Indiana University Press. It is the first Hughes book prepared by someone other than himself and the first to be published by an academic press.
Summer	Hughes's anthology *Poems from Black Africa, Ethiopia and Other Countries,* the culmination of his efforts to help non-American black writers gain broader audiences, is published by Indiana University Press.
3 November	The musical *Tambourines to Glory* premieres in New York.

1964

12 January	*Jerico-Jim Crow* opens in New York to enthusiastic reviews.
10 June	Hughes is awarded an honorary degree by Western Reserve University in Cleveland, Ohio.
Fall	*New Negro Poets USA,* an anthology Hughes edited to help young black poets establish their careers, is published by Indiana University Press.

1965

20 May	*The Prodigal Son* premieres in New York.

1966

8 January	Hughes publishes his final "Simple" column in the *New York Post.*
1 February	*The Book of Negro Humor* is published by Dodd, Mead.
Spring–Summer	Hughes travels to Africa, where he is honored at the First World Festival of Negro Arts in Dakar, Senegal. After the festival he tours Africa as a speaker for the U.S. State Department.
Winter	Hughes begins working on his last volume of poems, *The Panther and the Lash.*

1967

Winter	*The Best Short Stories by Negro Writers: An Anthology from 1899 to the Present* is published by Little, Brown.
12 May	Hughes undergoes surgery for an enlarged prostate gland at New York Polyclinic Hospital.
22 May	Langston Hughes dies from complications following surgery. Many posthumous editions of his work are published after his death, including his final book of poems, *The Panther and the Lash: Poems of Our Times,* published by Knopf in July 1967. From 2001 to 2004 the sixteen-volume *Collected Works of Langston Hughes* is published by the University of Missouri Press.

A Poet of the People: 1902 – 1929

James Mercer Langston Hughes, the second son of James Nathaniel Hughes and Carolina "Carrie" Mercer Langston Hughes, was born on 1 February 1902 in Joplin, Missouri, a city in the southwest corner of the state at the edge of the Ozarks. The couple's first child had died in infancy, and Langston, as he would come to be known, grew up an only child. Frustrated with the limited opportunities for African Americans in the United States at the turn of the century, Hughes's father left his family in 1903 to seek his fortune in Mexico. That same year Carrie Hughes took her son to Lawrence, Kansas, to live with her mother, Mary Langston. In 1907 his parents tried to save their marriage and reunite the family in Mexico, but after experiencing an earthquake Carrie Hughes returned to the United States, and her son grew up largely without a father's influence. His childhood years were not ideal, as his mother frequently moved in search of work, but through the strong influence of his maternal grandmother, with whom Langston mainly lived until her death in 1915, he entered adolescence with a broad understanding of African American history and a firm sense of the possibilities and resources of black culture in the United States.

Hughes's literary career might be said to have begun in the eighth grade when white classmates, evoking the old racial stereotype that African Americans possessed an inherent sense of rhythm, elected him class poet. As a student at Central High School in Cleveland, Ohio, Hughes pursued his literary apprenticeship more seriously, publishing his first poems and short stories in the *Monthly,* the literary magazine for the school. While his early writings show the immaturity of youth, they also indicate Hughes's interest in serious topics, such as World War I, and anticipate his poetic experiments with black vernacular speech. One of his high-school poems, "When Sue Wears Red," demonstrates clearly Hughes's talent as a poet and love for black culture.

Carrie Hughes with her son, Langston, in 1902 (Langston Hughes Papers, James Weldon Johnson Collection in the Yale Collection of American Literature, Beinecke Rare Book and Manuscript Library)

After graduation in 1920 Hughes left Cleveland to visit his father in Toluca, Mexico. While the journey stirred up negative feelings in the young writer—he believed that his father hated African Americans and their culture, though James Hughes was himself black—it proved to be crucial to his development as an artist. Rejecting his father's attitude and embracing the admirable and heroic qualities in black life, Hughes wrote a draft of "The Negro Speaks of Riv-

*Mary Langston, the grandmother who mainly raised Hughes
(Langston Hughes Papers, James Weldon Johnson
Collection in the Yale Collection of American
Literature, Beinecke Rare Book and
Manuscript Library)*

Living with Mary Langston

Of Native American, French, and African ancestry, Mary Patterson Leary Langston was first married to Lewis Sheridan Leary, who participated and was killed in John Brown's attack on Harpers Ferry, and then was the wife and widow of Charles Langston, a leader of the black community in Lawrence, Kansas.

Hughes found escape from the loneliness of growing up with his grandmother in Lawrence by reading: "Then it was that books began to happen to me, and I began to believe in nothing but books and the wonderful world in books—where if people suffered, they suffered in beautiful language, not in monosyllables, as we did in Kansas." Nevertheless, his grandmother, as he remembers in his first autobiographical volume, was a major influence on him.

You see, my grandmother was very proud, and she would never beg or borrow anything from anybody. She sat, looking very much like an Indian, copper-cobred with long black hair, just a little gray in places at seventy, sat in her rocker and read the Bible, or held me on her lap and told me long, beautiful stories about people who wanted to make the Negroes free. . . .

Through my grandmother's stories always life moved, moved heroically toward an end. Nobody ever cried in my grandmother's stories. They worked, or schemed, or fought. But no crying. When my grandmother died, I didn't cry, either. Something about my grandmother's stories (without her ever having said so) taught me the uselessness of crying about anything.

She was a proud woman—gentle, but Indian and proud. I remember once she took me to Osawatomie, where she was honored by President Roosevelt—Teddy—and sat on the platform with him while he made a speech; for she was then the last surviving widow of John Brown's raid.

—*The Big Sea: An Autobiography* (New York: Knopf, 1940), pp. 16, 17

ers," the poem that helped to define his aesthetic sensibilities, identify his thematic commitments, and launch his professional writing career.

Only eighteen years old, Hughes had gained the attention of Jessie Redmon Fauset—the literary editor of the youth-oriented *Brownies' Book* as well as the influential *Crisis,* the organ for the National Association for the Advancement of Colored People (NAACP)—with several poems written for children that he submitted for publication in fall 1920. Fauset was impressed with the submissions, promised to publish one poem in an upcoming issue of *Brownies' Book,* and inquired whether he had written any children's articles or stories about Mexico. Hughes responded by sending a brief piece on Mexican games, an essay about daily life in Toluca, and a

third article about a Mexican volcano, all of which Fauset accepted and published, respectively, in the January, April, and December 1921 issues of *Brownies' Book.* Fauset published a fourth essay by Hughes, "The Virgin of Guadalupe," in the December issue of *The Crisis.*

Hughes began to establish himself as a distinctive voice in African American literature with the publication of "The Negro Speaks of Rivers," which first appeared in the June 1921 issue of *The Crisis.* With its blend of self-revelation and historical consciousness, the poem revealed a young writer with a firm control of the English language and a deep appreciation of his culture and material. The poem also served to introduce Hughes to important contacts in New York City. Having arrived in New York in

*Hughes at age three and as a youth (Langston Hughes Papers, James Weldon Johnson Collection in the
Yale Collection of American Literature, Beinecke Rare Book and Manuscript Library)*

September 1921 to enroll for classes at Columbia University, Hughes was invited by Fauset to visit the offices of the NAACP and to meet Dr. W. E. B. Du Bois, whose eloquent words of strength, protest, and defiance in *The Souls of Black Folk* (1903) and in his *Crisis* editorials were among the earliest Hughes remembered from his childhood. Fauset and Du Bois were important to Hughes at the start of his career, publishing his writings in the *Crisis* and introducing him to NAACP dignitaries, some of whom, such as James Weldon Johnson and Walter F. White, were part of the intellectual community at the center of the Harlem Renaissance.

One of a few black students allowed to live in a dormitory, Hughes was unhappy at Columbia and withdrew after his first year, preferring manual labor to the stuffy classrooms and institutionalized racism of the university. In June 1923, partly to satisfy his wanderlust and partly to feed his growing fascination with the genesis of African American culture, Hughes signed on as a sailor and boarded the *West Hesseltine,* a freighter bound for the west coast of Africa. Arriving at the port of Dakar in Senegal in July 1923, Hughes remained in Africa for nearly three months. In February 1924, aboard the freighter

New Arrangements

After the death of his grandmother, Hughes lived with kindly friends of hers in Lawrence for a time.

When I went to live with Auntie Reed, whose house was near the depot, I used to walk down to the Santa Fe station and stare at the railroad tracks, because the railroad tracks ran to Chicago, and Chicago was the biggest town in the world to me, much talked of by the people in Kansas. I was glad when my mother sent for me to come to Lincoln, Illinois, where she was then living, not far from Chicago. I was going on fourteen. And the papers said the Great War had begun in Europe.

My mother had married again. She had married a chef cook named Homer Clark. But like so many cooks, as he got older he couldn't stand the heat of the kitchen, so he went to work at other things. Odd jobs, the steel mills, the coal mines. By now I had a little brother. I liked my step-father a great deal, and my baby brother, also; for I had been very lonesome growing up all by myself, the only child, with no father and no mother around.

But ever so often, my step-father would leave my mother and go away looking for a better job. The day I graduated from grammar school in Lincoln, Illinois, he had left my mother, and was not there to see me graduate.

– The Big Sea, pp. 23–24

Hughes with his mother, Carrie Clark, in March 1916. In summer 1915 Hughes had joined his mother and her second husband, Homer Clark, in Lincoln, Illinois (Langston Hughes Papers, James Weldon Johnson Collection in the Yale Collection of American Literature, Beinecke Rare Book and Manuscript Library).

Hughes with his family in Lincoln. Left to right: Hughes; an unidentified friend; his stepfather, Homer Clark; Gwyn "Kit" Clark, Homer Clark's son from a previous marriage; and his mother (Langston Hughes Papers, James Weldon Johnson Collection in the Yale Collection of American Literature, Beinecke Rare Book and Manuscript Library).

McKeesport, he jumped ship in Holland and traveled to France, where he worked as a kitchen helper in a Paris nightclub for several months; then he visited Italy, and finally returned to New York in November. More than simply satisfying an adventurous spirit, these experiences abroad shaped the poetry and prose that Hughes published during the Harlem Renaissance.

By 1925 Hughes was one of the most celebrated writers of the artistic and literary movement centered in Harlem, a predominantly black section of New York City. (Although scholars have labeled this movement the Harlem Renaissance, many black writers and artists lived outside New York; Hughes, for example, spent much of 1925 living with his mother in Washington, D.C.) He began to get his writings published frequently in prominent black journals such as *The Crisis* and *Opportunity: A Journal of Negro Life,* and in May 1925 his poem "The Weary Blues" garnered him first prize in a literary contest sponsored by *Opportunity.* The poem also led Carl Van Vechten, a white novelist and patron of the arts, to approach Hughes and request to see other examples of his work. Van Vechten urged his own publisher, Alfred A. Knopf, to consider Hughes's manuscript. The result was Hughes's first book of poems, *The Weary Blues,* published by Knopf in 1926 to nearly unanimous critical acclaim. The following year Knopf published Hughes's second book, *Fine Clothes to the Jew,* and while some critics responded harshly both to the title of the book and the themes of the poems, Hughes's reputation as the "Poet Laureate of Harlem" was firmly established.

In June 1929 Hughes graduated from Lincoln University, Pennsylvania, and by mid August he had completed a second draft of his first novel, *Not Without Laughter.* He seemed well positioned for the start of another productive decade as a professional writer. The stock market crash in October 1929 and the beginning of the Great Depression, however, curbed much of the excitement surrounding the intellectual and artistic activities of the Harlem Renaissance. As the nation struggled with economic collapse, Hughes began an artistic shift away from the jazz- and blues-influenced writings that had characterized the first period of his career and toward a more socially conscious, radical aesthetic.

Hughes on Central High School

Homer Clark moved his family from Illinois to Cleveland, where he had found work in a steel mill. Hughes attended Central High School from 1916 to 1920.

Central was the high school of students of foreign-born parents—until the Negroes came. It is an old high school with many famous graduates. It used to be long ago the high school of the aristocrats, until the aristocrats moved farther out. Then poor whites and foreign-born took over the district. Then during the war, the Negroes came. Now Central is almost entirely a Negro school in the heart of Cleveland's vast Negro quarter.

When I was there, it was very nearly entirely a foreign-born school, with a few native white and colored American students mixed in. By foreign, I mean children of foreign-born parents. Although some of the students themselves had been born in Poland or Russia, Hungary or Italy. And most were Catholic or Jewish.

Although we got on very well, whenever class elections would come up, there was a distinct Jewish-Gentile division among my classmates. That was perhaps why I held many class and club offices in high school, because often when there was a religious deadlock, a Negro student would win the election. They would compromise on a Negro, feeling, I suppose, that a Negro was neither Jew nor Gentile!

—*The Big Sea,* pp. 29–30

Hughes in his uniform for the Central High track-and-field team (Langston Hughes Papers, James Weldon Johnson Collection in the Yale Collection of American Literature, Beinecke Rare Book and Manuscript Library)

Hughes on the grounds of Central High School in Cleveland and posing with friends (Langston Hughes Papers, James Weldon Johnson Collection in the Yale Collection of American Literature, Beinecke Rare Book and Manuscript Library)

Hughes's inscription on a keepsake from his high school (Langston Hughes Papers, James Weldon Johnson Collection in the Yale Collection of American Literature, Beinecke Rare Book and Manuscript Library)

THE MONTHLY

LITERARY

SEVENTY-FIVE DOLLARS.

PRIMROSE Street was a most dejected looking thoroughfare. It was one of the poorest and ugliest strets in the poor district and contained not a single beautiful thing. From its beginning at Detroit Avenue to its end at the edge of a big ravine where the neighborhood threw empty tin cans and other refuse, Primrose Street was simply a jumble of delapidated frame houses monotonously alige, all the same dull color. A few of them had tumble-down fences in front and one or two had porches, but most of the houses were both fenceless and porchless. Landlords spent little money on their property in that vicinity. Since every house contained from one to a dozen children, the main thoroughfare was always rubbish strewn, as it was their only playground, but to the residents of Primrose Street, filth and squalor mattered little. The gaunt gray wolf of hunger was their most formidable enemy.

The last house on the street, a narrow two story frame on which the paint had long since faded, had a more dejected air than all the rest of the houses. It was situated on the edge of the ravine and its windows gave an extensive view of the tin cans and rubbish in the hollow. To-day, however, the worn shades were drawn and a wreath with a wisp of black crepe hung on the door. Death had visited Primrose Street.

In the afternoon the neighbors came to the house and the priest delivered the last rites over the dead.

"Poor woman," said Mrs. Mahoney as they watched the little funeral procession going toward Detroit Avenue. "Poor woman, and what will the six children be a-doin' without neither mother nor father?"

"It's hard," said Mrs Cohn. "Awful hard."

"Yes, it is hard," repeated Mrs. Mahoney. "It's hard the way she's worked and struggled to take care of them children after her husband died. All day in the factory and then she'd come home and wash and iron and cook for 'em. Only three's big enough to take care of themselves. She tried so hard to keep the little ones in the grades and to help Joe finish high school. The other two big ones quit school, but Joe always did have a hankerin' after education and his mother wanted to give it to him. That poor woman just worked herself to death. It was too much for her."

"Yes," said Mrs. Cohn. "She got so thin."

"And to think she had to die and leave the children! Poor dears! I'd take one myself if I didn't have seven of me own and Mr. Mahoney with none too much work to do. I guess the burden 'll fall on Martha now. She's been a-workin' at Weinbolt's store for over a year and maybe if Joe and the biggest boy helps she can manage to take care of the little tots. Maybe somehow they can get along."

"Maybe they can, somehow," said Mrs. Cohn.

That evening the parentless children

3

First page of Hughes's short story in the January 1919 issue of the Central High School Monthly *(Langston Hughes Papers, James Weldon Johnson Collection in the Yale Collection of American Literature, Beinecke Rare Book and Manuscript Library)*

Living the Blues

In this excerpt from the first volume of his autobiography, Hughes recounts his often conflicted feelings toward his parents and how his father's racial prejudice led to the genesis of "The Negro Speaks of Rivers," the poem that launched his professional writing career.

I've Known Rivers

That November the First World War ended. In Cleveland, everybody poured into the streets to celebrate the Armistice. Negroes, too, although Negroes were increasingly beginning to wonder where, for them, was that democracy they had fought to preserve. In Cleveland, a liberal city, the color line began to be drawn tighter and tighter. Theaters and restaurants in the downtown area began to refuse to accommodate colored people. Landlords doubled and tripled the rents at the approach of a dark tenant. And when the white soldiers came back from the war, Negroes were often discharged from their jobs and white men hired in their places.

The end of the war! But many of the students at Central kept talking, not about the end of the war, but about Russia, where Lenin had taken power in the name of the workers, who made everything, and who would now own everything they made. "No more pogroms," the Jews said, "no more race hatred, no more landlords." John Reed's *Ten Days That Shook the World* shook Central High School, too.

The daily papers pictured the Bolsheviki as the greatest devils on earth, but I didn't see how they could be that bad if they had done away with race hatred and landlords—two evils that I knew well at first hand.

My father raised my allowance that year, so I was able to help my mother with the expenses of our household. It was a pleasant year for me, for I was a senior. I was elected Class Poet and Editor of our Year Book. As an officer in the drill corps, I wore a khaki uniform and leather puttees, and gave orders. I went calling on a little brownskin girl, who was as old as I was—seventeen—but only in junior high school, because she had just come up from the poor schools of the South. I met her at a dance at the Longwood Gym. She had big eyes and skin like rich chocolate. Sometimes she wore a red dress that was very becoming to her, so I wrote a poem about her that declared:

When Susanna Jones wears red
Her face is like an ancient cameo
Turned brown by the ages.

Hughes's father, James Nathaniel Hughes Jr. (Langston Hughes Papers, James Weldon Johnson Collection in the Yale Collection of American Literature, Beinecke Rare Book and Manuscript Library)

Come with a blast of trumpets,
Jesus!

When Susanna Jones wears red
A queen from some time-dead Egyptian night
Walks once again.

Blow trumpets, Jesus!

And the beauty of Susanna Jones in red
Burns in my heart a love-fire sharp like pain.

Sweet silver trumpets,
Jesus!

I had a whole notebook full of poems by now, and another one full of verses and jingles. I always tried to keep verses and poems apart, although I saw no

I've known rivers:
I've known rivers ancient as the world
and older than the flow of human blood
in human veins!

My soul has grown deep like the rivers.
I bathed in the Euphrates when dawns
    were young.
I built my hut beside the Congo and
    it lulled me to sleep.
I looked upon the Nile and raised the
    pyramids above it.
I heard the singing of the Mississippi
    when Abe Lincoln went down
    to New Orleans,
and I've seen its muddy bosom
    turn all golden in the sunset
I've known rivers:
ancient, dusky rivers.

My soul has grown deep
    like the rivers.

From memory to read
on radio show —
    Langston Hughes

A copy of "The Negro Speaks of Rivers" Hughes made for a reading (Langston Hughes Papers, James Weldon Johnson Collection in the Yale Collection of American Literature, Beinecke Rare Book and Manuscript Library)

harm in writing verses if you felt like it, and poetry if you could.

June came. And graduation. Like most graduations, it made you feel both sorry and glad: sorry to be leaving and glad to be going. Some students were planning to enter college, but not many, because there was no money for college in most of Central's families.

My father had written me to come to Mexico again to discuss with him my future plans. He hinted that he would send me to college if I intended to go, and he thought I had better go.

I didn't want to return to Mexico, but I had a feeling I'd never get any further education if I didn't, since my mother wanted me to go to work and be, as she put it, "of some use to her." She demanded to know how I would look going off to college and she there working like a dog!

I said I thought I could be of more help to her once I got an education than I could if I went to work fresh out of high school, because nobody could do much on the salary of a porter or a bus boy. And such jobs offered no advancement for a Negro.

But about my going to join my father, my mother acted much as she had done the year before. I guess it is the old story of divorced parents who don't like each other, and take their grievances out on the offspring. I got the feeling then that I'd like to get away from home altogether, both homes, and that maybe if I went to Mexico one more time, I could go to college somewhere in some new place, and be on my own.

So I went back to Toluca.

My mother let me go to the station alone, and I felt pretty bad when I got on the train. I felt bad for the next three or four years, to tell the truth, and those were the years when I wrote most of my poetry. (For my best poems were all written when I felt the worst. When I was happy, I didn't write anything.)

The one of my poems that has perhaps been most often reprinted in anthologies, was written on the train during this trip to Mexico when I was feeling very bad. It's called "The Negro Speaks of Rivers" and was written just outside St. Louis, as the train rolled toward Texas.

It came about in this way. All day on the train I had been thinking about my father and his strange dislike of his own people. I didn't understand it, because I was a Negro, and I liked Negroes very much. One of the happiest jobs I had ever had was during my freshman year in high school, when I worked behind the soda fountain for a Mrs. Kitzmiller, who ran a refreshment parlor on Central Avenue in the heart of the colored neighborhood. People just up from the South used to come in for ice cream and sodas and watermelon. And I never tired of hearing them talk, listening to the thunderclaps of their laughter, to their troubles, to their discussions of the war and the men who had gone to Europe from the Jim Crow

South, their complaints over the high rent and the long overtime hours that brought what seemed like big checks, until the weekly bills were paid. They seemed to me like the gayest and the bravest people possible—these Negroes from the Southern ghettos—facing tremendous odds, working and laughing and trying to get somewhere in the world.

I had been in to dinner early that afternoon on the train. Now it was just sunset, and we crossed the Mississippi, slowly, over a long bridge. I looked out the window of the Pullman at the great muddy river flowing down toward the heart of the South, and I began to think what that river, the old Mississippi, had meant to Negroes in the past—how to be sold down the river was the worst fate that could overtake a slave in times of bondage. Then I remembered reading how Abraham Lincoln had made a trip down the Mississippi on a raft to New Orleans, and how he had seen slavery at its worst, and had decided within himself that it should be removed from American life. Then I began to think about other rivers in our past—the Congo, and the Niger, and the Nile in Africa—and the thought came to me: "I've known rivers," and I put it down on the back of an envelope I had in my pocket, and within the space of ten or fifteen minutes, as the train gathered speed in the dusk, I had written this poem, which I called "The Negro Speaks of Rivers":

I've known rivers:
I've known rivers ancient as the world and older than the
*　　flow of human blood in human veins.*

My soul has grown deep like the rivers.

I bathed in the Euphrates when dawns were young.
I built my hut near the Congo and it lulled me to sleep.
I looked upon the Nile and raised the pyramids above it.
I heard the singing of the Mississippi when Abe Lincoln
*　　went down to New Orleans, and I've seen its muddy*
*　　bosom turn all golden in the sunset.*

I've known rivers:
Ancient, dusky rivers.

My soul has grown deep like the rivers.

No doubt I changed a few words the next day, or maybe crossed out a line or two. But there are seldom many changes in my poems, once they're down. Generally, the first two or three lines come to me from something I'm thinking about, or looking at, or doing, and the rest of the poem (if there is to be a poem) flows from those first few lines, usually right away. If there is a chance to put the poem down then, I write it down. If not, I try to remember it until I get to a pencil and paper; for poems are like rainbows: they escape you quickly.

　　　　　　　　　　　　　　　　　　　—The Big Sea, pp. 51–56

* * *

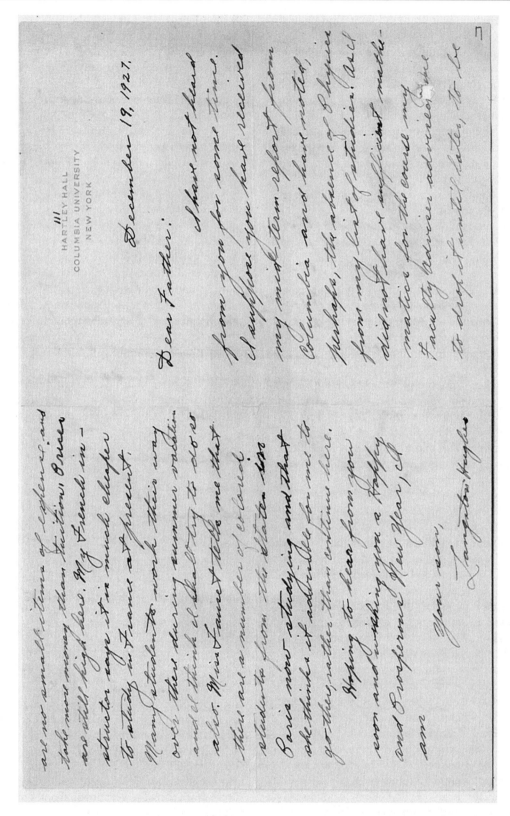

A letter Hughes wrote to his father after his first semester at Columbia University. Hughes quit the school after completing his second semester (Langston Hughes Papers, James Weldon Johnson Collection in the Yale Collection of American Literature, Beinecke Rare Book and Manuscript Library).

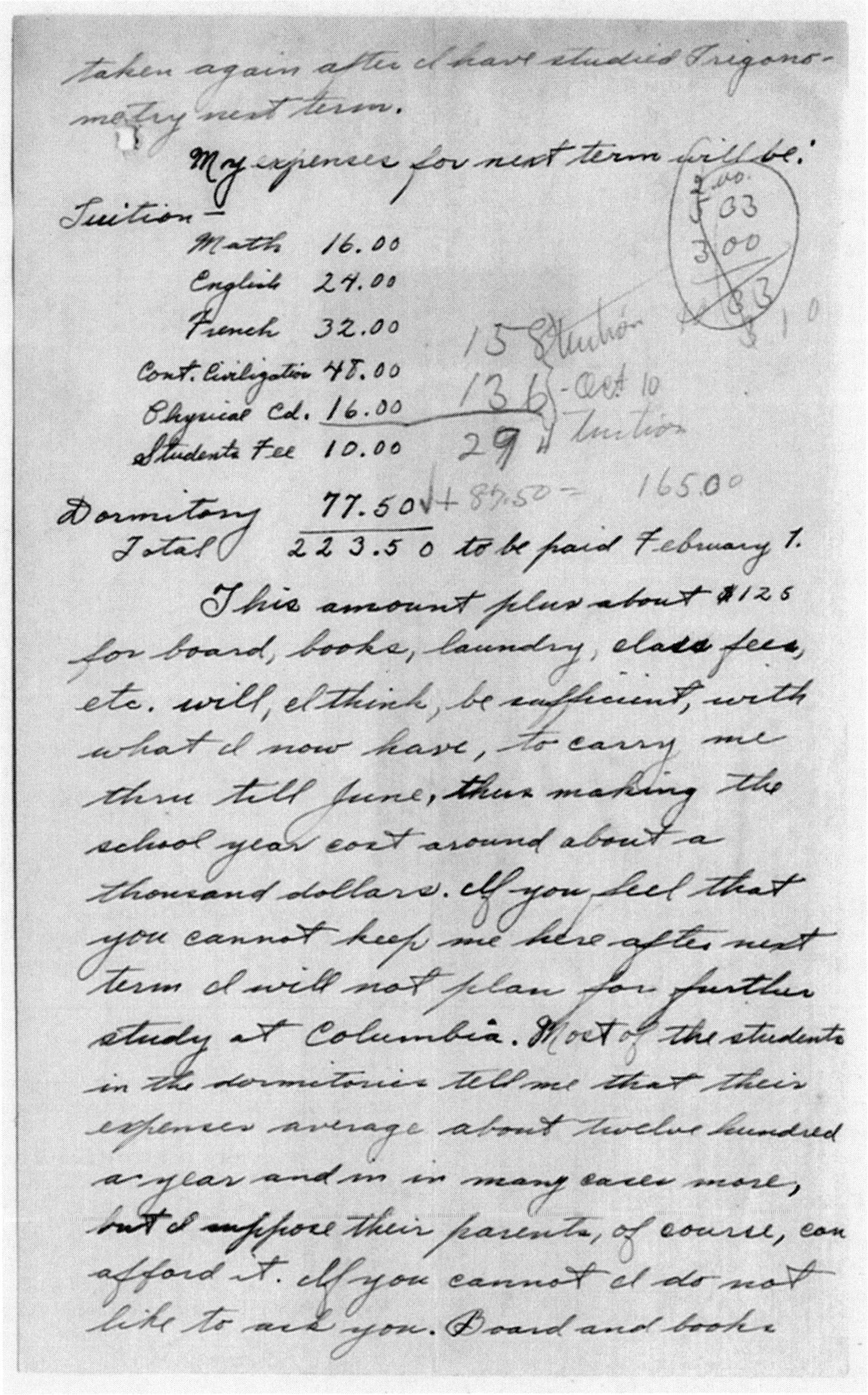

taken again after I have studied Trigonometry next term.

My expenses for next term will be:

Tuition—

Math	16.00
English	24.00
French	32.00
Cont. Civilization	48.00
Physical Ed.	16.00
Students Fee	10.00
Dormitory	77.50
Total	223.50 to be paid February 1.

15 Stuition
136 - Oct 10 Tuition
29
+ 85.50 = 165.00

This amount plus about $125 for board, books, laundry, class fees, etc. will, I think, be sufficient, with what I now have, to carry me thru till June, thus making the school year cost around about a thousand dollars. If you feel that you cannot keep me here after next term I will not plan for further study at Columbia. Most of the students in the dormitories tell me that their expenses average about twelve hundred a year and in in many cases more, but I suppose their parents, of course, can afford it. If you cannot I do not like to ask you. Board and books

Hughes's reply to a business associate of his father. Danley had written to Hughes of his father's stroke and had urged him to come to Mexico. James Hughes recovered from his illness and lived until 1934 (Langston Hughes Papers, James Weldon Johnson Collection in the Yale Collection of American Literature, Beinecke Rare Book and Manuscript Library).

A Letter from Africa

Hughes wrote this letter to his mother onboard the West Hesseltine, *the freighter on which he traveled to Africa. He informs his mother of his intention to "get the monk" in the Congo, a reference to "Jocko," the monkey he brought back to the United States.*

Hughes to Carrie Clark, 21 July 1923

Dearest Mother:

We are at Lagos, British Nigeria, now, just eight ports from the end of our trip. This is the first town since Dakar at which we have had shore leave or a chance to mail letters.

I'm having a delightful trip and, you won't believe it, but it's cool over here, really cool. This is the rainy season and the weather is fine, and at sea always a continuous breeze.

We've about a hundred and fifty on board now,—our regular crew and passengers, and a gang of African helpers—Kruboys. I have two, both about the age of Gwyn—but wonderful little workers—and smart! Their father is a head-man. The kids aren't paid, but the men get two shillings a day, and each and every human consumes about ten pounds each of rice a meal!

Our one colored passenger is getting off here. He is a tailor and enthusiastic about business prospects in Africa. He is going to open a shop here and a school. The white missionaries are going clear down to the Congo, about two weeks yet. There we are going to load mahogony logs and palm oil and start back. I'm going to get the monk there, too. There are two on board already doing all sorts of pranks. I'll write you again soon. Hope you got all my letters. Lots of love to you. One kiss.

Langston

—Langston Hughes Papers, James Weldon Johnson Collection in the Yale Collection of American Literature, Beinecke Rare Book and Manuscript Library

Remembering a Paris Romance

Scholars and critics have speculated about Hughes's sexuality, some calling him heterosexual, others proclaiming him homosexual, and still others describing him as asexual. In the first volume of his biography The Life of Langston Hughes *(1986), Arnold Rampersad describes Hughes's relationship with Anne Marie Coussey, a black woman educated in England whom he met and fell in love with in 1924 in Paris.*

Hughes and Coussey maintained an occasional correspondence thereafter. At points in this letter to "My very dear Langston," written from her home in Hampstead, England, not long before her engagement and marriage, Coussey recalls their time together in Paris.

Anne Marie Coussey to Hughes, 3 June 1926

Thank you so much for your letter it was so interesting, and your description of the American spring made me long to seize an umberella and come at once, over here it only rains; really you would die in this climate, believe me dear it beats Paris into a frazell, and you know how the skies wept there. to day is Derby Day, and it is pouring cats and dogs.

I sat down with the intention of writing and telling you all about myself, but now that I have started there seems nothing to tell you that wont bore you frightfully, running a flat is not very romantic or interesting, you do the same old thing in the same old way, there is little or no kick in housekeeping. I concluded long ago that it is waste of life, and yet it has to be done.

. . . .

When are you going to write a book, you must you know, something really to make peoples hair stand up, and make bishops blush, a real scorcher, it would be such a success, and sell for years and years and YEARS. then you would be able to buy me all the Violets that you wanted to buy in gay Paree= 'after all the Weary Blues is only the beginning, there are greater things to come. Why did you not send me a copy of Vanity Fair? I have not seen a copy of the Crisis for a very long time, have they printed some of your things lately? and how is Miss Fauset? was her second book a success and what did she call it?

Are'nt you coming over this year? why not? men folk can always travel painting their way round the world, or waiting their passages, after all it does not matter so long as one *does* travel, it must be wonderful think of the topping time we should have, I could show you this dear little town History to last you all the days of your life. even Hampstead where I live was once the home of Romney, Keats, Constable, du Maurier, and lots of other people, you really must come.

. . . .

Do please send me those photos, I really will send you that one of myself, I think I would have sent it long ago if I were very beautiful, but when you have a face

Anne Marie Coussey in 1924 (Langston Hughes Papers, James Weldon Johnson Collection in the Yale Collection of American Literature, Beinecke Rare Book and Manuscript Library)

that gives you a nasty shock I dont think you would be able to stand it knocking around for more than a few minutes, however a promise is a promise isnt it, but I warn you, be prepared for the worst.

I really must stop, and you will excuse a typed letter wont you dear?

I wonder if you really did love me when we were in Paris, I think not, you would not even kiss me goodbye when I was coming away, do you remember? and you have never looked on me as a real Pal not even when you were having a hard time in Genoa, and I was the only soul near enough to you to help you. I think sometimes too of that Spring time, I think I have always loved you without knowing it, but you know I am always rather cynical. I have just finished reading a book about a girl who wanted to love a man Soul to Soul, then one day she discovered that she had a Body, then concluded that there was no such thing as love, it was all Sex. maybe she is right' what do you think?

Goodbye dear Langaton write to me soon, and keep on keeping on and selling lots of your book, Come over if you can I want to see you too.

Always your sincere,
Anne

–Langston Hughes Papers, James Weldon Johnson Collection in the Yale Collection of American Literature, Beinecke Rare Book and Manuscript Library

In 1924 Hughes left New York, where he had resided on and off since September 1921, to live with his mother in Washington, D.C. After working briefly as an advertisement salesperson at a black newspaper, an attendant at a wet-wash laundry, and a pantryman at an oyster house, Hughes found employment doing odd jobs for Dr. Carter G. Woodson, editor of the Journal of Negro History. *Hughes lived in Washington for fourteen months and was introduced to members of the city's elite African American society. He recounted his mixed feelings about Washington life in the following essay, which appeared in* Opportunity *after Hughes's first two books of poems had been published. In a brief preface, the editor introducing Hughes noted that he had been "proclaimed many times over the poet of the masses of his people."*

Our Wonderful Society: Washington

As long as I have been colored I have heard of Washington society. Even as a little boy in Kansas vague ideas of the grandeur of Negro life in the capitol found their way into my head. A grand-uncle, John M. Langston, had lived there during and after the time of colored congressmen and of him I heard much from my grandmother. Later, when I went to Cleveland, some nice mulatto friends of ours spoke of the "wonderful society life" among Negroes in Washington. And some darker friends of ours hinted at "pink teas" and the color line that was drawn there. I wanted to see the town. "It must be rich and amusing and fine," I thought.

Four or five years passed. Then by way of Mexico and New York, Paris and Italy, through a season of teaching, a year at college, and a period of travel, I arrived at Washington. "Of course, you must meet the best people," were almost the first words I heard after greetings had been exchanged. "That is very important." And I was reminded of my noble family ties and connections. But a few days later I found myself a job in a laundry, carrying bags of wet-wash. The dignity of one's family background doesn't keep a fellow who's penniless from getting hungry.

It was not long, however, before I found a better place in the office of a national Negro organization. There I opened up in the morning, did clerical work, took care of the furnace, and scrubbed the floors. This was termed a "position," not a "job." And I began to meet some of the best people. The people themselves assured me that they were the best people,—and they seemed to know. Never before, anywhere, had I seen persons of influence,—men with some money, women with some beauty, teachers with some education,—quite so audibly sure of their own importance and their high places in the community. So many pompous gentlemen never before did I meet. Nor so many ladies with chests

John Mercer Langston, Hughes's grand-uncle, one of the most prominent black Americans of the nineteenth century. Professor of law, college president, and minister to Haiti, he was elected to Congress from Virginia (Langston Hughes Papers, James Weldon Johnson Collection in the Yale Collection of American Literature, Beinecke Rare Book and Manuscript Library).

swelled like pouter-pigeons whose mouths uttered formal sentences in frightfully correct English. I admit I was awed by these best people.

Negro society in Washington, they assured me, was the finest in the country, the richest, the most cultured, the most worthy. In no other city were there so many splendid homes, so many cars, so many A. B. degrees, or so many persons with "family background." Descendants of distinguished Negroes were numerous, but there were also those who could do better and trace their ancestry right on back to George Washington and his colored concubines: "How lucky I am to have a congressman for grand-uncle," I thought in the presence of these well-ancestored people.

She is a graduate of this . . . or, he is a graduate of that . . . frequently followed introductions. So I met many men and women who had been to colleges,—and seemed not to have recovered from it. Almost all of them appeared to be deeply affected by education in one way or another, and they, too, had very grand manners. "Surely," I thought when I saw them, "I'll never be important unless I get a degree." So I began to spend ten cents for lunch instead of fifteen,–putting the other nickle away for college.

Then I met some of the younger colored people, sons and daughters of the pompous gentlemen and pouter-pigeons ladies, some of them students at Northern colleges or at Howard. They were not unlike youth everywhere today,–jazzy and loud. But, "They are the hope of the race," I was told. Yet I found that their ideals seemed most Nordic and un-Negro and that they appeared to be moving away from the masses of the race rather than holding an identity with them. Speaking of a fraternity dance, one in a group of five college men said proudly, "There was nothing but pinks there,–looked just like 'fay women. Boy, you'd have thought it was an o'fay dance!" And several of the light young ladies I knew were not above passing a dark classmate or acquaintance with only the coolest of nods, and sometimes not even that. "She's a dark girl but nice," or similar apologies were made by the young men for the less than coffee-and-cream ladies they happened to know. These best young people had, too, it seemed, an excessive admiration for fur coats and automobiles. Boasts like this were often to be heard! "There were more fur coats in our box at the Thanksgiving game than in anybody else's." Or concerning the social standing of a young lady: "Her father owns two cars." Or of a sporty new-comer in town: "He's got a raccoon coat just like a 'fay boy." Or as the criterion of success: "He's one of our leading men. He has a Packard and a chauffeur."

But cars or fur coats or fine houses were not more talked about, however, than was culture. And the members of Washington society *were* cultured. They themselves assured me frequently that they were. Some of those who could pass for white even attended down-town theatres when "The Scandals" or Earl Carrol's "Vanities" came to town. But when a concert series of Negro artists including Abbie Mitchell and other excellent musicians, was put on at a colored theatre, the audiences were very small and most of the members of cultured society were absent.

I knew that Jean Toomer's home was Washington and I had read his book "Cane" and talked about it with other readers in New York and Paris and Venice. I wanted to talk about it in Washington, too, because I had found it beautiful and real. But the cultured colored society of the capital, I mean those persons who always insisted that they were cultured, seemed to know little about the book and cared less. And when the stories of Rudolph Fisher (also a colored Washingtonian) appeared in *The Atlantic Monthly*, what I heard most was, "Why didn't he write about nice people like us? Why didn't he write about cultured folks?" I thought it amazing, too, that a young playwright of ability and three or four poets of promise were living in Washington unknown to the best society. At least, I saw nothing being done to encourage these young writers, for the leading women's clubs appeared to be founded solely for the purpose of playing cards, and the cultured doctors and lawyers and caterers and butlers and government messengers had little concern for poets or playwrights. In supposedly intellectual gatherings I listened to conversations as arid as the sides of the Washington monument.

There appeared, also, to be the same love of scandal among the best folks as among the lower classes. Sometimes I heard how such-and-such a pompous gentleman had struck his wife or how this or that refined couple had indulged in physical combat,–all of which was very amusing but hardly compatible with a society which boasted of its gentility. Such consciously nice people ought never to let down the bars, I thought, but they did.

———

Washington is one of the most beautiful cities in the world. For that I remember it with pleasure. Georgia Douglass Johnson conversed with charm and poured tea on Saturday nights for young writers and artists and intellectuals. That, too, I remember with pleasure. Seventh Street was always teemingly alive with dark working people who hadn't yet acquired "culture" and the manners of stage ambassadors, and pinks and blacks and yellows were still friends without apologies. That street I remember with pleasure. And the few fine and outstanding men and women I met who had seemingly outgrown "society" as a boy outgrows his first long trousers,–those men and women I remember with pleasure. But Washington society itself,–perhaps I am prejudiced toward it. Perhaps I had heard too much about it before hand and was disappointed. Or perhaps I didn't really meet the best society after all. Maybe I met only the snobs, and the high-yellows, and the lovers of fur coats and automobiles and fraternity pins and A. B. degrees. Maybe I'm all wrong about everything.–Maybe those who said they were the best people had me fooled.–Perhaps they weren't the best people,–but they looked tremendously important. Or, perhaps they *were* the best people and it's my standard of values that's awry . . . Well, be that as it may, I have seen Washington, of which city I had heard much, and I have looked at something called "society" of which I had heard much, too. Now I can live in Harlem where people are not quite so ostentatiously proud of themselves, and where one's family background is not of such great concern. Now I can live contentedly in Harlem.

–*Opportunity: A Journal of Negro Life*, 5 (August 1927): 226–227

An Award-Winning Poem

Hughes considered "The Weary Blues," first published in the May 1925 issue of Opportunity, *his "lucky poem" because it won the literary contest the journal sponsored. Written in the African American vernacular tradition, the poem pays homage to the blues singers he remembered hearing while growing up in Kansas. The reference in the fourth line to Lenox Avenue sets the poem at the heart of Harlem.*

The Weary Blues

Droning a drowsy syncopated tune,

Rocking back and forth to a mellow croon,

    I heard a Negro play.

Down on Lenox Avenue the other night

By the pale dull pallor of an old gas light

    He did a lazy sway. . . .

    He did a lazy sway. . . .

To the tune o' those Weary Blues.

With his ebony hands on each ivory key

He made that poor piano moan with melody.

    O Blues!

Swaying to and fro on his rickety stool

He played that sad raggy tune like a musical fool.

    Sweet Blues!

Coming from a black man's soul.

    O Blues!

In a deep song voice with a melancholy tone

I heard that Negro sing, that old piano moan–

    "Ain't got nobody in all this world,

    Ain't got nobody but ma self.

    I's gwine to quit ma frownin'

    And put ma troubles on the shelf."

Thump, thump, thump, went his foot on the floor.

He played a few chords then he sang some more–

    "I got the Weary Blues

    And I can't be satisfied.

    Got the Weary Blues

    And can't be satisfied–

    I ain't happy no mo'

    And I wish that I had died."

And far into the night he crooned that tune.

The stars went out and so did the moon.

The singer stopped playing and went to bed

While the Weary Blues echoed through his head.

He slept like a rock or a man that's dead.

      –*The Weary Blues* (New York: Knopf, 1926),
                    pp. 23–24

James Weldon Johnson, a poet, novelist, songwriter, and NAACP executive, read "The Weary Blues" at the 1 May 1925 Opportunity *awards banquet (photograph by Carl Van Vechten, 3 December 1932; Library of Congress, Prints & Photographs Division, Carl Van Vechten Collection, courtesy of Carl Van Vechten Trust)*

A First Book

On 10 November 1924, the evening of the day that he returned from Europe by working on a freighter, Hughes attended a benefit cabaret party at a Harlem nightclub sponsored by the NAACP, where he was warmly greeted by admirers of his poems that had been appearing regularly in journals and first met the music critic and novelist Carl Van Vechten. The two men met again the following year at a 1 May 1925 Opportunity awards banquet, where Hughes was given the first prize in a literary contest for "The Weary Blues." Hughes and Van Vechten became close friends and soon began a lifelong correspondence. In large part because of Van Vechten's assistance and his strong relationship with the Knopf publishing house, Hughes's first book was soon accepted for publication.

In this letter Hughes responds to Van Vechten's request for information about the blues. He refers to Van Vechten's novels Peter Whiffle *(1922) and* The Blind Bow-Boy *(1923).*

Hughes to Carl Van Vechten, 17 May 1925

Sunday

Dear Carl,

I am sending you today the poem that I promised, The Fascination of Cities, and some old verses of the Blues. I hope you will find them all interesting. You will excuse me for sending you a carbon of Cities. I wanted to copy it for you but time moved faster than I did and I had to meet an engagement. Do you get the bull fight I am trying to describe in Mexico? By the way, I wish I'd have known you two years ago. I had a very beautiful pair of banderillos that I left in my room at Columbia when I went to sea. They might have gone well with the Spanish fan in your apartment. They were special ones that Gaona, the great Mexican matador, used in a festival fight at Easter. They were burnt orange, with tiny fruits of silk and tinselled gold. He had them made to contrast with his suit of mauve-grey. I got them while the blood was still fresh on them, with bits of the bull's hair stuck to the hilt. They were beautiful things to torture an animal with.

I know very little to tell you about the Blues. They always impressed me as being very sad, sadder even than the spirituals because their sadness is not softened with tears but hardened with laughter, the absurd, incongruous laughter of a sadness without even a god to appeal to. In the Gulf Coast Blues one can feel the cold northern snows, the memory of the melancholy mists of the Louisianna low-lands, the shack that is home, the worthless lovers with hands full of gimme, mouths full of much oblige, the eternal unsatisfied longings.

There seems to be a monotonous melancholy, an animal sadness running through all Negro jazz that is almost terrible at times. I remember hearing a native jazz-band playing in the Kameroon in Africa while two black youths stamped and circled about a dance hall floor, their feet doing exactly the same figures over and over to the monotonous rhythm, their bodies turning and swaying like puppets on strings. While the two black boys, half-grinning mouths never closed, went round and round the room, the horns cried and moaned in monotonous weariness,—like the weariness of days ever coming, going; like the weariness of the world moving always in the same circle,—while the drums kept up a deep-voiced laughter for the dancing feet. The performance put a damper on the evening's fun. It just wasn't enjoyable. The sailors left and went to a French whorehouse.

Perhaps the reason the Blues seem so melancholy to me is that I first heard them sung as a child by a blind orchestra that used to wander about the streets of the slums and the red-light district in Kansas City, singing for nickels or pennies, a fish sandwich, or anything one chose to give. The ribald verses, the music that seemed to cry when the words laughed, the painted girls from the houses of ill-fame in their gingham dresses, and the invariable verse about

Goin' to the river
And sit down

made me feel that there was no music in the world sadder than the Blues. But I was a kid then.

I wish that I could write you every day if it meant getting your delightful notes in return. Thank you very much for the books. I liked your lovely first chapter on Paris in Peter Whiffle. I am sorry I didn't first see Paris as you saw it. I caught only the gloomy coldness of it. When I arrived I had come down from the North a chill grey morning in February. It was snowing as the train passed the Belgian frontier, and the snow had turned to rain in Paris. And it seems to me that it rained steadily the whole seven months I was there! And I was never quite warm until July . . . But I did have one perfect week in Venice and, later, one glorious time in Catania.

(Request: Could you find out for me the name of that Italian song they sing after the fiesta in Pauline Lord's "They Knew what they Wanted?" I want to get it on a record.)

The Blind Bow-Boy again. I knew a colored girl, a cabaret singer in Paris, almost exactly like Zimbule. I had thought of writing a story about her and calling it The Golden Creature. That last chapter of the Bow-Boy is delightful. Oh! That adorable Campaspe.

I am afraid it is going to take me a long time to write you a "biography." Not that there is anything so intricate, or interesting, or deep about it. But I hate to think backwards. It isn't amusing. Today I sat half the morning wondering what the difference in me would have been had my father brought me up in Mexico instead of my aunt and grandmother in Kansas. And I wrote nothing. Wouldn't you be satisfied with an outline? I am still too much enmeshed in the affects of my young life to write clearly about it. I haven't yet escaped into serenity and grown old yet. I wish I could. What moron ever wrote those lines about "carry me back to the scenes of my childhood"?

Jessie Fauset wrote me about the little dinner and the pleasant evening with you. Has she introduced you to her cat, Stevie? I know him better than I do Sch . . . arazade. (Can't spell it.) You ought to meet my most ordinary kitten, —Mutt.

As 'tis said in Spanish,—Hasta luego. Vaya usted con dios,—some happy god I hope.

Sincerely,
Langston
1749 S Street, N.W.
Washington, D.C.

—Remember Me to Harlem: The Letters of Langston Hughes and Carl Van Vechten, 1925–1964, *edited by Emily Bernard (New York: Knopf, 2001), pp. 11–13*

* * *

BORZOI
BOOKS

ALFRED·A·KNOPF·Inc
730 FIFTH AVENUE
New York

May 18th, 1925.

Langston Hughes, Esq.,
1749 S Street, N. W.
Washington, D.C.

Dear Mr. Hughes,

Mr. Van Vechten has sent us your manuscript and we like it very much. It is very delightful verse and I am glad to tell you that we want to publish it. I am enclosing a contract that I should like you to sign and return so that I may send you a copy for your own files. It is very long and probably confusing as it was drawn up by B. H. Stern, lawyer for the Authors' League of America and in done in the usual language of a lawyer. If there is anything in it that you do not understand, do let me know and I shall be glad to explain.

Yours   sincerely,

Mrs. Alfred A. Knopf.

BWK/MAM

*Letter from Blanche Knopf that accompanied the publishing contract for Hughes's first book of poems
(Langston Hughes Papers, James Weldon Johnson Collection in the Yale Collection of American
Literature, Beinecke Rare Book and Manuscript Library)*

July 2 5, 1925

Dear Claude:

I feel most much like writing you this afternoon
altho I don't believe I have a thing exciting to
say. First, thanks for your letter and all those
cards you've been sending me. They were sort of
like meeting you on the corner every other day or
so and saying Hello. Did you run into Clarissa
Scott in Bordeaux? She must have landed there a-
bout the time you wrote me from there. Charming
girl going to Italy, Germany, then into Paris.
She's "society", but nice....If you see Davis
give him an interview. It's good publicity in the
colored papers...I saw you mentioned very well in
some new book or magazine the other day, but can't
remember just where now. You are still the best of
the colored poets and probably will be for the
next century and for me you are the one and only.

I am going to send you some more magazines after
pay day. That's the first. My Weary Blues is still
being republished in the big magazines,- echos of
the prize contest. Palms has taken another poem of
mine, and Van Vechten quotes a whole letter of mine
about the Blues in this month's Vanity Fair. Good
advertising. Next month they're using four of my
things, not however, the full page that they'd first
promised, and I've started to work on my first book
of prose. Now I think I'll have to move over southwest where the bootleggers live in order to escape
the "I've been so anxious to meet you"'s of Washington's darker intelligenzia. They're not sophisticated enough to visit an artist if he lives in
the slums. And I'm afraid they wouldn't be that low-
down. They're such "nice" people. My God!

Any news from your book? I hope it's good news.

Toomer's back in Washington for a while so I hear.
I've got to look him up. I don't know a thing about
the new group in New York you mention. I get very
little news from there. And I haven't been up since
May....Write to me.

                    Bien a toi,

                    Langston

*A letter from Hughes to Claude McKay, the Jamaican writer with whom Hughes frequently corresponded but had not yet met.
Hughes credited McKay for inspiring his prosocialist writings (Langston Hughes Papers, James Weldon Johnson Collection
in the Yale Collection of American Literature, Beinecke Rare Book and Manuscript Library).*

EDITORIAL ROOMS OF

THE CRISIS

69 FIFTH AVENUE, NEW YORK, N. Y.

NATIONAL ASSOCIATION

FOR THE   W. E. BURGHARDT DU BOIS

ADVANCEMENT OF COLORED PEOPLE

August 6, 1925

Mr. Langston Hughes
Y. M. C. A.
12th St. between S & T Sts, N. W.
Washington, D. C.

My dear Mr. Hughes:

Enclosed is an
invitation. We are
going to award you on
this night the second
prize of $30 for essays
on your essay "The
Fascination of Cities".
Can you be present?

Can you rush us
a recent photograph?

Very sincerely yours,

W. E. B. Du Bois
per J. F.

WEBD/KF

*Keep this quiet until the night of the award, but
be sure to come. Did you get my letter of earlier
in the week? J. F.*

Letter to Hughes from W. E. B. Du Bois, editor of the NAACP magazine The Crisis, which published Hughes's early
poems and prose. The letter is signed by Jessie Fauset, the magazine's literary editor (Langston Hughes Papers,
James Weldon Johnson Collection in the Yale Collection of American Literature,
Beinecke Rare Book and Manuscript Library).

Hughes as a busboy at a Washington hotel, a job he preferred to the "position" he had held at the Journal of Negro History. *Hughes added the annotation: top, "First newspaper photograph, U. & U. Syndicate"; right, "Published with interview in Washington Star, Dec. 13, 1950"; bottom, "Langston Hughes, Wardman Park Hotel, Washington, 1925"; left, "Day after 'discovery' by Vachel Lindsay, as a poet" (Langston Hughes Papers, James Weldon Johnson Collection in the Yale Collection of American Literature, Beinecke Rare Book and Manuscript Library).*

On Being Discovered

When Hughes received the proofs of The Weary Blues *from Knopf, he was working as a busboy. In his autobiography Hughes recalls his November 1925 encounter with poet Vachel Lindsay, well known for such collections as* General William Booth Enters into Heaven and Other Poems *(1913),* The Congo and Other Poems *(1914), and* The Chinese Nightingale and Other Poems *(1917).*

. . . I am glad I went to work at the Wardman Park Hotel, because there I met Vachel Lindsay. Diplomats and cabinet members in the dining room did not excite me much, but I was thrilled the day Vachel Lindsay came. I knew him, because I'd seen his picture in the papers that morning. He was to give a reading of his poems in the little theater of the hotel that night. I wanted very much to hear him read his poems, but I knew they did not admit colored people to the auditorium.

That afternoon I wrote out three of my poems, "Jazzonia," "Negro Dancers," and "The Weary Blues," on some pieces of paper and put them in the pocket of my white bus boy's coat. In the evening when Mr. Lindsay came down to dinner, quickly I laid them beside his plate and went away, afraid to say anything to so famous a poet, except to tell him I liked his poems and that these were poems of mine. I looked back once and saw Mr. Lindsay reading the poems, as I picked up a tray of dirty dishes from a side table and started for the dumb-waiter.

The next morning on the way to work, as usual I bought a paper—and there I read that Vachel Lindsay had discovered a Negro bus boy poet! At the hotel the reporters were already waiting for me. They interviewed me. And they took my picture, holding up a tray of dirty dishes in the middle of the dining room. The picture, copyrighted by Underwood and Underwood, appeared in lots of newspapers throughout the country. It was my first publicity break.

—The Big Sea, p. 212

Dust jacket for Hughes's first published volume of poems, designed
by Miguel Covarrubias, a popular caricaturist whose work
regularly appeared in Vanity Fair and The New
Yorker (Langston Hughes Papers, James Weldon
Johnson Collection in the Yale Collection of
American Literature, Beinecke Rare
Book and Manuscript Library)

*The Weary Blues was published in January 1926.
The 109-page book, of which Knopf initially printed 1,200 copies, included 69 poems grouped into 7 thematic sections. Hughes
was delighted when Van Vechten, who had asked Alfred A.
Knopf to publish the book, offered to write the preface, though he
later worried that black readers might find Van Vechten's tone
patronizing.*

Introducing Langston Hughes to the Reader

I

At the moment I cannot recall the name of any
other person whatever who, at the age of twenty-three,
has enjoyed so picturesque and rambling an existence
as Langston Hughes. Indeed, a complete account of his
disorderly and delightfully fantastic career would make
a fascinating picaresque romance which I hope this
young Negro will write before so much more befalls

him that he may find it difficult to capture all the salient
episodes within the limits of a single volume.

Born on February 1, 1902, in Joplin, Missouri, he
had lived, before his twelfth year, in the City of Mexico, Topeka, Kansas, Colorado Springs, Charlestown,
Indiana, Kansas City, and Buffalo. He attended Central
High School, from which he graduated, at Cleveland,
Ohio, while in the summer, there and in Chicago, he
worked as delivery- and dummy-boy in hat-stores. In
his senior year he was elected class poet and editor of
the Year Book.

After four years in Cleveland, he once more
joined his father in Mexico, only to migrate to New
York where he entered Columbia University. There,
finding the environment distasteful, or worse, he
remained till spring, when he quit, broke with his father
and, with thirteen dollars in cash, went on his own.
First, he worked for a truck-farmer on Staten Island;
next, he delivered flowers for Thorley; at length he partially satisfied an insatiable craving to go to sea by signing up with an old ship anchored in the Hudson for the
winter. His first real cruise as a sailor carried him to the
Canary Islands, the Azores, and the West Coast of
Africa, of which voyage he has written: "Oh, the sun in
Dakar! Oh, the little black girls of Burutu! Oh, the blue,
blue bay of Loanda! Calabar, the city lost in a forest;
the long, shining days at sea, the masts rocking against
the stars at night; the black Kru-boy sailors, taken at
Freetown, bathing on deck morning and evening; Tom
Pey and Haneo, whose dangerous job it was to dive
under the seven-ton mahogany logs floating and bob-
bing at the ship's side and fasten them to the chains of
the crane; the vile houses of rotting women at Lagos;
the desolation of the Congo; Johnny Walker, and the
millions of whisky bottles buried in the sea along the
West Coast; the daily fights on board, officers, sailors,
everybody drunk; the timorous, frightened missionaries we carried as passengers; and George, the Kentucky
colored boy, dancing and singing the Blues on the
after-deck under the stars."

Returning to New York with plenty of money
and a monkey, he presently shipped again—this time for
Holland. Again he came back to New York and again
he sailed—on his twenty-second birthday: February 1,
1924. Three weeks later he found himself in Paris with
less than seven dollars. However, he was soon provided for: a woman of his own race engaged him as
doorman at her *boîte de nuit*. Later he was employed,
first as second cook, then as waiter, at the Grand Duc,
where the Negro entertainer, Florence, sang at this
epoch. Here he made friends with an Italian family who
carried him off to their villa at Desenzano on Lago di
Garda where he passed a happy month, followed by a
night in Verona and a week in Venice. On his way

Carl Van Vechten in 1934 (Library of Congress, Prints &
Photographs Division, Carl Van Vechten Collection,
courtesy of Carl Van Vechten Trust)

back across Italy his passport was stolen and he became a beach-comber in Genoa. He has described his life there to me: "Wine and figs and *pasta*. And sunlight! And amusing companions, dozens of other beach-combers roving the dockyards and water-front streets, getting their heads whacked by the Fascisti, and breaking one loaf of bread into so many pieces that nobody got more than a crumb. I lived in the public gardens along the water-front and slept in the Albergo Populare for two lire a night amidst the snores of hundreds of other derelicts. . . . I painted my way home as a sailor. It seems that I must have painted the whole ship myself. We made a regular 'grand tour': Livorno, Napoli (we passed so close to Capri I could have cried). Then all around Sicily—Catania, Messina, Palermo—the Lipari Islands, miserable little peaks of pumice stone out in the sea; then across to Spain, divine Spain! My buddy and I went on a spree in Valencia for a night and a day. . . . Oh, the sweet wine of Valencia!"

He arrived in New York on November 10, 1924. That evening I attended a dance given in Harlem by the National Association for the Advancement of Colored People. Some time during the course of the night, Walter White asked me to meet two young Negro poets. He introduced me to Countée Cullen and Lang-

ston Hughes. Before that moment I had never heard of either of them.

II

I have merely sketched a primitive outline of a career as rich in adventures as a fruit-cake is full of raisins. I have already stated that I hope Langston Hughes may be persuaded to set it down on paper in the minutest detail, for the bull-fights in Mexico, the drunken gaiety of the Grand Duc, the delicately exquisite grace of the little black girls at Burutu, the exotic languor of the Spanish women at Valencia, the barbaric jazz dances of the cabarets in New York's own Harlem, the companionship of sailors of many races and nationalities, all have stamped an indelible impression on the highly sensitized, poetic imagination of this young Negro, an impression which has found its initial expression in the poems assembled in this book.

And also herein may be discerned that nostalgia for color and warmth and beauty which explains this boy's nomadic instincts.

> "We should have a land of sun,
> Of gorgeous sun,
> And a land of fragrant water
> Where the twilight
> Is a soft bandanna handkerchief
> Of rose and gold,
> And not this land where life is cold,"

he sings. Again, he tells his dream:

> "To fling my arms wide
> In the face of the sun,
> Dance! whirl! whirl!
> Till the quick day is done.
> Rest at pale evening. . . .
> A tall, slim tree. . . .
> Night coming tenderly,
>   Black like me."

More of this wistful longing may be discovered in the poems entitled *The South* and *As I Grew Older*. His verses, however, are by no means limited to an exclusive mood; he writes caressingly of little black prostitutes in Harlem; his cabaret songs throb with the true jazz rhythm; his sea-pieces ache with a calm, melancholy lyricism; he cries bitterly from the heart of his race in *Cross* and *The Jester;* he sighs, in one of the most successful of his fragile poems, over the loss of a loved friend. Always, however, his stanzas are subjective, personal. They are the (I had almost said informal, for they have a highly deceptive air of spontaneous improvisation) expression of an essentially sensitive and subtly illusive nature, seeking always to break through the veil that obscures for him, at least in some degree, the ultimate needs of that nature.

Blanche and Alfred Knopf (photograph by Carl Van Vechten, 4 April 1932; Library of Congress, Prints & Photographs Division, Carl Van Vechten Collection, courtesy of Carl Van Vechten Trust)

To the Negro race in America, since the day when Phillis Wheatley indited lines to General George Washington and other aristocratic figures (for Phillis Wheatley never sang "My way's cloudy," or "By an' by, I'm goin' to lay down dis heavy load") there have been born many poets. Paul Laurence Dunbar, James Weldon Johnson, Claude McKay, Jean Toomer, Georgia Douglas Johnson, Countée Cullen, are a few of the more memorable names. Not the least of these names, I think, is that of Langston Hughes, and perhaps his adventures and personality offer the promise of as rich a fulfillment as has been the lot of any of the others.

CARL VAN VECHTEN.
New York.
August 3, 1925.

–*The Weary Blues* (New York: Knopf, 1926), pp. 9–13

* * *

Countee Cullen and Langston Hughes were the most celebrated poets of the Harlem Renaissance, though their aesthetics differed greatly. In this review Cullen questions Hughes's decision to blend jazz poetry with more traditional lyrics.

Poet on Poet
Review of *The Weary Blues*

Here is a poet with whom to reckon, to experience, and here and there, with that apologetic feeling of presumption that should companion all criticism, to quarrel.

What has always struck me most forcibly in reading Mr. Hughes' poems has been their utter spontaneity and expression of a unique personality. This feeling is intensified with the appearance of his work in concert between the covers of a book. It must be acknowledged at the outset that these poems are peculiarly Mr. Hughes' and no one's else. I cannot imagine his work as that of any other poet, not even of any poet of that particular group of which Mr. Hughes is a member. Of course, a microscopic assiduity might reveal derivation and influences, but these are weak undercurrents in the flow of Mr. Hughes' own talent. This poet represents a transcendently emancipated spirit among a class of young writers whose particular battle-cry is freedom. With the enthusiasm of a zealot, he pursues his way, scornful, in subject matter, in photography, and rhythmical treatment, of whatever obstructions time and tradition have placed before him. To him it is essential that he be himself. Essential and commendable surely; yet the thought persists that some of these poems would have been better had Mr. Hughes held himself a bit in check. In his admirable introduction to the book, Carl Van Vechten says the poems have a *highly deceptive air of spontaneous improvisation.* I do not feel that the air is deceptive.

If I have the least powers of prediction, the first section of this book, *The Weary Blues,* will be most admired, even if less from intrinsic poetical worth than because of its dissociation from the traditionally poetic. Never having been one to think all subjects and forms proper for poetic consideration, I regard these jazz poems as interlopers in the company of the truly beautiful poems in other sections of the book. They move along with the frenzy and electric heat of a Methodist or Baptist revival meeting, and affect me in much the same manner. The revival meeting excites me, cooling and flushing me with alternate chills and fevers of emotion; so do these poems. But when the storm is over, I wonder if the quiet way of communing is not more spiritual for the God-seeking heart; and in the light of reflection I wonder if jazz poems really belong to that dignified company, that select and austere circle of high literary expression which we call poetry. Surely, when in *Negro Dancers* Mr. Hughes says

> Me an' ma baby's
> Got two mo' ways,
> Two mo' ways to do de buck!

he voices, in lyrical, thumb-at-nose fashion the happy careless attitude, akin to poetry, that is found in certain types. And certainly he achieves one of his loveliest lyrics in *Young Singer.* Thus I find myself straddling a fence. It needs only *The Cat and the Saxophone,* however, to knock me over completely on the side of bewilderment, and incredulity. This creation is a *tour de force* of its kind, but is it a poem:

> EVERYBODY
> Half-pint,–
> Gin?
> No, make it
>
> LOVES MY BABY
>
> corn. You like
> don't you, honey?
> BUT MY BABY . . . .

Countee Cullen, who was twenty-one years old when he inscribed this photograph. His first book, Color *(1925), established his reputation as a traditional lyric poet (Yale Collection of American Literature, Beinecke Rare Book and Manuscript Library).*

In the face of accomplished fact, I cannot say *This will never do,* but I feel that it ought never to have been done.

But Mr. Hughes can be as fine and as polished as you like, etching his work in calm, quiet lyrics that linger and repeat themselves. Witness *Sea Calm:*

> How still,
> How strangely still
> The water is today.
> It is not good
> For water
> To be so still that way.

Or take *Suicide's Note:*

> The Calm,
> Cool face of the river
> Asked me for a kiss.

Then crown your admiration with *Fantasy in Purple*, this imperial swan-song that sounds like the requiem of a dying people:

> *Beat the drums of tragedy for me,*
> *Beat the drums of tragedy and death.*
> *And let the choir sing a stormy song*
> *To drown the rattle of my dying breath.*
>
> *Beat the drums of tragedy for me,*
> *And let the white violins whir thin and slow,*
> *But blow one blaring trumpet note of sun*
> *To go with me to the darkness where I go.*

Mr. Hughes is a remarkable poet of the colorful; through all his verses the rainbow riots and dazzles, yet never wearies the eye, although at times it intrigues the brain into astonishment and exaggerated admiration when reading, say something like *Caribbean Sunset:*

> *God having a hemorrhage,*
> *Blood coughed across the sky,*
> *Staining the dark sea red:*
> *That is sunset in the Caribbean.*

Taken as a group the selections in this book seem one-sided to me. They tend to hurl this poet into the gaping pit that lies before all Negro writers, in the confines of which they become racial artists instead of artists pure and simple. There is too much emphasis here on strictly Negro themes; and this is probably an added reason for my coldness toward the jazz poems—they seem to set a too definite limit upon an already limited field.

Dull books cause no schisms, raise no dissensions, create no parties. Much will be said of *The Weary Blues* because it is a definite achievement, and because Mr. Hughes, in his own way, with a first book that cannot be dismissed as merely *promising,* has arrived.

—*Opportunity: A Journal of Negro Life,*
4 (February 1926): 73–74

* * *

W. C. Handy, the "Father of the Blues," who in an 8 February 1926 letter to Hughes commended his "entirely original" treatment of the blues in his first book (photograph by Carl Van Vechten, 17 July 1941; Library of Congress, Prints & Photographs Division, Carl Van Vechten Collection, courtesy of Carl Van Vechten Trust)

Journalist and theater critic Theophilus Lewis wrote this review.

Euterpe Learns the Charleston
Review of *The Weary Blues*

Lyric poetry—and I am almost persuaded to Edgar Allan Poe's opinion that there is no other kind of poetry—springs from the core of the mind where the emotional kinship of races is close enough to make the imagery of each intelligible to all. It sprouts from the youth of humanity, the race or the poet and, as youth is parent to maturity, it reveals the mold or pattern from which the more spiritual and intellectual arts will later develop. While the bard whose songs flow unalloyed from the universal human emotions usually wins quicker recognition, he will, unless he is a master of musical speech, inevitably be surpassed by the vigor and arresting originality of the poet bearing the unmistakable mark of his race. If anybody asserts this is simply an expression of my well-known chauvinism, I reply "Bushwah!" Differientiation is always a step forward in the process of evolution.

The "Blues" poems which make up the first part of the book, "The Weary Blues," reveal Langston Hughes as a poet of the latter type. On second thought I see no valid reason why the "Blues" should be distinguished from the earlier poems. They are merely an emphatic expression of the mood discernible in his work from the beginning. To people who think a poet is a man who repeats in verse what he reads in books or newspapers, these poems, all of them, will appear either gauche monstrosities or clever innovations, happily or lamentably, according to whether one likes them or not, destined to live no longer than the current cabaret vogue. Which view marks the failure, or perhaps the inability, to understand the function of an artist.

Langston Hughes has gone direct to life for his themes and he has embodied its ironies and vagous harmonies in his verse. He has not consulted life of 1890 as observed and recorded by Theodore Dreiser and Rudyard Kipling; he has caught life in its current incandescence as it roars and blazes in the bosoms of the new race of American blacks. Six lines of his are painted on a six-foot sign in the lobby of the Harlem Y. M. C. A. and this is no mere coincidence. It is one of the indications that this pagan poet is fast becoming a religious force. By this expression I do not mean he has invented a novel way to chant halleluiahs to a Jewish Jehovah, a standardized Christ and a Central Islip Holy Ghost. I mean that in giving concrete and definite expression to the incoherent feelings and impulses of his people he is functioning as a unifying spiritual agent. This is the chief work of the artist—this and to crystallize the beauty of his people in stone or verse or enduring drama and so leave behind [an] impressive tombstone when the civilization of which he is a part has trod the road to dusty death.

As no man can read vivid and thoughtful literature without showing the effects of it, there are places, here and there, where his verse faintly smells like the Public Library, as—

> He did a lazy sway . . .
> He did a lazy sway . . .

which suggests the rhythm of the Chinese Nightingale, or "To the Black Beloved," with its subdued elegance which somehow carried the mind back to the Song of Solomon. But these reminders of book lore, faint as they are, are few and far between. What we usually hear is the shuffle of happy feet as in:—

> Me an' ma baby's
> Got two mo' ways,
> Two mo' ways to do de buck!

Or Bessie Smith's robust contralto moaning a seductive ululation like:—

> My man's done left me,
> Chile, he's gone away.
> My good man's left me,
> Babe, he's gone away.
> Now the cryin' blues
> Haunts me night and day.

In "Cross" he takes his theme from the bio-sociological riot of the Aframerican's background and the first line, which establishes its rhythm, comes straight from the guts of 133rd Street, which cries out against the restraints of the Ten Commandments and the factory system in the Rabelaisian couplet beginning

> "My old man is a man like this."

It almost tempts one to write him a personal letter demanding something inspired by that other jewel of levity, the quatrain which opens:

> "I wish I had ten thousand bricks."

And Hughes, the craftsman, is quite as deft as Hughes the artist is original. His poems which at first sound as simple as the theme of Beethoven's Sixth Symphony on closer examination reveal a good deal

To Midnight Nan at Leroy's

Strut and wiggle,
Shameless gal.
Wouldn't no good fellow
Be your pal.

Hear dat music. . . .
Jungle night.
Hear dat music. . . .
And the moon was white.

Sing your Blues song,
Pretty Baby.
You want lovin'
And you don't mean maybe.

Jungle lover. . . .
Night black boy. . . .
Two against the moon
And the moon was joy.

Strut and wiggle,
Shameless Nan.
Wouldn't no good fellow
Be your man.

—*The Weary Blues*, p. 30

---

of the complexity of that master's music. As an example, I point of Midnight Nan at Leroy's. You will travel a long day's journey before you find another contemporary poem in which the fundamental poignancy and superficial gayety of life are so effectively blended. Note how skillfully he employs paired iambics to make the Charleston rhythm dance blithely down the surface of the poem while an excess of short feet and weak vowels form an undertow which establishes a final melancholy mood. I can think of no poet since Poe capable of weaving such and intricate tapestry [of] antithetical feelings.

Hughes is not a solitary figure, of course; there are at least two other poets producing work quite as authentic. But I know of no other poet who keeps in such close contact with life in its molten state or who is as capable of getting expression out of gaseous feelings without waiting for them to cool off. If he doesn't stop to mark time now he will certainly grow into a spiritual force of major significance.

—*The Messenger,* 8 (March 1926): 92

* * *

DuBose Heyward, whose novel Porgy *(1925) was the basis for George Gershwin's award-winning folk opera* Porgy and Bess, *wrote this review.*

The Jazz Band's Sob
Review of *The Weary Blues*

A little over a year ago the brilliant Negro journal "Opportunity" awarded a prize for a poem, "The Weary Blues," by Langston Hughes. Shortly thereafter "The Forum" reprinted the poem. Previous to the appearance of this poem very few were aware of the existence of the author, although he had been writing for seven years; an apprenticeship the results of which are evident in the pages of this volume, to which his prize poem gives its name.

"The Weary Blues" challenges more serious consideration than that generally accorded a "first book." Langston Hughes, although only twenty-four years old, is already conspicuous in the group of Negro intellectuals who are dignifying Harlem with a genuine art life. And, too, his use of syncopation in his prize poem suggested the possibility of a conflict in the rhythms of poetry paralleling that which is taking place between the spiritual and jazz exponents of Negro music.

Let it be said at once then that this author has done nothing particularly revolutionary in the field of rhythm. He is endowed with too subtle a musical sense to employ the banjo music of Vachel Lindsay, but he is close kin to Carl Sandburg in his use of freer, subtler syncopation. In fact, he has wisely refused to be fettered by a theory and has allowed his mood to select its own music. Several of the short free verse poems might have been written by Amy Lowell.

But if he derives little that is new in rhythm from his "Blues" he has managed to capture the *mood* of that type of Negro song, and thereby has caught its very essence. When he is able to create a minor, devil-may-care music, and through it to release a throb of pain, he is doing what the Negroes have done for generations, whether in the "Blues" of the Mississippi region or a song like "I Can't Help from Cryin' Sometimes," as sung by the black folk of the Carolina low country.

As he says in his "Cabaret":

"Does a jazz band ever sob?
They say a jazz band's gay.
Yet as the vulgar dancers whirled
And the wan night wore away,
One said she heard the jazz band sob
When the little dawn was gray."

That Langston Hughes has not altogether escaped an inevitable pitfall of the Negro intellectual is to be regretted. In one or two places in the book the artist is obscured by the propagandist. Pegasus has been made a pack-horse. It is natural that the Negro writer should feel keenly the lack of sympathy in the South. That the South is a great loser thereby brings him small comfort. In the soul of a poet, a revolt so born may be transmuted through the alchemy of art into poetry that, while it stings the eyes with tears, causes the reader to wonder.

But far more often in the volume the artist is victor:

"We have to-morrow
Bright before us
Like a flame.

Yesterday
A night-gone thing,
A sun-down name.

And dawn to-day
Broad arch above the road we came."

And in "Dream Variation" youth triumphs:

"To fling my arms wide
In some place of the sun,
To whirl and to dance
Till the white day is done.
Then rest at cool evening
Beneath a tall tree
While the night comes on gently,
Dark like me–
That is my dream!"

It is, however, as an individual poet, not as a member of a new and interesting literary group, or as spokesman for a race, that Langston Hughes must stand or fall, and in the numerous poems in "The Weary Blues" that give poignant moods and vivid glimpses of seas and lands caught by the young poet in his wanderings I find an exceptional endowment. Always intensely subjective, passionate, keenly sensitive to beauty and possessed of an unfaltering musical sense, Langston Hughes has given us a "first book" that marks the opening of a career well worth watching.
–*New York Herald Tribune Books*, 1 August 1926, pp. 4–5

* * *

Journalist and critic James Rorty wrote this review for the radical journal New Masses, *to which Hughes contributed frequently during the 1930s. Rorty refers to the Jamaican-born Marcus Garvey, who rose to prominence in New York during the 1920s with a political agenda emphasizing racial separatism.*

Off with the Black-Face!
Review of *The Weary Blues*

Creatively, New York is not much better than an ache and an appetite. It is the monstrous overgrown belly-plexus of a monstrous, overgrown competitive civilization. It doesn't make anything except money and its greed is enormous. It must live, it says, although of course it would be much better to have an earthquake up-end the whole idiot's carnival and let the healed earth go quietly back to sumach and timothy.

But New York must live and its wants are multitude. It wants girls–not the worn and jaded local product, but fresh and shapely beauties from the provinces; Mr. Florenz Ziegfeld caters astutely to this need. It wants rustics, eccentrics, lumberjacks, cowboys,–James Stevens, Will Rogers. It wants art–and the writers and painters and sculptors of a continent pour their hoarded gains of life and desire, thought and feeling, into the dry veins of the metropolis. It wants pottery from Czecho-Slovakia, hooked rugs from New England, idols from Africa, cults from India. New York will pay, liberally, and in cash, the only currency it recognizes.

New York is liberal, sophisticated, enlightened. New York draws no color line. It *wants* the Negro. It wants his dark uncorrupted flesh. It wants his jazz, his songs. It wants his laughter–New York's lips are split with its own wise-cracks. Despite the subways, the elevated trains, the rushing traffic, there is a terrible silence in New York, a white, death-house silence that aches to be filled.

Well, for five or six years now, New York has had the Negro. The black tides have poured north into Harlem. The black jazzers and singers are stars on Broadway. The sharp Jews and Nordics who run the cabarets have found a new decoy–painted black–and how it does pay! The black poets are published by the best publishers. The Negro renaissance. Carl Van Vechten has told us all about it, and New York is amused.

But how about the Negro in all this? I, for one, am sick of black-face comedians, whether high-brow or low-brow. I am sick of the manumitted slave psychology and I should think the Negroes themselves would be twice as sick. I, for one, am waiting and hoping for a new titillation. I want the Negroes to stop entertaining the whites and begin to speak for themselves. I am waiting for a Negro poet to stand up and say "I–I am *not* amused."

Langston Hughes doesn't say anything like this. Nothing as bitter, nothing as masterful, nothing as savage. Why not? Why do the Negroes express so little beyond this black-white relation? Why don't they speak forthrightly as free, untamed *human beings*. Are Negroes really savages? One hopes so, but one doubts. So many of them look, talk and write like sophisticated, tamed, adapted, behavioristic white men, and if that is what they want to be, it is nothing in the way of an aspiration.

Nevertheless, Hughes is a poet, with a curiously firm and supple style, half naive and half sophisticated, which is on the whole more convincing than anything which has yet appeared in Negro poetry. Here and there in the volume there are pieces startling in their effectiveness.

WHEN SUE WEARS RED

When Susanna Jones wear red
Her face is like an ancient cameo
Turned brown by the ages.
Come with a blast of trumpets, Jesus!
When Susanna Jones wear red
A queen from some time-dead Egyptian night
Walks once again.
Blow trumpets, Jesus!
And the beauty of Susanna Jones in red
Burns in my heart a love-fire sharp like pain.
Sweet silver trumpets,
*   Jesus!*

There are others the effect of which is much less pleasing. For example:

All the tom-toms of the jungle beat in my blood.
And all the wild hot moons of the jungles shine in my soul.
I am afraid of this civilization—
*   So hard,*
*   So strong,*
*   So cold.*

I hope and trust Hughes doesn't mean this. If he does, I'd rather have Garvey, who may not be intelligent, but who at least seems more angry than afraid.

–New Masses, 1 (October 1926): 26

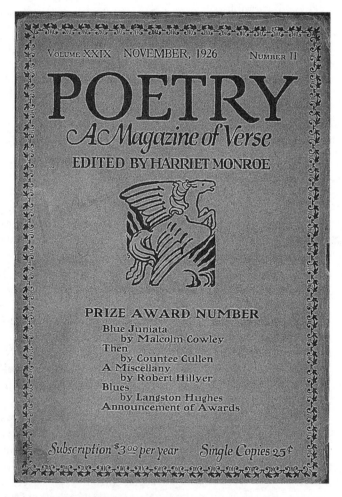

Cover for the issue of Poetry *that included four poems by Hughes, three of which appeared in his second volume of poetry,*
Fine Clothes to the Jew *(1927). Founded in 1912 by Harriet Monroe,* Poetry *published modernist poets such as*
T. S. Eliot, Ezra Pound, and Marianne Moore (Kenneth Spencer Research Library, University of Kansas Libraries).

An Argument of Art and Race

In the middle of the year in which The Weary Blues *was published, the iconoclastic black journalist George S. Schuyler, a columnist for the* Pittsburgh Courier, *wrote an essay for* The Nation *attacking the foundation of the aesthetic that Hughes had developed. The managing editor of the magazine, Freda Kirchwey, sent proofs of Schuyler's essay to Hughes in hopes of provoking a response. Hughes not only wrote a letter to the editor but also one of his most important essays.*

Schuyler's essay is reprinted below.

The Negro-Art Hokum

Negro art "made in America" is as non-existent as the widely advertised profundity of Cal Coolidge, the "seven years of progress" of Mayor Hylan, or the reported sophistication of New Yorkers. Negro art there has been, is, and will be among the numerous black nations of Africa; but to suggest the possibility of any such development among the ten million colored people in this republic is self-evident foolishness. Eager apostles from Greenwich Village, Harlem, and environs proclaimed a great renaissance of Negro art just around the corner waiting to be ushered on the scene by those whose hobby is taking races, nations, peoples, and movements under their wing. New art forms expressing the "peculiar" psychology of the Negro were about to flood the market. In short, the art of Homo Africanus was about to electrify the waiting world. Skeptics patiently waited. They still wait.

True, from dark-skinned sources have come those slave songs based on Protestant hymns and Biblical texts known as the spirituals, work songs and secular songs of sorrow and tough luck known as the blues, that outgrowth of ragtime known as jazz (in the development of which whites have assisted), and the Charleston, an eccentric dance invented by the gamins around the public market-place in Charleston, S.C. No one can or does deny this. But these are contributions of a caste in a certain section of the country. They are foreign to Northern Negroes, West Indian Negroes, and African Negroes. They are no more expressive or characteristic of the Negro race than the music and dancing of the Appalachian highlanders or the Dalmatian peasantry are expressive or characteristic of the Caucasian race. If one wishes to speak of the musical contributions of the peasantry of the South, very well. Any group under similar circumstances would have produced something similar. It is merely a coincidence that this peasant class happens to be of a darker hue than the other inhabitants of the land. One recalls the remarkable likeness of the minor strains of the Russian mujiks to those of the Southern Negro.

George S. Schuyler (photograph by Carl Van Vechten, 2 July 1941; Library of Congress, Prints & Photographs Division, Carl Van Vechten Collection, courtesy of Carl Van Vechten Trust)

As for the literature, painting, and sculpture of Aframericans—such as there is—it is identical in kind with the literature, painting, and sculpture of white Americans: that is, it shows more or less evidence of European influence. In the field of drama little of any merit has been written by and about Negroes that could not have been written by whites. The dean of the Aframerican literati is W. E. B. Du Bois, a product of Harvard and German universities; the foremost Aframerican sculptor is Meta Warwick Fuller, a graduate of leading American art schools and former student of Rodin; while the most noted Aframerican painter, Henry Ossawa Tanner, is dean of American painters in Paris and has been decorated by the French Government. Now the work of these artists is no more "expressive of the Negro soul"—as the gushers put it—than are the scribblings of Octavus Cohen or Hugh Wiley.

This, of course, is easily understood if one stops to realize that the Aframerican is merely a lampblacked Anglo-Saxon. If the European immigrant after two or three generations of exposure to our schools, politics, advertising, moral crusades, and restaurants becomes indistinguishable from the mass of

Americans of the older stock (despite the influence of the foreign-language press), how much truer must it be of the sons of Ham who have been subjected to what the uplifters call Americanism for the last three hundred years. Aside from his color, which ranges from very dark brown to pink, your American Negro is just plain American. Negroes and whites from the same localities in this country talk, think, and act about the same. Because a few writers with a paucity of themes have seized upon imbecilities of the Negro rustics and clowns and palmed them off as authentic and characteristic Aframerican behavior, the common notion that the black American is so "different" from his white neighbor has gained wide currency. The mere mention of the word "Negro" conjures up in the average white American's mind a composite stereotype of Bert Williams, Aunt Jemima, Uncle Tom, Jack Johnson, Florian Slappey, and the various monstrosities scrawled by the cartoonists. Your average Aframerican no more resembles this stereotype than the average American resembles a composite of Andy Gump, Jim Jeffries, and a cartoon by Rube Goldberg.

Again, the Aframerican is subject to the same economic and social forces that mold the actions and thoughts of the white Americans. He is not living in a different world as some whites and a few Negroes would have us believe. When the jangling of his Connecticut alarm clock gets him out of his Grand Rapids bed to a breakfast similar to that eaten by his white brother across the street; when he toils at the same or similar work in mills, mines, factories, and commerce alongside the descendants of Spartacus, Robin Hood, and Erik the Red; when he wears similar clothing and speaks the same language with the same degree of perfection; when he reads the same Bible and belongs to the Baptist, Methodist, Episcopal, or Catholic church; when his fraternal affiliations also include the Elks, Masons, and Knights of Pythias; when he gets the same or similar schooling, lives in the same kind of houses, owns the same makes of cars (or rides in them), and nightly sees the same Hollywood version of life on the screen; when he smokes the same brands of tobacco and avidly peruses the same puerile periodicals; in short, when he responds to the same political, social, moral, and economic stimuli in precisely the same manner as his white neighbor, it is sheer nonsense to talk about "racial differences" as between the American black man and the American white man. Glance over a Negro newspaper (it is printed in good Americanese) and you will find the usual quota of crime news, scandal, personals, and uplift to be found in the average white newspaper—which, by the way, is more widely read by the Negroes than is the Negro press. In order to satisfy the cravings of an inferiority complex engen-

Bert Williams and his partner George Walker, stars of black vaudeville. Schuyler argued that such entertainers gave white audiences a skewed impression of black culture (Yale Collection of American Literature, Beinecke Rare Book and Manuscript Library).

dered by the colorphobia of the mob, the readers of the Negro newspapers are given a slight dash of racialistic seasoning. In the homes of the black and white Americans of the same cultural and economic level one finds similar furniture, literature, and conversation. How, then, can the black American be expected to produce art and literature dissimilar to that of the white American?

Consider Coleridge-Taylor, Edward Wilmot Blyden, and Claude McKay, the Englishmen; Pushkin, the Russian; Bridgewater, the Pole; Antar, the Arabian; Latino, the Spaniard; Dumas, *père* and *fils,* the Frenchmen; and Paul Laurence Dunbar, Charles W. Chesnut, and James Weldon Johnson, the Americans. All Negroes; yet their work shows the impress of nationality rather than race. They all reveal the psychology and culture of their environment—their color is incidental. Why should Negro artists of America vary from the national artistic norm when Negro artists in other countries have not done so? If we can foresee what kind of white citizens will inhabit this neck of the woods in the next generation by studying the sort of education and environment the children are exposed to now, it should not be difficult to reason that the adults of today are what they are because of the education and environment they were exposed to a generation ago. And that education and environment were about the same for blacks and whites. One contemplates the popularity of the Negro-art hokum and murmurs, "How come?"

This nonsense is probably the last stand of the old myth palmed off by Negrophobists for all these many years, and recently rehashed by the sainted Harding, that there are "fundamental, eternal, and inescapable differences" between white and black Americans. That there are Negroes who will lend this myth a helping hand need occasion no surprise. It has been broadcast all over the world by the vociferous scions of slaveholders, "scientists" like Madison Grant and Lothrop Stoddard, and the patriots who flood the treasury of the Ku Klux Klan; and is believed, even today, by the majority of free, white citizens. On this baseless premise, so flattering to the white mob, that the blackamoor is inferior and fundamentally different, is erected the postulate that he must needs be peculiar; and when he attempts to portray life through the medium of art, it must of necessity be a peculiar art. While such reasoning may seem conclusive to the majority of Americans, it must be rejected with a loud guffaw by intelligent people.

–*The Nation*, 122 (16 June 1926): 662–663

* * *

Hughes's fully developed counterargument to Schuyler's denunciation of African American art became a manifesto of the Harlem Renaissance. The promising young poet Hughes refers to is probably Countee Cullen. Hughes and Cullen had been friends but had become literary rivals.

The Negro Artist and the Racial Mountain

One of the most promising of the young Negro poets said to me once, "I want to be a poet—not a Negro poet," meaning, I believe, "I want to write like a white poet"; meaning subconsciously, "I would like to be a white poet"; meaning behind that, "I would like to be white." And I was sorry the young man said that, for no great poet has ever been afraid of being himself. And I doubted then that, with his desire to run away spiritually from his race, this boy would ever be a great poet. But this is the mountain standing in the way of any true Negro art in America—this urge within the race toward whiteness, the desire to pour racial individuality into the mold of American standardization, and to be as little Negro and as much American as possible.

An Absurd Contention

Hughes's first response to Schuyler's essay was probably the following letter, dated 14 June but not published in The Nation *until August, under the title "American Art or Negro Art?" Hughes refers to* Nize Baby *(1926), a popular book by cartoonist Milt Gross based on his illustrated columns for the* New York World *that featured stereotypical conversations between Jewish mothers.*

To the Editor of the Nation:

Sir: For Mr. Schuyler to say that "the Negro masses . . . are no different from the white masses" in America seems to me obviously absurd. Fundamentally, perhaps, all peoples are the same. But as long as the Negro remains a segregated group in this country he must reflect certain racial and environmental differences which are his own. The very fact that Negroes do straighten their hair and try to forget their racial background makes them different from white people. If they were exactly like the dominant class they would not have to try so hard to imitate them. Again it seems quite as absurd to say that spirituals and blues are not Negro as it is to say that cowboy songs are not cowboy songs or that the folk ballads of Scotland do not belong to Scotland. The spirituals and blues are American, certainly, but they are also very much American Negro. And if one can say that some of my poems have no racial distinctiveness about them or that "Cane" is not Negro one can say with equal truth that "Nize Baby" is purely American.

From an economic and sociological viewpoint it may be entirely desirable that the Negro become as much like his white American brother as possible. Surely colored people want all the opportunities and advantages that anyone else possesses here in our country. But until America has completely absorbed the Negro and until segregation and racial self-consciousness have entirely disappeared, the true work of art from the Negro artist is bound, if it have any color and distinctiveness at all, to reflect his racial background and his racial environment.

–*The Nation* (18 August 1926): 151

But let us look at the immediate background of this young poet. His family is of what I suppose one would call the Negro middle class: people who are by no means rich yet never uncomfortable nor hungry—smug, contented, respectable folk, members of the Baptist church. The father goes to work every morning. He is a chief steward at a large white club. The mother sometimes does fancy sewing or supervises parties for the rich families of the town. The children go to a mixed school. In the

Cover for the only issue of Fire!!, *published in November 1926,
a journal that Hughes and other young artists conceived as
an avant-garde quarterly intended as a corrective to
conservative representations of black life in art and
literature (Kenneth Spencer Research Library,
University of Kansas Libraries)*

home they read white papers and magazines. And the mother often says "Don't be like niggers" when the children are bad. A frequent phrase from the father is, "Look how well a white man does things." And so the word white comes to be unconsciously a symbol of all the virtues. It holds for the children beauty, morality, and money. The whisper of "I want to be white" runs silently through their minds. This young poet's home is, I believe, a fairly typical home of the colored middle class. One sees immediately how difficult it would be for an artist born in such a home to interest himself in interpreting the beauty of his own people. He is never taught to see that beauty. He is taught rather not to see it, or if he does, to be ashamed of it when it is not according to Caucasian patterns.

For racial culture the home of a self-styled "high-class" Negro has nothing better to offer. Instead there will perhaps be more aping of things white than in a less cultured or less wealthy home.

The father is perhaps a doctor, lawyer, landowner, or politician. The mother may be a social worker, or a teacher, or she may do nothing and have a maid. Father is often dark but he has usually married the lightest woman he could find. The family attend a fashionable church where few really colored faces are to be found. And they themselves draw a color line. In the North they go to white theaters and white movies. And in the South they have at least two cars and a house "like white folks." Nordic manners, Nordic faces, Nordic hair, Nordic art (if any), and an Episcopal heaven. A very high mountain indeed for the would-be racial artist to climb in order to discover himself and his people.

But then there are the low-down folks, the so-called common element, and they are the majority—may the Lord be praised! The people who have their nip of gin on Saturday nights and are not too important to themselves or the community, or too well fed, or too learned to watch the lazy world go round. They live on Seventh Street in Washington or State Street in Chicago and they do not particularly care whether they are like white folks or anybody else. Their joy runs, bang! into ecstasy. Their religion soars to a shout. Work maybe a little today, rest a little tomorrow. Play awhile. Sing awhile. O, let's dance! These common people are not afraid of spirituals, as for a long time their more intellectual brethren were, and jazz is their child. They furnish a wealth of colorful, distinctive material for any artist because they still hold their own individuality in the face of American standardizations. And perhaps these common people will give to the world its truly great Negro artist, the one who is not afraid to be himself. Whereas the better-class Negro would tell the artist what to do, the people at least let him alone when he does appear. And they are not ashamed of him—if they know he exists at all. And they accept what beauty is their own without question.

Certainly there is, for the American Negro artist who can escape the restrictions the more advanced among his own group would put upon him, a great field of unused material ready for his art. Without going outside his race, and even among the better classes with their "white" culture and conscious American manners, but still Negro enough to be different, there is sufficient matter to furnish a black artist with a lifetime of creative work. And when he chooses to touch on the relations between Negroes and whites in this country with their innumerable overtones and undertones, surely, and especially for literature and the drama, there is an inexhaustible supply of themes at hand. To these the Negro artist can give his racial individuality, his heritage of rhythm and warmth, and his incongruous humor that so often, as in the Blues, becomes ironic laughter mixed with tears. But let us look again at the mountain.

A prominent Negro clubwoman in Philadelphia paid eleven dollars to hear Raquel Meller sing Andalusian popular songs. But she told me a few weeks before she would not think of going to hear "that woman," Clara Smith, a great black artist, sing Negro folksongs. And many an upper-class Negro church, even now, would not dream of employing a spiritual in its services. The drab melodies in white folks' hymnbooks are much to be preferred. "We want to worship the Lord correctly and quietly. We don't believe in 'shouting.' Let's be dull like the Nordics," they say, in effect.

The road for the serious black artist, then, who would produce a racial art is most certainly rocky and the mountain is high. Until recently he received almost no encouragement for his work from either white or colored people. The fine novels of Chestnutt go out of print with neither race noticing their passing. The quaint charm and humor of Dunbar's dialect verse brought to him, in his day, largely the same kind of encouragement one would give a sideshow freak (A colored man writing poetry! How odd!) or a clown (How amusing!).

The present vogue in things Negro, although it may do as much harm as good for the budding colored artist, has at least done this: it has brought him forcibly to the attention of his own people among whom for so long, unless the other race had noticed him beforehand, he was a prophet with little honor. I understand that Charles Gilpin acted for years in Negro theaters without any special acclaim from his own, but when Broadway gave him eight curtain calls, Negroes, too, began to beat a tin pan in his honor. I know a young colored writer, a manual worker by day, who had been writing well for the colored magazines for some years, but it was not until he recently broke into the white publications and his first book was accepted by a prominent New York publisher that the "best" Negroes in his city took the trouble to discover that he lived there. Then almost immediately they decided to give a grand dinner for him. But the society ladies were careful to whisper to his mother that perhaps she'd better not come. They were not sure she would have an evening gown.

The Negro artist works against an undertow of sharp criticism and misunderstanding from his own group and unintentional bribes from the whites. "O, be respectable, write about nice people, show how good we are," say the Negroes. "Be stereotyped, don't go too far, don't shatter our illusions about you, don't amuse us too seriously. We will pay you," say the whites. Both would have told Jean Toomer not to write "Cane." The colored people did not praise it. The white people did not buy it. Most of the colored people who did read "Cane" hate it. They are afraid of it. Although the critics gave it good reviews the public remained indifferent. Yet (excepting the work of Du Bois) "Cane" contains the finest prose written by a Negro in America. And like the singing of Robeson, it is truly racial.

But in spite of the Nordicized Negro intelligentsia and the desires of some white editors we have an honest American Negro literature already with us. Now I await the rise of the Negro theater. Our folk music, having achieved worldwide fame, offers itself to the genius of the great individual American Negro composer who is to come. And within the next decade I expect to see the work of a growing school of colored artists who paint and model the beauty of dark faces and create with new technique the expressions of their own soul-world. And the Negro dancers who will dance like flame and the singers who will continue to carry our songs to all who listen—they will be with us in even greater numbers tomorrow.

Most of my own poems are racial in theme and treatment, derived from the life I know. In many of them I try to grasp and hold some of the meanings and rhythms of jazz. I am sincere as I know how to be in these poems and yet after every reading I answer questions like these from my own people: Do you think Negroes should always write about Negroes? I wish you wouldn't read some of your poems to white folks. How do you find anything interesting in a place like a cabaret? Why do you write about black people? You aren't black. What makes you do so many jazz poems?

But jazz to me is one of the inherent expressions of Negro life in America: the eternal tom-tom beating in the Negro soul—the tom-tom of revolt against weariness in a white world, a world of subway trains, and work, work, work; the tom-tom of joy and laughter, and pain swallowed in a smile. Yet the Philadelphia clubwoman is ashamed to say that her race created it and she does not like me to write about it. The old subconscious "white is best" runs through her mind. Years of study under white teachers, a lifetime of white books, pictures, and

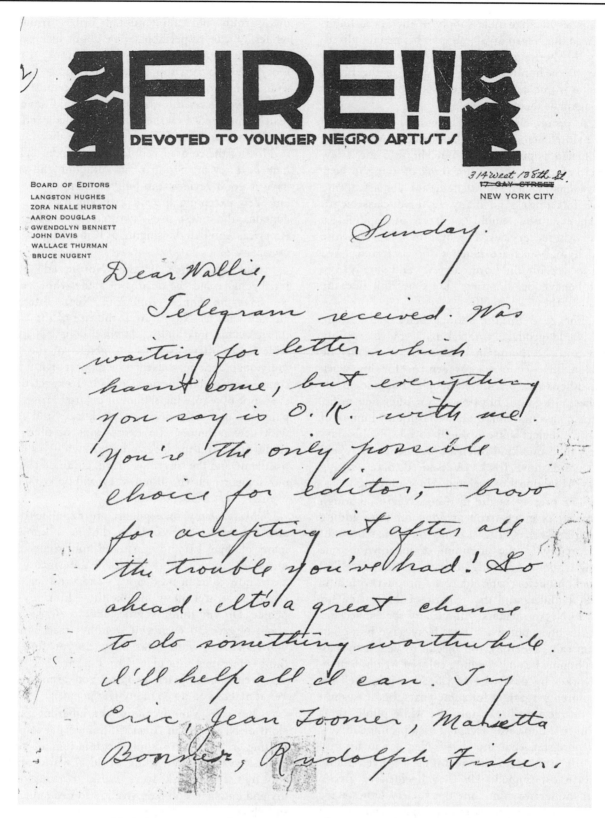

Hughes's letter to Wallace Thurman, circa 1926. Thurman arrived in Harlem in 1925 and quickly established himself as an editor, novelist, and playwright (Langston Hughes Papers, James Weldon Johnson Collection in the Yale Collection of American Literature, Beinecke Rare Book and Manuscript Library).

photographs wheather we use em or not. and she can introduce Fire!!! to best Parisian society. And lets hope we can get some really good poetry... "Fire Burns" should really be kept burning, a department of clever, sartirical comment on the vices and stupidities of the race. Make it hot! .... See if Aaron will do all covers, keeping same style and same black on red, but different each time. Try Willis Richardson for short play. Wish we could get a good personal estimate of some leading Negro, sort of sharp, keen biographical sketch, say of Du Bois, or Morton, or Locke. Maybe Fauset could do something like that if he's not afraid.... Might publish some reproductions of Locke's African sculptu Maybe he'd pay for cuts as publicity. How'd you come out with Brentano's, Lord & Taylor's? Blaze, boy!! Langs

Might publish art photos of Roberson for enterprise cover, etc. Send Joe three copies of Fire!!! at Folies Bergère, Paris, and ask publicity man for pictures. It's a good ad boy to get some beauty

papers, and white manners, morals, and Puritan standards made her dislike the spirituals. And now she turns up her nose at jazz and all its manifestations—likewise almost everything else distinctly racial. She doesn't care for the Winold Reiss portraits of Negroes because they are "too Negro." She does not want a true picture of herself from anybody. She wants the artist to flatter her, to make the white world believe that all Negroes are as smug and as near white in soul as she wants to be. But, to my mind, it is the duty of the younger Negro artist, if he accepts any duties at all from outsiders, to change through the force of his art that old whispering "I want to be white," hidden in the aspirations of his people, to "Why should I want to be white? I am a Negro—and beautiful!"

So I am ashamed for the black poet who says, "I want to be a poet, not a Negro poet," as though his own racial world were not as interesting as any other world. I am ashamed, too, for the colored artist who runs from the painting of Negro faces to the painting of sunsets after the manner of the academicians because he fears the strange un-whiteness of his own features. An artist must be free to choose what he does, certainly, but he must also never be afraid to do what he might choose.

Let the blare of Negro jazz bands and the bellowing voice of Bessie Smith singing Blues penetrate the closed ears of the colored near-intellectuals until they listen and perhaps understand. Let Paul Robeson singing Water Boy, and Rudolph Fisher writing about the streets of Harlem, and Jean Toomer holding the heart of Georgia in his hands, and Aaron Douglas drawing strange black fantasies cause the smug Negro middle class to turn from their white, respectable, ordinary books and papers to catch a glimmer of their own beauty. We younger Negro artists who create now intend to express our individual dark-skinned selves without fear or shame. If white people are pleased we are glad. If they are not, it doesn't matter. We know we are beautiful. And ugly too. The tom-tom cries and the tom-tom laughs. If colored people are pleased we are glad. If they are not, their displeasure doesn't matter either. We build our temples for tomorrow, strong as we know how, and we stand on top of the mountain, free within ourselves.

–*The Nation*, 122 (23 June 1926): 692–694

Reviews of *Fine Clothes to the Jew*

Fine Clothes to the Jew, *Hughes's second book of poems, was published in a printing of 1,500 copies in January 1927 by Knopf, which registered objections to the title but nevertheless let it stand upon Van Vechten's urging. Dedicated to Van Vechten, the book signaled a departure from Hughes's approach in* The Weary Blues, *for in the new book he used more authentic representations of common black vernacular. He included "A Note on the Blues" as a preface:*

> The first eight and the last nine poems in this book are written after the manner of the Negro folk-songs known as *Blues*. The *Blues*, unlike the *Spirituals*, have a strict poetic pattern: one long line repeated and a third line to rhyme with the first two. Sometimes the second line in repetition is slightly changed and sometimes, but very seldom, it is omitted. The mood of the *Blues* is almost always despondency, but when they are sung people laugh.

Selling the least copies of any of Hughes's books, Fine Clothes to the Jew *was attacked by some critics who found the language and subject matter vulgar.*

Critic Dewey R. Jones wrote this review for the Chicago Defender, *the respected black newspaper for which Hughes later in his career wrote a weekly column.*

Songs of the Lowly

> When hard luck overtakes you
>   Nothin' for you to do.
> When hard luck overtakes you
>   Nothin' for you to do.
> Gather up you' fine clothes
>   An' sell 'em to the Jew.

And thus the second book of poems by this young singer and student makes its bow. Not unlike "The Weary Blues" in many of its passages, "Fine Clothes" is more subtle, if possible, therefore more intriguing than his first book, printed early last year and now said to be in its third edition.

"Fine Clothes to the Jew" is a combination of typical chain-gang chants, blues songs heard all over the South today and in the large cities of the North since the war, "down home" Baptist church services, and plaints of the person lowest down everywhere. There are also scattered among these reproductions the author's own plaintive note against conditions as he finds them.

When "The Weary Blues" made its curtsy to America I expressed the belief that it heralded the approach of the real poet of the Race. "Fine Clothes to the Jew" only accentuates that belief. We have needed

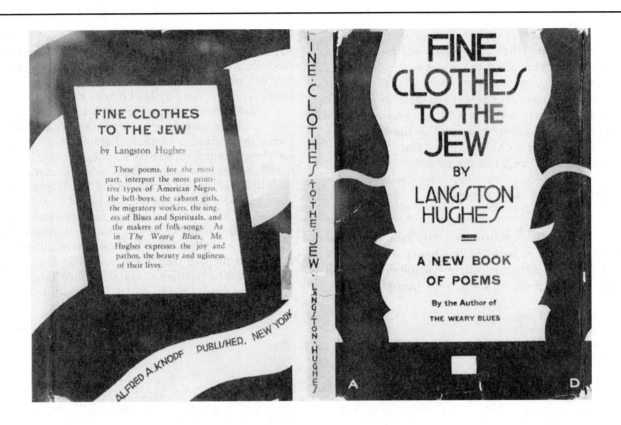

Dust jacket for Hughes's second volume of poetry (Yale Collection of American Literature, Beinecke Rare Book and Manuscript Library)

someone to interpret the emotions—the inner feelings— the dreams, even, of the great masses of us who are so far down in the scale of things. Dunbar treated of the same subjects as they applied in his day. And with his passing there was no one to take up the songs an igno- rant "black gal" sings down on Rampart St., for instance. There was no one who dared go beneath the surface of things and express in poetry the little witti- cisms of the convict—the gambler—the idler, or the "pimp." White men tried it and failed, and young poets of our Race studiously eschewed the subject. The reason, presumably the fear of antagonizing the white man who must print, and who must read the book, if it is to pay for itself.

Langston Hughes, with master strokes and fear- lessness, rips into the problem and lays it bare for all the world to see. The section of "Fine Clothes" devoted to the blues I passed over with almost cursory atten- tion. I know the blues fairly well, having heard them in their various ramifications practically all my life. My experience is that of the average person of my Race. To white readers of the book, however, I venture to say that this section and that devoted to "Hallelujahs" will bring real revelations and even thrills. For their sakes I am glad Langston Hughes included them.

But for me and for others of my Race there is real enjoyment—a sort of personal pride in those songs from Georgia Roads, the Railroad Avenue group and the Beale Street love. Perhaps no work in the entire book gives a clearer impression of the depth of feeling Mr. Hughes has on his subject than the sketch of "Ruby Brown." Here he gives vent to a feeling of long-suppressed (it seems), deep-burning, but calm resentment at conditions faced by young women of our Race in every small southern community today.

She was young and beautiful,
And golden like the sunshine,
That warmed her body,
And because she was Colored
Mayville had no place to offer her,
Nor fuel for the clean flame of joy
That tried to burn within her soul.

Well, Miss Ruby sits down one day and thinks out her problem, the results of which land her in a bordello where she is the toast of white men who

Pay more money to her now
Than they ever did before,
When she worked in their kitchens.

Ruby's case is typical. But for that matter, so are most of the other cases mentioned by Langston Hughes in "Fine Clothes." He has the faculty of transporting you into the midst of those about whom he is discoursing—you see them in their rollicking "Saturday night" at a "drag," and you dance along with the rest—or you stand on the bank of the Mississippi river with the "Ruined Gal" and sympathize with her even when she says:

Damn ma black old mammy's soul
For ever havin' a daughter.

What is more true to our lives than Mr. Hughes' "Feet of Jesus"? Who hasn't sat in one of our primitive churches where worshipers give full play to their emotions, and has not heard:

At de feet o' Jesus,
Sorrow like a sea.
Lordy, let yo' mercy
Come driftin' down on me.

At de feet o' Jesus,
At yo' feet I stand.
O, ma little Jesus,
Please reach out yo' hand.

Or this "prayer":

I ask you this:
Which way to go?
I ask you this:
Which sin to bear?
Which crown to put
Upon my hair?
I do not know,
Lord God,
I do not know.

Then comes what I consider the boldest, yet the most effective bit in the entire collection, "Mulatto."

I am your son, white man!
Georgia dusk
And the turpentine woods.
One of the pillars of the temple fell.

You are my son!
Like hell!

I wish I could quote the entire poem, but of course I can't. Mr. Hughes caught the very heart of the situation in that plaintive note of the "little yellow bastard boy" crying out in desperation, pointing an accusing finger at the slinking, shrinking, yet domineering thing that gave him being. I am your son, white man.

Commenting on his book in a letter to me, Mr. Hughes says: "It's harder and more cynical than my

first, and it's limited to an interpretation of the so-called 'lower classes,' the ones to whom life is least kind. I try to catch the hurt of their lives, the monotony of their 'jobs,' and the veiled weariness of their songs. They are the people I know best."

And they are the people we all know best, however much we seek to get away from them and submerge them under a blanket of aloofness. I am glad for "Fine Clothes" (in spite of its title), because I know it will be read by many, many white persons who can't help feel the real seriousness of Mr. Hughes' purpose, and who, consequently, will be led to wonder if after all these people, whom they are wont to despise, do think, dream, fight and love as the rest of them do. They may be led to look a little more tolerantly upon those who prepare their foods for them—even those who clean their "spittoons" and shine their shoes.

—*Chicago Defender*, part 2, 5 February 1927, p. 1

* * *

Bessie Smith, "The Empress of the Blues," one of the inspirations for Hughes's blues poems. In The Big Sea, he remembered her remark, "The trouble with white folks singing blues is that they can't get low down enough" (photograph by Carl Van Vechten, 3 February 1936; Library of Congress, Prints & Photographs Division, Carl Van Vechten Collection, courtesy of Carl Van Vechten Trust).

Walter F. White, a novelist and the assistant secretary of the NAACP, wrote this review.

The Growth of a Poet

It is probable that most of the sophisticated and near-sophisticated have by now heard Bessie or Clara Smith sing either in the flesh or on phonograph records one or more of the infinite number of songs known as "blues." If the prospective reader of Langston Hughes's "Fine Clothes to the Jew" (just published by Alfred A. Knopf) or his earlier "The Weary Blues" has not heard at least one of these songs as sung by a Negro singer, I urgently recommend that he do so before tackling the poems. For the blues are strictly limited both as to poetic pattern and meaning. As the name implies, blues are sung as plaintive expressions of utter despondency. Almost always there is expressed some idea of suicide through drowning or "laying ma head on de railroad track." Inevitably the repetition of a single emotion in time grows monotonous, and often triteness cannot be avoided because there are few changes to be rung on the blues theme. The human voice of a Bessie Smith is needed to transmute and vary the subtle overtones and in that manner give the needed variety.

So, too, is the form rigidly fixed, one line repeated and a third line to rhyme with the first two. In a paragraph Mr. Hughes explains that "sometimes the second line in repetition is slightly changed and sometimes, but very seldom, it is omitted. The mood of the Blues is almost always despondency, but when they are sung people laugh." Frequently a beautiful bit of imagery darts through one of these songs or a poignant catching up of a profound emotion in a single line. Take, for example, two stanzas of Mr. Hughes's "Homesick Blues" in which both of these gifts are seen:

De railroad bridge's
A sad song in de air.
De railroad bridge's
A sad song in de air.
Ever time de trains pass
I wants to go somewhere.

Homesick blues, Lawd,
'S a terrible thing to have,
Homesickness blues is
A terrible thing to have.
To keep from cryin'
I opens ma mouth and laughs.

———

Walter F. White, whose first novel, The Fire in the Flint *(1924), was one of the books that drew Van Vechten to African American culture (photograph by Carl Van Vechten, 12 July 1938; Yale Collection of American Literature, Beinecke Rare Book and Manuscript Library, courtesy of Carl Van Vechten Trust)*

It may be questioned, however, how much further blues can be utilized as poetry because of its rigid limitations. Out of the blues form it is possible and probable that a more inclusive poetic form may develop but that form would not be blues as the term is now interpreted. It will be interesting to watch these changes as they are developed by Mr. Hughes and others who may follow him in the growth of either a more universal medium of expression or a broadening of the scope of the moods themselves. Mr. Hughes's friends and admirers may perhaps have some apprehension that too diligent working of this vein may cramp him or lessen the fine, flowing, ecstatic sense of rhythm which he so undoubtedly possesses.

For he has seen the immense store of material for poetry which is in the life of the Negro. When he leaves the more confining form of the blues Mr. Hughes evokes magnificently stirring emotions from the life of Negro porters and prostitutes and others of humble estate. For example, take the last ten lines of this poem, "Brass Spittoons":

Hey, boy!
A bright bowl of brass is beautiful to the Lord.
Bright polished brass like the cymbals
Of King David's dancers,
Like the wine cups of Solomon.
    Hey, boy!
A clean spittoon on the altar of the Lord,
A clean bright spittoon all newly polished–
At least I can offer that.
    Com' mere, boy!

———

I would like to quote several other poems and give in Mr. Hughes's own words the fine flavor of his new book–poems like "Ruby Brown," "Porter," "Prayer Meeting," "Magnolia Flowers," "Song for a Dark Girl," "Laughers," or two or three others equally fine. But that would be fair neither to Mr. Hughes nor his publisher for then there would be some who would not buy the book. It is a book that should be bought and one that will grow upon its readers in its evocation of beauty and rhythm and color and warmth. And if the reader has heard Clara or Mamie Smith croon and moan the blues, the first eight and the last nine poems in "Fine Clothes to the Jew" won't seem as monotonous as they perhaps might otherwise be judged.

–*New York World,* 6 February 1927, p. 9M

* * *

Critic William M. Kelley wrote this review for the New York Amsterdam News, *an influential black weekly that had been published since 1909. Hughes responded specifically to the criticism of "Red Silk Stockings" in his essay "These Bad New Negroes: A Critique on Critics."*

Langston Hughes–The Sewer Dweller

About 100 pages of trash, that is about all we can say of "Fine Clothes to the Jew," by Langston Hughes. It is not even the kind of trash made by an accumulation of excelsior or straw or waste paper. Instead, it reeks of the gutter and sewer.

After reading it one feels that he has just passed through one of those Parisian sewers so well described by Victor Hugo in Les Miserables. True, on the way one passes openings where a little light and fresh air are permitted to penetrate the under-

ground passage, such as when one reads the nine poems grouped under the chapter heading Glory Hallelujah, and "Dressed Up" in the group, Beale Street Love, which shows that Mr. Hughes has both imagination and talent.

I had ma clothes cleaned
Just like new.
I put 'em on but
I still feels blue.

I bought a new hat,
Sho is fine,
But I wish I had back that
Old gal o' mine.

I got new shoes,–
They don't hurt ma feet,
But I ain't got nobody
For to call me sweet.

It is true that even the sewer is necessary, but we do not understand why so promising a poet as Hughes prefers to linger there and write the kind of dribble that characterizes his "Weary Blues" and the present volume.

We do not maintain that all poetry should be uplifting, or that it should deal exclusively with subjects foreign to everyday existence, but we do not believe that it should debase merely for the sake of debasing–to satisfy the morbid tendencies of a jazz-crazed world–as is done in "Red Silk Stockings."

Put on yu' red silk stockings,
Black gal.
Go out an' let de white boys
Look at yo' legs.

Ain't nothin' to do for you, no-how,
Round this town,–
You's too pretty.
Put on yo' red silk stockings, gal.
An' tomorrow's chile'll
Be a high yaller.

Go out an' let de white boys
Look at yo' legs.

If poetry of this type is the only kind white publishers will accept it may be that the world–both the black and the white world–would be just as well off without it.

–*New York Amsterdam News,* 9 February 1927, p. 22

* * *

Playwright, poet, and critic Margaret Larkin, who also worked as a publicist for labor organizations, wrote this review.

A Poet for the People

In casting about for a precise category in which to identify the work of Langston Hughes, I find that he might be acclaimed a new prophet in several fields, and very likely he does not think of himself as belonging to any of them.

There is still a great deal of talk about "native American rhythms" in poetic circles, and the desirability of freeing poetry from the stiff conventions which Anglo Saxon prosody inflicted upon it. In turning to the rhythm pattern of the folk "blues," Langston Hughes has contributed something of great value to other poets, particularly since he uses the form with variety and grace.

"De po' house is lonely,
An' de grave is cold.
O, de po' house is lonely,
De graveyard grave is cold.
But I'd rather be dead than
To be ugly an' old."

This apparently simple stuff is full of delicate rhythmic variety through which the long ripple of the form flows boldly. The "blues" are charming folk ballads and in the hands of this real poet present great possibilities for beauty.

Ever since I first heard Langston Hughes read his verse, I am continually wanting to liken his poems to those of Bobby Burns. Burns caught three things in his poems: dialect, speech cadence, and character of the people, so that he seems more Scotch than all of bonnie Scotland. It is a poet's true business to distil this pure essence of life, more potent by far than life ever turns out to be, even for poets. I think that Hughes is doing for the Negro race what Burns did for the Scotch—squeezing out the beauty and rich warmth of a noble people into enduring poetry.

In hearing a group of young poets reading their new poems to each other recently, I was struck with their common tendency to intricacy, mysticism, and preoccupation with brilliant technique. Their poems are competent and beautiful, and the antithesis of simple. To any but other poets, skilled in the craft, they are probably as completely mysterious as though in a foreign tongue. The machine age and the consequent decline of the arts has driven many poets and artists into the philosophy that art is the precious possession of the few initiate. Poets now write for the appreciation of other poets, painters are scornful of all but painters, even music, most popular of all the arts, is losing the common touch. Perhaps this is an inevitable development. Yet the people perish. Beauty is not an outworn ideal, for they still search for it on Fourteenth street. While the poets and artists hoard up beauty for themselves and each other, philosophizing upon the "aristocracy of art," some few prophets are calling for art to come out of rich men's closets and become the "proletarian art" of all the people.

Perhaps Langston Hughes does not relish the title of Proletarian Poet, but he deserves it just the same. "Railroad Avenue," "Brass Spittoons," "Prize Fighter," "Elevator Boy," "Porter," "Saturday Night," and the songs from the Georgia Roads, all have their roots deep in the lives of workers. They give voice to the philosophy of men of the people, more rugged, more beautiful, better food for poetry, than the philosophy of the "middle classes."

This is a valuable example for all poets of what can be done with simple technique and "every day" subjects, but it is particularly valuable, I believe, for other Negro poets. Booker T. Washington's adjuration to "educate yourself" has sunk too deep in the Race philosophy. As in all American life, there is a strong urge to escape life's problems by reaching another station. "The life of a professional man must surely be happier than that of a factory worker," America reasons. "A teacher must surely find greater satisfaction than a farmer." Poets, influenced by this group sentiment, want to write about "nicer" emotions than those of the prize fighter who reasons

Only dumb guys fight."
If I wasn't dumb
I wouldn't be fightin'
I could make six dollars a day
On the docks,
And I'd save more than I do now.
Only dumb guys fight."

or the pondering on circumstance of the boy who cleans spittoons

"Babies and gin and church
and women and Sunday
all mixed up with dimes and
dollars and clean spitoons
and house rent to pay.
  Hey, boy!
A bright bowl of brass is beautiful to the Lord.
Bright polished brass like the cymbals
Of King David's dancers,
Like the wine cups of Solomon.
  Hey, boy!"

Yet this, much more than the neurotic fantasies of more sophisticated poets, is the stuff of life.

There is evidence in this book that Langston Hughes is seeking new mediums, and this is a healthy sign. If he were to remain the poet of the ubiquitous "blues" he would be much less interesting. He will find new forms for himself, and I do not believe that he will lose his hold on the simple poignancy that he put into the "blues" as he adds to his poetic stature. The strong, craftsmanlike handling of "Mulatto," one of the best poems in the book, the delicate treatment of "Prayer," the effective rhythm shifts of "Saturday Night" are promises of growing power.

Not all of the poems of *Fine Clothes to the Jew* are of equal merit. Many of them are the product of too great facility. To be able to write easily is a curse that hangs over many a poet, tempting him to produce good verse from which the fine bead of true poetry is lacking. But even the most demanding critic cannot expect poets to publish perfect volumes. It ought to be enough to find one exquisite lyric like the "New Cabaret Girl" surcharged with an emotion kept in beautiful restraint,

"My God, I says,
You can't live that way!
Babe, you can't
Live that way!"

and here are many such.

—*Opportunity: A Journal of Negro Life*,
5 (March 1927): 84–85

On Critics

Hughes responded to conservative critics in an essay that was published in the 16 April 1927 issue of the Pittsburgh Courier. *The text for the following essay is the original typescript that Hughes mailed to Carl Van Vechten on 22 March. On the first page he added a handwritten note: "Dear Carlo, Here's the article I did for the Pittsburgh Courier at their request. Thought you might like to see it. Langston."*

These Bad New Negroes: A Critique on Critics

Tired of living penniless on bread and figs in Genoa, I found myself a job on a ship bound for New York in the fall, 1924. When, after many days of scrubbing decks on my part, the boat reached Manhattan there was a letter waiting for me from my mother saying, "We're living in Washington now. Come home." And I went.

I'd never been in Washington before but I found it a city as beautiful as Paris and full of nice colored people, many of them nice looking and living in nice houses. For my mother and me, the city was a sort of ancestral shrine of which I had heard much. The great John M. Langston, senator, educator, and grand-uncle of mine had once lived there. Indeed, I was to stop with descendants of his and, of course, I would meet the best people. And I did.

But since this is to be an article on literature and art, I must get on into the subject. For two years, working at sea and travelling, I had been away from books. Many of my own I had thrown into the ocean because I found life more attractive than the printed word. But now I wanted to read again and talk about literature so I set out to borrow, in good Negro fashion, a copy of Jean Toomer's Cane. "What!" said the well-bred Washington folk. "Cane?" they repeated, not many having heard of it. Then I was soon given to understand by the female heads of several nice families that Cane was a vulgar book and that no one read it. "Why do you young folks write that way?" they asked. I offered no protest for I had not heard the question before and I am not much at answering questions quickly. But, amazed, I thought how a prophet is without honor in his own country, since Jean Toomer was born and had lived in Washington. Cane had received critical recognition all over America, and even in Europe, as a beautiful book, yet in the society of the author's own home-town it was almost unknown. And those who knew it thought it something low and indecent. Whenever Cane was mentioned the best Washingtonians posted this question: "Why doesn't Jean Toomer write about nice people?" And I began to think they wanted to add, "Like ourselves."

When Rudolph Fisher's City of Refuge appeared in the Atlantic Monthly (Washington is Fisher's home-town, too) the best persons again asked the same thing: "Why can't you young folks write about nice people? Rudolph Fisher knows decent folks." And then I knew the "nice people" meant themselves.

Then Alain Locke's New Negro appeared on the scene with stories by Toomer, Fisher, Eric Waldron, Zora Hurston, Matheus, and none of them were nice stories in the Washington sense of the word. "Too bad," they said. But the storm broke on the Reiss drawings. They were terrible! And anyone defending them had to answer questions like these: "Why does he make his subjects so colored?" (As though they weren't colored.) And of the two school teachers pictured in the book: "Couldn't he find any better looking school teachers to paint than these two women?" (As though all teachers should resemble the high-yellow ladies dominating the Washington school system.) And always: "Does he call this art?" I said it was art and that the dark-skinned school teachers were beautiful. But one day a nice old grandmother, with whom I disliked to disagree, summed up everybody's aversion to Fisher, Toomer, Waldron, and the Reiss drawings in one indefinite but pregnant remark, "Lord help these bad New Negroes!"

Now that there has appeared in the colored press a definite but rather uncritical aversion to much of the work of the younger Negro writers and particularly myself; and because the Negro press reflects to a certain extent the minds of its readers, it is time to attempt to uncover the reasons for this dislike toward the "New Negro." I present these as possible solutions:

1. The best Negroes, including the newspaper critics, still think white people are better than colored people. It follows, in their minds, that since the drawings of Negroes do not look like the drawings of white people they are bad art.

2. The best Negroes believe that what white people think about Negroes is more important than what

Alain Locke, editor of the anthology The New Negro *(1925), which included ten poems by Hughes (Yale Collection of American Literature, Beinecke Rare Book and Manuscript Library)*

Negroes think about themselves. Then it follows that because a story by Zora Hurston does not tend to make white people think all Negroes good, then said story by Zora Hurston is a bad story.

3. Many of the so-called best Negroes are in a sort of nouveau riche class, so from the snobbishness of their positions they hold the false belief that if the stories of Fisher were only about better-class people they would be better stories.

4. Again, many of the best Negroes, including the newspaper critics, are not really cultured Negroes after all and, therefore, have little appreciation of any art and no background from which to view either their own or the white man's books or pictures.

Perhaps none of these reasons are true reasons but I offer them for consideration. Now I shall proceed to the defense.

Art is a reflection of life or an individual's comment on life. No one has labeled the work of the better known younger Negro writers as untrue to life. It may be largely about humble people, but three-fourths of the Negroes are humble people. Yet I understand these "best" colored folks when they say that little has been written about them. I am sorry and I wish some one would put them into a nice story or a nice novel. But I fear for them if ever a really powerful work is done about their lives. Such a story would show not only their excellencies but their pseudo-culture as well, their slavish devotion to Nordic standards, their snobbishness, their detachment from the Negro masses, and their vast sense of importance to themselves. A book like that from a Negro writer, even though true and beautiful, would be more thoroughly disliked than the stories of low-class Negroes now being written. And it would be more wrathfully damned than Nigger Heaven, at present vibrating throughout the land in its eleventh edition.

It seems to me too bad that the discussions of Mr. Van Vechten's novel in the colored press finally became hysterical and absurd. No book could possibly be as bad as Nigger Heaven has been painted. And no book has ever been better advertised by those who wished to damn it. Because it was declared obscene everybody wanted to read it and I'll venture to say that more Negroes bought it than ever purchased a book by a Negro author. Which is all very fine because Nigger Heaven is not a bad book. It will do nice people good to read it and maybe it will broaden their minds a bit. Certainly the book is true to the life it pictures. There are cabarets in Harlem and both white and colored people who are nationally known and respected can be found almost any night at Small's. I've seen ministers there,—nobody considers cabaret-going indecent any longer. And college boys, as you know, do have affairs with loose women. Some are even given allowances and put through medical school by such gen-

*Dust jacket for Carl Van Vechten's controversial 1926 novel,
which Hughes defended (Yale Collection of American
Literature, Beinecke Rare Book
and Manuscript Library)*

erous females. But nowhere in the novel does the author represent his college boy as a typical Negro college boy. And nowhere does he say he is writing about the whole Negro race. I admit I am still at a loss to understand the yelps of the colored critics and the reason for their ill-mannered onslaught against Mr. Van Vechten. The sincere, friendly, and helpful interest in things Negro of this sophisticated author, as shown in his published reviews and magazine articles, should at least have commanded serious, rather than vulgar, reviews of his book.

That many of the Negro write-ups of my own new collection of poems, Fine Clothes to the Jew, were unfavorable was not surprising to me. And to be charged with painting the whole Negro race in my poems did not amaze me either. Colored critics are given to accusing all works of art touching on the Negro of portraying and representing all Negro life. Porgy, about a beggar in Charleston, is said by them to picture all Negroes as beggars, yet nowhere does Du Bose Heyward imply such a thing. Newspaper critics, of course, came to the same amazing conclusion about Nigger Heaven picturing all

Negroes as cabaret goers. And now Fine Clothes to the Jew "low-rates" everybody of color, in their opinion.

In analyzing their reviews of my book their main objections against my work seem to be based on the reasons I am listing below with my own comments following:

1. White people will gain a bad impression of Negroes from my poems. This then implies that a Negro artist should create largely for the benefit of and for the approval of white people. In answering this I ask these questions: Does George Bernard Shaw write his plays to show Englishmen how good the Irish are? Do any of the great Russian writers write novels for the purpose of showing the perfections of the Russians? Does any true artist anywhere work for the sake of what a limited group of people will think rather than for the sake of what he himself loves and wishes to interpret? It seems to me that there are plenty of propagandists for the Negro, but too few artists, too few poets, too few interpreters and recorders of racial life, whether of the masses or of the best people.

2. My poems are indelicate. But so is life.

3. I write about "harlots and gin-bibers." But they are human. Solomon, Homer, Shakespeare, and Walt Whitman were not afraid or ashamed to include them.

4. "Red Silk Stockings." An ironical poem deploring the fact that in certain southern rural communities there is little work for a beautiful colored girl to do other than the selling of her body,—a fact for one to weep over rather than disdain to recognize.

5. I do not write in the conventional forms of Keats, Poe, Dunbar, or McKay. But I do not write chiefly because I'm interested in forms,—in making a sonnet or a rondeau. I write because I want to say what I have to say. And I choose the form which seems to me best to express my thoughts. I fail to see why I should be expected to copy someone else's modes of expression when it amuses me to attempt to create forms of my own. Certainly the Shakespearean sonnet would be no mould in which to express the life of Beale Street or Lenox Avenue. Nor could the emotions of State Street be captured in a rondeau. I am not interested in doing tricks with rhymes. I am interested in reproducing the human soul, if I can.

6. I am prostituting my talent. But even the income from a very successful book of poems is not worth the prostitution of one's talent. I make much more money as a bell-hop than as a poet.

7. I deal with low life. But I ask this: Is life among the better classes any cleaner or any more worthy of a poet's consideration?

8. Blues are not poetry. Those who have made a more thorough study of Negro folk verse than I, and who are authorities in this field, say that many Blues are excellent poetry. I refer to James Weldon Johnson, Dorothy Scarborough, Carl Van Vechten and H. O. Osgood in their published writings.

Jessie Redmon Fauset, Hughes, and Zora Neale Hurston at the entrance to Tuskegee Institute in Alabama. Hughes turned an invitation to read his poems at the June 1927 commencement of Fisk University into an extended summer tour of the South. He met Hurston in Mobile, Alabama, and traveled with her to Tuskegee, where Fauset was an invited speaker at a summer-school session (Langston Hughes Papers, James Weldon Johnson Collection in the Yale Collection of American Literature, Beinecke Rare Book and Manuscript Library).

Only the Best

As this letter indicates, Hughes was increasingly aware of his developing reputation as a literary artist.

Hughes to W. E. B. Du Bois, 11 February 1928

Dear Dr. Du Bois:

Please, if you have any old poems of mine in your office, do not print them in *The Crisis* as I'm afraid they're not up to the things I'm doing now. When I have some new poetry finished I shall be pleased to submit some of it to you. I'm always proud of *The Crisis* and proud when you print me there, that's why I want it to be my best poetry in your pages and not old things written years ago. Some months ago I asked for my old manuscripts in your office, but they couldn't be found. I was hoping they were really lost, but lately some of the poems have been in *The Crisis,* and I don't think they are quite good enough to be there so please throw them in your waste basket if there are any.

Sincerely,
Langston Hughes

—The Correspondence of W. E. B. Du Bois, Volume 1, Selections, 1877–1934, edited by Herbert Aptheker (Amherst: University of Massachusetts Press, 1973), p. 374

W. E. B. Du Bois (photograph by Carl Van Vechten, 18 July 1946; Library of Congress, Prints & Photographs Division, Carl Van Vechten Collection, courtesy of Carl Van Vechten Trust)

9. I am "supposed to be representative of Negro progress in the literary arts." To which I can only answer that I do not pretend, or ask anyone to suppose, that I officially represent anybody or anything other than myself. My poems are my own personal comments on life and represent me alone. I claim nothing more for them.

If the colored newspaper critics (excepting Dewey Jones and Alice Dunbar Nelson) choose to read only the words I write and not their meaning, if they choose to see only what they call the ugliness of my verse and not the protest against ugliness which my poems contain, what can I do? Such obtuse critics existed in the days of Wordsworth, Shelley, Burns, and Dunbar,—great poets with whose work I dare not compare my own. Burns was maligned because he did not write of Scottish nobles. And as Miss Nannie Burroughs says, "to come down to the nasty now," Jean Toomer is without honor in Washington. But certainly my life has been enlivened by the gentle critics who called me a "gutter-rat" and "sewer-dweller" right out in print! Variety, even in the weekly press, is the spice of criticism.

Since I am said to be the "baddest" of the bad New Negroes, I may as well express my own humble opinion on my young contemporaries, although I may vary with the race newspapers and the best Negroes. To me the stories of Rudolph Fisher are beautiful although he deals with common folks. To me it seems absurd to say that they are not elevating to the race. The stories of Sherwood Anderson deal largely with people of the same classes but white America calls him one of the greatest of the moderns. If Rudolph Fisher can write beautifully about a poor Negro migrant from the South, more power to him. A well-written story, no matter what its subject, is a contribution to the art of the Negro and I am amazed at the educated prudes who say it isn't. Jean Toomer is an artist to be proud of. Wallace Thurman, Countee Cullen with his marvellous command of technique and his poems of passion and free love, Zora Hurston with her fine handling of Negro dialect, Edward Silvera and the newer poets, all are contributing something worthwhile to the literature of the race. To me it seems that we have much to be proud of in the work of these younger colored writers whom the old lady in Washington so dissapprovingly called the "bad New Negroes."

–Langston Hughes Papers, James Weldon Johnson Collection in the Yale Collection of American Literature, Beinecke Rare Book and Manuscript Library

A Man of Letters

Hughes attended Lincoln University in Pennsylvania, one of the oldest black colleges, from February 1926 until his graduation in June 1929. In The Big Sea, *he writes that he was a student there at "the height of the Negro Renaissance," noting that he spent his "week-ends and holidays in New York." As his letters to correspondents such as the Jamaican-born writer Claude McKay and Wallace Thurman show, Hughes remained very much involved in the Harlem literary scene.*

Claude McKay's first novel, Home to Harlem *(1928), presented a gritty portrait of the black working class, emphasizing prostitution, gambling, and cabaret nightlife rather than the more polite world of the Harlem intelligentsia. Hughes wrote this letter from Lincoln University.*

Hughes to Claude McKay, 5 March 1928

Dear Claude,

I was mighty pleased to have your letter and right on the heels of it came your book,—which is the most exciting thing in years. Undoubtedly, it is the finest thing "we've" done yet, and I don't mean limited by the "we." It's a very fine novel,—as fine as Baroja writing about Madrid, or Ibañez in his early stories of the poor of Valencia, or Carco in Paris….Lord, I love the whole thing. It's so damned real!….Has there ever been another party anywhere in literature like Gin-Head Susy's? I thought that was marvellously well-done….Jake and Ray and Rose and the landladies, and the dining car folks are all too alive to be in a book….I'm enclosing what I wrote to Ruth Raphael about it as publicity comment. I hope it will be a great sales success, too….It's going to be amusing reading what the colored papers will say about it. They will want to tear you to pieces, I'm sure, but since they used up all their bad words on <u>Nigger Heaven</u>, and the rest on me,—I don't know what vocabulary they have left for you….Didn't Keats say "Beauty is truth"?….But I don't suppose a one of the Negro editors will see that <u>Home to Harlem</u> is Beauty….But maybe you've done it so well that they can't help themselves. I hope so.

I suppose you'll have a deluge of letters for the next few months, but if you can write me before summer, let me know where you are. I may be over when school closes. Not certain yet, though….I guess you know most of the literary news over this way: a Marin novel due; Bud Fisher novel, comedy vein, for fall; Nella Imes novel, slight and delicate, this spring; a play and novel by Wallace Thurman next season, I think….and God knows how many books by white people about Negroes due soon, and due to be due……Your novel ought to give a second youth to the Negro vogue. Some said it would die this season.....Have you seen Walter White around your way? What you doing from now on,–still remaining an expatriot?...Couldn't you do a play, maybe? Our theatre's way behind the rest of our world. Are you all healthy again and happy? You deserve to be....Wish I were in town so I could send you papers and magazines once in a while. We're two hours and more from Philly so I only see them in the library. The colored press is always amusing. But the best thing lately has been an interview which Ethel Waters gave to a white paper in Cleveland in which she said (quite truthfully) that the most successful Negroes on the American stage got to be that way by playing just what they are,–darkies....Of course, the best people are about to expire over that. They are so delicate! Locke is at Fisk for a term....artist from Chicago, Motley, is holding the first Negro one-man show in a down town gallery. His pictures are selling....Countee in this month's Opportunity says it isn't always good to tell the truth....He's to be married at Easter. I'm going to be an usher with a swallow-tail coat on. It'll be grand.....Enjoy yo' damn self!

Sincerely,
Langston

From note to Ruth Raphael:

"Home to Harlem is amazingly real and true to the life it pictures. What Pio Baroja has done for Madrid and Francis Carco for Paris, Claude McKay in this novel, does for Harlem,–that is, he makes alive and singing, alive and terrible, the movements of the lower classes at work and at play and at love. Beautiful because it is true and fascinating because it is so vividly alive, this book is, to my mind, the first real flower of the Negro Renaissance."

–L.H.
–Langston Hughes Papers, James Weldon Johnson
Collection in the Yale Collection of American
Literature, Beinecke Rare Book
and Manuscript Library

* * *

In this letter, typed at Lincoln University, Hughes brings McKay up to date on literary and cultural events in New York. He uses the word "Niggerati," a term coined by Zora Neale Hurston for the writers, artists, and intellectuals of the Harlem Renaissance.

Hughes to McKay, 13 September 1928

Dear Claude,

I am always sorry I answer letters so badly. I think of you so often and write you so seldom,–which seems to be my way with all the people I care anything about! Letters from people I never heard of always get answered regularly and promptly,–but I take all that as a part of helping my publishers sell my books,–which I have discovered is much more work than writing them.....I no longer read my poetry to ladies clubs, Y. W. C. A., and the leading literary societies in places like Columbus,–as I did for two winters. I began to hate my own stuff as much as I do Browning or Longfellow. And being "an example" to little kids in schools and listening to teachers telling what a model to pattern after I am rather shamed me,–because I have never felt like a good example,–and am worse at making inspirational speeches than I am at answering letters. I like to read to kids, though. They always strike me as having much more sense than grownups, but I don't like being exhibited before them like a prize dog. Did you ever have to go through anything like that when you were first published? I don't suppose you'd have stood it, would you? I don't see how I did it either, but sometimes I wanted the fifty dollars and sometimes I thought I was helping charity or race relations or some other dull cause, or again I didn't like to say "No" to a friend or old schoolmate. And last summer it was the only way I could discover to get my fare paid into the South,–but once there I threw my books away and lived in New Orleans almost a month before anybody who wore a necktie discovered I was there,–and when they did I got a job to Cuba on a tramp and failed to appear at the club meeting called in my honor.....Did you ever visit the Chinatown in Havana where thousands of them sleep on shelfs in warehouse-like boarding places waiting for a chance to come to the States? Or visit the whore-houses like kids visit the zoo, standing for hours in groups gazing at one woman and then moving on to the next doorway to gaze for a while at another?.....You've been at Tuskegee, haven't you? Do you remember the power house dynamo that can be heard at night beating and pulsing like a hidden tom-tom at the heart of the place? And the nice Negroes living like parasites on the body of a dead dream that was alive once for Booker Washington? I want to do an article, or even a novel, about that place. I suppose it will be a great university sometime with the Veterans Hospital for a med school.....This summer I went North for awhile,–Provincetown and Boston. I liked the beaches at Cape Cod and the clams,–but the artists are awful!.....In Boston I didn't go anear Harvard,– although I went there largely to see what the old place looked like,–but I met a colored lady who looked like she possessed six degrees, wore nose glasses and all,– and had been in jail eighteen times and in the pen once for robbing her clients,–Chinese laundrymen and white clerks,–but she was still operating undaunted. I never saw so dignified a daughter of joy before, but she said she had always worn pince-nez, and Boston has a cultural atmosphere,–even if the cops don't want colored ladies to associate with white gentlemen!

I've just come from New York so I'll give you the news. I may hit something that Thurman or some of the other guys haven't told you yet.....Anyway, the white woman who took Josephine Baker to Europe is now after Paul Robeson with the law because he refuses to come back from London to be in a revue which I once wrote for her years ago and which I can't much blame him for not wanting to perform in. However, she has him under contract,–but their social success in London, according to Mrs. Robeson has been amazing,–teas with duchesses and cocktails with Lords,–so they don't want to come back. The show is all being done over a la Broadway, anyhow, and I can't stay in town to work on it now that college is open so I suppose I'll have little left in it when it is produced, if ever it is produced, so I don't particulary care wheather Paul comes back or not......Porgy opens in London Easter Monday after a winter tour here. Almost every production on Broadway has a Negro or two in it these days and almost anybody who looks niggerish can get a job.....But leading men must still be white blacked up, if the play calls for their speaking to white ladies on the stage. Such is the case in "Goin' Home", laid in France after the war when the colored troups were on their way back leaving the little Francaises behind. The play is pure hokum done in chocolate, but rather amusing and simple minded.....The New York theatre, the part that isn't gone black, has gone in for gangwar and underworld stuff, and is producing some amazingly life-like and tremendously entertaining pictures of modern Chicago and Tenth Avenue scarcely less melodramatic than the reality.....The papers are full of real gangwar stuff this week. And THE GRAPHIC seems to be always on the spot with its cameras whenever a victim is popped off. Yesterday the whole front page was devoted to a picture of a falled crook dying in a saloon door.....A troup of colored actors have gone to the coast, too, and the rumor is that all the big companies are planning a colored production or so soon.....Grant Still has set a song of mine called THE BREATH OF A ROSE that is so modern that nobody can sing it.....VOODOO, a Negro opera by Freeman, opened Monday. Everybody in Harlem expected it to be punk like most of Freeman's former things, but the SUN gave it an amazing review, so maybe it's good. Anyway I hope so. This Johnny Spielt Auff or whatever it is that the Met is putting on this winter sounds awful,–but it's supposed to be a jazz opera. I can't imagine those fat singers at the Met waddling around in a jazz opera made in Berlin. But if it isn't good, I guess it will at least be funny.....Did you like Bud Fischer's book? Too much surface,–is the verdict of the niggerati. They expected better things of Bud, they say, and the colored papers don't seem to have gotten insulted over it yet. Or maybe you killed all the critics with your brick. Nella Larsen is said to have finished another novel; Walter White a book on lynching; Eric his Panama canal volumn; and Wallie his "The Blacker the Berry" which is due out in January.....Harlem cabarets are disgracefully white. The only way Negroes get in nowadays is to come with white folks, whereas it used to be the other way around.....Too bad you missed Countee and Harold. Locke was in Spain but I guess you didn't see him.....The phonographs are turning out some marvellous Negro records this year. Have you got a vic over there?? I hope you aren't bothered with radios very much. All the lunch rooms and restaurants in Harlem have them now so one no longer eats in peace. They let them run wide open, picking up anything from the Buffalo Jazzers to the lectures on the correct way to write a social letter.....The prohibition war over here is too funny for words,–and the licker is too bad to drink! I don't think it's worth the raids,–but the cops seem to like it. They take all they can get for themselves.....Niggers and machines,–whats going to happen when they really get acquainted? Have you read Paul Morand's MAGIE NOIRE? I just got it.....Did you ever discover if Carco was really rotten or not as a writer? Do you like bull fights? I loved them.....Do you want to come back to New York? I imagine it would bore you sick now.....I don't quite know why I'm so tired of it.....This is my last year at Lincoln. You see, I didn't go to Howard while I was in Washington, so with only a year at Columbia, I had to do three more here. I don't mind it so much, since I have nothing more amusing to do anyway. There's no self-discipline to it,–no more than it takes for me to remain anywhere six months straight.....I don't suppose you mind what Du Bois says? Who does? Some of the things the CRISIS does are too stupid to repeat,–so I'm not amazed at your poem story. After I had asked for the return of all my kid poetry they kept right on printing it. And after a second request for its return they even printed one poem with ––'s in place of my name! It amused me so much that I didn't get angry. They must have needed it badly or something. But it was so awful....I suppose you saw Allison Davis's article last month. I had to send a letter about that,–not that I cared what he said about me or my work,–but I didn't think he ought to blame Mr. Van Vechten for my defects because if I'm ruined, I ruined myself, and nobody else had a hand in it, and certainly not Mr. Van Vechten whom I hadn't met when many of the poems were already old.....But otherwise who cares what people say about your work?

When I'm done with a poem or a book I can't be bothered arguing over it forever. I imagine if I ever wrote a
play I would be bored sick if I ever had to look at it
more than once.....I don't see how artists stand their
own pictures on their own walls. I like to create things
but I don't like them around afterwards.....Writing is
like travelling,—it's wonderful to go somewhere but you
get tired of staying, and I've never stayed six months in
any one place I've ever wanted to go back to,—except
New York and if there were any other place at all like
it, I wouldn't want to go there again.....Did HOME
TO HARLEM come out in England, too? I was
awfully glad about its success. It's so alive! I love it as
much as any book I know.....I imagine your second
one will be great. When does it come out? Do you
know yet? And where are you going from Barcelona?
And why?

I'm doing a dozen or so short stories and some
articles which I may sell later on. I wrote a few poems
this summer, too, but I seem to enjoy prose more now.

Thurman is married, too,—a very nice girl who
was teaching at Hampton,—and a very efficient typist,
which isn't a bad combine for a literary man who
doesn't like to copy his own manuscripts.....There
seems to have been some hold up on Wallie's play but
I'm hoping it will be put on soon because it sounds like
a good one. And he has two others on the road to completion to bring forward if the first one is a hit.

Best of luck to you. I'm anxiously awaiting the
new novel.

Sincerely,

Langston

—Langston Hughes Papers, James Weldon Johnson
Collection in the Yale Collection of American
Literature, Beinecke Rare Book
and Manuscript Library

* * *

*In this undated letter that was likely written in 1929,
Hughes responds to the publication of Thurman's* The Blacker
the Berry. *He refers to awards made by the Harmon Foundation, established in 1922 by a white real-estate developer, William E. Harmon, to recognize African American achievements in
the arts, music, literature, and other fields of endeavor. Hughes
won a Harmon award—$400 and a gold medal—for achieve-
ment in literature in 1931.*

Hughes to Wallace Thurman, circa 1929

Dear Wallie,
It's a gorgeous book that nobody but a brand new nigger would dare write and I am sure it will complicate
things immeasurably for all the associations, leagues,

and federations, as well as for the seal-of-high-and-holy-
approval Harmon Awards and even reverberate in the
midst of the Nations and Worlds Any Other Day But
This.....And what with two more plays and another
novel, you yourself are a great and nobel example to the
Negro race, going in boldly for a literary career and not
deigning to hit a tap of any other kind of work—with or
without the doctor's orders! May the Gods preserve you
in your thorny way and give you extra appendages like
Mercury so that you may tread with winged heels and
so avoid the rocks and stones. For deep are the pits
thereof for he who falls in mud......And you are only
21 or is it 23 and Youth and Blackness ought to make
you the marvel of the age, especially since Aunt Hagar
has now knocked down all the old ones, and you still
have fifty years yet in which to be a young and new
Negro yourself.....I really do like the book very much
and shall use it for prescribed reading for every English
class I ever teach, as well as for Christmas presents for
the next decade. When is it due to appear?....I didn't
find a great many things to correct (that I could detect)
and I'm sending you my notes on it, bit by bit. I enjoyed

*Langston Hughes and Wallace Thurman, probably in Carmel,
California, May 1935 (Langston Hughes Papers, James
Weldon Johnson Collection in the Yale Collection of
American Literature, Beinecke Rare Book and
Manuscript Library)*

Hughes with his mother at his Lincoln University graduation,
June 1929 (Yale Collection of American Literature,
Beinecke Rare Book and Manuscript Library)

AFTER ALL THESE YEARS and have given away half my clothes (my few clothes) to the village boys because I'm too lazy to start packing them. Besides who wants the same old clothes forever! I used to feel like that about books, too, and once threw my entire library into the sea book by book after I left Columbia. (However, this is not a suit by suit performance; rather only a shirt by shirt.) I am undecided as to whether I should throw away my valuable correspondance during my collegiate years or not–leaving the autographs and slanders to posterity, or tug them by the suit case load to the eastern shores or where ever else I go. Would you, for example, care to see your noble letters in the HARLEM LITERARY MUSEUM fifty years after my death, all open to the public, at least twenty years before your own demise? Or in the hands of some rich autograph collector?....But I do not think I can carry them this hot weather, and I don't think I can burn them either because it would take too long to sort them out and see which ones are not from people that I might later want to blackmail....so I think I shall continue to play AFTER ALL THESE YEARS....It seems that I had something of importance to tell you in this letter but I can't for the life of me think what it was....Anyhow, will you kindly come on back to Harlem so that you can be lynched personally by W. E. B. D. when Aunt Hager finishes her assalt on all the high males still virgin in their innocence of what cometh upon them. Indeed the second renaissance beginneth with this tearing of the veil.

I'll be seeing you–
Lang
–Langston Hughes Papers, James Weldon Johnson
Collection in the Yale Collection of American
Literature, Beinecke Rare Book
and Manuscript Library

* * *

In the following letter, Hughes discusses the downside of life at Lincoln University and muses on the poor health of the "Niggerati."

Hughes to Thurman, 29 July 1929

Monday July 29, 1929 (full date for benifit of literary historian) Lincoln University, Pa., Box 36, (full place, ditto) Signed by my own hand. L.H.

Dear Wallie,
I am sorry to hear about your being ill–but anyway I see you're still able to use the typewriter so that's something. Zora has been sick in a Florida hospital, too. Thought it was her stomach but discovered it was her liver, at the last moment, so she's on the road to recovery now. Two

reading it greatly. A bee stung me in the left eye today as I was watching honey being removed from the eaves of the house where I board, so forgive me if I seem a little caustic in the latter passages, since my sight is limited.....If you'll be so kind, maybe I'll send you something to razz for me some day soon.....As it is now, I'm about to fold my tents and steal away into the fastnesses of Maryland and points both south and north, so unless you answer immediately, write me hereafter through Knopf as my address will be in my hat band for the next month or so, or year or so, I don't know. I've got plenty of amusing things I want to do, but between what one *has* to do and what one wants to do there is often a terrible tangle, is there not? However, quien sabe? I usually manage to come out having done in some fashion just what I wanted to do, although sometimes mired in it long after I've ceased the wanting. Nevertheless, I know quite well one must pay prices, and have long been able to calculate in advance.....I've done nothing all week but play a marvellous old record by Ethel Waters called

July 15, 1929

Therein lies the difference perhaps between talent and genius — talent is pathetic, genius is tragic when most intense. Pathos belongs to talent, true tragedy to genius alone. ⸺

Talent picks up the obvious and uses it cleverly. Genius creates anew out of the earth.

August 1, 1929

To create a Negro culture in America — a real, solid, sane, racial something growing out of the folk life, not copied from another, even though surrounding, race.

August 2, 1929

Thank them for what they did — and forget what they failed tot do.

Page from Hughes's journal, which he kept irregularly while working on his first novel (Langston Hughes Papers, James Weldon Johnson Collection in the Yale Collection of American Literature, Beinecke Rare Book and Manuscript Library)

of my friends and classmates who graduated with me, immediately had a nervous breakdown the week following and are still suffering. I have tried in vain for two years to have one and can't—so that I could rest. I recall with ever recuring pleasure my three weeks in the hospital that time I got mad at my father in Mexico and all my red corpulses turned white. I never enjoyed myself so much before nor since, being waited on and wheeled about by lovely nurses, and having nothing, absolutely nothing, to do. Not even the neccessity of being bored. I don't suppose I shall ever be in a hospital again for so trivial a cause. It seems that I can't get anything worng with my heart either. Nothing will fail me. I'm trying now to cough every morning, but without much success. I think a nice long hospital would do me so much good. There being no more nice, long colleges to do nothing in......Poor Locke had a heart attack, lay on the floor all night, and missed his sailing. I think I told you. It seems that all the niggeratti's going under—then going off and resting. He's on his way to Manheim now to take the cure (plus baths), you're in Salt Lake being cared for, hand and foot, no doubt by a darling grandmother....And here am I broken hearted—not even in love any more. She's gone home to her people taking several of my books and one ring (that someone else had given me.).....Even my kid brother refused to go to summer school, as dumb as he is, because he felt that he needed the outdoor air of a Massachusetts summer camp. And my mother has wearied her ankles working, so she is going home to Kansas day after tomorrow!.....I think I shall sit out in the sun for the next week and get a sun-stroke, then see if the black intelligentzia will rally to the aid of a poor New Negro (still quite young.) I'm doing my best to keep literary.....Did I tell you that someone tried to rob, assualt, or otherwise molest me when I first returned from N. Y.? I live in the oldest, largest, darkest, and most remote dormitory on the campus, third floor north-east corner, by myself. (Said residence donated to me by the University for literary purposes). Well, I hadn't been here anytime before, about midnight one evening while I was still up, some prowler or other by unlocking the door tried to get into my room, but in reality the door was already unlocked so what they did in turning the key was really to lock it, and when I got up and yelled hearing the key turn, they fled leaving the key in the lock and I was locked in all night, until next morning I called the campus janitor to let me out. (Wasn't anxious to get out beforehand, anyway.) You see, the villagers think I'm rich because I spend the summer here and do nothing, so maybe they planned, whoever it was, to take my cash, my typewriter, or my I know not what. But anyway I now lock up quite securely every night and play Bessie Smith on the victrola so I wouldn't hear

them if they came.....In the day time I occassionally practice on prose technique while waiting for imformation, (I mean inspiration) to descend upon me like a dove and lift me above mere writing. But the appearance of two or three nice checks recently from book reviews and German translations of Blues (God knows how they did it—perhaps if I could read them, I *would* get sick) lead me to think of seeking the sea shore or the mountain heights for the rest of the season. Or the eastern shore of Maryland across the Chesapeak Bay, which they tell me is like Georgia, it's so remote, and it's Negroes are so nappy headed. And they eat oysters all the year around. It's not far away. All one does is go to Baltimore and take a Jim Crow boat to the land of miscegenation where every colored lady has at least six little half-breads for practice before she gets married to a Negro. And where the word Mammy is still taken seriously, and the race is so far back that it has an illimitable potential— like me!.....Yes, I do intend to teach in the remote future when hunger and old age and dire neccessity come upon me. (The fall is quite remote!) And as for Harlem, alas, all the cabarets have gone white and the Sugar Cane is closed and everybody I know is either in Paris or Hollywood or sick. And Bruce wears English suits!.....Finish your talkie, if need be, but for crying out loud, don't die if cod liver oil can save you. I destest talkies, but funerals are even worse. I think I shall be creamated and put in a jar, and then sent on a trans-Atlantic flight......Will you kindly write more about the renaissance of the race in the West, and who's connected with which in the Hollywood scramble....Or will I have to come out there to see for myself?.....God what a child I have been.....(When?).....The German papers say I'm still quite young.....But I'm in no mood to wax eloquent over trifles and I can only think about what I wouldn't write if the doctor would let me.....Who is a nice family doctor in New York? I may need one.....How much do divorces cost and what are the grounds? (Why must it be grounds— Oh, Lord, the bitter dregs!—says he who drains the cup.)....I believe I'll go to Canada instead of Maryland where licker's still what it used to be. Even the owner of Small's Paradise summers in Quebec.....I think my nerves need wine.....Are you taking the waters at the Salt Lake......Don't be like that!

If you need anything I can send you, let me know.

(This last is real!)

Sincerely, your
friend,
Langston
(Hughes—for the sake of literary history.
This letter guaranteed
authentic—price
to museums
$15,000
cash
!

Turning to the World: 1930 – 1939

In February 1930 Hughes submitted the manuscript of his first novel, *Not Without Laughter,* to Blanche Knopf, who had accepted his first volume of poems for publication. Another strong woman who had taken an interest in the writer's career, Charlotte van der Veer Quick Mason, a wealthy philanthropist and patron of the arts, had financially supported Hughes during his work on the novel. For his part, Hughes provided the elderly woman with companionship and shared with her his developing artistic sensibilities and works in progress. Mason also helped fund Hughes's trip to Cuba, which he arranged upon completion of the novel.

Upon his arrival in Havana on 25 February 1930, Hughes began making contacts with Cuban artists and intellectuals. José Antonio Fernández de Castro, a newspaper editor, introduced Hughes to the poet Nicolás Guillén. The two poets established an enduring friendship based on their mutual admiration for one another's work and their desire to create a distinctly racial art. (Guillén later became a central figure of the *Négritude* movement, which shifted the concept of "blackness" from a position of subjugation and negativity to one of power and beauty.) Invigorated by the artistic and intellectual camaraderie he found in Cuba, Hughes returned home in early March to pursue new writing projects.

Hughes, as photographed by Carl Van Vechten, 29 February 1936 (Library of Congress, Prints & Photographs Division, Carl Van Vechten Collection, courtesy of Carl Van Vechten Trust)

Hughes spent much of spring 1930 working with Zora Neale Hurston on the folk opera *Mule Bone*. Hurston, whom Hughes befriended during the heyday of the Harlem Renaissance, had not yet established herself in the literary world to the degree that Hughes had, and she believed that the collaboration would benefit the two writers financially and enhance her own artistic development and reputation. Charlotte Mason, who provided financial support to Hurston as well as Hughes, encouraged the project, for she believed a folk opera provided a perfect means of exploring her fascination with the "primitive." The collaboration between the writers soured, however, and the collapse of the project was quickened by the painful dissolution of the Hughes-Mason relationship. "Godmother," as Mason liked to be called, was displeased with Hughes's work ethic and the direction in which he seemed to be heading aesthetically. Hughes, for his part, resented the control Mason tried to exercise over his life and art. By the end of the year, Hughes's relationships with Hurston and Mason were effectively over. Even the summer publication and subsequent positive reception of *Not Without Laughter* could do little to ease the pain Hughes felt from these ruptures.

After spending the first three months of 1931 with his mother in Cleveland, Hughes in early April set out with artist Zell Ingram on a road trip to Florida. At Key West the two friends booked passage to Cuba, seeing Havana and Santiago before continuing on to their ultimate destination, Haiti. At Port-au-Prince, Hughes observed both extreme poverty and immense wealth and was struck by the degree to which the U.S. military occupation of the small island had promoted segregationist practices. While he enjoyed exploring the culture of Haiti and was pleased to meet poet Jacques Roumain, Hughes was deeply affected by the suffering he witnessed. The trip resulted in some of his most politically charged writings, which he published in the *Crisis* and the communist magazine *New Masses*.

In July 1931 Hughes returned to Florida, where he met with the educator and activist Mary McLeod Bethune, who encouraged him to make a reading tour through the South. Supported by a fellowship from the Rosenwald Fund, Hughes began his four-month tour that November, visiting historically black schools and taking notes on the state of race relations. Hughes was particularly troubled by the case of the "Scottsboro Boys," in which nine black youths who had been accused of raping two white women in Alabama had been sentenced by all-white juries to the electric chair. His January 1932 visit with the accused youths in their Birmingham prison cells led Hughes to publish bold works of poetry, prose, and drama about the case in journals such as *New Masses* and *Contempo*.

Further affirming his commitment to the radical Left, Hughes sailed for the Soviet Union in June 1932 to make a never-completed movie about U.S. race relations for the Meschrabpom film company. He remained abroad for a year, traveling throughout Soviet Central Asia and writing his impressions for the Soviet newspaper *Izvestia*. While he was abroad Knopf published *The Dream Keeper and Other Poems* that summer to generally positive reviews. In fall 1932 *Popo and Fifina,* a children's book he co-authored with Arna Bontemps, was published by Macmillan, and in December the magazine *Negro Worker* featured his controversial poem "Goodbye Christ."

In June 1933 Hughes left the Soviet Union to travel to Korea, China, and Japan; in August he returned to the United States, where he took up residence in Carmel, California, at the home of his friend Noel Sullivan. He worked steadily on his short stories, which Knopf published the following spring in the collection *The Ways of White Folks,* and attended meetings of the John Reed Club to support workers engaged in the International Longshoremen's Association strike. Upon receiving news of his father's death in October 1934, he traveled that winter to Mexico; he returned to California in June 1935 and was back in New York in September to attend the opening of his play *Mulatto* on Broadway.

Hughes began his final sojourn abroad of the decade when he sailed to Europe in summer 1937 to speak against Fascism at the Second International Writers' Congress in Paris and to report on the Spanish Civil War for the *Afro-American* newspapers. Supporting the troops loyal to the anti-fascist Spanish Republic, Hughes traveled with Guillén and wrote steadily at the center in Madrid that housed the Alianza de Intelectuales Antifascistas, an organization composed of artists and intellectuals who used their various talents to disseminate pro-Loyalist information throughout Spain. Hughes befriended Ernest Hemingway while he sent dispatches to the United States. After returning to the United States in January 1938, Hughes worked with his friend Louise Thompson to launch the Harlem Suitcase Theatre, which premiered his play *Don't You Want to Be Free?* in April. That spring the communist International Workers Order published his small book of poems *A New Song*.

During the last year and a half of the decade, Hughes faced personal difficulties, begining with the death of his mother on 3 June 1938. The following year his screenplay for the movie *Way Down South*, which he had co-authored with actor Clarence Muse, was attacked for perpetuating the worst stereotypes of African Americans. Undeterred, however, Hughes at the end of the decade was back at Sullivan's home in Carmel, working on his autobiography.

Laughin' Just to Keep from Cryin'

In this excerpt from his autobiography, Hughes remembers the period from February 1926 to spring 1930, in which he accepted the support of two wealthy white women. Hughes and Amy Spingarn, the wife of NAACP executive Joel Spingarn, had begun a long-term friendship after their first meeting in 1925. Without seeking to direct Hughes, she helped him with his expenses at Lincoln University and sometimes invited him to her estate. Hughes's second patron, Charlotte Mason, whom Hughes first visited at her Manhattan home in April 1927, became involved in his life to an extraordinary degree. Without giving the name of his benefactor, Hughes describes the range of Mason's generosity and the tensions that attended his acceptance of her assistance.

Patron and Friend

While I was at Lincoln, I spent several pleasant weekends in the spring or fall with Joel and Amy Spingarn at their country place, Troutbeck, that had once been the old farm of John Burroughs, the naturalist, where his trout pool is still preserved. I met the Spingarn sons and daughters, who were also in college or prep school. And I saw the beautiful medieval virgin in wood that Mrs. Spingarn had brought from Europe. She had there, too, a tiny hand press, and later published a small volume of my poems, in a limited edition on hand-made paper, a collection of lyrics called *Dear Lovely Death*.

The Spingarns were charming, quiet people. Joel Spingarn told me much about the early days of the National Association for the Advancement of Colored People, in which he had a great interest as one of the founders and later as its President. He told me, too, about his long acquaintanceship with Dr. DuBois and other Negro leaders. And his brother, Arthur, who has one of the largest collections of Negro books in America, often spoke of the work of the older Negro authors like Chesnutt, my fellow Clevelander, and of others at the beginning of our literary history, of whom, until then, I had never heard.

During my years at Lincoln, on one of my week-end visits to New York, a friend took me to call on a distinguished and quite elderly white lady who lived on Park Avenue in a large apartment, with attendants in livery at the door and a private elevator-landing. I found her instantly one of the most delightful women I had ever met, witty and charming, kind and sympathetic, very old and white-haired, but amazingly modern in her ideas, in her knowledge of books and the theater, of Harlem, and of everything then taking place in the world.

Amy Spingarn at Troutbeck, her estate in Duchess County, New York (Arnold Rampersad, The Life of Langston Hughes. *Volume I: 1902–1941: I, Too, Sing America [1986]; Bruccoli Clark Layman Archives)*

Her apartment was many floors above the street and there was a view of all New York spread out beneath it. Her rooms were not cluttered with furniture or objects of art, but every piece was rare and beautiful. When I left, after a delightful evening, she pressed something into my hand. "A gift for a young poet," she said. It was a fifty-dollar bill.

From Lincoln, I wrote her and thanked her for the gift. In reply, she asked me to dine with her and her family on my next trip to New York. At dinner we had duck and wild rice. And for dessert, ice cream on a large silver platter, surrounded by fresh strawberries. The strawberries were served with their green stems still on them, the tiny red fruit being very pretty around the great mound of ice cream on the silver platter.

Carefully, I removed the green stems and put them on the side of my plate. But when I had finished eating the berries and ice cream, I noticed that no one else at the table had left any stems on the plates. Their ice cream and all was gone. I couldn't imagine what

*Charlotte Mason, whom Hughes affectionately called "Godmother"
(photograph by James Weldon Johnson; Yale Collection
of American Literature, Beinecke Rare Book and
Manuscript Library)*

they had done with their stems. What did one do with strawberry stems on Park Avenue? Or were these a very special kind of strawberry stem that you could eat? Or had I committed some awful breach of etiquette by removing my strawberry stems by hand and putting them in plain view of everyone on the side of my plate? I didn't know. I was worried and puzzled.

As the Swedish maids warmed the finger bowls, my curiosity got the best of me and I asked my hostess what had everyone else done with the strawberry stems. She smiled and replied that no one else had taken any—since they were all allergic to strawberries!

In the living room after dinner, high above Park Avenue with the lights of Manhattan shining below us, my hostess asked me about my plans for

the future, my hopes, my ambitions, and my dreams. I told her I wanted to write a novel. She told me she would make it possible for me to write that novel. And she did by covering the expenses of my summer, so that I need do no other work during vacation.

That was the summer when I wrote a draft of *Not Without Laughter*. Then I went for a short vacation at Provincetown, where I saw the Wharf Players performing a version of Donald Ogden Stewart's *Parody Outline of History*. I liked the wide sandy beaches of Cape Cod, but I did not like Provincetown very much, because it was hard for a Negro to find a place to sleep, and at night the mosquitoes were vicious.

During my senior year at Lincoln, I rewrote my novel. And at graduation I was given a generous monthly allowance by my patron, who had read both drafts of the book, had helped me with it, and found it good. Then began for me a strange and wonderful year of economic freedom, starting with a boat trip up the Saguenay River to see the northern lights. (The boat trip would have been pleasant had I not been the only Negro on board in the midst of a crowd of Middle-Westerners and Southerners. The steward refused to give me a sitting in the dining-saloon except after all the whites had eaten. So I got off the boat somewhere in the wilds of Canada and came back to Montreal by train. The company refunded my money.)

In the fall I spent a few weeks with Jasper Deeter at Hedgerow Theater, writing my first play, *Mulatto*. Then I settled in Westfield, New Jersey, near New York, where I made the final revisions of my novel.

My patron (a word neither of us liked) was a beautiful woman, with snow-white hair and a face that was wise and very kind. She had been a power in her day in many movements adding freedom and splendor to life in America. She had had great sums of money, and had used much of it in great and generous ways. She had been a friend of presidents and bankers, distinguished scientists, famous singers, and writers of world renown. Imposing institutions and important new trends in thought and in art had been created and supported by her money and her genius at helping others. Now she was very old and not well and able to do little outside her own home. But there she was like a queen. Her power filled the rooms. Famous people came to see her and letters poured in from all over the world.

I do not know why or how she still found time for me, and many others like me, young and just starting out on the big sea of life. Or how she arranged her very full day to include so many people

XXI.

HEY, BOY!

In the lobby of the Drummer's Hotel there were six ~~big bright red~~ *large*
brass spitoons, one in the center of the place, one in each corner,
and one near the clerk's desk. ~~and nine there~~ It was Sandy's duty
to clean these spitoons. Every evening *that winter*/after school he came in~~to~~ the
back door of the hotel, put his books in the ~~little~~ closet where he
kept his brooms and cleaning rags, ~~then~~ swept the lobby and dusted,
swept the two short upper halls and the two flights of stairs; then
took the spitoons, emptied their slimy contents into the alley, rinsed
them out, ~~and then in the inside of~~
~~them out you~~ and polished them until they shone as brightly as if they
were made of gold. Except for the stench of the emptying *of them* ~~of them~~
that proceeded the shining, Sandy rather liked this job. He always
felt very proud of himself when, about six o'clock, he could look
around the dingy, old *but freshly swept,* lobby and see *the* six gleaming brass bowls catching
the glow of the electric lamps on their shining surfaces before ~~they~~ *they*
~~when~~ were again covered with spit. The thought that he had created this
~~cleanliness and this~~ brightness with his own hands aided by ~~a can of~~ *of*
~~can—polished with~~ brass polish never failed to make Sandy happy.
He liked to clean things, to make them look ~~more~~ beautiful, to make
them shine. Aunt Hager ~~was that way~~ *did*, too. When she wasn't washing
clothes, she was always cleaning something about the house, dusting
something, polishing the ~~old~~ range, *or* scrubbing the kitchen floor until
it was *white*~~clean~~ enough to eat from like ~~box~~ *a* table. To ~~her~~ *Hager* a clean thing .
was ~~a~~ beautiful. ~~thing~~ And so, Sandy, ~~was~~ proud of his six ~~shining~~ *unblemished* brass
spitoons. ~~But~~ *Yet* every day when he came to work ~~again~~ they were covered *anew*
with tobacco juice, cigarette butts, wads of chewing gum, *phlem* and
saliva. ~~phlem.~~ But to make them clean *again was* ~~no~~ ~~for him to do and it was~~
Sandy's job. *and when they were clean they were beautiful.*
Charlie *Nutter* was right, there was nothing very hard about the ~~job~~ *work* and ~~he~~
~~Sandy~~ liked it for awhile. The new kinds of life which he saw in the

Page from the second draft of Not Without Laughter *(Langston Hughes Collection, Schomburg Center for Research in Black Culture, New York Public Library)*

and so many things. Or how she never forgot the tiniest detail of what she had worked for or planned with anyone. She was an amazing, brilliant, and powerful personality. I was fascinated by her, and I loved her. No one else had ever been so thoughtful of me, or so interested in the things I wanted to do, or so kind and generous toward me.

For years this good woman had been devoted in a mild way to the advancement of the Negro and had given money to Negro schools in the South. Now she had discovered the New Negro and wanted to help him. She was intensely excited about each new book, each new play, and each new artist that came out of the Negro world.

Everything born to Negroes in those days of the '20's, she knew about. For a woman as old as my grandmother would have been had she lived, she still kept up with everything from Duke Ellington to the budding Marian Anderson.

Still, Negroes occupied but one corner in that vast and active mind of hers. She was deeply interested in a great many things other than Negroes. One of the outstanding American achievements of this century, heralded on the front pages of the world's newspapers, came into being partly through this woman's aid. But, due to her own wish, her name was nowhere mentioned in connection with it, for she never permitted a credit line concerning anything she did, or a dedication to herself of any book she helped to bring to being.

Concerning Negroes, she felt that they were America's great link with the primitive, and that they had something very precious to give to the Western World. She felt that there was mystery and mysticism and spontaneous harmony in their souls, but that many of them had let the white world pollute and contaminate that mystery and harmony, and make of it something cheap and ugly, commercial and, as she said, "white." She felt that we had a deep well of the spirit within us and that we should keep it pure and deep.

In her youth she must have been an amazing person, indeed—and certainly one of America's finest representatives of great wealth. I cannot write about her more fully now because I have no right to disclose her name, nor to describe in detail her many and varied activities. I can only say that those months when I lived by and through her were the most fascinating and fantastic I have ever known.

Out of a past of more or less continued insecurity and fear, suddenly I found myself with an assured income from someone who loved and believed in me, an apartment in a suburban village for my work, my brother in school in New England

and no longer a financial difficulty to my mother, myself with boxes of fine bond paper for writing, a filing case, a typist to copy my work, and wonderful new suits of dinner clothes from Fifth Avenue shops, and a chance to go to all the theaters and operas and lectures, no matter how expensive or difficult securing tickets might be. All I needed to say was when and where I wished to go and my patron's secretary would have tickets for me.

That season I went to the Metropolitan, to concerts at Carnegie Hall, to the hit plays and latest musicals, often with my patron. Together we heard *Sadko,* saw the first *Little Show, Berkeley Square,* and *Blackbirds.* We heard Madame Naidu speak, and General Smuts. We saw the Van Goghs. We drove through Central Park in the spring to see the first leaves come out.

It was all very wonderful. Park Avenue and Broadway and Harlem and New York! But when I had finished my novel and it went to press, I didn't feel like writing anything else then, so I didn't write anything. I was tired and happy, having completed a book, so I stopped work.

I didn't realize that my not writing a while mattered so much to the kind and generous woman who was caring for my welfare. I didn't realize that she was old and wanted quickly to see my books come into being before she had to go away. She hadn't told me that I must always write and write, and I felt sure she knew that sometimes for months, a writer does not feel like writing. That winter I did not feel like writing because I was happy and amused. (I only really feel like writing when I am unhappy, bored or else have something I need very much to say, or that I feel so strongly about I cannot hold it back.) That winter I didn't seem to need to say anything. I had had my say in the novel—spread over almost two years in the saying. Now I was ready for the first time in my life really to enjoy life without having to be afraid I might be hungry tomorrow.

Of course, I felt bad sometimes because I couldn't share my new-found comfort as fully as I might have wished with my mother, who was working as a cook in a rest home in Atlantic City. And in Cleveland we had relatives who were having a pretty hard time getting along at all, for the depression had come. But at least the burden of my kid brother's care had been lifted from my mother. He was happy and well fed in New England, not running the back alleys of Atlantic City.

I always felt slightly bad, too, when I was riding in the long town-car that belonged to my Park Avenue patron—and most other Negroes (and white folk) were walking. I would never occupy the car alone if I could help it. But sometimes she would insist, if it were very late, that I be driven to Harlem—or to the ferry, if I were going to Jersey—in her car. At such times I felt specially bad, because I knew the chauffeur did not like to drive me.

He was a rather grim and middle-aged white man, who, probably in all his career as a chauffeur, had never before been asked to drive a Negro about. At least, I felt that in his attitude toward me when I was alone in the deep, comfortable back seat of the car (where I didn't want to be) with him driving me to Harlem. I would have preferred to ride in front with him, talk with him, and get to know him, but he never gave me a chance. He was always coldly polite and unsmiling, drawing ceremoniously up to the curb in front of my Harlem rooming house, getting out and opening the door for me, but never looking pleasant, or joking, or being kind about it. I felt bad riding with him, because I knew he *hated* to drive me, and I knew he had to do it if he wanted to keep his job. And I dislike being the cause of anyone's having to do anything he doesn't want to do just to keep a job—since I know how unpleasant that is. So often, I would ask my patron's chauffeur simply to drop me at the nearest subway entrance.

But I remember once an amusing situation developed on a certain occasion when I was going out of town on a mid-winter lecture trip. I had been delayed at luncheon on Park Avenue, and so was late getting to the train. There was a terrific blizzard with heavy snow, and, fearing that in a taxi I might be too late for the train, my hostess sent not only her car and chauffeur with me to the station, but her secretary as well to help me get my ticket and have the baggage checked.

The secretary was a tall New England spinster, very efficient and pleasant, and not at all ungracious like the chauffeur. But the funny thing was that when the long town-car drew up to the ramp in the Pennsylvania Station and a dozen colored red caps that I had gone to college with rushed up to take the baggage and saw me get out with the secretary—as a white chauffeur held the door—the red caps were gleefully amazed.

As the secretary rushed ahead to get the Pullman reservation, several of the red caps I knew shook hands and asked me where I was going, and my college friends slapped me on the back in their usual friendly manner and demanded: "Since when the swell chariot, Lang?" But the chauffeur closed the door with a bang, jumped back into the car, and whirled away.

New York began to be not so pleasant that winter. People were sleeping in subways or on newspa-

pers in office doors, because they had no homes. And in every block a beggar appeared. I got so I didn't like to go to dinner on luxurious Park Avenue—and come out and see people hungry on the streets, huddled in subway entrances all night and filling Manhattan Transfer like a flop house. I knew I could very easily and quickly be there, too, hungry and homeless on a cold floor, anytime Park Avenue got tired of supporting me. I had no job, and no way of making a living.

During the winter Zora Hurston came to Westfield from one of her many trips into the deep South, and there began to arrange her folk material, stacks and stacks of it—some of which later appeared in *Mules and Men*. Together we also began to work on a play called *Mule Bone,* a Negro folk comedy, based on an amusing tale Miss Hurston had collected about a quarrel between two rival church factions. I plotted out and typed the play based on her story, while she authenticated and flavored the dialogue and added highly humorous details. We finished a first draft before she went South again, and from this draft I was to work out a final version.

Zora, a very gay and lively girl, was seriously hemmed in in village-like Westfield. But those backing her folk-lore project felt that she should remain quietly in a small town and not go galavanting gaily about New York while engaged in the serious task of preparing her manuscripts. So she was restless and moody, working in a nervous manner. And we were both distressed at the growing depression—hearing of more and more friends and relatives losing jobs and becoming desperate for lack of work.

In the midst of that depression, the Waldorf-Astoria opened. On the way to my friend's home on Park Avenue I frequently passed it, a mighty towering structure looming proud above the street, in a city where thousands were poor and unemployed. So I wrote a poem about it called "Advertisement for the Waldorf-Astoria," modeled after an ad in *Vanity Fair* announcing the opening of New York's greatest hotel. (Where no Negroes worked and none were admitted as guests.)

The hotel opened at the very time when people were sleeping on newspapers in doorways, because they had no place to go. But suites in the Waldorf ran into thousands a year, and dinner in the Sert Room was ten dollars! (Negroes, even if they had the money, couldn't eat there. So naturally, I didn't care much for the Waldorf-Astoria.) The thought of it made me feel bad, so I wrote this poem, from which these excerpts are taken:

Advertisement from the July 1931 issue of Vanity Fair. *Hughes's poem "Advertisement for the Waldorf-Astoria" was first published in the December 1931 issue of* New Masses *(Thomas Cooper Library, University of South Carolina).*

ADVERTISEMENT FOR THE
WALDORF-ASTORIA

Fine living à la carte!!

LISTEN, HUNGRY ONES!

Look! See what *Vanity Fair* says about the
new Waldorf-Astoria:
"All the luxuries of private home. . . ."
Now, won't that be charming when the last flop-house
has turned you down this winter?
Furthermore:
"It is far beyond anything hitherto attempted in the
hotel world. . . ." It cost twenty-eight million dollars.
The famous Oscar Tschirky is in charge of banquet-
ing. Alexandre Gastaud is chef. It will be a distinguished background for society.
So when you've got no place else to go, homeless and
hungry ones, choose the Waldorf as a background
for your rags—
(Or do you still consider the subway after midnight
good enough?)

ROOMERS

Take a room at the new Waldorf, you down-and-
outers—sleepers in charity's flop-houses.
They serve swell board at the Waldorf-Astoria. Look at
this menu, will you:

GUMBO CREOLE
CRABMEAT IN CASSOLETTE
BOILED BRISKET OF BEEF
SMALL ONIONS IN CREAM
WATERCRESS SALAD
PEACH MELBA

Have luncheon there this afternoon, all you jobless.
Why not?
Dine with some of the men and women who got rich
off of your labor, who clip coupons with clean white
fingers because your hands dug coal, drilled stone,
sewed garments, poured steel to let other people
draw dividends and live easy.
(Or haven't you had enough yet of the soup-lines and
the bitter bread of charity?)
Walk through Peacock Alley tonight before dinner,
and get warm, anyway. You've got nothing else to
do.

NEGROES

Oh, Lawd! I done forgot Harlem!
Say, you colored folks, hungry a long time in 135th
Street—they got swell music at the Waldorf-Astoria.
It sure is a mighty nice place to shake hips in, too.
There's dancing after supper in a big warm room.
It's cold as hell on Lenox Avenue. All you've had
all day is a cup of coffee. Your pawnshop over-
coat's a ragged banner on your hungry frame. You
know, downtown folks are just crazy about Paul

Robeson! Maybe they'll like you, too, black mob
from Harlem. Drop in at the Waldorf this afternoon
for tea. Stay to dinner. Give Park Avenue a lot of
darkie color—free—for nothing! Ask the Junior
Leaguers to sing a spiritual for you. They probably
know 'em better than you do—and their lips won't
be so chapped with cold after they step out of their
closed cars in the undercover driveways.
Hallelujah! Undercover driveways!
Ma soul's a witness for de Waldorf-Astoria!
(A thousand nigger section-hands keep the roadbeds
smooth so investments in railroads pay ladies with
diamond necklaces staring at Cert murals.)
Thank Gawd A'mighty!
(And a million niggers bend their backs on rubber plan-
tations, for rich behinds to ride on thick tires to the
Theatre Guild tonight.)
Ma soul's a witness!
(And here we stand, shivering in the cold, in Harlem.)
Glory be to Gawd—
De Waldorf-Astoria's open!

EVERYBODY

So get proud and rare back; everybody! The new
Waldorf-Astoria's open!
(Special siding for private cars from the railroad yards.)
You ain't been there yet?
(A thousand miles of carpet and a million bathrooms.)
What's the matter?
You haven't seen the ads in the papers? Didn't you get
a card? Don't you know they specialize in American
cooking? Ankle on down to 49th Street at Park Ave-
nue. Get up off that subway bench tonight with the
Evening Post for cover! Come on out o' that
flop-house! Stop shivering your guts out all day on
street corners under the El.
Jesus, ain't you tired yet?

"It's not you," my benefactor said when she
had read that far. "It's a powerful poem! But it's not
you."

I knew she did not like it.

I began that winter to feel increasingly bad,
increasingly worried and apprehensive. Not all at
once, but gradually I knew something was wrong. I
sensed it vaguely, intuitively—the way I felt in Mexico, when my father would come home and find the
bookkeeping not added up right, and I could feel
before he got home that it wasn't added up right,
even though I had worked on it all the afternoon! So
it was hard eating dinner with him in his bare, tiled
dining room in Toluca, just as it became hard eating
dinner on Park Avenue with people who had freshly
cut flowers on the table while the snow fell outside.
—*The Big Sea* (New York: Knopf, 1940), pp. 311–324

* * *

The most positive development of 1930 for Hughes was the publication of Not Without Laughter *in July and the good notices it then received. This introduction to the novel, which was written by Arna Bontemps two years after Hughes's death, provides biographical and social context for a novel being republished almost forty years after it first appeared. Bontemps originally met Hughes in 1924 when he moved from Los Angeles to Harlem. The two men became lifelong friends and collaborators.*

"Next Thing to Camelot"
Introduction to *Not Without Laughter*

The Harlem Renaissance, as it is now remembered, had risen to a climax in 1930, the year in which *Not Without Laughter* first appeared. Langston Hughes, whose poetry had been quickening pulse beats since 1921, had clearly identified himself as a writer to watch. Sooner or later, many readers felt, and some actually said, the young author of *The Weary Blues* and *Fine Clothes to the Jew* would write a novel, and when he did it would have to be read.

Actually it was overdue, because the wandering poet had been inveigled into returning to school. Otherwise it might have been published as early as 1927. But 1930 was an auspicious year for such a novel, even though the stock market had crashed a few months earlier and terror was beginning to spread. Hope had not yet been completely destroyed. Nostalgia, to some extent, had been intensified in a generation that was beginning to close its eyes to looming disasters.

Hughes had created a small sensation among black intellectuals four years earlier when he published in *The Nation* an article called "The Negro Artist and the Racial Mountain." Included in the piece was a statement that had come to be regarded by many black intellectuals and artists as a kind of manifesto:

> We younger Negro artists who create now intend to express our individual dark-skinned selves without fear or shame. If white people are pleased we are glad. If they are not, it doesn't matter. We know we are beautiful. And ugly too. The tom-tom cries and the tom-tom laughs. If colored people are pleased, we are glad. If they are not, their displeasure doesn't matter either. We build our temples for tomorrow, strong as we know how, and we stand on top of the mountain free within ourselves.

The poets had become bellwethers, and protest organizations and friends of the blacks were following almost as if transfixed. Crusading civil-rights

leaders suddenly decided that a touch of magic had been found. They paused and began writing novels and poems themselves. W. E. B. Du Bois, James Weldon Johnson and Walter White all picked up the cue, but it was easy to recognize that the special new note was being sounded by their juniors, even though there was no tendency, such as became noticeable in the 1960s, to downgrade the elders.

Many eyes were watching the young poet when he accepted scholarship aid from a patron and selected Lincoln University in Pennsylvania as his alma mater. He had tried Columbia University as a freshman, years earlier, and turned away feeling miserable, as he recalls in the first part of his autobiography. Perhaps Columbia was not ready for Langston Hughes at that date. Lincoln put him at his ease. He soon felt at home as a contemporary of Thurgood Marshall, a friend of many students and faculty members and a fan of Cab Calloway. He joined a fraternity, wrote a lyric for one of its songs, studied enough to meet requirements and conducted a survey to determine whether or not the black Lincoln men would like to have some black teachers—which they did *not* at the time. This undergraduate investigation seemed somewhat indelicate under the circumstances. The survey agitated the campus, as might have been expected, but tremors from it appear to have been felt elsewhere in black education.

Its more immediate result for Hughes, however, was to delay the novel he knew, and his readers knew, he had to write. But in his senior year he got the work under way. Weekends and during breaks he would return to New York's Harlem. To a few of us he showed parts of the manuscript in progress. I for one never doubted that the mood of his effortless, unaffected poetry would be sustained in his fiction, and I was not disappointed in 1930. Nor am I disappointed in it now, nearly forty years later, when his first novel is again reissued. By the date of his first book of prose Hughes had become for many a symbol of the black renaissance. By 1969 the black renaissance of the 1920s had become a symbol of awakening awareness to blacks everywhere.

The Harlem Renaissance can be more precisely dated from 1917, the year in which certain seeds were planted. Then while Claude McKay and Jean Toomer were writing and putting together the poems and stories that were to transmit this mood in 1922 and 1923 respectively, Marcus Garvey came to the United States and awakened pride in blackness and a conviction that black is beautiful with unprecedented vigor and drama. Poetry had been the first to catch the beat, and the names of Langston Hughes and Countee Cullen appeared like unannounced stars in the small gray dawn.

Show business being what it is, some of the more established American playwrights and promoters were quick to recognize the basic excitement of the awakening in Harlem and to plug into the impulse, as it were. They did not start it, create it or direct it, but they publicized it and profited by it, sometimes spectacularly. With ready-made access to the wider media, they were able to extend the black influence to Broadway, and in one way and another the country gradually became aware of a happening in Harlem.

The period of the renaissance was then, roughly, the 1920s. Significant points in its beginnings, aside from the books by McKay and Toomer, the parades and the rapturous oratory of Marcus Garvey, may be marked by the concert debut of Roland Hayes in Carnegie Hall and the opening of a now almost legendary musical show called *Shuffle Along* near New York's theater district. Books could be written about either of these events. In any case, it was then that the stars began to fall on Harlem and Broadway.

A documentation of the era began when a special issue of *The Survey Graphic,* edited by Alain Locke, was published in March 1925 and when *Opportunity, A Journal of Negro Life,* edited by Charles S. Johnson for the National Urban League, began offering prizes and encouragement to black writers that same year. Considered either as a link-up or a break-through, what followed in relation to the established media of expression may be said to have ended the comparative segregation of black writers and artists and performers in the creative life of the nation.

Not surprisingly, this was the period in which jazz won acceptance and Jelly Roll Morton, W. C. Handy and Duke Ellington arrived in New York. The beat was firm. Harlem rocked. Bessie Smith and Ethel Waters sang in dark underground places where one could buy gin in those prohibition years. Afternoons as well as midnights kids on Lenox and Seventh Avenues invented camel walks, black bottoms and Charlestons. It was next thing to Camelot to be young and a poet in the Harlem of those days, and by the time he wrote *Not Without Laughter,* Langston Hughes was strolling among his kind like a happy prince whose time had come.

—"Introduction," in *Not Without Laughter* (New York: Macmillan, 1969), pp. ix–xiii

* * *

In this, the fifth chapter of Not Without Laughter, *Hughes shows how the popularity of the blues variously affects Aunt Hager's family.*

Guitar

> Throw yo' arms around me, baby,
> Like de circle round de sun!
> Baby, throw yo' arms around me
> Like de circle round de sun,
> An' tell yo' pretty papa
> How you want yo' lovin' done!

Jimboy was home. All the neighborhood could hear his rich low baritone voice giving birth to the blues. On Saturday night he and Annjee went to bed early. On Sunday night Aunt Hager said: "Put that guitar right up, less'n it's hymns you plans on playin'. An' I don't want too much o' them, 'larmin' de white neighbors."

But this was Monday, and the sun had scarcely fallen below the horizon before the music had begun to float down the alley, over back fences and into kitchen-windows where nice white ladies sedately washed their supper dishes.

> Did you ever see peaches
> Growin' on a watermelon vine?
> Says did you ever see peaches
> On a watermelon vine?
> Did you ever see a woman
> That I couldn't get for mine?

Long, lazy length resting on the kitchen-door-sill, back against the jamb, feet in the yard, fingers picking his sweet guitar, left hand holding against its fingerboard the back of an old pocket-knife, sliding the knife upward, downward, getting thus weird croons and sighs from the vibrating strings:

> O, I left ma mother
> An' I cert'ly can leave you.
> Indeed I left ma mother
> An' I cert'ly can leave you,
> For I'd leave any woman
> That mistreats me like you do.

Jimboy, remembering brown-skin mamas in Natchez, Shreveport, Dallas; remembering Creole women in Baton Rouge, Louisiana:

> O, yo' windin' an' yo' grindin'
> Don't have no effect on me,
> Babe, yo' windin' an' yo' grindin'
> Don't have no 'fect on me,
> 'Cause I can wind an' grind
> Like a monkey round a coconut-tree!

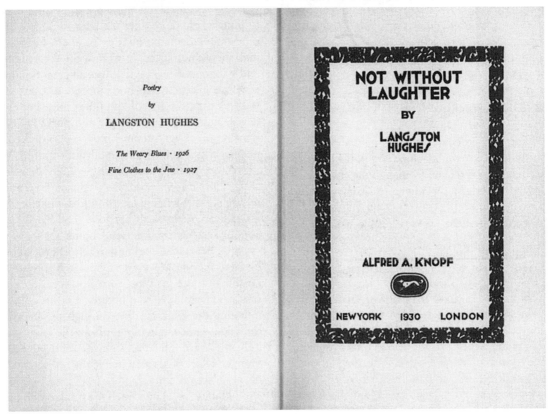

Dust jacket, list of previous books, and title page for Hughes's first novel (Yale Collection
of American Literature, Beinecke Rare Book and Manuscript Library)

Then Harriett, standing under the ripening apple tree, in the back yard, chiming in:

> Now I see that you don't want me,
> So it's fare thee, fare thee well!
> Lawd, I see that you don't want me,
> So it's fare–thee–well!
> I can still get plenty lovin',
> An' you can go to–Kansas City!

"O, play it, sweet daddy Jimboy!" She began to dance.

Then Hager, from her seat on the edge of the platform covering the well, broke out: "Here, madam! Stop that prancin'! Bad enough to have all this singin' without turnin' de yard into a show-house." But Harriett kept on, her hands picking imaginary cherries out of the stars, her hips speaking an earthly language quite their own.

"You got it, kid," said Jimboy, stopping suddenly, then fingering his instrument for another tune. "You do it like the stage women does. You'll be takin' Ada Walker's place if you keep on."

"Wha! Wha! . . . You chillen sho can sing!" Tom Johnson shouted his compliments from across the yard. And Sarah, beside him on the bench behind their shack, added: "Minds me o' de ole plantation times, honey! It sho do!"

"Unhuh! Bound straight fo' de devil, that's what they is," Hager returned calmly from her place beside the pump. "You an' Harriett both–singin' an' dancin' this stuff befo' these chillens here." She pointed to Sandy and Willie-Mae, who sat on the ground with their backs against the chicken-box. "It's a shame!"

"I likes it," said Willie-Mae.

"Me too," the little boy agreed.

"Naturally you would–none o' you-all's converted yet," countered the old woman to the children as she settled back against the pump to listen to some more.

The music rose hoarse and wild:

> I wonder where ma easy rider's gone?
> He done left me, put ma new gold watch in pawn.

It was Harriett's voice in plaintive moan to the night sky. Jimboy had taught her that song, but a slight, clay-colored brown boy who had hopped bells at the Clinton Hotel for a couple of months, on his way from Houston to Omaha, discovered its meaning to her. Puppy-love, maybe, but it had hurt when he went away, saying nothing. And the guitar in Jimboy's hands echoed that old pain with an even greater throb than the original ache itself possessed.

Approaching footsteps came from the front yard.

"Lord, I can hear you-all two blocks away!" said Annjee, coming around the house, home from work, with a bundle of food under her left arm. "Hello! How are you, daddy? Hello, ma! Gimme a kiss Sandy. . . . Lord, I'm hot and tired and most played out. This late just getting from work! . . . Here, Jimboy, come on in and eat some of these nice things the white folks had for supper." She stepped across her husband's outstretched legs into the kitchen. "I brought a mighty good piece of cold ham for you, hon', from Mis' Rice's."

"All right, sure, I'll be there in a minute," the man said, but he went on playing *Easy Rider,* and Harriett went on singing, while the food was forgotten on the table until long after Annjee had come outdoors again and sat down in the cool, tired of waiting for Jimboy to come in to her.

Off and on for nine years, ever since he had married Annjee, Jimboy and Harriett had been singing together in the evenings. When they started, Harriett was a little girl with braided hair, and each time that her roving brother-in-law stopped in Stanton, he would amuse himself by teaching her the old Southern songs, the popular rag-time ditties, and the hundreds of varying verses of the blues that he would pick up in the big dirty cities of the South. The child, with her strong sweet voice (colored folks called it alto) and her racial sense of rhythm, soon learned to sing the songs as well as Jimboy. He taught her the *parse me la,* too, and a few other movements peculiar to Southern Negro dancing, and sometimes together they went through the buck and wing and a few taps. It was all great fun, and innocent fun except when one stopped to think, as white folks did, that some of the blues lines had, not only double, but triple meanings, and some of the dance steps required very definite movements of the hips. But neither Harriett nor Jimboy soiled their minds by thinking. It was music, good exercise–and they loved it.

"Do you know this one, Annjee?" asked Jimboy, calling his wife's name out of sudden politeness because he had forgotten to eat her food, had hardly looked at her, in fact, since she came home. Now he glanced towards her in the darkness where she sat plump on a kitchen-chair in the yard, apart from the others, with her back to the growing corn in the garden. Softly he ran his fingers, light as a breeze, over his guitar strings, imitating the wind rustling through the long leaves of the corn. A rectangle of light from the kitchen-door fell into the yard striking sidewise across the healthy orange-yellow of his skin above the unbuttoned neck of his blue laborer's shirt.

"Come on, sing it with us, Annjee," he said.

"I don't know it," Annjee replied, with a lump in her throat, and her eyes on the silhouette of his long, muscular, animal-hard body. She loved Jimboy too much, that's what was the matter with her! She knew there was nothing between him and her young sister except the love of music, yet he might have dropped the guitar and left Harriett in the yard for a little while to come eat the nice cold slice of ham she had brought him. She hadn't seen him all day long. When she went to work this morning, he was still in bed—and now the blues claimed him.

In the starry blackness the singing notes of the guitar became a plaintive hum, like a breeze in a grove of palmettos; became a low moan, like the wind in a forest of live-oaks strung with long strands of hanging moss. The voice of Annjee's golden, handsome husband on the door-step rang high and far away, lonely-like, crying with only the guitar, not his wife, to understand; crying grotesquely, crying absurdly in the summer night:

> I got a mule to ride.
> I got a mule to ride.
> Down in the South somewhere
> I got a mule to ride.

Then asking the question as an anxious, left-lonesome girl-sweetheart would ask it:

> You say you goin' North.
> You say you goin' North.
> How 'bout yo' . . . lovin' gal?
> You say you goin' North.

Then sighing in rhythmical despair:

> O, don't you leave me here.
> Babe, don't you leave me here.
> Dog-gone yo' comin' back!
> Said don't you leave me here.

On and on the song complained, man-verses and woman-verses, to the evening air in stanzas that Jimboy had heard in the pine-woods of Arkansas from the lumber-camp workers; in other stanzas that were desperate and dirty like the weary roads where they were sung; and in still others that the singer created spontaneously in his own mouth then and there:

> O, I done made ma bed,
> Says I done made ma bed.
> Down in some lonesome grave
> I done made ma bed.

It closed with a sad eerie twang.

"That's right decent," said Hager. "Now I wish you-all'd play some o' ma pieces like *When de Saints Come Marchin' In* or *This World Is Not Ma Home*—something Christian from de church."

"Aw, mama, it's not Sunday yet," said Harriett.

"Sing *Casey Jones*," called old man Tom Johnson. "That's ma song."

So the ballad of the immortal engineer with another mama in the Promised Land rang out promptly in the starry darkness, while everybody joined in the choruses.

"Aw, pick it, boy," yelled the old man. "Can't nobody play like you."

And Jimboy remembered when he was a lad in Memphis that W. C. Handy had said: "You ought to make your living out of that, son." But he hadn't followed it up—too many things to see, too many places to go, too many other jobs.

"What song do you like, Annjee?" he asked, remembering her presence again.

"O, I don't care. Any ones you like. All of 'em are pretty." She was pleased and petulant and a little startled that he had asked her.

"All right, then," he said. "Listen to me:"

> Here I is in de mean ole jail.
> Ain't got nobody to go ma bail.
> Lonesome an' sad an' chain gang bound—
> Ever' friend I had's done turned me down.

"That's sho it!" shouted Tom Johnson in great sympathy. "Now, when I was in de Turner County Jail . . ."

"Shut up yo' mouth!" squelched Sarah, jabbing her husband in the ribs.

The songs went on, blues, shouts, jingles, old hits: *Bon Bon Buddy, the Chocolate Drop; Wrap Me in Your Big Red Shawl; Under the Old Apple Tree; Turkey in the Straw*—Jimboy and Harriett breaking the silence of the small-town summer night until Aunt Hager interrupted:

"You-all better wind up, chillens, 'cause I wants to go to bed. I ain't used to stayin' 'wake so late, nohow. Play something kinder decent there, son, fo' you stops."

Jimboy, to tease the old woman, began to rock and moan like an elder in the Sanctified Church, patting both feet at the same time as he played a hymn-like, lugubrious tune with a dancing overtone:

> Tell me, sister,
> Tell me, brother,
> Have you heard de latest news?

Then seriously as if he were about to announce the coming of the Judgment:

> A woman down in Georgia
> Got her two sweet-men confused.

How terrible! How sad! moaned the guitar.

One knocked on de front do',
One knocked on de back–

Sad, sad . . . sad, sad! said the music.

Now that woman down in Georgia's
Door-knob is hung with black.

O, play that funeral march, boy! while the guitar
laughed a dirge.

An' de hearse is comin' easy
With two rubber-tired hacks!

Followed by a long-drawn-out, churchlike:

Amen . . . !

The Break with Mason

Hughes's relationship with his patron became strained after the completion of Not Without Laughter. *The decisive quarrel that signaled the end of the relationship occurred in May 1930, when Hughes went against Mason's wishes that he stay home and write and traveled instead to Washington, D.C.*

Not Primitive

That winter I had been in Cuba looking for a Negro composer to write an opera with me, using genuinely racial motifs. The lady on Park Avenue thought that Amadeo Roldan might do, or Arturo Cartulo. I could not find Cartulo, and Roldan said he wasn't a Negro. But Miguel Covarrubias had given me a letter to José Antonio Fernandez de Castro, person extraordinary of this or any other world. And José Antonio saw to it that I had a rumba of a good time and met everybody, Negro, white and mulatto, of any interest in Havana–from the drummers at Marianao to the society artist and editor of *Social,* Masaguer.

But I came back to New York with no Negro composer who could write an opera.

More and more tangled that winter became the skein of poet and patron, youth and age, poverty and wealth–and one day it broke! Quickly and quietly in the Park Avenue drawing-room, it broke.

Great wealth had given to a woman who meant to be kind the means to power, and a technique of power, of so mighty a strength that I do not believe she herself knew what that force might become. She possessed the power to control people's lives–pick them up and put them down when and where she wished.

She wanted me to be primitive and know and feel the intuitions of the primitive. But, unfortunately, I did not feel the rhythms of the primitive surging through me, and so I could not live and write as though I did. I was only an American Negro–who had loved the surface of Africa and the rhythms of Africa–but I was not Africa. I was Chicago and Kansas City and Broadway and Harlem. And I was not what she wanted me to be. So, in the end it all came back very near to the old impasse of white and Negro

again, white and Negro–as do most relationships in America.

Then, too, I knew that my friend and benefactor was not happy because, for months now, I had written nothing beautiful. She was old and it took a great deal of strength out of her to worry about me, and she was, I think, a bit impatient with men who are not geniuses. (She knew so many great people.) So I asked kindly to be released from any further obligations to her, and that she give me no more money, but simply let me retain her friendship and good will that had been so dear to me. That I asked to keep. But there must have been only the one thread binding us together. When that thread broke, it was the end.

I cannot write here about that last half-hour in the big bright drawing-room high above Park Avenue one morning, because when I think about it, even now, something happens in the pit of my stomach that makes me ill. That beautiful room, that had been so full of light and help and understanding for me, suddenly became like a trap closing in, faster and faster, the room darker and darker, until the light went out with a sudden crash in the dark, and everything became like that night in Kansas when I had failed to see Jesus and had lied about it afterwards. Or that morning in Mexico when I suddenly hated my father.

Physically, my stomach began to turn over and over–and then over again. I fought against bewilderment and anger, fought hard, and didn't say anything. I just sat there in the high Park Avenue drawing-room and didn't say anything. I sat there and listened to all she told me, closed my mouth hard and didn't say anything.

I do not remember clearly what it was she said to me at the end, nor her face as the door closed, nor the elevator dropping down to the street level, nor my final crossing of the lobby through a lane of uniformed attendants.

But I do remember the winter sunshine on Park Avenue and the wind in my face as I went toward the subway to Harlem.

–*The Big Sea* (New York: Knopf, 1940),
pp. 324–326

Then with rapid glides, groans, and shouts the instrument screamed of a sudden in profane frenzy, and Harriett began to ball-the-jack, her arms flopping like the wings of a headless pigeon, the guitar strings whining in ecstasy, the player rocking gaily to the urgent music, his happy mouth crying: "Tack 'em on down, gal! Tack 'em on down, Harrie!"

But Annjee had risen.

"I wish you'd come in and eat the ham I brought you," she said as she picked up her chair and started towards the house. "And you, Sandy! Get up from under that tree and go to bed." She spoke roughly to the little fellow, whom the songs had set a-dreaming. Then to her husband: "Jimboy, I wish you'd come in."

The man stopped playing, with a deep vibration of the strings that seemed to echo through the whole world. Then he leaned his guitar against the side of the house and lifted straight up in his hairy arms Annjee's plump, brown-black little body while he kissed her as she wriggled like a stubborn child, her soft breasts rubbing his hard body through the coarse blue shirt.

"You don't like my old songs, do you, baby? You don't want to hear me sing 'em," he said, laughing. "Well, that's all right. I like you, anyhow, and I like your ham, and I like your kisses, and I like everything you bring me. Let's go in and chow down." And he carried her into the kitchen, where he sat with her on his knees as he ate the food she so faithfully had brought him from Mrs. J. J. Rice's dinner-table.

Outside, Willie-Mae went running home through the dark. And Harriett pumped a cool drink of water for her mother, then helped her to rise from her low seat, Sandy aiding from behind, with both hands pushing firmly in Aunt Hager's fleshy back. Then the three of them came into the house and glanced, as they passed through the kitchen, at Annjee sitting on Jimboy's lap with both dark arms tight around his neck.

"Looks like you're clinging to the Rock of Ages," said Harriett to her sister. "Be sure you don't slip, old evil gal!"

But at midnight, when the owl that nested in a tree near the corner began to hoot, they were all asleep–Annjee and Jimboy in one room, Harriett and Hager in another, with Sandy on the floor at the foot of his grandmother's bed. Far away on the railroad line a whistle blew, lonesome and long.

–*Not Without Laughter* (New York: Knopf, 1930), pp. 50–61

* * *

Mary Ross wrote this review for the Sunday book section of the New York Herald Tribune Books.

A Little Colored Boy Grows Up
Review of *Not Without Laughter*

To the white man, by and large, Negroes have been people who could cook or launder or sing and play jazz; who were lazy or faithful or religious; or sometimes, in a manner especially surprising because they were of another color, showed talent or even genius in one of the arts, which seemed important initially because it was Negro, and only secondarily because the products were beautiful in themselves. Negroes, even to those whose intellectual protestations were liberal, have not often been accepted as just people, aside from the qualities or defects which are sweepingly attributed to their race as a whole. That racial pot-pourri which goes by the name of American occasionally comes up against a similar indiscrimination in Europe, for example, when some one announces dogmatically that Americans are merely money-grabbers or that their chief ideal in life is sanitary plumbing.

And on the other side of the color line, that wavering but very real barrier between the two races, there has been in these past years of growing economic and educational attainment by Negroes a wholly understandable tendency to "cash in" on the gifts for which the domineering caste expressed admiration. If they are willing to pay royally for being amused in night clubs by the songs and dancing that they could see without a penny on the sideless streets of Charleston or Harlem, let them pay. All they can pay and more would do little enough to wipe out the debt of agony that produced the spirituals, and then, in a more secular generation, the blues. Personal integrity must have been hard to maintain before this fluctuation from contempt to almost maudlin admiration, which throughout so often has been entirely impersonal–treating the performer, whether in the arts or the professions or merely the economic maelstrom, as though he were no more than a racial puppet. Little wonder that there has grown up one counter-pride, which attempted to deny everything allegedly "Negro" and to imitate the life of the more fortunate whites; another pride, which denied the whites any virtue, and took out in bitterness and in the racial magnification to which subject peoples always are driven the indignities to which their loyalties made them prey. The pendulum has swung fitfully from martyrdom to sterile isolation or boastful mastery.

In this first novel Langston Hughes, already distinguished for his volumes of poetry, achieves the difficult equilibrium of showing Negroes who are essentially human beings. Like the other creatures who aspire to this title, they are molded by limitations from within and without; and for them, that which overpowers all else in

Acknowledged
and answered
July 28 – 1930

Box 94
Westfield, N. J.
July 12, 1930

My dear Mr. Johnson:

      I was sorry to have missed you the other
day when you were in town. I went past your house
and also tried to get in touch with you at Knopf's
by phone to find out where you would be. I suppose
Mr. Smith told you. Better luck next time.

      I would be very happy to have you use any
of the published poems of mine which you think worthy
to be included in your Book of American Negro Poetry.
In Jazz Band in a Parisian Cabaret, as published in
my book, one of the two German words therein is not
spelled correctly (so a magazine critic pointed out
in a review). Since I don't know German, I can't
exactly tell which word it is, but if you are going
to republish the poem, maybe you could find out and
correct it. I expect you will know anyway.

      I am sorry I haven't any new unpublished
poems that I could let you see. I have been working
on one or two things recently but I am not at all
sure of them yet. The other day, however, I mailed
you at your town address some copies of the recent
translations I have been doing of two young Cuban
Negro poets. I don't know if you would be interested
in using any of the Cubans in your anthology or not,
but I think some of the contemporary black poets
there are very good. The Once Beloved by Guillén
has been taken by Irita Van Doren for Books, and two
of his other poems have been accepted by Opportunity.
Pedroso has some marvelous semi-mystical poems which
I hope to translate some time soon. Anyway I would
like to know what you think of these translations.

      When I came back from Cuba I sent Fernandez
de Castro, leading Cuban journalist and translator,
a copy of your Autobiography of an Ex-Colored Man. He
has written me enthusiastically about it. Sorry I
haven't the letter with me at the moment or I would
quote to you what he said. He has just sent me his
essay on the great Russian poet who recently committed
suicide, addressed to you in my care, so I am sending it

A letter Hughes wrote to James Weldon Johnson, whose anthology The Book of American Negro Poetry *was first published
in 1922 and enlarged in 1931. Hughes refers to Johnson's novel* The Autobiography of an Ex-Colored Man *(1912)
and his recently published nonfiction study* Black Manhattan *(Langston Hughes Papers, Yale Collection
of American Literature, Beinecke Rare Book and Manuscript Library).*

-2-

on to you. Fernandez de Castro does book reviews and
articles for the leading Latin American publications,
so if you would like some Caribbean publicity on
Black Manhattan, he would be the fellow to whom a copy
should be sent. His address is

       17 Numero 180, Vedado
       Havana, Cuba

       I hope your book goes well. I am sure it will.
Many thanks to you for the copy which you left for me
at the Knopf offices. I haven't seen it yet, but they
said they would mail it to me at once. I had you on my
list for a copy of the novel, which I was hoping to
autograph for you when you were in town the other day.
Mr. Smith said he gave it to you. I hope the reading of
it won't bore you too much.

       Here's hoping you are having a delightful summer
in the country.

       With my kindest regards to Mrs. Johnson, I am
as ever

         Sincerely yours,

         Langston

LH:LT

I was at the library last night for their Book Review evening. They had a copy of Black Manhattan on display — and those who had read it were enthused about it. I'm glad we're getting some Negro books out that colored people themselves will like!

power, is the fact of their being colored, and the attitudes which that circumstance engenders. But "Not Without Laughter" should not, I think, be called "The Negro novel." It has no need to trade on the color of its characters or the race of its author. Because it is a story of a little boy growing up in a Negro family, with an outlook which no white reader could experience in full for himself, but more especially because it is written with understanding, tolerance and beauty, it lays special claim to the attention of those who love life and its mirroring in fiction.

Langston Hughes, not yet thirty, comes of a generation which was spared some of the need for bitterness by which cultured members of his race, like the early feminists, had to cut through the bigotry of an earlier day. He was born in Missouri, his father a lawyer, his mother a school teacher; and his twenty-odd years have seen life in Mexico City, Topeka, Colorado Springs, Kansas City, Buffalo, Cleveland, New York and Washington, as well as capitals of Europe and voyages to the Canary Islands, the Azores and the West Coast of Africa. As a beachcomber in Genoa, a doorman in a Paris cabaret, a busboy in a Washington hotel, a friend of poets and writers and singers, he has had a chance to see his own people–and the whites–from angles that a lifetime often fails to compass. And it is this richness of observation, this joy in experience, that he brings to a simple story of a little colored boy living with his grandmother–who was a laundress–in a Kansas town.

This story of Aunt Hager Williams, who had known slavery, and her three daughters and one little grandson gives play for some of the attitudes, white and Negro, which I tried to sketch above. One daughter, Tempy, marries modest riches, becomes genteel in her tastes, deserts the Baptists for the Episcopalians, and draws her skirts aside from all that has been known as "Negro." The second, Annjee, hangs her whole life on her love for her wandering man, Jimboy, and worn out by her unremitting toil to support him and their child, fails to keep before her, as did the old grandmother, the ideal that Sandy must get the education for which he thirsts. The third, gay little Harriett, refusing to accept her mother's faith that she must wait till the next world for the joys denied her in this, goes her dancing and blues-singing way, hating the whites, taking from them what she can get, but generous and loyal to her own people. And wise old Aunt Hager herself saw beyond her children to the possibilities for her grandchild. "For mighty nigh seventy years I been knowin' both of 'em, an' I ain't never had no room in ma heart to hate neither white nor colored. When you starts hatin' people you gets uglier than they is–an' I ain't never had no time for ugliness, b'cause that's where de devil comes in–in ugliness."

Occasionally, as perhaps in the speech just quoted, a bit of philosophizing seems to take one a little outside the story itself, to make its people more mouthpieces or examples than individuals. But to an extent unusual in any novel which deals with issues so cutting and tangled, this is a story of the poignant joys and griefs of a little boy, and the group of women and men who were his life. In places it is cruelly touching–when the colored children in school were placed at the back of the room; when they got to the amusement park with their newspaper coupons for a party for "all the children of Stanton," agog for a ride on the roller coaster, only to be told it was a party for white children only; when Santa Claus didn't bring the Golden Flyer sled. But this is no mawkish pathos, nor is there, even in Harriett's story, the disfiguring touch of rancor–but only regret. Rather it is the simple pleasures, the gayety and good humor of these people, that triumph, and make the whites seem, by contrast, as anemic in spirit as in color. Looking at old Uncle Dan Givens, the town's champion boaster, Sandy thought: "No matter how belligerent or lewd their talk was, or how sordid the tales they told–of dangerous pleasures and strange perversities–these black men laughed. That must be the reason why poverty-stricken old Negroes like Uncle Dan Givens lived so long–because to them, no matter how hard life might be, it was not without laughter."

–*New York Herald Tribune Books,* 27 July 1930, p. 5

* * *

Wallace Thurman's friendship with Hughes did not prevent him from offering honest criticism in his review of Not Without Laughter *for the* New York Evening Post.

"An Enviable First Performance"
Review of *Not Without Laughter*

Langston Hughes's novel, "Not Without Laughter," will confound many soothsayers and prematurely pessimistic critics. For the poet has proven that he can write prose adequate for the story he has to tell, and he has not concerned himself either with Harlem's Midnight Nans or the southland's cottonfield sweet men. He has depicted, rather, as the blurb on the jacket so conveniently states, a "deeply human picture of a simple people, living in a typical Kansas town, meeting, as best they can, the problems of their destructive, complex environment." He has done this, that is, for 249 pages of his 308-page novel. Remember this reservation for future reference.

Aunt Hagar Williams is an aged Negro woman, a pious, homespun, ample-bosomed individual, beloved by all with whom she comes into frequent contact. She lives her simple life, immersed in the steam and suds of her washtubs, dedicated to the welfare of her children, to the grace of God, and to the service of her neighbor should he be in need of her assistance. And, as a reward for this exemplary conduct, makes such an impression upon the community in which she lives that notice of her death merits, "in small type on its back page," the following paragraph from the Daily Leader:

> Hagar Williams, aged colored laundress, of 419 Cypress Street, passed away at her home last night. She was known and respected by many white families in the community. Three daughters and a grandson survive.

One of these surviving daughters, Tempy, is a victim of that lamentable American disease for which there seems to be no antitoxin: Keeping up with the Joneses, the Joneses in Tempy's case being bourgeois whites. With a smattering of what she believes to be culture, a few parcels of income property, and a husband who works for the Government, Tempy spends her time trying to convince herself and the world at large that she is neither part nor parcel of the peasant environment in which she happened to be born. While Tempy sounds as if she might be interesting, she is actually the most poorly delineated character in the novel. The reason is obvious. Being constantly surrounded by a legion of Tempy's prototypes, Mr. Hughes has not been as objective in this portrayal as he might have been had Tempy, like most of his other characters, been more indigenous to the novel's milieu.

The youngest daughter, Harriett, is a native hedonist, early and easily seduced by flashy clothes, torrid dancing, spontaneous song fests, stimulating beverages and amorous dalliance. Frustrating all efforts to keep her in school or make her amenable to menial labor, she gleefully, if not always successfully, defies the wrath of Aunt Hagar's God and Charlestons down a gaudy, primrose path.

———

The other daughter, Annjee, is the mother of Hagar's one grandchild, Sandy. Annjee is distressingly normal. She works hard, complains but seldom, has no desire to be either a Tempy or a Harriett, and loves her husband, the irresponsible Jimboy, intensely, constantly, albeit, he is subject to the "travelin' blues," and walks off from Annjee and her child whenever the spirit so moves him.

It is with Sandy, the son of this haphazard union, whom "Not Without Laughter" primarily concerns itself. Around him most of the action is woven, through his eyes much of the story is reflected, and it is the problem of Sandy's adjustment to his environment, a problem more or less peculiar to the maturing Negro child, which occupies many pages of the novel.

It is not Sandy, however, but Aunt Hagar, Harriett, Jimboy and Annjee who remain alive in the reader's mind once the novel is completed. And of these Aunt Hagar is by far the most indelible, a fact which explains the reference made to page 249 some paragraphs ago. For when Aunt Hagar dies and crosses over Jordan, the reader is hard put to retain his former high pitch of interest. Simultaneously with her death, Harriett, Jimboy and Annjee also fade into the background. It is too great a bereavement. Either the novel should have managed to end itself at this point or Aunt Hagar's demise should have been postponed. Certainly her heav'nly home could have done without her for a few more years. Her presence is vitally necessary to the more mundane "Not Without Laughter."

Following the death of his grandmother, Sandy is forced to sojourn with the dicty Tempy, his mother having decided to trail the truant Jimboy. Tempy keeps him in school, urges him to abjure bad company, and, being a myopic disciple of Dr. W. E. B. DuBois, attempts to invest him with ideals diametrically opposed to those disseminated and held dear by his dead grandmother, a loyal, if vague, disciple of Booker T. Washington. Sandy seems destined to pursue a middle course, and we leave him optimistically facing the future, appropriately misunderstood by Annjee, obligingly relieved of Tempy, and, surprisingly enough, encouraged and aided by Harriett, whose aversion to the straight and narrow path has brought her a measure of fame and fortune on the stage.

———

"Not Without Laughter" is an enviable first performance. Belonging to a more decorous school, it lacks the dramatic intensity, the lush color, and tropical gusto of Claude McKay's "Home to Harlem." It also lacks the pallid insipidity and technical gaucheries of certain other contemporary novels by Negroes which are best left unnamed and forgotten. But it does present a vivid, sincerely faithful and commendable picture of peasant Negro life in a small American town, a town which vacilates uncertainly, spiritually and physically, from one side of the Mason Dixon line to the other.

In a moment of post-college exuberance, while considering Mr. Hughes's first book of poems, "The Weary Blues," the present reviewer stridently declaimed that its author was possessed of "an unpredictable and immeasurable potential." After five years, the language might be more simple and more choice, but the spirit of the

10

ALFRED A. KNOPF, *Inc.*
730 FIFTH AVENUE
New York

July 29, 1930.

Dear Mr. Hughes,

You may be interested in the following comment on "Not Without Laughter" from Benjamin Brawley.

A few days ago you were so good as to send me for review "Not Without Laughter", by Mr. Langston Hughes. I regret after an examination that I cannot review this book, at least not without calling attention to its very unpleasant tone, and that I should prefer not to do. The book is being returned to-day. I have sometimes had to wonder how such an excellent firm as yours brings out such books as this, but I guess you know best what you want to publish.

What can we do with a mind like Professor Brawley's?

Yours faithfully,
ALFRED A. KNOPF, Inc.

bs:er   Publicity Dep't.

Langston Hughes, Esq.
P.O.Box 94
Westfield, New Jersey.

A letter from Bernard Smith, quoting scholar Benjamin Brawley, the author of The Negro in Literature and Art *in the United States (1918). In his 1927 essay "The Negro Literary Renaissance," Brawley had characterized Hughes as "a sad case of a young man of ability who has gone off on the wrong track altogether" (Langston Hughes Papers, Yale Collection of American Literature, Beinecke Rare Book and Manuscript Library).*

phrase would remain unchanged. For, as in his poetry Mr. Hughes carried a beacon light for Negro poets, he now, with this volume, advances to the vanguard of those who have recourse to the novel in an earnest endeavor to depict the many faceted ramifications of Negro life in America.

–*New York Evening Post,* 28 July 1930, p. 7

* * *

Sterling A. Brown, a poet and the author of The Negro in American Fiction *(1937), reviewed* Not Without Laughter *for* Opportunity.

"The Simplicity of Great Art"
Review of *Not Without Laughter*

We have in this book, laconically, tenderly told, the story of a young boy's growing up. Let no one be deceived by the effortless ease of the telling, by the unpretentious simplicity of *Not Without Laughter*. Its simplicity is the simplicity of great art; a wide observation, a long brooding over humanity, and a feeling for beauty in unexpected, out of the way places, must have gone into its makeup. It is generously what one would expect of the author of *The Weary Blues* and *Fine Clothes to the Jew*.

Not Without Laughter tells of a poor family living in a small town in Kansas. We are shown intimately the work and play, the many sided aspects of Aunt Hager and her brood. Aunt Hager has three daughters: Tempy, Annjee and Harriett. Tempy is doing well; having joined the Episcopalian Church she has put away "niggerish" things; Annjee is married to a likeable scapegrace, Jimboy, guitar plunker and rambling man; Harriett, young, full of life and daring, is her heart's worry. She has a grandchild, Sandy, son of Anjee and Jimboy. And about him the story centers.

Sandy with his wide eyes picking up knowledge of life about the house; Sandy listening to his father's blues and ballads in the purple evenings, watching his Aunt Harriett at her dancing; Sandy at school; Sandy dreaming over his geography book; Sandy at his job in the barbershop and hotel; Sandy at his grandmother's funeral; Sandy learning respectability at Aunt Tempy's,– and learning at the same time something of the ways of women from Pansetta; Sandy in Chicago; Sandy with his books and dreams of education–so run the many neatly etched scenes.

But the story is not Sandy's alone. We see Harriett, first as a firm fleshed beautiful black girl, quick at her lessons; we see her finally a blues singer on State Street. The road she has gone has been rocky enough. She has been maid at a country club where the tired business men made advances; she has been with a carnival troupe, she has been arrested for street walking. We follow Annjee in her trials, and Jimboy, and Tempy. And we get to know the wise, tolerant Aunt Hager, beloved by whites and blacks; even by Harriett who just about breaks her heart. Lesser characters are as clearly individualized and developed. We have Willie Mae, and Jimmy Lane, and Joe Willis, "white folks nigger," and Uncle Dan, and Mingo, and Buster, who could have passed for white. The white side of town, the relationships of employers with laundresses and cooks, all these are adequately done. The book, for all of its apparent slightness, is fullbodied.

One has to respect the author's almost casual filling in of background. The details are perfectly chosen; and they make the reader *see*. How representative are his pictures of the carnival, and the dance at which "Benbow's Famous Kansas City Band" plays, and the gossip over back fences! How recognizable is Sister Johnson's "All these womens dey mammy named Jane an' Mary an' Cora, soon's dey gets a little somethin', dey changes dey names to Janette or Mariana or Corina or somethin' mo' flowery than what dey had."

As the title would suggest the book is not without laughter. Jimboy's guitar-playing, Harriett's escapades, the barber shop tall tales, the philosophizing of the old sheep "who know de road," all furnish something of this. Sandy's ingenuousness occasionally is not without laughter. But the dominant note of the book is a quiet pity. It is not sentimental; it is candid, clear eyed instead–but it is still pity. Even the abandon, the fervor of the chapter called *Dance,* closely and accurately rendered (as one would expect of Langston Hughes) does not strike the note of unclouded joy. We see these things as they are: as the pitiful refuges of poor folk against the worries of hard days. It is more the laughter of the blues line–*laughin' just to keep from cryin'.*

The difference between comedy and tragedy of course lies often in the point of view from which the story is told. Mr. Hughes' sympathetic identification with these folk is so complete that even when sly comic bits creep in (such as Madame de Carter and the Dance of the Nations) the laughter is quiet–more of a smile than a Cohen-like guffaw. But even these sly bits are few and far between. More than Sandy's throwing his boot-black box at the drunken cracker, certainly a welcome case of poetic justice, one remembers the disappointments of this lad's life. Sandy went on Children's Day to the Park. "Sorry," the man said. "This party's for white kids." In a classroom where the students are seated alphabetically, Sandy and the other three colored children sit behind Albert Zwick. Sandy, in the white folks' kitchen, hears his hardworking mother reprimanded by her sharp tempered employer. And while his mother wraps several little bundles of food to carry to Jimboy, Sandy cried. These scenes are excellently done, with restraint, with irony, and with compassion.

Sandy knows the meaning of a broken family, of poverty, of seeing those he loves go down without being able to help. Most touching, and strikingly universal, is the incident of the Xmas sled. Sandy, wishful for a Golden Flyer sled with flexible rudders! is surprised on Christmas Day by the gift of his mother and grandmother. It is a sled. They had labored and schemed and sacrificed for it in a hard winter. On the cold Christmas morning they dragged it home. It was a home-made contraption—roughly carpentered, with strips of rusty tin along the wooden runners. "It's fine," Sandy lied, as he tried to lift it.

Of a piece with this are the troubles that Annjee knows—Annjee whose husband is here today and gone tomorrow; Annjee, who grows tired of the buffeting and loses ground slowly; and the troubles of Aunt Hager who lives long enough to see her hopes fade out, and not long enough to test her final hope, Sandy. . . . Tempy, prosperous, has coldshouldered her mother; Annjee is married to a man who frets Hager; Harriett has gone with Maudel to the sinister houses of the bottom. "One by one they leaves you," Hager said slowly. "One by one yo' chillen goes."

Unforgettable is the little drama of Harriett's rebellion. It is the universal conflict of youth and age. Mr. Hughes records it, without comment. It is the way life goes. Harriett, embittered by life, wanting her share of joy, is forbidden to leave the house. The grandmother is belligerent, authoritative, the girl rebellious. And then the grandmother breaks. . . . "Harriett, honey, I wants you to be good." But the pitiful words do not avail; Harriett, pitiless as only proud youth can be, flings out of doors—with a cry, "You old Christian Fool!" A group of giggling shreiks welcomes her.

Of all of his characters, Mr. Hughes obviously has least sympathy with Tempy. She is the *arriviste,* the worshipper of white folks' ways, the striver. "They don't 'sociate no mo' with none but de high toned colored folks." The type deserves contempt looked at in one way, certainly; looked at in another it might deserve pity. But the point of the reviewer is

this: that Mr. Hughes does not make Tempy quite convincing. It is hard to believe that Tempy would be as blatantly crass as she is to her mother on Christmas Day, when she says of her church "Father Hill is so dignified, and the services are absolutely refined! *There's never anything niggerish about them—so you know, mother, they suit me."*

But, excepting Tempy, who to the reviewer seems slightly caricatured, all of the characters are completely convincing. There is a universality about them. They have, of course, peculiar problems as Negroes. Harriett, for instance, hates all whites, with reason. But they have even more the problems that are universally human. Our author does not exploit either local color, or race. He has selected an interesting family and has told us candidly, unembitteredly, poetically of their joy lightened and sorrow laden life.

Langston Hughes presents all of this without apology. Tolerant, humane, and wise in the ways of mortals, he has revealed beauty where too many of us, dazzled by false lights, are unable to see it. He has shown us again, in this third book of his—what he has insisted all along, with quiet courage:

Beautiful, also, is the sun.
Beautiful, also, are the souls of my people. . . .

—*Opportunity,* 8 (September 1930): 279–280

Greetings to Soviet Workers

Not Without Laughter, first novel by Langston Hughes, parts of which first appeared in *New Masses* a few months ago, has been published recently in this country and is now being issued in several foreign translations.

In Soviet Russia, the book is being published by the State Publishing Company "Land and Factory." On request, the following greetings were sent by the author to Soviet readers, to be included in the first edition:

"All over the world Negroes are robbed, and poor. In the name of their misery I salute the Russian people. I send my greetings to the great Soviet ideal, to its true realization in your own land, and to its sunrise hope for the downtrodden and oppressed everywhere on earth."

—*New Masses,* 6 (December 1930): 23

The Story of *Mule Bone*

In spring 1930 Hughes worked with Zora Neale Hurston on Mule Bone, *but bitter arguments between the two writers prevented the play from being published or produced during their lifetimes. In this essay Henry Louis Gates Jr. charts the history of Hughes and Hurston's ill-fated collaboration during the Harlem Renaissance.* Mule Bone: A Comedy of Negro Life *(1991), edited by George Houston Bass and Gates, provides the most complete accounting of the* Mule Bone *controversy yet published.*

A Tragedy of Negro Life

This play was never done because the authors fell out.

–LANGSTON HUGHES, 1931

And fall out, unfortunately, they did, thereby creating the most notorious literary quarrel in African-American cultural history, and one of the most thoroughly documented collaborations in black American literature. Langston Hughes published an account entitled "Literary Quarrel" as the penultimate chapter—indeed, almost as a coda or an afterthought—in his autobiography, *The Big Sea* (1940). Robert Hemenway, Zora Neale Hurston's biographer, published a chapter in his biography entitled "Mule Bone," and Arnold Rampersad, Hughes's biographer, presents an equally detailed account in volume one of his *The Life of Langston Hughes*. Only Zora Neale Hurston, of the two principals, did not make public her views of the episode. But she did leave several letters (as did Hughes) in which she explains some of her behavior and feelings. In addition, Hurston left the manuscript of the short story, "The Bone of Contention," upon which the play was based. These documents—letters, the short story, Hughes's account, and two accounts from careful and judicious scholars—as well as a draft of the text of the play, *Mule Bone: A Comedy of Negro Life,* comprise the full record of the curious history of this brilliant collaboration between two extraordinarily talented African-American writers. We have assembled this archival and published data here to provide contemporary readers with the fullest possible account of a complex and bizarre incident that will forever remain impossible to understand completely, beclouded in inexplicable motivation.

In a sense, this is a casebook of a crucial–and ugly–chapter in the history of the Harlem Renaissance, that extraordinarily rich period in American cultural history that witnessed the birth of jazz, the

Zora Neale Hurston, who from the 1930s through the 1960s was among the most prolific black women writing in America (photograph by Carl Van Vechten; Library of Congress, Prints & Photographs Division, Carl Van Vechten Collection, courtesy of Carl Van Vechten Trust)

coming to fruition of the classic blues, and the first systematic attempt to generate an entire literary and cultural movement by black Americans. The Harlem Renaissance, also called "The New Negro Renaissance," is generally thought to have begun in the early 1920s and ended early on in the Great Depression, about the time when Hughes and Hurston had their dispute. The origins of the Renaissance are, of course, complex and have been written about extensively. It is clear, however, that the production of a rich and various black art, especially the written arts and the theatre, could very well help to reshape the public image of black people within American society and facilitate thereby their long struggle for civil rights, a struggle that commenced almost as soon as the last battle of the Civil War ended. As James Weldon Johnson put it in the "Preface" to his *Book of American Negro Poetry* (1922):

A people may be great through many means, but there is one by which its greatness is recognized and acknowledged. The final measure of the greatness of all peoples is the amount and standard of the literature and art they produced. The world does not know that a people is great until that people produces great literature and art. No people that has produced great literature and art has ever been looked upon by the world as distinctly inferior.

If, then, African-Americans created a recognizable and valued canon of literature, its effect would have enormous political ramifications: "The status of the Negro in the United States," Johnson concluded, "is more a question of national mental attitude toward the race than of actual conditions. And nothing will do more to change that mental attitude and raise his status than a demonstration of intellectual parity by the Negro through the production of literature and art."

Johnson, by 1922 one of the venerable figures of the black literary and theatrical traditions, effectively issued a call to arms for the creation of a literary movement. Soon, political organizations such as the National Association for the Advancement of Colored People (NAACP) and the National Urban League, through their magazines, *The Crisis* and *Opportunity,* began to sponsor literary competitions, judged by prominent members of the American literati, with the winners receiving cash prizes, publication in the journals, and often book contracts. At the prompting of Charles Johnson, the editor of *Opportunity,* Hurston submitted two short stories—"Spunk" and "Black Death"—and two plays—*Color Struck* and *Spears*—for consideration in *Opportunity*'s annual literary contests in 1925 and 1926. While "Spunk" and *Color Struck* won second-place prizes, *Spears* and "Black Death" won honorable mention. Two other short stories, "Drenched in Light" and "Muttsy" would be published in *Opportunity,* along with "Spunk." It was at the 1925 annual awards dinner that she met another award winner, Langston Hughes, who took third prize jointly with Countee Cullen and first prize for his great poem, "The Weary Blues." It was a momentous occasion, attended by "the greatest gathering of black and white literati ever assembled in one room," as Arnold Rampersad notes, and included among its judges Eugene O'Neill, John Farrar, Witter Bynner, Alexander Woolcott, and Robert Benchley. Hughes was quite taken with Hurston, Rampersad tells us: She "'is a clever girl, isn't she?' he soon wrote to a friend; 'I would like to know her.'" Eventually, he would know her all too well.

II

Between 1925 and their collaboration on the writing of *Mule Bone* between March and June 1930,

Hughes and Hurston came to know each other well. As Rampersad reports, by mid-summer of 1926, the two were planning a black jazz and blues opera. Hemenway calls it "an opera that would be the first authentic rendering of black folklife, presenting folk songs, dances, and tales that Hurston would collect." By the end of that summer, the two (along with Wallace Thurman, John P. Davis, Gwen Bennett, Bruce Nugent, and Aaron Douglass, all members of what was jokingly called "The Niggerati") decided to found a magazine, called *Fire!!,* the title taken from a Hughes poem. The following year, in July 1927, Hughes and Hurston met quite by accident in Mobile, Alabama, and decided to drive together to Manhattan in her car, "Sassy Susie." "I knew it would be fun travelling with her," Rampersad reports Hughes writing. "It was." The trip lasted about a month, with the two sharing notes on hoodoo, folktales, and the blues along the way, and even meeting Bessie Smith, the great classic blues singer. Shortly after this trip, Hughes introduced Hurston to his patron, Charlotte van der Veer Quick Mason, who would contribute about $75,000 to Harlem Renaissance writers, including $15,000 to Hurston. While Hughes received $150 per month, Hurston received $200. Ironically, their subsidies would end just about the time of their feud over *Mule Bone;* although Hurston's contract ended March 30, 1931, she received "irregular" payments until September 1932; Hughes and she fell out late in 1930, just before his confrontation with Hurston in Cleveland.

A more natural combination for a collaboration among the writers of the Harlem Renaissance, one can scarcely imagine—especially in the theatre! Hurston wrote to Hughes often during the early period of her research in the South, collecting black folklore as part of her doctoral research in anthropology at Columbia under Franz Boas; Hemenway describes her correspondence as "frequent and conspiratorial," providing "an unintentional documentary of the expedition." In April 1928, she shared with Hughes her plans for a culturally authentic African-American theatre, one constructed upon a foundation of the black vernacular: "Did I tell you before I left about the new, the *real* Negro theatre I plan? Well, I shall, or rather we shall act out the folk tales, however short, with the abrupt angularity and naivete of the primitive 'bama Nigger. Quote that with native settings. What do you think?" They would share the burdens and the glory: "Of course, you know I didn't dream of that theatre as a one man stunt. I had you helping 50-50 from the start. In fact, I am perfectly willing to be 40 to your 60 since you are always so much more practical than I. But I know it is going to be *glorious!* A really new departure in the drama." Despite their enthusiasm for this idea, however, Mrs. Mason

("Godmother") disapproved; as Hurston wrote to Alain Locke, the veritable dean of the Harlem Renaissance and another beneficiary of Mrs. Mason's patronage: "Godmother was very anxious that I should say to you that the plans–rather the hazy dreams of the theatre I talked to you about should never be mentioned again. She trusts her three children [Hurston, Hughes, and Locke] to never let those words pass their lips again until the gods decree that they shall materialize."

Not only did the two share the dream of a vernacular theatre and opera, but both had established themselves as creative writers and critics by underscoring the value of black folk culture, both of itself and as the basis for formal artistic traditions. By 1930, when, at last, the two would write *Mule Bone*, Hughes had published two brilliant, widely acclaimed, experimental books of poetry that utilized the blues and jazz as both form and content. And Hurston, though yet to publish a novel, had published sixteen short stories, plays, and essays, in prestigious journals such as *Opportunity, Messenger,* and the *Journal of Negro History,* and was pursuing a Ph.D. thesis in anthropology which was to be built around her extensive collection of Afro-American myths. With Hurston's mastery of the vernacular and compelling sense of story, and Hughes's impressive sense of poetic and theatrical structure, it would have been difficult to imagine a more ideal team to construct "a real Negro theatre." For, at ages twenty-eight and twenty-nine respectively,* Hughes and Hurston bore every promise of reshaping completely the direction of the development of African-American literature away from the blind imitation of American literature and toward a bold and vibrant synthesis of formal American literature and African-American vernacular.

III

The enormous potential of this collaborative effort was never realized, we know, because, as Hughes wrote on his manuscript copy of the text, "the authors fell out." Exactly *why* they "fell out" is not completely clear, despite the valiant attempts of Hemenway and Rampersad to reconstruct the curious series of events that led to such disastrous consequences. While we do know that Hughes and Hurston wrote acts one and three together, and, as Hemenway reports, "at least one scene of the second act," it is impossible to ascertain who wrote what. Hurston had conceived the plot, based as it was on her short story, "The Bone of Contention" (published here for the first time). Hughes would write that he "plotted out and typed the play based on her story," and that Hurston "authenticated and flavored the dialogue and added highly humorous details." Rampersad's estimate is probably the most

accurate: "Hurston's contribution was almost certainly the greater to a play set in an all-black town in the backwoods South (she drew here on her childhood memories), with an abundance of tall tales, wicked quips, and farcical styles of which she was absolute master and Langston not much more than a sometimes student. . . . Whatever dramatic distinction the play would have, Hurston certainly brought to it." But, just as surely, it was Hughes who shaped the material into a play, into comic drama, with a plot, a dramatic structure, and a beginning, middle, and end. While Hurston had published a play, and Hughes had not yet completed his first play, Hughes was the superior dramatist. Neither, however, would ever achieve the results that they did, in close collaboration, with *Mule Bone*.

While we cannot explain Hurston's motivation for denying Hughes's collaboration, which caused the dispute and the ending of their friendship, we can re-create the strange series of events through the following chronology, which is based on the accounts of Hemenway and Rampersad, printed in this book:

Late February–early March 1930: Hughes meets Theresa Helburn of the Dramatists Guild at a party; Helburn complains about the lack of real comedies about blacks.

April–May 1930: Hughes and Hurston write the first draft of "Mule Bone" in Westfield, New Jersey. Complete acts one and three and at least scene one of act two, dictating to Louise Thompson.

May 1930: Hughes's relation with patron, Mrs. Mason, begins to collapse.

June 1930: Hurston returns to the South, ostensibly to complete the trial scene of act two.

September 1930: Hurston returns, apparently without the scene completed.

October 1930: Hurston files for copyright of *Mule Bone* as sole author.

December 1930–January 1931: Hughes ends relationship with "Godmother," Mrs. Mason.

January 1931: Hughes returns to his mother's home in Cleveland, has tonsillectomy.

Winter 1930–31: Hurston gives Carl Van Vechten copy of play. Van Vechten sends it to Barrett Clark, reader for the Theatre Guild. Clark, an employee of Samuel French, the theatrical producer, contacts Rowena Jelliffe and sends script.

January 15, 1931: Hughes visits Rowena and Alexander Jelliffe, directors of the settlement playhouse "Karamu House," home of the black theatre troupe the Gilpin Players. Rowena Jel-

*Title page annotated by Hughes (Yale Collection of American Literature,
Beinecke Rare Book and Manuscript Library)*

liffe explains that she has obtained the rights to a play entitled *Mule Bone* by Zora Neale Hurston.

January 16, 1931: Hughes phones Hurston to protest her action. Hurston denies knowledge of play being sent to French or to Jelliffe. Hughes incredulous.

January 16, 1931: Hughes writes to Carl Van Vechten asking for his advice.

January 17, 1931: Louise Thompson arrives in Cleveland, in her capacity as official of the American Interracial Seminar.

January 18, 1931: Hurston visits Van Vechten, and "cried and carried on no end."

January 19, 1931: Hughes mails copy of play to U.S. copyright office, in name of Hurston and himself. Received January 22.

January 20, 1931: Hughes receives Hurston's letter denying joint authorship and complaining about Louise Thompson's compensation.

January 20, 1931: French's company wires Jelliffe refusing Hurston's permission to authorize production. Demands return of script.

January 20–21, 1931: Hurston sends three telegrams reversing her decision; authorizes the production and agrees to collaborate with Hughes.

January 21, 1931: Hughes receives Hurston letter of January 18, denying Hughes's collaboration and revealing resentment over Hughes's friendship with Louise Thompson.

January 21–26, 1931: Hurston agrees to come to Cleveland to collaborate with Hughes on rewrites; first performance scheduled for February 15.

"Flinging a Final Mule Bone"

In this letter Hughes describes the incident that ended his collaboration with Hurston. Those mentioned include Rowena Jelliffe, who, as director of the settlement playhouse "Karamu House," had initially agreed to produce the play, and Louise Thompson, a Mason protégée who had served as the typist for the play.

Hughes to Carl Van Vechten, 4 February 1931

Dear Carlo—

This is not an answer to your swell letter at all. Here, I'm only flinging a final mule bone at you: Zora's come and gone! I was flat on my back with tonsilitus, but got up against the doctor's orders to talk with her—and am in bed again as a result. She made such a scene as you cannot possibly imagine—right before the Jelliffe's, my mother, and a new boy friend Zora brought with her. This final performance took place at my house yesterday afternoon. It was mostly about Miss Thompson. Zora laid her out. Also laid out the Jelliffe's. Also me. She pushed her hat back, bucked her eyes, ground her teeth, and shook manuscripts in my face, particularly the third act which she claims she wrote alone by herself while Miss Thompson and I were off doing Spanish together. (and the way she said Spanish meant something else.) She admitted that we had worked jointly, and that certain characterizations were mine, but she dared and defied me to put my finger on a line that was my own. One line at the end of the 1st act had been mine, but she took that out, she said. Anyway, she had written a "new" play by herself; she hadn't come to Cleveland to be made a fool of, nor to submit to any sly tricks such as she felt Mrs. Jelliffe had pulled by having the nerve to put my name with hers on the play. Her agent had said the Jelliffes were honorable people—but now—why she couldn't even bear the sight of their Set-

tlement House, it was so muddy and dirty in the yard, etc! etc! in an absolutely crazy vein, until Mr. Jelliffe asked his wife to no longer remain to be further insulted—whereupon they all left, Zora in a rage without even saying Goodbye to me or mother. I haven't told you the half of it—but I've just finished six typed pages to Mr. Spingarn, and couldn't go into detail again today. I guess this is the end of Mule-Bone. But nine-tenths of Zora's talk here was not about the play at all, but Madame Thurman—the very thought of whom seemed to infuriate Zora. The play was a mere side-issue, but when it did come up Zora tried to make it appear that I wanted to steal it from her—(as if I began any of this Cleveland business!) and in all cases the stenographer was a hussy! . . . So I guess there is no more Mule-Bone. . . . What probably helped to make Zora so angry was that Sunday night, only a few hours before she arrived, the Gilpin Players voted to drop the production, as they had been unable to get any word from either Zora or her agent in regard to terms, and they felt that to go any further would make the risk too great as they had requested an answer by Feb. first, and none had come. Zora's defense was that she herself had intended to be here for the Sun. meeting, but, she said, she had stopped in Pittsburgh all night Saturday so that the boy she was driving with could buy a present for his aunt! . . . Do you think she is crazy, Carlo?

Thanks for the birthday stallions.

Langston

–Langston Hughes Papers, James Weldon Johnson Collection in the Yale Collection of American Literature, Beinecke Rare Book and Manuscript Library

MULEBONE   A COMEDY OF NEGRO LIFE IN THREE ACTS   Page (1)

BY LANGSTON HUGHES and ZORA HURSTON

CHARACTERS: JIM WESTON: Guitarist, Methodist, slightly arrogant, aggress-
                 ive, somewhat self-important, ready with his tongue.

DAVE CARTER: Dancer, Baptist, soft, happ-go-lucky character, slightly
                 dumb and unable to talk rapidly and wittily.

DAISY TAYLOR: Methodist, domestic servant, plump, dark and sexy, self-
                 conscious of clothes and appeal, fickle.

JOE CLARK: The Mayor, storekeeper and postmaster, arrogant, ignorant
                 and powerful in a self-assertive way, large, fat man;
                 Methodist.

ELDER SIMMS: Methodist minister, newcomer in town, ambitious, small and
                 fly, but not very intelligent.

ELDER CHILDERS: Big, loose-jointed, slow-spoken but not dumb. Long resident
                 in the town, calm and sure of himself.

KATIE CARTER: Dave's aunt, a little old wizened dried-up lady.

MRS. MATTIE CLARK: The Mayor's wife, fat and flabby mulatto, high-pitched voice.

MRS. SIMMS: Reverend Simms wife. Large and aggressive.

MRS. CHILDERS: Just a wife who thinks of details. Rev. Childers's wife.

LUM BOGER: Young town marshall about twenty, tall, gangly, with big
                 flat feet, liked to show off in public.

TEET MILLER: Village vamp who is jealous of DAISY.

LIGE MOSELY: A village wag.

WALTER TOMAS: Another village wag.

ADA LEWIS: A promiscuous lover.

DELLA LEWIS: Baptist, poor housekeeper, mother of ADA.

BOOTSIE PITTS: A local vamp.

MRS. DILCIE ANDERSON: Village housewife, Methodist.

WILLIE NIXON: Methodist, short runt.

SETTING: The raised porch of JOE CLARK'S store and the street in front
                 Porch stretches almost completely across the stage, with a
                 plank bench at either end. At the center of the porch three
                 steps leading from street. Rear of porch, center, door to the
                 store. On either side are single windows on which signs:
                 left, "POST OFFICE", and at right, "GENERAL STORE" are paint-
                 ed. Soap boxes, axe handles, small kegs, etc., on porch on
                 which townspeople sit and lounge during action. Above the
                 roof of the porch the "false front", or imitation second story
                 of the shop is seen with large sign painted across it "JOE
                 CLARK'S GENERAL STORE". Large kerosine street lamp on post
                 at right in front of porch.

TIME: Saturday afternoon and the villagers are gathered around the
                 store. Several men sitting on boxes at edge of porch chewing
                 sugar cane, spitting tobacco juice, arguing, some whittling,
                 others eating peanuts. During the act the women all dressed
                 up in starched dresses parade in and out of store. People
                 buying groceries, children playing in the street, etc. Gen-
                 eral noise of conversation, laughter and children shouting.

                 (Page 1)

First page of the Mule Bone *typescript (Yale Collection of American Literature,*
Beinecke Rare Book and Manuscript Library)

February 1, 1931: Hughes's twenty-ninth birthday. Hurston arrives in Cleveland, meets with Hughes, resolves differences, misses scheduled meeting with Gilpin Players. That evening, the Gilpin Players meet and vote to cancel play, but reconsider. All seems set for a Cleveland opening and a Broadway run.

February 2, 1931: Hurston learns that Louise Thompson has visited Cleveland and seen Hughes. Hurston berates Mrs. Jelliffe.

February 3, 1931: Hurston visits Hughes at his home and rudely cancels production.

August 1931: Wallace Thurman (estranged husband of Louise Thompson) hired to revise *Mule Bone.* Hughes writes to Dramatists Guild declaring joint authorship.

1940: Hughes publishes account in *The Big Sea.*

1964: Hughes publishes act three in *Drama Critique.*

This, in barest outline, is an account of the bizarre events of an extremely ugly affair. As Hemenway and Rampersad make clear, Hurston justified her denial of Hughes's collaboration by claiming anger over Hughes's apparent proposal that Louise Thompson be given a share of all royalties, and that she be made the business manager of any Broadway production that might evolve. In Hurston's words:

> In the beginning, Langston, I was very eager to do the play with you. ANYthing you said would go over big with me. But scarcely had we gotten underway before you made three propositions that shook me to the foundation of myself. First: that three way split with Louise. Now Langston, nobody has in the history of the world given a typist an interest in a work for typing it. Nobody would think of it unless they were prejudiced in favor of the typist.

If this seems scant reason, sixty years later, for Hurston's protest over Thompson's financial role to assume such an extreme form, her behavior was no doubt also motivated, as Hemenway and Rampersad argue, by Hughes's deteriorating relationship with Mrs. Mason and Hurston's desire to continue hers, even if at Hughes's expense. Hurston kept Mrs. Mason abreast of these developments over the play, and even sent her copies of Hughes's letters to her, all the while denying his claims to Mason. What seems clear, however, is that Hurston's behavior was not justified by her anger over Hughes's friendship with Thompson, and that her claim of sole authorship should not have been made. As Hughes concluded, "our art was broken," as was both their

friendship and the promise of a new and bold direction in black theatre.

IV

Certainly one tragic aspect of the failure of Hughes and Hurston to produce and publish *Mule Bone* was the interruption of the impact that it might have had on the shape and direction of Afro-American theatre. Among all of the black arts, greater expectations were held for none more than for black theatre. As early as 1918, W. E. B. Du Bois, writing in *The Crisis,* argued that "the value of [a sustained Afro-American theatre] for Negro art can scarcely be overestimated." In 1925, Du Bois would help to found Krigwa, a black theatre group in Harlem, dedicated to drama that is "by," "for," "about," and "near *us*," a self-contained and self-sustaining Afro-American theatre. Du Bois was just one of many critics who felt that the drama was the most crucial form of all of the arts for the future of black artistic development, and that it was precisely in this area that blacks had most signally failed. As Alain Locke put it, "Despite the fact that Negro life is somehow felt to be particularly rich in dramatic values, both as folk experience and as a folk temperament, its actual yield, so far as worthwhile drama goes, has been very inconsiderable." And, in another essay published in 1927, Locke wrote:

> In the appraisal of the possible contribution of the Negro to the American theatre, there are those who find the greatest promise in the rising drama of Negro life. Others see possibilities of a deeper, though subtler influence upon what is after all more vital, the technical aspects of the arts of the theatre. Until very recently the Negro influence upon American drama has been negligible, whereas even under the handicaps of second-hand exploitation and restriction to the popular amusement stage, the Negro actor has already considerably influenced our stage and its arts. One would do well to imagine what might happen if the art of the Negro actor should really become artistically lifted and liberated. Transpose the possible resources of Negro song and dance and pantomime to the serious stage, envisage an American drama under the galvanizing stimulus of a rich transfusion of essential folk-arts and you may anticipate what I mean. ("The Negro and the American Theatre")

There can be little doubt that Locke here voices the theory of black drama that Hurston and Hughes sought to embody in their unwritten black opera and in *Mule Bone.* (Hurston had, by the way, once described the relationship among the three as that of a triangle, with Hughes and her forming the base, and Locke the apex.)

There are many reasons for the supposed primacy of the theatre among the arts of the Harlem Renaissance. Many scholars date the commencement of the Renaissance itself to the phenomenal and unprecedented success of Eubie Blake's and Noble Sissle's all-black Broadway musical, *Shuffle Along,* which opened in 1921. (Blake and Sissle did the score, and Aubrey Lyles and Flournoy Miller did the book.) As Bruce Kellner informs us, "Often the week's first run business was so heavy that the street on which it was playing had to be designated for one-way traffic only." Josephine Baker, Florence Mills, and Paul Robeson were just a few of the performers who played in this musical.

Predictably, the success of *Shuffle Along* spawned a whole host of imitators, including *Alabama Bound, Bandana Land, Black Bottom Revue, Black Scandals, Blackbirds, Chocolate Blondes, Chocolate Browns, Chocolate Dandies, Darktown Scandals, Darktown Strutters, Goin' White, Lucky Sambo, North Ain't South, Raisin' Cane, Strut Miss Lizzie, Seven-Eleven, Dixie to Broadway,* and *Runnin' Wild* (which introduced "The Charleston"), to list just a few. Jazz, the dance, acting, and an extraordinarily large white and sympathetic audience made the theatre an enormously promising venue for a black art that would transform the public image of the Negro. Its effect was both broad and immediate; there was not the sort of mediation necessary between artist and audience as is the case with a printed book. What's more, theatre as a combination of several arts—poetry, narrative, music, the dance, acting, the visual arts—allowed blacks to bring together the full range of their traditions, vernacular and formal, rather than just one. The great potential of the theatre was hard to resist.

Resistance, however, arose from tradition itself. The roots of black theatre in the twenties were buried in the soil of minstrelsy and vaudeville. Musicals such as *Shuffle Along* did indeed reach tens of thousands more Americans than would any book before *Native Son* (1940). But what image did they represent, and at what cost? Reviews of *Shuffle Along* often turned on phrases such as "extreme energy," "the sun of their good humor." Especially notable were the dancers' "jiggling," "prancing," "wiggling," and "cavorting." In other words, what this sort of black theatre did was to reinforce the stereotype of black people as happy-go-lucky, overly sensual bodies. And while it was (and remains) difficult to disrupt the integrity of jazz and Afro-American dance, even in association with quasi-minstrel forms, it is difficult to imagine how the *intelligence* of these artistic traditions could shine through the raucous humor of this kind of theatre. Broadway, in other words, stood as the counterpoint to the sort of written art that Hughes and Hurston were determined to create, even if they envied Broadway's potential and actual market. Accordingly, they decided to intervene, to do for the drama what Hughes had done for poetry and what Hurston would do (in *Jonah's Gourd Vine* [1934] and *Their Eyes Were Watching God* [1937]) for the novel, which was to shape a formal written art out of the vast and untapped black vernacular tradition.

Mule Bone was based on a Hurston short story, "The Bone of Contention," which Hurston never published. For the Hurston scholar, it is particularly fascinating as a glimpse into Hurston's manner of revising or transforming the oral tradition (she had collected the story in her folklore research) and because of its representation of various characters (such as Eatonville, an all-black town where Hurston was born, Joe Clarke and his store, the yellow mule and his mock burial) who would recur in subsequent works, such as *Mule Bone* and *Their Eyes Were Watching God.*

The story's plot unfolds as follows: Dave Carter and Jim Weston are hunting turkeys one evening. Carter claims to have shot a turkey, while Weston is loading his gun. Weston claims that it is his shot that killed the turkey. They struggle. Jim Weston strikes Dave Carter on the head with "de hockbone" of a mule, Carter alleges, and steals his turkey.

The remainder of the plot depicts the trial, held at the Baptist Church and presided over by Mayor Joe Clarke. Weston is a Methodist while Clarke is a Baptist, and the townspeople are equally divided between the two denominations. They are also fiercely competitive, bringing a religious significance to the quarrel. In fact, Carter and Weston would be represented in court by their ministers, Rev. Simms (Methodist) and Elder Long (Baptist). "The respective congregations were lined up behind their leaders," the text tells us.

The resolution of the dilemma turns on traditional African-American biblical exegesis: can a mule-bone be a weapon? If it can, then it follows that its use could constitute a criminal act. Using Judges 15:16, Elder Long proves that since a donkey is the father of a mule, and since Samson slew one thousand Philistines with the jaw-bone of an ass, and since "de further back on a mule you goes, do mo' dangerous he gits," then "by de time you gits clear back tuh his hocks hes rank pizen." Jim Weston is banished from town.

The plot of *Mule Bone* is very similar. The play consists of three acts, and includes Jim Weston and Dave Carter (best friends), Joe Clarke, but now Daisy Taylor, over whom Weston and Clarke will, inevitably, quarrel. Weston will strike Carter with the hock-bone of "Brazzle's ole yaller mule," during an argument over Daisy on the front porch of Clarke's store. Weston is arrested, Carter is rushed off to be treated, leaving Daisy alone wondering who's going to walk her home.

Act Two consists of two scenes. The first reveals the subtext of the trial—the struggle between Joe Clarke and Elder Simms for mayor, and the class tension between the Baptists and the Methodists. Scene Two occurs mostly in the Macedonia Baptist Church, newly transformed into a courthouse, with Joe Clarke presiding. As in the short story, the Methodists and Baptists seat themselves on opposite sides, even singing competing hymns (Baptists, "Onward Christian Soldiers" and the Methodists, "All Hail the Power of Jesus's Name") when the mayor asks that the proceedings commence with a hymn. Act Two proceeds as does the short story, with Judges 18:18 coming to bear in exactly the same manner as had Judges 15:16. Jim Weston, found guilty, is banished from town for two years.

Act Three depicts the reconciliation of Jim and Dave, and Jim's return to Eatonville, following their joint rejection of Daisy, who as it turns out, wants her husband to "work for her white folks." What is most interesting about this scene is that the tension between Dave and Jim is resolved in a witty and sustained verbal dual, in which the two trade cleverly improvised hyperbolic claims of their love for Daisy, in an elaborate ritual of courtship. As Hemenway puts it:

> When Dave asks Jim how much time he would do for Daisy on the chain gang, Jim answers, "Twenty years and like it." Dave exults, "See dat, Daisy, Dat nigger ain't willin to do no time for you. I'd beg de judge to gimme life."
>
> Again a significant stage direction interrupts the dialogue. By telling us that "both Jim and Dave laugh," Hurston and Hughes were trying to show the sense of verbal play and rhetorical improvisation characteristic of Eatonville generally, and Joe Clark's store-front porch specifically. . . . The contest is a ritual, designed to defuse the violence implicit in the conflict, to channel the aggression into mental rather than physical terms. The manner in which the courting contest ends suggests its ritualistic nature: Dave says to Daisy, "Don't you be skeered, baby. Papa kin take keer o you [To Jim: suiting the action to the word] Countin from de finger back to de thumb. . . . Start anything, I got you some." Jim is taken aback: "Aw, I don't want no more fight wid you, Dave." Dave replies, "Who said anything about fighting? We just provin who love Daisy de best."

This courtship ritual, like so much of the verbal "signifying" rituals in which the characters engage throughout the play, are both reflections of historical folk rituals practiced by African Americans as well as their extensions or elaborations. As Hemenway shows so carefully in his essay appended to this volume, often the characters' dialogues are taken directly from the black vernacular tradition. As often, however, Hughes and Hurston are *imitating* that tradition, improvising upon a historical foundation of ritualized oral discourse, which Hurston had been collecting as part of her graduate research in anthropology with

Franz Boas. Hughes and Hurston, in other words, were drawing upon the black vernacular tradition both to "ground" their drama in that discourse but also to "extend" the vernacular itself.

Mule Bone, then, was not a mere vehicle for black folklore, rather, black folklore served as the basis, the foundation, for what they hoped would be a truly new art form: an art form that would stand in relation to traditional American drama in the way that Hughes's "blues poetry" stood to American poetry and Hurston's vernacular fictions stood to the American novel. *Mule Bone,* in other words, was meant to be the dramatic embodiment of James Weldon Johnson's demand that "the colored poet in the United States needs to do . . . something like what Synge did for the Irish; he needs to find a form that will express the racial spirit by symbols from within rather than by symbols from without, such as the mere mutilation of English spelling and pronunciation. He needs a form that is freer and larger than dialect, but which will still hold the racial flavor; a form expressing the imagery, the idioms, the peculiar turns of thought, and the distinctive humor and pathos, too, of the Negro, but which will also be capable of voicing the deepest and highest emotions and aspirations, and allow of the widest range of subjects and the widest scope of treatment." Dialect, Johnson continued, was doomed by its racist textual heritage:

> Negro dialect is at present a medium that is not capable of giving expression to the varied conditions of Negro life in America, and much less is it capable of giving the fullest interpretation of Negro character and psychology. This is no indictment against the dialect as dialect, but against the mould of convention in which Negro dialect in the United States has been set.

Mule Bone was also a refutation of Johnson's claim that "Negro dialect" "is an instrument with but two full stops, humor and pathos," because of the racist minstrel and vaudeville representations of black characters and their language. This is what they meant when they subtitled their play "A Comedy of Negro Life" and when they claimed that *Mule Bone* was "the first real Negro folk comedy."

By using the vernacular tradition as the foundation for their drama—indeed, as the basis for a new *theory* of black drama—Hughes and Hurston succeeded quite impressively in creating a play that implicitly *critiqued* and explicitly *reversed* the racist stereotypes of the ignorant dialect-speaking darky that had populated the stages of the minstrel and vaudeville traditions. Indeed, we can only wonder at the effect that a successful Broadway production of *Mule Bone* might have had on the subsequent development

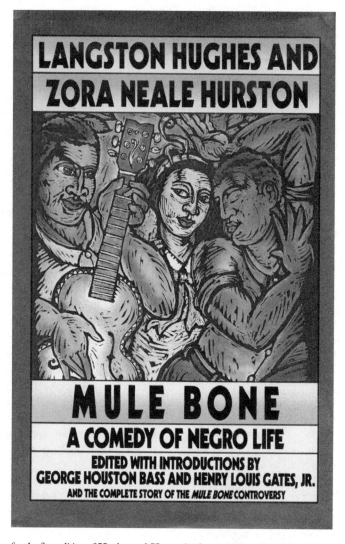

Dust jacket for the first edition of Hughes and Hurston's play, published in 1991, sixty years after their friendship terminated (Richland County Public Library)

of black theatre, given the play's sheer novelty and freshness of language.

With their turn to the vernacular, however, Hurston and Hughes also seem at times to reinscribe the explicit sexism of that tradition, through the discussions of physical abuse and wife-beatings as agents of control, which the male characters on Joe Clarke's store-front porch seem to take for granted as a "natural" part of sexual relations. These exchanges are quite disturbing for our generation of readers, demanding as they do a forceful critique by the reader. Daisy's representation in a triangle of desire as the *object* of her lovers' verbal dueling rather than as one who duels herself, a mode of dueling that demands great intelligence, is also a concern, even if this concern is tempered somewhat by the fact that it is she who controls their complex relationship all along, as demonstrated when she dismisses them both

when they will not accede to her demands that they get jobs and provide support for her own efforts at self-sufficiency: "Both of you niggers can git yo' hat on yo' heads and git on down de road. Neither one of y'all don't have to have me. I got a good job and plenty men beggin' for yo' change." Despite this, however, the depiction of female characters and sexual relations in *Mule Bone* almost never escapes the limitation of the social realities that the vernacular tradition reflects.

Mule Bone was never completed. Hurston, in a frantic attempt to demonstrate to Hughes's lawyer, Arthur Spingarn, that she had indeed been the play's sole author, sent him more handwritten revisions of large sections of the play, creating still another version. We have reprinted here, however, the last version on which Hughes and Hurston collaborated. Despite its limitations as a work-in-progress, it stands as a daring attempt to resurrect black poetic language from the burial grounds of racist stereotypes. Had it been performed, the power of its poetic language could very well have altered forever the evolution of African-American drama enabling the theatre to fulfill its great–and still unfulfilled–potential among the African-American arts.

–Langston Hughes and Zora Neale Hurston, *Mule Bone: A Comedy of Negro Life,* edited by Henry Louis Gates Jr. and George Houston Bass (New York: HarperCollins, 1991), pp. 5–24

——

*Hurston, the scholar Cheryl Wall discovered, shaved ten years from her age. Actually, in 1930, she would have been thirty-nine, not twenty-nine, as she claimed.

Selected Bibliography

Baker, Houston A., Jr. *Modernism and the Harlem Renaissance.* Chicago: University of Chicago Press, 1987.

Du Bois, W. E. B. "Can the Negro Save the Drama?" *Theatre Magazine* XXXVIII (July 1923): 12, 68.

Du Bois, W. E. B. "The Krigwa Players Little Negro Theatre." *Amsterdam News* (October 5, 1927) and *Crisis* XXXII, No. 3 (July 1926): 134–36.

Du Bois, W. E. B. "The Negro and the American Stage." *Crisis* XXVIII, No. 2 (June 1924): 55–60.

Du Bois, W. E. B. "The Negro Theatre." *Crisis* XV (February 1918): 165.

Fabre, Geneviève. *Drumbeats, Masks, and Metaphors: Contemporary Afro-American Theatre.* Cambridge, Mass.: Harvard University Press, 1983.

Hemenway, Robert. *Zora Neale Hurston: A Literary Biography.* Urbana, Ill.: University of Illinois, 1977.

Huggins, Nathan Irvin. *Harlem Renaissance.* New York: Oxford University Press, 1971.

Johnson, James Weldon. "Preface." In *The Book of American Negro Poetry.* New York: Harcourt, Brace, Jovanovich, 1931.

Kellner, Bruce. *The Harlem Renaissance: A Historical Dictionary of the Era.* New York: Methuen, 1987.

Lewis, David Levering. *When Harlem Was in Vogue.* New York: Alfred A. Knopf, 1981.

Locke, Alain. "The Drama of Negro Life." *Theatre Arts Monthly* 10 (October 1926): 701–6.

Locke, Alain. "The Negro and the American Stage." *Theatre Arts Monthly* 10 (February 1926): 112–20.

Rampersad, Arnold. *The Life of Langston Hughes. Vol. 1: 1902–1941: I, Too, Sing America.* New York: Oxford University Press, 1986.

Haiti and the South

In April, Hughes left Cleveland to travel to Haiti via Florida and Cuba with his friend Zell Ingram, an artist who specialized in prints. In this letter, written from St. Marc, Haiti, he shares some of his experiences.

Hughes to Amy Spingarn, 14 May 1931

Dear Mrs. Spingarn,

Some days ago we started from Port au Prince to Cap Haitien and the Citadel by camion (a sort of open-air bus, or rather a truck with very hard seats in it). But when we reached St. Marc we learned that the river had risen flooding the whole central plain, and that nobody could pass. So here we have been for nearly a week waiting for the water to go down. The camion went on back to Port au Prince, promising to pick us up when the flood is over. We are in a little native hotel facing the beach, with only the street and a field of yellow flowers between us and the sea. You can smell the flowers all night and hear the surf on the sand; and on Saturday and Sunday, the Congo drums, beating for the dance, sound all around. But there are so many Haitian dogs and fighting cocks that often the nights are so full of barking and crowing that not even the drums can be heard. It seems that the dogs here sleep all day in the sun and bark all night. Occassionally people wake up and throw a brick at them, but it does but momentary good. . . . In the midst of the yellow flowers a dozen cannons lie half-buried between the road and the beach. There used to be an old fort there, they say, to defend the town from pirates and other enemies, but it must have been carried away stone by stone, leaving only the cannons, too heavy to move. It was on this very beach, I believe, that Christophe tore the white from the French flag, leaving only the red and blue, which is the flag of free Haiti, and now the cannons lie quite useless among the flowers, and the planes of the American marine corp hum overhead every day. . . . There seem to be a great many marines in Port au Prince. One sees them everywhere. But here in St. Marc, I haven't seen any so far. Port au Prince is an ugly, ramshackle port-town, dirty and badly lighted. I didn't like it. As soon as we could, we started for the North, so I didn't go to meet any of the poets, or other people of whom Walter White and Arthur Spingarn told me. I shall do that when I come back. . . . St. Marc is quite pretty at the foot of great mountains with the sea in front. The people are friendly and the water is fine for bathing, but if one goes out too far there are sharks. The streets are very wide and they have no lights at all at night–only the moon, when there is one. It is a great coffee center, and in the hills all around there are bananas, mangoes, coconuts, and wild oranges. The peasant huts are thatched, and look quite African. The country people

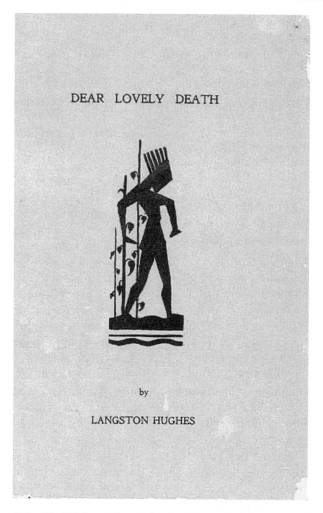

DEAR LOVELY DEATH

by

LANGSTON HUGHES

Cover designed by Zell Ingram for a 1931 chapbook printed by Amy Spingarn at her
Troutbeck Press in a signed, numbered edition of one hundred copies (courtesy of
Kenneth Spencer Research Library, University of Kansas Libraries)

are much cleaner than those of the towns, and very nice, although they scarcely understand any French, and I've learned only a few words of Creole so far. . . . One sees Voodoo shrines about, but nobody in the towns will talk much about them—the "better" people being officially Catholic. . . . In Cuba I saw a swell nañigo (or devil-dance) out of doors, but they do not allow any but members of the group to see the indoor ceremonies, altho every one may come to the dancing. It lasts all night and all day from sunset to sunset, and is very jolly, people laughing and kidding, as well as imitating, the drummers and the dancers. Nevertheless, every step and every note has a meaning. . . . We stayed three weeks in Havana where Zell (the other fellow) made two heads, one in Cuban wood and one in plaster, to be cast later. Then we came across Cuba by bus and Ford, changing conveyances several times, and once sleeping on the road all night, as every machine we got in broke down at some time or other. (They do not seem to keep their cars up down here. The bus to St. Marc

stopped on the road every half hour to repair something.). . . . At Santiago de Cuba we took passage on deck for Haiti, and rode in the open for three days with the sugar-cane workers returning home. We went to several little Hatian ports on the way. The last night, a storm came up and we had to sleep down in the hole with the sailors—but most of the people got wet. . . . It seems that I have been travelling continuously since we left Jersey in the Ford, so I don't much mind being held up here by the water, as it is a nice place to rest and write some letters. We have decided to stay in Haiti, and not do any of the other islands this time. Just passing through places, one doesn't learn much. You have to get acquainted with the people first—and the weeks go very fast. And Haiti seems delightful enough for a long stay—if one can learn the dialect, so if we can find a cheap place in Cap Haitien we'll probably put up there. The Citadel is only 20 miles away. One can go by bus to the foot of the mountain, and then make the climb on foot or horseback. I'll write you all about it. . . . Zell did not like the wood cuts he made for the book of poems, so he has made the enclosed ink design to be put at one side of the cover page. (I guess it is supposed to be Death.) So if you like it, you may use it. I have gone over the poems, and am enclosing slightly revised copies of some, and changed titles. I hope (and believe) it will make an interesting little book. If I can help any more about it, please let me know. . . . I've had one letter from Mrs. Peeples, at Havana. Jimmy was all right. School is out in Westfield June 24th, I understand–so that would leave the month of June to pay for–$33.34. After school he says he will start to California. If you would like to send his June check to me Poste Restante, at Cap Haitien, I will forward it back to Mrs. Peeples. Or if you'd rather send it direct, her address is: Mrs. F. L. Peeples, 514 Downer Street. I think he has profited by his winter there, and if he continues in school elsewhere, he will at least have a transfer not marked "Colored Orphan's Home." It has been mighty good of you to help him out. My royalties are payable this month, so I shall see that he has some pocket money to start out with. It should not be hard for him to find work through the country on the way. . . . I have an anthologie of Haitien poetry, but I don't find much there that I would care to translate–as it all seems to be weak French rather than Negro, or even Haitien–excepting two or three of the poets like Oswald Durand who wrote of Haiti, and often in Creole. . . . I was sorry I couldn't get back to New York that week for you to finish my picture. We left as we had planned and had a fine trip through the South, without punctures or anything unpleasant, except that at Miami they refused to sell us tickets to Havana on the grounds of color, but at Key West I got boat passage without any trouble, asking for it in Spanish. And there were no difficulties in landing at Havana. I was greatly surprised to find a large group of friends, and newspaper men and photographers waiting for us on the dock there. And the following morning our pictures came out on the front page of the morning paper, Diario de la Marina. . . . Cuba is very near a revolution. Soldiers with drawn bayonets guard the schools and public buildings. In Santiago mounted calvary patrol the main streets and one cannot sit down in the parks. Everyone says Machado's days are numbered. . . . Today I am going to the country to eat mangos. The father of our hotel keeper has a "jardin" there, and his trees are loaded with fruit. . . . I hope the spring is nice in New York and that you are well and happy.

Sincerely, Langston
–Langston Hughes Papers, James Weldon Johnson Collection in the Yale Collection of American Literature, Beinecke Rare Book and Manuscript Library

* * *

The United States occupied Haiti from 1915 to 1934. Hughes wrote about the conditions of Haitian society for New Masses.

People without Shoes

Haiti is a land of people without shoes–black people, whose bare feet tread the dusty roads to market in the early morning, or pat softly on the bare floors of hotels, serving foreign guests. These barefooted ones care for the rice and cane fields under the hot sun. They climb high mountains picking coffee beans, and wade through surf to fishing boats in the blue sea. All of the work that keeps Haiti alive, pays for the American Occupation, and enriches foreign traders–that vast and basic work–is done there by Negroes without shoes.

Yet shoes are things of great importance in Haiti. Everyone of any social or business position must wear them. To be seen in the streets barefooted marks one as low-caste person of no standing in the community. Coats, too, are of an importance equal

Hughes in Haiti, 1931 (Langston Hughes Papers, Yale Collection of American Literature, Beinecke Rare Book and Manuscript Library)

l/17

Cap Haitien, Haiti,
June 30, 1931.

Dear Father,

I was most happy to have your letter, as well as the book
which you sent me. It was good to have direct news of you.
Some years ago I wrote you, c/0 **of** the American Consulate
in Mexico City, but the letter finally came back. I saw
Aunt Sallie in Indianapolis (1716 Blvd. Place) a few years
back, and I hear from her occassionally. She always asks
about you, and I know she would be glad to hear from you,
if you wanted to write her......I was interested in what you
had to say about my novel. It had a great critical success,
the reviews in both the English and American press being almost uniformly good. The sales exceeded those of the average
first novel, my January first statement showing a sale of some
five thousand copies for the first five months of publication.
It was published in Moscow this spring, and will probably appear in Paris in the fall as the French translation rights
have been sold......In one way or another, directly or indirectly, enough money has come to me from my books to live,
but to make a good steady income from literature takes a long
time, as one must slowly build up a buying public, or else
sell a great deal to the magazines, or the movies.....I am
certainly sorry to hear that you have had such a difficult
time with your health, and I wish that something could be
done about it. I was sorry I couldn't come to you that time
when you first became ill, but I wanted to make my own way

Hughes's response to a rare letter from his father, who had found Not Without Laughter *"very amusing"*
(Langston Hughes Papers, Yale Collection of American Literature,
Beinecke Rare Book and Manuscript Library)

in the world——which has proven quite exciting, although I have
nothing to show for it except three books and practically no money.
I have travelled quite a lot, however——as you advised me. Last
March I started on a trip through the West Indies with another fellow, but so far, we have gotten no farther than Haiti, where we have
been for two months here in the shadow of the Citadel built by the
black king Christophe. Twenty miles away on a mountain top, it stands
a magnificent ruin, the grandest thing in Haiti——for the people today are asleep in the sun. The Marines are here, and all the money
goes into white pockets.....The news which you give me of Mexico is
very interesting. Miguel Covarrubias, the Mexican artist, is a good
friend of mine in New York, and he tells me, too, of the progress
which the country is making...I would like very much to read that
book on the American Negro. You must sent it to me when I get back
to the States in August. Please do not destroy the books you say
you do not want, as I would like to have them.....Have you seen the
magazine OPPORTUNITY, and a new one called ABBOTTS MONTHLY, published by the man who owns the Chicago Defender? They are both interesting, and I will send you copies when I get back, also any other books
or papers which you feel you would like to have. You must have a
great deal of time on your hands now to read, so if there is anything
from the States you want, let me know.....You ask me several questions
I can't answer. I don't know about Dr. Sweet. The Binga Bank, it
seems, went down in the general crash with hundreds of other small
banks in the country caught in the depression——frozen assets, etc.
When I left the States the papers said a reorganization was on foot.
The DuBois-Cullen match seemed to have been a marriage without love,
the two concerned not being very friendly on the day of the wedding,
so they probably had little intention of living together long. No
one in New York knows why they married, xx unless pressure had been
brought to bear on the part of one or the other of the parents as
the engagement had been so long announced.....Rhinelander married
Alice, knowing her to be the daughter of a colored coachman. His
parents forced a separation. There were counter-divorce suits.
She came out best, receiving a large settlement of money.....Do you
know the Murray's in Mexico City, a colored family from New York?
Mrs. Murray is the sister-in-law of Walter White, head of the N. A.
A. C. P. She was in New York on a visit just before I left.....I
have been in Havana twice in the last two years. My poems are well
known there, many of them having been translated in their magazines
and papers.....Give my love to the Patiños,
and write to me whenever you have the time. You can always reach
me c/o of my publishers, Alfred A. Knopf, Inc., 730 Fifth Avenue,
New York. That is the best address. If I make a lot of money
from my next book I will come down and see you.....Thanks for all
the good advice. I'm sure you're right.

                         Affectionately,

                              Langston

Will send later.
Left in Port au Prince.

Educator Mary McLeod Bethune, who inspired Hughes to launch a reading tour of predominantly black schools and colleges throughout the South (photograph by Carl Van Vechten, 6 April 1949; Yale Collection of American Literature, Beinecke Rare Book and Manuscript Library, courtesy of Carl Van Vechten Trust)

Reading at Coulter Academy

Upon returning from his trip to Haiti in July 1931, Hughes and Ingram, in need of money, managed to pay for enough gas to reach Daytona Beach, Florida, where they met with Mary McLeod Bethune, the founder and president (1904–1942, 1946–1947) of a school for girls that became Bethune-Cookman College. Bethune cashed Hughes's check and then surprised the travelers by deciding to ride north with them. As Hughes recalled, "Colored folks all along the Eastern seaboard spread a feast whenever Mary McLeod passed their way. Zell and I ate well on that trip. We didn't have to spend a penny for food or lodging." The idea for Hughes's reading tour of the South was born on this journey.

We arrived one day at Cheraw, South Carolina, just before noon. Mrs. Bethune said, "Let's stop at Coulter Academy and dine with the teachers, Langston, and you read some of your poems for the students."

We pulled up before a large frame building. As soon as the teachers and students saw Mrs. Bethune getting out of the car, word spread and commotion began. Classes greeted her with applause and an assembly for the whole school was ordered. She made a warm-hearted little talk, then introduced me as a poet whom she wanted the South to know better. I read the students a few of my poems, and was gratified at the warm response they received.

"You see," said Mrs. Bethune as we drove away, "you must go all over the South with your poems. People need poetry."

–I Wonder as I Wander: An Autobiographical Journey (New York & Toronto: Rinehart, 1956), p. 41

Financing a Reading Tour

Looking for support for his proposed reading tour through the South, Hughes wrote this letter from his room at the Y.M.C.A. in New York. His application for a Rosenwald Fund fellowship was successful, and he was awarded $1,000.

Hughes to James Weldon Johnson, 14 August 1931

Dear Mr. Johnson,

Just recently back from Haiti, and I found your note with the enclosure waiting for me the other day when I went after my mail. I have a lot to tell you about my impressions of the Black Republic. Would also like to talk over with you a reading tour of the South which I hope to do this fall and winter if dates and a Ford can be procured. In a Ford we came all the way from Miami for less than $20.00, so I know such a tour by car could be done cheaply. I want to help build up a public (I mean a Negro public) for Negro books, and, if I can, to carry to the young

people of the South interest in, and aspiration toward, true artistic expression, and a fearless use of racial material. I am asking the Rosenwald Fund if it wishes to help me in that and in the writing of some of the many things I have in mind to do. I would appreciate it immensely if you would allow me to use your name should they ask me for recomendations, etc., as I suppose they will. . . . I hope your summer has been an enjoyable one. I know I remember with delight the afternoon I spent at your lovely place last year with Amy Spingarn. . . . I send all good wishes and best regards to Mrs. Johnson.

Sincerely,

Langston

–Langston Hughes Papers, James Weldon Johnson Collection in the Yale Collection of American Literature, Beinecke Rare Book and Manuscript Library

Hughes on Negro Art

Hughes wrote a few brief statements in the early 1930s on African American art and the responsibility of the artist for The New Sign, *a newsletter published weekly by the West 135th Street (Harlem) Branch of the Y.M.C.A. of the City of New York. Hughes was listed as one of two feature editors on the masthead of* The New Sign.

Negro Art and–Its Audience

That Negro Art means nothing to the masses of our people in this country may be due to a combination of many different causes: our general poverty, and the high cost of books, pictures, and concert tickets; lack of education and the power to appreciate the so-called finer arts; complete ignorance of the fact that there is Negro Art; and the further fact that maybe something is wrong with Negro Art itself, and that the practitioners of said art, the Paul Robesons, Aaron Douglases, and Claude McKays (all in white Europe at the moment) may be lacking in the power and ability to ever create for themselves a large personal following among their black contemporaries, no matter how much admiration the white world gives them. Certainly poor people whose salaries average less than twenty dollars a week can't very often pay two or three dollars for a book or an evening of song; certainly uneducated folks in Georgia can't appreciate *Cane* or decorations in the most modern manner; and certainly black artists who have had the adulation of the "best white folks," through the press, and in the great cities of the world, can hardly be expected to care much about poor colored folks in Selma, Alabama, or points South. Negro Art, like white art in this bourgeois world, is high priced, high-hat, and lacking in any special aim toward having a dark mass appeal. Bessie Smith, who never received a Spingarn medal, is the great singer of the Negro masses. Paul Lawrence Dunbar, long dead but still recited, holds a place in the racial heart that none of the younger and more widely heralded poets will be likely to take away soon. The men who make the pictures on the calendars the butcher gives away at Christmas is just as great an artist as any one of the recent winners of the Harmon Award–in the eyes of the people. But before modern Negro Art can stand soundly on its own feet and mean something great, it must have its own public. What can be done then to make our art mean something to the Negro people–and to whom must it be done–to the artist or the people? Must Negro Art remain as it is now, largely entertainment for the white world–or will it become truly significant to the dark world as well?

–*The New Sign,* 13 (26 September 1931): 1

Negro Art and–Publicity Value

Whereas modern American Negro Art and Literature may not yet have sunk deeply into the dark waters of the black soul at home, it has spread in an ever-widening circle to the Caucasian world of intellect and culture in this country and Europe, and has served to make the troubles and problems of the race known where they were not known before. It has become a sort of glorified exhibitionism for the world outside itself, and our artists are paid performers for a strange people. Books from *Cane* to *Black No More,* shows interpreted by Negro actors, from *Shuffle Along* to *The Green Pastures,* the Harmon Awards and Art exhibits, the lectures of Dr. Alain Locke, have all put themselves on display to an interested but alien world. Hayes, Robeson, Josephine Baker in Europe, the German anthology of Negro verse, *Africa Sings,* the foreign editions of racial books, the movie *Hallelujah,* the *Blackbirds* in London and Paris, *Porgy,* and other entertainments, have all taken the native black man into rich homes and castles abroad where his natural feet would never have gained him entrance, and where his cries of oppression would never otherwise have been heard. There picturesque and new, he has been put on display. And Negro Art has become a kind of exotic banner–making everybody look to see what black parade it heads. The question is, does it head any parade? Without doubt, Negro artists are splendid publicity men for the race. They have succeeded in attracting the attention of the globe to themselves–and thus to their black people. But what direct and vital influence have they had, so far, on their people? Now, with the ears of Europe and America listening, if we could only turn our backs and talk directly to ourselves, to our own black masses, forgetting outsiders for awhile–write, paint, sing for Negroes–something truly great and fundamental might come out of this New Negro Renaissance in Art. Born from the contact of the colored artist with his own dark audience, a stronger, finer Negro Art should come. And its publicity value would then be greater than ever.

–*The New Sign,* 12 (3 October 1931): 1

to footwear. In a country where the climate would permit everybody to go naked with ease, officials, professional men, clerks, and teachers swelter in dignity with coats buttoned about their bellies on the hottest days.

Strange, bourgeois, and a little pathetic is this accent on clothes and shoes in an undeveloped land where the average wage is thirty cents a day, and where the sun blazes like fury. It is something carried over, perhaps, from the white masters who wore coats and shoes long ago, and then had force and power; or something remembered, maybe, as infinitely desirable–like leisure and rest and freedom. But articles of clothing for the black masses in Haiti are not cheap. Cloth is imported, as are most of the shoes. Taxes are high, jobs are scarce, wages are low, so the doubtful step upward to the dignity of leather between one's feet and the earth, and a coat between one's body and the sun, is a step not easily to be achieved in this island of the Caribbean.

Practically all business there is in the hands of white foreigners, so one must buy one's shoes from a Frenchman or a Syrian who pays as little money as possible back into Haitian hands. Imports and exports are in charge of foreigners, too, German often, or American, or Italian. Haiti has no foreign credit, no steamships, few commercial representatives abroad. And the government, Occupation controlled, puts a tax on almost everything. There are no factories of any consequence in the land, and what few there are largely under non-Haitian control. Every ship brings loads of imported goods from the white countries. Even Haitian postage stamps are made abroad. The laws are dictated from Washington. American controllers count their money. And the military Occupation extracts fat salaries for its own civilian experts and officials.

What then, pray, have the dignified native citizens with shoes been doing all the while–those Haitians, mulattoes largely, who have dominated the politics of the country for decades, and who have drawn almost as sharp a class line between themselves and their shoeless black brothers as have the Americans with their imported color line dividing the Occupation from *all* Haitians? How have these super-class citizens of this once-Republic been occupying themselves? Living for years on under-paid peasant labor and lazy government jobs, is one answer. Writing flowery poetry in the manner of the French academicians, is another. Creating bloody civil wars and wasteful political-party revolutions, and making lovely speeches on holidays. Borrowing government money abroad to spend on themselves– and doing nothing for the people without shoes,

building no schools, no factories, creating no advancements for the masses, no new agricultural developments, no opportunities–too busy feeding their own pride and their own acquisitiveness. The result: a country poor, ignorant, and hungry at the bottom, corrupt and greedy at the top–a wide open way for the equally greedy Yankees of the North to step in, with a corruption more powerful than Paris-cultured mulattoes had the gall to muster.

Haiti today: a fruit tree for Wall Street, a mango for the Occupation, coffee for foreign cups, and poverty for its own black workers and peasants. The recently elected Chamber of Deputies (the Haitian Senate) has just voted to increase its salaries to $250.00 a month. The workers on the public roads receive 30¢ a day, and the members of the gendarmerie $2.50 a week. A great difference in income. But then–the deputies must wear shoes. They have dignity to maintain. They govern.

As to the Occupation, after fifteen years, about all for which one can give the Marines credit are a few decent hospitals and a rural health service. The roads of the country are still impassable, and schools continue to be lacking. The need for economic reform is greater than ever.

The people without shoes cannot read or write. Most of them have never seen a movie, have never seen a train. They live in thatched huts or rickety houses; rise with the sun; sleep with the dark. They wash their clothes in running streams with lathery weeds–too poor to buy soap. They move slowly, appear lazy because of generations of undernourishment and constant lack of incentive to ambition. On Saturdays they dance to the Congo drums; and on Sundays go to mass,–for they believe in the Saints and the Voodoo gods, all mixed. They grow old and die, and are buried the following day after an all-night wake where their friends drink, sing, and play games, like a party. The rulers of the land never miss them. More black infants are born to grow up and work. Foreign ships continue to come into Haitian harbors, dump goods, and sail away with the products of black labor–cocoa beans, coffee, sugar, dye-woods, fruits, and rice. The mulatto upper classes continue to send their children to Europe for an education. The American Occupation lives in the best houses. The officials of the National City Bank, New York, keep their heavy-jawed portraits in the offices of the Banque d'Haiti. And because black hands have touched the earth, gathered in the fruits, and loaded ships, somebody–across the class and color lines–many somebodies become richer and wiser, educate their children to read and write, to travel, to be ambitious, to be superior, to create armies, and to build banks. Somebody wears coats and shoes.

On Sunday evening in the Champs de Mars, before the Capital at Port au Prince, the palace band plays immortally out-worn music while genteel people stroll round and round the brilliance of the lighted bandstand. Lovely brown and yellow girls in cool dresses, and dark men in white suits, pass and repass.

I asked a friend of mine, my first night there, "Where are all the people without shoes? I don't see any."

"They can't walk here," he said, "The police would drive them away."

—*New Masses*, 12 (October 1931): 12

* * *

Brown, who in 1929 had begun his long career as an English professor at Howard University, wrote this letter to Hughes from Cambridge, Massachusetts, where he was pursuing his Ph.D. at Harvard. Southern Road *was Brown's first collection of poems. He responds here to several works by Hughes. The play Brown refers to is probably* Scottsboro Limited, *which was published as* Scottboro Limited: Four Poems and a Play in Verse *by Golden Stair Press in 1932.*

Sterling A. Brown to Hughes, 7 December 1931

Dear Langston,

I suppose that by this time you realize that I am the world's worst correspondent. When your interesting pamphlet came I was in the midst of preparing my book of poems for a trip to the publishers, then when the New Masses came in, I wanted to get a letter off immediately—but fell by the wayside under the load these birds up here have thrown on me. I'm wrestling here with such stuff as Old French, Old English—everything old—I'm getting to feel right old. I'm back up here, partly for reasons of expediency—our colleges being afflicted with the P.h.Disease—and partly because I wanted a great deal to step out of a grind that I haven't let up on for nine years. But the philology I'm forced to take

Ain't no work o' mine
Lawd, ain't no work o' mine!

The book has been accepted—It's to be called Southern Road and will be out in the spring, Harcourt and Brace bringing it out. There are a handful of poems in it that you haven't seen—Since the acceptance I've done four or five others; I think my good luck will give me an added urge to write.

I am very glad to see your latest work. The Scottsboro poem, in Opportunity is great, and up to your best. It is straight forward, moving—it goes underneath—says a lot.

The play absolutely hit me squarely between the eyes. You've done a fine thing there. It is raw, harsh, sardonic—the bits dealing with boys on the freight—just right—and you've got those two whores exactly—There's not much I can say about it—It's mighty well done—

With the "booklet", I'm not so well satisfied. I hope I can make myself clear. I hope too that I don't descend even lower in the ranks of the "bourgeois intellectuals".— Now your purpose you achieve—i.e. to write simply for people to whom most poetry is a closed book. This is a creditable move, surely, an education of the masses—well an education in poetry—or a giving poetry to those of the masses—(as distinguished from the "intellectuals")—who don't have their own in Bessie Smith, Blind Lemon Jefferson, etc.— The subject matter of the poetry is what you want to indoctrinate them with, or stir them to thinking about—or give an articulation denied to them. O.K. estimable motives.—

But what I don't quite like is your doing this. That is, I believe that they are readers of your poetry who cannot all be contemptuously discarded as quotation marks intellectuals. They too have their needs. And I believe that reaching them is as important as reaching Sunday Schools—high schools, clubs, etc.— That is, a poet of your caliber can get more results from matured minds than from this other popularization. I hope this won't make me out to seem an apostle of the cult of unintelligibility. I want intelligibility, simplicity; that's what I've admired greatly in your work—in your poetry, and in Not Without Laughter. The Taos poem I never quite got—but regardless of my own stupidity—I did not feel it to be representative. This does not mean that there is no overtone to your representative work—I hope I won't seem that stupid. What I mean is that directness and simplicity in the best poetic sense have never been strangers to your work.—

I think the best of the pamphlet is where you speak out in your old vein of bitter irony—The part I don't like is where certain banalities creep in, for the rhyme, or some other reason. What remains is this: after all, the book isn't such a departure after all—and there are some poems and some stanzas in other poems that are very good—up to the best in Weary Blues and Fine Clothes To The Jew.

I've run on about the pamphlet, which I didn't completely like, and not about the other two things on Scottsboro which I did, immensely—If I seem stupid—remember that after all I teach English, and that's sholy a heavy burden for anybody to carry—

dups

THE GOLDEN STAIR PRESS

Announces the publication of

THE NEGRO MOTHER

*A booklet of six dramatic recitations
in rhymed verse by*

LANGSTON HUGHES

Author of THE WEARY BLUES and NOT WITHOUT LAUGHTER

With appropriate decorations by

PRENTISS TAYLOR

These ballads, titled *The Colored Soldier, Broke, The Black Clown, The Big-Timer, The Negro Mother*, and *Dark Youth*, passionately lyrical presentations of widely known and well-beloved Negro characters delineated in a broadly popular manner not associated with Negro poetry since the death of Paul Lawrence Dunbar, are suitable for recitation by amateurs in schools, churches, and clubs.

The booklet containing the six poems, illustrated, sells for twenty-five cents the copy. ✹ ✹ ✹ Four of the poems

No. 1. THE NEGRO MOTHER   3. BROKE

2. THE BLACK CLOWN   4. THE BIG-TIMER

are printed separately in broadside form convenient for framing, or pinning to the wall, at ten cents the copy. A limited number of the booklets, with hand-colored illustrations, will be issued at seventy-five cents each, and a number of the broadsides at twenty-five cents each.

Both the booklet and the broadsides may be ordered through

THE CRISIS, 69 Fifth Avenue, New York City

OPPORTUNITY, 1133 Broadway, New York City

THE GOLDEN STAIR PRESS, 23 Bank Street, New York City

20% should be added to all orders for postage.

Ready October 2nd

Advertisement and cover for the 1931 chapbook published by the Golden Stair Press, a short-lived imprint founded by Hughes, Carl Van Vechten, and Prentiss Taylor (Langston Hughes Collection, Schomburg Center for Research in Black Culture, New York Public Library)

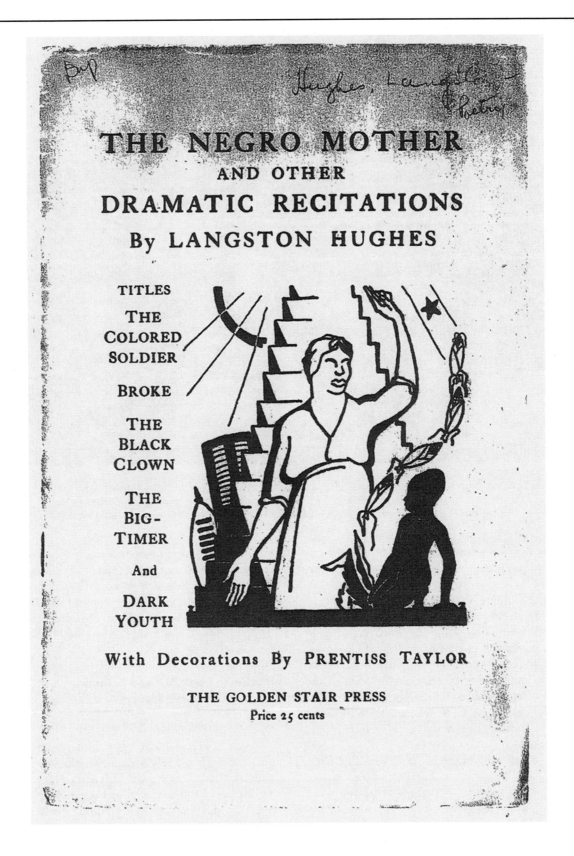

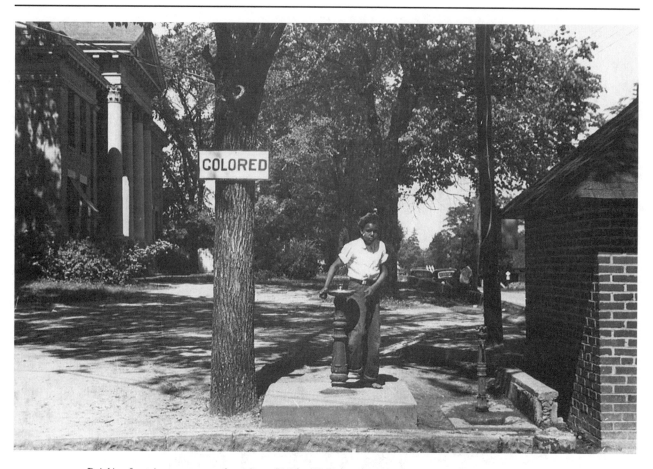

Drinking fountain on county courthouse lawn, Halifax, North Carolina, April 1938. Hughes encountered many such reminders of segregation on his reading tour of Southern schools and colleges (photograph by John Vachon for the Farm Security Administration; courtesy of Library of Congress, Prints & Photographs Division).

I was doing a poem on Scottsboro when yours came in–I've put it aside–Maybe I'll get it down sometime.

Waring Cuney is in Boston; I see him whenever I go to the Sandwich Shop–which isn't often–but he, true Bostonian, won't cross the Charles River.

I am sending this to the press–I don't have your address. I had one or two, but they're lost, and I believe that you do ramble. I'm ordering three copies of the booklet, and single copies of <u>The Negro Mother,</u> <u>The Black Clown,</u> and <u>Broke.</u> I'm sending down to you a check for one dollar twenty five cents, which covers postage as well.–

Best of luck, and forgive my tardiness in writing.

Sincerely yours,
Sterling A. Brown.

–Langston Hughes Papers, James Weldon Johnson Collection in the Yale Collection of American Literature, Beinecke Rare Book and Manuscript Library

* * *

Hughes read at a benefit for Bethune-Cookman Institute in Daytona Beach, Florida, in January 1932. He and Mrs. Bethune had evidently then discussed the need for a book on Bethune's life, the main subject of this letter that Hughes wrote from Tuskegee Institute in Alabama. Hughes marked the copy of the letter "draft," so it may not have been sent. He did not do any work on a Bethune biography.

Hughes to Mary McLeod Bethune,
15 February 1932

Dear Mrs. Bethune:

Of course I have been thinking about you a great deal since I left Bethune-Cookman. I am sure you must have known how I hated to leave so pleasant a place. I did not even feel like telling you goodbye that day in the dining room. I felt more like staying.

My lecture schedule has been pretty strenuous for the last month. Among other things I did ten days through Mississippi over some of the worst roads in the world, but meeting some of the most

Vachel Lindsay: Incident

Washington, 1925. Noon-time. The crowded dinning room of
the Wardman Park Hotel: senators, baseball players, army men, rich
old ladies, ambassadors from abroad, society women, oil magnates,
naval officers——and at a small table near the wall, Vachel Lindsay
and his wife. I am a bus boy. I know him from his pictures. The
morning papers ~~have said~~ say he will give a recital of his poems in the
little theatre of the hotel that evening. As I pass with trays of
~~some~~ dishes on my shoulder, I look at him in admiration and awe.

During the afternoon I copied three of my poems, and in
the evening as he sat at dinner, I put them down beside his plate,
muttered frightened admiration for his work, and went away quickly.
I stayed in the pantry until he had/left the dinning/room.

That night he read my poems to his ~~own~~ distinguished audience.
The next day the reporters came. They took my picture holding a bus
boy's tray. Papers published the story. Guests wanted to see/all my poetry.
Notes arrived from strange people. Dinners asked the head waiter, "Where
is that bus boy who writes poetry?"

Embarrassed by the curious eyes of people at tables, I stayed
home for three days. When I went back to work, Vachel Lindsay had gone.
I never saw him again, but he had left for me at the desk a package and
a written word of encouragement. The package contained Amy Lowell's
Life of John Keats, his gift ~~to a~~ to a young, Negro poet.

Vachel Lindsay's life, I understand, was full of such instances of generousity and kindness. His ~~story~~ work was a living encouragement of the original and the American in ~~the~~ creation of beauty.

Langston Hughes

Thousands feel now a sense of personal loss. We miss him as we miss
a friend. A fine poet, and a great heart, has left us for the universe
of stars.

Fort Valley,
Georgia,
Re January 18,
1932.

*Draft of a tribute to poet Vachel Lindsay that Hughes wrote during his reading tour of the South.
Lindsay died 5 December 1931 (Langston Hughes Papers, Yale Collection of American
Literature, Beinecke Rare Book and Manuscript Library).*

responsive groups of Negro students it has been my pleasure to read before.

At Fisk I had a long talk with James Weldon Johnson about your book and about possible people who might assist you in bringing it to pass. As to Mr. Johnson himself, there are several reasons why he cannot undertake the task. One is that he has considerable work of his own already in progress—enough, he says, for the next two or three years; another is that he feels that a woman writer might be able to do your book with greater sympathy and understanding. He suggests very strongly that you think about Jessie Faucet in connection with the matter. He feels that Miss Faucet has a thorough mastery of her style and the proper touch for an inspirational autobiography such as yours should be. Of course, she has a name in the literary world and her last book, THE CHINABERRY TREE, has been receiving splendid reviews from some of the papers. I think he might be right in his suggestion concerning your consideration of her as a person to write your book or else to work with you in doing it. Mr. Johnson feels that it would be a splendid thing to have a book about one great Negro woman by another Negro woman who has made a name for herself as a writer.

I don't know what you will think about this yourself. I have been turning over in my mind the thought of your book in relation to myself, and whether or not I might be able to do it. This is what I think: that I could not do your book as an impersonal study of your life and do it well and with complete objectivity. I am afraid, too, that if I did it, having a personal style and tone of my own, people might expect to find the personal flavor and my own analyses of your work and your position therein. You know, of course, that I have tremendous admiration for you, but a life such as yours connected so closely with the general problems of Negro education would, if I wrote about it directly and personally, demand from me, I feel, a critical treatment that, while not in any way touching your own splendid position, might hold up to too unpleasant a criticism our entire American system of philanthropic and missionary education for the Negro, since I am becoming very critical of that system from my observation on this tour. Not that it isn't doing good; it is. But I feel it a great pity that any group of people should have to beg for their education, and it is a worse defect in our public educational systems, of course.

I feel, however, that if you would like to do your book as your own under your own name, for example, with such a title as this:

MARY McLEOD BETHUNE
MY STORY

with, if you wish, a note or sub-title perhaps stating "as recounted to Langston Hughes", (or whoever did most of the actual writing), that I could be of help to you in that way. The advantage of this method would be that the whole story of your life and work would have the effect of coming from your own lips and could then carry as much of the flavor of your own powerful and inspiring personality as your speeches have when you stand before an audience. At least I hope it could be written in a fashion which would convey your own force, simplicity and great sincerity. It would be then much like Jane Ad[d]ams' books, and I think, would perhaps have even more value to the youth than if it were written as a study of your life by someone else. Many autobiographies, you know, are not actually written by the subjects themselves. Sometimes credit is given to the actual writer, and sometimes not. In my own case, if I were to do your book in that way, it would be entirely up to you as to whether you thought it wise to name myself or not. In any case, believe me only too happy to be of service to you, if I can, in any way that I can, and certainly I hope that your book will get under way soon.

Please let me know what you think of these two ideas and whether or not you are planning to get in touch with Miss Faucet. Perhaps should the book be done in the personal manner (as your own story) Miss Faucet might be, even then, the person to do it. Being a woman, perhaps she would have greater power of putting into words some situations in your life which maybe only a woman could truly understand. Anyway I would [be] happy to know what you yourself think about all this.

I am enclosing my forwarding addresses for the two weeks, so that you can write me without writing through New York if you would like to.

I shall never forget the cordial reception accorded me on your campus, and I send my regards to my many friends there.

With my love, I am

Sincerely yours,

—Langston Hughes Papers, James Weldon Johnson Collection in the Yale Collection of American Literature, Beinecke Rare Book and Manuscript Library

* * *

In January 1932 Hughes visited the Scottsboro boys at the Kilby State Penitentiary near Montgomery, Alabama, an experience he recounted in the following piece for Opportunity.

Brown America in Jail: Kilby

The steel doors closed. Locked. Here, too, was Brown America. Like monkeys in tiered cages, hundreds of Negroes barred away from life. Animals of crime. Human zoo for the cast-offs of society. Hunger, ignorance, poverty: civilization's major defects woven into a noose for the unwary. Men in jail, months and months, years and years after the steel doors have closed. Vast monotony of guards and cages. The State Penitentiary at Kilby, Alabama, in the year of our Lord, 1932.

Our Lord . . . Pilate . . . and the thieves on the cross.

For a moment the fear came: even for me, a Sunday morning visitor, the doors might never open again. WHITE guards held the keys. (The judge's chair protected like Pilate's.) And I'm only a nigger. Nigger. Niggers. Hundreds of niggers in Kilby Prison. Black, brown, yellow, near-white niggers. The guards, WHITE. Me–a visiting nigger.

Sunday morning: In the Negro wing. Tier on tier of steel cells. Cell doors are open. Within the wing, men wander about in white trousers and shirts. Sunday clothes. Day of rest. Cards, checkers, dice, story telling from cell to cell. Chapel if they will. One day of rest, *in jail*. Within the great closed cell of the wing, visiting, laughing, talking, *on Sunday*.

Hughes's congratulatory telegram for Wallace Thurman's new novel Infants of the Spring *(1932), with a handwritten note, probably by Carl Van Vechten (Langston Hughes Papers, Yale Collection of American Literature, Beinecke Rare Book and Manuscript Library)*

The young black men who were falsely accused of raping two young white women aboard a freight train near Scottsboro, Alabama, on 25 March 1931 (Langston Hughes Papers, Yale Collection of American Literature, Beinecke Rare Book and Manuscript Library)

But in the death house, cells are not open. You enter by a solid steel door through which you cannot see. White guard opens the door. White guard closes the door, shuts out the world, remains inside with you.

THE DEATH HOUSE. Dark faces peering from behind bars, like animals when the keeper comes. All Negro faces, men and young men in this death house at Kilby. Among them the eight Scottsboro boys. *Sh-s-s-s!* Scottsboro boys? SCOTTSBORO boys. SCOTTS-BORO BOYS! (Keep silent, world. The State of Alabama washes its hands.) Eight brown boys condemned to death. No proven crime. Farce of a trial. Lies. Laughter. Mob. Music. Eight poor niggers make a country holiday. (Keep silent, Germany, Russia, France, young China, Gorki, Thomas Mann, Roumain Rolland, Theodore Dreiser. Pilate washes his hands. Listen Communists, don't send any more cablegrams to the Governor of Alabama. Don't send any more telegrams to the Supreme Court. What's the matter? What's all this excitement about, over eight young niggers? Let the law wash its hands in peace.)

There are only two doors in the death house. One from the world, in. The other from the world, out—to the electric chair. To DEATH. Against this door the guard leans. White guard, watching Brown America in the death house.

Silence. The dark world is silent. Speak! Dark world:

> Listen, guard: Let the boys out.
> Guard with the keys, let 'em out.
> Guard with the law books, let them out.
> Guards in the Supreme Court! Guards in the White House!
> Guards of the money bags made from black hands sold in the cotton
>   fields, sold in mines, sold on Wall Street:
> Let them out!

Daily, I watch the guards washing their hands.

The world remembers for a long time a certain washing of hands. The world remembers for a long time a certain humble One born in a manger—straw, manure, and the feet of animals—standing before Power washing its hands. No proven crime. Farce of a trial.

Dust jacket for the 1932 Golden Stair Press publication of Hughes's first produced play, which had premiered in Los Angeles on 8 May 1932 (courtesy of Kenneth Spencer Research Library, University of Kansas Libraries)

Lies. Laughter. Mob. Hundreds of years later Brown America sang: *My Lord! What a morning when the stars began to fall!*

For eight brown boys in Alabama the stars have fallen. In the death house, I heard no song at all. Only a silence more ominous than song. All of Brown America locked up there. And no song.

> *Even as ye do unto the least of these, ye do it unto Me.*
> White guard.
> The door that leads to DEATH.
> Electric chair.
> No song.

> *—Opportunity,* 10 (June 1932): 174

Writing for Children

*From early in his career Hughes believed that black children needed to have positive representations of people of color in poetry and fiction. His first books for children–*The Dream Keeper and Other Poems *and* Popo and Fifina, *which he co-authored with Arna Bontemps–were published in 1932. The poetry collection was put together by Effie Lee Powers, a white Cleveland librarian, who in 1931 had asked Hughes to select poems for young people from his previous work.*

Poet Horace Gregory, who in 1930 had published his first book, Chelsea Rooming House, *reviewed* The Dream Keeper and Other Poems *for the* New York Evening Post.

Sandburg of Negro Verse
Review of *The Dream Keeper*

About five years ago Countee Cullen published an anthology of Negro poetry. In this collection over thirty-five living Negro poets were represented. Here was a sudden renaissance of Negro literature and its results were often more than merely promising. So much for the movement at full tide. It was inevitable that a reaction should set in, a reaction not unlike the lull that followed the American poetry renaissance of 1912–1916. Today one hears almost nothing of the general movement, but a few names survive: Charles Weldon Johnson, Claude McKay, Stirling A. Brown, Countee Cullen and Langston Hughes.

In some respects Langston Hughes is the most interesting figure in the group. When "The Weary Blues," his first book of poems, was published, the vogue for Negro jazz was at its height. His poetry, which employed many of the dominant elements of jazz music, struck the ear with the conviction that here was something extraordinarily fresh and invigorating. Langston Hughes never disguised his purpose: first of all he was a Negro poet and in that sense a propagandist quite without the usual apologies for being so. He had overcome the initial stages of self-consciousness and could afford to speak out loud. From the very start his poetry had an air of outdoor health and vitality. His work had something of the same physical charm that we associate with the singing of Paul Robeson.

The present volume, a collection of verse made for young people from the ages of twelve to sixteen, is an admirable example of editing. The poems are selected from his two early books and are supplemented by a group of new poems so as to complete a feeling of unity. It has been a long time since any book of verse for children has been so attractively presented. Langston Hughes's charm is here with its best foot forward and each page is deftly illustrated with a design by Helen Sewell. The little poems and the drawing seem to merge into an inseparable unit which is a rare accident in modern book illustration.

Frontispiece and title page for the 1954 edition of Hughes's collection of poems for children, originally published by Knopf in 1932 (courtesy of Kenneth Spencer Research Library, University of Kansas Libraries)

Glancing through this book one might almost say that Langston Hughes is the Carl Sandburg of Negro poetry. Surely his attraction for children springs from the same source that makes Carl Sandburg one of the few contemporary poets whose verse continues to demand attention from younger people. The direct speech and the simple image evoke an instantaneous response. Take the first stanza of "Homesick Blues":

De railroad bridge's
A sad song in de air.
De railroad bridge's
A sad song in de air.
Every time de trains pass
I wants to go somewhere.

Or the poem called "The Negro," which contains these stanzas:

I've been a slave:
Caesar told me to keep his doorsteps clean.
I brushed the boots of Washington.
I've been a worker:
Under my hand the pyramids arose.
I made mortar for the Woolworth Building.

There is a kind of emotional validity in these lines that gives them genuine, unforced power and a quality of frankness that deserves respect. Miss Effie L. Power, director of work with children at the Cleveland Public Library, is responsible for suggesting that this selection be made into a book. Her choice was a wise one and I believe that her enthusiasm for Langston Hughes as a poet for children will be shared by hundreds of young people throughout the country.

–*New York Evening Post*, 2 August 1932, p. 9

* * *

This excerpt is chapter 4 from Popo and Fifina, *Hughes's best-known children's book.*

By the Sea

One afternoon, when there was no work to do and the day was bright with golden sun, Popo and Fifina went down to the beach.

Behind their house there was a gentle slope of about one hundred yards. At the end of the slope there was the large tree with the gnarled serpentlike roots curled above the ground. And a few feet beyond, along the water's edge, were the large rocks of the wave line.

Looking up and down the long curved coast, Popo could see that the harbor of Cape Haiti was shaped roughly like a horseshoe. He could see that almost all the way around mountains rose sharply out of the sea, rocks jutted out of the water itself, and almond trees grew among the rocks.

Popo and Fifina sat side by side on a large rock and looked out across the bay. Away out, some big steamships were anchored, and with them there were a large number of sailing boats.

"Aren't they fine!" Popo exclaimed.

"They are," Fifina agreed.

"But look at these tiny little boats pulling away from the shore. What are they?"

"They are sculling boats," Fifina said. "Those things behind them that the men wiggle like tails are what Papa Jean calls sculls. They are as good as oars, he says."

Popo was looking at a little craft no longer than a good-sized skiff. Three half-naked black men, standing at the end of the boat, were working the sculls back and forth, back and forth, very leisurely, very much indeed like tails. And somehow the motion of these tails sent the boat forward.

"Look," Popo said. "Look at that one near the shore. The men are wading in the water and pushing it."

"Yes," said Fifina. "But do you see what they are carrying in the boat?"

Sitting in the bow of the small craft was a boy about Popo's size. He was naked, and he held under each arm a game chicken. In addition to the boy with the chickens, the boat held a basket of mangoes, two bunches of bananas, and a tiny green parrot tied by the foot and sitting on one of the sculls.

Popo jumped to his feet and threw up his hands, waving at the other youngster. When he saw that the boy was looking at him, he called at the top of his voice, "Say, where are you going with the chickens?"

The boy smiled broadly.

"We are going out to the ships to sell them," he shouted back.

The men who had been pushing the boat out into the deeper water jumped aboard and began working the sculls; and promptly the little bark with its curious cargo drifted out into the blue bay.

Popo stretched out on the rock, rested his chin in his hand, and began daydreaming. He wondered what kind of boat Papa Jean had gone out in, and where he might be at that very moment. Was he selling things to the steamers anchored near the horizon? Or was he out beyond the harbor on the big tossing waves with his net cast in the deep water? Either of these seemed to Popo a fine occupation, and he longed with all his heart to be with Papa Jean. But some day they would have a boat of their own, Papa

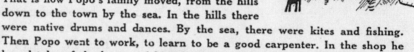

Advertisement for Hughes and Arna Bontemps's popular children's novel (Langston Hughes Papers, Yale Collection of American Literature, Beinecke Rare Book and Manuscript Library)

Jean had promised that, and then he would go out like the youngster with the chickens. Ah, wouldn't that be a life!

Meanwhile Fifina was hopping from rock to rock. Sometimes she stopped to look down into the shallow clear water. She would stand very still for a moment or two, and then she would start leaping and climbing again. Suddenly she came to a quick stop and called very loudly: "Popo! Oh, Popo, come here quick!"

Popo did not wait to ask what she wanted but jumped up and ran around to the rock where she was standing. The rock was under an almond tree that hung over the water, and it was so far out in the water that it could be reached only by stepping on another rock and making a little jump.

"What is it? What is it?" Popo whispered breathlessly as he stood by his sister's side.

"There. See." She pointed to the water near the base of the rock.

"Oh, yes!"

Popo slid down on his stomach, his head hanging over the edge of the rock. Fifina knelt beside him, supporting herself by her hands as she peered into the clear transparent water.

Down near the white sandy bottom they could see a host of lovely red, blue, and yellow parrot fish darting about excitedly. They looked as bright and pretty as sticks of candy, and neither Popo nor Fifina had ever seen any living creatures half so vivid.

"Do you think we could catch some of them?" Popo asked eagerly.

Fifina shook her head.

"We have nothing to catch them with," she said. "Besides, what would we do with them if we did?"

"We might have Mamma Anna cook them for our supper."

"It would be a shame to eat them," Fifina said. "They are such darlings."

Popo thought a moment and then calmly agreed. They were too pretty to eat. And maybe it would be just as well not to frighten them.

"You are right," he whispered.

"But we might catch a few crabs and carry them home with us," she suggested. "Mamma Anna loves them."

They climbed back over the rocks and came down to the water's edge at another place and began digging in the sand and scratching in the water with switches.

"Here, Fifina," Popo called presently. "I have the first one. And a beauty he is too. Just look."

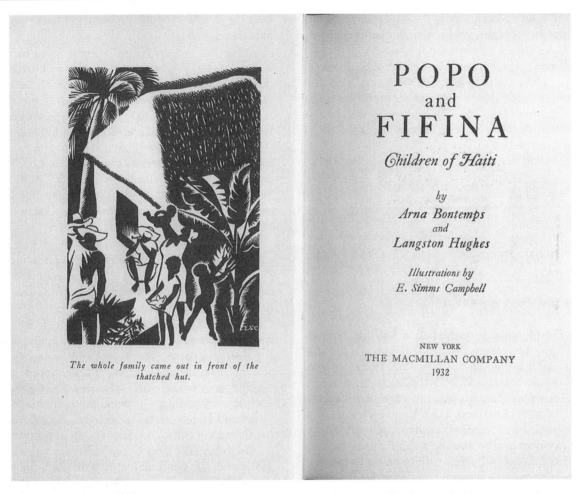

The whole family came out in front of the thatched hut.

POPO
and
FIFINA
Children of Haiti

by
Arna Bontemps
and
Langston Hughes

Illustrations by
E. Simms Campbell

NEW YORK
THE MACMILLAN COMPANY
1932

Frontispiece and title page for the children's book that was called "a model of its kind" in the 23 October 1932 issue of
The New York Times Book Review *(courtesy of the University of Illinois Libraries)*

He held up a large greenish-red crab, holding it carefully so as not to be snapped by its claws.

"Well, put a rock on him till I get one," Fifina said. "Then we can fasten their legs together so that they can't crawl away."

A few moments later, she caught a crab of her own, and they attached the claws together. Then they continued their search, digging separately. Soon the string of crabs was nearly a yard long, and Fifina suggested that they had enough for one day.

But before they started for home a boat slid up near the bank and Papa Jean with several other men got out and waded ashore. At first Popo was surprised. He had not supposed that it was time for boats to be returning. But here indeed was his father, and out in the bay were many other small craft, taking advantage of the land breeze for their return. Scores of small white sails flashed in the rays of the western sun. They were a sight to remember. And here was Papa Jean, standing

with his bare feet wide apart, his pants rolled up to the knees, his ragged and sleeveless shirt hanging open in front, and a string of sparkling glasslike fish in his hand. The fish were hung on a switch that went through their gills.

"What will we do with so many fish?" Fifina asked as she looked first at Papa Jean's string and then at the crabs.

"Some of them we'll eat," he said. "Some of them we'll sell in the market. And if we have any left I'll carry them to your Uncle Jacques, who lives at the other end of rue Bord de la Mer. We have not gone to visit him since we moved to town, and I'd like to take him a present."

"May I go too?" Popo asked hurriedly.

"Not to-night," Papa Jean said. "It will be too late when I get back. But maybe another time. . . . Hello!" He suddenly noticed the string of crabs at his feet on the ground. "Well, just look at these! I see I have two bright children. Won't Mamma Anna be happy to see these! Some day I'm going to give you a treat. Maybe next Sunday I'll take you for a walk to the lighthouse."

Popo put his shoulders back. He felt as big as a man. And the promise of a trip to the lighthouse made him forget for the moment that he had just been denied the trip to Uncle Jacques's home. He followed Papa Jean and Fifina up the slope, dragging his string of crabs just as proudly as Papa Jean carried his sparkling fish.

—Popo and Fifina (New York: Macmillan, 1932), pp. 26–32

* * *

An outspoken advocate for children's literacy throughout his career, Hughes wrote this essay for Children's Library Yearbook.

Books and the Negro Child

Albert Einstein, in his message to American Negroes in The Crisis for January 1932, says, "It seems to be a universal fact that minorities, especially when their individuals are recognizabel because of physical differences, are treated by the majorities among whom they live as an inferior class. The tragic part of such a fate, however, lies not only in the automatically realized disadvantages suffered by these minorities in economic and social relations, but also in the fact that those who meet such treatment themselves, for the most part, acquiesce in this prejudiced estimate because of the suggestive influence of the majority, and come to regard people like themselves as inferior."

Overcoming this racial inferiority complex is, undoubtedly, one of the greatest tasks of the teachers of Negro children. To make their little charges feel that they will be men and women, not "just niggers," is a none too easy problem when textbooks are all written from a white standpoint. Geographies picturing the African natives as bushy headed savages with no culture of their own; civics describing Negro neighborhoods as the worst quarters in our cities; histories that note the backwardness of the Negro South but none of its amazing progress in only three score years of freedom; all of the bad, depressing phases of racial life set before the black child—none of the achievements; these are what the school books usually give. A Negro pilot with Columbus; black Crispus Attucks, first citizen to fall in the American Revolution; a colored Benjamin Banneker creating the first clock made in this country—none of these is mentioned.

Only when one is no longer ashamed of one's self can one feel fully American, and capable of contributing proudly to the progress of America. To drive out false shame, then, with its companions, timidity and fear, is one of the duties of all grown-ups toward the Negro child. Teachers, authors, and librarians can help greatly in this,

once they understand the problem and books are made available.

For so long, the Negro folk-tales, often in difficult dialect even for Negroes, have been the only kind of stories directly appealing to the life-background of the colored child. So far, the children's booklets on Negro themes, other than the folktales have been of the pickaninny variety, poking fun (however innocently) at the little youngsters whose skins are not white, and holding up to laughter the symbol of the watermelon and the chicken. Perhaps Topsy set the pattern; Sambo and the others came along—amusing undoubtedly to the white child, but like an unkind word to one who has known too many hurts to enjoy the additional pain of being laughed at.

The need today is for books that Negro parents and teachers can read to their children without hesitancy as to the psychological effect on the growing mind, books whose dark characters are not all clowns and whose illustrations are not merely caricatures.

There are a few volumes on Negro life that librarians can recommend to colored children without apology. For older youngsters, Vandercook's Black majesty, a tale of the Haitian kings, is excellent. Elizabeth Ross Haynes' Unsung heroes, and Arthur Fauset's For freedom can teach the achievements of black character. Mary White Ovington's Hazel and her more recent Zeke are two stories for dark youth by a white woman of sympathy and understanding. But there is a need for many more books still unwritten in this field; and after the books are written, a need for Negro library facilities throughout the South where most dark people still live.

The main public libraries in the cities of the South, are not open to Negro readers. Some of the larger towns (but far too few) have branch libraries for their colored citizens, but these branches are understaffed, often with only a single librarian who is sometimes janitress as well, and usually poorly supplied with books, perhaps a collection of dog-eared volumes turned over to the Negro branch when too badly worn for further use by the whites.

Few of these Negro branch libraries in the South can afford or have the books or space to allow separate children's departments. Many of the libraries in the Negro schools and colleges are pitifully lacking in books, too. Fortunately, the Rosenwald Fund has done something to remedy this for the schools—but much more needs to be done, in both schools and cities, for through the written word a people may find themselves.

Faced too often by the segregation and scorn of a surrounding white world, America's Negro children are in pressing need of books that will give them back their souls. They do not know the beauty they possess.

—Children's Library Yearbook, 4 (1932): 108–110

Hughes (first row standing, third from right) on the Europa, *bound for the Soviet Union, June 1932. Others shown include Louise Thompson (sitting on deck, left) and writer Dorothy West (sitting on deck, right) (Langston Hughes Papers, Yale Collection of American Literature, Beinecke Rare Book and Manuscript Library).*

The Soviet Union and Asia

In June 1932 Hughes traveled to the Soviet Union with a group of twenty-two young African Americans to make Black and White, *a motion picture commissioned by the Meschrabpom Film Corporation of the Workers' International Relief that was never completed. Hughes remained in the Soviet Union for one year and wrote about his experiences.*

In this letter, the "new manuscript of poems" Hughes refers to was titled "Good Morning Revolution"; it was sent to Knopf in early March and rejected by Blanche Knopf. The firm did publish the short stories Hughes mentions, as The Ways of White Folks *(1934). Hughes refers also to "my book about Central Asia";* A Negro Looks at Soviet Central Asia *was a book-length essay divided into six sections in which Hughes discusses how the Revolution had affected life and culture in Soviet Central Asia. It was published in Moscow in 1934 by the Co-Operative Publishing Society of Foreign Workers in the U.S.S.R., but it was not published in the United States until 2002, when it was included in volume nine of* The Collected Works of Langston Hughes.

Hughes to Spingarn, 20 March 1933

Dear Amy Spingarn,
I've been meaning to write you for the longest. I've been back in Moscow for more than a month from Central Asia, and awfully busy getting settled again: room, food cards, and all the various papers one needs here where

money isn't of nearly as much importance as the proper papers. For 3 rubles with a card, one gets a meal that would otherwise cost 20, a pack of ciggarettes for 1.50 that would otherwise cost 7, and so on. So there's a great difference. I eat now in one of the best writers' restaurants and live in a splendid hotel overlooking the Kremlin. Each time, in Moscow, I've been fortunate in living within a block of the Red Square, which is just about the center of things and near all the best theatres. . . . There are some tremendously interesting new plays. The one by Gorky is grand and marvellously acted at the Vocktangov. It's about the decay of a merchant family, and covers from the beginning of the Great War to the eve of the Revolution. Another hit this winter is a play about the trials and tribulations of a Soviet factory manager. It's called MY FRIEND, and is done entirely against a background of steel cables on which moving screens slide up and down indicating change of place. But the most advanced theatre of all here (even outdoing Meyerhold) is the Red Presni where the audience sits in the middle and the play goes on all around one, things happening in front and behind you, and even on a circular runway over your head. It's most exciting, and a place where one could never go to sleep. It gives the effect of being in the very midst of the thing itself. For each play the whole inside of the theatre must be rebuilt. Tomorrow, I am going to see Gorky's MOTHER there, and see what they do with it. . . . The new movies this winter are not so good. None of them

TO THE PRESS:

    Newspaper reports that I and the members of
the Negro film group with which I am connected
are "adrift" in Moscow without funds are absolutely untrue. Our contracts and salaries with
the Meschrabpom Film continue until October 20.
Return passage to America is guaranteed. Several
members of the group intend to remain in Moscow,
and some have already secured work here. The
film BLACK AND WHITE is to be made in the spring.

                                        LANGSTON HUGHES
                                        Moscow,
                                        Aug. 31, 1932.

Hughes released this statement after newspaper reports of the collapse of the movie project. He was responding in particular to a headline in the 12 August 1932 issue of the New York Herald Tribune: *"Negroes Adrift in 'Uncle Tom's' Russian Cabin" (Langston Hughes Papers, Yale Collection of American Literature, Beinecke Rare Book and Manuscript Library).*

yet come up to many of the old ones that we have seen in New York. One, however, is effective and has some stirring music in it. In Russian it's called MY MOTH-ERLAND and is about the Red Army on the Chinese border. They use the Red Partisan song, a marching melody, very beautiful, that one often hears the Red Army men singing here in Moscow as they go through the streets. . . . Have you seen photographs of the Red Army men? They're probably the best dressed soldiers in the world with their long coats and pointed hats with the star in front. And almost always, they sing as they march. . . . I've been working pretty hard. Just lately sent off to Knopf's a new manuscript of poems. And have done 6 short stories, all about various nuances of the color line in America with white and colored characters. And my book about Central Asia is coming along. I want to get it done before I leave in May. . . . I hope to come home by way of China and California. I liked it on the coast, and was there too short a time last spring. . . . When I come back, I must get that second novel done. And I want to do another child's book. This time about Soviet Asia which is a fascinating subject. . . . You would love the museums here. The Picasso's, the Gauguin's, and the Cezanne's at the Western Art are enough to bowl one over. In Leningrad I didn't get to go to the Hermitage there, but I may go up there for a day or so before I leave. But there's so much still I want to see in the Soviet Union, it would take another year, I'm sure. . . . I can't make out what is happening in America. Every letter I get from home seems to be worse and worse. What's going on anyway? About a dozen people have written me lately wanting to come over here and work. Some of the fellows who graduated with me at Lincoln haven't had a steady job yet—and that's been nearly four years ago. One boy writes me that he works 16 hours a day for a dollar, and only twice a week at that, in a market. Terrible, isn't it? . . . I saw several of Glikencamp's swell woodcuts reproduced somewhere recently. I liked them a lot. . . . Have you done any new pictures lately? . . . I asked some of our group who returned last fall to bring Arthur Spingarn a copy of my novel in Russian for his collection. I wonder if they did? Please ask him, and if he never received it, I will try sending it through the post. I can't find any other Negro books here. All books are sold out here almost as soon as they are printed. It's impossible to find Claude

Hughes and Arthur Koestler at a cotton collective in Soviet Central Asia, 1932 (Langston Hughes Papers,
Yale Collection of American Literature, Beinecke Rare Book and Manuscript Library)

McKay or Walter White any more, as they came out some years back. I've been looking through the old bookshops on a chance that I might find them there, but nothing doing so far. . . . I've got some rather good prints of Pushkin and a medallion for the Negro collection at the Harlem branch library. They want me to try and find some old programs of Ira Aldridge. After all these years, I'm afraid it can't be done. . . . The papers say Robeson will be here next season, and probably do Othello in Russian at the Great Theatre. He would probably be a great success here, as the Russian are intensely interested in everything Negro. UNCLE TOM'S CABIN and O'Neil's ALL GOD'S CHILLUN (NEGRO here) are played regularly. And at the Children's Theatre, where I've not been yet, there is a piece called THE NEGRO AND THE MONKEY which all the kids talk about. They've recently made a swell little cartoon film from Mayakovsky's poem BLACK AND WHITE, which is the first serious cartoon film I've seen. It's about the exploitation in Cuba. . . . My mother writes me that she has a role in Hall Johnson's new play which was to open early in March. I haven't learned yet if it opened or not. (Or if it closed or not.) I hope it's good enough to have a run, as mother has been out of work for the longest time; but almost nothing seemed to last on Broadway nowadays. . . . One of the girls from the Roxy ballet was in the hotel here the other day. She

was speaking of the disappointment on the part of the dancers at the new Radio City Music Hall. They thought it was going to run forever, and it seems it only lasted a week, and either closed, or cut down the performers terribly. This girl wanted to get into one of the theatres here. But there's a new ruling here now that people coming on a tourist visa cannot be accepted for work, so lots of people have had to go home who wanted to remain recently. Formerly, lots of tourists used to get work, remain in their hotel rooms, and thus keep the hotels so full there was scarcely any place for travellers—so something had to be done about it. And to get a room outside a hotel is some job. Although there are new apartments all over the place, building hasn't been able to keep ahead of the number of people who want to live in Moscow and refuse to leave. It's like the lure of New York to the mid-westerners, I guess. . . . I hope you are O.K. and that you will write soon. . . . With regards and greetings to Joel Spingarn,

sincerely,
Langston
—Langston Hughes Papers, James Weldon Johnson
Collection in the Yale Collection of American
Literature, Beinecke Rare Book
and Manuscript Library

* * *

Hughes wrote this essay about the city where he spent most of his time during his sojourn in the Soviet Union.

Moscow and Me

"If you can't carry from New York, then buy in Berlin. Everything: Canned goods, sugar, soap, toilet paper, pencils, ink, winter clothes, can openers, tooth-brushes, shoestrings, and so on, and so on, and so on. Otherwise you will go hungry, dirty and ragged in Moscow," thus good friends earnestly advised me.

"You will be guided, guarded and watched all the time in Moscow—the G.P.U.," they warned me.

"The peasants and poor folks have control and they're the stupidest people on earth. You will be sadly disappointed in Moscow," estimable gentlemen who had especially studied the "Russian experiment" told me.

"Oh, and what might happen to your poetry! There's only propaganda in Moscow," charming ladies with artistic souls exclaimed.

"They only want to make Communists out of you-all, you and the rest of these Negroes going in that group—and get you slaughtered when you come back home—if the American government lets you come back," genteel colored people told me. "You'd better stay home."

"Can't," I said. "I want to see Moscow."

So when the Europa sailed from New York on June 14 in the year of our one-time Lord 1932, there I was in a group of 22 Negroes going to the Soviet Union to make a film, *Black and White!*

Moscow met us at Leningrad—in the persons of some of the officials of the Meschrabpom for whom we were to work. And among them was a Negro! None of these men from Moscow appeared pale and undernourished or in need of the canned goods we had brought. And certainly colored Comrade White-man didn't look anything like

A motherless chile
A long ways from home.

And he has lived in Moscow for years.

The banquet they spread for us at the October Hotel in Leningrad ran all the way from soup on through roast chicken and vegetables right down to ice cream and black coffee. And an orchestra playing dinner music. All of which was

Better, better, than I gets at home.

The speeches were short and warm with proletarian greetings and the orchestra played the *Internationale:*

Arise, ye prisoners of starvation.

But we were all a little too full of good food at the moment to give that line its real meaning

Arise, ye slaves no more in thrall.

We did better on that; we Negroes: Moscow and freedom! The Soviet Union! The dream of all the poor and oppressed—like us—come true.

You have been naught,
You shall be all.

We slept on the Express roaring through the night toward Moscow. In the morning we emerged from the train to the clicking of a battery of newspaper cameras and the greetings of a group of Moscovites come to meet us. And among them were two more Negroes! One was Emma Harris who's lived in Russia for thirty years, sings, and makes the best apple pies in the world. And the other was a grandly black boy whom we thought was from Africa—but who turned out to be from Chicago. His name was Bob.

Our hands were shaken. We were hugged and kissed. We were carried along in the crowd to the bright sunshine of the street outside. And there a flock of long shiney cars waited for us—Buicks and Lincolns—that swept us through the Moscow boulevards making as much time as the taxis in Central park. We drove across the Red Square past Lenin's Mausoleum and the towers and domes of the Kremlin—and stopped a block away at the Grand Hotel.

Our rooms were ready for us—clean and comfortable, with hot and cold water, homelike settees and deep roomy chairs. Courteous attendants there were, baths and elevator, a book shop and two restaurants. Everything that a hotel for white folks at home would have—except that, quite truthfully, there was no toilet paper. And no Jim Crow.

Of course, we knew that one of the basic principles of the Soviet Union is the end of all racial distinctions. That's the main reason we had come to Moscow.

That afternoon another long table was spread in the hotel dining room, and we ate again. Around this welcoming board we met our first Russian friends. And learned to say, "Tovarish." And thus began our life in Moscow, the Red Capital.

Here there should follow several pages about how we made the movie that we had come to take part in—except that the movie was not made! Why?

Well, here's the inside dope. A few days after I got here, I was contracted to revise the dialogue so, with an interpreter, I sat in at most of the conferences. I listened to Pudovkin, Eck, and other famous kino experts analyze and dissect the proposed script for *Black and White* as prepared for filming. There were heated discussions on every scene and every line of dialogue. There were a dozen different disagreements. The defects of the plot and continuity were mercilessly exposed. And finally the production of a picture based on the scenario at hand was called off.

Moving picture studios all over the world are, after all, more or less alike. Pictures are listed and cancelled. Directors are hired and fired. Films are made and shelved. What happened to *Black and White* in Moscow, happens to many films in Hollywood. But between the studios of Hollywood and those of Moscow there is this difference: In Hollywood the production of films is quite frankly a business for the making of money. In Moscow the production of films is quite frankly an art for the advancement of certain ideas of social betterment. In Hollywood, too, writers, directors, and producers will squabble over a scenario for weeks, but in the end, if the artistic ideals of the writers are opposed to the money-making ideals of the producers, the artistic ideals go and box-office appeal takes their place. In Moscow, on the other hand, the profit-making motif is entirely absent. It has no need for being, as the films do not necessarily depend on the box office for their funds. And the endless arguments that go on between scenario writers, directors, and producers center rather around how to present with the greatest artistic force the ideals that will make for the betterment of the Soviet people. In Moscow, the aim is to create a socially important film. In Hollywood, it is to make money.

So when the best minds of the Soviet film industry declared the scenario of *Black and White* artistically weak and unsound; and when they said that they felt it could not do justice to the oppressed and segragated Negroes of the world, or serve to further enlighten Soviet movie audiences, there could hardly have been a better reason for the postponement of the film until a more effective scenario could be prepared. Nevertheless, a few of the members of our group, loath to leave the comforts of the Grand Hotel and return to Harlem, shouted loudly that the black race of the whole world had been betrayed, and they themselves had been cheated and disillusioned. Even after they had been paid in full for the four months of our contract, fare in dollars reimbursed, and sent home via Paris, some few still continued to weep in the Harlem papers about the evils of Moscow which housed a film company that would not make a bad picture from a weak scenario–so they could act in it. One can understand that attitude, however, so great is the urge to go in the movies, even among us Negroes. Many an aspirant has left Hollywood cursing Metro-Goldwyn-Mayer. But between leaving Hollywood and Moscow there is this difference: Many disappointed would-be screen stars depart from Hollywood hungry. Our Negro artists left Moscow well-fed, well paid, and well entertained, having been given free excursions that included Odessa, the Black Sea, Central Asia, Tiflis, and Dnieprostroy. They went home via London, Paris, or Berlin. Or they could have stayed (and several did) with offers of parts in other films or jobs in Moscow. But I hear from New York that a few are still mad because they could not immediately star in *Black and White,* be the scenario good or bad.

O, Movies. Temperaments. Artists. Ambitions. Scenarios. Directors, producers, advisors, actors, censors, changes, revisions, conferences. It's a complicated art–the cinema. I'm glad I write poems.

After three months of the movies, I was delighted to pack my bags and go off on a plain prose writing assignment to Central Asia for a study of the new life there around Bukhara and Samarkand–socialism tearing down the customs of ages: veiled women, concubines, mosques, Allah-worship, and illiteracy disappearing. When I came back to Moscow in the winter, those of our Negro group who had remained, seven in all, had settled down comfortably to life in the Soviet capital. Dorothy West was writing, Mildred Jones taking screen tests for a new picture. Long, tall Patterson who paints houses had married a girl who paints pictures, and together they have executed some of the finest decorations for the May Day celebration. Wayland Rudd was studying singing, fencing and dancing, and taking a role in a new Meyerhold play. McKenzie stayed in the films, working for Meschrabpom. And Homer Smith, as a special consultant in the Central Post Office, was supervising the installation of an American special delivery system for Moscow mail. So the Negroes made themselves at home. Some were getting fat.

After five months in Asia, I was glad to be back in Moscow again–great, bustling city comparable in some ways to Chicago, Cleveland or New York. But very different, too. For instance, in the American cities money is the powerful and respected thing. In Moscow, work is powerful–and

Cover for the radical magazine Masses, *to which Hughes was a frequent contributor of poetry and nonfiction during the 1930s (courtesy of Kenneth Spencer Research Library, University of Kansas Libraries)*

not money. One can have ever so many rubles and still find many places and pleasures closed to him. Food, lodging, theatre tickets, medical service, all the things that dollars buy at home, are easily available in Moscow only if one is a worker and has the proper papers from one's factory, shop, office or trade union. I was glad I belonged to the International Union of Revolutionary Writers. Credentials were far more important than rubles.

And another thing that makes Moscow different from Chicago or Cleveland, or New York, is that in the cities at home Negroes—like me—must stay away from a great many places—hotels, clubs, parks, theatres, factories, offices, and union halls—because they are not white. And in Moscow, all the doors are open to us just the same, of course, and I find myself forgetting that the Russians are white folks. They're too damn decent and polite. To walk into a big hotel without the doorman yelling at me (at my age), "Hey, boy, where're you going?" Or to sit at the table in any public restaurant and not be told, "We don't serve Negroes here." Or to have the right of seeking a job at any factory or in any office where I am qualified to work and never be turned down on account of color or a WHITE ONLY sign at the door. To dance with a white woman in the dining room of a fine restaurant and not be dragged out by the neck—is to wonder if you're really living in a city full of white folks (as is like Moscow).

But then the papers of the other lands are always calling the Muscovites red. I guess it's the red that makes the difference. I'll be glad when Chicago gets that way, and Birmingham.

For me, as a writer, Moscow is certainly different, too. It's the first city I've ever lived in where I could make my living entirely from writing. Not that I write more here than I do elsewhere, but I am paid better, and there is a wider market. In America the magazines in which one can frequently publish stories or poems about Negroes are very few, and most of these do not pay, since they are of a social service or proletarian nature. The big American bourgeois publications are very careful about what they publish by or about colored people. Exotic or humorous tales they will occasionally use. Stories that show Negroes as savages, fools, or clowns, they will often print. And once in a blue moon there may be a really sound and serious literary picture of black life in a big magazine—but it doesn't happen often enough to feed an author. They can't live on blue moons. Most colored writers find their work turned down with a note that the files are already

full of "Negro material," or that the subject is not suitable, or, as happened to me recently when I submitted a story about a more or less common situation in American inter-racial life—the manuscript was returned with regrets since the story was "excellently written, but it would shock our good middle-class audience to death." And thus our American publications shy away from the Negro problem and the work of Negro writers.

In Moscow, on the other hand, the editors welcome frank stories of American Negro life. They print them and pay for them. Book publishers welcome volumes by black writers, and, in spite of the paper shortage, a great many books of Negro life have appeared in translation in Moscow. Large audiences come to hear colored writers lecture on their work, and dinners and testimonials are given in their honor. There is no segregated Harlem of literature in Moscow.

As to writers in general, I feel safe in saying that members of the literary craft, on the whole, live better in the Soviet Union than they do in America. In the first place there is a tremendous reading public buying millions of books, papers, and magazines, in dozens of different languages. Translation rights of a Soviet writer's work here within the Union alone may bring in thousands of rubles. And there are, in Moscow and other cities, cooperative dining rooms for writers, specially built modern apartments with very low rents, excellent clubs and tennis courts and libraries—all for the workers in words.

As for me, I received for one edition of my poems in translation more money in actual living value than I have yet made from the several editions of my various volumes of poetry in America. For an edition in Uzbek, a minority language that most Americans never heard of (nor I either till I came here), I was paid enough to live in grand style for a year or modestly for two years—which is more than poetry alone ever did for me at home.

There is in Moscow a great curiosity for things American, and a great sympathy for things Negro. So, being both an American and a Negro, I am met everywhere with friendly questions from children and adults as to how we live at home. Is there really a crisis, with people hungry and ragged when there are in America so many factories, so much technique, so much wheat, and cotton and live stock? How can that be? Do they actually kill people in electric chairs? Actually lynch Negroes? Why?

The children in the Moscow streets, wise little city children, will ofttimes gather around you if you

Hughes in Moscow with the Russian translation of Not Without Laughter *(Langston Hughes Papers, Yale Collection of American Literature, Beinecke Rare Book and Manuscript Library)*

are waiting for a street car, or looking into a shop window. They will take your hand and ask you about the Scottsboro boys, or if you like the Soviet Union and are going to stay forever. Sometimes as you pass a group of children playing, they will stop and exclaim, "Negro!" But in wonder and surprise a long ways from the insulting derision of the word "Nigger" in the mouths of America's white children. Here, the youth in the schools are taught to respect all races. And at the Children's Theatre there is a sympathetic play being given of how a little Negro girl found her way from Africa to Moscow, and lived happily ever after.

Strangers in general meet with widespread curiosity from the citizens of Moscow. *Inastranyetz,* they will say, and let you go to the head of the line, if there is a crowd waiting at the stamp window in the post office, or standing in the queue for an auto bus, or buying tickets to the theatre. If you go alone to the movies, someone is sure to offer to translate for you, should they happen to know a little German or English. If you hand a written address to a citizen on a Moscow street, often said citizen will go out of his way to lead you to the place you are seeking. I have never lived in a more truly courteous city. True, there is not here anywhere in public places the swift and efficient directness of America. Neither is there the servile, tip-chasing, bowing and scraping service of Paris. But here there is friendliness. In Moscow there are often mountains and swamps of red tape that would drive you crazy, were it not for the gentle patience and kindness of the ordinary citizens and simple workers anxious to offer to strangers their comradely help and extend their services as hosts of the city. So in spite of the entirely new routine of life which Moscow offers it does not take one long to feel at home.

Of course, there is the room problem, for the city is the most over-crowded in the world. A foreigner coming to Moscow (unless as a tourist) should really bring a room with him. The great Eisenstein, maker of marvellous movies, lives in only one room. In spite of hundreds of new apartments that have been built, the growth of housing has not been able to keep up with the growth of the populace. A Moscow apartment is as crowded as a Harlem flat at the height of the great Negro migration from the South. Yet, with all their own housing difficulties, the Muscovite can listen patiently to irate foreign workers who are indignant at not immediately receiving on arrival a three room apartment with kitchenette and bath.

The Negroes whom I know in Moscow are all housed comfortably and are not as much given to complaints as certain other nationalities who come to the workers' capital with a greater superiority complex as to their world importance. The colored people in Moscow move easily in Russian circles, are well received, and cordially welcomed in private homes, in workers' clubs, and at demonstrations. There are always dark faces in the tremendous May Day demonstrations that move for hours through the Red Square. A great many Negroes took part in the gigantic Scottsboro Demonstration in the summer of 1932 at the Park of Rest and Culture. The pictures of Negro workers are often displayed in the windows of shops on the main Moscow streets. During the recent May holidays there was a huge picture of Robinson, the colored udarnik at the Ball Bearing Plant, on display in a busy part of Gorky Street. Moscow's black residents are well woven into the life of this big proletarian city, and they are received as comrades.

As for me, I've had a swell time. I've spoken at demonstrations, read poems at workers' clubs, met lots of poets and writers and artists and actors, attended all the leading theatres from the Opera to Ohlopkov's Realistic Theatre where the stage is all round the audience and you sit in the middle. I've seen the finest Gauguin's and Cezanne's in the world, have eaten soup with the Red Army, danced with the Gypsies, and lived excitingly well, and have done a great deal of writing.

I shall go back to America just as clean (there is soap here), just as fat (and food), just as safe and sound (and the G.P.U.) as I was when I left New

York. And once there, I'm thinking that I'll probably be homesick for Moscow. There's an old Negro song that says:

You never miss the water till the well runs dry. Those who ought to know, tell me that you never really appreciate Moscow until you get back again to the land of the bread lines, unemployment, Jim Crow cars and crooked politicians, brutal bankers and overbearing police, three per cent beer and the Scottsboro case.

Well, the Russian workers and peasants were awfully patient with the Tsar, but when they got rid of him–they really *got rid* of him. Now they have a right to be proud of their red flags flying over the Kremlin. They put them there. And don't let anybody in America kid you into believing what with talking about lack of soap and toilet paper and food and the G.P.U., that Moscow isn't the greatest city in the world today. Athens used to be. Then Rome. And more recently, Paris. Now they'll put you in jail in Alabama for even mentioning Moscow! That's one way of recognizing its leadership.

–*International Literature,* 3 (July 1933): 61–66

***

In June 1933 Hughes boarded the Trans-Siberian Express to begin his long trip back to the United States, in effect completing a round-the-world journey of fourteen months. He left the Soviet Union at Vladivostok and visited Korea, Japan, and China on the final leg of his trip. The following year he published his impressions of imperialism and military occupation in Asia in Fight against War and Fascism.

Swords over Asia

Recently, I took a Japanese boat from Vladivostok. At our first port of call in Korea, I heard the rattle of swords coming up the gangplank. The Japanese military came on board to inspect passports. They lined up the passengers, and looked us over. In each Korean port there was some form of inspection, whether you landed or not. If you went ashore for a walk, someone tailed a respectable distance behind you, always there.

At Tsuruga, where the boat docks in Japan, scarcely had I gotten to my hotel, before a representative of the military came to call to ask me about Soviet Russia, and to demand why I came to Japan.

Japan is covered with fortified zones, zones where you can't take pictures and where a foreigner shouldn't be. Upon checking out of a hotel, you

PORTION OF A SPEECH BY LANGSTON HUGHES BEFORE THE PAN-PACIFIC
CLUB OF TOKYO, JUNE 30, 1933, AS REPORTED IN THE JAPAN ADVERTISER
TOKYO, JULY 1, 1933.

LANGSTON HUGHES, NOTED NEGRO
POET, ALSO SPEAKS AND SAYS
HIS PEOPLE ARE OPPRESSED

Mr. Hughes, after recalling that tea had played a considerable
part in the beginnings of American history, said:

"I am an American, or as you can see, an American Negro, but
unfortunately for me and my people, American democracy has not meant
all that it has meant to the other inhabitants of my country. My
people were slaves for some 300 years. When we were freed we were
freed without benefit of land, money or education, and have remained
more or less in the power of our former masters. In America today
the Negroes, about 15,000,000, suffer all sorts of oppression and
discriminations that can by no means be called democracy. Economic,
political, and social oppression is our lot --- economic in that most
of the American factories and commercial enterprises are closed to
Negro workers; political in that half of the American Negroes cannot
vote or hold public office; social in that in the southern part of
America the educational system is more or less closed to us. In
many States there are intermarriage laws between Negroes and whites;
in theatres and restaurants and hotels there is discrimination against
us.

"But what has all this to do with our meeting today? A friend
of mine who gave me the invitation to this luncheon said I might
speak on the attitude of the American Negro to Japan. Most of the
darker peoples of the world have experienced the same sort of oppression that the American Negro has experienced, but Japan has not, because Japan has been strong against the powers of oppression and has
been able to stand alone and defend herself. The American Negroes
are proud of and have a feeling of sympathy and friendship for Japan.
We feel it is the only large group of dark people in the world who
are free and independent, and that means a lot for us psychologically,
because we feel there are in the world some dark people who are not
down and oppressed. So the American Negro is glad that Japan is
able to enjoy her ceremonial tea without the unwelcome intrusion
of the imperial powers of the West."

*Page from Hughes's speech before the Pan-Pacific Club of Tokyo, 30 June 1933 (Langston Hughes Papers,
Yale Collection of American Literature, Beinecke Rare Book and Manuscript Library)*

must inform your hotel keeper where you are going. To alight from any train at any station is dependent upon whether the military wish to allow your presence there or not. Foreigners living in Japan have permanent spies attached to them. Travelers have their temporary spies. The Japanese militarists are quite open about all this. They make no secret that they are shadowing you, and that they are suspicious of everyone.

Imperialist Dictatorship

In Tokio, my second night there, I thought I heard tractors going through the streets but they were tanks, more than a dozen of them. Where they were going down a big city street in the middle of the night, I do not know. But I read in the papers that day that three young men of Tokio had committed suicide rather than become a part of the yearly draft for the imperial army—for more than 11,000 young fellows have come back maimed for life from the recent wars in Manchuria. The three who killed themselves the day the tanks came by did not want to fight. In Japan there are thousands of other young men who do not want to fight either—but the present military dictatorship imprisons them, shames them through the press, drives them to suicide, or forces them at the point of a gun to shoulder arms.

In Shanghai, that vast international powder-keg of a city, the Japanese marines patrol the streets in fives, marching slowly and gravely, armed, swinging little sticks on constant patrol.

Guns, Guns Everywhere

Arms bristle everywhere, on everybody, on all nationalities—except the Chinese whose land the foreigners have taken. In Shanghai, the British are armed, guarding shops and banks. The French are armed, and their gendarmes, the Annamites. The Sikh police are armed. The White Russian mercenaries are armed. The American marines are armed. They all guard banks, important corners, consulates, and steel gates at the end of the foreign quarter's streets.

All kinds of gunboats mass in the harbor of Shanghai, too, facing one another, taking the best buoys away from commercial shipping. Up and down the Chinese rivers these foreign gunboats travel protecting investments and missionaries, shooting down Chinese who rebel against the graft and rapine going on in their own land.

Our American gunboats protect Standard Oil. They trail Standard Oil tankers like enormous flunkies. Our Admirals bow down to Standard Oil—shooting at Communists and letting opium runners pass, for opium is not dangerous to Standard Oil. Communists are dangerous. Hungry people are, too.

On the edge of Shanghai is Chapei, in blackened ruins, empty wall to wall, charred stone on stone, destroyed by the Japanese. In the canals of Shanghai, the bodies of babies dead from hunger float and rot. And in the poor streets of Tokio, young men drink poison rather than go to a stupid War. In the prisons of Nanking, students are slowly tortured to death for protesting against War, hunger, and foreign battleships. The President of China and the Emperor of Japan are one in killing and torturing the young and fearless.

Imperialists vs. Workers

In Asia the rich international bandits fight for spoils: England, France, Japan, America, and the traitors of the Kuomintang. If you don't own warships and bombing planes, you're out of luck. The fighting is crude and cruel—and the masses get their heads smashed and their hearts shot out.

Over Asia the swords rattle. Over Shanghai, over Tokio, over Nanking. The military dictators of China and Japan snarl and shake their bloody sticks. Meanwhile, the British guns prepare to bark, snarling, too. The French are oiling their pistols. The American cruisers maneuver. Everywhere steel prepares to point, to ram, to shoot, to cut, to kill. And overhead the airplanes zoom, steel bombs in their bodies.

WAR IN THE FAR EAST
FLEET MASSES AT HAWAII
PATRIOTS PREPARE

Mr. Rockefeller is our brother. Fight for Standard Oil! Carry civilization to the Orient! Swing another sword over Asia! Burn down another Chapei! The Japanese imperialists shall rule the world! Boom! The white race shall rule the world! Boom! Guns shall rule the world! Boom! Unless the workers pull down the War-makers—destroy their governments—and turn their battleships into yachts to use on summer holidays.

—*Fight against War and Fascism*, 1 (June 1934): 6

NATIONAL COMMITTEE

FOR THE DEFENSE OF POLITICAL PRISONERS

NORTHERN CALIFORNIA BRANCH ——— 2957 WASHINGTON STREET, SAN FRANCISCO, CALIF.

Phone: WEst 3799

SHERWOOD ANDERSON
WILLIAM ROSE BENET
MALCOLM COWLEY
FLOYD DELL
THEODORE DREISER
WALDO FRANK
SIDNEY HOWARD
EDNA ST. VINCENT MILLAY
ELMER RICE
MARK VAN DOREN
MARY HEATON VORSE
EDMUND WILSON

———

Members in California
——

GEORGE ANDERSEN
JOHN D. BARRY
RICHARD BRANSTEN
BENIAMINO BUFANO
PROF. JAMES R. CALDWELL
DR. ELEANOR K. CHAMBERS
CLARKSON CRANE
MIRIAM ALLEN DeFORD
MARGARET De PATTA
ALICE DeNAIR
DOROTHY W. ERSKINE
SARA BARD FIELD
MARTIN FLAVIN
PROF. FELIX FLUGEL
JOSEPH GAER
LEON GELBER
ELSA GIDLOW
CHARLES A. HOGAN
J. L. HOWARD
ADELAIDE HOWARD
HELEN HOYT
LANGSTON HUGHES
ORRICK JOHNS
EMILY OLGA JOSEPH
BEATRICE KINKEAD
DAVID KINKEAD
ELIZABETH LIVERMORE
JOAN LONDON
RELLA MANN
GEORGE MAURER
HELEN EVERETT MEIKLEJOHN
MRS. E. D. MINTON
DR. CAVENDISH MOXON
ANNA G. NEWELL
MADEFREY ODHNER
PROF. HUBERT PHILLIPS
ANNA PORTER
ELSIE ROBINSON
MARION R. ROTH
HELEN SALZ
JEAN SCUPHAM
MARIE SHORT
UPTON SINCLAIR
ADRIANA SPADONI
LINCOLN STEFFENS
JACK S. STRAUSS
NOEL SULLIVAN
ETHEL TURNER
J. KENNETH TURNER
MARIE De L. WELCH
EDWARD WESTON
ANITA WHITNEY
ELLA WINTER
JEAN WARD WOLFF
COL. C. E. S. WOOD
MARCY WOODS

Carmel, California
P. O. Box 1582
November 17, 1933

Dear Jean Toomer:

I am a writer also. I know what it means to receive continually by mail requests and appeals for aid. So, believe me, I would not write you now were it not of the utmost urgency. The nine Scottsboro boys are still under sentence of death in Alabama. The new trials come up this November. There is a great and immediate need for funds to see that their defense is carried through adequately and that, if necessary, further appeals be taken to the State and United States Supreme Court in order that lynch laws may not triumph, and that these boys, in spite of pronounced evidence of their innocence, are not again sentenced to death. They have already spent months in the house of electrocution at Kilby, and more months in jail at Birmingham. They are denied bail. They were boys when they left home that day nearly three years ago looking for work. They are growing into young manhood now in the prison hells of Alabama. I know the great sympathy which you have shown for the Negro peoples and the beauty you have given them in your writing. I feel that you would not want these nine Negro boys to die.

There are two things you can do that will aid greatly in their defense (and incidentally in the defense of justice in America). Send me at the above address, payable to this Committee, your check for as large an amount as you can afford for the defense of these nine imprisoned boys about whose black brothers and sisters in your books you have written so beautifully.

And then, if the spirit moves you to express in words what you feel about the plight of these young Negroes in a Birmingham jail, (and I hope you will be so moved), send me a short statement that we may release to the press of America. Any comment from you would be of inestimable value in arousing public opinion against hasty and unfair trials for Negroes, and in securing a fair hearing for these young black boys under the shadow of death in Alabama.

This letter is being sent to those American writers who have based their inspiration (or a portion of it) on the life of the Negro peoples. Please let me have your answer now, for to those sitting in prison, time seems very long.

Sincerely yours,

SCOTTSBORO DEFENSE FUND

Langston Hughes

LH:EB

LINCOLN STEFFENS, National Chairman   ●   DOROTHY W. ERSKINE, Exec.-Sec'y   ●   TOM WARD, Corresp. Sec'y and Treas.

Hughes's solicitation on behalf of the Scottsboro boys and Jean Toomer's reply
(Jean Toomer Collection, Fisk University Archives)

Dear LH

Your splendid appeal reached me here.

The New York papers are reporting the new difficulties
the defense is running up against down there.

All of it makes one realize that something must be done
now.

As soon as I read your letter I was moved to send a
check at once, and would have done so if it were not that
my own finances have been shot these past months, and I
am here attempting to do business. I can only pledge that
if something comes to me I shall send a portion of it
to you for the fund.

I can, however, send now a statement for the press,
and I hope it will xxxxx do good work. I'll put it on a
separate page.

best wishes,

Those who have been caught in a machine will sympathize
with the plight of the Scottsboro boys. Those who have freed
themselves will realize xxxxxxx how much they owe to the
help of others. So let us help these boys in every way we can,
for surely their xxxxxxxx suffering is greater than our own.

Justice aids life; law often takes it. That we need
less law and more justice has never been so true as it is
today. It would be an amazing thing for the world at large
and for the nine S boys in particular to have justice prevail
in their case. Those who have been caught in a machine, who
have gotten free, realize how much they owe to the help of
others. I for one feel that I may in some measure pay my
debt   I feel I must help these boys in every way I can.

Then let us, who are free today, help liberate
these boys who are caught.

Most of us at one time or an another have been
caught in a machine, though few have been in so painful a
plight as the S boys. How did we get free? Partly by our
own merit, largely owing to the help of others. The help of
others. So let our realization of this arouse us in turn
to help liberate these boys who merit to be as free as
any of us, who need our help.

A First Collection of Stories

Hughes's first book of short stories, The Ways of White Folks, *struck a more somber tone than his work of the 1920s, focusing on the social, economic, and psychological implications of racial prejudice and discrimination in the United States. Published in May 1934 to mostly strong reviews, the book sold poorly. In this story, the eighth in the fourteen-story collection, Hughes blends stream of consciousness and impressionistic narrative techniques to explore the effects of racist thinking on both blacks and whites.*

Red-Headed Baby

"Dead, Dead as Hell, these little burgs on the Florida coast. Lot of half-built skeleton houses left over from the boom. Never finished. Never will be finished. Mosquitoes, sand, niggers. Christ, I ought to break away from it. Stuck five years on same boat and still nothin' but a third mate puttin' in at dumps like this on a damned coast-wise tramp. Not even a good time to be had. Norfolk, Savannah, Jacksonville, ain't bad. Ain't bad. But what the hell kind of port's this? What the hell is there to do except get drunk and go out and sleep with niggers? Hell!"

Feet in the sand. Head under palms, magnolias, stars. Lights and the kid-cries of a sleepy town. Mosquitoes to slap at with hairy freckled hands and a dead hot breeze, when there is any breeze.

"What the hell am I walkin' way out here for? She wasn't nothin' to get excited over–last time I saw her. And that must a been a full three years ago. She acted like she was a virgin then. Name was Betsy. Sure ain't a virgin now, I know that. Not after we'd been anchored here damn near a month, the old man mixed up in some kind of law suit over some rich guy's yacht we rammed in a midnight squall off the bar. Damn good thing I wasn't on the bridge then. And this damn yellow gal, said she never had nothing to do with a seaman before. Lyin' I guess. Three years ago. She's probably on the crib-line now. Hell, how far was that house?"

Crossing the railroad track at the edge of town. Green lights. Sand in the road, seeping into oxfords and the cuffs of dungarees. Surf sounds, mosquito sounds, nigger-cries in the night. No street lights out here. There never is where niggers live. Rickety run-down huts, under palm trees. Flowers and vines all over. Always growing, always climbing. Never finished. Never will be finished climbing, growing. Hell of a lot of stars these Florida nights.

"Say, this ought to be the house. No light in it. Well, I remember this half-fallin'-down gate. Still fallin' down. Hell, why don't it go on and fall? Two or

three years, and ain't fell yet. Guess *she's* fell a hell of a lot, though. It don't take them yellow janes long to get old and ugly. Said she was seventeen then. A wonder her old woman let me come in the house that night. They acted like it was the first time a white man had ever come in the house. They acted scared. But she was worth the money that time all right. She played like a kid. Said she liked my red hair. Said she'd never had a white man before. . . . Holy Jesus, the yellow wenches I've had, though. . . . Well, it's the same old gate. Be funny if she had another mule in my stall, now wouldn't it? . . . Say, anybody home there?"

"Yes, suh! Yes, suh! Come right in!"

"Hell, I know they can't recognize my voice. . . . It's the old woman, sure as a yard arm's long. . . . Hello! Where's Betsy?"

"Yes, suh, right here, suh. In de kitchen. Wait till I lights de light. Come in. Come in, young gentleman."

"Hell, I can't see to come in."

Little flare of oil light.

"Howdy! Howdy do, suh! Howdy, if 'tain't Mister Clarence, now, 'pon my word! Howdy, Mister Clarence, howdy! Howdy! After sich a long time."

"You must-a knowed my voice."

"No, suh, ain't recollected, suh. No, suh, but I knowed you was some white man comin' up de walk. Yes, indeedy! Set down, set down. Betsy be here directly. Set *right* down. Lemme call her. She's in de kitchen. . . . You Betsy!"

"Same old woman, wrinkled as hell, and still don't care where the money comes from. Still talkin' loud. . . . She knew it was some white man comin' up the walk, heh? There must be plenty of 'em, then, comin' here now. She knew it was some white man, heh! . . . What yuh sayin', Betsy, old gal? Damn if yuh ain't just as plump as ever. Them same damn moles on your cheek! Com'ere, lemme feel 'em."

Young yellow girl in a white house dress. Oiled hair. Skin like an autumn moon. Gold-ripe young yellow girl with a white house dress to her knees. Soft plump bare legs, color of the moon. Barefooted.

"Say, Betsy, here is Mister Clarence come back."

"Sure is! Claren–Mister Clarence! Ma, give him a drink."

"Keepin' licker in the house, now, heh? Yes? I thought you was church members last time I saw yuh? You always had to send out and get licker then."

"Well, we's expectin' company some of the times these days," smiling teeth like bright-white rays of moon, Betsy, nearly twenty, and still pretty.

Three Characters IN SEARCH OF A

MAGAZINE THAT IS

Unhampered BY THE OLD *Taboos*

"A GOOD JOB GONE"

"Mr. Lloyd had plenty of money, liked his licker and his women young and pretty. Out of one of the Harlem night clubs he picked up Pauline, one of these golden browns like an Alabama moon. From then on the blondes didn't have a break. A sugar-brown had crowded the white babies out, and he loved her like a dog. But she had a colored boy-friend—a tall black good looking guy, a number writer on 135th Street. Mr. Lloyd found out about him and they had a hell of a quarrel." *Well, we mustn't spoil it by telling too much, but that little high brown told that rich white man that he could go to the devil. And that, both figuratively and literally, is just what he did.*

January, 1934

WE HAVE a story by Langston Hughes, brilliant young Negro author whose work has appeared in some of the country's leading magazines. But this is the kind of story that no commercial magazine would touch with a ten foot pole.

Now ESQUIRE is a commercial magazine — don't ever let anybody tell you different. And yet, ESQUIRE hates to fall into the old ruts that have been worn so deep by the formula-type stories that comprise the bulk of the fiction in the so-called "slick paper" magazines.

This is a man's magazine. It isn't edited for the junior miss. It isn't dedicated to the dissemination of sweetness and light. It is addressed to an adult male audience, and feels that its stories ought, therefore, to be allowed to depart from the beaten track.

The story in question is briefly sketched in the synopsis at the left. How about it? We'd like to print it. And we think, if you'll lay aside your old prejudices for five minutes, that you'll enjoy reading it. There ought to be one magazine in America in which a man can read stories like this. But it's entirely up to you. Tell us what you want ESQUIRE to be.

ESQUIRE's distribution is now completely national. If the yeas out-number the nays in thirty-six of the forty-eight states (or in that proportion, if all states are not heard from) then this story will appear in an early issue of ESQUIRE, and will be followed by others that are similarly at sixes and sevens with the usual run of magazine fiction. Address the Editor of ESQUIRE, 919 N. Michigan Ave., Chicago.

Promotional advertisement from the second issue of Esquire, *in which a story by Hughes is described (Thomas Cooper Library, University of South Carolina)*

First page of the story published in the April 1934 issue of Esquire *and collected in* The Ways of White Folks. *The promotion of the story in the January issue of the magazine provoked a surprisingly strong reaction from readers. In the March issue, editor Arnold Gingrich wrote that "The story was voted in by a ratio of yea's to nay's which stands, at this moment, at over nine to one" (courtesy of the University of Illinois Libraries).*

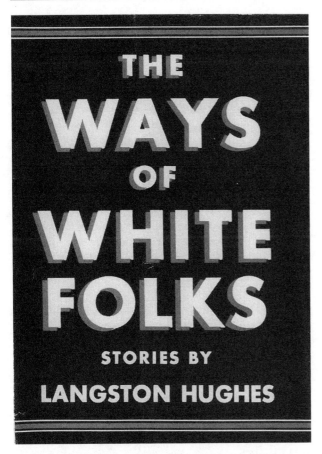

THE WAYS OF WHITE FOLKS

STORIES BY LANGSTON HUGHES

Dust jacket for Hughes's first book of short stories, published by Knopf in 1934 (Langston Hughes Papers, Yale Collection of American Literature, Beinecke Rare Book and Manuscript Library)

"You usin' rouge, too, ain't yuh?"

"Sweet rouge."

"Yal?"

"Yeah, man, sweet and red like your hair."

"Yal?"

No such wise cracking three years ago. Too young and dumb for flirtation then: Betsy. Never like the old woman, talkative, "This here rum come right off de boats from Bermudy. Taste it, Mister Clarence. Strong enough to knock a mule down. Have a glass."

"Here's to you, Mister Clarence."

"Drinkin' licker, too, heh? Hell of a baby, ain't yuh? Yuh wouldn't even do that last time I saw yuh."

"Sure wouldn't, Mister Clarence, but three years a long time."

"Don't Mister Clarence *me* so much. Yuh know I christened yuh. . . . Auntie, yuh right about this bein' good licker."

"Yes, suh, I knowed you'd like it. It's strong."

"Sit on my lap, kid."

"Sure. . . ."

Soft heavy hips. Hot and browner than the moon—good licker. Drinking it down in little nigger house Florida coast palm fronds scratching roof hum mosquitoes night bugs flies ain't loud enough to keep a man named Clarence girl named Betsy old woman named Auntie from talking and drinking in a little nigger house on Florida coast dead warm night with the licker browner and more fiery than the moon. Yeah, man! A blanket of stars in the Florida sky—outside. In oil-lamp house you don't see no stars. Only a white man with red hair—third mate on a lousy tramp, a nigger girl, and Auntie wrinkled as an alligator bringing the fourth bottle of licker and everybody drinking—when the door . . . slowly . . . opens.

"Say, what the hell? Who's openin' that room door, peepin' in here? It can't be openin' itself?"

The white man stares intently, looking across the table, past the lamp, the licker bottles, the glasses and the old woman, way past the girl. Standing in the door from the kitchen—Look! a damn red-headed baby. Standing not saying a damn word, a damn runt of a red-headed baby.

"What the hell?"

"You Clar— . . . Mister Clarence, 'cuse me! . . . You hatian, you, get back to you' bed this minute—fo' I tan you in a inch o' yo' life!"

"Ma, let him stay."

Betsy's red-headed child stands in the door looking like one of those goggly-eyed dolls you hit with a ball at the County Fair. The child's face got no change in it. Never changes. Looks like never will change. Just staring—blue-eyed. Hell! God damn! A red-headed blue-eyed yellow-skinned baby!

"You Clarence! . . . 'Cuse me, Mister Clarence. I ain't talkin' to you suh. . . . You, Clarence, go to bed. . . . That chile near 'bout worries de soul-case out o' me. Betsy spiles him, that's why. De po' little thing can't hear, nohow. Just deaf as a post. And over two years old and can't even say, 'Da!' No, suh, can't say, 'Da!'"

"Anyhow, Ma, my child ain't blind."

"Might just as well be blind fo' all de good his eyesight do him. I show him a switch and he don't pay it no mind—'less'n I hit him."

"He's mighty damn white for a nigger child."

"Yes, suh, Mister Clarence. He really ain't got much colored blood in him, a-tall. Betsy's papa, Mister Clarence, now he were a white man, too. . . . Here, lemme pour you some licker. Drink, Mister Clarence, drink."

Damn little red-headed stupid-faced runt of a child, named Clarence. Bow-legged as hell, too. Three shots for a quarter like a loaded doll in a County Fair. Anybody take a chance. For Christ's sake, stop him from walking across the floor! Will yuh?

"Hey! Take your hands off my legs, you lousy little bastard!"

"He can't hear you, Mister Clarence."

"Tell him to stop crawlin' around then under the table before I knock his block off."

"You varmint. . . ."

"Hey! Take him up from there, will you?"

"Yes, suh, Mister Clarence."

"Hey!"

"You little . . ."

"Hurry! Go on! Get him out then! What's he doin' crawlin' round dumb as hell lookin' at me up at me. I said, *me*. Get him the hell out of here! Hey, Betsy, get him out!"

A red-headed baby. Moonlight-gone baby. No kind of yellow-white bow-legged goggled-eyed County Fair baseball baby. Get him the hell out of here pulling at my legs looking like me at me like me at myself like me red-headed as me.

"Christ!"

"Christ!"

Knocking over glasses by the oil lamp on the table where the night flies flutter Florida where skeleton houses left over from boom sand in the road and no lights in the nigger section across the railroad's knocking over glasses at edge of town where a moon-colored girl's got a red-headed baby deaf as a post like the dolls you wham at three shots for a quarter in the County Fair half full of licker and can't hit nothing.

"Lemme pay for those drinks, will yuh? How much is it?"

"Ain't you gonna stay, Mister Clarence?"

"Lemme pay for my licker, I said."

"Ain't you gonna stay all night?"

"Lemme pay for that licker."

"Why, Mister Clarence? You stayed before."

"How much is the licker?"

"Two dollars, Mister Clarence."

"Here."

"Thank you, Mister Clarence."

"Go'bye!"

"Go'bye."

– *The Ways of White Folks* (New York: Knopf, 1934), pp. 121–128

* * *

In this review Herschel Brickell inaccurately cites the title of Hughes's novel and the number of stories in the collection.

Langston Hughes Produces a Remarkably Fine Book of Short Stories Review of *The Ways of White Folks*

Ever since the appearance of his novel, "No More Laughter," Langston Hughes has seemed to me the most genuinely talented of the Negro writers in America, and his volume of short stories, "The Ways of White Folks," completely confirms my opinion.

It is not that good and admirable work has not been done by others of his race, but that from the first in both his prose and poetry there has been a quality that challenged comparison with first-rate work by anybody, regardless of color.

So it is with the present book, from which at least half a dozen stories might be awarded the O. Henry Prize without disturbing the even temper of the reviewers, so sensitive in these matters. They are works of art, these tales that do not depend upon their material for their appeal, although the heartbreaking tragedy of race runs through them like a theme.

In general, as might be expected from the title, they are concerned with the relations of white and colored people from the angle of the Negro.

They do not depend upon background or dialect—in other words, they are not related to the familiar type of genre story that has grown into a convention,—but they are about human beings in a variety of situations and settings, ranging from our Middle West to New England and from the Deep South to Paris.

For the Anthologies

Mr. Hughes has a genuine gift for irony among other things, as may be seen from such stories as "Rejuvenation Through Joy," a most amusing and malicious satire on the goings-on of a cult based upon Negro music and dancing.

The irony of another of the best of the stories, "Poor Little Black Fellow," is of a different and more astringent quality. I am not sure this isn't my favorite of the fifteen stories, although it does not appear in the trio selected by Carl Van Vechten, author of the jacket blurb, as masterpieces. His choices are "A Good Job Gone," which I read in *Esquire* with an immediate realization of its excellence; "Cora Unashamed" and "Little Dog."

"A Good Job Gone" and "Little Dog" are technically perfect, particularly the latter. The former is, perhaps, a bit broad for the run of short-story anthologies, but if "Little Dog" doesn't find itself a permanent place in these collections it will certainly not be because of any lack of merit.

"Poor Little Black Fellow" is the story of a Negro boy who was brought up by a New England family after his father, their butler, had been killed in France. Grown up, he is taken to Paris for the sake of his education, where he meets a white girl from Rumania and introduces her to his "family." They are shocked beyond words and, after lecturing him severely, think of him as ungrateful for all their great generosity and kindness.

Plenty of Racial Pride

This is an unforgettably poignant story, from which there is no shade of pathos missing, and not a tear in sight, for there is no sentimentality in Mr. Hughes's writing. He can even write a Christmas story about a neglected little black boy and make it so sad that one is moved too deeply for wet eyes to be any relief.

There is no propaganda in the stories, but there are here an understanding of racial qualities and a proper pride therein, as may be seen in "The Blues I'm Playing," the story of a colored girl who was adopted by a rich white woman who wished to make a great pianist of her, but who decided she would rather marry her lover. It ends like this:

> Mrs. Ellsworth sat very still in her chair looking at the lilies trembling delicately in the priceless Persian vases, while Oceola made the bass notes throb like tom-toms deep in the earth.
>
> *O, if I could holler*
> sang the blues,
> *Like a mountain jack,*
> *I'd go up on de mountain*
> sang the blues,
> *And call my baby back.*
>
> "And I," said Mrs. Ellsworth rising from her chair, "would stand looking at the stars."

"The Ways of White Folks" is, I think, as distinguished a volume of short stories as has been published in this country within a decade, perhaps longer.

—*New York Post* (28 June 1934), p. 11

* * *

Poet and journalist Edwin Rolfe wrote this review for the Communist newspaper Daily Worker.

Change the World!
Review of *The Ways of White Folks*

Langston Hughes possesses a very rare talent—the ability to create living and altogether understandable characters and situations in every subject his pen touches. He has done this for many years and in many forms. First in his two volumes of poetry, "The Weary Blues" and "Fine Clothes to the Jew." Then in his novel "Not Without Laughter." Very frequently in his vigorous reportage—readers of the Daily Worker will recall his "Moscow and Me," published on this page more than six months ago. And now in his new book of short stories, "The Ways of White Folks" (Alfred A. Knopf. $2.50).

Unlike a host of other poets, novelists, writers of all kinds, Hughes is not afraid of sentiment or emotion. And their presence in his writings, even in his most subtle and restrained stories, his most delicate sketches, gives them the real qualities, the authenticity of life, so that the reading of his work is not merely an interesting exercise but an absorbing experience.

The fourteen stories in "The Ways of White Folks" are, as the title indicates, concerned with the feelings and doings of Negroes in relation to white people. The struggles of his own people concern Langston Hughes most in these stories, but it is the white people with whom they come in contact and among whom they live which in the majority of cases circumscribes and affects their lives. And, even though he portrays individuals for the greater part, in many of his stories these individual figures epitomize and symbolize the actions, plight, direction, of great masses of people.

The Struggles of the Toiling Negroes

Hughes very naturally writes of the Negro artists and intellectuals whom he knows so well, living in a land where the white bourgeoisie controls and directs all means of artistic and intellectual expression. And he writes of the white intellectuals as well—or of those white people of considerable wealth or weltschmerz who attempt to make up for their lack of talent and intellect by acting as sponsors and patrons and sycophants of the arts.

But he is also deeply concerned, in his stories as in his life, with the struggles of the great masses of toiling Negroes, particularly the sharecroppers and tenant farmers of the South upon whose shoulders the southern ruling class has built its backward and semi-feudal agricultural system—the entire southern economy which depends for its continued existence upon the oppression of the Negro people. Not a few of his stories are about such Negroes on large southern plantations, living side by side with the white landlords, subservient to them. And it is in the masterly depiction of the relations of these people, their struggles, aspirations, tragedies, that some of his best stories are built.

"Father and Son"

Such a story is "Father and Son," the very last in the book, which ends with the self-inflicted death of Bert Lewis, son of Colonel Norwood, a white plantation owner, and Coralee Lewis, his Negro housekeeper. Bert is Colonel Norwood's youngest and most handsome son, strongly resembling and just a shade darker of skin than his father. He is a boy who is sick of "white folks' niggers," sick of his people's oppression. Upon his return to the Norwood plantation he refuses to submit to the degradation, the slave behavior which is forced upon the Negro in the South. After the death of Colonel Norwood, he attempts to escape to the swamp but is driven back into the Norwood residence, where he shoots his white attackers and would-be lynchers with his white father's gun until but one bullet remains. His mother aids him:

"'No time to hide, Ma,' Bert panted. 'They're at the door now. They'll be coming in the back way, too. They'll be coming in everywhere. I got one bullet left, Ma. It's mine.'

"'Yes, son, it's your'n. Go upstairs in mama's room and lay down on ma bed and rest. I won't let 'em come up till you're gone. God bless you, chile.'

"Quickly they embraced. A moment his head rested on her shoulder."

Then the white men came:

"'Keep still, men,' one of the leaders said. 'He's armed. . . . Say where's that yellow bastard of yours, Cora—upstairs?'

"'Yes,' Cora said, 'Wait.'

"'Wait, hell!' the men cried. 'Come on, boys, let's go!'

"A shot rang out upstairs, then Cora knew it was all right."

"'Go on,' she said, stepping aside for the mob."

Knows Workers' Plight Under Capitalism

It is impossible to indicate in a brief discussion the consummate restraint and artistry with which Langston Hughes brings his Negroes and white folks to life. Or to give more than a suggestion of the depth and power of his stories. Of "Cora Unashamed" or of "Home," in which a young Negro violinist, returning to his southern home town after being "away seven or eight years," is lynched by white hoodlums for shaking the hand of a white woman, a friend, on the street. Or to give the full satiric flavor of "Rejuvenation Through Joy" or the quiet pathos of "Little Dog."

The last-named story, by the way, shows clearly that Langston Hughes is not trying to categorize "white folks" as a race of oppressors. He differentiates between the white worker, the white sufferer under capitalism, and the white boss and landlord, just as he distinguishes between black toilers and the black bourgeoisie. This story, permeated by a

tender and understanding sympathy for this tragic, middle-aged spinster-heroine, reveals Hughes' approach as essentially a class-approach, not a racial one.

What makes all fourteen stories so intensely alive and authentic, I submit, is the author's intimate knowledge not only of the members of his own race and the white people, but of their plight in capitalist America, in which their position as an oppressed national minority has its roots in their economic position and the attempt of the white ruling class to perpetuate this state in order to safeguard its own wealth, its own social and economic and political domination. This means terror, social subjugation, lynching for the Negro toilers, as well as similar degradation for the white workers.

"The Ways of White Folks" is the book of an extraordinarily gifted writer, and the working class movement in the United States may well be proud of the fact that Langston Hughes is "one of our own."

                                        –*Daily Worker* (10 July 1934): 5

*   * * *

Vernon Loggins wrote this review.

Jazz-Consciousness
Review of *The Ways of White Folks*

Negro literature in this country has been flowing in an uninterrupted stream since it had its beginning with the much written about Phillis Wheatley just before the American Revolution. For most of its long course it has been calm, turning up little that could interest any one except the historian or the sociologist. But there have been flood periods.

One came during the twenty years preceding the Civil War; another between the years 1895 and 1905. And about 1920 a third was ushered in that is upon us still, and which has corresponded with the so-called jazz age. The Negro indeed—whether rightly or wrongly does not matter—was pointed out as the creator of jazz. Naturally he was filled with pride and the spirit of self-assertion. Jazz-consciousness was for him another Emancipation Proclamation. As an artist he was no longer obliged to speak haltingly in the idiom of the whites. They themselves were aping the idiom which he had created.

Among the Negro authors of the present no one has been more jazz-conscious than Langston Hughes. A little less than ten years ago he began publishing poems. Right from the start his aim was to put into English words the pulse and verve of jazz. Imagery and idea were of minor importance; the meaning of the poem depended upon the jazz overtones. Often–especially in his numerous specimens of the blues, which he regards as a distinct pattern, as binding in its laws as the sonnet–he has been astoundingly successful. In 1930 he published his one novel, "Not Without Laughter." The tempo is again that of jazz; but, because of the large proportions, the effect is to a great extent lost.

Now he gives us what seems to us his strongest work–"The Ways of White Folks," a collection of fourteen stories, each an intense drama projected before the reader with the suavity and gliding grace of Cab Calloway conducting the Cotton Club orchestra. Each of the stories deals primarily with a white person–the mother who prefers her daughter's death to an illegitimate grandchild, the rich *roué* who goes insane over his thwarted love for a Harlem high-yellow, the old maid who unconsciously falls in love with her Negro janitor, the Southerner who is defied by his mulatto son, and ten other varying types. But while the force of the white person is felt, the drama of each story belongs to the Negro.

Perhaps the most satisfying tale in the volume is "The Blues I'm Playing," the chronicle of a wealthy patron of the arts who takes under her wing a black girl with extraordinary physical strength and a great talent for the piano. Mrs. Ellsworth instals the girl in a luxurious flat in Paris, engages Philippe to teach her, and makes her an interpreter of Beethoven and Brahms whom the European critics rush to praise. But to Oceola life means something else besides glory on the concert stage. Life means Pete, the Negro boy whom she has kept in her four-room apartment back in Harlem, whom she has lain in bed with planning a formal engagement and a wedding, whom she will join again when he is through with medical school. To the starved, rich Mrs. Ellsworth art lies in looking at the stars; to Oceola it lies in sitting at the piano and letting her fingers wander from Beethoven and Brahms to the blues–laughing and crying . . . white like you and black like me . . . like a man . . . like a woman . . . warm as Pete's kiss.

The story is ideal for Mr. Hughes's jazz touch. He has given it a superb telling. His cynicism, his sarcasm, his radicalism, and his urbane humor tumble and cavort throughout the volume. And there is scarcely a line in which his sophisticated jazziness is not felt. Reading the fourteen stories one after another is like listening with eyes closed to a Paul Whiteman concert of fourteen numbers.

–*The Saturday Review of Literature,*
10 (14 July 1934): 805

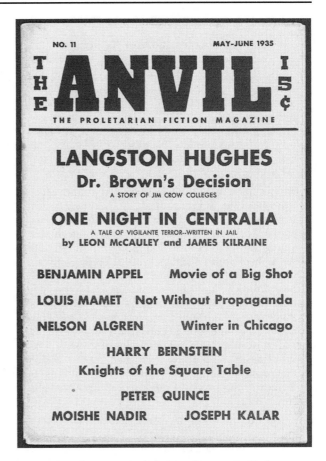

*Cover for a magazine featuring a short story by Hughes
(courtesy of Kenneth Spencer Research Library,
University of Kansas Libraries)*

The Uses of Words

The following is a transcript of a statement Hughes prepared for the first American Writers' Congress, a gathering of radical writers held in New York City in April 1935. Hughes was in Mexico at the time and asked that the statement be read in absentia. The essay includes an allusion to Cordie Cheek, a seventeen-year-old black youth from Nashville, Tennessee, who was abducted by a lynch mob, castrated, and hanged on 15 December 1933 after being falsely accused of assaulting a white woman.

To Negro Writers

There are certain practical things American Negro writers can do through their work.

We can reveal to the Negro masses, from which we come, our potential power to transform the now ugly face of the Southland into a region of peace and plenty.

We can reveal to the white masses those Negro qualities which go beyond the mere ability to laugh and sing and dance and make music, and which are a part

An Appeal for Jacques Roumain

During his trip to the West Indies in 1931, Hughes befriended the Haitian poet Jacques Roumain, a wealthy government executive whose poetry about Haiti's black masses had been inspired by Hughes's earlier writings. When Hughes learned of Roumain's imprisonment for alleged radical activity, he wrote this letter to The New Republic.

SIR: Jacques Romain, poet and novelist of color, and the finest living Haitian writer, has just been sentenced at Port-au-Prince, Haiti, to two years in jail for circulating there a French magazine of Negro liberation called Cri des Nègres. Jacques Romain is a young man of excellent European education who formerly occupied a high post in the Haitian government and is greatly respected by intellectuals as an outstanding man of letters. He is one of the very few upper-class Haitians who understands and sympathizes with the plight of the oppressed peasants of his island home and who has attempted to write about and to remedy the pitiful conditions of 90 percent of the Haitian people exploited by the big coffee monopolies and by the manipulations of foreign finance in the hands of the National City Bank of New York.

As a fellow writer of color, I call upon all writers and artists of whatever race who believe in the freedom of words and of the human spirit, to protest immediately to the President of Haiti and to the nearest Haitian Consulate the uncalled for and unmerited sentence to prison of Jacques Romain, one of the few, and by far the most talented, of the literary men of Haiti.

—The New Republic (12 December 1934): 130

of the useful heritage that we place at the disposal of a future free America.

Negro writers can seek to unite blacks and whites in our country, not on the nebulous basis of an inter-racial meeting, or the shifting sands of religious brotherhood, but on the *solid* ground of the daily working-class struggle to wipe out, now and forever, all the old inequalities of the past.

Furthermore, by way of exposure, Negro writers can reveal in their novels, stories, poems, and articles:

The lovely grinning face of Philanthropy—which gives a million dollars to a Jim Crow school, but not one job to a graduate of that school; which builds a Negro hospital with second-rate equipment, then commands black patients and student-doctors to go there whether they will or no; or which, out of the kindness of its heart, erects yet another separate, segregated, shut-off, Jim Crow Y.M.C.A.

Negro writers can expose those white labor leaders who keep their unions closed against Negro workers and prevent the betterment of all workers.

We can expose, too, the sick-sweet smile of organized religion—which lies about what it doesn't know, and about what it *does* know. And the half-voodoo, half-clown, face of revivalism, dulling the mind with the clap of its empty hands.

Expose, also, the false leadership that besets the Negro people—bought and paid for leadership, owned by capital, afraid to open its mouth except in the old conciliatory way so advantageous to the exploiters.

And all the economic roots of race hatred and race fear.

And the Contentment Tradition of the O-lovely-Negroes school of American fiction, which makes an ignorant black face and a Carolina head filled with superstition, appear more desirable than a crown of gold; the jazz-band; and the O-so-gay writers who make of the Negro's poverty and misery a dusky funny paper.

And expose war. And the old My-Country-'Tis-of-Thee lie. And the colored American Legion posts strutting around talking about the privilege of dying for the noble Red, White and Blue, when they aren't even permitted the privilege of living for it. Or voting for it in Texas. Or working for it in the diplomatic service. Or even rising, like every other good little boy, from the log cabin to the White House.

White House is right!

Dear colored American Legion, you can swing from a lynching tree, uniform and all, with pleasure—and nobody'll fight for you. Don't you know that? Nobody even salutes you down South, dead or alive, medals or no medals, chevrons or not, no matter how many wars you've fought in.

Let Negro writers write about the irony and pathos of the *colored* American Legion.

"Salute, Mr. White Man!"
"Salute, hell! . . . You're a nigger."

Or would you rather write about the moon?

Sure, the moon still shines over Harlem. Shines over Scottsboro. Shines over Birmingham, too, I reckon. Shines over Cordie Cheek's grave, down South.

Write about the moon if you want to. Go ahead. This is a free country.

Settling Matters in Mexico

Hughes's father died on 22 October 1934. This letter was mailed from Mexico City.

Hughes to Carrie Clark, 14 December 1934

Dearest mama,

I'm here at last, arrived yesterday, after having to stay three days at Nogales because my entrance papers did not state that I was colored. So, with getting the papers and all, it has taken me way over a month to get down here.

The Patiños are all three just the same, and send their love to you. Send them a Christmas card, if you can. I'm staying with them in the same room that my father had. You know how cold it gets at night down here, and they have no fire, so I am almost frozen, except in the middle of the day when the sun is shinning.

My father left a will made some years ago in which he bequeathed all his possessions to the Patiños in return for the care they have given him during these years of his illness, the property to be divided equally among the three of them. They, however, wish to divide it four ways, to include me. Since there isn't a great deal (as my father had sold everything before going to Germany) we will each apparently get only a few hundred dollars, and 20% of that must go to the government as a tax. So I'll probably have just about enough to pay Uncle John back for the trip. There are lots of details to attend to, and we have to go to Toluca to probate the will, so it will probably take 6 or 8 weeks yet, things move so slowly down here.

In today's mail, I got a check from my agent, (smaller than I had hoped but better than nothing) so I am sending it on to you for Christmas. I have written him that if any more checks come in for me, to send directly to you—but no telling whether he will sell any more stories soon or not. I hope so, as I'd like awfully to send you something else for the holidays. Don't try to send me any presents down here as the new Mexican laws put a heavy duty on everything. Lots of love to you and Gwyn. Write soon, Langston

—Langston Hughes Papers, James Weldon Johnson Collection in the Yale Collection of American Literature, Beinecke Rare Book and Manuscript Library

---

But there are certain very practical things American Negro writers can do. And must do. There's a song that says, "the time ain't long." That song is right. Something has got to change in America—and change soon. We must help that change to come.

The moon's still shining as poetically as ever, but all the stars on the flag are dull. (And the stripes, too.)

We want a new and better America, where there won't be any poor, where there won't be any more Jim Crow, where there won't be any lynchings, where there won't be any munition makers, where we won't need philanthropy, nor charity, nor the New Deal, nor Home Relief.

We want an America that will be ours, a world that will be ours—we Negro workers and white workers! Black writers and white!

We'll make that world!

—*American Writers' Congress*, edited by Henry Holt (New York: International Publishers, 1935), pp. 139–141

* * *

Hughes's Soul Gone Home, *published in the magazine* One-Act Play *in 1937, was first produced on 9 July 1953 at the Burlap Summer Theatre in New York City.*

Soul Gone Home
A One-Act Play

CHARACTERS

The MOTHER

Her SON

TWO MEN

SETTING: *Night. A tenement room, bare, ugly, dirty. An unshaded electric-light bulb. In the middle of the room a cot on which the body of a negro youth is lying. His hands are folded across his chest. He is a soul gone home.*

As the curtain rises: his MOTHER, *a large middle-aged woman in a red sweater, kneels weeping beside the cot.*

Draft of speech by Langston Hughes at the Second International Writers
Congress, Paris, July 16, 1937

TOO MUCH OF RACE

Members of the Second International Writers Congress,
comrades, and people of Paris, *especially the creators of your great and thrilling Popular Front.* I come from a land called
America, a democratic land, a rich land---and yet a land whose
democracy from the very beginning has been tainted with race
prejudice born of slavery, and whose richness has been poured
through the narrow channels of greed into the hands of the few.
And so I come to the Second International Writers Congress
re resenting my country, America, but most especially *representing* the Negro
peoples of America, and the poor peoples of America---because I
am both a Negro and poor. And that combination of color and of
poverty gives me the right then to speak for the most oppressed group
in America/ that group that has known so little of democracy,
the fifteen million Negroes who dwell within our borders.

We are the people who have long known in actual practice the
meaning of the word fascism---for the American attitude toward us
has always been one of economic and social discrimination: In many
States of our country Negroes are not permitted to vote or to hold
any kind of political office. In some sections freedom of
movement is greatly hindered, especially if they happen to *be* sharecroppers on the cotton *plantations* of the South. All over America we
know what it is to be refused admittance to certain schools and colleges,
to theatres and concert halls, to hotels and restaurants. We know
Jim-Crow cars, we know race riots, we know lynchings, we know the
sorrows of the nine Scottsboro boys, innocent young Negroes imprisoned
now six years in jail for a crime that even the trial judge boys
declares them not guilty of having committed. Negroes In
America do not have to told what fascism *is* in action. We know.
Its theories of Nordic supremacy and economic suppression have long
been realities to us. *We Negro writers know what it is to be unable to work in editorial offices or write for the motion pictures.*

*First page of a draft of a speech that Hughes concluded with a call for "friendship and brotherhood" among all the races:
"And the Fascists know that when there is no more race there will be no more capitalism, and no more war, and no
more money for the munitions makers—because the workers of the world will have triumphed" (Langston Hughes
Papers, Yale Collection of American Literature, Beinecke Rare Book and Manuscript Library)*

MOTHER: *(Loudly)* Oh, Gawd! Oh, Lawd! Why did you take my son from me? Oh, Gawd, why did you do it? He was all I had! Oh, Lawd, what am I gonna do? *(Looking at the dead boy and stroking his head)* Oh, son! Oh, Rannie! Oh, my boy, speak to me! Rannie, say something to me! Son, why don't you talk to your mother? Can't you see she's bowed down in sorrow? Son, speak to me, just a word! Come back from the spirit world and speak to me! Rannie, come back from the dead and speak to your mother!

SON: *(Lying there dead as a door-nail. Speaking loudly)* I wish I wasn't dead, so I *could* speak to you. You been a hell of a mama!

MOTHER: *(Falling back from the cot in astonishment, but still on her knees)* Rannie! Rannie! What's that you say? What you sayin' to your mother? *(Wild-eyed)* Is you done opened your mouth and spoke to me? What you said?

SON: I said you a hell of a mama!

MOTHER: *(Rising suddenly and backing away, screaming loudly)* Awo-OOO-o! Rannie, that ain't you talkin'!

SON: Yes, it is me talkin', too! I say you been a no-good mama.

MOTHER: What you talkin' to me like that, Rannie? You ain't never said nothin' like that to me before.

SON: I know it, but I'm dead now . . . and I can say what I want to say. *(Stirring)* You done called on me to talk, ain't you? Lemme take these pennies off my eyes so I can see. *(He takes the coins off his eyes, throws them across the room, and sits up in bed. He is a very dark boy in a torn white shirt. He looks hard at his* MOTHER*)* Mama, you know you ain't done me right.

MOTHER: What you mean, I ain't done you right? *(She is rooted in horror)* What you mean, huh?

SON: You know what I mean.

MOTHER: No, I don't neither. *(Trembling violently)* What you mean comin' back to hant your poor old mother? Rannie, what does you mean?

SON: *(Leaning forward)* I'll tell you what I mean! You been a bad mother to me.

MOTHER: Shame! Shame! Shame, talkin' to your mama that away. Damn it! Shame! I'll slap your face. *(She starts towards him, but he rolls his big white eyes at her, and she backs away)* Me, what bored you! Me, that suffered the pains o' death to bring you into this world! Me, what raised you up, what washed your dirty didies. *(Sorrowfully)* And now I'm left here mighty nigh prostrate 'cause you gone from me! Rannie, what you mean talkin' to *me* like that . . . what brought you into this world?

SON: You never did feed me good, that's what I mean! Who wants to come into the world hongry and go out the same way?

MOTHER: What you mean hongry? When I had money, ain't I fed you?

SON: *(Sullenly)* Most the time you ain't had no money.

MOTHER: 'Twarn't my fault then.

SON: 'Twarn't *my* fault neither.

MOTHER: *(Defensively)* You always was so weak and sickly, you couldn't earn nothin' sellin' papers.

SON: I know it.

MOTHER: You never was no use to me.

SON: So you just lemme grow up in the street, and I ain't had no manners nor morals, neither.

MOTHER: Manners and morals? Rannie, where'd you learn all them big words?

SON: I learnt 'em just now in the spirit-world.

MOTHER: *(Coming nearer)* But you ain't been dead no more'n an hour.

SON: That's long enough to learn a lot.

MOTHER: Well, what else did you find out?

SON: I found out that you was a hell of a mama puttin' me out in the cold to sell papers soon as I could walk.

MOTHER: What? You little liar!

SON: If I'm lyin', I'm dyin'! And lettin' me grow up all bowlegged and stunted from undernourishment.

MOTHER: Under-nurse-mint?

SON: Undernourishment. You heard what the doctor said last week?

MOTHER: Naw, what'd he say?

SON: He said I was dyin' o' undernourishment, that's what he said. He said I had T.B. 'cause I didn't have enough to eat never when I were a child. And he said I couldn't get well, nohow, eating nothin' but beans ever since I been sick. Said I needed milk and eggs. And you said you ain't got no money for milk and eggs, which I know you ain't. *(Gently)* We never had no money, mama, not ever since you took to hustlin' on the streets.

MOTHER: Son, money ain't everything.

SON: Naw, but when you got T.B. you have to have milk and eggs.

MOTHER: *(Advancing sentimentally)* Anyhow, I love you, Rannie!

SON: *(Rudely)* Sure you love me . . . but I am dead.

MOTHER *(Angrily)* Well, damn your hide, you ain't even decent dead. If you was, you wouldn't be sittin' there jawin' at your mother when she's sheddin' ever' tear she's got for you tonight.

SON: First time you ever did cry for me, far as I know.

MOTHER: Tain't! You's a lie! I cried when I bored you . . . you was such a big child . . . ten pounds.

SON: Then I did the cryin' after that, I reckon.

MOTHER: *(Proudly)* Sure, I could of let you die, but I didn't. Naw, I kept you with me . . . off and on. And I lost the chance to marry many a good man, too . . . if it weren't for you. No man wants to take care o' nobody else's child. *(Self-pityingly)* You been a burden to me, Randolph.

SON: *(Angrily)* What did you have me for then, in the first place?

MOTHER: How could I help havin' you, you little bastard? Your father ruint me . . . and you's the result. And I been worried with you for sixteen years. *(Disgustedly)* Now, just when you get big enough to work and do me some good, you have to go and die.

SON: I sure am dead!

MOTHER: But you ain't decent dead! Here you come back to hant your poor old mama, and spoil her cryin' spell, and spoil the mournin'. *(There is the noise of an ambulance gong outside. The MOTHER goes to the window and looks down into the street. Turns to SON)* Rannie, lay down quick! Here comes the city's ambulance to take you to the undertaker's. Don't let them white men see you dead, sitting up here quarrelin' with your mother. Lay down and fold your hands back like I had 'em.

SON: *(Passing his hand across his head)* All right, but gimme that comb yonder and my stocking cap. I don't want to go out of here with my hair standin' straight up in front, even if I is dead. *(The MOTHER hands him a comb and his stocking cap. The SON combs his hair and puts the cap on. Noise of MEN coming up the stairs)*

MOTHER: Hurry up, Rannie, they'll be here in no time.

SON: Aw, they got another flight to come yet. Don't rush me, ma!

MOTHER: Yes, but I got to put these pennies back on your eyes, boy! *(She searches in a corner for the coins as her SON lies down and folds his hands, stiff in death. She finds the coins and puts them nervously on his eyes, watching the door meanwhile. A knock)* Come in. *(Enter TWO MEN in the white coats of City Health employees)*

MAN: Somebody sent for us to get the body of a Rannie Bailey?

MOTHER: Yes, sir, here he is! *(Weeping loudly)* He's my boy! Oh, Lawdy, he's done gone home! His soul's gone home! Oh, what am I gonna do? Mister! Mister! The Lawd's done took him home. *(As the MEN unfold the stretchers, she continues to weep hysterically. They place the BOY's thin body on the stretchers and cover it with a rubber cloth. Each*

MAN *takes his end of the stretcher silently. They walk out the door as the MOTHER wails)*

MOTHER: Oh, my son! Oh, my son! Come back, come back, come back! Rannie, come back! *(One loud scream as the door closes)* Awo-OOO-o! *(As the footsteps of the MEN die down on the stairs, the MOTHER becomes suddenly quiet. She goes to a broken mirror and begins to rouge and powder her face. In the street the ambulance gong sounds fainter and fainter in the distance. The MOTHER takes down an old fur coat from a nail and puts it on. Before she leaves, she smooths back the quilts on the cot from which the dead boy has been removed. She looks in the mirror again, and once more whitens her face with powder. She dons a red hat. From a handbag she takes a cigarette, lights it, and walks slowly out the door. At the door she switches off the light. The hallway is dimly illuminated. She turns before closing the door, looks back in the room, and says)* Tomorrow, Rannie, I'll buy you some flowers . . . if I can pick up a dollar tonight. You was a hell of a no-good son, I swear!

THE CURTAIN FALLS

—One-Act Play, 1 (July 1937)

* * *

Hughes traveled to Spain in 1937 as a correspondent for the Afro-American *newspapers. The following piece is the first in a series of thirteen essays on the Spanish Civil War that he published in the* Baltimore Afro-American.

Hughes Bombed in Spain

I came down from Paris by train. We reached Barcelona at night. The day before there had been a terrific air raid in the city, killing almost a hundred persons in their houses and wounding a great many more. We read about it in the papers at the border: AIR RAID OVER BARCELONA.

"Last night!" I thought. "Well, tonight I'll be there."

There's a tunnel between France and Spain, a long stretch of darkness through which the trains pass. Then you come out into the sunlight again directly into the village of Port Bou on the Spanish side of the mountain, with a shining blue bay below where children are swimming.

But as you leave the train, you notice that the windows of the station are almost all broken. Several nearby houses are in ruins, gutted by bombs. And in the winding streets of the village there are signs, REFUGIO, pointing to holes in the mountains in case of air-raids. That is wartime Spain. A little town by the blue Mediterranean where travellers change trains.

Cuban poet Nicolás Guillén, with whom Hughes traveled in Spain during the Spanish Civil War (Langston Hughes Papers, Yale Collection of American Literature, Beinecke Rare Book and Manuscript Library)

Working in the Fields

In the country they were harvesting the wheat and, as we rode southward, we saw men and women working with their scythes in the fields. The Barcelona train was very crowded. I was travelling with Nicolas Guillen, the colored poet from Havana, and a Mexican writer and his wife.

Rapid-Fire Talk

They kept up a rapid fire of Spanish in various accents all around me. Guillen and I were the only colored on the train, so I thought, until at one of the stations when we got out to buy fruit, we noticed a dark face leaning from the window of the coach ahead of us. When the train started again, we went forward to investigate.

He was a young brown-skin boy from the Canary Islands. He wore a red shirt and blue beret. He had escaped from the fascists who now control his island by the simple expedient of getting into his fishing boat with the rest of her crew and sailing toward Africa.

The Canary Islands belong to Spain, but the fishermen do not like the fascists who have usurped power there, and so many of them sail their boats away and come to fight on the mainland with the Spanish government. This young man had come to fight.

Spoke Dialect

He spoke a strange Spanish dialect which was hard for us to understand, but he made it clear to us that he did not like fascism with its crushing of the labor unions and the rights of working people like himself. He told us that a great many folks who live in the Canary Islands are colored, mixed with African and Spanish blood.

It was almost midnight when we got to Barcelona. There were no lights in the town, and we came out of the station into pitch darkness. A bus took us to the hotel. It was a large hotel several stories high which, before the Civil War, had been a fashionable stopping place for tourists.

We had rooms on an upper floor. The desk clerk said that in case of air-raids we might come down into the lobby, but that a few floors more or less wouldn't make much difference. The raids were announced by a siren, but guests would be warned by telephone as well. That night there was no bombing, so we slept in peace.

The next day Guillen and I were sitting in a side-walk cafe on the tree-lined boulevard called Las Ramblas, when a dark young colored man came by.

Remembered Meeting

He looked at us, then turned and spoke. He recognized me, he said, because he had heard me speak in New York. He was a Puerto Rican who had come from Harlem to serve as interpreter in Spain. His name was Roldan. He invited us to go with him to the Mella Club where Cubans and West Indians gather in Barcelona.

The Mella Club, named after Julio Antonio Mella, famous Cuban student leader assassinated in Mexico, occupies the whole second floor of a large building near the center of the town. It has a beautiful courtyard for games and dancing, and a little bar where Cuban drinks are mixed. We were invited to a dance that afternoon given in honor of the soldiers on leave, and here we met a number of Cubans, both colored and white, and a colored Portuguese, all taking an active part in the Spanish struggle against the fascists.

Find New Freedom

And all of them finding in loyalist Spain more freedom than they had known at home—for most of

Hughes, Mikhail Koltsov, Ernest Hemingway, and Nicolás Guillén in Madrid, 1937 (Langston Hughes Papers,
Yale Collection of American Literature, Beinecke Rare Book and Manuscript Library)

the West Indian Islands are burdened by colonial or semi-fascistic types of dictatorships such as Batista's in Cuba, and Vincent's in Haiti. And all of them draw the color-line between colored and whites.

In Spain, as one could see at the dance that afternoon, there is no color line, and Catalonian girls and their escorts mingled gaily with the colored guests.

That night, back at the hotel, one knew that it was war-time because, in the luxurious dining room with its tuxedoed waiters, there was only one fixed dinner menu, no choice of food. It was a good dinner of soup, fish, meat, one vegetable, and fruit, but nothing elaborate. Later, as one often does in Europe, we went to a sidewalk cafe for coffee.

No Lights

Until midnight, we sat at our table watching the crowd strolling up and down the broad Ramblas. The fact that Barcelona was lightless did not seem to keep people home on a warm evening. A few wan bulbs from the interior of the cafes cast a dull glow on the sidewalks, but that was the only visible light, save for the stars shining brightly above.

The buildings were great grey shadows towering in the night, with windows shuttered and curtains drawn. There must be no light on any upper floors to guide enemy aviators.

Hears Sirens Wail

At midnight, the public radios began to blare forth the war-news, and people gathered in large groups on corners to hear it. Then the cafe closed and we went to the hotel. I had just barely gotten to my room and had begun to undress when the low extended wail of the siren began, letting us know that the fascist planes were coming. (They come from Mallorca across the sea at a terrific speed, drop their bombs, and circle away into the night again.)

Quickly, I put on my shirt, passed Guillen's room, and together we started downstairs. Suddenly all the lights went out in the hotel, but we heard people rushing down the halls and stairways in the dark. A few had flashlights with them to find the way. Some were visibly frightened. In the lobby two candles were burning, casting weird, giant-like shadows on the walls.

In an ever increasing wail the siren sounded louder and louder, droning its deathly warning. Suddenly it stopped. By then the lobby was full of people, men, women, and children, speaking in Spanish, English, and French.

In the distance we heard a series of quick explosives.

Anti-Aircraft Guns

"Bombs?" I asked.

A NEW PLAY BY
LANGSTON HUGHES DIR.
APRIL 24, — ~ ~ ~ 8:30 P.M.
HARLEM I.W.O. COM. CENTER
317 WEST 125 ST.   ADM. 35¢

Poster for the first play performed at the Harlem Suitcase Theatre, which was sponsored by the International Workers' Order. Hughes served as executive director (Langston Hughes Papers, Yale Collection of American Literature, Beinecke Rare Book and Manuscript Library).

"No, anti-aircraft gun," a man explained.

Everyone was very quiet. Then we heard the guns go off again.

"Come here," the man called, leading the way. Several of us went out on the balcony where, in the dark, we could see the searchlights playing across the sky. Little round puffs of smoke from the anti-aircraft shells floated against the stars. In the street a few women hurried along to public bomb-proof cellars.

Planes Driven Away

Then for a long while nothing happened. After about an hour, the lights suddenly came on in the hotel again as a signal that the danger had ended. Evidently, the enemy planes had been driven away without having dropped any bombs. Everyone went back upstairs to bed. The night was quiet again. I put out my light, opened the window, and went to sleep.

Being very tired, I slept soundly without dreaming. The next thing I knew, the telephone was ringing violently in the dark, the siren screaming its long blood-curdling cry again, and the walls of the building shaking.

BOOM! Then the dull roar of a dying vibration. And another BOOM! Through my window I saw a flash of light. I didn't stay to look again. Down the hall I went, clothes in my arms, sensing my way toward the staircase in the dark.

No Foolin' This Time

This time the air-raid was on for sure. When I got to the lobby, the same people as before were gathered there in various stages of dress and undress. Children crying, women talking hysterically, men very quiet. Nobody went out on the balcony now.

In the street an ambulance passed, its bell ringing into the distance. The anti-aircraft guns kept up their rapid fire. The last BOOM of the enemy bombs was a long way off. The planes, with their cargo of death partially emptied, were driven away. But for a long time nobody left the lobby.

When I went back to bed, dawn was coming in at my open window. Below, in the cool light, the rooftops of Barcelona were grey and lonely. Soon a little breeze blew in from the sea and the red of the rising sun stained the sky. I covered up my head to keep out the light, but I couldn't go to sleep for a long time.

—Baltimore Afro-American, 23 October 1937, pp. 1–2

* * *

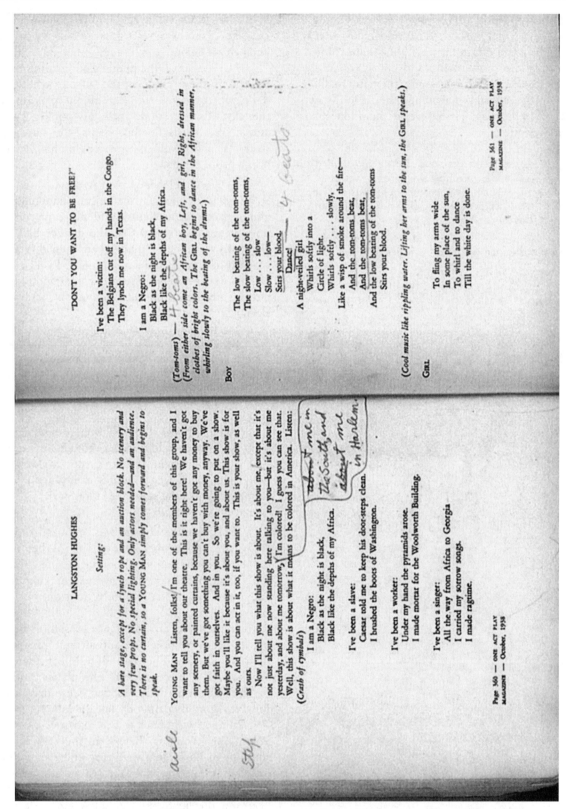

Pages with Hughes's notes for his play Don't You Want To Be Free?: A Poetry Play: From Slavery Through
the Blues to Now–and then some!–with Singing, Music and Dancing. *The verses here were originally
published in* Crisis *and collected in* The Weary Blues *(courtesy of Kenneth Spencer
Research Library, University of Kansas Libraries).*

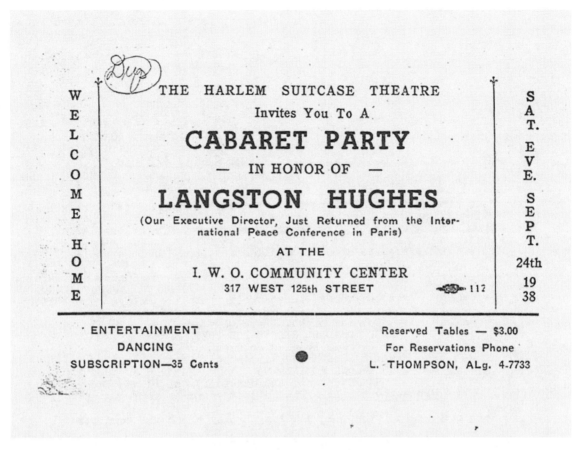

Invitation for a Harlem Suitcase Theatre celebration. Hughes resigned as director of the theater the following year (Langston Hughes Papers, Yale Collection of American Literature, Beinecke Rare Book and Manuscript Library).

After the first season of the Harlem Suitcase Theatre ended, Hughes traveled to Paris to speak at a meeting of the International Writers' Association for the Defense of Culture on 25 July 1938.

Writers, Words and the World

Words have been used too much to make people doubt and fear. Words must now be used to make people believe and do. Writers who have the power to use words in terms of belief and action are responsible to that power not to make people believe in the wrong things. And the wrong things are, as surely everyone will agree, death instead of life, suffering instead of joy, oppression instead of freedom, whether it be freedom of the body or of the mind.

Words put together beautifully, with rhythm and meaning, are as the branches and roots of a tree—if that meaning be a life meaning—such words can be of more value to humanity than food to the hungry or garments to the cold. For words big with the building of life rather than its destruction, filled

with faith in life rather than doubt and distress, such words entering into the minds of men last much longer than today's dinner in the belly or next year's overcoat on the back. And such words, even when forgotten, may still be reflected in terms of motives and actions, and so go out from the reader to many people who have never seen the original words themselves.

Writers have power. The better the writer the greater that power to impel people toward the creation of a good life. We know that words may be put together in many ways: in beautiful but weak ways having meaning only for the few, worldly-wise and capable of understanding; or in strong and sweeping ways, large and simple in form, like yesterday's Walt Whitman or today's Theodore Dreiser.

The best ways of word-weaving, of course, are those that combine music, meaning and clarity in a pattern of social force.

One's own creative talents must supply the music of the words, one's background and experience, the meaning, and one's ability to study, sim-

*Apart is a mild word. I mean
ASUNDER!

1379 E. Washington Blvd.,
Los Angeles, California,
July 25, 1939.

Darling Dorothy,

Back here again, and liking it! What with sunshine, palm trees, cool nights, and a theatre to worry me, who wouldn't like it? This theatre also is about to split apart, but I refuse to let it. DON'T YOU WANT TO BE FREE is still selling out Sunday nights, but to keep everybody busy, we are going into production on a bill of one-act plays Tuesday night. Here they are:
                    FRED DOUGLASS STARTS FOR FREEDOM
                    by Georgia Douglas Johnson
                    MAYBE SOMEDAY by Vincent Williams
                    SOUL GONE HOME by Me
                    JOHN HENRY sung and danced by our blues singers
An All Negro Authors bill. How does it sound to you? To open in September. After that, a full length play which the committee is now in process of choosing. So to that end, kindly send on FRONT PORCH so they can give it the once over.....And please ask Tommy Richardson to let Perry Watkins see his copy of FRONT PORCH as I think it is the only one of mine he hasn't seen.....WAY DOWN SOUTH got off to a good preview, swell press the next day. I could stand to see it again, so you know it must be better than MULATTO. Our songs are sung in grand style, which pleased me! I guess it will be released in August.....Local SWING MIKADO opens Sunday. They've already got one on the coast at the Fair.....Otherwise no news, except that I have an offer of a sort from one of the companies making Negro movies. Am waiting to hear about the money-end, which is slightly important. In any case, shortly, I go into seclusion to finish my book......Send me news of the SUITCASE. And of you.

                    Un abrazo,
                              Langston

Hughes's letter to Dorothy Peterson, who was acting in the Harlem Suitcase Theatre production of Don't You
Want To Be Free? *(Langston Hughes Papers, Yale Collection of American Literature,*
Beinecke Rare Book and Manuscript Library)

Hughes with Arna Bontemps and family in Chicago, 1939 (Langston Hughes Papers, Yale Collection of American Literature, Beinecke Rare Book and Manuscript Library)

plify and understand, the clarity. To understand being the chief of these.

To understand! In one way the whole world situation today is very simple: greed against need. But within that simplicity there are many complexities and apparent contradictions. The complexities of race, of capital and labour, of supply and demand, of the stock exchange and the bowl of rice, of treaties that lie and bombs that tell the truth. And all these things are related to creative writing, and to the man or woman who writes. The shortest poem or story— let us say about a child playing quietly alone in a courtyard—and such a poem or story will be a better one if the author understands the relationship of his child to the Tokio war-machine moving against China. Why? Because the Tokio war-machine—if its lines be traced clearly back to Paris or London or Berlin or New York—the Tokio war-machine touches that very child in our simple little story, no matter in whose yard the child may be playing.

Because our world is like that today, so related and inter-related, a creative writer has no right to neglect to understand clearly the social and eco-

nomic forces that control our world. No matter what his country or what his language, a writer, to be a good writer, cannot remain unaware of Spain and China, of India and Africa, of Rome and Berlin. Not only do the near places and the far places influence, even without his knowledge, the very subjects and material of his books, but they affect their physical life as well, their actual existence and being. For there are two depositories for books today: on democratic shelves or in reactionary bonfires. That is very simple. Books may live and be read, or be burned and blown away.

So there may still be those who use words to make people doubt and wonder, to remain inactive, unsure of the good in life, and afraid to struggle for it. But we must use words to make them believe in life, to understand and attempt to make life better. To use words otherwise, as decent members of society, we have no right.

–Langston Hughes Papers, James Weldon Johnson Collection in the Yale Collection of American Literature, Beinecke Rare Book and Manuscript Library

Adventures as a Social Writer: 1940 – 1949

Two major events marked the year 1940 for Hughes. The publication of his autobiography *The Big Sea* was a high point for the thirty-eight-year-old author, who had accumulated more than enough remarkable experiences to fill the pages of a sizable book. While reviews of *The Big Sea* were generally favorable, more than one critic pointed out the absence of the radical political sentiment that characterized much of his writings of the 1930s. The author's detractors, however, had not forgotten his procommunist rhetoric, and the year was notable, too, as Hughes first became a target for right-wing critics. In Pasadena, at an event in which he was to speak, Hughes was picketed by a crowd of angry protesters, the followers of evangelist Aimee Semple McPherson, whom he had disparaged in his 1932 poem "Goodbye Christ." A circular that included that poem, which had been handed out on the street at the event, was published without Hughes's permission in *The Saturday Evening Post*, greatly magnifying the public-relations disaster.

In January 1941 Hughes distanced himself from the radicalism of "Goodbye Christ" by sending to friends, publishers, and foundations a statement that reaffirmed his opposition to racial and class oppression but dismissed the poem as a work of his youth. Perhaps as a follow-up gesture, he commemorated his twentieth anniversary as a contributor to *The Crisis* with an essay that was decidedly conservative. In "The Need for

Hughes signing autographs during Negro History Week in Atlanta, Georgia, 1947 (photograph by Griffith J. Davis; Langston Hughes Papers, Yale Collection of American Literature, Beinecke Rare Book and Manuscript Library)

JULIUS ROSENWALD FUND
4901 ELLIS AVENUE
CHICAGO

Application and accompanying documents should be filed as early as possible for the convenience of the Fellowship Committee, preferably during the early autumn. No application can be considered by the Committee unless the completely filled-out blank and all of the materials requested reach the Director for Fellowships by January 5, 1941.

Negro ☒   White Southerner ☐

Name in full......James Langston Hughes......................................

Present address ...Hollow Hills Farm,.......Monterey,.........California.......
                                              City   State

Permanent address 634 St. Nicholas Avenue, c/o Harper, New York, N. Y........
                                              City   State

Present position (be specific)....Unemployed...................................

   Institution or organization...Annual salary...............

   Address ....
                                              City   State

Specific Field ...Playwright and poet...

   Concise statement of plan of work.casts.and.simple.sets.suitable.for.production by
Negro high schools, colleges, and amateur group s, or on the air; the
plays to each be built around an outstanding Negro historical character
and written especially in such a way as to allow production in the South
where the need for such material is great; to pproceed the writing of
these plays by three or four months of reading of the necessary background material for historical accuracy and inspiration; the whole project to aid in providing the current need of Negro youth for the inspirational and heroic out of their own background and history, and to provide the various Negro little theatre groups with material stemming from
their own racial roots.

What institution do you wish to attend?..

Have you been admitted?.............For what degree will you work?..............

Under whose supervision?.................................Department of..........

Dates of period for which grant is desired....March 1941-March 1942...........

What is your estimate of the total duration of the proposed project?....One year

Will you return to your present position?........If not, for what position do you seek further training?...For.

possible teaching position in Southern college; or extensive work.......

with theatre group. And, as always, further writing.

First page of Hughes's application for a fellowship from the Julius Rosenwald Fund. He was eventually awarded $1,500 (Langston Hughes Papers, Yale Collection of American Literature, Beinecke Rare Book and Manuscript Library).

Heroes," which was published in the June 1941 issue, Hughes emphasized a moral responsibility among African American writers to celebrate the strongest individuals and best achievements of the past and present, rather than the faults and defeats of black America, a theme he revisited often in his writings throughout the remainder of his career.

On 7 December 1941 Hughes was busy checking page proofs for *Shakespeare in Harlem,* his new volume of poems, when he heard the news that Japan had attacked Pearl Harbor. In the following year, the publication of the new collection, the New York premiere of his play *The Sun Do Move,* and his residency at Yaddo artists' colony buoyed his spirits, but like many Americans, war weighed heavily on his mind. Eager to reach a wider audience and to comment on important events, Hughes on 21 November 1942 published his first column for the *Chicago Defender,* beginning a twenty-year career with the black newspaper. His popular "Here to Yonder" columns began to be even more widely read after he introduced readers to Jesse B. Semple, a fictional barroom philosopher, in 1943. "Simple," as he came to be known, blended folk wisdom, wit, and charm to comment incisively on the pressing issues of the times; the character became both a regular fixture in the *Defender* and one of the best-known literary creations in African American letters.

In fall 1943 Hughes's chapbook of poems on the struggle for civil rights, *Jim Crow's Last Stand,* was published by the Negro Publication Society of America. He also addressed civil rights issues in a series of essays published in *Common Ground, Negro Digest,* and the *Journal of Educational Sociology* in 1943 and 1944, with titles such as "What Shall We Do about the South?" and "The Case Against Segregation." Hesitant to champion radical socialism after the announcement of the Nazi-Soviet Nonaggression Pact of 1939 and yet undeterred by the knowledge that he was under surveillance by the Federal Bureau of Investigation (which had started a file on him in 1940), Hughes wrote with a keen sense of his audience and message, framing his criticism of society in the rhetoric of American democratic idealism and arguing that the status of African Americans was a barometer for the progress and future of America itself.

In the latter half of the decade Hughes pursued a diverse range of writing projects and collaborated with other writers. Notable among his collaborations was his work with Mercer Cook on a translation of Haitian writer Jacques Roumain's novel *Masters of the Dew* (1947) and his partnership with Elmer Rice and Kurt Weill on the musical *Street Scene,* based on Rice's Pulitzer Prize–winning play of the same name, which made its Broadway debut on 9 January 1947. Later that

month he began a semester-long position as visiting professor of creative writing at Atlanta University–a new role for him that he embraced with his typical enthusiasm and sense of humor. Halfway through the semester another book of his poems, *Fields of Wonder,* received a mixed critical reception. Far more laudatory were reviews of *Cuba Libre* (1948), a book of poems by Nicolás Guillén that Hughes translated with Ben Frederic Carruthers. Hughes did not fare well with his last major publication of the decade, *One Way Ticket,* brought out by Knopf in 1949, which struck many reviewers as too formulaic and at times simplistic. The decade ended with another disappointment, as Blanche Knopf declined his proposal for a book-length experimental poem titled "Montage of a Dream Deferred." The refusal marked the beginning of a ten-year hiatus in the relationship between Hughes and the firm that had been his publisher for the first twenty-three years of his career.

───────── ✦ ─────────

Ellison and Wright on *The Big Sea*

After its publication in August 1940, The Big Sea *was reviewed by two writers who became major African American novelists: Ralph Ellison, whose masterpiece,* Invisible Man *(1952), was a dozen years from publication, and Richard Wright, whose most influential novel,* Native Son, *had been published earlier in 1940.*

Well before he gained literary celebrity with the publication of Invisible Man, *Ellison had earned a reputation as an essayist and an exacting critic of serious literature. He wrote this review for* The New Masses.

Stormy Weather

Langston Hughes' autobiography, *The Big Sea,* is a story of the writer's life from his birth in 1902 up to 1930. It is a highly exciting account of a life which in itself has encompassed much of the wide variety of Negro experience (even within the Jim-Crow-flanked narrowness of American Negro life there is much variety). Before he was twenty-seven, Langston Hughes had lived in Kansas, Missouri, Ohio, New York, and Washington, D. C., on this side of the world; and on the other side he had lived in France and Italy and he had visited Africa. He had known the poverty of the underprivileged Negro family and the wealth of his successful businessman father. He had taught school in Mexico, gone to college at Columbia, shipped to Africa on a freighter, worked as a doorman in Paris, combed the beaches of Genoa, bussed dishes in a Washington hotel, and had

Ralph Ellison. The inscription reads: "To Langston: the Dream Keeper, in sincerity and admiration. from Ralph W. Ellison, 4-28-37" (Yale Collection of American Literature, Beinecke Rare Book and Manuscript Library).

Richard Wright (photograph by Carl Van Vechten, 23 June 1939; Library of Congress, Prints & Photographs Division, Carl Van Vechten Collection, courtesy of Carl Van Vechen Trust)

received the encouragement of Vachel Lindsay for the poetry he was making of these experiences.

Hughes' family background is no less broad. It winds and spreads through the years from a revolutionary grandmother whose first husband had died with John Brown, to include a great-uncle who was a Reconstruction congressman from Virginia, US minister to Haiti, and the first dean of Howard Law School. Hughes' early life was marked by economic uncertainty, while his father, who left his wife and child to seek freedom in Mexico, was a rich man. Despite its revolutionary source there was even room on Hughes' family tree to include a few bourgeois Washington snobs. This wide variety of experience and background is enough in itself to make *The Big Sea* an interesting book and to recommend it as an important American document. It offers a valuable picture of the class divisions within the Negro group, shows their traditions and folkways and the effects of an expanding industrial capitalism upon several generations of a Negro family.

But *The Big Sea* is more than this. It is also a story told in evocative prose of the personal experiences of a sensitive Negro in the modern world.

In the wake of the last war there appeared that phenomenon of literary and artistic activity among Negroes known as the Negro Renaissance. This movement was marked by the "discovery" of the Negro by wealthy whites, who in attempting to fill the vacuum of their lives made the 1920's an era of fads. Negro music, Negro dancing, primitive Negro sculpture, and Negro writing became a vogue. The artificial prosperity brought by the war allowed these whites to indulge their bohemian fancies for things Negroid. Negro writers found publishing easier than ever before. And not strange to the Marxist is the fact that the same source which furnished the money of the period had also aroused the group energy of the Negro people and made for the emergence of these writers. But this in a different way.

The wave of riots and lynchings released by the war ushered in a new period in the struggle for Negro liberation. Under this pressure Negroes became more militant than ever before in attacking the shortcomings of American democracy. And in the sense that the American Negro group is a suppressed nation, this new spirit was nationalistic. But despite its national charac-

TELLURIDE ASSOCIATION
ITHACA, NEW YORK

On tour,
Cornell College,
February 29, 1940

Dear Dick,

I've been reading "Native Son" on the train. It is a tremendous performance! A really great book which sets a new standard for Negro writers from now on. Congratulations and my very best wishes for a great critical and sales success. Judging from the "New Yorker's" early review

Hughes's letter congratulating Wright on the publication of his first novel (Langston Hughes Papers,
Yale Collection of American Literature, Beinecke Rare Book and Manuscript Library)

you're bound to have both.

I wonder what the Chicago critics (and the colored ones) will say about it? It will be fun to see.

Hastily, but

Sincerely,

Langston

P.S. I've been ballyhooing the book at all my lectures. Several folks want to book you to speak (naturally) but I told them I didn't think you were engageable right now — but to write ℅ Harper's.

ter, the group was not without its class divisions. It happened that those who gave artistic expression to this new spirit were of the Negro middle class, or, at least, were under the sway of its ideology. In a pathetic attempt to reconcile unreconcilables, these writers sought to wed the passive philosophy of the Negro middle class to the militant racial protest of the Negro masses. Thus, since the black masses had evolved no writers of their own, the energy of a whole people became perverted to the ends of a class which had grown conscious of itself through the economic alliances it had made when it supported the war. This expression was further perverted through the bohemian influence of the white faddists whom the war had destroyed spiritually, and who sought in the Negro something primitive and exotic; many writers were supported by their patronage.

Into this scene Langston Hughes made his first literary steps. Two older writers, Claude McKay and James Weldon Johnson, have treated the movement in their autobiographies. But neither has given a realistic account of the period or indicated that they knew just what had happened to them. Hughes himself avoids an analysis, but his candid and objective account of his personal experience in the movement is far more realistic than theirs. For the student of American letters it should offer valuable material.

There are many passages in *The Big Sea* in which Hughes castigates the Negro bourgeoisie, leaving no doubt as to what he thought of its value. Declining its ideological world, he gained his artistic soul: he is one of the few writers who survived the Negro Renaissance and still has the vitality to create. While his contemporaries expressed the limited strivings of this class, Hughes' vision carried him down into the black masses to seek his literary roots. The crystallized folk experience of the blues, spirituals, and folk tales became the stuff of his poetry. And when the flood of 1929 wrecked the artistic houses of his fellows, his was balanced firm upon its folk foundation. The correctness of his vision accounts for his development during that period of his life which follows the close of this book, and which we hope will be made the material of a forthcoming volume.

In his next book, however, we hope that besides the colorful incidents, the word pictures, the feel, taste, and smell of his experiences, Langston Hughes will tell us more of how he felt and thought about them. For while the style of *The Big Sea* is charming in its simplicity, it is a style which depends upon understatement for its more important effects. Many NEW MASSES readers will question whether this is a style suitable for the autobiography of a Negro writer of Hughes' importance; the national and class position of the writer should guide his selection of techniques and method, should influence his

style. In the style of *The Big Sea* too much attention is apt to be given to the esthetic aspects of experience at the expense of its deeper meanings. Nor—this being a world in which few assumptions may be taken for granted—can the writer who depends upon understatement to convey these meanings be certain that they do not escape the reader. To be effective the Negro writer must be explicit; thus realistic; thus dramatic.

The Big Sea has all the excitement of a picaresque novel with Hughes himself as hero. This gives the incidents presented a unity provided by a sensitive and unusual personality; but when Hughes avoids analysis and comment, and, in some instances, emotion, a deeper unity is lost. This is that unity which is formed by the mind's brooding over experience and transforming it into conscious thought. Negro writing needs this unity, through which the writer clarifies the experiences of the reader and allows him to re-create himself. Perhaps its lack of this unity explains why *The Big Sea* ends where it does.

For after 1930 Hughes was more the conscious artist. His work followed the logical development of the national-folk sources of his art. Philosophically his writings constitute a rejection of those aspects of American life which history has taught the Negro masses to reject. To this is accountable the power of such poems as *Ballad of Lenin, Letter to the Academy, Elderly Race Leaders, Ballad of Ozzie Powell,* and *Let America Be America Again.* It is the things which he rejects in American life that make for the strength of the Negro writer. This amounts to the recognition of the new way of life postulated by the plight of the Negro and other minorities in our society. In accepting it the writer recognizes the revolutionary role he must play. Hughes' later work, his speeches before the International Congress of Writers for the Defense of Culture at Paris and his presence in Madrid during the Spanish war, shows his acceptance of that role.

Because he avoided the mistakes of most Negro writers of the twenties, Hughes' responsibility to younger writers and intellectuals is great. They should be allowed to receive the profound benefits of his experiences, and this on the plane of conscious thought. Then, besides the absorbing story of an adventurous life, we would be shown the processes by which a sensitive Negro attains a heightened consciousness of a world in which most of the odds are against his doing so—in the South the attainment of such a consciousness is in itself a revolutionary act. It will be the spread of this consciousness, added to the passion and sensitivity of the Negro people, that will help create a new way of life in the United States.

–*The New Masses,* 37 (24 September 1940): 20–21

* * *

Wright wrote this review for The New Republic.

Forerunner and Ambassador

The double role that Langston Hughes has played in the rise of a realistic literature among the Negro people resembles in one phase the role that Theodore Dreiser played in freeing American literary expression from the restrictions of Puritanism. Not that Negro literature was ever Puritanical, but it was timid and vaguely lyrical and folkish. Hughes's early poems, "The Weary Blues" and "Fine Clothes to the Jew," full of irony and urban imagery, were greeted by a large section of the Negro reading public with suspicion and shock when they first appeared in the middle twenties. Since then the realistic position assumed by Hughes has become the dominant outlook of all those Negro writers who have something to say.

The other phase of Hughes's role has been, for the lack of a better term, that of a cultural ambassador. Performing his task quietly and almost casually, he has represented the Negroes' case, in his poems, plays, short stories and novels, at the court of world opinion. On the other hand he has brought the experiences of other nations within the orbit of the Negro writer by his translations from the French, Russian and Spanish.

How Hughes became this forerunner and ambassador can best be understood in the cameo sequences of his own life that he gives us in his sixth and latest book, "The Big Sea." Out of his experiences as a seaman, cook, laundry worker, farm helper, bus boy, doorman, unemployed worker, have come his writings dealing with black gals who wore red stockings and black men who sang the blues all night and slept like rocks all day.

Unlike the sons and daughters of Negro "society," Hughes was not ashamed of those of his race who had to scuffle for their bread. The jerky transitions of his own life did not admit of his remaining in one place long enough to become a slave of prevailing Negro middle-class prejudices. So beneficial does this ceaseless movement seem to Hughes that he has made it one of his life principles: six months in one place, he says, is long enough to make one's life complicated. The result has been a range of artistic interest and expression possessed by no other Negro writer of his time.

Born in Joplin, Missouri, in 1902, Hughes lived in half a dozen Midwestern towns until he entered high school in Cleveland, Ohio, where he began to write poetry. His father, succumbing to that fit of disgust which overtakes so many self-willed Negroes in the face of American restrictions, went off to Mexico to make money and proceeded to treat the Mexicans just as the whites in America had treated him. The father yearned to educate Hughes and establish him in business. His

---

Wright Wins the Spingarn Medal

Although he strikes an enthusiastic tone in this letter, Hughes, according to his biographer Arnold Rampersad, was highly envious of Wright's being awarded the Spingarn Medal, the highest honor bestowed by the National Association for the Advancement of Colored People (NAACP). Hughes received the award in 1960. Writing from the estate of his friend and patron Noel Sullivan–Hollow Hills Farm in Monterey, California–Hughes refers to "How Bigger was Born," a lecture about the genesis of Wright's fictional character "Bigger Thomas" that Wright delivered at Columbia University shortly after Native Son *was published. He also refers to the Hollywood Theatre Alliance (HTA), a leftist, largely white organization, and to the dramatization of* Native Son, *which premiered in New York on 24 March 1941.*

Hughes to Richard Wright, 15 February 1941

Dear Dick,

Delighted with the fact that the Spingarn Medal goes to you this year! Your statement to the press in acceptance was very well said indeed......I've meant to thank you for a long time for sending me HOW BIGGER WAS BORN, but before the holidays was head over heels in the HTA Negro revue in Los Angeles, writing and re-writing songs and sketches, my own and dozens of others, as they expected to go into rehearsal the first of the year, but (as is usual in show business, left, right, colored, or white, amateur or professional) various hitches developed. I came here for the holidays, got ill with the flu and general disgustedness, got up too soon and had a relapse, went to the hospital, and so am just now up and about a bit, but still house-bound.....I was sorry to learn of the downfall of the Playwrights. It takes a teriffic amount of money to run a theatre, even an amateur one, let alone professional–and cullud have got no money. This system is hardly designed to let us get much either. So for a real Negro theatre, looks like we will have to wait until!.....Me I am going back to words on paper and not on the stage. But I wish Ted and the rest of you playwrights well. May your dramatization of your book be a wow–as it should be if done well. Hope I'll be East to see it......Federal Music Projects combined white and colored units are doing mine and Still's opera, TROUBLED ISLAND, about the Haitian slave revolts, in Los Angeles in April, chorus of a hundred, orchestra of seventy, Still himself conducting. With all those voices, they ought to sing up a breeze.

Best to you,

Sincerely,

Langston

–Langston Hughes Papers, James Weldon Johnson Collection in the Yale Collection of American Literature, Beinecke Rare Book and Manuscript Library

Dust jacket for the first translation of The Big Sea, *published in Buenos Aires in 1944 (courtesy of Kenneth Spencer Research Library, University of Kansas Libraries)*

favorite phrase was "hurry up," and it irritated Hughes so much that he fled his father's home.

Later he entered Columbia University, only to find it dull. He got a job on a merchant ship, threw his books into the sea and sailed for Africa. But for all his work, he arrived home with only a monkey and a few dollars, much to his mother's bewilderment. Again he sailed, this time for Rotterdam, where he left the ship and made his way to Paris. After an interval of hunger he found a job as a doorman, then as second cook in a night club, which closed later because of bad business. He went to Italy to visit friends and had his passport stolen. Jobless in an alien land, he became a beachcomber until he found a ship on which he could work his way back to New York.

The poems he had written off and on had attracted the attention of some of his relatives in Washington and, at their invitation, he went to live with them. What Hughes has to say about Negro "society" in Washington, relatives and hunger are bitter poems in themselves. While living in Washington, he won his first poetry prize; shortly afterwards Carl Van Vechten submitted a batch of his poems to a publisher.

The rest of "The Big Sea" is literary history, most of it dealing with the Negro renaissance, that astonishing period of prolific productivity among Negro artists that coincided with America's "golden age" of prosperity. Hughes writes of it with humor, urbanity and objectivity; one has the feeling that never for a moment was his sense of solidarity with those who had known hunger shaken by it. Even when a Park Avenue patron was having him driven about the streets of New York in her town car, he "felt bad because he could not share his new-found comfort with his mother and relatives." When the bubble burst in 1929, Hughes returned to the mood that seems to fit him best. He wrote of the opening of the Waldorf-Astoria:

Now, won't that be charming when the last flophouse
has turned you down this winter?

Hughes is tough; he bends but he never breaks, and he has carried on a manly tradition in literary expression when many of his fellow writers have gone to sleep at their posts.

–*The New Republic*, 103 (28 October 1940): 600–601

The "Goodbye Christ" Controversy

Hoping to publicize The Big Sea *at a 15 November 1940 luncheon in Pasadena, California, Hughes encountered an angry crowd of the followers of Aimee Semple McPherson, the head of the fundamentalist Temple of the Four Square Gospel in Los Angeles, who were handing out circulars featuring Hughes's poem "Goodbye Christ" (1932). After* The Saturday Evening Post *reproduced a copy of the circular in its 21 December 1940 issue, Hughes wrote the the following explanation, dated 1 January 1941, to mail to friends, publishers, and foundations.*

Concerning "Goodbye, Christ"

Almost ten years ago now, I wrote a poem in the form of a dramatic monologue entitled "Goodbye, Christ" with the intention in mind of shocking into being in religious people a consciousness of the admitted shortcomings of the church in regard to the condition of the poor and oppressed of the world, particularly the Negro people.

Just previous to the writing of the poem, in 1931 I had made a tour through the heart of our American Southland. For the first time I saw peonage, million-dollar high schools for white children and shacks for Negro children (both of whose parents work and pay taxes and are Americans). I saw vast areas in which Negro citizens

Aimee Semple McPherson and an illustration for an Octavus Roy Cohen story in The Saturday Evening Post.
Hughes criticized both McPherson and the magazine in his poem "Goodbye Christ" (top, Los Angeles
Examiner *Collection, Regional History Collection, University of Southern California;*
bottom, Thomas Cooper Library, University of South Carolina).

were not permitted to vote, I saw the Scottsboro boys in prison in Alabama and colored citizens of the state afraid to utter a word in their defense, I crossed rivers by ferry where the Negro drivers of cars had to wait until all the white cars behind them had been accommodated before boarding the ferry even if it meant missing the boat. I motored as far North as Seattle and back across America to New York through towns and cities where neither bed nor board was to be had if you were colored, cafes, hotels, and tourist camps were closed to all non-whites. I saw the horrors of hunger and unemployment among my people in the segregated ghettos of our great cities. I saw lecture halls and public cultural institutions closed to them. I saw the Hollywood caricatures of what pass for Negroes on the screens that condition the attitudes of a nation. I visited state and religious colleges to which no Negroes were admitted. To me these things appeared unbelievable in a Christian country. Had not Christ said, "Such as ye do unto the least of these, ye do it unto Me."? But almost nobody seemed to care. Sincere Christians seeking to combat this condition were greatly in the minority.

Directly from this extensive tour of America, I went to the Soviet Union. There it seemed to me that Marxism had put into practical being many of the precepts which our own Christian America had not yet been able to bring to life, for, in the Soviet Union, meagre as the resources of the country were, white and black, Asiatic and European, Jew and Gentile stood alike as citizens on an equal footing protected from racial inequalities by the law. There were no pogroms, no lynchings, no Jim Crow cars as there had once been in Tzarist Asia, nor were the newspapers or movies permitted to ridicule or malign any people because of race. I was deeply impressed by these things.

It was then that I wrote "Goodbye, Christ." In the poem I contrasted what seemed to me the declared and forthright position of those who, on the religious side in America (in apparent actions toward my people) had said to Christ and the Christian principles, "Goodbye, beat it on away from here now, you're done for." I gave to such religionists what seemed to me to be their own words merged with the words of the orthodox Marxist who declared he had no further use nor need for religion.

I couched the poem in the language of the first person, I, as many poets have done in the past in writing of various characters other than themselves. The I which I pictured was the newly liberated peasant of the state collectives I had seen in Russia merged with those American Negro workers of the depression period who believed in the Soviet dream and the hope it held out for a solution of their racial and economic difficulties. (Just as the I pictured in many of my blues poems is the

poor and uneducated Negro of the South–and not myself who grew up in Kansas.) At the time that "Goodbye, Christ" first appeared, many persons seemed to think I was the characterized I of the poem. Then, as now, they failed to see the poem in connection with my other work, including many verses most sympathetic to the true Christian spirit for which I have always had great respect–such as that section of poems, "Feet Of Jesus," in my book, The Dream Keeper, or the chapters on religion in my novel, Not Without Laughter which received the Harmon Gold Award from the Federated Council of Churches. They failed to consider "Goodbye, Christ" in the light of various of my other poems in the ironic or satirical vein, such as "Red Silk Stockings"–which some of my critics once took to be literal advice.

Today, accompanied by a sound truck playing "God Bless America" and bearing pickets from the Aimee Semple McPherson Temple of the Four Square Gospel in Los Angeles, my poem of ten years ago is resurrected without my permission and distributed on handbills before a Pasadena Hotel where I was to speak on Negro folk songs. Some weeks later it was reprinted in The Saturday Evening Post, a magazine whose columns, like the doors of many of our churches, has been until recently entirely closed to Negroes, and whose chief contribution in the past to a better understanding of Negro life in America has been the Octavus Roy Cohen stories with which most colored people have been utterly disgusted.

Now, in the year 1941, having left the terrain of "the radical at twenty" to approach the "conservative of forty," I would not and could not write "Goodbye, Christ," desiring no longer to épater le bourgeois. However, since those at present engaged in distributing my poem do not date it, nor say how long ago it was written, I feel impelled for the benefit of persons reading the poem for the first time, to make the following statement:

"Goodbye, Christ" does not represent my personal viewpoint. It was long ago withdrawn from circulation and has been reprinted recently without my knowledge or consent. I would not now use such a technique of approach since I feel that a mere poem is quite unable to compete in power to shock with the current horrors of war and oppression abroad in the greater part of the world. I have never been a member of the Communist party. Furthermore, I have come to believe that no system of ethics, religion, morals, or government is of permanent value which does not first start with and change the human heart. Mortal frailty, greed, and error, know no boundary lines. The explosives of war do not care whose hands fashion them. Certainly, both Marxists and Christians can be cruel.

ATTENTION CHRISTIANS ! !

Be sure to attend the Book & Author Luncheon
At
VISTA DEL ARROYO HOTEL,
Pasadena, California

FRIDAY, NOVEMBER 15TH, 1940—at 12:15 Promptly

Hear the Distinguished Young Negro Poet

LANGSTON HUGHES

Author of the following poem, and member of the
American section of Moscow's

"INTERNATIONAL UNION OF REVOLUTIONARY WRITERS"

"GOODBYE CHRIST"

"Listen, Christ,
  You did all right in your day, I reckon—
  But that day's gone now.
  They ghosted you up a swell story too,
  Called it Bible—
  But its dead now.
  The popes and the preachers 've
  Made too much money from it.
  They've sold you to too many

"Kings, generals, robbers and killers—
  Even to the Czar and the Cossacks,
  Even to Rockefeller's church,
  Even to THE SATURDAY EVENING
    POST.
  You ain't no good no more.
  They've pawned you
  Till you've done wore out.

"Goodbye,
  Christ Jesus Lord God Jehova,
  Beat it on away from here now.
  Make way for a new guy with no religion
    at all—
  A real guy named
  Marx Communist Lenin Peasant Stalin
    Worker *ME*—

"I said, *ME!*

"Go Ahead on now,
  You're getting in the way of things, Lord.
  And please take Saint Ghandi with you
    when you go,
  And Saint Pope Pius,
  And Saint Aimie McPherson,
  And big black Saint Becton
  Of the Consecrated Dime.
  And step on the gas, Christ!
  The world is mine from now on—
  Move!
  Don't be so slow about movin'!
  And nobody's gonna sell ME
  To a king, or a general,
  Or a millionaire."

ATTEND THE LUNCHEON CHRISTIANS
And Hear
GEORGE PALMER PUTNAM
Introduce the author of the above "poem,"
MR. LANGSTON HUGHES
Distinguished young Negro poet—and eat, *if you can.*

Broadside reproduced in the 21 December 1940 issue of The Saturday Evening Post *without Hughes's permission. It was originally distributed in Pasadena in early November (Thomas Cooper Library, University of South Carolina).*

Would that Christ came back to save us all. We do not know how to save ourselves.

–Langston Hughes Papers, James Weldon Johnson
Collection in the Yale Collection of American
Literature, Beinecke Rare Book
and Manuscript Library

* * *

This letter is one of those Hughes mailed out with "Concerning 'Goodbye, Christ.'" Hughes had met Malcolm Cowley, the literary editor of The New Republic *from 1929 to 1944, in Spain during the Spanish Civil War. Hughes wrote from Hollow Hills Farm.*

Hughes to Malcolm Cowley, 2 January 1941

Dear Malcom,

Aimee McPherson's followers issued on a handbill and distributed in Pasadena an old poem of mine, GOOD-BYE CHRIST long ago withdrawn from circulation. This, without rhyme or reason, was reprinted without my permission in the SATURDAY EVENING POST of December 21. Accordingly, I have issued the enclosed statement regarding the poem which, should you feel it of interest to the readers of THE NEW REPUBLIC, I would be pleased to have you print entirely or in part, particularly the final paragraph, since the POST apparently does not open its columns to comment. As you know, I am not and have never been a member of the Communist Party, but Mrs. McPherson's move coincided with an autumn wave of red-baiting in Los Angeles, and with the aid of the POST may be an opening step toward taking advantage of the current reaction to intimidate into silence the protests of Negroes regarding certain very obvious defects in our democracy concerning the colored peoples. For that reason it seems to me important to attempt to clarify the mood of such a poem as my own, now woefully outdated, of course, but brought back to life by those who, in the past, have been the least friendly to colored people.

With my very best wishes to you for a Happy New Year, I am

Sincerely yours,
Langston Hughes

–Langston Hughes Papers, James Weldon Johnson
Collection in the Yale Collection of American
Literature, Beinecke Rare Book and
Manuscript Library

The Third Collection of Poems

Shakespeare in Harlem, Hughes's third major volume of poetry for adults, was published on 16 February 1942 to mixed reviews. Hughes had protested what he perceived to be stereotypical illustrations for the book drawn by E. McKnight Kauffer, but Knopf ignored his concerns and included the drawings. Poet and critic Ruth Lechlitner wrote this review.

To Croon, Shout, Recite or Sing
Review of *Shakespeare in Harlem*

Several years ago a book of verse, "The Weary Blues," brought considerable attention to the work of a young Negro writer, Langston Hughes. Recently a wider audience learned more about him through his exciting autobiography, "The Big Sea." His first collection of poems since 1932, "Shakespeare in Harlem," continues, in mood and form–but with greater variety and deeper perception–those dynamic songs on the thoughts and doings of his people as first set down in "The Weary Blues."

Mr. Hughes himself calls these syncopated verses "blues, ballads and reels to be read aloud, crooned, shouted, recited and sung. Some with gestures, some not–as you like. None with a faraway voice." The last phrase implies both their characteristic keynote of emotional immediacy and that ever-present, general conflict between the black and the "great white race." The poems built simply upon individual experience are done with so sure a touch and an insight so genuine as to make that experience universal. In first-person speech of casual idiom–not dialect–Mr. Hughes shows the combination of illogical, big-talk childlike imagination ("Just by ifing I have a good time") and the checkrein of adult reality and despair. "Seven Moments of Love" is the ordinary moods of a black boy whose wife, after a spat, has walked out on him. His are the humanly universal alternate moods of don't care, I'm free now, and aching loneliness–a universality pointed by

> I wonder if white folks ever feel bad,
> Getting up in the morning lonesome and sad?

Making these verses memorable, too, is the humor that almost always surmounts near tragedy. It is never read in from the outside, but inherent in the Negro's ability to objectify his own situation, to laugh at himself. Further, the Negro's genuine feeling for poetry has its own way with an image. He doesn't say he's jobless and hungry, but

> This mornin' for breakfast
> Chawed de mornin' air.
> But this evenin' for supper
> I got evenin' air to spare.

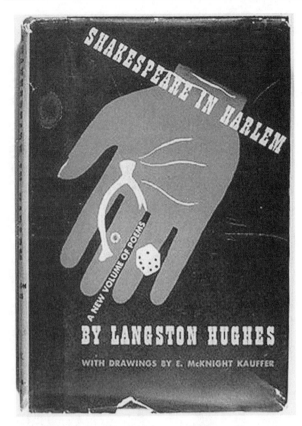

Dust jacket for Hughes's book of poems published by Knopf on 16 February 1942

Or he will say

Night like a reefer man
Slipped away.

There is an occasional luscious-colored lyric, such as "Harlem Sweeties," in the early Countee Cullen manner; in contrast the rollicking, somewhat synthetic ballad of Arabella Johnson and the Texas Kid, or the rowdy high spirits of "Hey Hey Blues." But in almost all the poems—whether the theme be love, work, or death—we sense a black world never free from the heavy intrusion of the white: the lynchers, the boss-man who takes the share-cropper's money, and—no less sinister—the white woman in the ermine cape at "Dixie's" in Harlem, who

Looked at the blacks and
Thought of a rope,
Looked at the blacks and
Thought of a flame—
And thought of something
Without a name.

However, this collection of Hughes's poems does not have the bitterly stressed social angle one finds in the work of other Negro poets, such as Robert Hayden. But the lighter scoring is no less poignant when an old

situation is given a new turn; the colored child at the carnival, for instance, looking for the "Jim Crow" section on the merry-go-round. Mostly it is a matter of economics—the underlying eternal poverty—that shapes and directs the action in Mr. Hughes's ballads: the killer boy who robs a bank to get money for his girl; the pawnbroker, asked to lend on life itself; the struggle of the poor to get enough cash together for a burial:

I wonder what makes
A funeral so high?
A poor man ain't got
No business to die.

The book is designed and illustrated with several striking portrait drawings, in white on black, by C. McKnight Kauffer.
    —*New York Herald Tribune Books,* 3 May 1942, p. 2

* * *

Poet and dramatist Owen Dodson wrote this review.

"Unworthy of the Author"
Review of *Shakespeare in Harlem*

This Shakespeare still rolls dice in Harlem, grabs a wishbone, makes a wish for his sweet mamma, long gone, long lost; still lies in bed in the noon of the day. This Shakespeare is lazy, unpoetic, common and vulgar. In short Mr. Langston Shakespeare Hughes is still holding his mirror up to a gold-toothed, flashy nature. It is the same mirror he has held up before but somehow the glass is cracked and his deep insight and discipline has dimmed. There is no getting away from the fact that this book, superior in format, is a careless surface job and unworthy of the author Mr. Van Vechten calls the "Negro Poet Laureate," who loves his race and reports and interprets it feelingly and understandingly to itself and other races. His verse resounds with the exultant throb of Negro pain and gladness.

Once Mr. Hughes wrote

Because my mouth
Is wide with laughter
You do not hear
My inner cry;
Because my feet
Are gay with dancing
You do not know
I die.

In this volume we merely hear the laughter: loud, lewd, unwholesome and degenerate. We see and hear a cartoon doing a black-face, white-lip number, trying terribly to please the populace. None of the inner struggle is revealed, no bitter cries, no protests, no gentleness, no ladders of hope being climbed. These things are hard to say about a poet I very much admire. But they must be said.

Mr. Hughes states at the beginning of the book that this is "light verse. Afro-Americana in the blues mood. Poems syncopated and variegated in the colors of Harlem, Beal[e] Street, West Dallas, and Chicago's South Side. Blues, ballads and reels to be read aloud, crooned, shouted, recited and sung. Some with gestures, some not—as you like. None with a far-away voice." This statement screens a thousand sins. Because verse is "light" it doesn't therefore follow that anything goes. The technique of light verse is as exacting as that of serious verse, almost more so.

If this were Mr. Hughes' first book we would say, here is some promise but in a few years he will deepen this stream, he will broaden this stream. But as this is his fourth volume of verse all I can say is that he is "backing into the future looking at the past" to say nothing of the present.

Eight sections make up the book: "Seven Moments of Love", "Declarations", "Blues for Men", "Death in Harlem", "Mammy Songs", "Ballads", "Blues for Ladies", "Lenox Avenue".

The section called "Death in Harlem" has, perhaps, some of his better work

> They done took Cordelia
> Out to stony lonesome ground.
> Done took Cordelia
> To stony lonesome,
> Laid her down.

Another poem in this section that has a haunting and poetic shine is "Crossing".

The real "nitty gritty" is a poem in the "Lenox Avenue" section called "Shakespeare in Harlem"

> Hey ninny neigh!
> And a hey nonny no!
> Where, oh, where
> Did my sweet mama go?
>
> Hey ninny neigh!
> With a tra-la-la-la!
> They say your sweet mama
> Went home to her ma.

But the "cup" is poems like "Hey-Hey Blues", and "Little Lyric". Whoever drinks will choke on these.

After hearing some of these poems read aloud a fellow who hadn't heard of Mr. Hughes said: "that Langston Hughes must be a cracker." Lord have mercy!

–*Phylon,* 3 (Third Quarter 1942): 337–338

Hughes, 11 June 1942 (photograph by Carl Van Vechten; Yale Collection of American Literature, Beinecke Rare Book and Manuscript Library)

Writing for the *Chicago Defender*

Hughes wrote the following essay, dated 24 August 1942, for the Chicago Defender, *urging black writers to draw connections between the war against imperialism and fascism and the struggle of blacks to gain fair treatment in the United States. Shortly after its publication, Metz T. P. Lochard, the editor in chief of the* Defender, *offered Hughes a weekly column in the newspaper. This text follows Hughes's original typescript.*

Hughes makes many topical allusions, decrying Southern politicians such as Georgia governor Eugene Talmadge, Mississippi representative John Elliot Rankin, and Alabama governor Frank Murray Dixon as he endorses President Franklin Delano Roosevelt's call for four essential human freedoms: "freedom of speech and expression"; "freedom of every person to worship God in his own way"; "freedom from want"; and "freedom from fear."

Negro Writers and the War

There is an old story almost everyone has heard. The version I remember is this:

Hughes with Katherine Anne Porter (second from right) at Yaddo artists' colony in Saratoga Springs, New York, 1942
(Langston Hughes Papers, Yale Collection of American Literature, Beinecke Rare Book and Manuscript Library)

During slavery time on a certain big plantation, the slaves were very meagrely fed. Although master's bins and smoke-houses were bursting with food, the field hands had only cow peas, corn pone, and bitter molasses day after day. One night, sitting in her cabin, an old slave woman said, "Huh! I <u>do</u> wish I had some ham!"

From his pallet in the corner, her grandson commented, "Old Massa's smoke-house is just full of hams. I could sneak in there some evening and steal one, Granny—then we all could eat."

"Un-huh!" cried the old woman stearnly. "That's wicked! Satan done put that thought in your head. Wouldn't nobody but the Devil steal a ham. Stop that talk and go to sleep, boy!"

The boy went to sleep, but he dreamed about a great big juicy ham, dozens of great big old juicy hams hanging from the rafters in Massa's well-stocked smoke-house. Grandma dreamed about hams, too, perhaps. When the good things of life are consistently denied folks, they often think about them over much, even in their sleep.

A few nights later, as Granny bent above the fireplace putting together a meagre supper—a hoe-cake in the ashes, two tin plates of molasses—she heard bare feet running toward the house in the darkness. Suddenly, as the feet went past, through the open window a ham sailed, a great big old juicy ham. It fell ker-plunk in front of the fire as her grandson fled in the dusk. The old woman stooped down and picked up the ham.

"Hallelujah!" she cried, shouting. "Thank God for this ham—even if the Devil did bring it!"

That is the way a lot of colored people feel about democratic gains and the war. They feel that Executive Order 8802 opening defense plants to all without discrimination, the abolition of Jim Crow seating on the Washington-Virginia busses, and other similar advances are a kind of ham that indirectly the Japanese and the Germans have thrown them—by forcing democracy to recognize belatedly some of its own failings in regard to the Negro people. The trouble is that many colored folks do not think as strongly as they should that the Germans and the Japanese are <u>really</u> devils, and very dangerous ones, at that. Some colored people mistakenly think Talmadge, Rankin, and Dixon are more devilish because they are closer at hand and holler so loud. The truth of the matter is, of course, that they are <u>all</u> devils—Hitler, Mussolini, and Hirohito abroad, plus their Klan-minded followers at home. It is the duty of Negro writers to point out this fact. But since all Negroes recognize deviltry at home, the stress should be laid on those devils abroad whom we are now engaged in fighting–so that our race will fully realize how dangerous they are and how, in triumph, they would merely back up the worst of our enemies at home.

That in large areas of this country deplorable racial conditions exist, nobody can deny. But that some attempts at improvement have been set in motion by our government since the war is also true. Also that great newspapers like PM in New York, great Americans like Vice-President Wallace, Eleanor Roosevelt, Paul Robeson, and Pearl Buck openly fight our battles as a part of democracy's, and that even in the traditionally Jim Crow city of Washington, Jim Crowism has begun ever so slowly and weakly, but slightly, to crack–these are facts of great importance. That huge pro-democracy, anti-Jim Crow meetings of Negroes have been held from New York to Los Angeles in recent weeks is of great importance. And the fact that the Negro press, our several hundred valiant colored newspaper[s] have been clearer on the war aims and the real meaning of world democracy than any similar number of white newspapers is also of very great importance. Negro editors know what democracy is about because they haven't got much of it–and they want it.

But we do have in America freedom of press and of speech denied, for instance, to Jews–and Negroes–in Germany. In Berlin now a Negro can no longer even blow a trumpet in a jazz band–silenced musically as well as verbally. In Japan under the current militarist regime nobody, no matter what color they are, can speak out for any liberal cause. It's the same in Italy. The Axis is out to crush the little people all over the world, to dominate by force of arms everything from labor to radio, from women in kitchens (where the Axis likes them) to jazz bands. The fact that the Japanese have slapped a few white faces in Hong Kong to the delight of American Negroes who have been maltreated by Jim Crow, does not mean that the Japanese are friends of ours. The Japanese militarists are more nearly friends of Dixon and Talmadge. They use the same tactics to keep down subject peoples under them–and to submerge their own liberals and intellectuals, as well. Japanese militarism is a reactionary force, like the German, that respects nobody else's face, white or colored.

Therefore, it is the duty of Negro writers to point out quite clearly that it is an error to think of World War II in terms of race–in spite of the apparent determination of the British imperialists in India to force peo-

ple to think that way. We have to remember that English imperialism, for as long as it could, treated the Irish about the same as they do the Indians–and the Irish are white. Imperialism does not run by color. Korea under Japan has today a kind of Asiatic Jim Crow. Imperialism everywhere dies hard. Africa is still enchained and needn't even read the Atlantic Charter. But the pro-democratic forces who are fighting this war for the Allies will have to consider the freedom of Africa at the peace table–or go right back where they started to economic chaos and further war.

It is the duty of Negro writers to reveal the international aspects of our problems at home, to show how these problems are merely a part of the great problem of world freedom everywhere, to show how our local fascists are blood brothers of the Japanese fascists–though they speak with a Dixie drawl, to show how on the great battle front of the world we must join hands with the crushed common people of Europe, the Soviet Union, the Chinese, and unite our efforts–else we who are American Negroes will have not only the Klan on our necks in intensified fashion, but the Gestapo, as well. (And the Nazis, I am sure, could teach the Klan a few things, for the Germans do not bother with silly crosses and childish nightshirts. Death and the concentration camp are more effective.)

But for Negro writers to point out merely the negative reasons for full Negro co-operation in the war effort–merely that we should fight because, although Alabama is bad, the Axis is worse, is to throw out of perspective the basic reasons why all oppressed peoples must take part in the current struggle to overcome the devils of the world. The reasons are that Hitlerism, Fascism, and Japanese imperialism are but intensifications and bu[t]tresses of all that is bad, indeed all the worst, left over from barbarism in world politics and government today. They represent the old techniques of force and robbery carried out in their boldest form without even lip service to decency. They represent racial oppression as a means of economic oppression without even pretending to do otherwise. The Axis represents organized gangsterism lifted to government. Against their bombs and machine guns–their frank and deadly Jim Crow–the darker millions of the world, including ourselves, could be for generations helpless.

Negro journalists have so far been the best writers among us since December 7th. They have been clear, brave, and hard-hitting. They have sometimes written movingly and with great effect–their articles on the death of Waller, the slugging of Roland Hayes. The journalists have beaten the creative writers, poets, essayists, and novelists all hollow of late. They have pleaded, cajoled, explained the need of, and demanded democracy for the fourteen million sub-citizens of this

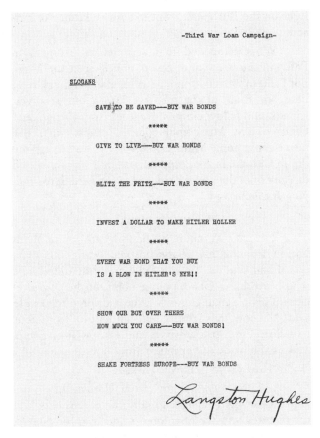

-Third War Loan Campaign-

SLOGANS

SAVE TO BE SAVED----BUY WAR BONDS

*****

GIVE TO LIVE----BUY WAR BONDS

*****

BLITZ THE FRITZ----BUY WAR BONDS

*****

INVEST A DOLLAR TO MAKE HITLER HOLLER

*****

EVERY WAR BOND THAT YOU BUY
IS A BLOW IN HITLER'S EYE!!

*****

SHOW OUR BOY OVER THERE
HOW MUCH YOU CARE----BUY WAR BONDS!

*****

SHAKE FORTRESS EUROPE---BUY WAR BONDS

Langston Hughes

*Slogans for war bonds, probably written in 1942. Hughes served
on the advisory board of the Writers' War Committee, later the
Writers' War Board, from spring 1942 to summer 1945
(Langston Hughes Papers, Yale Collection of American
Literature, Beinecke Rare Book and
Manuscript Library).*

country week by week. They deserve great praise. If creative writers, during the course of the war, get into their poems, stories, novels, and plays, half the hard-hitting fire of Negro weekly journalism, very likely the great novel, or great poem of World War II–like a flaming dream of democracy–will come from the pen of a Negro–a Richard Wright, a Sterling Brown, or a Margaret Walker.

Unfortunately, however, our journalists have written almost entirely for publications read exclusively by Negroes. The creative writers then, who publish in the general American magazines, have a task before them of great positive value to carry out. It is their duty to explain to our white American brothers why it is urgently necessary that we now and immediately take steps in this country–for all our sakes–to wipe out all forms of public discrimination against minorities within our borders. Great masses of white people are even yet only vaguely aware of the enormous discrimination against Negroes. They do not realize how difficult it is

for us to earn a decent living, nor how essential it is that Order 8802 really be carried out ALL over America. They do not realize the indignities of the Jim Crow car on Southern railways, nor how hungry–not to speak of angry–a Negro soldier can get coming home on furlough penned up in the black coach and denied service in the public dining cars of Dixie trains. They do not realize how, when Negro soldiers march through a colored community with all white officers at their head, Negroes mutter, "The white man's always boss. Won't even let us lead our own troops out to die."

A great many white people still accept the false grinning charicatures of the movies as being true of colored people–Negroes are happy-go-lucky, they always smile, they always sing, they don't care what happens to them, they're not sensitive about persecution or segregation. Probably the British and the Dutch thought that about the Malayans, too–but the Malayans welcomed the Japanese when they came. Maybe now the British think the Indians do not mind a declaration of war in which they have no part–but they do mind. Just as maybe our Southern whites think Negroes do not mind being unable to vote in most of the South–but they do mind. Fear and intimidation may keep them from saying so. It is the duty of our writers to express what these voiceless people cannot say, and to relate their longings for decency and fairness to the world aims of the President's Four Freedoms for everybody.

Furthermore, we must study methods for the practical working out of these democratic aims at home now, and present concrete plans to our white brothers with whom we have to work as to how we may create a fully democratic America. We must show them that it will not injure them to be fair to us. It will instead help them. We must stress the fact that in this coming world of international co-operation, no one group within a country or without, can work alone. That all of us might live, let's be decent to one another. Our white fellow citizens must be made to realize that Jim Crow and all it symbolizes–meagre educational facilities, discrimination in industries, lynchings–is not decent. It is an anachronism in American life that, especially for the sake of the war effort, must be gotten rid of–and soon. After all, this is a war for freedom. It's logic must be straight in order for it to be successful. It is not logical to speak of freedom for Poland and forget Georgia. These things Negro writers must tell America. After all, it embarasses us to see our white folks acting foolish.

–Langston Hughes Papers, James Weldon Johnson
Collection in the Yale Collection of American
Literature, Beinecke Rare Book
and Manuscript Library

* * *

Hughes signed on as a weekly columnist for the Chicago Defender *in 1942, eager to write for the broad readership of the newspaper that billed itself as "The World's Greatest Weekly." Founded by the African American businessman Robert S. Abbott in 1905, the* Defender *was the most influential black weekly newspaper in the nation, reaching an estimated readership of more than 500,000 people at its peak. He began his "Here to Yonder" column, which he wrote until 1962, as a straight commentary on topical events and issues. In this, his first column, Hughes refers to the lynching of Charlie Lang and Ernest Green, who had been hanged beneath the Shubuta Bridge over the Chicasawhay River in Mississippi on 12 October 1942.*

Why and Wherefore

Things that happen away off yonder affect us here. The bombs that fall on some far-off Second Front in Asia rattle the dishes on your table in Chicago or New Orleans, cut down on your sugar, coffee, meat ration, and take the tires off your car. Right now Hitler is about to freeze your salary or your work, although his activities at the moment are centered around Stalingrad. But it is not so far from here to yonder.

For the last 20 years, half writer and half vagabond, I have travelled from here to yonder around the world and back again, up and down the African coast, through Russia, through Asia, back and forth across America and, in general, from pillar to post. One thing I learned is that Alabama and Africa have the same problems. Stalingrad and Chicago fight the same gangsters. Two 14-year-old boys are lynched at Shubuta Bridge and Harlem shudders—also Chungking.

What happens at the post affects the pillar, and vice versa. Here is yonder, and yonder is here. When you do wrong, it affects me. If I don't behave myself, it hurts you. When you do good it helps me. When I do good, I hope it aids you. When white folks do wrong, in the long run it lays as heavy a burden on them as it does on us. Witness India, witness Malaya, witness the poverty of the South and the sorry spectacle of Shubuta Bridge.

A year before the war in Paris, the summer of Munich, I saw the left and right literally—I mean factually—thumbing their noses at each other, shouting curses back and forth in the Place de l'Opera in the heart of the French capital—the workers and the fascists openly displaying that woeful gulf between them that brought about the fall of France and the Vichy collaboration that now sends your son, your brother, your friends, mine—and probably me—to

fight on the European front to restore France to herself.

What happened that summer at Munich, in Paris, in the betrayal of Spain, and later at the Maginot Line—way over yonder—will make YOU cry right here, for some of the men we know, our relatives, friends, and fellow citizens, Negroes from Harlem and Chicago and Mississippi—some of those men will never come home again. Some will die way over yonder in Europe, in Asia, and Africa—thus forcefully and directly does the yonder reach into the here. It touches you. It touches me.

Guns, Not Shovels

The cat was taking his first physical, standing in line in front of me at the hospital where our draft board had sent us. He was talking and he didn't care who heard him. (Chalk up one point for the democracies—at least a man can talk, even a colored man.) He said, "I know they gonna send all us cats to a labor battalion. I'm a truck driver, and I know they gonna make me a truck driver in the army."

"How do you know?" I asked.

"All the guys I know from Harlem," he said, "have gone right straight to labor battalions. Look at the pictures you see of colored soldiers in the papers, always working, building roads, unloading ships, that's all. Labor battalions! I want to be a fighter!"

"I know a fellow who's gone to Officers School," I said. "And another one learning to fight paratroopers."

"I don't know none," he said. "And besides, if they don't hurry and take this blood test, I'm liable to lose my job. That Italian I work for don't care whether the draft board calls you or not, you better be to work on time. He ain't been in this country but six or seven years and owns a whole fleet of trucks, and best I can do is drive one of 'em for him. Foreigners can get ahead in this country. I can't."

"Some colored folks get ahead some," I said.

"You have to be a genius to do it," he argued.

Another man in the line spoke up, older, dark brownskin, quiet. "Between Hitler and the Japanese," the other man said, "these white folks are liable to change their minds. They're beginning to find out they need us colored people."

It was that third fellow who took the conversation all the way from the here of Manhattan Island to the yonder of Hitler, the Japanese, and the arena of struggle—that far-off yonder—including Africa, India and China, Gandhi and Chiang Kai Chek—that yonder that, in spite of all, is changing our world in Harlem, on State street, and maybe even in Mississippi.

There was no chance to talk any more for the line moved on. He went in to the little room where the doctors were, had his blood drawn, and hurried off. I do not know his name. Probably our paths will never cross again. But I hope, since he wants to be a fighter, Uncle Sam will give him a gun, not a shovel or a truck. A gun would probably help his morale a little—now badly bent by the color line.

Your Folks and Mine

The afternoon paper that I bought as I came out of the hospital reported an unconfirmed rumor that Josephine Baker is slowly dying of consumption way over yonder in Casablanca on the coast of North Africa. That hit me almost as hard as the war news. I hope the report is not true for the dusky brown girl from St. Louis is one of our greatest ambassadors of charm and beauty to the world.

Aubrey Pankey, young Negro singer from Sugar Hill, is giving concerts this week in Rio de Janeiro.

Chatwood Hall, former colored postal clerk from Minneapolis, is in Kuibyshev, U.S.S.R.

Arna Bontemps in Chicago is writing a new book. These are folks I know and shall write about in future columns.

I know lots of folks, whose names have never been in the newspapers—as interesting as those whose names have been in the papers. I shall write about them, also. Your folks and mine—as colored as me—scattered all over the world from here to yonder. From week to week, they—and you—shall be the subjects of this column. I got a feeling that you are me. And I know dog-gone well, HERE is YONDER. I even expect that in due time white will be black. Amen!

—*Chicago Defender,* 21 November 1942, p. 14

* * *

In his 13 February 1943 column, Hughes surprised his regular Chicago Defender *readers by introducing a fictional barroom philosopher, Jesse B. Semple. "Simple," as he came to be called, became a semiregular feature in Hughes's newspaper columns through the early 1960s.*

Conversation at Midnight

My simple minded Friend said, "Day time sure is a drag. I like night time a lot better."

"I do too," I said. "Day time hurts my eyes. I was born at midnight, but my mama told me I didn't start crying until morning. After that, I hollered and cried every morning straight for two years."

"I could holler and cry every morning now when I have to get up and go to work."

"That's why you don't get ahead in the world," I said. "The people who get ahead in the world are the ones who get up early."

"I get up early," said my Simple Minded Friend. "But I don't get ahead. Besides, what you say is not necessarily right. Joe Louis likes to sleep—and he got ahead."

"I'll bet he doesn't sleep in the army, though."

"I'll bet he does," said my Simple Minded Friend, "'cause he's always on furlough. How come Joe Louis is always on furlough?"

"I can't answer you that," I said, "but I guess it's because he's doing Special Services."

"Naw! It's because Joe said, 'We're on God's side.' White folks like religious Negroes."

"Well, we are on God's side, aren't we? Naturally, God's against the Nazis."

"Who made the Nazis?"

"Are you trying to blame Hitler on God?"

"Who made Hitler?"

"Well, who did make him?" I asked.

"God," said my Simple Minded Friend.

"Then He must have made him for some purpose."

"Sure, He did," declared my Simple Minded Friend. "God made Hitler to be a thorn in the side of our white folks."

"Aw, you're crazy!" I said. "Hitler would stick a bigger thorn in your side, if he could get hold of you."

Why Not Shakespeare

"He ain't going to get hold of me," said my Simple Minded Friend. "I'm gonna fight him. I been reclassified in 1-A."

"Good! When you hear that bugle blow in the mornings, and get up with all that outdoor air in your lungs, you'll feel swell. The army will make you like rising early."

"Nothing can make me like rising early," said my Simple Minded Friend. "Nothing."

"Then why don't you go to bed at some decent hour at night?" I asked.

"Why don't you?" demanded my Simple Minded Friend in return.

"I'm a writer," I said, "and I don't have to get up until noon. But if I had a job, I would go to bed on time. Here it is after midnight."

"And I am just really waking up good now, after midnight. You know, it's a shame for a man to have to go to bed when he is just waking up good. Say, do you really believe this is God's war?"

"There's a divinity that shapes our ends," I said, "rough hew them though we may."

"Did you write that?"

"No, Shakespeare."

"Shakespeare wrote that play Paul Robeson was playing in last summer, too, didn't he?"

"Othello. He wrote 'Merchant of Venice,' too. Also 'Hamlet'."

"Killer! Why don't you write something like 'Hamlet'?"

"Because I'm not Shakespeare. Why don't you be the World's Heavyweight Champion?"

"I wish I was, so I could get into Special Services. I sure don't want to be sent down South! Soon as I'm drafted, I bet they'll send me down South. Do you reckon God will look after me down South?"

Right to Stay Up Late

"Sure, God'll look after you down South. All you have to do is just obey those Jim Crow laws."

"I don't want to obey no Jim Crow laws. I don't think they are right."

"Of course, they're not right. But if you don't obey them, they'll put you in jail."

"It hurts my soul," said my Simple Minded Friend. "To be Jim Crowed hurts my soul. To have on my uniform and have to be Jim Crowed."

"If you beat Hitler, though, you'll be helping to beat Jim Crow."

"I want to beat Jim Crow first," said my Simple Minded Friend. "Hitler's over yonder, and Jim Crow is here."

"But if the Nazis ever got over here, and Hitler and Jim Crow ever got together, you would have an awful time beating the two of them. In fact, you would be hog-tied. They would have curfew laws for Negroes—just like they have curfew laws for Jews in Germany. And you couldn't stay up after nine."

"You mean I'd have to go to bed early, whether I wanted to or not?"

"That is exactly what I mean. They do let you stay up late down South, If you want to."

"They do, don't they? That is worth fighting for," said my Simple Minded Friend. "The right to stay up late! That is really worth fighting for."

"The fascists won't let Negroes stay up late."

"Then I will fight the fascists," said my Simple Minded Friend. "I will even get up early to fight for the right to stay up late. Damned if I won't!"

–Chicago Defender, 13 February 1943, p. 14

On America's Democracy

Hughes had been a prominent supporter and spokesperson for the League of American Writers–an organization of politically committed, antifascist writers on the Left–since the mid 1930s. He resigned as vice president of the league on 26 May 1941 and gave notice that he would not attend its fourth congress in June 1941 in New York, but he sent this statement, drafted 13 May 1941, to be read at the congress.

Democracy, Negroes, and Writers

Writing is the urge to tell folks about it. About what? About what hurts you inside. Colored folks, through the sheer fact of being colored, have got plenty hurting them inside. You see, we, too, are one of those minority races the newspapers are always talking about. Except that we are here in America, not in Europe, fourteen million of us–a rather large minority, but still a minority.

Now, what's hurting us? Well, Jim Crow is hurting us. Ghettos, and segregation, and lack of jobs is hurting us. Signs up: COLORED TRADE NOT DESIRED, and dirty names such as the Jews know under Hitler hurt us. So those of us who are writers have plenty to tell the world about.

To us democracy is a paradox, full of contradictions. Sure, in the North Negroes can vote, but we can't work in airplane factories and various other defense industries supported with our tax money as well as that of other citizens. In the South we can't vote, but we can howl to high heaven about it in our newspapers–and run the risk of lynching and the Ku Klux Klan for howling. In Mississippi the state spends nine times as much for the education of each white child as it does to educate a Negro child, yet the Negro population equals the white, and the wealth of the state is based on the labor of Negroes in the sun of the cotton fields. We give and others take. That's what makes us mad. So we feel bad and have to write about it.

The color line runs right on down from capital through labor, although labor is waking up a bit. But in many industries today the factories won't hire us because they say the unions won't admit us, and the unions won't admit us because they say the factories won't hire us: a vicious circle into which a swastika fits perfectly. We can sweep a floor almost anywhere if a white man doesn't need the job, but even if we graduate from Massachusetts Institute of Technology, we still are not permitted to run a machine in the average American Factory. A great many Negroes work, study, and learn, and then are frustrated by the blind alley of color-segregation in American industry. That color line runs all the way through culture and the arts, as well.

First page for a song that Hughes wrote to support the U.S. war effort (courtesy of Kenneth Spencer Research Library, University of Kansas Libraries)

There are world-famous and very great American Negro singers, some of whom have appeared in opera abroad, but not one had been asked to appear at the Metropolitan. And in many cities where they sing, their own people, the Negro concert goers, are Jim Crowed and segregated. There are some excellent Negro writers in this country, too, but, to my knowledge, none is employed at present in Hollywood where the real money for writers lies. All along the line, we suffer economic discrimination of a discouraging and arbitrary sort, be we artisan or artist.

The League of American Writers, meeting in their Fourth Writer's Congress in New York on June 6th, has been one of the few cultural organizations to take up the fight for the artistic and economic equality of the Negro writer. Another stand of equal importance to Negro, and all writers, is the League's position on freedom of speech and publication. To colored people in the United States this is of particular importance as the trend toward suppression and censorship is growing and already there is a tendency to attempt to prevent Negro newspapers, with their editorials against discrimination in defense industries and the Jim Crow set-up of our army and navy, from being read by Negro soldiers and draftees in the army camps. From this it is but a step to the actual suppression of Negro papers, or else the censorship of their articles and editorials.

Negroes, like all other Americans, are being asked at the moment to prepare to defend democracy. But Negroes would very much like to have a little more democracy to defend. And democracy is achieved only through constant vigilance, struggle, and the educational processes of the written and spoken word. For Negro writers it is vital that the channels of free press and publication be kept open. It is necessary to the well-being of the creative soul that the harsh and ugly aspects of our life be exposed to public view in order that they might be changed and remedied in accordance with the democratic ideals for which we are urged to be ready to die. But ideals on paper mean very little. They must be put into practice. Writers must be free to call for and work toward the realization of full democracy in regard to peoples of all colors, else the light will rapidly go out for everyone of us, white or Negro, gentile or Jew, for if we wish to preserve democracy, we must not only defend it but extend it.

–Langston Hughes Papers, James Weldon Johnson
Collection in the Yale Collection of American
Literature, Beinecke Rare Book
and Manuscript Library

* * *

Concerned about accusations from right-wing groups that he was a subversive, Hughes published an article in the February 1943 issue of the Journal of Educational Sociology *in which he reaffirmed his love for the American democratic ideal while still addressing how that ideal was compromised by racial prejudice. Hughes wrote this expanded version of that article for* What the Negro Wants *(1944).*

My America

This is my land, America. Naturally, I love it–it is home–and I am vitally concerned about its *mores,* its democracy, and its well-being. I try now to look at it with clear, unprejudiced eyes. My ancestry goes back at least four generations on American soil and, through Indian blood, many centuries more. My background and training is purely American–the schools of Kansas, Ohio, and the East. I am old stock as opposed to recent immigrant blood.

Yet many Americans who cannot speak English–so recent is their arrival on our shores–may travel about our country at will securing food, hotel, and rail accommodations wherever they wish to purchase them. *I may not.* These Americans, once naturalized, may vote in Mississippi or Texas, if they live there. *I may not.* They may work at whatever job their skills command. *But I may not.* They may purchase tickets for concerts, theatres, lectures wherever they are sold throughout the United States. *Often I may not.* They may repeat the Oath of Allegiance with its ringing phrase of "Liberty and justice for all," with a deep faith in its truth–as compared with the limitations and oppressions they have experienced in the Old World. I repeat the oath, too, but I know that the phrase about "liberty and justice" does not fully apply to me. I am an American–*but I am a colored American.*

I know that all these things I mention are not *all* true for *all* localities *all* over America. Jim Crowism varies in degree from North to South, from the mixed schools and free franchise of Michigan to the tumbledown colored schools and open terror at the polls of Georgia and Mississippi. All over America, however, against the Negro there has been an economic color line of such severity that since the Civil War we have been kept most effectively, as a racial group, in the lowest economic brackets. Statistics are not needed to prove this. Simply look around you on the Main Street of any American town or city. There are no colored clerks in any of the stores–although colored people spend their money there. There are practically never any colored street-car conductors or bus drivers–although these public carriers run over streets for which we pay taxes. There are no colored girls at the switchboards of the telephone company–but millions of Negroes have

Eugene Talmadge (top) and Ellis Arnall, political rivals and governors of Georgia in the 1930s and 1940s. They were two of the men who personified the Jim Crow South for Hughes (top, photograph by Tony Linck/Time Life Pictures/Getty Images; bottom, photograph by William C. Shrout/Time Life Pictures/Getty Images).

phones and pay their bills. Even in Harlem, nine times out of ten, the man who comes to collect your rent is white. Not even that job is given to a colored man by the great corporations owning New York real estate. From Boston to San Diego, the Negro suffers from job discrimination.

Yet America is a land where, in spite of its defects, I can write this article. Here the voice of democracy is still heard—Wallace, Willkie, Agar, Pearl Buck, Paul Robeson, Lillian Smith. America is a land where the poll tax still holds in the South—but opposition to the poll tax grows daily. America is a land where lynchers are not yet caught—but Bundists are put in jail, and majority opinion condemns the Klan. America is a land where the best of all democracies has been achieved for some people—but in Georgia, Roland Hayes, world-famous singer, is beaten for being colored and nobody is jailed—nor can Mr. Hayes vote in the State where he was born. Yet America is a country where Roland Hayes *can* come from a log cabin to wealth and fame—in spite of the segment that still wishes to maltreat him physically and spiritually, famous though he is.

This segment, the South, is not all of America. Unfortunately, however, the war with its increased flow of white Southern workers to Northern cities, has caused the Jim Crow patterns of the South to spread *all* over America, aided and abetted by the United States Army. The Army, with its policy of segregated troops, has brought Jim Crow into communities where it was but little, if at all, in existence before Pearl Harbor. From Camp Custer in Michigan to Guadalcanal in the South Seas, the Army has put its stamp upon official Jim Crow, in imitation of the Southern states where laws separating Negroes and whites are as much a part of government as are Hitler's laws segregating Jews in Germany. Therefore, any consideration of the current problems of the Negro people in America must concern itself seriously with the question of what to do about the South.

The South opposes the Negro's right to vote, and this right is denied us in most Southern states. Without the vote a citizen has no means of protecting his constitutional rights. For Democracy to approach its full meaning, the Negro *all over* America must have the vote. The South opposes the Negro's right to work in industry. Witness the Mobile shipyard riots, the Detroit strikes fomented by Southern whites against the employment of colored people, the Baltimore strikes of white workers who objected to Negroes attending a welding school which would give them the skill to rate upgrading. For Democracy to achieve its meaning, the Negro like other citizens must have the

right to work, to learn skilled trades, and to be upgraded.

The South opposes the civil rights of Negroes and their protection by law. Witness lynchings where no one is punished, witness the Jim Crow laws that deny the letter and spirit of the Constitution. For Democracy to have real meaning, the Negro must have the same civil rights as any other American citizen. These three simple principles of Democracy—the vote, the right to work, and the right to protection by law—the South opposes when it comes to me. Such procedure is dangerous for *all* America. That is why, in order to strengthen Democracy, further the war effort, and achieve the confidence of our colored allies, we must institute a greater measure of Democracy for the eight million colored people of the South. And we must educate the white Southerners to an understanding of such democracy, so they may comprehend that decency toward colored peoples will lose them nothing, but rather will increase their own respect and safety in the modern world.

I live on Manhattan Island. For a New Yorker of color, truthfully speaking, the South begins at Newark. A half hour by tube from the Hudson Terminal, one comes across street-corner hamburger stands that will not serve a hamburger to a Negro customer wishing to sit on a stool. For the same dime a white pays, a Negro must take his hamburger elsewhere in a paper bag and eat it, minus a plate, a napkin, and a glass of water. Sponsors of the theory of segregation claim that it can be made to mean equality. Practically, it never works out that way. Jim Crow always means less for the one Jim Crowed and an unequal value for his money—no stool, no shelter, merely the hamburger, in Newark.

As the colored traveller goes further South by train, Jim Crow increases. Philadelphia is ninety minutes from Manhattan. There the all-colored grammar school begins its separate education of the races that Talmadge of Georgia so highly approves. An hour or so further down the line is Baltimore where segregation laws are written in the state and city codes. Another hour by train, Washington. There the conductor tells the Negro traveller, be he soldier or civilian, to go into the Jim Crow coach behind the engine, usually half a baggage car, next to trunks and dogs.

That this change to complete Jim Crow happens at Washington is highly significant of the state of American democracy in relation to colored peoples today. Washington is the capital of our nation and one of the great centers of the Allied war effort toward the achievement of the Four Freedoms. To a southbound Negro citizen told at Washington to change into a segregated coach the Four Freedoms have a hollow sound, like distant lies not meant to be the truth.

The train crosses the Potomac into Virginia, and from there on throughout the South life for the Negro, by state law and custom, is a hamburger in a sack without a plate, water, napkin, or stool—but at the same price as the whites pay—to be eaten apart from the others without shelter. The Negro can do little about this because the law is against him, he has no vote, the police are brutal, and the citizens think such caste-democracy is as it should be.

For his seat in the half-coach of the crowded Jim Crow car, a colored man must pay the same fare as those who ride in the nice air-cooled coaches further back in the train, privileged to use the diner when they wish. For his hamburger in a sack served without courtesy the Southern Negro must pay taxes but refrain from going to the polls, and must patriotically accept conscription to work, fight, and perhaps die to regain or maintain freedom for people in Europe or Australia when he himself hasn't got it at home. Therefore, to his ears most of the war speeches about freedom on the radio sound perfectly foolish, unreal, high-flown, and false. To many Southern whites, too, this grand talk so nobly delivered, so poorly executed, must seem like play-acting.

Liberals and persons of good will, North and South, including, no doubt, our President himself, are puzzled as to what on earth to do about the South—the poll-tax South, the Jim Crow South—that so shamelessly gives the lie to Democracy. With the brazen frankness of Hitler's *Mein Kampf,* Dixie speaks through Talmadge, Rankin, Dixon, Arnall, and Mark Ethridge.

In a public speech in Birmingham, Mr. Ethridge says: "All the armies of the world, both of the United States and the Axis, could not force upon the South an abandonment of racial segregation." Governor Dixon of Alabama refused a government war contract offered Alabama State Prison because it contained an anti-discrimination clause which in his eyes was an "attempt to abolish segregation of races in the South." He said: "We will not place ourselves in a position to be attacked by those who seek to foster their own pet social reforms." In other words, Alabama will not reform. It is as bull-headed as England in India, and its governor is not ashamed to say so.

As proof of Southern intolerance, almost daily the press reports some new occurrence of physical brutality against Negroes. Former Governor Talmadge was "too busy" to investigate when Roland Hayes and his wife were thrown into jail, and the great tenor beaten, on complaint of a shoe salesman over a dispute as to what seat in his shop a Negro should occupy when buying shoes. Nor did the governor of Mississippi bother when Hugh Gloster, professor of English at Morehouse College, riding as an inter-state passenger, was illegally ejected from a train in his state, beaten, arrested, and fined because, being in an overcrowded Jim Crow coach, he asked for a seat in an adjacent car which contained only two white passengers.

Legally, the Jim Crow laws do not apply to inter-state travellers, but the FBI has not yet gotten around to enforcing that Supreme Court ruling. En route from San Francisco to Oklahoma City, Fred Wright, a county probation officer of color, was beaten and forced into the Texas Jim Crow coach on a transcontinental train by order of the conductor in defiance of federal law. A seventy-six-year-old clergyman, Dr. Jackson of Hartford, Connecticut, going South to attend the National Baptist Convention, was set upon by white passengers for merely passing through a white coach on the way to his own seat. There have been many similar attacks upon colored soldiers in uniform on public carriers. One such attack resulted in death for the soldier, dragged from a bus and killed by civilian police. Every day now, Negro soldiers from the North, returning home on furlough from Southern camps, report incident after incident of humiliating travel treatment below the Mason-Dixon line.

It seems obvious that the South does not yet know what this war is all about. As answer Number One to the question, "What shall we do about the South?" I would suggest an immediate and intensive government-directed program of pro-democratic education, to be put into the schools of the South from the first grades of the grammar schools to the universities. As part of the war effort, this is urgently needed. The Spanish Loyalist Government had trench schools for its soldiers and night schools for its civilians even in Madrid under siege. America is not under siege yet. We still have time (but not too much) to teach our people what we are fighting for, and to begin to apply those teachings to race relations at home. You see, it would be too bad for an emissary of color from one of the Latin American countries, say Cuba or Brazil, to arrive at Miami Airport and board a train for Washington, only to get beaten up and thrown off by white Southerners who do not realize how many colored allies we have—nor how badly we need them—and that it is inconsiderate and rude to beat colored people, anyway.

Because transportation in the South is so symbolic of America's whole racial problem, the Number Two thing for us to do is study a way out of the Jim Crow car dilemma at once. Would a system of first, second, and third class coaches help? In Europe, for-

*Pearl S. Buck and Erskine Caldwell, two of the writers whom Hughes proposed could accompany Negro
speakers in the South (top, photograph by Peter Stackpole/Time Life Pictures/Getty Images;
bottom, photograph by John Florea/Time Life Pictures/Getty Images)*

merly, if one did not wish to ride with peasants and tradespeople, one could always pay a little more and solve that problem by having a first class compartment almost entirely to oneself. Most Negroes can hardly afford parlor car seats. Why not abolish Jim Crow entirely and let the whites who wish to do so, ride in coaches where few Negroes have the funds to be? In any case, our Chinese, Latin American, and Russian allies are not going to think much of our democratic pronunciamentos as long we keep compulsory Jim Crow cars on Southern rails.

Since most people learn a little through education, albeit slowly, as Number Three, I would suggest that the government draft all the leading Negro intellectuals, sociologists, writers, and concert singers from Alain Locke of Oxford and W. E. B. Du Bois of Harvard to Dorothy Maynor and Paul Robeson of Carnegie Hall and send them into the South to appear before white audiences, carrying messages of culture and democracy, thus off-setting the old stereotypes of the Southern mind and the Hollywood movie, and explaining to the people without dialect what the war aims are about. With each, send on tour a liberal white Southerner like Paul Green, Erskine Caldwell, Pearl Buck, Lillian Smith, or William Seabrook. And, of course, include soldiers to protect them from the fascist-minded among us.

Number Four, as to the Army—draftees are in sore need of education on how to behave toward darker peoples. Just as a set of government suggestions has been issued to our soldiers on how to act in England, so a similar set should be given them on how to act in Alabama, Georgia, Texas, Asia, Mexico, and Brazil—wherever there are colored peoples. Not only printed words should be given them, but intensive training in the reasons for being decent to everybody. Classes in democracy and the war aims should be set up in every training camp in America and every unit of our military forces abroad. These forces should be armed with understanding as well as armament, prepared for friendship as well as killing.

I go on the premise that most Southerners are potentially reasonable people, but that they simply do not know nowadays what they are doing to America, or how badly their racial attitudes look toward the rest of the civilized world. I know their politicians, their schools, and the Hollywood movies have done their best to uphold prevailing reactionary viewpoints. Heretofore, nobody in America except a few radicals, liberals, and a handful of true religionists have cared much about either the Negroes or the South. Their sincere efforts to effect a change have been but a drop in a muddy bucket. Basically, the South needs universal suffrage, economic stabilization, a balanced diet, and vita-

mins for children. But until those things are achieved, on a lesser front to ameliorate—not solve—the Negro problem (and to keep Southern prejudice from contaminating all of America) a few mild but helpful steps might be taken.

It might be pointed out to the South that the old bugaboo of sex and social equality doesn't mean a thing. Nobody as a rule sleeps with or eats with or dances with or marries anybody else except by mutual consent. Millions of people of various races in New York, Chicago, and Seattle go to the same polls and vote without ever co-habiting together. Why does the South think it would be otherwise with Negroes were they permitted to vote there? Or to have a decent education? Or to sit on a stool in a public place and eat a hamburger? Why they think simple civil rights would force a Southerner's daughter to marry a Negro in spite of herself, I have never been able to understand. It must be due to some lack of instruction somewhere in their schooling.

A government sponsored educational program of racial decency could, furthermore, point out to its students that cooperation in labor would be to the advantage of all—rather than to the disadvantage of anyone, white or black. It could show quite clearly that a million unused colored hands barred out of war industries might mean a million weapons lacking in the hands of our soldiers on some foreign front—therefore a million extra deaths—including Southern white boys needlessly dying under Axis fire—because Governor Dixon of Alabama and others of like mentality need a little education. It might also be pointed out that when peace comes and the Southerners go to the peace table, if they take there with them the traditional Dixie racial attitudes, there is no possible way for them to aid in forming any peace that will last. China, India, Brazil, Free French Africa, Soviet Asia and the whole Middle East will not believe a word they say.

Peace only to breed other wars is a sorry peace indeed, and one that we must plan now to avoid. Not only in order to win the war then, but to create peace along decent lines, we had best start *now* to educate the South—and all America—in racial decency. That education cannot be left to well-meaning but numerically weak civilian organizations. The government itself should take over—and vigorously. After all, Washington is the place where the conductor comes through every southbound train and tells colored people to change to the Jim Crow car ahead.

That car, in these days and times, has no business being "ahead" any longer. War's freedom train can hardly trail along with glory behind a Jim Crow coach. No matter how streamlined the other cars may be, that coach endangers all humanity's hopes for a peaceful tomorrow. The wheels of the Jim Crow car are about to come off and the walls are going to burst wide open. The wreckage of Democracy is likely to pile up behind that Jim Crow car, unless America learns that it is to its own self-interest to stop dealing with colored peoples in so antiquated a fashion. I do not like to see my land, America, remain provincial and unrealistic in its attitudes toward color. I hope the men and women of good will here of both races will find ways of changing conditions for the better.

Certainly it is not the Negro who is going to wreck our Democracy. (What we want is more of it, not less.) But Democracy is going to wreck itself if it continues to approach closer and closer to fascist methods in its dealings with Negro citizens–for such methods of oppression spread, affecting other whites, Jews, the foreign born, labor, Mexicans, Catholics, citizens of Oriental ancestry–and, in due time, they boomerang right back at the oppressor. Furthermore, American Negroes are now Democracy's current test for its dealings with the colored peoples of the whole world of whom there are many, many millions–*too many* to be kept indefinitely in the position of passengers in Jim Crow cars.

–*What the Negro Wants,* edited by Rayford W. Logan (Chapel Hill: University of North Carolina Press, 1944), pp. 299–307

* * *

Hughes wrote this article for The New Republic *following race riots that occurred in West Harlem in summer 1943.*

Down Under in Harlem

If you are white and are reading this vignette, don't take it for granted that all Harlem is a slum. It isn't. There are big apartment houses up on the hill, Sugar Hill, and up by City College–nice high-rent houses with elevators and doormen, where Canada Lee lives, and W. C. Handy, and the George S. Schuylers, and the Walter Whites, where colored families send their babies to private kindergartens and their youngsters to Ethical Culture School. And, please, white people, don't think that all Negroes are the same. They aren't.

Last year's Harlem riots demonstrated this clearly. Most of the people on Sugar Hill were just as indignant about the riots as was Mayor LaGuardia. Some of them even said the riots put the Negro race back fifty years. But the people who live in the riot area don't make enough money really to afford the high rents and the high prices merchants and landlords charge in Harlem, and most of them are not

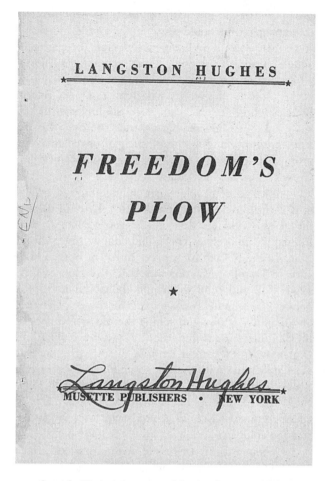

Cover for Hughes's long poem celebrating America, published in 1943 (courtesy of Kenneth Spencer Research Library, University of Kansas Libraries)

acquainted personally–as are many Sugar Hillites–with liberals like Pearl Buck and John Haynes Holmes. They have not attended civic banquets at the Astor, or had luncheon with emancipated movie stars at Sardi's. Indeed, the average Harlemite's impression of white folks, democracy and life in general is rather bad.

Naturally, if you live on nice, tree-lined, quiet Convent Avenue, even though you are colored, it would never occur to you to riot and break windows. When some of the colored leaders whose names are often in the white newspapers, came out of their elevator houses and down into Harlem during the riots, to urge, with the best intentions in the world, that the mobs stop breaking windows and go home, lots of the rioters did not even know who they were. And others of them said, "Boo-oo-o! Go home yourself."

It is, I should imagine, nice to be smart enough and lucky enough to be among Dr. DuBois' "talented tenth" and be a race leader and go to the symphony concerts and live on that attractive rise of bluff and parkway along upper Edgecombe Avenue overlooking the Polo Grounds, where the plumbing really works and the ceilings are high and airy. For just a few thousands a year one can live very well on Sugar Hill in a house with a white-tiled hall.

But under the hill on Eighth Avenue, on Lenox, and on Fifth there are places like this—dark, unpleasant houses with steep stairs and narrow halls, where the rooms are too small, the ceilings too low and the rents too high. There are apartments with a dozen names over each bell. The house is full of roomers. Papa and mama sleep in the living room, the kids in the dining room, lodgers in every alcove, and everything but the kitchen is rented out for sleeping. Cooking and meals are rotated in the kitchen.

In vast sections below the hill, neighborhood amusement centers after dark are gin mills, candy stores that sell King Kong (and maybe reefers), drug stores that sell geronimoes—dope tablets—to juveniles for pepping up cokes, pool halls where gambling is wide open and barbecue stands that book numbers. Sometimes, even the grocery stores have their little side rackets without the law. White men, more often than Negroes, own these immoral places where kids as well as grown-ups come.

The kids and the grown-ups are not criminal or low by nature. Poverty, however, and frustration have made some of them too desperate to be decent. Some of them don't try any more. Slum-shocked, I reckon.

One Saturday night last winter, I went into a barbecue stand where the juke-box was loud and the air thick with smoke. At the tables there were mostly young folks—nice, not very pretty girls dressed in their best, with young men who had cleaned up after work. Some of the young men still wore their last spring's artificial camel's-hair coats—a top coat in winter with the snow outside—but they were trying to look nice, to be nice in the Harlem slums.

A half-dozen teen age boys came in and stood around listening to the records on the juke-box. Shortly, a quarrel began among them. Almost immediately knives were drawn and switch-blades flashed, and one youngster let a blackjack a foot long slide out of his sleeve.

The woman at the counter who served my sandwich said, "Somebody ought to call the cops." (As though cops could solve the problems of poverty and delinquency in Harlem.) The white proprietor behind the beer bar paid no attention to the turmoil. Short of murder or destruction, white proprietors in Harlem seldom mix in Negro squabbles—just as they never belong to neighborhood committees to improve conditions, either.

"I just don't want 'em to fight in here," the woman said, "that's all!"

The boys didn't fight. They simply milled around, showed their weapons, bluffed and cursed each other.

But their language frightened some of the quiet, not-very-pretty girls at the tables with the young men in their thin near-camel's-hair coats, out on a Saturday night trying to look nice and have a nice quiet time.

Louis Jordan on the juke-box, loud. Over the music the woman behind the counter said, "This time of night, all these young boys ought to be home."

"That's right," I said.

Home. A dozen names on the bell. Roomers all over the house. No place for a kid to bring his friends. Only the pool halls open, the candy stores that bootleg liquor, the barbecue stands where you can listen to the juke-box even if you're broke and don't want to buy anything, and the long Harlem streets outside dimmed out because Hitler might send his planes overhead some dark night.

Should the planes come, their bombs most certainly would be louder than the juke-boxes, and their flying fragments of metal sharper than the cheap steel of drug-store switch-blades in the hands of kids who have no homes where they can bring their friends. A piece of bomb can hit harder than a boy with a blackjack up his sleeve.

Hitler in Berlin. Bad kids in Harlem. Indignation in the Mayor's office. Also on Sugar Hill. Louis Jordan's records:

> *I'm gonna move . . .*
> *. . . outskirts of town . . .*

Barbecued ribs, a quarter. Sign:

> DON'T ASK FOR CREDIT—HE'S DEAD!!!

Riots. Long discussions downtown about forming more committees to make more surveys for more reports for more detailed study by more politicians before taking action on conditions in Harlem.

Sign over the barbecue counter:

> WE CAN'T PAY OUR BILLS WITH TRUST!
> CAN YOU?

That sign, of course, is in reference to credit for sandwiches. It has nothing to do with the democratic system. It simply means that if you haven't got a quarter, you don't eat. There has been a sort of permanent scarcity of quarters in Harlem, so that sign might very well serve the committees as a motto for their surveys.

—*The New Republic,* 110 (27 March 1944): 404–405

From *Jim Crow's Last Stand* to *One-Way Ticket*

Carter G. Woodson, director of the Association for the Study of Negro Life and History, wrote this review.

"Fearlessly Presenting His Case"
Review of *Jim Crow's Last Stand*

Langston Hughes has written another book of poems. It is a slender volume of only 29 poems. The publication comes from the press of the Negro Publication Society of America in New York City. This collection of poems is No. 2 of the "Race Culture Series" brought out by this society whose purpose is to "publish and promote the publication of literary and scientific works giving instruction in and interpreting the history and contributions of the Negro people of American life." The launching of this effort is justified by the belief that

"certainly in times like these, America needs to draw on the experience of one tenth of the population whose efforts to help make the country 'one nation, indivisible, with liberty and justice for all,' are thwarted by the forces of ignorance and racial intolerance."

These poems are written in the spirit of this declaration. The first poem, "The Black Man Speaks," boldly says that if we are fighting for democracy we must get rid of "Old Jim Crow." The second poem, "Democracy," expresses the impatience with the "friends" of the Negro who caution waiting to let things take their course. The poet does not want freedom when he is dead because he cannot live on tomorrow's bread. On "Freedom," the poet says further that some folks are wrong in thinking that they imprison freedom by burning books and imprisoning reformers and that by lynching a Negro they lynch freedom. "Freedom stands up in their face and says, 'You'll never kill me.'" On the "Red Cross" the poet says "An angel of mercy got her wings in the mud,

---

A Proposal for an Anthology

This letter concerns a proposal for a collection of poems that was not published, in part because of the deaths of Countee Cullen in 1946 and Claude McKay in 1948. Hughes wrote from Yaddo artists' colony.

Hughes to Countee Cullen, 23 July 1943

Dear Countee,

I am back at Yaddo for the summer. Came to the city for the week-end, dropped by the Y but Claude was out, and failed to get by your house, so maybe we can make a few plans about our proposed book by mail—advance details, at any rate, and then when I'm next in town, around mid-August, if you and Claude are there, we can get together for discussion.

I brought up with me all my poems—several hundred—and will make a selection of hitherto unpublished in book form ones for our volume. If you-all think wise, I'll stick to lyric and poetic kind of poetry and exclude the folk forms this time. The two don't mix very well, and blues and such would probably throw the whole book out of key.

My proposal is this: That each of us submit our poems to the other two for elimination. In other words, you and I would look over Claude's selection and suggest which ones are not up to his best standards, and which we would advise including. Claude and I would do the same for yours. And you and Claude would act as jury on mine. Then from the lot left intact, we would arrange a sequence for a section of a book. How does that strike you?

I suppose the book would be in three sections, perhaps alphabetical in order:

COUNTEE CULLEN
LANGSTON HUGHES
CLAUDE MCKAY

Next thing to [do] is to think of a good title. You and Claude start thinking.

As I remember, Claude had some very beautiful sonnets he once sent back from Europe to Locke that I've never seen in print anywhere. I hope he still has them on hand. Ask him. And if convenient, kindly show him this letter and get his reactions to these proposals. If you like the two man jury idea, I could post my poetry down to you anytime, and you two could initial the ones that you like best and think should be in the volume, then while I'm up here where it is quiet and there's time for work, if you'd send them back, I could make a sequence arrangement for the book and bring it down around the 15th when I come. We could then meet and possibly tentatively put the book together. Let me know?

There's a pleasant group here this summer: Agnes Smedley, Margaret Walker, Rebecca Pitts, Karen Michailis, and seven others.

Best regards to your wife. As ever,

Sincerely,

Langston

—Langston Hughes Papers, James Weldon Johnson Collection in the Yale Collection of American Literature, Beinecke Rare Book and Manuscript Library

and all because of Negro blood." "The Bitter River" is dedicated to the memory of Charlie Lang and Ernest Green, the fourteen-year-old boys who were lynched beneath the Shubuta Bridge over the Chicasawhay River in Mississippi on October 12, 1942. "October 16" deals with John Brown at Harpers Ferry. He died for a cause. What about you? In "Motherland" Africa is imprisoned in bitter sorrow. In "Brothers" appears the kinship of all Negroes whether from West or East, from the United States or the West Indies, from America or Africa, "We are brothers—you and I." In Captain Mulzac, Negro skipper of the *The Booker T. Washington,* the poet sees a symbol of a captain conducting the ship "Victory" which will triumph over the enemies of freedom, brotherhood and democracy."

After dealing thus with the political questions now moving the Negro to radical action the poet looks at the shacks in the "Blackbelt" and gives us the "Ballad of the Landlord," who is attacked in trying to enforce an eviction. Next we have "Big Buddy" at hard labor, unrequited toil, and then the "Ballad of Sam Solomon" who is not afraid of the Ku Klux Klan. The poet looks next at the "Commercial Theatre" which takes our blues and spirituals to make money, and the way they are rendered "they don't sound like me," but "some day somebody'll stand up and talk about me, and write about me— . . . I reckon it'll be me myself! It'll be me." "Daybreak in Alabama" prophesies that some of these days a colored composer will give a new picture in a new song of Alabama and Negroes triumphant will be in that song. "Me and My Song" is more prophecy of the day that is breaking. In "Good Morning Stalingrad" there is the herald of a new ally in the struggle for freedom. The picture closes with "Jim Crow's Last Stand." Jim Crow cannot fight for democracy, and it must go.

These poems bring additional evidence of the self-assertion of the subordinated Negro. Books of which this one is typical show how rapidly Negroes have advanced in recent years. Formerly the Negro ran from the aggressor. Now the Negro runs to him. The battle of the Negro for freedom is no longer defensive. The Negro is now on the offensive. He sees a difference between dying to secure democracy for others and dying to secure it for himself. He prefers death in the latter case. The point to be observed also is that the Negro of today is fearlessly expressing his thought and backing up with action what he says. He is not looking for trouble, but he is not running from it.

Looking back over the last seventy years, the historian cannot escape the stages in the development of the Negro. Immediately after emancipation, the freedmen were nominally free only. Their former masters actually reenslaved them through the black codes of 1865. The minds of the freedmen were still enslaved, and nothing

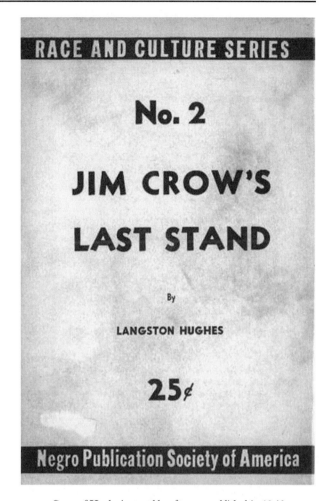

Cover of Hughes's pamphlet of poems, published in 1943
(Courtesy of University of Delaware
Library Special Collections)

else could have been expected. Federal troops stationed in the South undertook to secure the freedom of the Negro through a new plan of reconstruction at the point of the bayonet, but as soon as the troops were withdrawn the Negroes were reduced immediately to chattel slavery with a status like that of the free Negroes in the South before the Civil War. There the Negroes remained under an appeasement leadership until the First World War. One result of that rather short conflict was the awakening of the Negroes almost to the point of self-assertion but the capitalistic forces of the country were too strong, and when they joined with the plantation aristocracy to keep the Negro down he could do nothing about it. Today in the midst of a world upheaval when capitalism has been shaken and exploitation is yielding ground to cooperation in a world brotherhood, the Negro is fearlessly presenting his case before a new tribunal.

—*Journal of Negro History,* 28 (October 1943): 492–494

* * *

2nd draft,
New York,
June 14, 1945.

TRUMPETER

The kid
With the trumpet at his lips
Has dark moons of weariness
Beneath his eyes
And the memory of deep holes
Of slave ships
And the crack of whips
About his thighs.

The kid
With the trumpet at his lips
Has ~~jungle~~ vibrant hair/slicked down
And patented-leathered/till it gleams/
Like jet---were jet a crown.

The music
From the trumpet at his lips
Is honey/mixed with liquid fire.
The music
From the trumpet at his lips
Is extasy/distilled from old desire---
Desire/that is longing for the moon
When the moonlight's but a spot light
In your eyes,
Desire/that is longing for the sea
When the sea is but a bar-glass
Reduced size.

TRUMPETER

Drafts of the poem Hughes published as "Trumpet Player: 52nd Street" in the 1947 collection Fields of Wonder
(Langston Hughes Papers, Yale Collection of American Literature, Beinecke Rare Book and Manuscript Library)

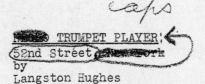

caps

~~NEGRO~~ TRUMPET PLAYER
52nd Street ~~New York~~
by
Langston Hughes

Revised June 27, 1945

The ~~big~~ *negro*

With the trumpet at his lips

Has dark moons of weariness

Beneath his eyes

Where the smoldering memory

Of slave ships

Blazes to the crack of whips

About his thighs.

The ~~kid~~ *negro*

With the trumpet at his lips

Has a head of vibrant hair

Tamed down

And patented-leathered now

Until it gleams

Like jet

Were jet a crown.

The music

From the trumpet at his lips

Is honey

Mixed with liquid fire,

And the rhythm

From the trumpet at his lips

Is ecstasy

Distilled from old desire——

Hughes to Arna Bontemps, 2 May 1946

How was Chicago and did you get my letter there? Glad Palfi got a Rosenwald. She has run me down to the ground about that book she wants to do with me! She intends going to California so will be there when YOU get there. (Like Marion Oswald whom I thought I had escaped a few years ago when I went Westward–but no sooner had I got to Hollywood than she too called up from one of them hilltops and said, "C'est Marianne!")

Dick Wright and wife and also child have gone to Paris.

Now as to your piece on me. You should have an invite by now. It is an "Arts and Letters Grant" from The American Academy of Arts and Letters–One Thousand Dollars. (Cash.)

2. 15 lectures in fall, and 40 since New Years, not counting freebies–I'd say about 75 all told this season including the schools they drug me by against my will sleepy and just off the train. My first was in Washington in 1924, so in 22 years I'd estimate from Mississippi to Moscow and Chicago to Shanghai well over a thousand public appearances reading my poems. There are seldom less than a hundred people in an audience, average I'd say five hundred, often a thousand, and high school or college assemblies frequently 2 to 3 thousand, so I'd say at least 500,000 or a half million folks have heard me read *Rivers* myself in person. (Although I doubt if the Chinese understood it.)

Six cross country tours, and up and down and back between times, so probably have travelled at least 100,000 miles in this country alone. Recent cross country tour as you know entirely by air.

More Negro audiences and sponsors in America than white, but white sponsors growing all the time. This season from Town Hall, New York, to Parent-Teachers Association (colored) Tupelo, Mississippi, fashionable Oak Park Nineteenth Century Women's Club to Colored Community Center, Anderson, Indiana, the University of Colorado to Lanier High School, Jackson, Mississippi, the sixth grades assembly of Kalamazoo, Michigan to the Brooklyn Academy of Arts and Sciences–all within a year. And reading the *same* poems from kids on up to whoever goes to Town Hall or Brooklyn at 11 A.M., same poems in Mississippi as in Boston, to colored or white or mixed–which proves something or other!

3. Translated into Uzbek among other languages. . . . . . Singers of my songs range from Lawrence Tibbett to Josh White, Marian Anderson to Marion Oswald. . . . . I got two sets of fan letters, some to me, some to Simple. . . . . Hobbies: Collecting House Rent Party cards and attending Gospel Song Battles. . . . . . In only one railroad wreck in all my travels. Got an overcoat out of that, and nary a scratch. . . . . Sometimes sleep 15 hours at a time. . . Lately (more and more) am invited to deliver the Sunday morning message at churches (Paid). Recently Community Church of Boston and Unity Church, Unitarian, of Montclair, N. J. . . . . Did Tour USO's and army camps during war. . . . . Enormous fan mail from soldiers overseas re Defender column and Bedside Esquire story, "A Good Job Gone" which by the way brought Esquire its largest mail in pre-publication controversy. . . . . . Have only received one threatening communication–about ten years ago from Ku Klux Klan. . . . . As you know, have no mechanical sense. Took me eight years to learn to close vegetable bin in Aunt Toy's kitchen. Never turn on right burner on a gas stove. Still can't close a folding table (much). . . . . . Have a long head, but just recently learned I should always buy an oval shaped hat. Even then they get out of shape quick. . . . . Give away as many books as I sell. All of my books (except *Fine Clothes*) still in print. *Weary Blues* never out of print in twenty years. . . . . . . Try to answer every letter I receive at least once, but in recent years unable to keep up steady correspondences. (Haven't yet read all the mail that accumulated during my recent winter tour–a suitcase full still unread. Have only *part time* secretary–but two portable typewriters–one of which has been around the world with me and is over twenty years old. . . . Like to eat. Gain weight on tour from the good dinners folks fix. . . . . Get sick if get mad. . . . Have several hundred unpublished poems as far as book form goes. . . . . Read slowly. . . . . Read books I like over and over, but don't read many new ones. . . . . Never had a thousand dollars all at once until I was forty. Haven't had two thousand dollars all at once yet. . . . . . Pay bills promptly. . . . . Arrested once in Cuba for defying Jim Crow at Havana Beach. Put out of Japan for visiting Madame Sun Yat Sen in China . . . . . . Picketed by Gerald L. K. Smith's Mothers of America at Wayne College in Detroit. . . . . By Aimee Semple McPherson in Pasadena. Never sued. . . . . Never married, but once reported engaged to Elsie Roxborough in public press (niece Joe's manager) . . . . . . Friends include Mrs. Bethune and Bricktop, Diego Rivera and Bootsie's creator, Ollie Harrington, Paul Robeson and Willie Bryant, Still and Duke, Margot and Butterbeans and Susie, Hemingway and Roy Wilkins! . . . . .

. . . Hey, now! . . . . . Love kids. . . . . . Love dogs. . . . . Hate parsnips, narrative poems, bridge, breakfast invitations, Jim Crow cars, and people who recite poetry in a far-away voice . . . . . Also "Trees" sung just before I am introduced. . . . . Chain smoker. . . . . Height of ambition to live in Arizona. Love that there sun. . . . . Also to have plenty time to just stand on the street and loaf like street corner colored do. . . . . Also to have enough wall space to hang all the pictures and paintings friends give me. . . . . . And shelves to pile the records I own. . . . And time to write another novel.

C'est tout.

Josh Logan (Director *Annie Get Your Gun*) told Kurt Weill your show is wonderful. (I told him, too.)

Sincerely,
Langston

—*Arna Bontemps–Langston Hughes Letters, 1925–1967*,
edited by Charles H. Nichols (New York:
Dodd, Mead, 1980), pp. 205–207

* * *

Hughes greatly admired Walt Whitman and felt a sense of kinship for the poet, believing Whitman to be one of the nation's great chroniclers of the democratic ideal. He wrote this introduction for I Hear the People Singing: Selected Poems of Walt Whitman *(1946).*

The Ceaseless Rings of Walt Whitman

Walt Whitman, greatest of American poets, was born on a farm owned by his father near West Hills, Long Island, New York, on the last day of May, 1819. He died in a tiny little old house of his own on Mickle Street in Camden, New Jersey, at the end of March, 1892. The span of his life ran from American slavery through the Civil War to American freedom and the approaching dawn of the twentieth century.

Whitman did not fight in the War Between the States. He hated war and killing, but he devoted much of his time to nursing and caring for the wounded, both Northern and Southern, white or Negro, Yankee or Rebel. At Culpeper, Virginia, a staging area, he saw enough of combat to sicken him against war. But on

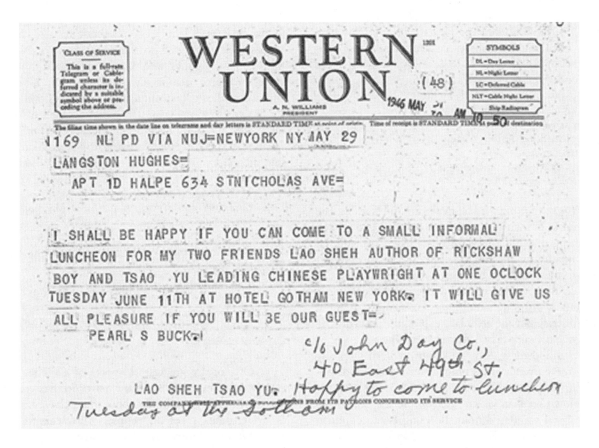

Telegram from the author of The Good Earth *(1931) and other novels about China. Hughes served with Buck on the editorial board of* Common Ground *magazine (Langston Hughes Papers, Yale Collection of American Literature, Beinecke Rare Book and Manuscript Library).*

errands of mercy, he went out to the battlefields and into field hospitals. From his friends he solicited money to buy cookies, candies, ice cream, magazines, and papers for the wounded. He tended them, read to them, wrote letters home for those who could not write, and cheered them with stories. He helped those with leg injuries to learn to walk again.

In 1864, assisting a surgeon in an amputation, Walt Whitman was accidentally cut with a gangrenous scalpel. An infection set in which caused him health complications in later life. While carrying on this voluntary nursing among the wounded in and near Washington, Whitman held a job as a clerk in the Indian Office. The attacks of narrow-minded readers on his poetry caused him to lose this job. But, through the help of friends, he secured a place in the Attorney General's office. In the late night hours, he continued to write his poems of democracy, articles, and letters for the papers.

His position in the Indian Office was not the first that Whitman had lost because of his liberal views. He had been an editor of the Brooklyn *Eagle,* but was fired there in 1848 because he refused to support Governor Cass of Michigan who advocated the continuation of slavery. Whitman called people like Cass "Dough Faces," because of their condonance of Southern slavery. Whitman abhorred slave catchers and those who gave them aid or supported their political beliefs. In the New York *Evening Post,* Whitman wrote:

We are all docile dough-faces,
They knead us with the fist,
They, the dashing Southern Lords,
We labor as they list.
For them we speak—or hold our tongue,
For them we turn and twist.

There had been a half-dozen or so slaves on the ancestral Whitman farm, and young Walt had played with them as a child. Perhaps that is where he acquired his sympathy for the Negro people and his early belief that all men should be free—a belief that grew to embrace the peoples of the whole world, expressed over and over throughout his poems, encompassing not only America but the colonial peoples, the serfs of tsarist Russia, the suppressed classes everywhere.

In our own land, Walt Whitman lived intensely within the currents of his time, absorbed in the democratic strivings growing in America and taking root like wind-blown seeds in varied soils around the world. His physical self wandered from the Long Island countryside to the Brooklyn Ferries and Broadway trolley cars, from urban foundries and shops to Mississippi river boats and the fields of battle during the Civil War. His spiritual self roamed the earth wherever the winds of freedom blow however faintly, keeping company with

the foiled revolutionaries of Europe or the suppressed coolies of Asia.

Because the vast sweep of democracy is still incomplete even in America today, because revolutionaries seeking to break old fetters are still foiled in Europe and Asia, because the physical life of the Brooklyn ferries and the Broadway street cars and the Mississippi river banks and the still fresh battlefields of World War II continue to pulse with the same heartbeats of humanity as in Whitman's time, his poetry strikes us now with the same immediacy it must have awakened in its earliest readers in the 1850's.

The good gray poet of democracy is one of literature's great faith-holders in human freedom. Speaking simply for people everywhere and most of all for the believers in our basic American dream, he is constantly growing in stature as the twentieth century advances and edition after edition of his poems appears.

Walt Whitman wrote without the frills, furbelows, and decorations of conventional poetry, usually without rhyme or measured prettiness. Perhaps because of his simplicity, timid poetry lovers over the years have been frightened away from his *Leaves of Grass,* poems as firmly rooted and as brightly growing as the grass itself. Perhaps, too, because his all-embracing words lock arms with workers and farmers, Negroes and whites, Asiatics and Europeans, serfs, and free men, beaming democracy to all, many academic-minded intellectual isolationists in America have had little use for Whitman, and so have impeded his handclasp with today by keeping him imprisoned in silence on library shelves. Still his words leap from their pages and their spirit grows steadily stronger everywhere:

. . . I give the sign of democracy.
By God! I will accept nothing which all cannot have their counterpart of on the same terms . . .

So there is no keeping Whitman imprisoned in silence. He proclaims:

I ordain myself loosed of limits . . . .
Going where I list . . . .
Gently, but with undeniable will, divesting myself of the holds that would hold me.

One of the greatest "I" poets of all time, Whitman's "I" is not the "I" of the introspective versifiers who write always and only about themselves. Rather it is the cosmic "I" of all peoples who seek freedom, decency, and dignity, friendship and equality between individuals and races all over the world.

The best indication of the scope of Whitman's poems might be found in his own SONG OF THE ANSWERER where he writes about poetry:

Cover of musical score for an opera that opened in Philadelphia on 16 December 1946 and premiered on Broadway on 9 January 1947 (courtesy of Kenneth Spencer Research Library, University of Kansas Libraries)

The words of true poems give you more than poems,
They give you to form for yourself poems, religions, politics, war,
peace, behavior, histories, essays, daily life and everything else,
They balance ranks, colors, races, creeds, and the sexes . . . .
They bring none to his or her terminus or to be content and full,
Whom they take they take into space to behold the birth of stars, to
learn one of the meanings,
To launch off with absolute faith, to sweep through the ceaseless rings
and never be quiet again.

In this atomic age of ours, when the ceaseless rings are multiplied a millionfold, the Whitman spiral is upward and outward toward a freer, better life for all, not narrowing downward toward death and destruction. Singing the greatness of the individual, Whitman also sings the greatness of unity, cooperation, and understanding.

> *. . . all the men ever born are also my brothers, and the women my sisters . . . .*

As an after-thought he adds:

> *(I am large, I contain multitudes).*

Certainly, his poems contain us all. The reader cannot help but see his own better self therein.
—*I Hear the People Singing: Selected Poems of Walt Whitman* (New York: International Publishers, 1946), pp. 7–10

* * *

Hughes met Russell and Rowena Jelliffe in 1917 at Karamu House, the interracial community center for neighborhood children that the married couple founded in their Cleveland home. Interested in fostering awareness of African American arts, the Jelliffes encouraged promising young artists such as Hughes, whose book Fields of Wonder *they reviewed for the* Cleveland News Week-End Review.

**Langston Hughes Fulfills Promise
of Great Destiny in New Book
Review of *Fields of Wonder***

Langston Hughes came from a little town in Kansas to live in Cleveland (at the age of 13) in the same year that we came to Cleveland, tucked ourselves in a little rear cottage on E. 38th St. and set about the building of Karamu House. Books and theories were now behind us and we began to learn from people. Among that first group of children from whom we learned so much, upon whose lives our Karamu program came to be based, was Langston Hughes.

The debt we owe to him and to other children of that period can scarcely be defined, much less repaid. Here we learned from a child's unfolding. He was one

of a score or more whom we watched and interpreted as honestly as we knew how, searching for the thing which would meet the basic need. This searching shaped Karamu.

In Langston Hughes the outstanding thing to see was his wonder at the world. It shone through his deep hurt, his struggle to understand, his gaiety, his fine sense of humor, his sensitiveness to beauty and his deep liking for people.

There are outstanding moments to treasure. There was the moment when his wondering eyes fell upon a little brown girl in a red dress and he fell in love with her. One of his poems is written to her. There were the times when he fell asleep over books in our living room. We have the memory of his eager invitation to come to his home to see his Grandfather Leary's shawl with the bullet holes, the shawl which his grandfather had worn when he fell beside John Brown at Harper's Ferry. He became one of our first volunteers and drew and painted with a group of younger children.

In his adult years again he came very close to us at Karamu through his plays, most of which are unpublished. He has written for Karamu Theater more plays than any other one playwright. Six of his plays we premiered, though but one of these, *Mulatto,* has so far reached Broadway. None is more beloved, by both children and adults at Karamu, than he, and he returns to us just often enough to implant that same love in each generation of people.

It seems altogether fitting and logical to us that this last book of poems should be one of lyric poems, and further that it should bear the name *Fields of Wonder.* We have through it a sense of seeing his own destiny approaching its fulfillment, of a fine maturing, of the coming to fruition of the best of those things of which he gave promise a good many years ago. Surely he is one of those rare people given rare vision to see all nature and man alike very truly indeed and to crystallize that seeing into poetic form with an honesty and a simplicity that is deeply moving.

Repeatedly in this volume he sings of a sense of order, of peace, of triumph.

> Walls have been known
> To fall
> Dusk turn to dawn
> And chains to be gone.

Knowing the life and the honest searching of this man one can but respond confidently to his abstract conclusions, to his ideology, for he has not rushed madly toward these concepts through any wish to escape the storm of living, through a willful b[l]inding of his eyes to the sordid and the ugly. Rather, he has in

Rowena and Russell Jelliffe in 1951 (photograph by Francis Miller/Time Life Pictures/Getty Images)

the past written of these things sharply, concisely, sometimes bitterly, always honestly.

Sometimes Negroes have disapproved of his writing, feeling that he is not enough concerned about putting forth the best racial foot for the world at large to see. Somewhere back of this misunderstanding is his deep conviction that either foot is very good indeed and that all art should be used to reveal life, to hunt out its truths about all men, humble as well as great, rather than to conceal it with superficial drapings. For the people he is most concerned about there is a poem called "Prayer" in which he says—

> Gather up
> In the arms of your love
> Those who expect
> No love from above.

In *Fields of Wonder* he sings of many of the things about which he has sung before. He writes of life in a night club, of the southern cabin, of the wail and ache of jazz, of old sailors, of the secrets of Harlem, of the Mexican market place and the Cuban bar, of children at play, of the religious shout, of black motherhood, of the Mother, Africa, of the waste and sting of segregation, of night and sunrise, of the sea and the desert, of human destiny, of God, of immortality.

Of all these things he has written before. But it is as though the path of his life had been that of a spiral (a spiral with a very wide base indeed) and that now, when the same point is viewed, it is from a higher level, with a wider vision, through a clearer atmosphere. While there is maturing, there is no withdrawing from life and there is the unvarying basis of honesty. It is as though he had long ago made a pact with himself and his readers always to tell so truly what he sees.

When this poet was growing up his greatest pleasure came from his writing. He glowed from it. Years later he said to us, "I never quite escape the feeling of guilt about taking money for my poems. It doesn't seem decent to earn money from anything that you enjoy so much. Maybe I ought to make my living some other way."

As there was, during his adolescence, the need to reach very often within himself for pleasant experience (for his real life was not easy) he wrote abundantly. He wrote for the Central High School paper, which he loved so much, as well as his numerous "letters to God." It interests us deeply to note that in this current collection is a reference again to these "letters." He writes—

In an envelope marked
Personal
God addressed me a letter
In an envelope marked
Personal
I have given my answer.

But if the final achievement of his writing gave him pleasure, that prior period, when a thought was twisting through his being but had not yet gotten itself into words, was one of haunting misery. Thus he describes it under the caption, "Burden."

It is not weariness
That bears me down
But sudden nearness
To song without sound.

At the moment he is no doubt best known as the writer of the lyrics to Elmer Rice's *Street Scene,* now running on Broadway, and for which Kurt Weill wrote the music. Here are lyrics so sensitive and true to character they seem to rise at the instant of hearing spontaneously from the heart of the singer, so true are they to the character they portray. Likewise are they true to the culture and emotions of America.

If it is true, as it seems to us to be, that in this group of poems, Langston Hughes rounds out and approaches the sensitiveness which his childhood promised, it is true also that another and larger destiny is here attained. It has to do with the destiny of his race as he sensed it long before he put it into words.

Long ago he saw that in those values in which we, as the American people, are weak, the Negro was strong. The emotive, esthetic values of life, the rich enjoyment of life as the goal of living, he knew to be strong and deep within his race. That America, which this poet so deeply loves, needs this element more strongly woven into her life he also knew. Well aware of the predominant emphasis which we in this country give to economic, political, technological and practical

matters and of the gap that is there in the realm of the esthetic, he knew that along the latter line the Negro will achieve his fullest giving.

That he himself has here and in this way given to us more fully than ever before is evident. That here he fulfills a racial as well as a personal destiny seems equally true.

—Cleveland News Week-End Review,
30 (29 March 1947): 1, 8

* * *

This essay includes Hughes's fullest description of the intimidation he endured from right-wing critics. Hughes consistently denied being affiliated with the Communist Party.

My Adventures as a Social Poet

Poets who write mostly about love, roses and moonlight, sunsets and snow, must lead a very quiet life. Seldom, I imagine, does their poetry get them into difficulties. Beauty and lyricism are really related to another world, to ivory towers, to your head in the clouds, feet floating off the earth.

Unfortunately, having been born poor—and also colored—in Missouri, I was stuck in the mud from the beginning. Try as I might to float off into the clouds, poverty and Jim Crow would grab me by the heels, and right back on earth I would land. A third floor furnished room is the nearest thing I have ever had to an ivory tower.

Some of my earliest poems were social poems in that they were about people's problems—whole groups of people's problems—rather than my own personal difficulties. Sometimes, though, certain aspects of my personal problems happened to be also common to many other people. And certainly, racially speaking, my own problems of adjustment to American life were the same as those of millions of other segregated Negroes. The moon belongs to everybody, but not this American earth of ours. That is perhaps why poems about the moon perturb no one, but poems about color and poverty do perturb many citizens. Social forces pull backwards or forwards, right or left, and social poems get caught in the pulling and hauling. Sometimes the poet himself gets pulled and hauled—even hauled off to jail.

I have never been in jail but I have been detained by the Japanese police in Tokyo and by the immigration authorities in Cuba—in custody, to put it politely—due, no doubt, to their interest in my written words. These authorities would hardly have detained me had I been a writer of the roses and moonlight school. I have never known the police of any country to show an interest in lyric poetry as such. But when poems stop talking about the moon and begin to mention poverty, trade unions, color lines, and colonies, somebody tells the police. The history of world literature has many examples of poets fleeing into exile to escape persecution, of poets in jail, even of poets killed like Placido or, more recently, Lorca in Spain.

My adventures as a social poet are mild indeed compared to the body-breaking, soul-searing experiences of poets in the recent fascist countries or of the resistance poets of the Nazi invaded lands during the war. For that reason, I can use so light a word as "adventure" in regard to my own skirmishes with reaction and censorship.

My adventures as a social poet began in a colored church in Atlantic City shortly after my first book, *The Weary Blues,* was published in 1926. I had been invited to come down to the shore from Lincoln University where I was a student, to give a program of my poems in the church. During the course of my program I read several of my poems in the form of the Negro folk songs, including some blues poems about hard luck and hard work. As I read I noticed a deacon approach the pulpit with a note which he placed on the rostrum beside me, but I did not stop to open the note until I had finished and had acknowledged the applause of a cordial audience. The note read, "Do not read any more blues in my pulpit." It was signed by the minister. That was my first experience with censorship.

The kind and generous woman who sponsored my writing for a few years after my college days did not come to the point quite so directly as did the minister who disliked blues. Perhaps, had it not been in the midst of the great depression of the late '20's and early '30's, the kind of poems that I am afraid helped to end her patronage might not have been written. But it was impossible for me to travel from hungry Harlem to the lovely homes on Park Avenue without feeling in my soul the great gulf between the very poor and the very rich in our society. In those days, on the way to visit this kind lady I would see the homeless sleeping in subways and the hungry begging in doorways on sleet-stung winter days. It was then that I wrote a poem called "An Ad for the Waldorf-Astoria," satirizing the slick-paper magazine advertisements of the opening of that de luxe hotel. Also I wrote:

PARK BENCH

I live on a park bench.
You, Park Avenue.
Hell of a distance
Between us two.

I beg a dime for dinner—
You got a butler and maid.
But I'm wakin' up!
Say, ain't you afraid

That I might, just maybe,
In a year or two,
Move on over
To Park Avenue?

In a little while I did not have a patron any more.

But that year I won a prize, the Harmon Gold Award for Literature, which consisted of a medal and four hundred dollars. With the four hundred dollars I went to Haiti. On the way I stopped in Cuba where I was cordially received by the writers and artists. I had written poems about the exploitation of Cuba by the sugar barons and I had translated many poems of Nicholas Guillen such as:

CANE

Negro
In the cane fields.
White man
Above the cane fields.
Earth
Beneath the cane fields.
Blood
That flows from us.

This was during the days of the dictatorial Machado regime. Perhaps someone called his attention to these poems and translations because, when I came back from Haiti weeks later, I was not allowed to land in Cuba, but was detained by the immigration authorities at Santiago and put on an island until the American consul came, after three days, to get me off with the provision that I cross the country to Havana and leave Cuban soil at once.

That was my first time being put out of any place. But since that time I have been put out of or barred from quite a number of places, all because of my poetry—not the roses and moonlight poems (which I write, too) but because of poems about poverty, oppression, and segregation. Nine Negro boys in Alabama were on trial for their lives when I got back from Cuba and Haiti. The famous Scottsboro "rape" case was in full session. I visited those boys in the death house at Kilby Prison, and I wrote many poems about them. One of these poems was:

CHRIST IN ALABAMA

Christ is a Nigger,
Beaten and black—
O, bare your back.

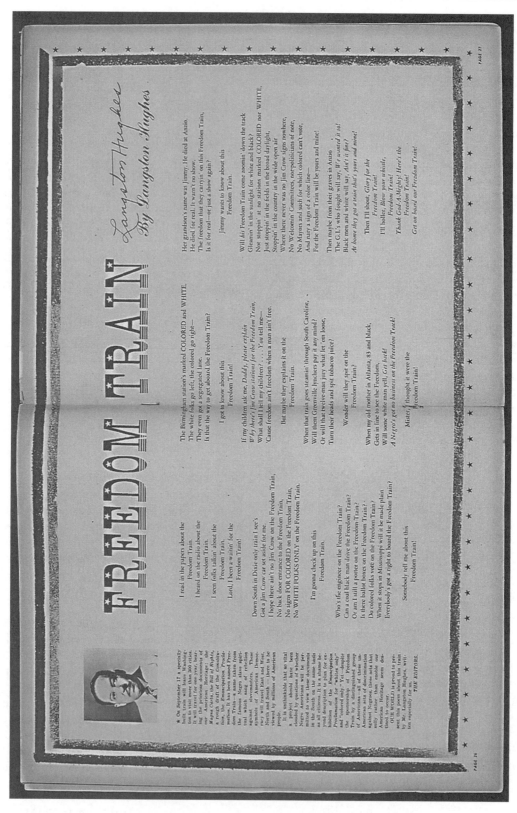

Hughes's poem celebrating the American Freedom Train project was featured in the October 1947 issue of Our World
(courtesy of Kenneth Spencer Research Library, University of Kansas Libraries).

Mary is His Mother—
Mammy of the South.
Silence your mouth.

God's His father—
White Master above,
Grant us your love.

Most holy bastard
Of the bleeding mouth:
Nigger Christ
On the cross of the South.

Contempo, a publication of some of the students at the University of North Carolina, published the poem on its front page on the very day that I was being presented in a program of my poems at the University in Chapel Hill. That evening there were police outside the building in which I spoke, and in the air the rising tension of race that is peculiar to the South. It had been rumored that some of the local citizenry were saying that I should be run out of town, and that one of the sheriffs agreed, saying, "Sure, he ought to be run out! It's bad enough to call Christ a *bastard.* But when he calls him a *nigger,* he's gone too far!"

The next morning a third of my fee was missing when I was handed my check. One of the departments of the university jointly sponsoring my program had refused to come through with its portion of the money. Nevertheless, I remember with pleasure the courtesy and kindness of many of the students and faculty at Chapel Hill and their lack of agreement with the anti-Negro elements of the town. There I began to learn at the University of North Carolina how hard it is to be a white liberal in the South.

It was not until I had been to Russia and around the world as a writer and journalist that censorship and opposition to my poems reached the point of completely preventing me from appearing in public programs on a few occasions. It happened first in Los Angeles shortly after my return from the Soviet Union. I was to have been one of several speakers on a memorial program to be held at the colored branch Y. M. C. A. for a young Negro journalist of the community. At the behest of white higher-ups, no doubt, some reactionary Negro politicians informed the Negro Y. M. C. A. that I was a Communist. The secretary of the Negro Branch Y then informed the committee of young people in charge of the memorial that they could have their program only if I did not appear.

I have never been a Communist, but I soon learned that anyone visiting the Soviet Union and speaking with favor of it upon returning is liable to be so labeled. Indeed when Mrs. Roosevelt, Walter

White, and so Christian a lady as Mrs. Bethune who has never been in Moscow, are so labeled, I should hardly be surprised! I wasn't surprised. And the young people's committee informed the Y secretary that since the Y was a public community center which they helped to support, they saw no reason why it should censor their memorial program to the extent of eliminating any speaker.

Since I had been allotted but a few moments on the program, it was my intention simply to read this short poem of mine:

Dear lovely death
That taketh all things under wing,
Never to kill,
Only to change into some other thing
This suffering flesh—
To make it either more or less
But not again the same,
Dear lovely death,
Change is thy other name.

But the Negro branch Y, egged on by the reactionary politicians (whose incomes, incidentally, were allegedly derived largely from gambling houses and other underworld activities), informed the young people's committee that the police would be at the door to prevent my entering the Y on the afternoon of the scheduled program. So when the crowd gathered, the memorial was not held that Sunday. The young people simply informed the audience of the situation and said that the memorial would be postponed until a place could be found where all the participants could be heard. The program was held elsewhere a few Sundays later.

Somebody with malice aforethought (probably the Negro politicians of Uncle Tom vintage) gave the highly publicized California evangelist, Aimee Semple McPherson, a copy of a poem of mine, "Goodbye, Christ." This poem was one o[f] my least successful efforts at poetic communication, in that many persons have misinterpreted it as an anti-Christian poem. I intended it to be just the opposite. Satirical, even ironic, in style, I meant it to be a poem against those whom I felt were misusing religion for worldly or profitable purposes. In the poem I mentioned Aimee Semple McPherson. This apparently made her angry. From her Angelus Temple pulpit she preached against me, saying, "There are many devils among us, but the most dangerous of all is the red devil. And now there comes among us a red devil *in a black skin!*"

She gathered her followers together and sent them to swoop down upon me one afternoon at an unsuspecting and innocent literary luncheon in Pasadena's Vista del Arroyo Hotel. Robert Nathan, I believe, was one of the speakers, along with a number of other authors. I was to have five minutes on the program to read a few poems from my latest collection of folk verses, *Shakespeare in Harlem,* hardly a radical book.

When I arrived at the hotel by car from Los Angeles, I noticed quite a crowd in the streets where the traffic seemed to be tangled. So I got out some distance from the front of the hotel and walked through the grounds to the entrance, requesting my car to return at three o'clock. When I asked in the lobby for the location of the luncheon, I was told to wait until the desk clerk sent for the chairman, George Palmer Putnam. Mr. Putnam arrived with the manager, both visibly excited. They informed me that the followers of Aimee McPherson were vehemently picketing the hotel because of my appearance there. The manager added with an aggrieved look that he could not have such a commotion in front of his hotel. Either I would have to go or he would cancel the entire luncheon.

Mr. Putnam put it up to me. I said that rather than inconvenience several hundred guests and a half dozen authors, I would withdraw—except that I did not know where my car had gone, so would someone be kind enough to drive me to the station. Just then a doorman came in to inform the manager that traffic was completely blocked in front of the hotel. Frantically the manager rushed out. About that time a group of Foursquare Gospel members poured into the lobby in uniforms and armbands and surrounded me and George Palmer Putnam, demanding to know if we were Christians. Before I could say anything, Mr. Putnam lit into them angrily, saying it was none of their business and stating that under our Constitution a man could have any religion he chose, as well as freedom to express himself.

Just then an old gentleman about seventy-two who was one of the organizers of the literary luncheon came up, saying he had been asked to drive me to the station and get me out of there so they could start the luncheon. Shaking hands with Mr. Putnam, I accompanied the old gentleman to the street. There Aimee's sound truck had been backed across the roadway blocking all passage so that limousines, trucks, and taxis were tangled up in all directions. The sound truck was playing "God Bless America" while hundreds of pickets milled about with signs denouncing Langston Hughes—atheistic Red. Rich old ladies on the arms of their chauffeurs were trying to get through the crowd to the luncheon. Reporters were dashing about.

None of the people recognized me, but in the excitement the old gentleman could not find his car. Finally he hailed a taxi and nervously thrust a dollar into the driver's hand with the request that I be driven to the station. He asked to be excused himself in order to get back to the luncheon. Just as I reached out the door to shake hands in farewell, three large white ladies with banners rushed up to the cab. One of them screamed, "We don't shake hands with niggers where we come from!"

The thought came over me that the picketing might turn into a race riot, in which case I did not wish to be caught in a cab in a traffic jam alone. I did not turn loose the old gentleman's hand. Instead of shaking it in farewell, I simply pulled him into the taxi with me, saying, "I thought you were going to the station, too."

As the pickets snarled outside, I slammed the door. The driver started off, but we were caught in the traffic blocked by the sound truck lustily playing "God Bless America." The old gentleman trembled beside me, until finally we got clear of the mob. As we backed down a side street and turned to head for the station, the sirens of approaching police cars were heard in the distance.

Later I learned from the afternoon papers that the whole demonstration had been organized by Aimee McPherson's publicity man, and that when the police arrived he had been arrested for refusing to give up the keys to the sound truck stalled midway the street to block the traffic. This simply proved the point I had tried to make in the poem—that the church might as well bid Christ goodbye if his gospel were left in the hands of such people.

Four years later I was to be picketed again in Detroit by Gerald L. K. Smith's Mothers of America—for ever since the Foursquare Gospel demonstration in California, reactionary groups have copied, used and distributed this poem. Always they have been groups like Smith's, never known to help the fight for democratic Negro rights in America, but rather to use their energies to foment riots such as that before Detroit's Sojourner Truth housing project where the Klan-minded tried to prevent colored citizens from occupying government homes built for them.

I have had one threatening communication signed *A Klansman.* And many scurrilous anonymous anti-Negro letters from persons whose writing did not always indicate illiteracy. On a few occasions, reactionary elements have forced liberal sponsors to cancel their plans to present me in a reading of my poems. I recall that in Gary, Indiana, some years ago the colored teachers were threatened with the loss of

"HATE CHRIST"
Is the Slogan of the Communists

One of the most notorious propagandists for the lovers of Stalin is Langston Hughes, a Negro poet. This Negro moves in the circles of the high-toned (?) whites. He has conferred with and addressed groups to whom Eleanor Roosevelt has spoken and with whom she has cooperated. He moves in the circles of mongrelizers and race mixers. He has been paid large fees for addressing many tax-supported and state-owned universities and colleges. The following poem is one of his most popular among his Red followers:

This hymn of hate is designed to persuade the simple Christian, whether he be black or white, to throw down Christ, to say goodbye to Christ, and embrace Marx, Lenin and Stalin.

LANGSTON HUGHES

Notorious Negro Stalin lover who
wrote the revolutionary song
"Goodbye Christ."

ATTENTION: Extra copies of this sheet may
be had at the following rates:

25 copies	$ 1.00
100 copies	2.00
1000 copies	15.00

Address your request to Gerald L. K. Smith,
P. O. Box D4, Central Station, St. Louis 1, Mo.

GOODBYE CHRIST

Listen, Christ,
You did all right in your day, I reckon—
But that day's gone now.
They ghosted you up a swell story, too.
Called it the Bible—
But it's dead now.
The popes and the preachers 've
Made too much money from it.
They've sold you to too many
Kings, generals, robbers, and killers—
Even to the Tzar and the Cossacks,
Even to Rockefeller's Church,
Even to the Saturday Evening Post.
You ain't no good no more.
They've pawned you
Till you've done wore out.
Goodbye.
Christ Jesus Lord God Jehovah,
Beat it on away from here now.
Make way for a new guy with no religion at all—
A real guy named
Marx Communist Lenin Peasant Stalin Worker ME—
I said, ME!
Go ahead on now,
You're getting in the way of things, Lord,
And please take Saint Ghandi with you when you go,
And Saint Pope Pius,
And Saint Aimee McPherson,
And big black Saint Becton
Of the Consecrated Dime.
And step on the gas, Christ!
Move!
Don't be so slow about movin'!
The world is mine from now on—
And nobody's gonna sell ME
To a king, or a general,
Or a millionaire.

     * * *

Goodbye Christ, good morning Revolution!

THE CROSS AND THE FLAG, a monthly magazine edited by Gerald L. K. Smith, is the official organ for the crusade of Christian Nationalism. This dynamic magazine is devoted exclusively to the most fearless and deadly issues of the hour. Subscription rate: 1 year, $2.00; 6 months, $1.00. Subscriptions should be addressed to Gerald L. K. Smith, Editor, Post Office Box D4, Central Station, St. Louis 1, Mo.

Page from a 1947 issue of the racist and anti-Semitic newspaper The Cross and the Flag, *edited by Gerald L. K. Smith.*
In "My Adventures as a Social Poet," Hughes recalls that four years after he was picketed by Aimee Semple McPherson's
followers in Pasadena, Smith's Mothers of America mounted a protest against him in Detroit (Langston Hughes
Papers, Yale Collection of American Literature, Beinecke Rare Book and Manuscript Library).

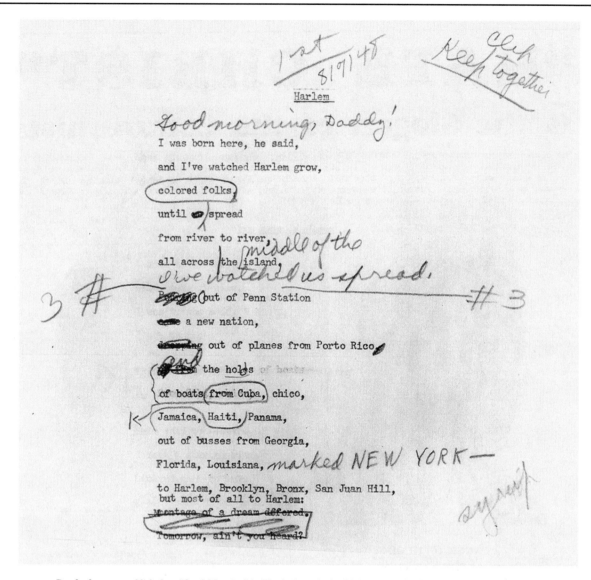

Draft of a poem published as "Good Morning" in Hughes's 1951 book Montage of a Dream Deferred *(Langston Hughes Papers, Yale Collection of American Literature, Beinecke Rare Book and Manuscript Library)*

their jobs if I accepted their invitation to appear at one of the public schools. In another city a white high school principal, made apprehensive by a small group of reactionary parents, told me that he communicated with the F. B. I. at Washington to find out if I were a member of the Communist Party. Assured that I was not, with the approval of his school board, he presented me to his student body. To further fortify his respectability, that morning at assembly, he had invited all of the Negro ministers and civic leaders of the town to sit on the stage in a semi-circle behind me. To the students it must have looked like a kind of modern minstrel show as it was the first time any Negroes at all had been invited to their assembly.

So goes the life of a social poet. I am sure none of these things would ever have happened to me had I limited the subject matter of my poems to roses and moonlight. But, unfortunately, I was born poor—and colored—and almost all the prettiest roses I have seen have been in rich white people's yards—not in mine. That is why I cannot write exclusively about roses and moonlight—for sometimes in the moonlight my brothers see a fiery cross and a circle of Klansmen's hoods. Sometimes in the moonlight a dark body swings from a lynching tree—but for his funeral there are no roses.

—Phylon, 8 (Third Quarter 1947): 205–212

* * *

Cuba Libre

Poems by Nicolás Guillén

Translated from the Spanish by
Langston Hughes *and* Ben Frederic Carruthers

Illustrated by Gar Gilbert

Anderson & Ritchie : The Ward Ritchie Press
Los Angeles, California : 1948

Title page for a collection of fifty translated poems (Langston Hughes Papers, Yale Collection of American Literature, Beinecke Rare Book and Manuscript Library)

The poetry collection One-Way Ticket *was published in January 1949 by Knopf. The critic and scholar J. Saunders Redding wrote this review.*

Old Forms, Old Rhythms, Old Words
Review of *One-Way Ticket*

It is a tribute to Langston Hughes's earlier accomplishments that his reputation continues undimmed by verse which of late is often jejune and iterative. Intellectual recognition of the thinning out of his creativeness is inescapable, but emotional acceptance of the fact comes hard. An old loving admiration simply will not die. It is not easy to say that a favorite poet's latest book is a sorry falling off. It is not easy to declare that "One-Way Ticket" is stale, flat, and spiritless.

The reason for this dull level of lifelessness has a simple explanation: Hughes harks back to a youthful-

ness that is no longer green. He has long since matured beyond the limited expressive capacity of the idiom he uses in "One-Way Ticket." It is many a year since he was the naive and elemental lyrist of "The Weary Blues" and the folklike story-teller of "The Ways of White Folks." In mind, emotion, and spirit (and in time, space, and event as well) he has traveled a "far piece," and he has not traveled in circles. The old forms, the old rhythms, the old moods cannot encompass the things he sees and understands and loves and hates now.

While Hughes's rejection of his own growth shows an admirable loyalty to his self-commitment as the poet of the "simple, Negro common-folk"–the peasant, the laborer, the city slum-dweller–, it does a disservice to his art. And of course the fact is that Langston Hughes is not now, nor ever truly was one of the simple, common people. Back in the Twenties and Thirties, his sympathy for them had the blunt, passionate forthrightness of all youthful outpourings of emotion, but lately that sympathy seems a bit disingenuous and a bit strained, like a conversation between old acquaintances who have had no mutual points of reference in a dozen years.

As an example of the artful use of folk idiom and folk rhythm, "One-Way Ticket" will interest those who know only this volume of the author's work, but it will disappoint those who remember the beauty and brilliance of "The Dream Keeper" and "Fields of Wonder."

–The Saturday Review of Literature,
32 (22 January 1949): 24

* * *

Journalist Abner W. Berry wrote this review for a communist newspaper.

'One Way Ticket,' New Book of Poems
by Langston Hughes

Langston Hughes, 20 years ago, was the eloquent singer of "New Negro." His Weary Blues, a slender volume published in the late 'twenties, established Hughes as the poetic spokesman of the Negro people. Using blues rhythms, blank verse and the folk imagery and idiom of a people then moving into a political struggle for their full rights, Hughes caught in his poems the mood and aspirations of America's oppressed and neglected darker brothers.

Hughes functioned in poetry as Duke Ellington did in music and as Aaron Douglas did in the graphic arts, to mention only two of the important cultural contributors

Alfred·A·K₁

P U B L I S H E R   O F

Cables: KNOPF NEW YORK
Telephones: PLAZA 3-4761

An Announcement to Friends of Langston Hughes –

You will be pleased to hear that today is Publication Day for
Langston Hughes's first collection of poems on Negro subjects since
SHAKESPEARE IN HARLEM.

Today we are publishing ONE-WAY TICKET.

Here the man whom Carl Van Vechten calls "the Negro Poet
Laureate" brings together the happy lyrics, dirges, dramatic soliloquies,
and love songs that have made Hughes an enduringly popular poet.

> "He loves his race," Van Vechten says
> of Mr. Hughes, "and reports and interprets
> it feelingly and understandingly to itself
> and to the other races. His verse re-
> sounds with the exultant throb of Negro
> pain and gladness."

ONE-WAY TICKET is beautifully illustrated by the distinguished
young American Negro painter, Jacob Lawrence. We think you will find
that Mr. Lawrence has caught the spirit of Langston Hughes's work.

We are sure that you will want to read and own this readable
and exciting new book. Just fill out and mail the enclosed self-
addressed order card and we will send you ONE-WAY TICKET by return mail
postpaid. (Price $2.75)

Sincerely yours,

Richard C. Ernst

P.S. Arna Bontemps says, "ONE-WAY TICKET is that rare thing – a book of
contemporary poetry that gets up and goes."

*Announcement for a book of poems that received generally poor reviews (Langston Hughes Collection,
Schomburg Center for Research in Black Culture, New York Public Library)*

Cover for the libretto of an opera about the Haitian revolutionary Jean-Jacques Dessalines, based on a play Hughes wrote in 1938. The opera premiered in New York City on 30 March 1949 (courtesy of Kenneth Spencer Research Library, University of Kansas Libraries).

of the times. But One-Way Ticket, unfortunately does not build further upon the well-established foundation.

———

In One Way Ticket, Hughes shows that he still possesses the magic of transferring the blues rhythm to literature; he has the magic of the colloquial usage blended with simple and dramatic imagery. For example in his little poem:

> I pick up my life
> And take it with me
> And put it down in
> Chicago, Scranton,
> Any place that is
> North and East—
> And not Dixie. . . .
>
> I am fed up
> With Jimcrow laws,

> People who are cruel
> And afraid. . . .
> I pick up my life
> And take it away
> On a one way ticket—
> Gone up North
> Gone out West,
> Gone!

———

Hughes here seems to be speaking for himself. No struggle. No hope of victory. No reflection of the Negro people—the Negro workers especially—who are today utilizing the blues and the spiritual and the beautiful and sometimes terrifying imagery of the sermon as weapons in their fight for their rights—in Dixie. The Negro people have carried on since 1928. Hughes, in his own personal expressions, has shown himself to be a part of this carrying on. But his poetry

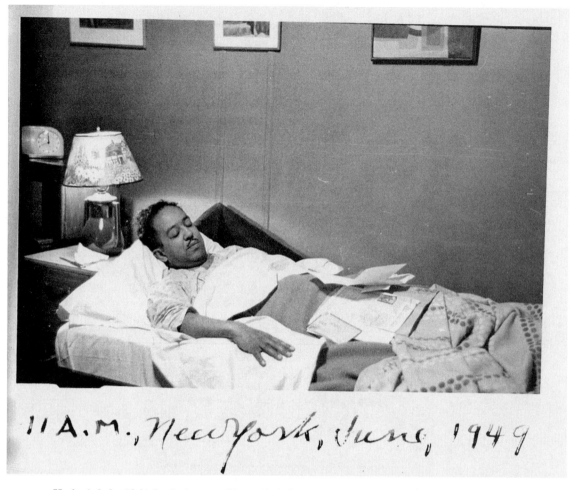

11 A.M., NewYork, June, 1949

Hughes in bed, with his handwritten note. He was fond of working late and sleeping in (Langston Hughes Papers, Yale Collection of American Literature, Beinecke Rare Book and Manuscript Library).

here misses by a mile the mood and the temper of the people for whom he has been so virile a spokesman.

His "Madam" poems in the present volume, despite their mood, are static pictures of static people caught in an inescapable net of exploitation. Some of them border on the rejected stereotype. In other poems there is an echo of the "Bigger Thomas" school of Richard Wright in which he envisions a blind struggle: "Wind / In the cotton fields, / Gentle breeze: / Beware the hour / It uproots trees." And except in one poem the Negro is placed in isolation–black against white. The one exception is October 16, dedicated to John Brown.

———

The poem to John Brown, I would say, is the only one with perspective. The rest, although worth while reading for their craft and the charm with which they are suffused, are "tame" pieces, minor recordings of minor doings in the ghetto. There is none of the social insight which Hughes' readers have known in his "White Worker, Here's My Hand," or "Let America Be America Again," or "The Freedom Train."

If Hughes were a new poet and if One Way Ticket were his new work, we could say that here is a star full of promise which will rise. But with 20 years of activity behind him, we must say of Hughes that One Way Ticket indicates a waning of his star. He was once the booming and beautifully defiant voice of the Negroes' spokesman in North America, matching that of Nicholas Guillen, the Afro-Cuban, in Latin America. One Way Ticket is the well-turned product, though, of a charming singer of little songs. Langston Hughes is capable of better.

–*Daily Worker,* 13 February 1949,
p. 13

A Citizen of Harlem: 1950 – 1959

The 1950s began positively for Hughes with the 18 January 1950 premiere of his and Jan Meyerowitz's opera *The Barrier* at Columbia University to favorable reviews. Hughes scored another success that year when *Simple Speaks His Mind,* a book based on his *Chicago Defender* column, was published on 14 April. The popularity of Hughes's character Jesse B. Semple was shown by nearly fourteen thousand prepublication sales. Most reviewers were charmed by Semple's folksy wisdom.

Hughes spent the early part of 1951 giving readings and lecturing in the South, ending his brief tour to attend celebrations for *Montage of a Dream Deferred,* his experimental, book-length poem published by Holt on 19 February. Hughes had not let Blanche Knopf's rejection of the manuscript the previous year curb his enthusiasm for the book, and many of the reviews were indeed positive. A notable exception, however, was fellow poet Babette Deutsch, who castigated Hughes in the 6 May 1951 issue of

Langston Hughes and neighborhood children at the Children's Garden, Harlem, 1955 (photograph by Don Hunstein; Langston Hughes Papers, Yale Collection of American Literature, Beinecke Rare Book and Manuscript Library)

213

The New York Times Book Review for not rising above the limitations of folk art and making more rigorous use of his talents. Undeterred, Hughes in April began working on another "Simple" book and in June readied translations of Federico García Lorca's *Gypsy Ballads*–for which he had done most of the work while living in Madrid during the Spanish Civil War–for publication in the fall *Beloit Poetry Chapbook.*

In January 1952 Hughes's second collection of short stories, *Laughing to Keep from Crying,* was published to generally positive reviews. Composed mainly of stories that had been previously published in magazines, the book served for several critics as a reminder of traits they had always found compelling in his work. That same year Hughes wrote *The First Book of Negroes,* the first of five educational children's books in the "First Book" series for the publisher Franklin Watts. Hughes also agreed to write *Famous American Negroes,* the first of three books for adolescents published by Dodd, Mead.

Despite Hughes's attempts to position himself as politically moderate, he was subpoenaed in March 1953 to appear before Senator Joseph R. McCarthy's Senate Permanent Subcommittee on Investigations to explain and account for his "un-American" past. In his testimony on 24 March 1953 at a closed executive session of the hearings, Hughes argued that his radical writings should be read in the context of the historical struggle of African Americans to gain basic civil and social rights in the United States. Near the end of the public hearing held on 26 March, Hughes satisfied his interrogators–at the risk of alienating his many friends on the Left–by repudiating the poem "Goodbye Christ," "a very young, awkward poem" that "does not express my views or my artistic techniques today." He was dismissed by McCarthy after assuring the senator that he "was agreeably surprised at the courtesy and friendliness" with which he was received by the committee.

After the McCarthy hearings Hughes returned to the routine of his writing. In May 1953 the second volume of Simple stories, *Simple Takes a Wife,* was published to excellent reviews. He completed manuscripts for *The First Book of Rhythms* (1954) and *Famous American Negroes* (1954). In July 1954 he began work on his second autobiography and also began collaborating with the photographer Roy DeCarava on a photo-narrative of Harlem life, which was published as *The Sweet Flypaper of Life* in 1955. Although finan-

cial worries sometimes compelled Hughes to take on projects that clearly did not add to his reputation as a serious artist, he evidently sincerely enjoyed working on books such as *The First Book of Jazz* (1955), *Famous Negro Music Makers* (1955), and *The First Book of the West Indies* (1956).

In November 1956 two works by Hughes were published to good reviews: his collaborative effort with Milton Meltzer, *A Pictorial History of the Negro in America,* and, more significant, his second volume of autobiography, *I Wonder as I Wander.* Hughes then worked on *Simply Heavenly,* a musical based on the Simple books, which premiered in New York on 21 May 1957 and opened on Broadway on 20 August. His third Simple book, *Simple Stakes a Claim,* was warmly received in fall 1957.

Hughes spent the remainder of 1957 polishing the manuscript of *Famous Negro Heroes of America* (1958) and determining the contents of *The Langston Hughes Reader,* which was published in spring 1958. In October 1958 he embarked on a reading tour that included stops in Lawrence, Kansas, where he spent much of his childhood, and Joplin, Missouri, where he was born, as well as towns in California, Ohio, and Pennsylvania, returning to New York in time for a party honoring the publication of his second novel, *Tambourines to Glory* (1958). In a notable exception to the generally enthusiastic reviews, poet LeRoi Jones asserted that "if a book of similar literary worth were to be written by another author it would not be reviewed (probably it would have never gotten published)."

In 1959 Hughes continued pursuing a rigorous travel and lecture schedule. The major event of the year was the publication in March of *Selected Poems of Langston Hughes* by Knopf, the publisher of his first book and his main publisher for the first fifteen years of his career. Hughes's pleasure in the book was tempered by James Baldwin's negative review in *The New York Times.* The young writer–himself a rising literary star–admitted to being "very fond of" at least one poem in the book, but it was the opening sentence of his review that Hughes feared would stick in readers' minds: "Every time I read Langston Hughes I am amazed all over again by his genuine gifts–and depressed that he has done so little with them."

The McCarthy Hearings and
Right-Wing Critics

Hughes received a subpoena to appear before the Senate Permanent Subcommittee on Investigations, chaired by Senator Joseph R. McCarthy, on Saturday morning, 21 March 1953. He appeared in a closed executive session of the committee on 24 March and in a public session on 26 March. Early in Hughes's first appearance, Senator Everett M. Dirksen explained the ostensible reason for Hughes's being called before the committee:

Senator DIRKSEN. You see, last year Congress appropriated $86,000,000 against an original request of $160,000,000 for the purpose of propagandizing the free world, the free system, and I think you get the general idea of what I mean, the American system. In that $86,000,000, about $21,000,000 was allocated to the Voice of America. Some was allocated to the motion pictures. Some funds were used.

Mr. HUGHES. I am sorry, I did not understand that.

Senator DIRKSEN. Motion pictures and the Voice of America, did you get that?

Mr. HUGHES. Yes, I did.

Senator DIRKSEN. And then some funds were used to purchase books to equip libraries in many sections of the world, the idea being, of course, that if people in those countries have access to American books, which allegedly delineate American objectives and American culture, that it would be useful in propagandizing our way of life and our system. The books of a number of authors have found their way into those libraries. They were purchased, of course. The question is whether or not they subserve the basic purpose we had in mind in the first instance when we appropriated money or whether they reveal a wholly contrary idea. There is some interest, of course, in your writings, because volumes of poems done by you have been acquired, and they have been placed in these libraries, ostensibly by the State Department, more particularly, I suppose I should say, by the International Information Administration. So we are exploring that matter, because it does involve the use of public funds to require that kind of literature, and the question is, is it an efficacious use of funds, does it go to the ideal that we assert, and can it logically be justified.

So we have encountered quite a number of your works, and I would be less than frank with you, sir, if I did not say that there is a question in the minds of the committee, and in the minds of a good many people, concerning the general objective of some of those poems, whether they strike a Communist, rather than an anti-Communist note.

During the executive session, Hughes was grilled on his personal beliefs as well as on the meanings of some of his works

such as "Goodbye Christ" and "Good Morning, Revolution," which he had not collected in books. In this excerpt from his testimony, Hughes is questioned by Roy Cohn, McCarthy's chief counsel.

Testimony before the Executive Session, 24 March 1953

Mr. COHN. Do you remember writing this: "Good morning, Revolution. You are the very best friend I ever had. We are going to pal around together from now on."

Mr. HUGHES. Yes, sir, I wrote that.

Mr. COHN. Did you write this, "Put one more 'S' in the USA to make it Soviet. The USA when we take control will be the USSA then."[1]

Mr. HUGHES. Yes, sir, I wrote that.

Mr. COHN. Were you kidding when you wrote those things? What did you mean by those?

Mr. HUGHES. Would you like me to give you an interpretation of that?

Mr. COHN. I would be most interested.

Senator Everett M. Dirksen of Illinois, the only senator to question Hughes during the 24 March executive session of the McCarthy subcommittee (photograph by Yale Joel/Time Life Pictures/Getty Images)

Mr. HUGHES. Very well. Will you permit me to give a full interpretation of it?

Mr. COHN. Surely.

Mr. HUGHES. All right, sir. To give a full interpretation of any piece of literary work one has to consider not only when and how it was written, but what brought it into being. The emotional and physical background that brought it into being. I, sir, was born in Joplin, Missouri. I was born a Negro. From my very earliest childhood memories, I have encountered very serious and very hurtful problems. One of my earliest childhood memories was going to the movies in Lawrence, Kansas, where we lived, and there was one motion picture theater, and I went every afternoon. It was a nickelodeon, and I had a nickel to go. One afternoon I put my nickel down and the woman pushed it back and she pointed to a sign. I was about seven years old.

Mr. COHN. I do not want to interrupt you. I do want to say this. I want to save time here. I want to concede very fully that you encounter oppression and denial of civil rights. Let us assume that, because I assume that will be the substance of what you are about to say. To save us time, what we are interested in determining for our purpose is this: Was the solution to which you turned that of the Soviet form of government?

Mr. HUGHES. Sir, you said you would permit me to give a full explanation.

Mr. COHN. I was wondering if we could not save a little time because I want to concede the background which you wrote it from was the background you wanted to describe.

Mr. HUGHES. I would much rather preserve my reputation and freedom than to save time.

Mr. COHN. Take as long as you want.

Mr. HUGHES. The woman pushed my nickel back and pointed to a sign beside the box office, and the sign said something, in effect, "Colored not admitted." It was my first revelation of the division between the American citizens. My playmates who were white and lived next door to me could go to that motion picture and I could not. I could never see a film in Lawrence again, and I lived there until I was twelve years old.

When I went to school, in the first grade, my mother moved to Topeka for a time, and my mother worked for a lawyer, and she lived in the downtown area, and she got ready for school, being a working woman naturally she wanted to send me to the nearest school, and she did, and they would not let me go to the school. There were no Negro children there. My mother had to take days off from her work, had to appeal to her employer, had to go to the school

board and finally after the school year had been open for some time she got me into the school.

I had been there only a few days when the teacher made unpleasant and derogatory remarks about Negroes and specifically seemingly pointed at myself. Some of my schoolmates stoned me on the way home from school. One of my schoolmates (and there were no other Negro children in the school), a little white boy, protected me, and I have never in all my writing career or speech career as far as I know said anything to create a division among humans, or between whites or Negroes, because I have never forgotten this kid standing up for me against these other first graders who were throwing stones at me. I have always felt from that time on—I guess that was the basis of it—that there are white people in America who can be your friend, and will be your friend, and who do not believe in the kind of things that almost every Negro who has lived in our country has experienced.

I do not want to take forever to tell you these things, but I must tell you that they have very deep emotional roots in one's childhood and one's beginnings, as I am sure any psychologist or teacher of English or student of poetry will say about any creative work. My father and my mother were not together. When I got old enough to learn why they were not together, again it was the same thing. My father as a young man, shortly after I was born, I understand, had studied law by correspondence. He applied for permission to take examination for the Bar in the state of Oklahoma where he lived, and they would not permit him. A Negro evidently could not take the examinations. You could not be a lawyer at that time in the state of Oklahoma. You know that has continued in a way right up to recent years, that we had to go all the way to the Supreme Court to get Negroes into the law school a few years ago to study law. Now you may study law and be a lawyer there.

Those things affected my childhood very much and very deeply. I missed my father. I learned he had gone away to another country because of prejudice here. When I finally met my father at the age of seventeen, he said "Never go back to the United States. Negroes are fools to live there." I didn't believe that. I loved the country I had grown up in. I was concerned with the problems and I came back here. My father wanted me to live in Mexico or Europe. I did not. I went here and went to college and my whole career has been built here.

As I grew older, I went to high school in Cleveland. I went to a high school in a very poor neighborhood and we were very poor people. My friends and associates were very poor children and many of them were of European parentage or some of them had been brought here in steerage themselves from Europe, and many of these students in the Central High School in Cleveland–and this story is told, sir, parts of it, not as fully as I want to tell you some things, in my book, *The Deep Sea,* my autobiography[2]–in the Central High School, many of these pupils began to tell me about Eugene Debs, and about the new nation and the new republic. Some of them brought them to school. I became interested in whatever I could read that Debs had written or spoken about. I never read the theoretical books of socialism or communism or the Democratic or Republican party for that matter, and so my interest in whatever may be considered political has been non-theoretical, non-sectarian, and largely really emotional and born out of my own need to find some kind of way of thinking about this whole problem of myself, segregated, poor, colored, and how I can adjust to this whole problem of helping to build America when sometimes I can not even get into a school or a lecture or a concert or in the south go to the library and

get a book out. So that has been a very large portion of the emotional background of my work, which I think is essential to one's understanding.

When I was graduated from high school, I went to live with my father for a time in Mexico, and in my father I encountered the kind of bitterness, the kind of utter psychiatric, you might say, frustration that has been expressed in some Negro novels, not in those I have written myself, I don't believe. A man who was rabidly anti-American, anti-United States. I did not sympathize with that viewpoint on the part of my own father. My feeling was this is my country, I want to live here. I want to come back here I want to make my country as beautiful as I can, as wonderful a country as I can, because I love it myself. So I went back after a year in Mexico, and I went to Columbia.

At Columbia University in New York City where I had never been before, but where I heard there was practically no prejudice, by that time wanting to be a writer and having published some papers in Negro magazines in this country, I applied for a position on

Hughes with his lawyer, Frank Reeves (left), at the public hearing of the Senate Permanent Subcommittee on Investigations, 26 March 1953 (Associated Press)

the staff of the *Spectator* newspaper, I think that they had at the time, and I think they still do. Our freshman counselor told us the various things that freshmen could apply for and do on the Columbia campus, and I wanted to do some kind of writing, and I went to the newspaper office. I was the only Negro young man or woman in the group. I can not help but think that it was due to colored prejudice that of all the kinds of assignments, and there were various assignments, sports, theater, classroom activities, debating, of all the various assignments they could pick out to assign me to cover was society news. They very well knew I could not go to dances and parties, being colored, and therefore I could bring no news, and after a short period, I was counted out of the *Spectator* group at my college.

When I went into the dormitory my first day there, I had a reservation for a room. It had been paid for in the dormitory–the correct portion was paid for– it was Fardley Hall. I was not given the room. They could not find the reservation. I had to take all of that day and a large portion of the next one to get into the dormitory. I was told later I was the first to achieve that. In other words simple little things like getting a room in a university in our country, one has to devote extraordinary methods even to this day in our country in some parts.

I am thinking of the early 1920's. I did not stay at Columbia longer than a year due in part to the various kinds of little racial prejudices that I encountered.

Senator DIRKSEN. I think, Mr. Hughes, that would be adequate emotional background.

Mr. HUGHES. No, sir, that would not explain it all, how I arrive at the point that Mr. Cohn, I believe, has asked me about.

Mr. COHN. Could you make it briefer, please?

Senator DIRKSEN. Do you think we need more background to tell what you meant by USSA?

Mr. HUGHES. I think you do, sir. Because a critical work goes out of a very deep background, it does not come in a moment. I am perfectly willing to come back and give it to you later, if you are tired.

Mr. COHN. No, we will sit here as long as you want to go on. But you are missing the point completely. What we want to determine is whether or not you meant those words when you said them.

Mr. HUGHES. Sir, whether or not I meant them depends on what they came from and out of.

Mr. COHN. Did you desire to make the United States Soviet, put one more "S" in the USA to make it Soviet. "The USA, when we take control, will be the USSA."

Mr. HUGHES. When I left Columbia, I had no money. I had $13.

Mr. COHN. Did you mean those words when you spoke them? We know the background. I want to know now, did you mean the words when you spoke them? I am not saying you should not have meant them. I am asking you—

Mr. HUGHES. Yes, sir, and you gave me the permission to give the background.

Senator DIRKSEN. That answers the question.

Mr. HUGHES. I did not say "Yes" to your question. I said you gave me the chance to give you the background to the point.

Senator DIRKSEN. We have had enough background.

Mr. COHN. Would you tell us whether or not you meant those words?

Mr. HUGHES. What words, sir?

Mr. COHN. "Put one more 'S' in the USA to make it Soviet. The USA, when we take control, will be USSA then."

Mr. HUGHES. Will you read me the whole poem?

Mr. COHN. I do not have the whole poem. Do you claim these words are out of context?

Mr. HUGHES. It is a portion of a poem.

Mr. COHN. Do you claim that these words distort the meaning?

Mr. HUGHES. That is a portion of a poem and a bar of music out of context does not give you the idea of the whole thing.

Mr. COHN. At any time in your life did you desire to make the United States of America Soviet?

Mr. HUGHES. Not by violent means, sir.

Mr. COHN. By any means.

Mr. HUGHES. By the power of the ballot, I thought it might be a possibility at one time.

Mr. COHN. Did you want to do it? Did you desire that by the ballot, not by violent means? Would you give us a yes or no answer to that?

Mr. Hughes, you say you have changed your views. You say you no longer feel the way you did in 1949 when you made that statement in defense of the Communist leaders, and said the things we read you. Will you give us some evidence of that and be frank with this committee?

Mr. HUGHES. Evidence of what, sir?

Mr. COHN. Will you be frank with this committee and give us some straightforward answers? Did you ever in your life desire the Soviet form of government over here? That is a very simple question, Mr. Hughes, for a man who wrote the things you did, and we have just started.

Mr. HUGHES. You asked me about the poem, and I would like to hear it all.

Mr. COHN. I would like to know right now whether you ever desired the Soviet form of government in this country, and I would like it answered.

Mr. HUGHES. Would you permit me to think about it?

Mr. COHN. Pardon me? Mr. Hughes, you have belonged to a list of Communist organizations a mile long. You have urged the election to public office of official candidates of the Communist party. You have signed statements to the effect that the purge trials in the Soviet Union were justified and sound and democratic. You have signed statements denying that the Soviet Union is totalitarian. You have defended the current leaders of the Communist party. You have written poems which are an invitation to revolution. You have called for the setting up of a Soviet government in this country. You have been named in statements before us as a Communist, and a member of the Communist party.

Mr. Hughes, you can surely tell us simply whether or not you ever desired the Soviet form of government in this country.

Mr. HUGHES. Yes, I did.

Mr. COHN. The answer is yes. I think if you were a little more candid with some of these things, we would get along a little better, because I think I know enough about the subject so I am not going to sit here for six days and be kidded along. I will be very much impressed if you would give us a lot of straightforward answers. It would save us a lot of time. I know you do not want to waste it any more than we do. We know every man is entitled to his views and opinions. We are trying to find out which of these works should be used in the State Department in its information program.

In the course of finding that out, we want to know whether you ever desired the Soviet form of government in this country. I believe you have said just a minute ago your answer to that is yes, is that right?

Mr. HUGHES. I did desire it, and would desire—

Mr. COHN. That is an answer. That is what we want. I believe your statement before was that you desired it, but not by violent means, is that right?

Mr. HUGHES. Yes, sir. That would be correct.

Mr. COHN. What did you mean when you said "Good morning, Revolution, you are the very best friend I ever had. We are going to pal around together from now on."

Does not revolution imply violent means?

Mr. HUGHES. Not necessarily, sir. I think it means a change like the industrial revolution.

Am I Excused Now?

At the public session of his testimony on 26 March 1953, Hughes admitted to chief counsel Roy Cohn that there was a period of his life when he had believed in the Soviet form of government.

Mr. Cohn. And when did that period end?
Mr. Hughes. There was no abrupt ending, but I would say, that roughly the beginnings of my sympathies with Soviet ideology were coincident with the Scottsboro case, the American Depression, and that they ran through for some ten or twelve years or more, certainly up to the Nazi-Soviet Pact, and perhaps, in relation to some aspects of the Soviet ideology, further, because we were allies, you know, with the Soviet Union during the war. So some aspects of my writing would reflect that relationship, that war relationship.
Mr. Cohn. And, as a matter of fact, when would you say you completely broke with the Soviet ideology?
Mr. Hughes. I would say a complete reorientation of my thinking and emotional feelings occurred roughly four or five years ago.

Later, in an interchange with Senator McCarthy, Hughes admitted that some of his books purchased by the information program followed the Communist line and that he was "amazed" that they had been approved by the government. McCarthy had "Goodbye Christ" entered into the record but did not have it read aloud: "As far as I know, this was not in any of the books purchased by the information program. This is merely included in the record on request, to show the type of thinking of Mr. Hughes at that time, the type of writings which were being purchased." The hearing ended with Hughes's thanking the committee for its "courtesy and friendliness" and asking, "Am I excused now?"

Mr. COHN. That is an answer. When you used the word "revolution" you were using it in a very broad sense, and meaning a change, is that right?

Mr. HUGHES. That is right, sir. . . .
—*Executive Sessions of the Senate Permanent Subcommittee on Investigations of the Committee on Government Operations,* volume 2, Eighty-Third Congress, First Session (Washington: U.S. Government Printing Office, 1953), pp. 972–998

1. In the public hearing on March 26, Senator McClellan asked: "May I inquire of counsel if you are quoting from books or works of the author that are now in the library?"
MR. COHN. "No; this one poem I quoted, 'Put Another "S" in the USA to make it Soviet' is as far as we know not in any poems in the collection in the information centers."
2. Langston Hughes, *The Big Sea* (New York: Alfred A. Knopf, 1940).

* * *

Although Hughes's cooperation with Senator McCarthy temporarily blunted conservative criticism, he was never able to wholly distance himself from the radicalism of his youth. Detractors such as Elizabeth Staples continued to dredge up his allegedly subversive writings and activities in articles such as this for the January 1959 issue of American Mercury.

Langston Hughes: Malevolent Force

Two recent happenings prompt and justify definitive research on Langston Hughes, longtime contributor to publications in America.

One is that various denominations of Protestant churches are proceeding, as by a prearranged signal, to recommend Hughes' writings for intensive study by church groups. For example, the Methodist Church, strong arm of the National Council of Churches, urges specific supplemental reading from Langston Hughes in its official study book for WSCS classes, entitled *The Kingdom Beyond Caste,* by Liston Pope (published in 1957 by the Friendship Press, New York). This is but one of many similar recommendations by various sects, while some college

Senator Joseph R. McCarthy of Wisconsin (foreground) and his chief counsel, Roy Cohn (photograph by Hank Walker/Time Life Pictures/Getty Images)

courses have stamped this author with their seal of approval for undergraduate perusal. In view of these endorsements, friends of organized Protestantism and of higher education might well do a little independent investigating.

Concurrently, a 500-page book has popped off the Braziller Press, New York, about which some astonishing review opinion has been printed. Twitters one reviewer: "This versatile Negro . . . handsome cosmopolite . . . has earned the respect and admiration of both races." (From book review by Hermes Nye, p. 15, Roundup Section, *Dallas Times Herald,* July 27, 1958.)

The colorful jacket on the book reads, "*The Langston Hughes Reader*–Novels, Stories, Plays, Autobiographies, Poems, Songs, Blues, Pageant Articles, Speeches." The bulky volume is priced at $5.95.

We are not informed how many "Autobiographies" Hughes can boast, and must wonder if the *Reader* inadvertently omitted some of them. For unknown reasons, one notable excision is that of his celebrated *vers libre,* "Goodbye, Christ," which has been so widely circulated as not to need reproduction here. It may be found, produced in sworn testimony before the Special Committee on Un-American Activities, Vol. 2, page 1366; also in House Special Committee Report No. 2681, on Tax-Exempt Foundations, 83rd Congress, Second Session, pp. 293–294; and is referred to on pp. 41–42 of House Document No. 136, *One Hundred Things You Should Know About Communism.*

Is it possible that the publisher, or someone at the helm, decided that a little scrubbing-up of Hughes' literary offerings was in order? If so, an additional can of strong cleansing powder would have been a good investment.

We acknowledge perforce that the current mode of fiction, poetry, and plays call for loading the text, to varying degrees, with depravities, obscenities, and miscellaneous, malodorous barnyard dirt. Hughes goes far beyond the call of duty in piling filth on filth.

A critic is both embarrassed and handicapped in trying to assess the devious Langston Hughes expression. For daring to quote verbatim, one could justly be sued. He is master of the sly and wily innuendo–the remark that is either innocent or guilty, depending on the reader's "wised up" reaction. This, in the judgment of some mature yet not hidebound guardians of developing intellects, makes the most unworthy, most unrewarding type of reading matter which can be placed in the hands of inquiring youth.

Young readers, of course, are loath to let the *double entendre* go "over their heads." They will focus intently, in order to get "the point" (which random reading of a page or two in the *Reader* will convince them is lurking, veiled or unveiled, in almost every paragraph). After they have comprehended "the point," they are apt to plume themselves on being clever; thus the unwholesome interpretation will be impressed upon their plastic minds for keeps.

The part-time joy and jollity of Hughes, as exemplified particularly in his short stories, are thinly spread over bitter, thrice bitter, bedrock sarcasm and hatred. The Negroes he describes are singularly devoid of dignity and race pride.

In a portion of the "Autobiographies," Hughes tells of a trip he made to Africa, at age 21, as busboy on a freighter. He realistically conveys the thrill he felt on visiting the land of his forefathers. The excerpts, however, contain no record of his conclusions as to whether or not he thinks that several generations of American life have given him advantages over those enjoyed by his distant cousins who still inhabit the Dark Continent. To this obvious question, however, his agile mind must have had a ready answer.

He is quick to seize on the term "race relations" to prove that thoroughgoing "race relations" would rest on the prerequisite of mating and miscegenation.

His pageant, "The Glory of Negro History," omits a significant factor. When telling of the captive black men and women who, in the early seventeenth century, began to be transported from Africa as slaves, Hughes misses a good chance to inform his audience that those poor wretches were sold into bondage by their own greedy and cruel African chiefs, who rounded up unwanted and troublesome tribesmen and sold them as "blackbirds," thus constituting themselves first offenders in the opprobrious slave traffic.

Admittedly, Hughes presents a convincing picture, almost a documentary one, of the Negro and Negroid population in America. His fictional characters stride through the pages; they are real, not dreamed. But oh, what traits emerge! Quite matter-of-factly he records Negro qualities and outlook for Leftist critics to accept and rave over. Commonplace are such lines as, "He didn't remember his father," "In mid-June, her illegitimate kid was born," and "He's mighty damn white for a nigger chile." The tone thereby established as normal fits directly into the pattern of statism, wherein family ties, traditions and associations are hacked down to the irreducible minimum.

His short story, "Guitar," from the collection, *Not Without Laughter,* is a perfect reproduction of spontaneous musical utterance, done without bitterness and yielding up the very heart of transplanted primitive Negro artistry. It's a rare find for a folklorist, yet does not compensate for the viciousness and vulgarity of his work as a whole. And even in this almost-admirable fragment is embedded a violent slap at the minds of

"white folks" who will discern evil where it exists; of course the fault is in their own minds, even in the face of reality. This is a perverted conception if ever there was one. Apparently, he puts it over among a certain coterie of Langston Hughes promoters.

Much has been left out of this comprehensive volume.

Not mentioned is the long and constant pro-Communist record of Langston Hughes. His citations run into fantastic numbers. Here are a few:

The Daily Worker, September 14, 1932, named Hughes as one of the signers of a "Call for Support of the Communist Party National Elections and Its Candidates." The same newspaper, issue of February 7, 1949, reported that Langston Hughes, Negro people's poet, defends the Communist leaders on trial; and warns the Negro people that "they too are being tried," in his column in the current issue of the Chicago *Defender.* The article further quoted Hughes as declaring, "If the 12 Communists are sent to jail, in a little while they will send Negroes to jail simply for being Negroes, and to concentration camps just for being colored." (Quoted from "Tax-Exempt Foundations," House Report No. 2681.) The spirit of this broadside is clearly akin to that prevailing in his prose and poetry.

Langston Hughes endorsed the drive of Friends of the Abraham Lincoln Brigade, and went to Spain in 1937 as correspondent for a Cuban newspaper. His account of this trip in the *Reader* is openly sympathetic to the Loyalist-Communists and is found on pages 418–461.

Through the years his works have been enthusiastically reviewed by the *Daily Worker,* and his books have been advertised and sold by the Workers Book Shop.

He has been identified as a Communist Party member by Manning Johnson and by Louis Budenz, under oath. On July 8, 1953, Manning Johnson testified to that effect (pp. 2174, 2175, U.S. Government publication No. 33909, House Investigation of Communist Activities in New York City Area, Part 7. Verified on page 69, February 6, 1954, in Annual House Report No. 1192, on Un-American Activities).

An allegation of Hughes' Communist Party membership appears in the 1944 Appendix, Part IX, report of the Special House Committee on Un-American Committees, Martin Dies, chairman. On Page 261 the appendix states that "the National Citizens Political Action Committee has 141 members. Out of this number, 83 per cent have records of affiliation with Communist and Communist front organizations." On Page 262, the report goes on to say: "So far as is known, only one of Hillman's NCPAC members has been a card-holding member of the Communist Party: namely, Langston Hughes."

Hughes signed a "message" which called upon the United States Congress to oppose renewal of the House Un-American Activities Committee (p. 29, Eleventh Report, California Senate Investigating Committee on Education, 1953).

Hughes was one of a score of Communists and pro-Communists who gathered in New York in 1937 to celebrate the adoption of the new Constitution of Soviet Russia (p. 24, Fourteenth Report, California Senate Investigating Committee on Education, 1956).

House Report No. 378 on the Communist "Peace" Offensive, a "Campaign to Disarm and Defeat the United States, April 1, 1951, mentions Langston Hughes among individuals who have been affiliated with such a significant number of Communist fronts that they may be said to constitute a body of reliable and consistent supporters of Communist organizations."

As far back as March, 1949, Hughes had already been cited for affiliation in more than 70 Communist-front organizations, according to "Review of the Scientific and Cultural Conference for World Peace," released by the House Committee on Un-American Activities, March 25, 26 and 27, 1949, page 18.

In the testimony of G. Bromley Oxnam, July 21, 1953, at a Hearing before the House Committee on Un-American Activities, Hughes shows up as a member of the American League for Peace and Democracy (page 3639) and as a signer of the "message" to the House of Representatives opposing renewal of the Dies Committee (page 3661).

Also, Hughes rejoices in 25 separate listings for subversive or Communist-front activities in the 1948 volume, Fourth Report, Un-American Activities in California (indexed).

In tracing his affiliations, it is pitiable to note that Hughes is never an officer in these organizations, is seldom even a sponsor at a dinner party, but is just another member, another signer, another statistic—a mere private in the rear ranks. For so assiduous a worker, this would seem to betray a lack of proper recognition, perhaps even a touch of—ah, well, discrimination.

His friends, as claimed in the autobiographical data, include such well-known, many-splendored Left-Wingers as Paul and "Essie" Robeson, Theodore Dreiser, Rev. Clayton Powell, Mary McLeod Bethune, Pearl Buck, Clarence Darrow, Salvador Dali, Aaron Douglas (mentioned in the Jack McMichael Hearing), Zora Neale Hurston, Ralph Bunche, and many more—for Hughes is a name-dropper.

A United States Senate hearing on Government Operations, dated March 24, 25 and 26, 1953 (Government Document No. 33616), contains nine pages of Langston Hughes' testimony, in which he explains (apparently to the satisfaction of all) that some of his most un-American writings were placed in the utterances of his fictional character, Simple, therefore could not be construed as unpatriotic. He further states under oath that he "never actually joined the Communist Party," although he admits that he wrote some books which "very largely followed at times some aspects of the Communist line, reflecting my sympathy with them." (We trust that his listeners made due allowance for the fact that Langston Hughes is widely accepted as a top-flight humorist!) The foregoing testimony brings to a surprising climax events of his career.

        —American Mercury, 88 (January 1959): 46–50

Critic, Translator, and Teacher

In this interview for Phylon *Hughes discusses the opportunities the Harlem Renaissance created for African American writers, while noting that the television, movie, and radio industries largely ignore black talent.*

Some Practical Observations: A Colloquy

Editors: Mr. Hughes, very few Negro writers in America have chosen, or have felt themselves able to choose, writing as their sole occupation as you have. What has being a Negro meant for you as a writer?

Hughes: Well, for one thing, I think it's pretty obvious that the bulk of my work stems directly from the life of the Negro in America. Since the major aims of my work have been to interpret and comment upon Negro life, and its relations to the problems of Democracy, a major satisfaction for me has been the assurance given me by my readers that I have succeeded in some measure—especially in those areas lightly touched upon, if at all, by the writers who preceded me.

Editors: You certainly must have been asked this next question before: From this vantage point, and as one of the major figures in the "Negro Renaissance," what would you say as to the value of the "Renaissance?" Is there any real truth in the suggestion advanced by some that the "Renaissance" was in certain respects actually a harmful thing for the Negro writer?

Hughes: My feeling would be that the "Renaissance" represented a positive value mainly. It certainly helped a great deal by focusing attention on Negro writers and on literature about Negroes for some six or eight years. It provided a springboard for young Negro writers and for those who wanted to write about Negroes. That impetus in many cases has continued into the present.

Now there may have been certain false values which tended at the time to be over-stressed—perhaps

DODD, MEAD & COMPANY
432 FOURTH AVENUE · NEW YORK 16, N.Y.
PUBLISHERS

June 25, 1952

Dear Mr. Hughes:

We have a series of juvenile books
called the FAMOUS books. I am enclosing a tear
sheet from our catalog which will give you an
idea of them. They are short – they run about
30,000 words apiece and as a rule there is a
portrait photograph of each individual.

Now we are thinking it would be a good
idea to do one called FAMOUS NEGRO AMERICANS.
Would you be interested in authoring it? Or, if
you are too busy, would you like to suggest a
friend who might do the job? Of course it is not
necessary to have a Negro author. In some ways
it might be better not to, but, on the whole, I
think it would add to the effectiveness of the
book.

Yours sincerely,

Edward H. Dodd, Jr.

Mr. Langston Hughes,
20 East 127th Street,
New York, N. Y.

EHD/MCD

*Letter initiating the relationship between Hughes and Dodd, Mead. Hughes wrote three "Famous Negro" books for
children that were published by the company in the 1950s (Langston Hughes Collection, Schomburg
Center for Research in Black Culture, New York Public Library).*

Dust jacket for the first of Hughes's six books in the "First Book" series for Franklin Watts, published in 1952 (Langston Hughes Papers, Yale Collection of American Literature, Beinecke Rare Book and Manuscript Library)

The Famous Negro Books

Hughes responded quickly to the opportunity to write a children's book about prominent African Americans. Hughes published Famous American Negroes *in 1954 and two more such books for Dodd, Mead:* Famous Negro Music Makers *(1955) and* Famous Negro Heroes of America *(1958). According to biographer Arnold Rampersad, Hughes was troubled by the insistence of the company that he remove from the texts most references to overt racism and avoid figures who might be considered radical or subversive.*

Hughes to Edward H. Dodd Jr., 28 June 1952

Dear Mr. Dodd,

Thank you for thinking of me concerning your proposed book, FAMOUS AMERICAN NEGROES. I would indeed be interested in writing it.

I have recently done a book for Franklin Watts, Inc., as a part of their FIRST BOOKS series, THE FIRST BOOK OF NEGROES, for the 7 to 12 age group, which heads their fall catalogue. It's only 30 pages—running from ancient Africa to right now. So when Mrs. Piel, the Librarian at City and Country School read the manuscript for me, her main comment was regret that the book couldn't be larger and have more space devoted to great Negro personalities. Which is just what your book would permit.

Mrs. Piel feels that there is a real need, particularly on the part of teachers and librarians, for material on Negroes suitable for young people. And I know in the South, Negro teachers are always asking for additional books, particularly around Negro History Week time.

Would you like to have me come down and talk to you about this? If so, let me know when. I have to go up to Yale on Tuesday. But Thursday, July 3rd, is open. Or almost anytime after the 4th.

I've been in the country up to yesterday, so didn't have a chance to talk with you about Marion Palfi's book either—which we can do when I come down.

Arna Bontemps is in town at the Algonquin, just phoned me.

I'll be looking for a word from you. If you'd rather phone, best time is after two P.M.

Sincerely Yours,
Langston Hughes

—Langston Hughes Papers, James Weldon Johnson Collection in the Yale Collection of American Literature, Beinecke Rare Book and Manuscript Library

the primitivism and that business of the "color" of Negro life was overdone. But that kind of exaggeration is inevitable, and I doubt that any real harm was done. Those of us who were serious about writing weren't actually affected very much. We knew what we were doing and what we wanted to do. So we went ahead with our work, and whatever false emphasis there was didn't really disturb us.

Editors: You have behind you well over two decades of varied and substantial achievement. How would you say the general situation has changed for the Negro author in America since you began writing?

Hughes: Oh, in several ways, but the most striking change I would say has occurred in the magazine world. In the past twenty years—and in the case of some publications, in the past five years or so—the field of magazine writing has opened up considerably. For instance, when I first started writing, it was said that the *Saturday Evening Post* would not accept work written by Negroes. Whether or not the *Post* actually followed such a policy, it did seem to be true of certain other magazines. Yet in recent years the *Post* has run pieces by Zora Neale Hurston and Walter White, as well as some of my own work; and in many major magazines articles and stories which take something other than the Octavus Roy Cohen line now appear frequently.

Editors: Would you say that this is one of the gains which may in part be attributed to the "Renaissance"?

Hughes: I think so—though, of course, there are other factors in the picture, including two which I think are often overlooked in accounting for the increased activity among Negro writers and the widening audience to which these writers may address themselves. But it can hardly be disputed that the "Renaissance" did a great deal to make possible a public willing to accept Negro problems and Negro art.

Editors: You spoke just now of two factors which tend to be overlooked. What are they?

Hughes: The first of these is the international fame which Negroes in fields other than literature have won in the last fifteen years or so. The world renown won by such diverse figures as Joe Louis, Marian Anderson, Duke Ellington, and Ralph Bunche has created greater interest abroad in the American Negro. I think this has helped to bring about the present situation in which we find books by Negro writers in this country being translated into other languages and reaching an international audience.

Another factor which will, I believe, become increasingly important is the growth in the number of good Negro bookshops and efficient booksellers. Negroes operate at least four first-rate bookstores in New York; there is at least one such bookstore in Atlanta run by Negroes, and this is true of other cities. This, in my opinion, is one of the healthiest developments which could have occurred for the Negro writer and for the Negro reading public.

Editors: We are inclined to agree with you on that—though as difficult to analyze statistically as the influence of the labor and liberal movements in this country—the factors you cite must undoubtedly be recognized as gains for the Negro writer. Granted these and other gains and the access to a wider reading public, in which literary areas would you say Negroes have done the best work in recent years?

Hughes: In the novel and in poetry, I should think. We've had Wright, and Motley, and Ann Petry, and Yerby in the novel. And in addition to the older poets still writing there is a promising group coming along in Bruce McWright, Myron O'Higgins, Margaret Walker, and M. Carl Holman. And, of course, Gwendolyn Brooks, the Pulitzer poet. But here I'm thinking mainly of poets who haven't yet published books. There are three or four good young poets in this category, like Russell Atkins, whose work appeared in *The Poetry of the Negro.*

And in fiction, among those who haven't yet brought out books, there is a really significant talent in Ralph Ellison.

Editors: What about the theatre? You probably have done as much in the theatre as any other contemporary Negro writer. Why haven't there been more plays by Negro authors?

Hughes: We've had some plays, of course. There's Theodore Ward, whom you know of—though he hasn't had any real "success" yet. And George Norford, who had a comedy done by the Group Theatre last year. We haven't made too much progress as writers in the theatre—mainly because it's pretty hard to have professional contacts. Such contacts are indispensable to success in modern playwriting and it's difficult to make headway when the opportunities for achieving the contacts are so limited.

Editors: The lag then, if we may call it that, in playwriting seems due to this difficulty in getting "inside"—a problem which does not seem to be restricted to Negro playwrights alone. The difference may be one of degree.

But are there any other points at which the Negro writer seems not to be making any significant contribution?

Hughes: Well, let me put it this way: it seems to me that there is a crying need for good literary criticism. I can't give the reasons for it, but our great deficiency is this dearth of really good critics. We have almost no books of literary criticism—certainly not recent, competently-done books.

And it's not just literary essays, and books of criticism which are lacking. There is a need for good journalistic articles and for non-fiction works in many fields. In history and in sociology the record is better than elsewhere. Frazier, John Hope Franklin, Cayton, Drake, and others, have done fine work here. I hope to see more good writing in these and other fields.

Editors: The almost inevitable question in any discussion of this kind makes its appearance now: Are there any special problems which face the Negro writer here in America which the white writer is not likely to encounter?

Hughes: I think so. It's pretty clear by now, for example, that the Negro writer has to work especially hard to avoid the appearance of propaganda. Then there is the hypersensitivity arising from the Negro's situation in this country which causes him to take offense at certain realistic portrayals of Negro life.

Editors: There are those problems arising from his materials and his audience, then. But what of marketing problems? It has been suggested, for example, that Negro authors sometimes meet with special difficulties in selling manuscripts. It has even been charged that publishers have insisted on editing of the kind which was, in effect, censorship based on prejudice, or on the willingness to kowtow to the prejudiced reader in the interest of sales.

Hughes: That the Negro writer marketing the fruits of his talent meets with problems which the white writer does not face, I would agree. I would not agree that the field of book publishing is actually involved. Other experienced Negro writers would testify, I believe, that when a writer has done a good book, the publisher usually tends not to alter or limit it in any way—and certainly not with racial considerations in mind.

Editors: If the book publishers deserve a clean bill of health, then where does the Negro writer meet with his "special problems?"

Hughes: The real limitations are in the "tributary" fields where race is definitely a handicapping factor. Hollywood is the Number One example of this, using practically no Negroes as writers. Radio also is a very limited field for the author who happens to be a Negro. Television, while newer, seems no more likely to be hospitable to Negro writers.

All this means, of course, that unless he is fortunate enough to produce best-sellers the Negro who wishes to write must usually supplement his writing by some occupation which is generally not very closely related to writing. If Negro publications could be, or would be, more generous in the fees paid (or which they should pay) Negro writers, there would be an improvement in the quality of these publications and more Negro writers would be able to earn a living from writing, rather than from teaching and other activities. Failing that, the Negro writer turns in vain to the editorial staffs of other American magazines and of publishing houses. These almost never hire Negroes. Negro book reviewers—even for such publications as the *Times,* the *Herald-Tribune,* and the *Saturday Review of Literature*—are limited by the fact that they are usually given only books about Negroes or by Negroes to review.

Another important source of income for most authors—that of lecturing—is severely limited if the author happens to be a Negro. Only the most liberal women's clubs care to have Negro lecturers—so about seventy-five or eighty per cent of this field is closed. And you can count on your hands the white colleges in the southern and border states of this country which will invite Negroes to lecture.

Editors: What you have just said is good strong medicine. And it is certainly not with any desire to palliate it that we pose our final question: As you consider the Negro writer in the field of contemporary letters, what do you find most heartening?

Hughes: There are, as I think I have indicated by some of the things I said earlier, many encouraging aspects which were not present twenty, or ten, or even five years ago. The most heartening thing for me, however, is to see Negroes writing works in the general American field, rather than dwelling on Negro themes solely. Good writing can be done on almost any theme—and I have been pleased to see Motley, Yerby, Petry and Dorothy West presenting in their various ways non-Negro subjects. Dunbar, of course, and others, wrote so-called "white" stories, but until this particular period there have not been so many Negroes writing of characters not drawn from their own race.

Edna Ferber originally wrote stories of Jewish life, but she broadened her perspective and went on to write *So Big, Show Boat* and *Cimarron.* I think we are headed in the direction of similar and perhaps superior achievement.

—*Phylon,* 11 (Winter 1950): 307–311

* * *

Hughes wrote this introduction for a 1952 edition of Harriet Beecher Stowe's Uncle Tom's Cabin *(1852).*

Introduction to *Uncle Tom's Cabin*

The first publisher of *Uncle Tom's Cabin* was so fearful of not making his money back from the book that he wanted Harriet Beecher Stowe to share half the expenses of publication, offering in return to give her half the income, if any. The author's husband, however, insisted on what he felt to be a more businesslike arrangement, a ten per cent royalty to his wife. Mrs. Stowe, happy to have her book published at all, since another publisher had unequivocally turned it down as being unlikely to sell, simply sighed, "I hope it will make enough so I may have a silk dress."

Two days after its publication in Boston on March 20, 1852, the entire first edition of 5000 copies had been exhausted. Four months after publication Mrs. Stowe's royalties amounted to $10,000. Within a year 300,000 copies had been sold in America and 150,000 in England. Six months after the book's appearance, George L. Aiken's dramatization of *Uncle Tom's Cabin* opened in Troy and ran for 100 performances in that small town, moving on to New York City for 350 performances at the National Theatre. At one time as many as four companies were performing it simultaneously in New York, sometimes giving three shows a day, so great were the crowds. It continued to be presented by various companies throughout the country, as America's most popular play, each season for the next eighty years. Meanwhile the book, translated into every civilized language from Welch to Bengali, became the world's second best seller, outranked only by the Bible.

Uncle Tom's Cabin was the most cussed and discussed book of its time. Tolstoy termed it a great work of literature "flowing from love of God and man." George Sand was so moved by it that she voluntarily offered to write the introduction to its first French edition. Longfellow, Dickens, Macaulay, Heine praised it. But others damned it as vicious propaganda, bad art, cheap melodrama, and factually a tissue of lies. The truth of the matter is that *Uncle Tom's Cabin* in 1852 was not merely a book. It was a flash, as Frederick Douglass put it, to "light a million camp fires in front of the embattled hosts of slavery." It was an appeal to the consciences of all free men to look upon bondage as a crime. It was a call to action as timely as a newly printed handbill or a newspaper headline. During the Civil War, when Abraham Lincoln met Harriet Beecher Stowe at the White House he said, "So this is the little lady who started this big war." No doubt he smiled, but Lincoln knew that thousands of men who had voted for him had read *Uncle Tom's Cabin,* and many a Union soldier must have remembered it as he marched, for the book was a moral battle cry.

But in addition *Uncle Tom's Cabin* also happened to be a good story, exciting in incident, sharp in characterization, and threaded with humor. That is why it still lives. No reader ever forgets Simon Legree, Little Eva, Miss Ophelia, Eliza, or Uncle Tom. And Topsy, who in cartoons and theatre later became a caricature, is in the book not only funny but human. Harriet Beecher Stowe, who had six children, created out of mother love her Eva, her Topsy, Eliza's baby, Harry, and the other unforgettable children in her book. And perhaps because her father, Lyman Beecher, was a Congregational minister and she had grown up on the Bible, her novel, as Carl Sandburg has described it, became in essence the story of a gentle black Christ who turned the other cheek, Uncle Tom, with Golgotha a place south of the Ohio River, a whipping post instead of the Cross, and a plantation as the background of the passion and the death. Once when asked how her book came into being, Harriet Beecher Stowe said, "God wrote it."

The book began in 1851 in a series of sketches in a paper called *The National Era.* With a baby to nurse, other children to attend, and a house to manage, Mrs. Stowe wrote by sheer determination. Her husband was Professor of Natural and Revealed Religion at Bowdoin College in Maine. They were poor. Her friends and neighbors looked askance upon a woman who aspired to any sort of career outside the home, who took sides in national controversies, or participated in political issues. Slavery was a political issue. But Harriet Beecher Stowe had grown up in Cincinnati where she had seen slavery at first hand just across the river in Kentucky. She had helped her brother, Henry Ward Beecher, edit a paper which was forbidden in some parts of the South. She had once aided a Negro woman to escape from a pursuing master. So she had already taken sides.

When she was almost forty she wrote a friend, "I feel now that the time is come when even a woman or a child who can speak a word for freedom and humanity is bound to speak. The Carthaginian women in the last peril of their state cut off their hair for bow-strings to give the defenders of their country, and such peril and shame as now hangs over this country is worse than Roman slavery. I hope every woman who can write will not be silent." So she began to write *Uncle Tom's Cabin.*

When the book appeared in England Queen Victoria wrote Mrs. Stowe a note of gratitude, and in London an overflow meeting of 5000 persons greeted the author at Exeter Hall on her first trip abroad. But our American Ambassador, James Buchanan, frowned upon such anti-slavery demonstrations and did not consider Mrs. Stowe's appearance at the London meeting in the best interests of our country. At home Northern papers such as the New York *Journal of Commerce* and Southern papers like the *Alabama Planter* denounced the

SUICIDE AS A SOLUTION

This slave mother leaped into the Red River with her child rather than
see him traded for a keg of whiskey. Suicide was not uncommon among
slaves. On the voyage from Africa some captains never allowed their
cargo above decks for, chained together at the ankles as they were, one
or two might make for the rail, leap into the ocean, and drag a whole
group down with them. In the hole, having no other way to die, some
are reported to have swallowed their own tongues. Others starved themselves to death. Illustration by George Cruikshank for the English
edition of *Uncle Tom's Cabin*.

Hughes's text for an illustration in the 1952 edition of Uncle Tom's Cabin *he introduced*
(Thomas Cooper Library, University of South Carolina)

book. A free Negro in Maryland received ten years in prison for possessing it. A book dealer in Mobile was hounded from the city for selling it. When Mrs. Stowe and her husband returned to Brunswick, Maine, from Europe, they found hundreds of scurrilous and even obscene letters attacking both the book and its author. And one day Mrs. Stowe opened a package that came in the mails, and a black human ear tumbled out.

In 1853 Mrs. Stowe published *A Key to Uncle Tom's Cabin* documenting and giving sources for the material relating to the horrors of slavery in her book. But readers around the world and throughout the years have not needed this "Key" to understand her book, nor to be moved by it to laughter and to tears. The love and warmth and humanity that went into its writing keep it alive a century later from Bombay to Boston.

–"Introduction," in *Uncle Tom's Cabin* (New York: Dodd, Mead, 1952)

* * *

Published in early 1953, James Baldwin's first novel, Go Tell It on the Mountain, *treats a day in the lives of Harlem church members and, through flashbacks, the histories of their forebears. Hughes commented on the novel in this letter, at one point comparing Baldwin's writing to that of Willard Motley, an African American journalist, essayist, and novelist best known for his 1947 naturalistic novel,* Knock on Any Door.

Hughes to Arna Bontemps, 18 February 1953

Dear Arna,

If you'll tell me what Dick Wright's book is like (since I haven't it) I'll tell you about James Baldwin's *Go Tell It on the Mountain* which I've just finished: If it were written by Zora Hurston with her feeling for the folk idiom, it would probably be a *quite* wonderful book. Baldwin over-writes and over-poeticizes in images way over the heads of the folks supposedly thinking them–often beautiful writing in itself–but frequently out of character– although it might be as the people *would* think if they *could* think that way. Which makes it seem like an "art" book about folks who aren't "art" folks. That and the too frequent use of flashbacks (a la Lillian Smith's "Strange Fruit") slows the book down to a sleepy pace each time the story seems to be about to start to go somewhere. And everyone is so fear-ridden and frustrated and "sorry" that they might as well have all died a-borning. Out of all that religion SOMEbody ought to triumph somewhere in it, but nary soul does. If it is meant to show the futility of religion, then it should be sharper and clearer and not so muddy and pretty and poetic and exalted without being exalting. It's a low-down story in a velvet bag–and a Knopf binding. Willard Motley-like

writing without his heart-breaking characters fitting the poetry Motley weaves around them. As Motley's does, but Baldwin's don't. Has a feeling of writing-for-writing's-sake quality. I'd hoped it would be (and wish it were) a more cohesive whole with the words and the people belonging to each other. The words here belong more to the author. Although there are one or two VERY good sections, it is on the whole not unlike "John Brown's Body" (stage version, not the poem itself) which I saw last night and which nearly wore me down trying to bear up and look cultural in a hot crowded theatre 7th row orchestra with a party of folks who'd paid an ENORMOUS price for benefit tickets and had just et an enormous dinner starting with whole lobsters as just the first course, and running on down to demi tasses and brandy. With that and Baldwin's book, I've had my culture for the YEAR. When folks are dealing with God and John Brown there ought to be *fire* and FIREWORKS too, not just endlessly stretching taffy that lops over and pulls out again and declamation and taffy colored lights and heads held noble and all of it kind of sticky. If you've read it,* tell me what you think. Also about Dick's book.

Got your check for the London transcriptions, so will now pay that little bill. . . . Read and returned the "Simple" proofs. . . . . . Saw the Blacks yesterday at a cocktail party (heads of Doubleday) and they're still remembering our FINE "Poetry of the Negro" party that you missed. Also saw Buck Moon at a PEN party (did I tell you) and he's with Collier's. . . . . And did I tell you some Reading Circle in Midwest is buying 1500 "First Book of Negroes"? . . . . . And waded through my first big snow of season at Brandeis U. the other day where there are 7 Negroes amidst all those of "the other persuasion". Had a pleasant half hour with Ludwig Lewisohn at his place there. I have now uttered my last public word for the season–in fact, the whole YEAR. Folks will just have to buy my records the rest of 1953. . . . . . Jane White and Bill Marshall are getting ready to do "readings" of plays and things, too,–just like white folks–which delights me. But I swear I do not believe I am going–that is, not until the "far-away voice" in poetry is strangled. *Go Tell It on the Mountain* should go swell done that way. (At $8.80 a seat). But it ain't my meat. I wish he had collaborated with Zora.

Sincerely yours truly,
Lang

*Theme: It's one-day (his birthday) in-the-life-of-a-14-year-old boy–plus all the lives of those around him–set in and seen largely through the religious estascy of an all-night store-front church meeting.

–*Arna Bontemps–Langston Hughes Letters, 1925–1967,* edited by Charles H. Nichols (New York: Dodd, Mead, 1980), pp. 302–303

* * *

Begun 1 A.M. August 4m 1953.
FIRST DRAFT.

Langston Hughes

PHILLIS WHEATLEY

Whose ~~Poems~~ *Poetry* George Washington ~~Wrote~~ *Praised*

Born about 1753—Died 1784

Senegal.
She was born in/~~MMMMMMMM~~ We do not know what her African name was. She
in 1761 ~~MMMMMM~~
was only about seven years old when/she was brought to Boston/as a slave and sold
no one~~MMMM~~ spoke
to a tailor named John Wheatley. Since/~~MMMMM~~/in Boston ~~MMMMMMM~~/her language, nor
she English, so nobody in America what it was.
/she did not understand when asked her name,/~~MMMMMMM~~ ever knew. But the Wheatleys

called her Phillis, and gave her their last name, Wheatley. Before she was twenty-
her
one ~~MMM~~/name, Phillis Wheatley, was famous throughout the Colonies and in England.

She became one of the best known poets of her time.

Phillis
It happened that she had a kind mistress who, seeing that ~~MMM~~/was a bright little
her
girl, soon taught ~~MMMMMM~~/to read and write. In those days in many parts of America
it was against the law, and certainly contrary to custom, to teach slaves to read and
write. Nevertheless, a number of slaves did so learn. And some of them, even before
had
Phillis/published her poems, became known as writers. ~~MMMMMMMMMMMMMMMMMMMMMMM~~
verses, "Bars Fight", a
A colored woman named Lucy Terry wrote, among other/~~MMMMMMM~~ vivid rhymed account of
Deerfield, Massachusetts, Negro in bondage,
an Indian raid on/~~MMMMMMM~~ in 1746. ~~MMMMMMMMMMMM~~ Another ~~MMMMM~~/Jupiter MM

Hammond, began publishing his poems as broadsides in Queens Village, Long Island, MM

~~MMMMMMMMMMMMMMMMMMMMMMMMMMMMMMMMMMMMMMMMMMM~~ in 1760. And eighteen
whom he had never met
years later he paid tribute to a younger slave poet/in "A Poetical Address to Phillis

Wheatley".

with its
When the ship,~~MMMMMMMMMMM~~/cargo of slaves ~~MMMMMMMMMMMMM~~ that included

the little girl whose name was to be Phillis, dropped anchor in Boston harbor, the

~~MMMMMMMMMMMMMMMMMMMMMMMMMMMMMMMMMMMMMMMMMM~~ Thirteen Colonies
Soldiers of the~~MMMMMMMMM~~ *Praised*
were becoming ever more resentful of ~~British~~ domination. ~~When Phillis was in her~~
Soldiers of King Charles (?) patrolled the streets of Boston. When Phillis was in her
early teens, a group of citizens clashed with these/soldiers Near Fanueil Hall. Among
Bostonians *British*
the ~~Americans~~ was a Negro seaman named ~~MMMMMM~~ Crispus Attucks. When the ~~MMMMMMM~~

Redcoats fired, Crispus Attucks was the first to ~~MMMMMM~~ *fall.* Today there is *a*

monument to his memory in Boston Common as the first who died for American freedom.

Page from a draft of Hughes's Famous American Negroes *(Langston Hughes Collection, Schomburg Center for Research in Black Culture, New York Public Library)*

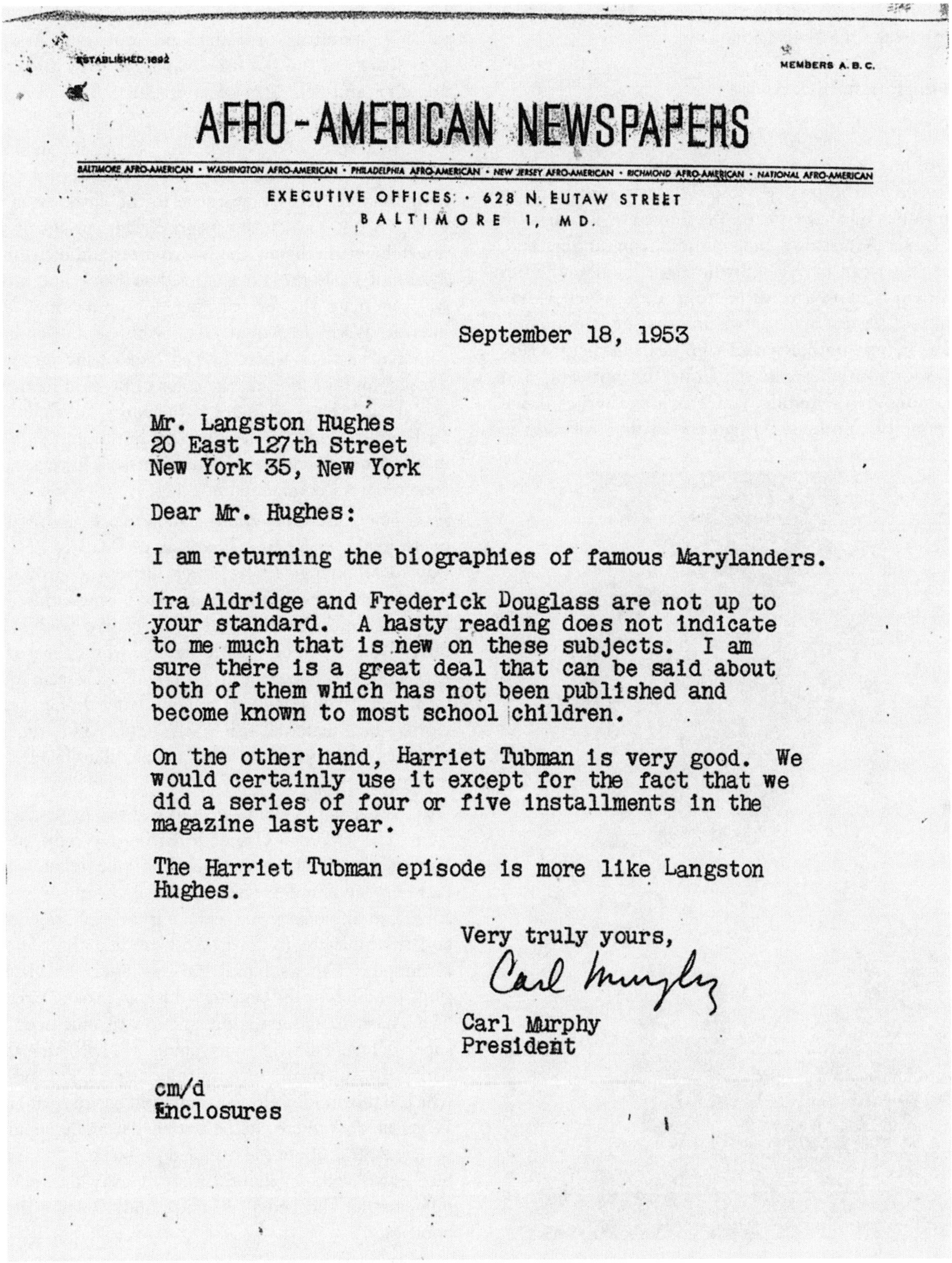

AFRO-AMERICAN NEWSPAPERS

BALTIMORE AFRO-AMERICAN · WASHINGTON AFRO-AMERICAN · PHILADELPHIA AFRO-AMERICAN · NEW JERSEY AFRO-AMERICAN · RICHMOND AFRO-AMERICAN · NATIONAL AFRO-AMERICAN

EXECUTIVE OFFICES · 628 N. EUTAW STREET
BALTIMORE 1, MD.

ESTABLISHED 1892

MEMBERS A.B.C.

September 18, 1953

Mr. Langston Hughes
20 East 127th Street
New York 35, New York

Dear Mr. Hughes:

I am returning the biographies of famous Marylanders.

Ira Aldridge and Frederick Douglass are not up to
your standard. A hasty reading does not indicate
to me much that is new on these subjects. I am
sure there is a great deal that can be said about
both of them which has not been published and
become known to most school children.

On the other hand, Harriet Tubman is very good. We
would certainly use it except for the fact that we
did a series of four or five installments in the
magazine last year.

The Harriet Tubman episode is more like Langston
Hughes.

Very truly yours,

Carl Murphy

Carl Murphy
President

cm/d
Enclosures

Letter rejecting essays Hughes culled from his book in progress, Famous American Negroes
*(Langston Hughes Collection, Schomburg Center for Research in
Black Culture, New York Public Library)*

Hughes wrote this review of James Baldwin's collection of essays, Notes of a Native Son.

From Harlem to Paris

I think that one definition of the great artist might be the creator who projects the biggest dream in terms of the least person. There is something in Cervantes or Shakespeare, Beethoven or Rembrandt or Louis Armstrong that millions can understand. The American native son who signs his name James Baldwin is quite a ways off from fitting such a definition of a great artist in writing, but he is not as far off as many another writer who deals in picture captions or journalese in the hope of capturing and retaining a wide public. James Baldwin writes down to nobody, and he is trying very hard to write up to

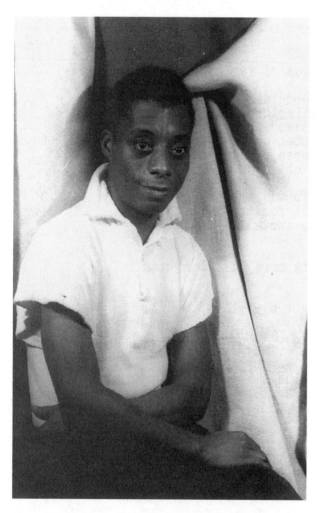

James Baldwin (photograph by Carl Van Vechten, 13 September 1955; Library of Congress, Prints & Photographs Division, Carl Van Vechten Collection, courtesy of Carl Van Vechten Trust)

himself. As an essayist he is thought-provoking, tantalizing, irritating, abusing and amusing. And he uses words as the sea uses waves, to flow and beat, advance and retreat, rise and take a bow in disappearing.

In "Notes of a Native Son," James Baldwin surveys in pungent commentary certain phases of the contemporary scene as they relate to the citizenry of the United States, particularly Negroes. Harlem, the protest novel, bigoted religion, the Negro press and the student milieu of Paris are all examined in black and white, with alternate shutters clicking, for hours of reading interest. When the young man who wrote this book comes to a point where he can look at life purely as himself, and for himself, the color of his skin mattering not at all, when, as in his own words, he finds "his birthright as a man no less than his birthright as a black man," America and the world might well have a major contemporary commentator.

Few American writers handle words more effectively in the essay form than James Baldwin. To my way of thinking, he is much better at provoking thought in the essay than he is in arousing emotion in fiction. I much prefer "Notes of a Native Son" to his novel, "Go Tell It on the Mountain," where the surface excellence and poetry of his writing did not seem to me to suit the earthiness of his subject-matter. In his essays, words and material suit each other. The thought becomes poetry, and the poetry illuminates the thought.

What James Baldwin thinks of the protest novel from "Uncle Tom's Cabin" to Richard Wright, of the motion picture "Carmen Jones," of the relationships between Jews and Negroes, and of the problems of American minorities in general is herein graphically and rhythmically set forth. And the title chapter concerning his father's burial the day after the Harlem riots, heading for the cemetery through broken streets— "To smash something is the ghetto's chronic need"—is superb. That Baldwin's viewpoints are half American, half Afro-American, incompletely fused, is a hurdle which Baldwin himself realizes he still has to surmount. When he does, there will be a straight-from-the-shoulder writer, writing about the troubled problems of this troubled earth with an illuminating intensity that should influence for the better all who ponder on the things books say.

—New York Times Book Review, 26 February 1956, p. 26

* * *

In February 1956, Bernard B. Perry, an editor for Indiana University Press, commissioned Hughes to select and translate a book of poems by the Nobel Prize–winning poet Gabriela Mistral, whom Hughes had never met. Hughes, who enlisted two Latin American students from Princeton University to help him with the translations, wrote this introduction for the volume.

Introduction to *Selected Poems of Gabriela Mistral*

She did not sign her poetry with her own name, Lucila Godoy y Alcayaga, because as a young teacher she feared, if it became known that she wrote such emotionally outspoken verses, she might lose her job. Instead she created for herself another name—taking from the archangel Gabriel her first name, and from a sea wind the second. When the poems that were quickly to make her famous, *Sonetos de la Muerte,* were published in 1914, they were signed Gabriela Mistral.

She was born in 1889 in the Chilean village of Vicuña on the River Elqui in a valley where the sweetest of grapes grow. She grew up in the little town of Montegrande where her father was a schoolmaster, and she in turn became a teacher in rural schools, sometimes walking miles into the country to meet her classes. Her father made up verses for village fiestas and, as a young woman, his daughter composed little poems for texts to help children learn to read. She met a young man, Romelio Ureta, with whom she fell in love, but they were never married. For reasons unrelated to their friendship, Ureta committed suicide. Out of love for him and of her desolation at his death came the first of a series of poems soon to be read throughout all Latin America. These included *Sonnets of Death, Prayer,* and the *Poem of the Son,* in whose stark beauty and intensity her personal tragedy "lost its private character and became a part of world literature. It was then that Lucila Godoy y Alcayaga became Gabriela Mistral."

As her renown as a poet grew, so grew her reputation as a teacher of children. The young woman who had no children of her own took her work as an educator very seriously, and explored what was for Chile and the times the most progressive methods of enlightening young minds—visual aids, extracts from great literature, games sometimes in place of books. At first in country schools and coastal villages, then in Santiago de Chile she became an influence in educational circles, and soon was given a government post in the Department of Education at the capital. A group of teachers brought about the publication of her first book—happily for us, in the United States. Federico de Onis, Professor of Spanish Literature at

Columbia University in New York, one day gave a talk about her and a reading of a few of her poems. This so inspired his students—most of whom were (or intended to be) teachers of Spanish—that they wanted to lay hands on more of her work. Then they learned that as yet no volume of her poems had been printed. Gabriela Mistral's first book, *Desolacion,* was published by the Spanish Institute of Columbia University in 1922. It has since been reprinted in various editions in South America, each time containing more poems as well as revised versions of previous work, for Gabriela Mistral rewrote often.

In Madrid in 1924 *Ternura* was published. In Buenos Aires in 1938 appeared a third small volume, *Tala,* the proceeds of whose sale went to the relief of the Basque orphans of the Spanish Civil War. In 1954 *Lagar* appeared in Chile, and there that same year a new edition of *Desolacion* was printed. In 1950 in Santiago the *Poemas de las Madres* (included in *Desolacion*) had appeared separately in a beautiful limited edition with drawings by Andre Racz. By then in Spanish speaking countries Gabriela's name (and almost everyone in referring to the poet said simply *Gabriela*) had long been a household word. She had become one of the most popular poets of her tongue. Although her first publication was achieved in our country, in Continental Europe her poems were more widely translated than in England or the United States. Even after she was awarded the Nobel Prize for Literature, why so little of Gabriela was translated into English, I do not know. Much of her poetry is simple and direct in language, never high-flown or flowery, and much easier, I think, to translate than most poets writing in Spanish. Since her poetry is so intensely feminine, however, I hesitated to attempt translations myself, hoping that a woman would do so. None did, in terms of a book. So when Bernard Perry of the Indiana University Press requested that I do so, it intrigued me to try—for the simple reason that I liked the poems.

For the most part I have selected from the various books those poems relating to children, motherhood, and love, including the famous *Poem of the Son* and *Prayer* written during her period of complete desolation, after the man for whom she cared so greatly had died by his own hand.

I have no theories of translation. I simply try to transfer into English as much as I can of the literal content, emotion, and style of each poem. When I feel I can transfer only literal content, I do not attempt a translation. For that reason I have not translated the three *Sonetos de la Muerte.* They are very beautiful, but very difficult in their rhymed sim-

"Even the Simplicity Defeats Him"

Poet and Harvard professor Edwin Honig, who was knighted by Spain and Portugal for his translations, wrote this review of the Selected Poems of Gabriela Mistral. *Hughes was angered by Honig's critique of his skills as a translator.*

Poet of Womanhood

In Latin America and Spain the poetry of Gabriela Mistral is as well known as Robert Frost's in the English-speaking world. Born Lucila Godoy y Alcayaga in 1889, she was a popular rural schoolteacher before entering the Chilean government service. Subsequently a widely sought consultant and educator in both Americas, she was variously a diplomat, professor, and delegate to the League of Nations and to the United Nations. In 1945 she was awarded the Nobel Prize for Literature, the first Latin American to be so honored; on her death, a year ago on Long Island, three days of mourning were decreed by the president of Chile.

Her first poems, "Sonnets of Death," appeared in 1914 under the name Gabriela Mistral, by which she presumably asserted her fondness for the archangel and for a famous wind. These sonnets and the poems "Prayer" and "Poem of the Son," all directly reflecting a very personal loss, established her reputation eight years before her first book, "Desolación," was published in New York. Two years later, in 1924, a second book, "Ternura," appeared in Madrid; then came "Tala," in Buenos Aires in 1938, and finally "Lagar," which appeared in Chile in 1954. Not a prolific poet, she was nonetheless a widely esteemed one, and certainly an international figure for many years.

The choice of poems for this first selection of Mistral's work to appear as a book in English heavily stresses only one of her many poetic subjects. They are poems about children and childbearing, about animals and things literally close to the earth, through which the poet speaks in a mother's voice. Mr. Hughes's selections reveal as much about his own lyrical sense as they do of Mistral's and yet without actually defining either hers or his own. Although he admits that "much of her poetry is simple and direct . . . and much easier, I think, to translate than most poets writing in Spanish," he has very few devices for rendering more than the poetry's literal content, and that often rather stiffly or flatly. But even the simplicity defeats him for he is compelled to exclude the famous three "Sonetos de la muerte" because they are "very difficult in their rhymed simplicity to put into an equivalent English form."

Shouldn't Mr. Hughes have called in some collaborator? Shouldn't he have worked harder and used other devices for rendering the poetry more exactly, and in this way have been able to include the three famous sonnets? And shouldn't he, finally, have turned out a more representative collection, one that would include the poet's other styles and subjects, her traditional ballads and coplas, more of the recent poems, and at least a few dealing with indigenous Latin American themes and myths?

As it happens, the most successful versions are the dozen or so prose poems from the early collection, "Desolación."

Gabriel Mistral was a dedicated woman. "One afternoon," she has written, "walking through a poor street in Temuco, I saw a quite ordinary woman sitting in the doorway of her hut. She was approaching childbirth, and her face was heavy with pain. A man came by and flung at her an ugly phrase that made her blush. At that moment I felt toward her all the solidarity of our sex, the infinite pity of one woman for another." And so, very early, with a sense of having to express something unique, Gabriela Mistral became a poet of womanhood and motherhood. This became her best known, although not her only, poetic subject. In such poetry man is the merest instrument of a nearly divine condition which he cannot experience but which it is woman's special joy to achieve. Of the child-to-come the poet writes, "Now my belly is as noble as my heart" and "one who rests gently in my being, like dew on the grass" and "all my body is a veil beneath which a child sleeps." Childbearing, then, approximates a mystic condition: it is like finding union with God. For Mistral the experience of gestating another life inside oneself is the supreme act of creation; it is a finding of union with natural being and with the earth–the only time when a human being may do so except when one dies.

The sources of such poetry are rich. Its subject and form are those of the traditional Spanish cradle song; the feeling it touches is that peculiar mixture (both pagan and Catholic) of the matriarchal Hispanic pride in childbearing and identification with the rhythms of earth. The voice in these poems is extremely personal and yet curiously objective and selfless (as though it were praying) in the joyfully painful reality it isolates and celebrates. Sentiment could not help but attach itself to such poetry, for the feeling is both fundamental and accurately expressed, as in Blake's "Songs." It is not the put-them-all-together-they-spell-mother kind of sentiment which expresses the guilty moralism of an urbanized society that has lost contact with its sources and that attempts murkily to stagger back to a penitential refuge in infantile emotion. Mistral's maternal voices are archetypes of engendering, self-enlightened sufferers, for whom mankind exists on a par with all animals and all products of the earth. There is nothing either clinical or arty about such identifications in the poetry; indeed when most effective the poetry seems to be the opposite of a formal literary artifice: it becomes the objective record of something both constant and passing, like the coiled and precise movement of a watch.

One is grateful to have the poetry in English, although these translations would have represented Gabriela Mistral better had they been more assiduously prepared and had they appeared in a bilingual edition.

–The Saturday Review of Literature,
41 (22 March 1958): 22

plicity to put into an equivalent English form. To give their meaning without their word music would be to lose their meaning.

The music of Gabriela's poetry started around the world a decade or more before she left her native Chile in the early thirties to begin her own travels, first to Mexico, which had asked her assistance in the organization of rural schools and libraries, then to become Chile's delegate to the League of Nations Institute of Intellectual Cooperation. And in 1931 Gabriela Mistral came to the United States as an instructor in Spanish history and civilization at Middlebury and Barnard colleges. Later she represented her government in various diplomatic posts in South America and Europe, and was a member of the United Nations Subcommittee on the Status of Women. For two years, at President Aleman's invitation, she lived in Mexico as a "guest of the nation." She was Chilean Consul in Brazil, Portugal, at Nice, and Los Angeles. Then after a year as Consul at Naples, in 1953 Gabriela Mistral came again to the United States and settled down in a charming house in Roslyn Harbor, Long Island, where she lived until her death. For twenty years before her death, Gabriela had been honored as Chile's only "life consul"–so appointed by a special enactment of the Chilean Congress–her consulate designated to be "wherever she finds a suitable climate for her health and a pleasant atmosphere to pursue her studies." In the end she chose Roslyn Harbor.

Early in the new year of 1957 Gabriela Mistral died. When the news reached Chile, President Ibañez decreed three days of national mourning. In the United Nations she was eulogized. And the press of the world paid her tribute. In an article at the center of a full page devoted to her memory in *The New York Times Book Review,* Mildred Adams wrote, "Gabriela's clarity and precision, her passion and that characteristic which can only be called her nobility of soul are accepted as ideals. She will not quickly vanish from the literary consciousness of those who value the Spanish tongue." And in *El Diario de Nueva York* Ramon Sender said, "There are poets who hide behind their verses. Others give themselves from their first poem, and so it was with Gabriela Mistral."

–"Introduction," in *Selected Poems of Gabriela Mistral* (Bloomington: Indiana University Press, 1957), pp. 9–12

* * *

Hughes wrote this introduction for a 1959 paperback edition of Mark Twain's Pudd'nhead Wilson *(1894).*

Introduction to *Pudd'nhead Wilson*

Mark Twain's ironic little novel, *Pudd'nhead Wilson,* is laid on the banks of the Mississippi in the first half of the 1800s. It concerns itself with, among other things, the use of fingerprinting to solve the mystery of a murder. But *Pudd'nhead Wilson* is not a mystery novel. The reader knows from the beginning who committed the murder and has more than an inkling of how it will be solved. The circumstances of the denouement, however, possessed in its time great novelty, for fingerprinting had not then come into official use in crime detection in the United States. Even a man who fooled around with it as a hobby was thought to be a simpleton, a puddenhead. Such was the reputation acquired by Wilson, the young would-be lawyer in the Missouri frontier town of Dawson's Landing. But Wilson eventually made his detractors appear as puddenheads themselves.

Although introduced early, it is not until near the end of the book that Wilson becomes a major figure in the tale. The novel is rather the story of another young man's mistaken identity–a young man who thinks he is white but is in reality colored; who is heir to wealth without knowing his claim is false; who lives as a free man, but is legally a slave; and who, when he learns the true facts about himself, comes to ruin not through the temporarily shattering knowledge of his physical status, but because of weaknesses common to white or colored, slave or free. The young man thinks his name is Thomas à Becket Driscoll, but it is really Valet de Chambre–a name used for twenty-three years by another who is held as a slave in his stead, but who, unknown to himself, is white–and therefore legally free.

Pudd'nhead Wilson is the man, who, in the end, sets things to rights. But for whom? Seemingly for the spectators only, not for the principals involved, for by that time to them right is wrong, wrong is right, and happiness has gone by the board. The slave system has taken its toll of all three concerned–mother, mammy, ward and child–for the mother and mammy, Roxana, matriarch and slave, are one. Roxy is a puppet whose at first successful deceits cause her to think herself a free agent. She is undone at the climax by the former laughing stock of the town, Pudd'nhead Wilson, whose long interest in the little swirls at the ends of the fingers finally pays off.

Hughes (fifth from left) at Lincoln University commencement, 8 June 1954 (Langston Hughes Papers, Yale Collection of American Literature, Beinecke Rare Book and Manuscript Library)

Years before he published *Pudd'nhead Wilson* Mark Twain had been hailed as America's greatest humorist. From *The Celebrated Jumping Frog of Calaveras County* in 1865 to *The Adventures of Huckleberry Finn* in 1884, most of his fiction—and his spoken words on the lecture platform—had been sure sources of laughter. But in this work of his middle years (Twain was 59) he did not write a humorous novel. Except for a few hilarious village scenes, and a phonetic description of a baby's tantrums, the out-loud laughs to be found in *Tom Sawyer* or *Huckleberry Finn* are not a part of *Pudd'nhead*. In this book the basic theme is slavery, seriously treated, and its main thread concerns the absurdity of man-made differentials, whether of caste or "race." The word *race* might properly be placed in quotes for both of Mark Twain's central Negroes are largely white in blood and physiognomy, slaves only by circumstance, and each only "by a fiction of law and custom, a Negro." The white boy who is mistakenly raised as a slave in the end finds himself "rich and free, but in a most embarrassing situation. He could

neither read nor write, and his speech was the basest dialect of the Negro quarter. His gait, his attitudes, his gestures, his bearing, his laugh—all were vulgar and uncouth; his manners were the manners of a slave. Money and fine clothes could not mend these defects or cover them up, they only made them the more glaring and pathetic. The poor fellow could not endure the terrors of the white man's parlour, and felt at home and at peace nowhere but in the kitchen."

On the other hand, the young dandy who thought his name was Thomas à Becket, studied at Yale. He then came home to Dawson's Landing bedecked in Eastern finery to lord it over black and white alike. As Pudd'nhead Wilson, who had the habit of penning little musings beneath the dates in his calendar, wrote, "Training is everything. The peach was once a bitter almond; cauliflower is nothing but cabbage with a college education." It took a foreigner with no regard for frontier aristocracy of Old Virginia lineage to kick Thomas à Becket right square in his sit-downer at a public meeting. In the ensuing free-for-all that breaks out, the hall is set afire. Here the sparkle of Twain's traditional humor bursts into hilarious flame, too, as the members of the nearby fire department—"who never stirred officially in unofficial costume"—donned their uniforms to drench the hall with enough water to "annihilate forty times as much fire as there was there; for a village fire company does not often get a chance to show off." Twain wryly concludes, "Citizens of that village . . . did not insure against fire; they insured against the fire-company."

Against fire and water in the slave states there was insurance, but none against the devious dangers of slavery itself. Not even a fine old gentleman like Judge Driscoll "of the best blood of the Old Dominion" could find insurance against the self-protective schemes of his brother's bond servant, Roxy, who did not like being a slave, but was willing to be one for her son's sake. Roxy was also willing to commit a grievous sin for her son's sake, palliating her conscience a little by saying, "white folks has done it." With "an unfair show in the battle of life," as Twain puts it, Roxy, as an "heir of two centuries of unatoned insult and outrage," is yet not of an evil nature. Her crimes grow out of the greater crimes of the slave system. "The man in whose favor no laws of property exist," Thomas Jefferson wrote in his *Notes on Virginia,* "feels himself less bound to respect those made in favor of others."

Roxy's fear of eventually receiving the same punishment as that threatened other servants for the thieving of a few dollars from their master, Percy Driscoll, was enough to start a chain of thought in her mind that led eventually to disaster. Even though her master was "a fairly humane man towards slaves and other animals," was he not a thief himself? Certainly he was, to one in bondage, "the man who daily robbed him of an inestimable treasury—his liberty." Out of the structure of slave society itself is fashioned a noose of doom. In *Pudd'nhead Wilson* Mark Twain wrote what at a later period might have been called in the finest sense of the term, "a novel of social significance." Had Twain been a contemporary of Harriet Beecher Stowe, and this novel published before the War between the States, it might have been a minor *Uncle Tom's Cabin.* Twain minces no words in describing the unfortunate effects of slavery upon the behavior of both Negroes and whites, even upon children. The little master, Thomas, and the little slave, Chambers, were both born on the same day and grew up together. But even in "babyhood Tom cuffed and banged and scratched Chambers unrebuked, and Chambers early learned that between meekly bearing it and resenting it, the advantage all lay with the

former policy. The few times his persecutions had moved him beyond control and made him fight back had cost him . . . three such convincing canings from the man who was his father and didn't know it, that he took Tom's cruelties in all humility after that, and made no more experiments. Outside of the house the two boys were together all through their boyhood. . . . Tom staked him with marbles to play 'keeps' with, and then took all the winnings away from him. In the winter season Chambers was on hand, in Tom's worn-out clothes . . . to drag a sled up the hill for Tom, warmly clad, to ride down on; but he never got a ride himself. He built snow men and snow fortifications under Tom's directions. He was Tom's patient target when Tom wanted to do some snowballing, but the target couldn't fire back. Chambers carried Tom's skates to the river and strapped them on him, then trotted around after him on the ice, so as to be on hand when wanted; but he wasn't ever asked to try the skates himself."

Mark Twain, in his presentation of Negroes as human beings, stands head and shoulders above the other Southern writers of his times, even such distinguished ones as Joel Chandler Harris, F. Hopkins Smith, and Thomas Nelson Page. It was a period when most writers who included Negro characters in their work at all, were given to presenting the slave as ignorant and happy, the freed men of color as ignorant and miserable, and all Negroes as either comic servants on the one hand or dangerous brutes on the other. That Mark Twain's characters in *Pudd'nhead Wilson* fall into none of these categories is a tribute to his discernment. And that he makes them neither heroes nor villains is a tribute to his understanding of human character. "Color is only skin deep." In this novel Twain shows how more than anything else environment shapes the man. Yet in his day behavioristic psychology was in its infancy. Likewise, the science of fingerprinting. In 1894 *Pudd'nhead Wilson* was a "modern" novel indeed. And it still may be so classified.

Although knowledge of fingerprinting dates back some two thousand years, and fingerprints are found as signatures on ancient Chinese tablets and Babylonian records, it was not until 1880 that the first treatise on the possible use of fingerprinting in criminal identification appeared in English. And it was sixteen years later (two years after the appearance of *Pudd'nhead Wilson*) before the International Association of Chiefs of Police meeting in Chicago in 1896 decided to set up a Bureau of Criminal Identification and, as a part of its program, study ways and means whereby fingerprint-

Sleeves for record albums based on Hughes's children's books (Langston Hughes Papers, Yale Collection of American Literature, Beinecke Rare Book and Manuscript Library; Langston Hughes Collection, Schomburg Center for Research in Black Culture, New York Public Library)

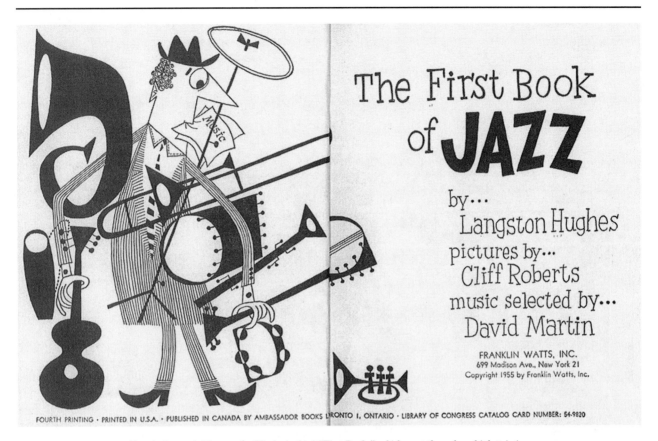

Frontispiece and title page for Hughes's third "First Book," which went through multiple printings
(courtesy of Kenneth Spencer Research Library, University of Kansas Libraries)

ing might supplement or perhaps supplant the Bertillon system of bodily measurements as a means of identifying criminals. So Mark Twain was well ahead of the international keepers of law and order when he devoted several pages in his novel to a description of how fingerprints might be used for the positive identification of a criminal who has neglected to put on gloves before committing a crime.

"Every human being," Twain has Pudd'nhead Wilson inform the court, "carries with him from his cradle to his grave certain physical marks which do not change their character, and by which he can always be identified—and that without shade of doubt or question. These marks are his signature, his physiological autograph, so to speak, and this autography cannot be counterfeited, nor can he disguise it or hide it away, nor can it become illegible by the wear and the mutations of time. . . . This autograph consists of the delicate lines or corrugations with which Nature marks the insides of the hands and the soles of the feet. If you will look at the balls of your fingers—you that have very sharp eyesight—you will observe that these dainty curving lines lie close together, like those that indicate the borders of oceans in maps, and that

they form various clearly defined patterns, such as arches, circles, long curves, whorls, etc., and that these patterns differ on the different fingers."

Curiously enough, as modern as *Pudd'nhead Wilson* is, its format is that of an old-fashioned melodrama, as if its structure were borrowed from the plays performed on the riverboat theatres of that period. Perhaps deliberately, Twain selected this popular formula in which to tell a very serious story. Moving from climax to climax, every chapter ends with a teaser that makes the reader wonder what is coming next while, as in Greek tragedy, the fates keep closing in on the central protagonists. And here the fates have no regard whatsoever for color lines. It is this treatment of race that makes *Pudd'nhead Wilson* as contemporary as Little Rock, and Mark Twain as modern as Faulkner, although Twain died when Faulkner was in knee pants.

The first motion picture was made in the year in which Twain wrote *Pudd'nhead Wilson*. As if looking ahead to the heyday of this medium, the author begins his story with a sweeping panorama of the river and Dawson's Landing, then briefly poses by name the cast of characters against it. Thereafter, he

Hughes leading a class at Fisk University, circa 1959 (Langston Hughes Papers, Yale Collection of American Literature, Beinecke Rare Book and Manuscript Library)

continues his tale in a series of visualizations, most of them growing logically one from another, but some quite coincidentally. A common dictum in Hollywood is, "Simply picture it on the screen, and the audience will believe it–because *there it is*." The advent of two handsome Italian twins in Dawson's Landing is pictured so vividly that the reader believes the men are there, and only briefly wonders *why*– although these two fellows immediately begin to figure prominently in the frightful march of events leading toward the novel's climax. But, to tell the truth, we do not need to know exactly why these ebullient twins came to Dawson's Landing. And they do brighten up the story considerably.

Additional, and what seem at first to be extraneous flashes of amusing brilliance in the novel (and at other times sober or ironic comment) are the excerpts that serve as chapter headings from *Pudd'nhead Wilson's Calendar*. "Few things are harder to put up with

than the annoyance of a good example." And another: "It is often the case that the man who can't tell a lie thinks he is the best judge of one." And an observation that would have almost surely, had there been a McCarthy Committee in Twain's day, caused the author to be subpoenaed before it: "*October 12– The Discovery*–It was wonderful to find America, but it would have been more wonderful to miss it." And a final admonition that might almost be Mark Twain himself concerned with the tight and astringent style of this smallest of his novels: "As to the Adjective: when in doubt, strike it out." *Pudd'nhead Wilson* marches along much too rapidly to be bothered with a plethora of adjectives.

–"Introduction," in *Pudd'nhead Wilson*, by Mark Twain (New York: Bantam, 1959), pp. vii-xiii

The Simple Story

In summer 1949, Hughes began the process of selecting from nearly two hundred Chicago Defender *columns that featured Jesse B. Semple and editing them for inclusion in the first and subsequent Simple books. Hughes followed the advice of Maria Leiper, his editor at Simon and Schuster, who suggested he use an anonymous narrator for the Simple pieces and focus on the women in Simple's life. The first Simple collection,* Simple Speaks His Mind, *was published on 14 April 1950 in hardback for $3 and in paperback for $1.*

Lloyd L. Brown, an African American labor organizer and journalist who wrote this review, was not the only critic to compare Hughes's work to that of Peter Finley Dunne, whose columns in the Chicago Evening Post *featured conversations between an Irish bartender, Martin Dooley, and his friend, Henessey, but most reviewers recognized Simple as a Harlem original.*

Not So Simple
Review of *Simple Speaks His Mind*

Langston Hughes' new book comes as something of a jolt to those of us who have insisted that the Man-on-the-Street is a myth. Since meeting his Jesse B. Semple—the nickname "Simple" was inevitable—I for one am ready to concede that the composite man really exists, at least in Harlem. Of course there are some 400,000 Negroes living in this world center of Negro life and among us there are all kinds of people; but when Simple speaks his mind he is truly speaking the mind of the common people of this community.

So I urge you: Don't miss reading this book. It is revealing, it is stimulating; you are sure to enjoy it. It is especially recommended for all who have been chilled by the cold war; here is a chance for them to warm

Hughes and cast members on the set of Just a Little Simple, *a series of skits adapted by Alice Childress from Hughes's* Simple Speaks His Mind. *The play was performed at Club Baron in New York City, September 1950 (Langston Hughes Papers, Yale Collection of American Literature, Beinecke Rare Book and Manuscript Library).*

their bones before the glow of Simple's humor, the humor of a people who have come through 300 *years* of cold war.

There are a number of unusual features to this work which consists of monologues in the Mr. Dooley tradition, with the author playing it straight, asking a few questions and occasionally trying, without much success, to get a word in edgewise.

Especially notable is the fact that Simple is talking to Negroes, the book being largely a compilation of columns which have appeared in the Negro press. Offered now to the general public, the special quality that results from this approach, the intimacy of uninhibited expression, is of unique value.

Of special interest too is that here Langston Hughes has tapped the bubbling wellsprings of authentic Negro humor, the wonderful quality of which is the direct opposite of that noxious sewer-flow with which Amos 'n' Andy and Octavus Roy Cohen have drenched the nation for too many years.

The humor of the Negro people, one of the most significant features of their national psychology, is not of the "gag" variety; it is subtle, compounded of double-meanings, indirection, allusions, colloquialisms. It has a bitter-sweet tone, this laughter in the shadows, that is difficult to describe and more difficult to render without distortion; that he succeeds so well in getting much of its elusive quality into print is further evidence that Langston Hughes retains his close touch with his people and his top place among Negro creative writers.

Simple speaks of many things, of almost everything: rents, prices, wages, baseball, the F.B.I., $2,000 fur coats for dogs, the Un-Americans, his landlady, why lingerie is pink, the police and courts ("I definitely do not like the Law"), the South, Congress, atom bombs, Negroes, white people, the Army, the last war, the cold war, his love life, literature—everything in Harlem and the rest of the world too; in fact, Simple looks forward to the coming Rocket Age and figures out what he will do in all the far-away places to which he'll zoom.

And through it all he wrestles with his implacable enemy, Jim Crow. For Simple is a militant Negro—though he would use the expression "race-man"—and if Judge Medina overheard his forceful talk he'd probably double his daily dose of dry Martinis. If Simple were to pray what was really on his mind, "the Lord would shut his ears and not listen to me at all."

Simple would have the Lord wipe out all the white people and let *him* rule a while. But as Simple goes on to outline the beneficent program he would install as world ruler, it seems there would still be white people around.

"First place, with white folks wiped out, I would stop charging such high rents—so my landlady would charge *me* less. Second place, I would stop hoarding up all the good jobs for white folks—so I could get ahead myself. Third place, I would make the South behave. . . ."

And lest somebody wrongly accuse him of being a reactionary nationalist for even thinking of this prayer which he didn't pray, I should hasten to add that Simple is a staunch union man and that he would not deny a white man his just reward—only he'd like to see, for once, a *black* general pinning a medal on a *white* soldier, instead of the other way around all the time.

I have heard it said that there are some people who are a little leery about the Simple language of this book; that eyebrows have been lifted because the idiom is other (I wouldn't say "less") than pure Churchillian. I've heard tell that some were even so mad about this that they forgot to be angry about the things that anger Simple—lynchings, police brutality, Red-baiting and the rest. At one place in the book his girl friend, Joyce, also accuses him of something like that, saying reproachfully, "You are acting just like a Negro." Well, he also *talks* like a Negro, or rather, like a great many Negroes talk; and as for me, I'd rather listen to his salty speech than to all the mush-mouthed sons of Marlborough in the King's own England.

Lambasting the ways of white folks, Simple does not fail to swing a few left-hooks at some of the Negro upper-crust. Joyce takes him to a banquet sponsored by Mrs. Sadie Maxwell-Reeves, who "lives so high up on Sugar Hill that people in her neighborhood don't even have roomers." He is filled with delight when the guest of honor, a venerable artist-writer whom they are feteing because the New York *Times* called him a genius, turns upon the assemblage and says:

"Now, to tell you the truth, I don't want no damned banquet. I don't want no honoring where *you* eat as much as me, and enjoy yourselves more, besides making some money for your treasury. If you want to honor me, give some young boy or girl who's coming along trying to create arts and write and compose and sing and act and paint and dance and make something out of the beauties of the Negro race—give that child some help . . . but don't come giving me, who's old enough to die and too near blind to create anything any more anyhow, a great big banquet that *you* eat up in honor of your *own* stomachs as much as in honor of me—who's toothless and can't eat. You hear me, I ain't honored!"

There are some weak spots in the book, and I have in mind particularly the treatment of Negroes in relation to foreigners. Simple inveighs against the situation where a new immigrant has rights that his people, "old Americans," are denied. The situation is real and that's how Simple sees it, but I was hoping that Author Hughes would butt in to indicate the danger of pitting Negroes against foreign-born and I was disappointed when he didn't. With all his wisdom, the Man-on-the-Street can be wrong too; folk-wisdom is not without its fallacies.

But in spite of such weaknesses and the limitations of this literary form, Jesse B. Semple is a splendid character, full of the zest for living and the spirit for fighting; he has nothing in common with the warped, frustrated and above all *doomed* Negro that Richard Wright, Chester Himes and others of that school have given us. That is because his creator, truly knowing his people, *loves* them. Loves them as they are, for what they are, and to hell with the white chauvinists.

No, there is nothing doomed about Simple, with all his troubles which he is quick to recite:

> "I have been underfed, underpaid, undernourished, and everything but *undertaken*. I been bit by dogs, cats, mice, rats, poll parrots, fleas, chiggers, bedbugs, granddaddies, mosquitoes, and a gold-toothed woman. . . . In this life I been abused, confused, misused, accused, false-arrested, tried, sentenced, paroled, blackjacked, beat, third-degreed, and near about lynched. . . ."

But listen to this—and here I come back to those people who have been gloomed by the way things are or seem to be: after going through the list of his grievances (which I have quoted only in part), Simple concludes by saying:

> *"—but I am still here. Daddy-o, I'm still here!"*

That's right, Simple is still here just the same; and he and his people are going to *be here* come A-bombs or H-bombs, McCarthys, Mundts and Trumans. So all of us who aim to be here too had better get acquainted with him now if we aren't already.

— *Masses and Mainstream*, 3 (June 1950): 81–84

* * *

John W. Parker of Fayetteville State Teachers College wrote this review. To "play the dozens," as Parker notes Simple does, is to engage in an African American verbal game—a test of originality, wit, and improvisational skills through an exchange of insults usually centering on the mothers of the two opponents.

"A Brilliant and Shockingly Accurate Exposé" Review of *Simple Speaks His Mind*

In his latest book, *Simple Speaks His Mind,* Langston Hughes returns to Harlem, the scene of his departure as a poet in 1922, and the spot that just a few decades back became the home of the much-discussed and not infrequently much-cussed "Negro Literary Renaissance." Although void of much of the glitter and the fanfare that it possessed during the Mid-Twenties, Harlem has remained a center of color and enchantment and has retained its firm hold on the popular imagination of the American people. *Simple Speaks His Mind* is a brilliant and shockingly accurate exposé of the social milieu of the Harlem dweller and of the accompanying frustration that results from his desperate struggle to make ends meet and from his recognition of his out-group status in a period of growing social awareness. Hughes' selection of the social and emotional situations that make up the volume attest to his familiarity with the Harlem scene and his adeptness in the artistic handling of the simple narrative as a literary medium. Everywhere the humor is that both of characterization and of situation; it is calculated for people who laugh *with* Negroes, not *at* them.

Simple Speaks His Mind began in 1942 as a series of stories written especially for readers of the *Chicago Defender,* and with the idea that none other than Negroes would ever see it. Hence, its amazing intimacy and its chit chat, Harlem style, that sometimes leaves the reader almost with a sense of eavesdropping. The collection divides into four parts—Summer Time, Winter Time, Hard Times, and Any Time—but these divisions are more formal than organic. It achieves its unity through the unity of action of Simple, who, symbolic of the "ordinary man in the street," laughs to keep from crying. Himself a Harlemite, Simple talks endlessly in a half-humorous, half-serious way about the goings-on Harlem dwellers are wont to discuss.

And as it turns out, Simple has a great deal to tell (or perhaps not to tell), for his character imperfections and his social rôle leave much to be desired. The Virginia bi-racial set-up has blurred his view of life; he is separated from his wife, but cannot afford the price of a divorce; he "plays the dozens" despite his impatience with others who do so; he resorts occasionally to clandestine association with Zarita, an "uncombed woman," who calls at his room; he is resigned to the four walls of a rented room, and with too many women on his hands, clocks to punch and landladies to dodge, Simple relaxes at parties and bars, and drinks incessantly because "I'm lonesome within myself."

While the author neither justifies nor condemns Simple's irregular conduct, it is obvious, even to Simple, that the forces at play in his life lead but to his undoing. Yet a return to the soil is unthinkable; for Simple, it is Harlem today, tomorrow, next week, and then, well, forget it. He confesses that

When I am a hundred and one,
If I'm still having fun,
I'll start all over again
Just like I begun.

Implicit in Hughes' study of the world's largest urban Negro center is an obvious irony and a tragedy that are part and parcel of the Negro ghetto in an urban community above the Mason-Dixon line.

But for the character, Simple, who is typical rather than distinctive, the array of characters in the volume are but sharply-etched sketches for the reason that the stories turn upon a central theme rather than upon character. And while individually the stories for the most part make absorbing reading, collectively they piece together the inner life of Simple, "the toughest Negro God's got," and constitute a definition of the situation for at least one social class in present-day Harlem. This attractively-bound book, which comes both in the one dollar and the three dollar editions, bears the characteristic Hughes trademarks—disdain for literary "Nice-Nellyism," an abiding faith in the common folk, and a clarion call for social justice for America's minority groups. All in all, the collection enhances Hughes' reputation as a story teller.

Somehow one cannot help wishing that Hughes would write a companion volume to *Simple Speaks His Mind,* that is, a book based upon Negroes who, even though they own fish-tail Cadillacs and live in ranch-style solar houses, see life steadily and as a whole. Such a study would serve to balance the present overdrawn picture of the Negro of no consequence, and to disclose the fact that sane, forward-looking Negroes do exist, even in Harlem. And it is conceivable that a few of them are worthy of literary treatment. At any rate, Langston Hughes is still fishing in the proverbial big sea of American literature, and his new book, *Simple Speaks His Mind,* represents another significant catch. It is a fresh and a thought-provoking contribution to the literature of the urban Negro community.

—*Journal of Negro History,* 36 (January 1951): 96–98

* * *

Arna Bontemps wrote this review.

That Not So Simple Sage, Mr. Simple
Review of *Simple Takes a Wife*

There is no convenient category for the Simple books. Like much of Langston Hughes' writing, they go a merry way without too serious a regard for form or fashion. "Simple Takes a Wife" is neither a novel nor a collection of stories. To call it humor is insufficient. A series of dialogues in the idiom of a transplanted Southerner, it is as outlandish as the hubbub in a Harlem bar, as noisy and startling as voices in a rooming house, but it has too much bite to be just funny. Categories aside, however, the new book bears a signature which is indeed unmistakable.

The character called Simple was first introduced in a weekly column of "The Chicago Defender," a Negro newspaper. He began his public

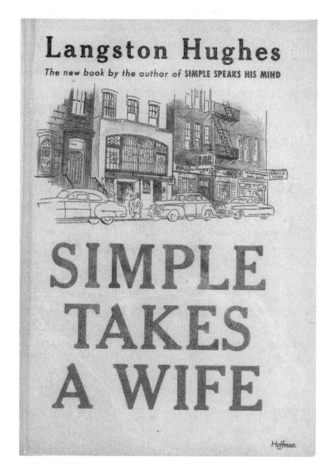

Dust jacket for the second collection of Hughes's Simple stories, published by Simon and Schuster in 1953 (courtesy of Kenneth Spencer Research Library, University of Kansas Libraries)

career, so to speak, as a bewildered observer of the war effort. Langston Hughes first employed his languid asides as a commentary on discrimination in defense plants. Once started, however, Simple would not be shushed. He became almost embarrassingly frank about his domestic problems. At the same time he revealed a certain sensitiveness to life's philosophic overtones and a tendency to let his moods overpower him:

I got the Dallas blues
And the Fort Worth heart's disease.

More important, he made friends fast. Readers of the column addressed letters to Simple instead of his author. One impetuous admirer sent a possum from Tennessee packed in dry ice. The first book in which these pieces were brought together was "Simple Speaks His Mind." To a considerable extent it represented a reworking of the material rather than a collection of columns from "The Defender." The second book goes still farther in this direction and it makes even better reading.

Between the time when Simple began to hanker for a divorce from the wife he had left in Baltimore and the day when he finally achieves freedom to marry his girl Joyce, almost everything happens, and most of it Simple reports in his own words to an interlocutor in Paddy's Bar. His troubles with his landlady are peculiarly disturbing, but scarcely more so than those precipitated by another landlady when he calls on Joyce and rings seven times for the third floor rear, as the instruction on the bell directs. When Joyce fails to respond to the first seven, he must ring seven more. At the end of a third such cluster the fat landlady comes out storming.

By then, of course, the complexity of Simple's life as a whole has been underscored, but he lives it to the hilt, nevertheless. As he pauses for beer, he has his say about ladies' hats, bed bugs, afternoon teas, be-bop music, grammar, college education, moving pictures, intermarriage, and a host of equally vital matters. He befriends an aspiring young nephew, sidesteps the party girl Zarita, and indulges a heavenly feeling as he heads for the City Hall with Joyce.

Harlem hasn't a more authentic citizen.

—*New York Herald Tribune Book Review*,
14 June 1953, p. 12

* * *

Abner Berry, an African American journalist and Communist Party member, wrote this review.

Not So Simple
Review of *Simple Takes a Wife*

Among the 66,000 furnished room dwellers who live in Harlem between the two rivers from 110th Street, on the south, to just beyond the Polo Grounds, on the north, is one Jesse B. Semple—called "Simple," for short, by his friends. We don't know Simple's exact address, but it appears from his salty comments on landladies, bars, upper class Negroes and patronizing whites that he lives in the "valley," in "Deep Harlem," east of Seventh Avenue in the 130's.

Simple and his neighbors, refugees from the sterner racism of the South, understand and denounce the jimcrow nuances of New York City with a fierce race consciousness. This rooming house set, whose addresses denote the place where they bathe, sleep and change clothes, and for whom their favorite tavern must serve as a living room, furnish the characters and the action in Langston Hughes' *Simple Takes a Wife*.

Hughes takes us with Simple as he moves among his friends, understanding their problems, discussing his own, working hard to get a divorce so that he can marry Joyce. To pay for this divorce from his estranged wife in Baltimore, Simple explains that it took "a whole lot of NOT having what you want, to get what you want most." But most of Simple's conversations range far from the purely personal. Simple doesn't think Negroes have made as much progress as some say. "I tell them," says Simple to his friend, "that white folks can measure their race problem by how far they have come. But Negroes measure ours by how far we have got to go." He then continues, hitting at the theory of Negro progress that is limited to advancing a few big shots:

"Them white folks are always telling me, 'Isn't it wonderful the progress that's been made amongst your people. Look at Dr. Bunche!'
"All I say is 'Look at me.'"

When it is pointed out to Simple that Negroes can now stay at the Waldorf-Astoria, he answers, "Mr. Semple cannot stay there right now—because Mr. Semple ain't able." And he will not accept the explanation that his disability is due to money and not race for "if I were not of the colored race, smart as I am, I would have money." Nor is Simple satisfied with two Negroes in Congress when "there ought to be *two dozen* colored Congressmen" who aren't there because southern Negroes are not allowed to vote. Reminded of the

Supreme Court mandate against voting restrictions, Simple asks rhetorically:

> "Can a Negro take time off from work to go running to the Supreme Court every time the Klan keeps him from voting? We can't enforce no laws by ourselves."

Simple has a word for the cops, too, and in saying it, he uses the Negro folk characteristic of treating a serious problem, like police brutality, with humorous derision. Be-Bop, says Simple, "makes plenty of sense," because it originated "from the police beating Negroes' heads, . . . beaten right out of some Negro's head into them horns and saxophones and piano keys . . ." Policemen, says Simple, are likely to question him any time about "what are you doing in this neighborhood?"

> "Then I have to go into my whole pedigree because I am a black man in a white neighborhood. And if my answers do not satisfy them, Bop! Mop! . . . Be-Bop! . . . If they do not hit me they have already hurt my soul."

In Simple, Hughes has found the perfect protagonist for the thousands of racial battles that are fought in conversations in every ghetto throughout the United States. It is a warm and human story of distant relatives arriving unexpectedly and sharing the cubicle of a room until they can get a foot on the ladder of New York life. We share the problems of a young couple falling in love, marrying and rearing their first child in their own one-room home. But we sense the quality of laughing at heartbreak, or being able to "escape" through the humor derived from commonplace situations, of bitterness which evades frustration. For Simple, the composite of Harlem's common man, is not defeated nor dejected, even though the road ahead is not clearly marked.

On one thing Simple is irrevocably determined: to be free from jim crow and to avenge the many insults the South has handed him and his people. He dreams one night he was a bird and wishes on awakening he could make the dream true for a while. Among the things he would like to do as a bird is to "just fly *over* the South, stopping only long enough to spread my tail feathers and show my contempt." And musing on the racist "blood theories," Simple twits their proponents:

> "Why is Negro blood so much more powerful than any other kind of blood in the world? If a man has Irish blood in him, people will say, 'He's *part* Irish.' If he has a little Jewish blood, they'll say, 'He's *half* Jewish.' But if he has just a small bit of colored blood in him, Bam!– '*He's a Negro!*' . . . Now, that is what I do not understand–why one drop is so powerful. . . ."

I suspect it is the author who steers Simple away from more basic political topics, keeping the discussions on the level of "race talk." For there was a much wider topical range in Hughes' first volume about Simple–*Simple Speaks His Mind*. Whereas in the first book, Simple had some sharp observations to make on the Un-American Activities Committee, he now limits his discussion of Congress to the absence of Negroes. And it should be remembered that Hughes, since the appearance of *Simple Speaks His Mind*, has been a "guest" of Sen. Joseph McCarthy.

It is also notable that Hughes before McCarthy did not fare nearly as well as did Simple before the Un-Americans, for Simple really "told off" that "old Georgia chairman" with some biting comments on jimcrow. Simple still has bite in discussing jimcrow, but he "talks at the big gate," out of earshot of the oppressors, to his anonymous friend. However, Simple remains a healthy representative of Negro ghetto dwellers continuing in every way they know to struggle for first class American citizenship.

I hope that in future stories, Hughes will let us see and hear Simple (who is a poorly-paid worker) in his relationships with other workers and his employers. So far we have only seen him after work, relaxing over a beer, discussing his and other Negroes' problems, within the relationship of Negro to Negro. Hughes should give us more of Simple's sides, for as one colloquy in *Simple Speaks His Mind* went:

> "'Life is not so simple,' cautioned his friend on one of Simple's propositions.
> "'Neither am I,' said Simple."

The present volume exhibits an artistic weakness: Hughes combines the reporter's eye, the novelist's ear, but misses the third dimension of the ghetto scene as reflected in the real characters of whom Simple is a composite. One feels that Simple and those around him can do little more than complain, futilely, of the oppressive jimcrow conditions under which they live. Despite the charm and the many nuggets of wisdom in this panorama of Harlem, the reader can conclude that Simple and his friends will remain as they are indefinitely.

It would be a mistake to say that this makes *Simple Takes a Wife* poor or insubstantial reading. On the contrary, with all of his weaknesses, Hughes has given us a vivid picture of Negro life and its richness, a picture which is sharply opposed to the "arty" degeneracy of writers like Richard Wright and Ralph Ellison. For even though he is held under wraps by the author, Simple is a healthy, probing, salty young Negro, a pleasant relief from Ellison's *Invisible Man* and Wright's fascistic killer in *The Outsider*. Simple may not show us the way to the future, but he certainly gives us a seldom seen and delightful picture of today.

–*Masses and Mainstream*, 6 (September 1953): 55–58

* * *

a community project. All the youngsters on the block help to plant and weed it.

"This is a rooming-house block and jammed with children. Their families just can't find housing. It's a shame—two and three children to a room. And if you apply for an apartment in a project, it takes three years and by that time there are two or three more children."

Hughes took me up to the top floor and his study at the back of the house, a square comfortable room with the sun shining in the windows through the trees. His new book, "Simple Stakes a Claim" (Rinehart, $2.50) is his 22d. The Simple dialogues (Jesse B. Semple and an "I" who sometimes speaks for Hughes and sometimes doesn't) have been running in the Chicago Defender for 15 years. "Simply Heavenly," the current Broadway play, is based on "Simple Takes a Wife."

"The character originated from a boy I met in a bar. It was in the early days of the war and I asked him where he worked and he said in a war plant and I asked him what they made and he said 'Cranks.' 'What kind?' I asked. 'Jeeps, trucks, planes?'

"'Just cranks,' he said. 'I don't know what them cranks cranks. You know white folks don't tell Negroes what cranks cranks.'

"Most of these things in the Simple books come out of actual incidents. Simple really represents a composite of the not too well educated Negro from the South in the urban community."

I asked Hughes if Simple would care to make a statement on Gov. Faubus. "Well, not just offhand. My feeling is half amazement, half wonder that people can behave that way. I have the greatest admiration for those Negro parents and particularly for those children, kids who walk through a mob. I remember when I was a kid, my first experience in school was not unlike what's going on now. That was in Topeka, Kansas.

"Just recently I went back to Kansas to visit an aunt and when the train got in I stopped at the counter in the station for breakfast. The hostess came up and said, 'I have a table for you' and then took me practically back to the kitchen. I said, 'I really don't need this table, I'll go back to the counter.' In a drug store when I tried to get a coke at the counter, they handed it to me in a paper container in a bag!

"Yes, that's in Kansas and it's that way more or less all over the Middle West. You can't be sure how

Melvin Stewart and Ethel Ayler as Simple and Zarita in Simply Heavenly. *Hughes collaborated with composer David Martin on this musical that opened on 21 May 1957 (photograph by Carl Van Vechten; Library of Congress, Prints & Photographs Division, Carl Van Vechten Collection, courtesy of Carl Van Vechten Trust).*

This interview article with journalist Martha MacGregor was published after Hughes's third Simple book, Simple Stakes a Claim *(1957). MacGregor asks about Orval E. Faubus, governor of Arkansas from 1955 to 1967, who defied a federal court order to integrate Little Rock Central High School by calling in the Arkansas National Guard to prevent black students from entering the school.*

Simple is Back

Langston Hughes lives in his Aunt Toy Harper's rooming-house on East 127th St., where I found him in the front garden. "The garden is a defense," said Hughes, laughing. "I couldn't keep the children off it, so I asked them if they'd like to make it

you'll be treated. Some places will take you in and some won't—you never know.

"In the South there are so many little nuances that are amusing, yet sad. At some of the airports the limousines will take you into town, but in some cities you have to get a taxi—and a Negro taxi, not a white taxi.

"I don't see why Negroes who can possibly get out stay in the South and that's God's truth. I go down South and read my poems and get back to Harlem as fast as I can.

———

"There are decent people on both sides; the tragedy is they're being kept apart. I was speaking at a white college down South where I happen to know a Negro writer in the town. I wanted to see her, and the people at the college said they would come along, they would like to meet her.

"So we drive up to this very nice Negro home—beautiful garden—and the students and professor go up on the porch and I introduce them to my friend. She said, 'How do you do and goodbye.' Just like that. 'How do you do and goodbye.'

"Later she told me that she simply could not invite those people into her home. One of the teachers at the college had arranged for a group of white students to visit her and see her library, and it had gotten all over town that she was socializing with whites. Bigots on both sides went into action and her husband almost lost his job and the teacher who brought the students was called on the carpet."

———

I asked Hughes what the ordinary well-meaning citizen could do to help. First, he said, be as decent as you can on the personal level. But personal good will is not enough. Do everything you can to support liberal legislation and the kind of candidates who will give us liberal legislation. And we must give money to the NAACP and other civil rights organizations. These injunctions are expensive. "Who has the money to go hire a lawyer every time they can't ride on a bus? But if you want justice you have to do it."

—*New York Post,* 15 September 1957, p. M11

* * *

While many critics found the production of Simply Heavenly *to be enjoyable if not highly polished, some of Hughes's friends were troubled by what they perceived to be its stereotypical or one-sided representations of African American life. In his biography of Hughes, Arnold Rampersad quotes a 7 June 1957 letter to* the author from William L. Patterson, a leader in the Communist Party: "To me, Lang, the play was political. But the politics suited my enemy's—Simple's enemy's—aims and purposes in describing the Negro."

Scenes from *Simply Heavenly*

ACT I
SCENE 1

A lonely guitar is playing in the darkness—it's the Blues . . . Simple's room. Early spring evening. Simple, just coming home from work, removes his jacket as he enters, but before he can hang it up, the voice of Madam Butler, his landlady, is heard calling up the stairs, through the half-open door.

LANDLADY. Mr. Semple! Oh, Mr. Semple!

SIMPLE. Yes'm?

LANDLADY. I heard you come in! Mr. Semple, would you mind taking Trixie out for a walk? My arthritis is bothering me.

SIMPLE. Madam Butler, please! I've got no time to walk no dog tonight. Joyce is waiting for me.

LANDLADY. From all I've heard, that girl's been waiting for you to marry her for years! A few minutes of waiting for you to show up tonight won't hurt.

SIMPLE. Madam, my private affairs ain't none of your business.

LANDLADY. Um-hum! Well, you don't need to take Trixie to no tree—just the nearest fireplug. (*Boyd, a fellow-roomer, peers in.*)

SIMPLE. Aw, I ain't hardly got home from work good, yet. . . . Hello, Boyd. Come on in. Landladies is a bodiddling! How come she never make none of the other roomers—or you—to walk her dog?

BOYD. She knows I won't do it, that's why.

SIMPLE. Don't you ever get behind in your rent?

BOYD. Not to the point of walking dogs. But you seem to walk Trixie pretty often.

SIMPLE. Mostly always.

LANDLADY. Did you say you would take the dog?

SIMPLE. Oh, hell, lemme go walk the bitch.

LANDLADY. No profanity in my house.

SIMPLE. Madam, that's a perfectly good word meaning a fine girl dog—bitch—for female dog.

LANDLADY. There'll be no bitches in my house—and that goes for your girl friend, Zarita, too.

SIMPLE. I'll thank you to leave my friends out of this.

LANDLADY. I'll thank you to keep your profanity to yourself. This is a decent house. Now, come on and walk my dog—else pay me my rent.

SIMPLE. I'll walk your dog—because I love Trixie, though, that's what! If I had a dog, I wouldn't keep it

From Jacket Design by Ben Feder Inc.

By Langston Hughes:

'Simple Stakes a Claim'

"The race problem in America," says Langston Hughes, "is serious business . . . But must it always be written about seriously?" The novelist-poet-playwright supplies his own answer: No. Humor, he says, is a weapon too, and he suggests that "since we have not been able to moralize [Dixiecrats and their kind] out of existence with indignant editorials, maybe we could laugh them to death." The story on this page is from Hughes' latest collection of tales, "Simple Stakes a Claim" (Rinehart). More excerpts will appear in subsequent editions of The Post Week-End Magazine.

Jazz, Jive and Jam

"It being Negro History Week," said Simple, "Joyce took me to a pay lecture to hear some Negro hysterian——"

"Historian," I corrected.

"Hy-terian speak," continued Simple, "and he laid our Negro race low. He said we was misbred, misread, and misled, also losing our time good-timing. Instead of time-taking and money-making, we are jazz-shaking. Oh, he enjoyed hisself at the expense of the colored race—and him black as me. He really delivered a lecture—in which, no doubt, there is some truth."

"Constructive criticism, I gather—a sort of tearing down in order to build up."

"He tore us down good," said Simple. "Joyce come out saying to me, her husband, that he had really got my number. I said, 'Baby, he did not miss you, neither.' But Joyce did not consider herself included in the bad things he said."

"She answers me back. 'How come your gullet has got to be so wet? You are sitting in this subway right now looking like you would like to have a beer.'"

"'Solid!' I said. 'I would. How did you guess it?'"

"'Married to you for three years, I can read your mind,' said Joyce. 'We'll buy a couple of cans to take home. I might even drink one myself.'"

"'Joyce, baby,' I said, 'in that case, let's buy three cans.'"

"Joyce says, 'Remember the budget, Jess.'"

"I says, 'Honey, you done busted the budget going to that lecture program which cost One Dollar a head, also we put some small change in the collection to help Negroes get ahead.'"

"'Small change?' says Joyce, 'I put a dollar.'"

"'Then our budget is busted real good,' I said, 'so

we might as well dent it some more. Let's get six cans of beer.'

"'All right,' says Joyce, 'go ahead, drink yourself to the dogs—instead of saving for that house we want to buy!'"

"'Six cans of beer would not pay for even the bottom front step,' I said. 'But they would lift my spirits this evening. That Negro high-speaking doctor done tore my spirits down. I did not know before that the colored race was so misled, misread, and misbred. According to him there is hardly a pure black man left. But I was setting in the back, so I guess he did not see me.'

"'Had you not had to go to sleep in the big chair after dinner,' says Joyce, 'we would have been there on time and had seats up front.'

"'I were near enough to that joker,' I said. 'Loud as he could holler, we did not need to set no closer. And he certainly were nothing to look at!'

"'Very few educated men look like Harry Belafonte,' said Joyce.

"'I am glad I am handsome instead of wise,' I said. But Joyce did not crack a smile. She had that lecture on her mind.

"'Dr. Conboy is smart,' says Joyce. 'Did you hear him quoting Aristotle?'

"'Who were Harry Stottle?' I asked.

"'Some people are not even misread,' said Joyce. 'Aristotle was a Greek philosopher like Socrates, a great man of ancient times.'

"'He must of been before Booker T. Washington then,' I said, 'because, to tell the truth, I has not heard of him at all. But tonight being Negro History Week, how come Dr. Conboy has to quote some Greek?'

"'There were black Greeks,' said Joyce. 'Did you not hear him say that Negroes have played a part in all history, throughout all time, from Eden to now?'

"'Do you reckon Eve was brownskin?' I requested.

"'I do not know about Eve,' said Joyce, 'but Cleopatra was of the colored race, and the Bible says Sheba, beloved of Solomon, was black but comely.'

"'I wonder would she come to me?' I says . . .

"'But by that time the subway had got to our stop. At the store Joyce broke the budget again, opened up her pocket purse, and bought us six cans of beer. So it were a good evening. It ended well—except that I ain't for going to any more meetings—especially interracial meetings.'

"'Come now! Don't you want to improve race relations?'

"'Sure,' said Simple, 'but in my opinion, jazz, jive and jam would be better for race relations than all this high-flown gab, gaff and gas the orators put out. All this talking that white folks do at meetings, and big Negroes, too, about how to get along together—just a little jam session would have everybody getting along fine without having to listen to so many speeches. Why, last month Joyce took me to a Race Relations Seminar which her club and twenty other clubs gave, and man, it lasted three days! . . .'

"'And you sat through all that?'

"'I did not set,' said Simple. 'I stood. I walked in and walked out. I smoked on the corner and snuck two drinks at the bar. But I had to wait for Joyce, and I thought them speeches would never get over! My wife

were a delegate from her club, so she had to stay, although I think Joyce got tired her own self. But she would not admit it. Joyce said, 'Dr. Hillary Thingabod was certainly brilliant, were he not?'

"'I said, 'He were not.'

"Joyce said, 'What did you want the man to say?'

"'I said, 'I wish he had sung, instead of said. That program needed some music to keep folks awake.'

"Joyce said, 'Our forum was not intended for a musical. It was intended to see how we can work out integration.'

"'I said, 'With a jazz band, they could work out integration in ten minutes. Everybody would have been dancing together like they do at the Savoy—colored and white—or down on the East Side at them Casinos on a Friday night where jam holds forth—and we would have been integrated.'

"Joyce said, 'This was a serious seminar, aiming at facts, not fun.'

"'Baby,' I said, 'what is more facts than acts? Jazz makes people get into action, move! Didn't nobody move in that hall where you were—except to jerk their head up when they went to sleep, to keep anybody from seeing that they was nodding. . . . Thank God, I did not have to set up there like you with the delegation. I would not be a delegate to no such gab-fest for nothing on earth.'

"'I thought you was so interested in saving the race!' said Joyce. 'Next time I will not ask you to accompany me to any cultural events, Jesse B., because I can see you do not appreciate them. That were a discussion of ways and means. And you are talking about jazz bands!'

"'There's more ways than one to skin a cat,' I said. 'A jazz band like Duke's or Hamp's or Basie's sure would of helped that meeting. At least on Saturday afternoon, they could have used a little music to put some pep into the proceedings. Now, just say for instant, baby, they was to open with jazz and close with jam—and do the talking in between. Start out, for example, with "The St. Louis Blues," which is a kind of colored national anthem. That would put every human in a good humor. Then play, "Why Don't You Do Right" which could be addressed to white folks. They could pat their feet to that. Then for a third number before introducing the speaker, let some guest star like Pearl Bailey sing "There'll Be Some Changes Made"—which, as I understand it, were the theme of the meeting, anyhow—and all the Negroes could say. Amen!

"'Joyce, I wish you would let me plan them interracial seminars next time. After the music, let the speechmaking roll for a while—with maybe a calypso between speeches. Then, along about five o'clock, bring on the jam session, extra-special. Start serving tea to "Tea For Two," played real cool. Whilst drinking tea and dancing, the race relationers could relate, the integraters could integrate, and the desegregators desegregate. Joyce, you would not have to beg for a crowd to come out and support your efforts then. Jam—and the hall would be jammed! Even I would stick around, and not be outside sneaking a smoke, or trying to figure how I can get to the bar before the resolutions are voted on. Resolved: that we solve the race problem! Strike up the band! Hit it, men! Aw, play that thing! "How High the Moon!" How high! Wheee-ee-e!'"

"'What did Joyce say to that?' I demanded.

"'Joyce just thought I was high,' said Simple."

Mr. Jesse B. Semple is the name Langston Hughes gave a real-life character he met in a Harlem gin mill one hot wartime evening. Fascinated at his bar companion's unorthodox outlook on the American scene, Hughes wrote a series of columns about him in The Chicago Defender, a Negro weekly. Enthusiastic readers immediately interpreted "Jesse B. Semple" to mean "Just Be Simple," and Hughes' character overnight became "Simple"—and eventually the hero of three published volumes, "Simple Speaks His Mind," "Simple Takes a Wife" and now "Simple Stakes a Claim."

A story from Simple Stakes a Claim *that was reprinted in the* New York Post *(Langston Hughes Collection, Schomburg Center for Research in Black Culture, New York Public Library)*

penned up in the house all day neither. Poor old thing, airless as she is.

LANDLADY. She's not hairless.

SIMPLE. I said *airless*, Madam! Shut up airtight, wonder Trixie don't get arthritis, too. Dogs and womens, dogs and womens! Damn! What am I gonna do?

BOYD. Good luck, pal. (*Simple and Boyd exit. BLACK-OUT. In the darkness, Trixie's bark is heard. Auto horns, street noises. Simple's voice addresses the barking dog.*)

SIMPLE. Now, Trixie, come on now. Come on, Trixie, do your duty. Leave that other dog alone, Trixie! Hound, get away from here! O.K., O.K., let's head on in the house. (*Bark.*) Now, go on to your madam. I guess you love her. Well, I love somebody, too! My choice, Joyce! She's the one I found—and that's where I'm bound. Trixie, that's where I am bound. (*The music of "Simply Heavenly" rises happily as the LIGHTS COME UP to reveal Joyce's room.*)

ACT I
SCENE 2

Joyce's room a bit later. Joyce is singing as, in a frilly dressing gown, she is putting her clothes away.

JOYCE.

Love is simply heavenly!
What else could it be?
When love's made in heaven
And you are made for me.
Love is simply heavenly!
What else can I say?
When love sends an angel
To hold me close this way.
Love is like a dream
That's too good to be true,
But when your lips kiss mine
The dream turns into you.
Yes, it's simply heavenly!
Our love's just divine—
For love is made in heaven
And you, my love, are mine!

Love is simply heavenly—

(*Voice of her Landlady calls from below stairs.*)

MRS. CADDY. Oo-oo-oo-oo! Miss Lane!

JOYCE. Yes?

MRS. CADDY. I'm letting Mr. Semple come up. OK?

JOYCE. Yes, indeed, Mrs. Caddy, I'm expecting him. (*Simple knocks lightly and enters grinning.*)

SIMPLE. Hey, Baby! (*He closes the door, to which Joyce objects.*)

JOYCE. Jess! No! Just a crack. . . .

SIMPLE. Aw, your old landlady's worse than mine. At least I can shut my door when I got company.

JOYCE. You're a man. I'm a— (*Simple hugs Joyce.*)

SIMPLE. Lady! Which is what I like about you. Joyce, morals is your middle name. But you can still be a lady behind closed doors.

JOYCE. I know, Jess, those are the landlady's rules. Besides, I respect Mrs. Caddy.

SIMPLE. She don't respect you if she thinks soon as the door is shut—

JOYCE. Sshhss! Come on, rest your jacket, honey. It's warm.

SIMPLE. I knowed there was something! I forgot to bring your ice cream! I passed right by the place, too!

JOYCE. We can walk out for a soda.

SIMPLE. Or a beer?

JOYCE. Tomorrow's communion Sunday, and I do not drink beer before communion.

SIMPLE. You just don't drink beer, period! Gimme a little sugar and we'll skip the beer.

JOYCE. Don't think I'll skip the ice cream.

SIMPLE. Let's set on the— (*He dances toward the studio bed.*)

JOYCE. There's a chair.

SIMPLE. Baby, what's the matter? Don't you trust me yet?

JOYCE. I don't mind you being close to me. But when you get close to a bed, too—

SIMPLE. Then you don't trust yourself.

JOYCE. Have you ever known me to—

SIMPLE. That's the trouble . . .

JOYCE. That goes with marriage, not courtship. And if you don't move on from courtship to engagement soon, Jess Semple, and do something about that woman in Baltimore.

SIMPLE. My wife! Isabel—she run me out—but she could claim I left her. She could find some grounds to get a divorce.

JOYCE. Since you're not together, why don't you get one?

SIMPLE. Joyce, I don't want to pay for no woman's divorce I don't love. And I do not love Isabel. Also, I ain't got the money.

JOYCE. I would help you pay for it.

SIMPLE. One thing I would not let you do, Joyce, is pay for no other woman's divorce. No!

JOYCE. Well, if you and I just paid for half of it, you'd only be paying for your part of the divorce.

SIMPLE. That woman wants me to pay for it all! And, Joyce, I don't love her. I love you. Joyce, do you want me to commit bigamy?

JOYCE. Five years you've been away from your wife—three years since you met me! In all that time you haven't reached a point yet where you can ask for my hand without committing bigamy. I don't know how my love holds out so long on promises. But now my friends

Program cover for the play based on Hughes's Simple stories (courtesy of Kenneth Spencer Research Library, University of Kansas Libraries)

are all asking when I'm going to get married. Even my landlady's saying it's a mighty long time for a man to just be "coming around calling," just sitting doing nothing.

SIMPLE. I agree, baby—when there ain't no action, I get kinder drowsy.

JOYCE. Well, to me, a nice conversation is action.

SIMPLE. Conversationing makes me sleepy.

JOYCE. Then you ought to go to bed early instead of hanging over Paddy's Bar until all hours. You have got to go to work just like I do.

SIMPLE. When I sleep, I sleep fast. Anyhow, I can't go to bed early just because you do, Joyce, until—unless—

JOYCE. Until what?

SIMPLE. Until we're married.

JOYCE. Simple!

SIMPLE. But, listen! It's Saturday night, fine outside. Spring in Harlem! Come on, let's us get some ice cream.

JOYCE. O.K., but, Jess, are you coming to church in the morning to see me take communion?

SIMPLE. You know I'll be there. We'll just take a little stroll down Seventh Avenue now and catch some air, heh?

JOYCE. And you'll bring me home early, so we can both get our rest.

SIMPLE. In a jiffy, then I'll turn in, too.

JOYCE. You don't mean into a bar?

SIMPLE. Baby, one thing I *bar* is bars.

JOYCE. Turn your back so I can dress.

SIMPLE. Don't stand over there. Anybody could be looking in.

JOYCE. There are no peeping-toms in this house. *(Simple turns his back as she dresses, but drops his pack of cigarettes on the floor, bends down to get it, then remains that way, looking at Joyce from between his legs.)* Baby, is your back turned?

SIMPLE. Yes'm. *(Joyce glances his way, clutches her dress to her bosom and screams.)*

JOYCE. Oh, Simple!

SIMPLE. I love it when you call me Simple. *(Head still down, he proceeds to turn a somersault, coming up seated on the floor with his back toward her.)* Now say my back ain't turned.

JOYCE. I didn't mean you had to turn inside out.

SIMPLE. That's the way you've got my heart—turned in . . . *(He turns his eyes to look at her.)*

JOYCE. Then turn your head so I can dress.

SIMPLE. O.K., Joyce. Now, is everything all right?

JOYCE. Everything is all right.

SIMPLE. So you feel O.K.?

JOYCE. Simply heavenly! Oh, Jess, it's wonderful to be in love.

SIMPLE. Just wonderful—wonderful—wonderful— *(As Joyce dresses, they sing.)*

BOTH.

Love is simply heavenly!
What else could it be?
When love's made in heaven
And you are made for me.
Love is simply heavenly!
What else can I say?
When love sends an angel
To hold me close this way.
Love is like a dream
That's too good to be true,
But when your lips kiss mine
The dream turns into you.
Yes, it's simply heavenly!
Our love's just divine—
For love is made in heaven
And you, my love, are mine!

SIMPLE.

Love is simply heavenly!
What else could it be?
When love is made in heaven
And you are made for me.

JOYCE.

Love is simply heavenly!
What else can I say?
When love sends me an angel
To hold me close this way.

SIMPLE.

Love is like a dream
That's too good to be true,
(Dressed now, Joyce emerges and Simple rises to embrace her.)

JOYCE.

But when your lips kiss mine
The dream turns into you.

BOTH.

Yes, it's simply heavenly!
Our love's just divine—
For love is made in heaven
And you, my love, are mine!

BLACKOUT

–Langston Hughes and David Martin, *Simply Heavenly* (New York: Dramatists Play Service, 1958), pp. 7–13

Who sang Cora in "The Barrier"
at Columbia University

Review published in the 19 January 1950 issue of the New York Herald Tribune. *Good reviews of the initial production led producers to take the play to Broadway (Langston Hughes Collection, Schomburg Center for Research in Black Culture, New York Public Library).*

Poetry and Prose

Montage of a Dream Deferred, a work Hughes conceived as a book-length poem in six sections, was published in February 1951 by Holt. Arthur P. Davis, one of the editors of The Negro Caravan: Writings by American Negroes *(1941), wrote this review.*

"A Sensitive and Fascinating Work"
Review of *Montage of a Dream Deferred*

Carl Van Vechten has called Langston Hughes the "Negro Poet Laureate," but this title, it seems to me, is too ambitious. I prefer to think of Hughes as the "Poet Laureate of Harlem." He has been associated with that community since the days of the Negro Renaissance; he has written about Harlem oftener and more fully than any other writer; and in this, his latest work, he gives a picture of that city, which in sympathy, depth and understanding has rarely been equalled.

In *Montage of a Dream Deferred,* Mr. Hughes has recaptured some of the magic of phrase and tone which characterized *Weary Blues* (1925), his first publication. Decidedly superior to *Shakespeare in Harlem* (1942), the

present volume is a sensitive and fascinating work. Sometimes tender and pathetic, sometimes playful and satiric, and sometimes profoundly moving, *Montage of a Dream Deferred* is, in some respects, the most mature verse that Hughes has yet produced.

In this volume, the poet has made effective use of a technique with which he has been experimenting since 1925. Mr. Hughes explains this technique in a brief prefatory note:

> In terms of current Afro-American popular music . . . this poem on contemporary Harlem, like be-bop, is marked by conflicting changes, sudden nuances, sharp and impudent interjections, broken rhythms, and passages sometimes in the manner of the jam session, sometimes the popular song, punctuated by the riffs, runs, breaks, and disc-tortions of the music of a community in transition.

According to this scheme, we are to consider the whole book of ninety-odd pieces as really one long poem, marked by the conflicting changes, broken rhythms, and sudden interjections characteristic of a jam session. This "jam session" technique is highly effective because it not only ties together fragmentary and unrelated segments in the work, but it also allows the poet, without being monot-

Hughes, Muriel Rahn, and Lawrence Tibbett on the set of The Barrier. *The play had a short run and disappointing reviews when it opened on Broadway at the Broadhurst Theatre on 2 November 1950 (Langston Hughes Papers, Yale Collection of American Literature, Beinecke Rare Book and Manuscript Library).*

onous, to return again and again to his over-all theme, that of Harlem's frustration. Like the deep and persistent rolling of a boogie bass—now loud and raucous, now soft and pathetic—this theme of Harlem's dream deferred marches relentlessly throughout the poem. Hughes knows that Harlem is neither a gay nor healthy but basically a tragic and frustrated city, and he beats that message home. Because of the fugue-like structure of the poem, it is impossible for the reader to miss the theme or to forget it.

Langston Hughes, as I have said above, knows and loves and understands Harlem. He can see the pathos in a Harlem night funeral or a fraternal parade. He understands the grim realism of poverty-stricken slum-dwellers who like war because it means money for them. He sympathizes with the Harlem wife who can play, *via* a dream book, the number suggested by her husband's dying remarks. He realizes the appeal which black celebrities have for white girls, and he knows the explosive possibilities of such alliances. He is conscious of Harlem's bitter anti-Semitism. He is aware that Harlem, white opinion to the contrary, is not one city but several; and he can, therefore, understand the bitterness of the Negro masses when they are snubbed by their Cadillac-riding professional men. But he also understands the shame of the "respectable" Harlemite when he sees the crudeness and the violence of the masses. All of these things and many more, Langston Hughes knows thoroughly, and he writes convincingly about them.

There are a few false notes in *Montage of a Dream Deferred*. Poems like "Not a Movie," "Ballad of a Landlord," and "Freedom Train," especially the last, seem alien to the mood of the work. Essentially, they are protest pieces of a type now definitely outmoded. Their tunes have been played so often and so long they have lost their power to move us. Even in a *montage* arrangement, they still impress me as being out of key with the mood and spirit of the rest of the work.

Each reader will pick his favorite poems from the *Montage of a Dream Deferred*, and he will have a wide and diversified field of choice. One of the loveliest poems in the book for me and one of the most delicate Hughes has ever done is "College Formal: Renaissance Casino." "Theme for English B" is also a moving presentation of the Negro's peculiar "Americanism," and "Night Funeral in Harlem" has the kind of folk pathos which is effective because it is genuine. The pieces in the work carrying the title-theme are generally well done and, as I have intimated above, serve admirably their purpose in this type of "jam session" presentation. Taken all in all, *Montage of a Dream Deferred* is a provocative and highly delightful work.

–*Journal of Negro History*, 36 (April 1951): 224–226

* * *

John W. Parker, who wrote this review, mistakenly attributed Ann Petry's novel The Street *(1946) to Hughes.*

Poetry of Harlem in Transition
Review of *Montage of a Dream Deferred*

With the recent publication of *Montage of a Dream Deferred,* his second book on the contemporary Harlem scene to appear within a year, Langston Hughes has rejuvenated the Harlem theme of the Mid-Twenties, and re-asserted his faith in popular verse, particularly that which draws upon popular Negro folk music. Implicit throughout the volume is a seriousness of purpose and a sense of awareness of times transhifting. And, like such previous studies as *The Weary Blues* (1926), *The Street* (1946), and even *Simple Speaks His Mind* (1950), *Montage of a Dream Deferred* runs the gamut of the ups and downs that constitute the way of life for present-day Harlem; unlike them, however, it betrays the inner conflict of Harlem's Brown Americans, and a consciousness of the steady pull exerted by this urban community in transition. It is a fast-moving story of a people who, despite their own imperfections and the bitter and corroding circumstances they face from day to day, have never relinquished their dream of a tomorrow that will be better. But it is a dream born out of a heartache, a dream much like life in dark Harlem—"all mixed up."

Montage of a Dream Deferred, Mr. Hughes' first book-length poem in his twenty-odd years of writing, is divided into six parts—"Boogie Segue to Bop," "Dig and Be Dug," "Early Bright," "Vice Versa to Bach," "Dream Deferred" and "Lenox Avenue Mural." A good many of these "poems within a poem" have appeared previously in such publications as *Tomorrow, Our World, Common Ground,* and *The Harlem Quarterly.* Scattered generously throughout the volume are poems written after the style of Negro folk songs known as boogie-woogie and be-bop. Of the manner in which he has appropriated popular Negro folk music to heighten the effectiveness of poetry that is equally popular, Hughes writes in the introductory statement: "In terms of current Afro-American popular music and the sources from which it has progressed—jazz, ragtime, swing, blues, boogie-woogie, and be-bop—this poem on contemporary Harlem, like be-bop, is marked by conflicting changes, sudden nuances, sharp and impudent interjections, broken rhythms, and passages sometimes in the manner of a jam session." Thus the reader is prepared for innovations he may find them—the occasional omission of the latter part of a line, the excessive employment of the dash for a sudden and sometimes unwarranted break in thought, the insertion of such otherwise meaningless expressions as "oop-pop-a-da," and, of course, "Figurine," a one-line poem that is limited to an even two words. By and large the measures throughout the book are cut to absolute simplicity, and the language, the imagery, and the easy flow of syllables enhance one of the collection's strong features— its popular appeal. Unlike the position taken by James Joyce a few years back, Hughes is convinced that comprehensibility in poetic expression is a virtue, not a vice.

The goings-on in Harlem as disclosed by *Montage of a Dream Deferred* leave much to be desired. The "bad nigger," who can out Herod Herod, proceeds from joint to joint; wide-eyed newcomers from the South encounter "bars at each gate"; the low and the high look, not across, but up and down at one another; pimps make the rounds at Lenox Avenue gin-mills while hustlers wait in dark doorways; and in the effort to get along on a "dime and a prayer," many sicken and die. It is the same old story of "dig and be dug" and of "trying to forget to remember the taste of day."

The nine-line poem, "Jam Session," which appears in the section, "Early Bright," defines a situation that is fraught with tragedy and comedy, hope and despair, faith and disillusionment, but one that reveals the black man's struggle to salt his dreams away:

Letting midnight
out of jail
          pop-a-da
having been
detained in jail
          oop-pop-a-da
for sprinkling salt
on a dreamer's tail
          pop-a-da

First and last, *Montage of a Dream Deferred,* like the six books of poetry that have preceded it, suggests the manner in which Mr. Hughes has gone on loving life and writing upon those aspects of it that have stirred his emotion deeply—"Negro life, and its relations to the problems of Democracy." Convinced that the writing of poetry about Brown Americans is serious business in these times of transition, he has remained indifferent to criticism sometimes levelled at his "predominantly-Negro themes," and at the extreme popular aspect of his poetic output. Likewise, he has shied away from the recent tendency on the part of some Negro writers in the direction of a "return to form" and of international and global perspective.

But that is Langston Hughes. And it is perhaps one of the reasons that his name has become synonymous with popular Negro poetry. With its freshness of approach, its powerful rhythm, and its moving quality, *Montage of a Dream Deferred* further justifies its author's claim to the title by which he is frequently designated in literary circles, "The Negro Poet Laureate."

                                   –*Phylon,* 12 (Second Quarter, 1951): 195–197

*   *   *

In January 1952 Holt published Hughes's second collection of non-Simple short stories, Laughing to Keep from Crying, *to generally positive reviews. The volume includes stories mainly written from the mid 1930s to early 1940s that had been previously published in periodicals, including* Esquire, American Spectator, The Crisis, *and* The New Yorker.

The thirteenth of twenty-four stories in the volume, "Professor" was originally published in the May–June 1935 issue of The Anvil.

Professor

Promptly at seven a big car drew up in front of the Booker T. Washington Hotel, and a white chauffeur in uniform got out and went toward the door, intending to ask at the desk for a colored professor named T. Walton Brown. But the professor was already sitting in the lobby, a white scarf around his neck and his black overcoat ready to button over his dinner clothes.

As soon as the chauffeur entered, the professor approached. "Mr. Chandler's car?" he asked hesitantly.

"Yes, sir," said the white chauffeur to the neat little Negro. "Are you Dr. Walton Brown?"

"I am," said the professor, smiling and bowing a little.

The chauffeur opened the street door for Dr. Brown, then ran to the car and held the door open there, too. Inside the big car and on the long black running board as well, the lights came on. The professor stepped in among the soft cushions, the deep rug, and the cut glass vases holding flowers. With the greatest of deference the chauffeur quickly tucked a covering of fur about the professor's knees, closed the door, entered his own seat in front beyond the glass partition, and the big car purred away. Within the lobby of the cheap hotel a few ill-clad Negroes watched the whole procedure in amazement.

"A big shot!" somebody said.

At the corner as the car passed, two or three ash-colored children ran across the street in front of the wheel, their skinny legs and poor clothes plain in the glare of the headlights as the chauffeur slowed down to let them pass. Then the car turned and ran the whole length of a Negro street that was lined with pawn shops, beer joints, pig's knuckle stands, cheap movies, hairdressing parlors, and other ramshackle places of business patronized by the poor blacks of the district. Inside the big car the professor, Dr. Walton Brown, regretted that in all the large Midwestern cities where he had lectured on his present tour in behalf of his college, the main Negro streets presented the same sleazy and disagreeable appearance: pig's knuckle joints, pawn shops, beer parlors—and houses of vice, no doubt—save that these latter, at least, did not hang out their signs.

The professor looked away from the unpleasant sight of this typical Negro street, poor and unkempt. He looked ahead through the glass at the dignified white neck of the uniformed chauffeur in front of him. The professor in his dinner clothes, his brown face even browner above the white silk scarf at his neck, felt warm and comfortable under the fur rug. But he felt, too, a little unsafe at being driven through the streets of this city on the edge of the South in an expensive car, by a white chauffeur.

"But, then," he thought, "this is the wealthy Mr. Ralph P. Chandler's car, and surely no harm can come to me here. The Chandlers are a power in the Middle West, and in the South as well. Theirs is one of the great fortunes of America. In philanthropy, nobody exceeds them in well-planned generosity on a large and highly publicized scale. They are a power in Negro edu-

cation, too. That is why I am visiting them tonight at their invitation."

Just now the Chandlers were interested in the little Negro college at which the professor taught. They wanted to make it one of the major Negro colleges of America. And in particular the Chandlers were interested in his Department of Sociology. They were thinking of endowing a chair of research there and employing a man of ability for it. A Ph.D. and a scholar. A man of some prestige, like the professor. For his *The Sociology of Prejudice* (that restrained and conservative study of Dr. T. Walton Brown's) had recently come to the attention of the Chandler Committee. And a representative of their philanthropies, visiting the campus, had conversed with the professor at some length about his book and his views. This representative of the Committee found Dr. Brown highly gratifying, because in almost every case the professor's views agreed with the white man's own.

Invitation to a party celebrating Hughes's second book of short stories (Langston Hughes Collection, Schomburg Center for Research in Black Culture, New York Public Library)

"A fine, sane, dependable young Negro," was the description that came to the Chandler Committee from their traveling representative.

So now the power himself, Mr. Ralph P. Chandler, and Mrs. Chandler, learning that he was lecturing at one of the colored churches of the town, had invited him to dinner at their mansion in this city on the edge of the South. Their car had come to call for him at the colored Booker T. Washington Hotel–where the hot water was always cold, the dresser drawers stuck, and the professor shivered as he got into his dinner clothes; and the bellboys, anxious for a tip, had asked him twice that evening if he needed a half pint or a woman.

But now he was in this big warm car and they were moving swiftly down a fine boulevard, the black slums far behind them. The professor was glad. He had been very much distressed at having the white chauffeur call for him at this cheap hotel in what really amounted to the red-light district of the town. But, then, none of the white hotels in this American city would house Negroes, no matter how cultured they might be. Marian Anderson herself had been unable to find decent accommodations there, so the colored papers said, on the day of her concert.

Sighing, the professor looked out of the car at the wide lawns and fine homes that lined the beautiful well-lighted boulevard where white people lived. After a time the car turned into a fashionable suburban road and he saw no more houses, but only ivy-hung walls, neat shrubs, and boxwoods that indicated not merely homes beyond but vast estates. Shortly the car whirled into a paved driveway, past a small lodge, through a park full of fountains and trees, and up to a private house as large as a hotel. From a tall portico a great hanging lantern cast a soft glow on the black and chrome body of the big car. The white chauffeur jumped out and deferentially opened the door for the colored professor. An English butler welcomed him at the entrance and took his coat, hat, and scarf. Then he led the professor into a large drawing room where two men and a woman were standing chatting near the fireplace.

The professor hesitated, not knowing who was who; but Mr. and Mrs. Chandler came forward, introduced themselves, shook hands, and in turn presented their other guest of the evening, Dr. Bulwick of the local Municipal College–a college that Dr. Brown recalled did *not* admit Negroes.

"I am happy to know you," said Dr. Bulwick. "I am also a sociologist."

"I have heard of you," said Dr. Brown graciously.

The butler came with sherry in a silver pitcher. They sat down, and the whites began to talk politely, to ask Dr. Brown about his lecture tour, if his audiences were good, if they were mostly Negro or mixed, and if there was much interest in his college, much money being given.

Then Dr. Bulwick began to ask about his book, *The Sociology of Prejudice,* where he got his material, under whom he had studied, and if he thought the Negro Problem would ever be solved.

Dr. Brown said genially, "We are making progress," which was what he always said, though he often felt he was lying.

"Yes," said Dr. Bulwick, "that is very true. Why, at our city college here we've been conducting some fine interracial experiments. I have had several colored ministers and high-school teachers visit my classes. We found them most intelligent people."

In spite of himself Dr. Brown had to say, "But you have no colored students at your college, have you?"

"No," said Dr. Bulwick, "and that is too bad! But that is one of our difficulties here. There is no Municipal College for Negroes–although nearly forty per cent of our population is colored. Some of us have thought it might be wise to establish a separate junior college for our Negroes, but the politicians opposed it on the score of no funds. And we cannot take them as students on our campus. That, at present, is impossible. It's too bad."

"But do you not think, Dr. Brown," interposed Mrs. Chandler, who wore diamonds on her wrists and smiled every time she spoke, "do you not think *your* people are happier in schools of their own–that it is really better for both groups not to mix them?"

In spite of himself Dr. Brown replied, "That depends, Mrs. Chandler. I could not have gotten my degree in any schools of our own."

"True, true," said Mr. Chandler. "Advanced studies, of course, cannot be gotten. But when your colleges are developed–as we hope they will be, and our Committee plans to aid in their development–when their departments are headed by men like yourself, for instance, then you can no longer say, 'That depends.'"

"You are right," Dr. Brown agreed diplomatically, coming to himself and thinking of his mission in that house. "You are right," Dr. Brown said, thinking too of that endowed chair of sociology and himself in the chair, the six thousand dollars a year that he would probably be paid, the surveys he might make and the books he could publish. "You are right," said Dr. Brown diplomatically to Ralph P. Chandler. But in the back of his head was that ghetto street full of sleazy misery he had just driven through, and the segregated hotel where the hot water was always cold, and the colored churches where he lectured, and the

Poster for a 1953 production of Hughes's one-act play about the conflicted relationship between a mother and her recently deceased son (Langston Hughes Papers, Yale Collection of American Literature, Beinecke Rare Book and Manuscript Library)

Jim Crow schools where Negroes always had less equipment and far less money than white institutions; and that separate justice of the South where his people sat on trial but the whites were judge and jury forever; and all the segregated Jim Crow things that America gave Negroes and that were never equal to the things she gave the whites. But Dr. Brown said, "You are right, Mr. Chandler," for, after all, Mr. Chandler had the money!

So he began to talk earnestly to the Chandlers there in the warm drawing room about the need for bigger and better black colleges, for more and more surveys of *Negro* life, and a well-developed department of sociology at his own little institution.

"Dinner is served," said the butler.

They rose and went into a dining room where there were flowers on the table and candles, white linen and silver, and where Dr. Brown was seated at the right of the hostess and the talk was light over the soup, but serious and sociological again by the time the meat was served.

"The American Negro must not be taken in by communism," Dr. Bulwick was saying with great positiveness as the butler passed the peas.

"He won't," agreed Dr. Brown. "I assure you, our leadership stands squarely against it." He looked at the Chandlers and bowed. "All the best people stand against it."

"America has done too much for the Negro," said Mr. Chandler, "for him to seek to destroy it."

Dr. Brown bobbed and bowed.

"In your *Sociology of Prejudice*," said Dr. Bulwick, "I highly approve of the closing note, your magnificent appeal to the old standards of Christian morality and the simple concepts of justice by which America functions."

"Yes," said Dr. Brown, nodding his dark head and thinking suddenly how on six thousand dollars a year he might take his family to South America in the summer where for three months they wouldn't feel like Negroes. "Yes, Dr. Bulwick," he nodded, "I firmly believe as you do that if the best elements of both races came together in Christian fellowship, we would solve this problem of ours."

"How beautiful," said Mrs. Chandler.

"And practical, too," said her husband. "But now to come back to your college–university, I believe you call it–to bring that institution up to really first-class standards you would need . . . ?"

"We would need . . ." said Dr. Brown, speaking as a mouthpiece of the administration, and speaking, too, as mouthpiece for the Negro students of his section of the South, and speaking for himself as a once ragged youth who had attended the college when its rating was lower than that of a Northern high school so that he had to study two years in Boston before he could enter a white college, when he had worked nights as redcap in the station and then as a waiter for seven years until he got his Ph.D., and then couldn't get a job in the North but had to go back down South to the work where he was now–but which might develop into a glorious opportunity at six thousand dollars a year to make surveys and put down figures that other scholars might study to get their Ph.D.'s, and that would bring him in enough to just once take his family on a vacation to South America where they wouldn't feel that they were Negroes. "We would need, Mr. Chandler, . . ."

And the things Dr. Brown's little college needed were small enough in the eyes of the Chandlers. The sane and conservative way in which Dr. Brown presented his case delighted the philanthropic heart of the Chandlers. And Mr. Chandler and Dr. Bulwick both felt that instead of building a junior college for Negroes in their own town they could rightfully advise local colored students to go down South to that fine little campus where they had a professor of their own race like Dr. Brown.

Over the coffee, in the drawing room, they talked about the coming theatrical season. And Mrs. Chandler spoke of how she loved Negro singers, and smiled and smiled.

In due time the professor rose to go. The car was called and he shook hands with Dr. Bulwick and the Chandlers. The white people were delighted with Dr. Brown. He could see it in their faces, just as in the past he could always tell as a waiter when he had pleased a table full of whites by tender steaks and good service.

"Tell the president of your college he shall hear from us shortly," said the Chandlers. "We'll probably send a man down again soon to talk to him about his expansion program." And they bowed farewell.

As the car sped him back toward town, Dr. Brown sat under its soft fur rug among the deep cushions and thought how with six thousand dollars a year earned by dancing properly to the tune of Jim Crow education, he could carry his whole family to South America for a summer where they wouldn't need to feel like Negroes.

–*Laughing to Keep from Crying* (New York: Holt, 1952), pp. 97–105

* * *

Lewis Gannett, a frequent reviewer for The Saturday Review of Literature *and the* New York Herald Tribune, *wrote this assessment.*

Books and Things
Review of *Laughing to Keep from Crying*

Langston Hughes has blues rhythms in his bones, and the blues that gives him the title for this book of color-line stories runs

When you see me laughing,
I'm laughing to keep from crying.

Between Laughter and Tears
In fact, few of these twenty-four evocative stories laugh aloud, and none of them cries; some of them merely record, and the best of them sing–sing in that

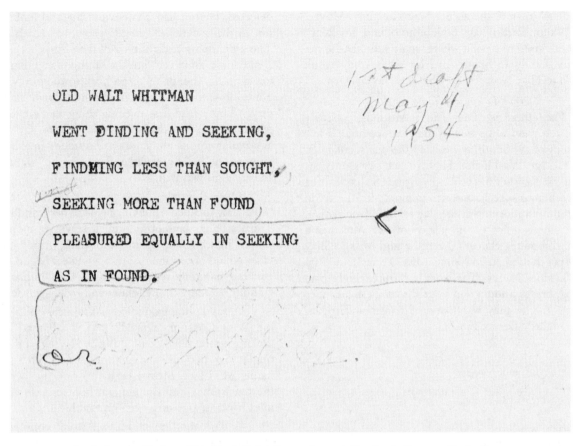

Draft of a poem Hughes published in the Beloit Poetry Journal Chapbook *(Langston Hughes Papers,*
Yale Collection of American Literature, Beinecke Rare Book and Manuscript Library)

minor blues key that is half-way between laughter and tears. Mr. Hughes has been around; he writes in many moods, but in his best stories, he catches conflict in the moods of a single moment.

Some of these are O. Henry stories with a Negro twist. There is the almost too neat tale of the two derelicts, one white, one black, insulting each other and fighting in a Hong Kong bar; then, in the gutter, becoming allies determined together to revenge themselves upon the Limey bartender who had had the temerity to throw two Americans out.

Still another tale pictures a white Harlem tourist, Edward Peedee McGill 3d, surviving a mugging with delight: "This is the first exciting thing that's ever happened to me," he says. "This is the first time in my life I've ever had a good time in Harlem. Everything else has been fake, a show. You know, something you pay for. This was real." Whereupon one of the black muggers says to the other: "What's the matter with rich white folks? Why you reckon they ain't happy?"

Along the Border Lines of Color

Mr. Hughes has followed the color line around the world. He tells a poignant tale of a brown-skinned boy in black Nigeria, who knows that his father will return to England and his mother's people will cast him out; he paints a weird scene in a Mexican bathhouse; reports a lively knifing in a Reno dive; recounts a Filipino experience in New Orleans. But the best of his stories are pictures of emotional border lines in what we call the border states of America. (The "border" sometimes reaches far into the North.)

"Big Meeting" tells of two dark boys contemptuously watching a revival meeting in which their mothers participate—until a white couple parks near by and echoes their own contempt. Langston Hughes subtly catches the dark eloquence of such Negro preaching—and the confusion in an "emancipated" man's reaction to its genuine emotion and piety.

"Professor" is another story of inner conflict. T. Walton Brown, professor of sociology at a Southern colored college, goes to dinner with the Ralph P. Chandlers, "liberal" philanthropists in a city somewhere on the latitude of Baltimore or St. Louis, where the local municipal college does not admit Negroes. Maybe the Chandlers will give generously to T. Walton Brown's college and provide scholarships to send boys from the

Chandlers' town to the deeper South to study. Maybe, if T. Walton Brown says nothing to offend, his salary might be raised to a point where, some summer, he can take his family to South America where they won't need to feel like Negroes. So what does he say?

'With Liberty and Justice for All'

Then there is "One Friday Morning," a story almost too good to be true. Nancy Lee, colored, a few years out of the South, has earned the one scholarship from George Washington High to her city's only art school. Her teacher has told her so; and she has written her acceptance speech, in warm gratitude for the credo repeated each morning in the flag salute–"One nation, indivisible, with liberty and justice for all." And then a higher committee changes the rules, and Miss O'Shay has a speech to make to Nancy. Miss O'Shay handles it well. So does Nancy. The story, heartbreakingly convincing, brings a lump into your throat. Perhaps, after reading it, you may recall one of Langston Hughes' poems, called "Border Line":

> I used to wonder
> About living and dying–
> I think the difference lies
> Between tears and crying.
>
> I used to wonder
> About here and there–
> I think the distance
> Is nowhere.

　　　　–New York Herald Tribune, 26 March 1952, p. 27

* * *

Bontemps wrote this review.

Black & Bubbling
Review of *Laughing to Keep from Crying*

Few people have enjoyed being Negro as much as Langston Hughes. Despite the bitterness with which he has occasionally indicted those who mistreat him because of his color (and in this collection of sketches and stories he certainly does not let up), there has never been any question in this reader's mind about his basic attitude. He would not have missed the experience of being what he is for the world.

The story "Why, You Reckon?," which appeared originally in *The New Yorker,* is really a veiled expression of his own feeling. Disguised as a young Park Avenue bachelor who comes with a group of wealthy friends for a night of colorful, if not primitive, entertainment in a Harlem night club, the Langston Hughes of a couple of decades ago can be clearly

detected. He too had come exploring and looking for fun in the unfamiliar territory north of 125th Street. The kidnapping and robbing of the visitor in the story is of course contrived, but the young man's reluctance to rejoin his friends or to go back to the safety of his home downtown reflects the author's own commentary. "This is the first exciting thing that's ever happened to me," he has the white victim say to the amazement of his abductors as he stands in a coal bin stripped of his overcoat and shoes, his wallet and studs. "This was real."

Over this tale, as over most of the others in "Laughing to Keep from Crying," the depression of the Thirties hangs ominously, and it serves as more than just an indication of the dates of their writing. It provides a kind of continuity. After a while it begins to suggest the nameless dread which darkens human lives without reference to breadlines and relief agencies.

A sailor, for example, makes a fast pick-up on the West Coast in jive talk ("Well, all reet! That's down my street! Name it!" "White Horse. Send it trotting!" "Set her up, and gimme a gin. What's your name, Miss Fine Brown Frame?") only to learn that the hard times and the general hopelessness of their lives frustrate pleasure even on that level.

A dark mother, in another story, consoles herself by attributing the prohibition-time ruin of her good-looking mulatto son to his Spanish blood. In another a rounder laughs at his misfortunes: "The next thing I knew I was in the hospital, shot everywhere but in my big toe. He fired on me point-blank– and barefooted. I was nothing but a target." And elsewhere a pushcart man becomes a sort of tape-recorder for grim, depression-shaded, Saturday night talk on Eighth Avenue; a blossoming girl painter is denied through prejudice a prize she had won; and in the occasionally anthologized Christmas story "On the Road" an unemployed black man, given a quick brush-off by a high-toned preacher, breaks into a church and sees a vision of Christ before the police arrest him and start breaking his knuckles with their sticks.

Langston Hughes has practised the craft of the short story no more than he has practiced the forms of poetry. His is a spontaneous art which stands or falls by the sureness of his intuition, his mother wit. His stories, like his poems, are for readers who will judge them with their hearts as well as their heads. By that standard he has always measured well. He still does.

　　　　　　　　–The Saturday Review of Literature,
　　　　　　　　35 (5 April 1952): 17

* * *

Sheet music for one of many songs Hughes wrote for Christmas pageants (Langston Hughes Collection, Schomburg Center for Research in Black Culture, New York Public Library)

The result of Hughes's collaboration with photographer Roy DeCarava, The Sweet Flypaper of Life *(1955) was one of his most critically acclaimed books. Hughes provided a monologue by the fictional Sister Mary Bradley as a narrative device for DeCarava's pictorial of Harlem life. Almena Lomax wrote this review.*

"The Why and Wherefore"
Review of *The Sweet Flypaper of Life*

This commentator has never been an admirer of Langston Hughes, except in the isolated instance, a poem here and there, and Part I of his biography, the title of which we have long since forgotten.

Trying to pin this disillusionment down, we think it is because he always seemed no more to us than a folklorist, a reporter and not an interpretative one, either, a photographer, maybe, a fellow who went around recording for Negroes what they said and were and did, without any more idea than his subjects of what it all meant, what it added up to, the why and wherefore.

It is ironic, therefore, that in the one book in which Langston Hughes has the forethought to arm himself with, not a camera, but better yet a marvelously articulate cameraman . . . in the book in which there is the least of Hughes, we should like him best, and feel that at last he has added up the why and wherefore and has emerged with something more than folklore, some of life, itself.

This is a charming little book, one which we can even imagine you, dear, dear *Tribune* readers, whose reading proclivities we frankly think nothing of, buying, reading, picking up again and again, perhaps never wholly tiring of. Such is the advantage over words of pictures, when they are "really real" and really life. They leap at you, smack you in the face, saying something with no effort on your part . . . which is something words do not do; also, they say something different each time. When they are good pictures, they are almost as multi-dimensional as live people. These, we might say, are great pictures.

EPIC OF LIFE IN HARLEM

This is a strictly Hughes story, really no more than a character sketch of an old woman, of the type whom we have come to know that Langston Hughes admires, above all men . . . somebody small, probably black, wiry, gutty, salty, gallant, philosophical . . . the "Life for me ain't been no crystal stair"-type, with a dash of Mehitable who had a "dance in the old girl, yet."

Possibly if you could read the manuscript, which is entirely a monologue, without the pictures, it might not be quite so complete a document of a woman's life.

But you can't read the words without looking at the pictures. . . . leastways we didn't try . . . who would want to? . . . and you end up having the complete epic of life in Harlem . . . the why, the wherefore . . . and something which we are not too sure Hughes has ever been able to say for himself, a relatedness of that life to life, itself.

This is not, we might point out, the dilemma summed up by Mr. George Lamming, the British West Indian writer of novels which we were never able to read. "The Castle of My Skin," for instance–lovely title, but we could never wade through the density of words, the fugues of words introspective, lovely sombre thoughts, funneling down into the hero until we felt as lost as Alice in Wonderland, falling through an endless tunnel in the earth.

Talking a commoner type of English to the students at Atlanta University last week than he has talked thus far in his novels, Mr. Lamming said the dilemma of the Negro writer is that he can't relate himself to the world he lives in.

This, you might say, has been the dilemma, particularly of Mr. Hughes, as a writer, and is the dilemma which has kept him the "laughing boy" of Negro literature for all the years of his writing career, dulling his talent with diffidence and self-deprecation, hinting at truths which he should have been expressing outright.

But there is nothing diffident, deprecatory, nor mute about "The Sweet Flypaper of Life". Here is a full lecture on life as it is lived in Harlem, and the lecture says of Harlem: . . . Life there is real, rounded, and fully packed . . . nothing shadowy, fragmentary, nor disoriented from the stuff of life, and none of the real living hemmed in appreciably by being black.

STARTS RIGHT ON COVER

The story begins right on the cover with the arrival of a telegram for "Sister Mary Bradley . . . at 113 W. 134th st., New York" from "The Lord", telling her to "'Come Home'" . . . a particular bit of ante-bellum corn, incidentally, which we wouldn't expect the new-found Hughes to rid himself of a tendency toward, all in one easy lesson.

Being a doughty old dame, Mary Bradley tells the Lord's messenger to take the Lord's wire on back because she isn't ready yet, "ain't no ways tired", and the rest of the book is sort of a decalogue on why Mary isn't ready, a recital which in spirit is so familiar that it will immediately put her "one" with all the women who know their little worlds hinge on them, and who can't take a trip . . . or who hope the baby won't come tonight and send them traipsing off to the hospital before they have fully prepared for all eventualities . . . or who, whether anybody writes a book about it or not, probably reject the summons of St. Peter with an "I'm not ready yet, Lord. There's so much here for me to do. . . . I'm needed around here so . . ."

Among the things Mary Bradley has to do is "look after Ronnie Bell", a winsome lass with big eyes whom you know Mary has identified with herself and wants to keep on scrubbing floors for, so she can give her "some of the advantages" she never had. . . . And she's got to set her mind to rest about Rodney, her easy-does-it "favorite grandson", whom everybody but her and his girl "downs", but about whom she knows "there's something". . . . How could she die not seeing what that "something" is?

You can see that she wants to stick around and help her youngest daughter Malinda, who has been "married four years and got five children. . . . Two is twins" . . . and who is "getting ready to populate the colored race again" . . . You can see that Malinda's particularly contented-looking baby who "never cries, except when it's not setting on a lap" . . . or Jerry, a blood-thirsty demon of two who "wants a gun that shoots both ways at once" . . . are all special concerns of Mary's, who leave her no time to die . . . as well as "this integration the Supreme Court has decreed", about whose workings she is curious, . . . particularly in South Carolina which she was planning to visit once more before she dies. . . . And last but not least, there is the mildly attractive proposition of the man downstairs, whose wife is dead, and "who's crazy about children" and "I kinder like him myself" . . . and "Do you reckon I'm too old to get married again?"

To make a long story short, says Mrs. Mary Bradley, standing by her "front stoop" in her "best clothes" and with the dignity of her mien in her black hat and black dress with the gold hoop earrings and thingamajig on her bosom, belying the veined, big knuckled testimony to humility and toil of her hands, "I got my feet caught in the sweet flypaper of life—and I'll be dogged if I want to get loose."

This is the story which we can sketch in for you, but the story of Mr. DeCarava's marvelous pictures defy description. Suffice to say that it is the first pictorial of the Harlems of the United States, whether found in the pages of a Negro newspaper, the motion picture, or newsreel, which made the writer glad to be alive, and not ashamed or set apart in the freakish, phony existence which people tell us is Negro life. Here is all of the realism and the redemption of a family album.

–*Los Angeles Tribune,* 11 November 1955, p. 9

* * *

In his autobiography I Wonder As I Wander, *published in November 1956 by Rinehart, Hughes continues the story of his life from where he had left off in* The Big Sea *(1940), charting his experiences from the stock market crash in 1929 through the Spanish Civil War in 1937. Jonathan F. Beecher wrote this review for the* Harvard Crimson, *the nation's oldest continuously published daily college newspaper.*

Hughes' *I Wonder as I Wander:* Reveries of an Itinerant Poet

"Most of my life from childhood on has been spent moving, traveling, changing places, knowing people in one school, in one town or in one group, or on one ship a little while, but soon never seeing most of them again," Langston Hughes writes in *I Wonder as I Wander.* The book, which he calls an autobiographical journey, describes Hughes' travelings from 1930 to 1937.

"When I was twenty-seven," he begins, "the stock-market crash came. When I was twenty-eight my personal crash came. Then I guess I woke up. So, when I was almost thirty, I began to make my living from writing." Hughes had been a long time getting through college. He graduated in 1929, and had worked in a hat store, on a truck farm, in a flower shop, and as a doorman, second cook, waiter, beachcomber, bum, and seaman, on the way. In that time he was writing poems too, and a novel, *Not Without Laughter,* which earned him a $400 award, which was what he had in 1929 when he lost his patron and decided to go to Haiti for a while.

He knew pretty well by then that he wanted to be a writer, but it was not so easy for a Negro to get a living out of writing. In Haiti he started to think about making poetry pay, and during the next few years which took him from Port au Prince to Havana, through the south via New York to San Francisco, and then to Moscow, Tashkent, Tokyo, Shanghai, Carmel, California, Mexico City, Harlem, Cleveland, Madrid, and finally Paris, he got along.

With stops in Russia during the "heroic days" of the second Five Year Plan and in Spain in 1937, Langston Hughes' journey from 1930 to 1937 paralleled those of many writers and journalists born around 1900. But Hughes' story is not much like those of such men as Stephen Spender, Louis Aragon, Louis Fischer, George Orwell, and Arthur Koestler.

The difference is that the travels of the latter group often served some carefully thought out intellectual purpose, and Hughes never cared much for ideology. Orwell chose to go down and out in Paris and London, and Koestler's trips to Palestine, Russia, and Spain were motivated by prior and (he thought) complete ideological commitments to Zionism, Communism, and finally the Popular Front. These men,

Hughes with his autobiography I Wonder As I Wander *at an authors' luncheon. Next to Hughes are Eartha Kitt,*
Henry Armstrong, and Pauli Murray (Langston Hughes Papers, Yale Collection of American
Literature, Beinecke Rare Book and Manuscript Library).

particularly those who joined the Communist Party, were afflicted, wherever they went by an all-embracing purpose which made it difficult for them to see anything except in relation to that purpose.

Hughes and Koestler met by chance in Ashkhabad in 1932, and it is interesting to compare their accounts of the weeks they spent together in Russian Central Asia. Koestler had come to inspect the accomplishments of the Soviet Five Year Plan in backward areas such as Ashkhabad, while Hughes was enjoying a free vacation at the expense of the Russians after the movie he had come to Russia to make had turned into a fiasco.

"As I lay on the sheetless bed," Koestler writes in *The Invisible Writing*–"enveloped by gloom and stench, counting the familiar stains on the wall which crushed bed-bugs leave behind, I heard the sound of a gramophone in the next room." It was Hughes, playing Sophie Tucker on his phonograph, not bothering to notice the dirt. While Koestler was disgusted by the

filth and unsanitary living habits, and only briefly amused by a local purge trial, Hughes was enjoying lavish Turk hospitality and occasionally reading the voluminous notes Koestler took each day. What Koestler found most everywhere failed to meet his expectations, and Hughes, having none, was mostly satisfied.

When Koestler described those days in 1953, he apologized, "I found it impossible to revive the naive enthusiasm of that period." This was not Hughes' way. His enthusiasm stayed fresh because it was for people and things, not ideas, which date faster. While he protested violently against the Scottsboro decision and later against Franco's bombing Madrid, his protest was not a Party member's, but always that of an individual. As he was convinced by the discovery of a swank little restaurant in Tashkent: "The system under which the successful live–left or right, capitalist or communists–did not seem to make much difference to that group of people, in every city around the globe, who managed by hook or crook to live well."

Though it was often by crook, Hughes usually managed to live well, or fully. Unlike those who distorted themselves and what they saw to correspond with prefixed ideas, Hughes was willing to take things pretty much as he found them and, if possible, to get fun out of them. In Russia for instance a free dental filling "seemed to me a minor miracle." "Moscow dental customs, the unveiling of the harem women in Turkestan, and the disappearance of the color line throughout Soviet Asia, are the three achievements I remember best of the whole USSR."

Of course he could never forget the barriers that faced a Negro at home; and it made him more tolerant of the Russians, for all their purge trials and liquidations. He said he felt about Communism as Frederick Douglass thought of abolition, "Whatever else it might be—it was not unfriendly to the slaves." "After all," he concluded, "I suppose how anything is seen depends on whose eyes look at it."

Hughes' willingness to take things as they came sometimes reached astonishing proportions. There was the day when he arrived in Shanghai, not knowing a soul, nor a word of the language: "Hardly had I climbed into a rickshaw than I saw riding in another along the Bund a Negro who looked exactly like a Harlemite. I stood up in my rickshaw and yelled, 'Hey man!' He stood up in his rickshaw and yelled, 'What ya sayin'?' We passed each other in the crowded street, and I never saw him again."

Hughes made few prejudgments about the people that passed his way, and knew that few judgments—least of all those one makes about oneself—are final. He was not so absorbed in his own purposes as not to notice what was going on around him. And often enough it was the funny side of things that got his attention, in besieged Madrid for instance, where Franco broadcasted each day the Falangists' dinner menus to the hungry loyalists, and where he and his friends would play Jimmie Lunceford's "Organ Grinder's Swing" all night to drown out the noise of the bombing.

What he saw in Madrid could only be wondered at—a girl practicing her piano the morning after a shell had passed through her house taking with it part of the living room wall and the top corner of the piano. "The will to live and laugh in this city of over a million people under fire, each person in constant danger, was to me a source of amazement." Langston Hughes is that kind of traveler who seeks after little, and, so, discovers much to wonder at.

—*Harvard Crimson,* 13 December 1956, p. 5

* * *

J. Saunders Redding wrote this review.

"A Personality Without Pretense"
Review of *I Wonder As I Wander*

Traveling is a drug to which one can quickly become addicted, especially if he happens to have all the equipment that goes into the making of a fine writer, and also especially if he begins to travel at that very early time before the possession of the equipment is realized as a responsibility.

Langston Hughes began early—out of necessity.

He has kept at it since out of habit and also probably because, like most of today's writers, he believes that traveling is good for him, for any writer.

(On this latter point though, I must say that there is room for argument.

Except for one brief trip to Belgium, Jane Austin never left her backyard; and all the traveling Anthony Trollope did was on a dinky commuters train from Barchester to his dinky job in the London Post Office; and all Leo Tolstoy did . . . etc. etc. Staying at home did not hurt them any.)

———

While still a schoolboy, Langston Hughes moved from one mid-western city to another, and on to Mexico where for a time he lived with his father and was cared for by three lovely and very religious ladies.

Still in his teens, he joined up as a merchant seaman and sailed half around the world.

At twenty-one or twenty-two he had seen more of "strange peoples and their stranger ways" than ten ordinary men see in a lifetime.

And much of what he had seen and done before he reached his legal majority made delightful and significant reading in the first volume of his autobiography, THE BIG SEA.

———

I WONDER AS I WANDER is the second volume. It begins in time approximately where the first volume ends.

Mr. Hughes went to college late, and his college days are over and the depression is on when I WONDER AS I WANDER opens.

He is beginning to feel the responsibility a writer has both to himself and the world.

It is pertinent to recall that among the things he did at the beginning of his career was to visit the Scottsboro Boys in the death house at Kilby prison, where he read them poetry.

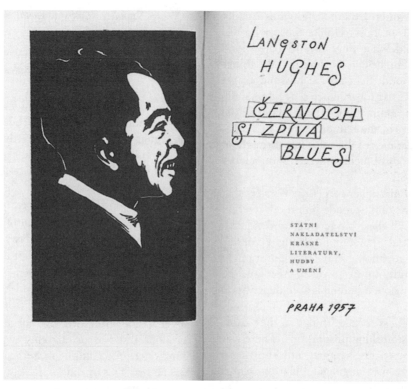

*Frontispiece and title page for a Czechoslovakian edition of Hughes's poems
(courtesy of Kenneth Spencer Research Library, University of Kansas)*

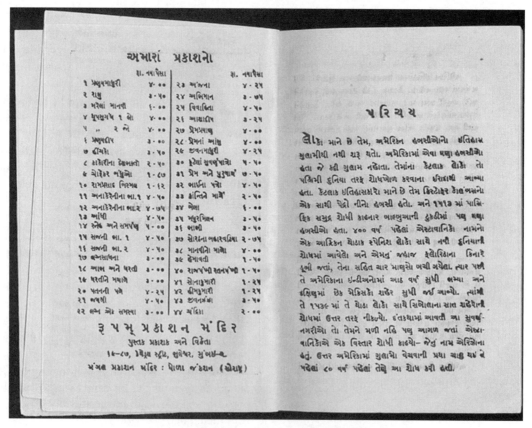

Pages from a 1958 Gujarati translation of Famous American Negroes
(courtesy of Kenneth Spencer Research Library, University of Kansas)

If the sense of responsibility had begun, so had the expressions of it which make Langston Hughes a particular delight.

———

But his visit to the Scottsboro Boys is only an incident in a long, long journey around the eastern half of the world, from Moscow to Ashkhabad, to Lashkent, Camarkand, to Hong Kong and Shanfhai–and eventually to Spain.

He went to Russia to write for Russian production of a film about American Colored people. When he got there, the film had already been written–and badly–by a famous Russian writer, but Mr. Hughes stayed on for a year in the USSR.

He went everywhere there and saw everything and had a delightful time, and his humor is such that even the misery he suffered is transmuted into pleasurable moments for the reader.

———

In Russia he met and traveled with Arthur Koestler, had Ivy Litvinoff for a friend, and Karl Radek for an editor. In Shanghai he met the fabulous Teddy Weatherford.

In Tokyo he brushed with the Japanese police. In Spain he drank with Ernest Hemingway. Such names naturally have a special attraction, but Langston Hughes does not give up the personalities that go with the names.

The one personality that shines through the pages of I WONDER AS I WANDER is Langston Hughes' own, and it is especially delightful, for it is a personality without pretense, or brass, or side. I WONDER AS I WANDER may not be a "significant book," but it is a fascinating one.

–*Baltimore Afro-American,* 12 January 1957, magazine section, p. 2

* * *

Nick Aaron Ford of Morgan State College, the author of The Contemporary Negro Novel: A Study in Race Relations *(1936) and editor of* Best Short Stories by Afro-American Writers, 1925–1950 *(1950), wrote this review.*

Odyssey of a Literary Man
Review of *I Wonder As I Wander*

In *I Wonder As I Wander* Langston Hughes has apparently attempted a four-fold task: to entertain, to present historical and cultural information about far-away places, to point out attitudes toward race and color in various parts of the world, and to reveal his philosophy of art and of life. This latest of his more

than twenty books is a grand mixture of autobiography, history, gossip, legend, sociology, travel guide, compendium of names of famous contemporary writers and artists, and poetry.

It is divided into eight chapters, each chapter containing from six to eighteen sub-divisions. The most successful chapters, in this reviewer's opinion, are "South to Samarkand," which deals with life, legends, customs, and human interest experience encountered in Soviet Central Asia; "Writing for a Living," which gives intimate glimpses into the heart and soul of the author as well as a thoroughly enjoyable discussion of the trials and tribulations he endured in the process of having his play *Mulatto* produced on Broadway; and "World Without End" which effectively dramatizes first-hand experiences of the Spanish Civil War.

This book begins where *The Big Sea* (1940) ended. Using the incident of his break with his wealthy patron, which had served as the climax of the earlier volume, he proceeds to relate his most notable experiences from 1929 to 1938. In addition to tours through the states to read his poetry, his travels during those years extended through Cuba, Haiti, Russia, China, Japan, Hawaii, France, and Spain. He tells intimate anecdotes of his association with such famous writers and artists as Arthur Koestler, Ernest Hemingway, Robinson Jeffers, Lincoln Steffens, Diego Rivera, and a host of others not so well known to the American public.

Assuming that I have rightly stated Hughes' four objectives in the writing of this book, I now address myself to the question of his success in accomplishing those objectives. On the whole, his peculiar wit, his humor, the content of his legends and anecdotes, and often his style and language make entertaining reading. But at times dull hunks of historical backgrounds of events and places get in the way. Sometimes the historical and cultural information appears to be extraneous, dragged in to demonstrate the author's knowledge. For the most part, this type of information is delightfully and successfully conveyed through legend and anecdote.

Almost every sub-chapter contains one or more incidents calculated to reveal attitudes toward race and color. The author makes it clear that he thoroughly enjoys associating with members of his own race and seeks them out wherever he goes. He makes it equally clear that for him friendship and camaraderie are not limited by race or color. He is impatient at discrimination and segregation of all kinds, but seldom bitter. He points with derision and pity at those who are committed to the doctrine of racial inferiority and superiority, some of whom he finds in every country.

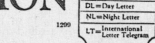

9

CLASS OF SERVICE
This is a fast message unless its deferred character is indicated by the proper symbol.

WESTERN UNION
TELEGRAM
W. P. MARSHALL, PRESIDENT

1299

SYMBOLS
DL=Day Letter
NL=Night Letter
LT=International Letter Telegram

The filing time shown in the date line on domestic telegrams is STANDARD TIME at point of origin. Time of receipt is STANDARD TIME at point of destination.

N190D4 5R NL PD

NEW YORK NY SEP 25 1958

LANGSTON HUGHES *LHB*

20 EAST 127 ST NYC

YOU ARE CORDIALLY INVITED TO ATTEND OUR BON VOYAGE

CHAMPAGNE PARTY TO BE GIVEN IN THE CAFE DE PARIS ROOM

ON THE PROMENADE DECK OF THE ILE DE FRANCE PIER 88

NORTH RIVER SATURDAY SEPTEMBER 27TH AT 945 AM SHARP

THIS LITTLE GET TOGETHER MARKS THE BEGINNING OF OUR

FIRST EUROPEAN TRIP IN NEARLY A DECADE KNOWING THAT

YOU WILL BE WITH US WILL MAKE US LOVE YOU MORE MADLY

TIME OF DEPARTURE IS SCHEDULED FOR 1130 AM

DUKE ELLINGTON

230A SEP 26

WIRE SENT, SEPP. 27, 1958:

    BON VOYAGE XXXXXX AND A WONDERFUL TRIP TO YOU AND ALL THE BAND

            LANGSTON HUGHES

THE COMPANY WILL APPRECIATE SUGGESTIONS FROM ITS PATRONS CONCERNING ITS SERVICE

Telegram exchange between Duke Ellington and Hughes (Langston Hughes Papers, Yale Collection of American Literature, Beinecke Rare Book and Manuscript Library)

His philosophy of art and of life shows up at intervals throughout the volume. He states his artistic credo thus: "I did not want to write for the pulps, or turn out fake 'true' stories to sell under anonymous names as Wallace Thurman did. I did not want to bat out slick non-Negro short stories in competition with a thousand other commercial writers trying to make *The Saturday Evening Post*. I wanted to write seriously and as well as I know how about Negro people, and make that kind of writing earn for me a living."

Stretching his philosophy beyond art to life, he says, "In the last few years I had been all around the embattled world and I had seen people walking tightropes everywhere–the tightrope of color in Alabama, the tightrope of transition in the Soviet Union, the tightrope of repression in Japan, the tightrope of the fear of war in France–and of war itself in China and in Spain–and myself everywhere on my tightrope of words. Anybody is liable to fall off a tightrope, in any land, I thought, and God help you if you fall the wrong way."

Despite the many favorable aspects, there are several shortcomings that cannot be ignored. First, the book is eighteen years too late. The material is topical, documentary, polemical, treated for the most part journalistically. If it had been published in 1938 or 1939 when it was written (or should have been) while the topical events were still fairly fresh, it could have had a powerful impact. But it takes more than humor and wit and a few philosophical comments to transform yesterday's news copy into today's literature.

Secondly, the overemphasis on the amatory experiences of the author is unfavorable. The normal reader expects to find sex in literature when it serves a necessary purpose, but for Hughes to relate intimate details of his own sex life, especially with other men's wives, seems in bad taste, to say the least. It appears that he is bragging about his virility or sex appeal or both.

Thirdly, his constant references to praise of his work by others and his reproduction of news items attesting to his notoriety suggest an immaturity that is not expected of serious writers.

Fourthly, there is too much serious attention given to gossip and hearsay.

Although these faults detract, they do not prevent *I Wonder as I Wander* from affording many moments of pleasure and profit to those who take the time to read it.

–*Phylon*, 18 (First Quarter, 1957): 88–89

* * *

John W. Parker wrote the following review of Hughes's novelistic adaptation of the gospel play Tambourines to Glory.

**Another Revealing Facet of the Harlem Scene
Review of *Tambourines to Glory***

Since the publication of *The Weary Blues,* poetic account of the enchantment, romance, and tragedy that was Harlem's back in the Twenties, Langston Hughes has maintained a healthy nostalgia for the Harlem scene, not only because it marks the point of his departure as a man of letters, but likewise because it remains a city within a city, a widely-discussed experiment in large-scale living in the urban ghetto. The impact of the Black Metropolis both as a place and a symbol is illuminated by such Hughes publications as *Shakespeare in Harlem* (1942), *Montage of a Dream Deferred* (1951), *Simple Takes a Wife* (1953), *The Sweet Flypaper of Life* (1955), and now *Tambourines to Glory*. A casual glance at the dates of these volumes attests to the fact that by and large each follows the other in rapid succession.

Tambourines to Glory is an urban folk tale which results from the skillful fusion of some thirty-six smaller segments into a whole more meaningful by far than any of the parts. Such organization as the book displays stems from its consistency in mood and atmosphere and from the unity of action exhibited by the characters. Artistically handled, too, is the selection and arrangement of the details in such a way as to assure suspense and movement. Starting as it does *in media res,* *Tambourines to Glory* has a middle, but scarcely a beginning or an end.

The volume turns mostly upon the sham and pretense of two attractive Harlem tenement women who, with their names on the relief rolls and time on their hands, set about to establish an independent, unorthodox church, the predominance of their own worldly interests notwithstanding. Only Essie's half-hidden seriousness of purpose and the power that sometimes stems from the singing of powerful hymns lighted up an otherwise drab, second-floor kitchenette in which the idea of a new church was crystalized.

These gospel racketeers, wisely enough, gauged their public utterances to the gullibility of unsuspecting people, and suppressed in their own hearts the knowledge that whiskey, loose women, the numbers game, and the Gospel of Christ make strange bedfellows. Just the same, the church prospered and before long the Reed Sisters (as they elected to designate themselves) moved the church from the corner block to a converted theater building with a thousand seats and their names in lights on the marquee.

The total situation, however, leaves much to be desired. The two-dollar down-payment on the Bible for the new church resulted from Laura's having hit the numbers. In the absence of proper credentials, Laura and Company found it necessary to produce cash periodically to keep back the law-enforcement officers. And with too many men on her hands and whiskey to buy, Laura frequently put in late appearances at the church services. Before long, however, tragedy settled down upon the enterprise. Laura finally stabbed her boy friend, Big-Eyed-Buddy, landed in prison, and left it to Essie and Birdie Lee to purify the church for the first time in its brief history.

Tambourines to Glory is in no sense a satire upon organized religion, or even upon cults as such, but rather a close-up exposé of the manner in which what sometimes passes as religion turns out to be nothing more than a commercial venture in the hands of unscrupulous racketeers.

Touched upon in this new novel are several themes treated elsewhere in Hughes' published writings. One observes, for instance, that the characters fall for the most part in the category of the nothings, not the dicties; that the author shuns sweetness and light and digs into the difficulties that aggravate men here and now; that an underlying Darwinian emphasis takes its toll upon conventional morality; and that fallen women, wandering irregularly from bar to bar, abound. Mr. Hughes cites facts, but does not draw conclusions; himself a Harlemite, he continues to laugh with the people, not at them.

All in all, *Tambourines to Glory* underscores a wide knowledge of the New York ghetto (and by implication others around the world) in a period of increasing racial awareness.

–Phylon, 20 (Spring 1959): 100–101

* * *

Poet and critic LeRoi Jones, a leading figure of the Black Arts Movement, wrote this review.

Langston Hughes' *Tambourines to Glory*

I suppose, by now, Langston Hughes's name is synonymous with "Negro Literature." For many, he is the only Negro in the world of books. This, of course, is unfortunate. But in quite another sense this is as it should be. Hughes is probably the last "major" Negro writer who will be allowed to write what could be called a "Negro Literature" (as differentiated from literature in general): to impose upon himself such staggering limitations.

Now, don't for a moment take this to be a plea for "assimilationist" literature (i.e., novels, etc. written by Negroes that assiduously avoid any portrayal of Negro life in much the same way that the "Black Bourgeoisie" avoid any attempt to connect them, even vicariously, with blues, jazz, "greens" or anything else even remotely "Negroid"). I am merely saying, that the Negro artist, and especially the Negro writer, A. E. (After Ellison), has come too far and has experienced so much that cannot be, even vaguely, attributed to the "folk tradition." And that to confine all of his thinking, hence all his writing to that tradition (with no thought as to where that tradition has got to; what significance that tradition has, say, in relation to the macrocosm of American life in general, or for that matter, man's life on earth) is to deny that there is any body of experience outside of that tradition. A kind of ethnic solipsism. Poet Robert Creeley says (in quite another context . . . but with the same general implications) . . . "A tradition becomes inept when it blocks the necessary conclusion: it says *we* have felt nothing, it implies others have felt more." This does not mean that the Negro writer, for instance, ought to stop using Negro Life In America as a theme; but certainly that theme ought only to be a *means*. For the Negro writer to confuse that means with the end (let us arbitrarily say that end is "art") is stultifying and dangerous. For these reasons, Hughes, to my mind, is a folklorist. He abdicated from the world of literature just after his second book of verse (*Fine Clothes to the Jew:* 1927); since then, he has sort of crept backwards and away from significant literature, until finally (with this book) he has gotten to a kind of meaningless ethnic name-dropping.

I am pretty well acquainted with the Negro in literature. I know of Hughes's early writing: his first novel (*Not Without Laughter,* 1930), his early poetry (some of it very beautiful, a rough mixture of spoken blues, Masters, and Imagists). I know of his affiliation with the "Harlem School" (Claude McKay, Jean Toomer, Countee Cullen, and a few others) and the importance and merit of the "School" (Toomer's novel *Cane* is among the three greatest novels ever written by a Negro in America. The others: Richard Wright's *Native Son*, Ralph Ellison's *Invisible Man*). I also know of the "School's" (or at least Hughes's) wonderful credo . . . "To express our individual dark-skinned selves without fear or shame. If the white people are pleased we are glad. If they are not, it doesn't matter . . . If colored people are pleased, we are glad. If they are not, their displeasure doesn't matter either." This credo almost singularly served to notify the world that the Negro artist had got to the point where he was ready to challenge that world solely on the basis of his art. Hughes's attitude, along with the even fiercer attitude of Claude McKay, and the more intellectually sound attitudes of Jean Toomer and Countee Cullen, was a far cry

C O P Y

SIMON AND SCHUSTER, PUBLISHERS   GET OTHER REPORTS BY...........................

630 FIFTH AVENUE • ROCKEFELLER CENTER • NEW YORK 20, N.Y.   **EDITORIAL DEPARTMENT REPORT**

Date Ms. Received.................. Ms. No................   Author..Avery..E...Kolb...............
Description of Ms. ..Author.:..........................
Submitted by ....Avery..E...Kolb,.................   Title.."..JIGGER"..OF..THE..BULL..RED..DICE......
Address................7618..Nancemond..Street,.........
................................Springfield,..Virginia...........
Special Instructions ..DEDICATED:.EN..."To..Jigger's   Report by ....Langston..Hughes...........
................comrades,..whose..courageous..story.........
Notification or decision to be sent to....has..yet..to..be..told."   Date of Report ......September..29,..1958.........
....
Recommended or Secured through......................   Postage..............

   It is a sweet little book that grows on you as you read.
It has its own quiet humor, unique charm, and a warmth of
characterization which makes even its fantasy fantastically human
enough to be real. It is easy to read. There is a pleasant
pictorial quality on most of its pages, and there are ocassionally
quite beautiful passages: page 107 of the troops marching to the
sea; page 179 of the gendarme and the thief; and then there is a
wonderful tribute to Paris---with which all who adore that city
will identify. The author has made Jigger a memorable little
fellow. I like the book very much.

   JIGGER being a lovable book, I would only wish that before
publication the author would tone down or perhaps remove some of
the long over-worked stereotypes relative to Negroes: dice,
chicken stealing, rabbits' feet. The hue and cry on the part of
colored people over the State Department sponsored world tour of
PORGY AND BESS stemmed largely from the interminable crap game
in its first act, right at the very opening (as this book opens)
since dice and Negroes are synonomous in the popular mind---as
likewise are rabbits' feet and chicken stealing---stemming probably from minstrel days. This well-characterized little book
does not need stereotypes to bolster its reality.

   If this were my book, specifically, I would:
1. Omit the phrase OF THE BULL RED DICE from the book's title.
2. Cut on page 24: "I ain't never stole hens."
3. Cut at least a couple of the stereotypes on page 76 where there
   are now four in a row: the zoot suit chain, the voodoo root,
   the rabbit foot, and a horseshoe. I'd surely drop the rabbit
   foot. The other soldiers in the outfit would probably have
   kidded or shamed Jigger out of carrying it anyway.
4. Since they have no particular dramatic or character value in
   this story---and Negro readers loath the words---I would cut
   all niggers and pickannies, except where Madden uses nigger
   in contempt. For example, there are 11 niggers on page 103;
   several on pages 108, 127, 128, 141, 169, 179, etc. Too many.
5. Equating Negroes with children just excites the ire of the NAACP.
   Where this occurs on page 110, I would cut the word pickaninnies.
   Likewise, I would omit this word from the title of Chapter 13:
   PICKANINNY ON PICCADILLY. This book will charm Negro readers, too,
   I believe, if these nuances are taken care of---with no loss to
   its verisimilitude.

                      [OVER]

REJECTED...............   ACCEPTED...............   O.K. for reading fee...............   Paid...............

Asked to Revise and Resubmit...............

First page of Hughes's reader's report for Simon and Schuster, the only such report he is known to have written
(Langston Hughes Papers, Yale Collection of American Literature,
Beinecke Rare Book and Manuscript Library)

from the "head patting" parochial "literature" of Chesnutt, Dixon, Dunbar and the so-called "Talented Tenth" of the 1890's. Hughes and the rest were interested in dispelling once and for all the Negro novel of apology. . . . (For example, from an early novel by a Negro, Charles Chesnutt; he relates an incident where "A refined Afro-American is forced to share a Jim Crow car with dirty, boisterous, and drunken Negroes.") . . . of fawning appeals for "an alliance between the better class of colored people and the quality white folks." The "School" was also reacting against the need for a Negro artist to be a pamphleteer, a social organizer, or, for that matter, anything else except an artist. This, of course, was the beginning of the Negro in literature; and the beginning of the end for a "Negro literature."

"Negro literature" is simply *folk literature,* in the sense I choose to take it. It has the same relationship to literature *per se* (that is, to that writing which can be fully significant to all the world's peoples) that any folk art has to art in general. It is usually too limited in its appeal, emotional nuances, intellectual intentions, etc. to be able to fit into the mainstream of world art. Of course, when a folk art does have enough breadth of intellectual, emotional, and psychological concern to make its presence important to those outside of its individual folk tradition, then it has succeeded in thrusting itself up into the area of serious art. And here, by "serious," I mean *anything* containing what Tillich calls an "Ultimate Concern" (God, Death; Life after—the concerns of art) and not as some people would have it, merely anything taught in a university. "Negro Literature" is only that; a literature of a particular folk. It is of value only to that particular folk and perhaps to a few scholars, and certain kinds of literary *voyeurs.* It should not make pretensions of being anything else.

Of course, utilizing the materials of a certain folk tradition to fashion a work of art (the artist, certainly, must work with what he has, and what is closest to him) can lead to wonderful results: Lorca, Villon, Joyce and Dublin, Faulkner, Ellison. But merely relying on the strength and vitality of that tradition, without attempting (either because one lacks talent or is insincere) to extend the beauty or meaning of that tradition into a "universal" statement cannot result in art. Bessie Smith is certainly in the folk tradition, but what she finally got to, through that tradition, is, as they say, "something else." *Nobody Knows You When You're Down And Out,* could almost be sung by Oedipus leaving Thebes. As Pound said of great literature, "language charged with meaning to the utmost possible degree." That is art. A work that never leaves or points to some human reference outside a peculiar folk tradition is at best only folklore.

Ralph Ellison is a Negro writer. His novel *Invisible Man* won the National Book Award as the best American novel of 1952. It is among the best books written by an American in the last twenty years. The novel clearly deals with what is superficially a "Negro theme." Its characters are primarily Negroes, and its protagonist is a Negro. And although it is this "Negro theme" that gives the book its special twist, the theme is no more than a point of departure for Ellison. It is no more a "folk tale" than Faulkner's *The Sound And The Fury.* Ellison's horrifying portrait of a man faced with the loss of his identity through the weird swinishness of American society is probably made more incisive by its concentration on one segment of that society. Ellison uses the folk materials; jazz, blues, church songs, the southern heritage, the whole phenomena of Harlem. But he "charges them with meaning," extending the provincial into the universal. He makes art. Ellison, by utilizing the raw materials of his environment and the peculiar cultural heritage of the Negro, has not written a "Negro novel" but a novel. Ellison is a Negro writing literature and great literature at that.

To get back to Langston Hughes. Hughes and the "Harlem School" proposed (the credo was written around 1926 in *The Nation*) essentially to resist writing mere folklore. They were to become "full-fledged" artists; though bringing in the whole of the Negro's life. Jean Toomer's novel *Cane* succeeded; some of Cullen's poetry, and Langston Hughes's early verse. Toomer's is perhaps the greatest achievement. His *Cane* was the most significant work by a Negro up until Richard Wright's *Native Son.* Cullen's failure to produce great art is not reproachable. He just wasn't talented enough perhaps. Perhaps Langston Hughes is not talented enough, either. But there are the poems of his early books. "The Negro Speaks Of Rivers" is a superb poem, and certainly there must be something else where that came from. And though he is never as good as a prose writer, *Not Without Laughter,* his first novel, with all its faults did have a certain poise and concern nowhere after so seriously approached. Some of the famous "Simple" pieces (started as a series of sketches for *The Chicago Defender*), at their best, contain a genuine humor; but most of them are crushed into mere half-cynical yelping (through a simulated laughter) at the almost mystical white oppressors. At any rate, Hughes has not lived up to his credo. Or perhaps the fault is that he has only lived up to a part of it. "To express our individual dark-skinned selves." Certainly, that is not the final stance of an artist. A writer must be concerned with more than just the color of his skin. Jesse B. Simple, colored man, has to live up to both sides of that title, the noun as well as the adjective.

Since this is a review of a particular book rather than a tract on the responsibilities of the Negro artist, as it must seem I have made it, I must mention the book, *Tambourines to Glory.* There's not much I can say about the book itself. Probably, if a book of similar literary worth were to be written by another author it would not be reviewed (probably, it would have never gotten published). But the Negro writer (especially Hughes, since he is so well known as such) raises certain peculiar questions that are not in the least "literary." I have tried to answer some of them. But the book is meaningless, awkward, and never gets past its horribly inept plot. In fact, were it not for, say, the frequent introduction of new characters within the book, it would be almost impossible to distinguish the novel, itself from the blurb summary on the jacket. "Laura Reed and Essie Belle Johnson, two attractive Harlem tenement women with time on their hands and no jobs, decide to start their own gospel church on a street corner. Laura wishes to make money. Essie honestly desires to help people." The characterizations don't get much past that.

Even as a folklorist Hughes leaves much to be desired. His use of Harlem slang is strained and rarely precise. When a Harlem con man "Big-Eyed Buddy," is trying to make little Marietta (from the South), he says hiply . . . "Men don't start asking a sharp little chick like you what school you're in." "Sharp?" Marietta replies incredulously. Buddy says, "Stacked, solid, neat-all-reet, copasetic, baby!" It reeks of the Cab Calloway–Cotton Club–zoot suit era. No self-respecting young Harlemite hipster would be caught dead using such passé, "uncool" language today. As they say, "Man, that stuff went out with pegs." At least a folk artist ought to get the tradition of the folk straight.

But there are so many other faults in the very structure and technical aspect of the novel, as to make faults in the writer's own peculiar stylistic device superfluous. None of the basic "novelistic devices" are used correctly. Any advance in the plot is merely stated, never worked into the general texture of the novel. By mentioning the landmarks of Harlem and its prominent persons, occasionally, and by having his characters use a "Negro" dialect to mouth continually old stock phrases of Negro dissatisfaction with white America, Hughes apparently hoped to at least create a little atmosphere and make a good folk yarn out of it. But he doesn't even succeed in doing that this time.

It's like a jazz musician who knows that if you play certain minor chords it sounds kind of bluesy, so he plays them over and over again; year in, year out. A kind of tired "instant funk." Certainly this kind of thing doesn't have anything much to do with jazz; just as Hughes's present novel doesn't really have anything to do with either literature *per se*, or, in its imperfect and shallow rendering, the folk tradition he has gotten so famous for interpreting.

– *Jazz Review*, 2 (June 1959): 33–34

* * *

While reviews of Selected Poems of Langston Hughes *were largely positive, the young novelist James Baldwin, who was becoming an increasingly important voice in the literary world, found Hughes's latest volume, a self-selected representation of his entire career as a poet, lacking in depth and of uneven quality. Baldwin's review of the book in* The New York Times Book Review *hurt Hughes deeply, for he had always made it a priority to help promote the careers of younger black writers.*

Sermons and Blues
Review of *Selected Poems of Langston Hughes*

Every time I read Langston Hughes I am amazed all over again by his genuine gifts—and depressed that he has done so little with them. A real discussion of his work demands more space than I have here, but this book contains a great deal which a more disciplined poet would have thrown into the waste-basket (almost all of the last section, for example).

There are the poems which almost succeed but which do not succeed, poems which take refuge, finally, in a fake simplicity in order to avoid the very difficult simplicity of the experience! And one sometimes has the impression, as in a poem like "Third Degree"—which is about the beating up of a Negro boy in a police station—that Hughes has had to hold the experience outside him in order to be able to write at all. And certainly this is understandable. Nevertheless, the poetic trick, so to speak, is to be within the experience and outside it at the same time—and the poem fails.

Mr. Hughes is at his best in brief, sardonic asides, or in lyrics like "Mother to Son," and "The Negro Speaks of Rivers." Or "Dream Variations":

To fling my arms wide
In some place of the sun,
To whirl and to dance
Till the white day is done.
Then rest at cool evening
Beneath a tall tree
While night comes on gently,
    Dark like me—
That is my dream!

To fling my arms wide
In the face of the sun.
Dance! Whirl! Whirl!
Till the quick day is done.
Rest at pale evening . . .
A tall, slim tree . . .
Night coming tenderly
    Black like me.

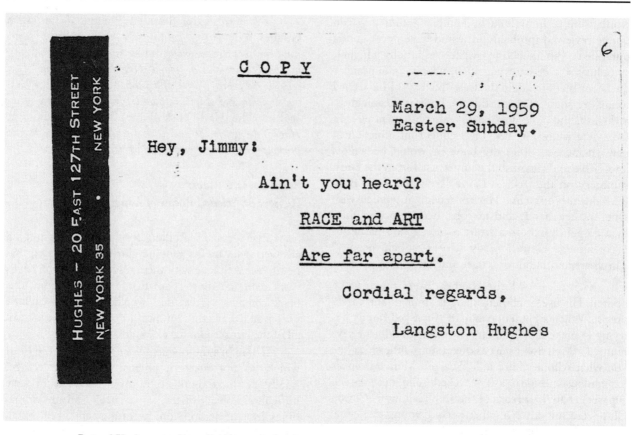

C O P Y

March 29, 1959
Easter Sunday.

Hey, Jimmy:

Ain't you heard?

RACE and ART

Are far apart.

Cordial regards,

Langston Hughes

HUGHES – 20 EAST 127TH STREET
NEW YORK
NEW YORK 35

Postcard Hughes sent to James Baldwin *on the day the younger writer's unfavorable review of* Selected Poems of Langston Hughes *was published in* The New York Times Book Review *(Langston Hughes Papers, Yale Collection of American Literature, Beinecke Rare Book and Manuscript Library)*

I do not like all of "The Weary Blues," which copies, rather than exploits, the cadence of the blues, but it comes to a remarkable end. And I am also very fond of "Island," which begins "Waves of sorrow / Do not drown me now."

Hughes, in his sermons, blues and prayers, has working for him the power and the beat of Negro speech and Negro music. Negro speech is vivid largely because it is private. It is a kind of emotional shorthand—or sleight-of-hand—by means of which Negroes express, not only their relationship to each other, but their judgment of the white world. And, as the white world takes over this vocabulary—without the faintest notion of what it really means—the vocabulary is forced to change. The same thing is true of Negro music, which has had to become more and more complex in order to continue to express any of the private or collective experience.

Hughes knows the bitter truth behind these hieroglyphics: what they are designed to protect, what they are designed to convey. But he has not forced them into the realm of art where their meaning would become clear and overwhelming. "Hey, pop! / Re-bop! / Mop!" conveys much more on

Lenox Avenue than it does in this book, which is not the way it ought to be.

Hughes is an American Negro poet and has no choice but to be acutely aware of it. He is not the first American Negro to find the war between his social and artistic responsibilities all but irreconcilable.

–The New York Times Book Review, 29 March 1959, p. 6

* * *

John Henrik Clarke, a founding member of the Black Academy of Arts and Sciences, wrote this review.

"Enduring Poems"
Review of *Selected Poems of Langston Hughes*

While emphatically disagreeing with James Baldwin's inept review of the *Selected Poems of Langston Hughes* in the *New York Times,* the writer Lloyd L. Brown gave a truer evaluation of Langston Hughes as a poet in the following excerpt from his letter to the book review editor of that paper:

276

This citation was presented to Hughes by the playwright Lorraine Hansberry at the Village Gate in New York City.

MANHATTAN ARTS THEATRE
CITATION
TO
LANGSTON HUGHES

Without the traditional whereases and therefores, we of the Manhattan Arts Theatre, a group of theatre minded folk who believe we have something to say and a lot of wonderful people to say it to, take this opportunity to say that we consider Langston Hughes not only the most—but the utmost.

We feel this way because for more than a quarter of a century Langston Hughes has been giving to the world his great gift of simplicity and eloquence through his poetry, his lyrics, his novels and plays and his being.

And also because we, who seek to establish a community theatre in Harlem, appreciate what Langston Hughes has done to help build the American Theatre and to help us by contributing his play "The Emperor of Haiti" to our group to launch our first effort to bring legitimate theatre to the uptown area.

In his poetry somewhere Langston Hughes has quoted one of his personalities as "wishing to dig and be dug in return."

We dig Langston Hughes. He has been "digging" people ever since.

Sunday, May 3rd, 1959   Citation Format prepared by
Gene Boland, Alfred Duckett,
Jackie Hayes

—Langston Hughes Papers, James Weldon Johnson Collection in the Yale Collection of American Literature, Beinecke Rare Book and Manuscript Library

"He is indeed the poet laureate of our people, and that is because in his writing he is a Negro, voicing with a rare genius the very heart of the Negro in America."

Unlike the small, though increasing group of alienated Negro writers, who spend so much of their time running from other Negroes and cursing God for making them black, Langston Hughes has never left home. The publication of his *Selected Poems,* thirty-three years after he made his debut with his first volume of poems *The Weary Blues,* was needed and welcome.

For more than a quarter of a century the steady and prolific pen of Langston Hughes has poured forth, with what seems to be untiring consistency.

Being our most versatile writer, he has the largest Negro reading audience and for many years he has also been universally read and appreciated.

No writer with the tremendous output and diversity of Langston Hughes can be expected to reach the heights of literary form with every effort. Some of his poems are weak and topical, others are strong and enduring. His most enduring poems can be found in this volume.

In his poems of protest, Langston Hughes has given us a dimension and a point of view not found elsewhere—a philosophical bitterness tempered with

Searching for a Star

As this letter indicates, Hughes had hoped to cast the singer and actress Pearl Bailey in the lead role of Tambourines to Glory, *a musical based on the black gospel tradition. Bailey declined the role for medical reasons. The play eventually opened in November 1963 at the Little Theater in New York with Hilda Simms cast in the lead role, but Hughes was criticized sharply for its stereotypical representations of black life.*

Hughes to Pearl Bailey, 6 December 1959

Dear Pearl Bailey:

I am just recently back from a lecture trip to Trinidad and find your kind note awaiting me. I very much hope that you are rested and feeling all O. K. again. I know how hard it is to create and maintain a career such as yours is—giving so generously and so happily to so many people. One has to take time out now and then to get one's breath back.

I am, of course, delighted to know that you might possibly be interested in my Theatre Guild play, TAMBOURINES TO GLORY; and certainly the leading role, that of LAURA, needs the sort of warmth, humor, and lovableness that you as an artist have. The Guild plans to give it an excellent supporting cast and a bang-up good singing chorus of at least 30 voices. And they want to get rolling as soon as possible, for a late winter opening in New York. Mr. Langner tells me that he is writing to you, and everyone in the Guild office thinks you would be ideal for the lead.

Certainly I envy you that California sunshine, and send you all my best wishes.

Sincerely yours,
Langston Hughes

—Langston Hughes Papers, James Weldon Johnson Collection in the Yale Collection of American Literature, Beinecke Rare Book and Manuscript Library

*Hughes with Ralph Ellison (left) and James Baldwin (right) at The Newport Jazz Festival in 1958
(Langston Hughes Papers, Yale Collection of American Literature,
Beinecke Rare Book and Manuscript Library)*

humor. His range as a poet extends far beyond his unique method of protest. He is also a poet who celebrates the joy of living.

Nearly all of his best known poems are included in this selection. "The Negro Speaks of Rivers," "Mother to Son," "The Weary Blues," and "Cross" show the early flourishing of his talent.

In utilizing Negro speech and idioms, he has shown us values in the thought patterns of Negro life that we had not previously considered.

I began this review by disagreeing with James Baldwin's evaluation of Langston Hughes as a poet. I am still of the same opinion. Speaking of Hughes in his *New York Times* review of March 29, 1959, Baldwin said: "He is not the first American Negro to find the war between his social and artistic responsibilities all but irreconcilable."

Quite the contrary, I think what Mr. Baldwin calls a war between the writer's social and artistic responsibilities is only a long bridge that every seriously minded writer will have to learn how to cross. For years, Langston Hughes has been crossing this bridge, in style.

—Chicago Defender (4 July 1959), p. 3

The Last Years: 1960 – 22 May 1967

By 1960 Hughes was one of the best-known African American writers in the world and continued to be in high demand on the reading and lecture circuit. He also regularly encountered fierce detractors; in February 1960 a bomb threat was made before his reading in Buffalo, New York, and that same month he canceled a reading in Grand Rapids, Michigan, after learning that conservative churchmen were protesting his upcoming visit. In 1960 two books by Hughes were published—*The First Book of Africa*, a children's book, and *An African Treasury: Articles, Essays, Stories, Poems by Black Africans*, which he edited—but the most significant event of the year for the author was being awarded the NAACP's prestigious Spingarn Medal.

In 1961 Hughes polished the manuscript of "Ask Your Mama," a long poem he had begun the previous year, and on 6 February, with piano backing, he introduced the poem to a receptive audience at a reading in Harlem. *Ask Your Mama: 12 Moods for Jazz* was published in the fall. On 24 May 1961, Hughes was inducted into the National Institute of Arts and Letters at a ceremony in New York. On 3 November he was a guest at a White House luncheon honoring Léopold Sédar Senghor, the president of Senegal. His play *Black Nativity*, which premiered on 11 December in New York, was well received on Broadway and in Lagos, Nigeria, at an African and African American arts festival held that month. Hughes, who had traveled to Nigeria, remained in the country for nearly a month before returning to New York in January.

In June 1962 Hughes traveled to Africa again to speak at a writers' conference in Kampala, Uganda. From there he made a brief visit to Egypt, attended productions of his plays *Shakespeare in Harlem* in Rome and *Black Nativity* in Spoleto, Italy, and then returned to Africa, where he made a speech at the opening ceremony for a new U.S. library in Accra, Ghana. He returned to the United States in time for the fall publication of *Fight for Freedom*, the official history of the NAACP that he had been commissioned to write.

Although his health and energy level showed signs of decline, Hughes began 1963 with January readings at Michigan State University and Wayne State University. While he was pleased with the publication of his books—*Something in Common and Other Stories* and *Poems from Black Africa, Ethiopia and Other Countries*, which he edited—as well as Webster Smalley's edition of *Five Plays by Langston Hughes*,

Hughes in Chicago, 1960 (photograph by Roy DeCarava; Langston Hughes Papers, Yale Collection of American Literature, Beinecke Rare Book and Manuscript Library)

Hughes welcomed a European vacation and Mediterranean cruise that summer. Well rested, he returned to New York in early September and worked on rewrites of the musical *Tambourines to Glory*, which premiered on 3 November to stinging criticism. The blow to Hughes's ego—and to his reputation in theater—was softened, however, when *Jerico-Jim Crow* earned enthusiastic praise upon its premiere in New York on 12 January 1964; the next year, *The Prodigal Son* was also well received when it opened in New York on 20 May 1965.

In late March 1966 Hughes left New York for Africa, an official appointee of President Lyndon Johnson to represent the United States at the First World Festival of Negro

Arts in Dakar, Senegal. He spent a month in Dakar and then traveled through Africa for two months on a tour sponsored by the U.S. State Department. After his return to the United States, he began work that winter on *The Panther and the Lash,* his final volume of poems.

In spring 1967 Hughes was preparing for a trip to Paris when his health began to deteriorate. Severe stomach pains finally compelled a visit to the emergency room at the New York Polyclinic Hospital, and on 12 May Hughes underwent prostate surgery. He appeared to be recuperating nicely on the day immediately following the surgery, but soon a bacterial infection caused his condition to worsen. Hughes died on 22 May 1967.

——— ✦ ———

A-Climbin' On

The first Spingarn Medal, created by NAACP chairman of the board Joel Elias Spingarn to recognize distinguished merit and achievement by African Americans, was awarded in 1915 to Ernest E. Just of the Howard University Medical School. Past literary recipients of the annual award include William Stanley Braithwaite (1918), James Weldon Johnson (1925), Charles Waddell Chesnutt (1928), and Richard Wright (1941). Hughes delivered this speech on 26 June 1960 upon receiving the medal.

Remarks in Acceptance of 45th Spingarn Medal

To the NAACP, the Members of the Spingarn Medal Committee, and to Arthur Spingarn for his genial presentation, my thanks. But it would indeed be of the utmost conceit were I to accept this Medal in my name alone; or in the name of literature, which is my field. I can accept it only in the name of the Negro people who have given me the materials out of which my poems and stories, plays and songs, have come; and who, over the years, have given me as well their love and understanding and support.

Without them, on my part, there would have been no poems; without their hopes and fears and dreams, no stories; without their struggles, no dramas; without their music, no songs.

Had I not heard as a child in the little churches of Kansas and Missouri, "Deep river, my home is over Jordan," or "My Lord, what a morning when the stars begin to fall," I might not have come to realize the lyric beauty of <u>living</u> poetry.

Had I not listened to a blind guitar player on a Kansas City street corner singing, "Going down to the railroad, lay my head on the track–but if I see the train a-coming, I'll jerk it back"–had I not listened to songs like these, the laughter and sadness of the blues might never have become a part of my own poetry.

Had I not heard as a child such folk verses as:

"What a wonderful bird the frog are: When he hop he fly almost
"When he sit he stand almost. He ain't got no sense hardly.
He ain't got no tail hardly neither where he sit–almost."

Had I not heard these, I might not have grasped the humor of the absurd in casing human as well as animal behavior.

Had I not listened to the old folks' memories of slavery told on front porches of a summer evening, there might not have been "The Negro Speaks of Rivers" written before I was twenty:

I've known rivers: I've known rivers ancient as the world
And older than the flow of human blood in human veins
My soul has grown deep like the rivers.
I bathed in the Euphrates when dawns were young
I built my hut near the Congo and it lulled me to sleep
I looked upon the Nile and raised the pyramids above it
I heard the singing of the Mississippi when Abe Lincoln went down to New Orleans
And I've seen its muddy bosom turn all golden in the sunset
I've known rivers: Ancient, dusky rivers. My soul has grown deep like the rivers.

Hughes at the Spingarn Medal ceremony in St. Paul, Minnesota, 26 June 1960. Arthur Spingarn is behind Hughes
(Langston Hughes Papers, Yale Collection of American Literature, Beinecke Rare Book and Manuscript Library).

In the years following my childhood, had I not listened to the State Street stories, the Vine Street annecdotes, the Central Avenue complaints, Paradise Valley comments, the fun of South Street jokes whose humor is deeper than fun, and the Lenox Avenue tales and observations that eventually combined to create a composite character–born in the South but urbanized in the North–there would have been no Simple stories, no "Simple Speaks His Mind," or "Simply Heavenly," or "Simple Dreams a Mighty Dream."

There is so much richness in Negro humor, so much beauty in black dreams, so much dignity in our struggle, and so much universality in our problems, in us–in each living human being of color–that I do not understand the tendency today that some American Negro artists have of seeking to run away from themselves, of running away from <u>us</u>, of being afraid to sing our own songs, paint our pictures, write about ourselves–when it is our music that has given America its greatest music, our humor that has enriched its entertainment media for the past 100 years, our rhythm that has guided its dancing feet from plantation days to the Charleston, the Lindy Hop, and currently the Madison. Our problems have given intriguing material to writers from "Uncle Tom's Cabin" to Faulkner, from "The Octoroon" to Eugene O'Neil. Yet there are some of us who say, "Why write about Negroes? Why not be <u>just a writer</u>?" And why not–if one wants to be "just a writer?" Negroes in a free world should be whatever each wants to be–even if it means being "just a writer."

Some quite famous Americans of color are "just writers," their pages reflecting nothing of their ethnic background. Well and good! On the other hand, there is such a wealth of untapped material for writing in the Negro group, that it would be a shame were most of us to become "just writers". It would be an even greater shame if such a decision were made out of fear or shame. There is nothing to be ashamed of in the strength and dignity and laughter of the Negro people. And there is nothing to be afraid of in the use of their material.

Could you possibly be afraid that the rest of the world will not accept it? Our spirituals are sung and loved in the great concert halls of the whole world. Our blues are played from Topeka to Tokyo. Harlem's jive talk delights Hong Kong and Paris. Those of our writers who have most concerned themselves with our very special problems are translated and read around the world. The local, the regional can–and does–become universal. Sean O'Casey's Irishmen are an example. So I would say to young Negro writers, do not be afraid of yourselves. <u>You</u> are the world.

A very local literary character of mine, Jesse B. Simple, has gone from the corner of 125th and Lenox in Harlem to speak his mind around the world. He's read in Johannesburg, recited on the London radio, recreated on European stages by white actors in languages Simple himself never heard of. A Harlemite–from a very specific locale, in a very specific corner of a very specific city, and of a very specific color–black–is accepted in foreign lands thousands of miles away from the corner of 125th and

Lenox as a symbol of the problems of the little man of any race anywhere.

I did not create Simple. He created himself. I merely transcribed him on paper. He is his own literature. In the South today—where children are going dangerously to school and teen-agers are sitting on stools before counters where no food is served them except the bitter herbs of hate—there is great material for literature. I hope there will soon be writers who will make great use of this material. Certainly in time, out of the Negro people there will come a great literature. Perhaps today the capital <u>P</u> with which some of us spell <u>problem</u>, is larger than the capital <u>A</u> with which others would spell <u>art</u>. Nevertheless, I think it permissible that a poem pose a problem. In the case of many of my poems, the problem is that which the NAACP is seeking to solve. Once I presented it through the eyes of a child in a poem called "Merry-Go-Round."

When I wrote it, I imagined a little colored girl perhaps six or seven years old, born in the Deep South where segregation is legal. When she was about school age, her parents moved to a Northern or Western city, perhaps looking for better jobs, or a better school for their child. At any rate, in this new town—maybe a town like Newark, New Jersey, or Oakland, California, or even St. Paul or Minneapolis—one day this little girl goes to a carnival and she sees a merry-go-round going around. She wants to ride. But, being a very little girl, and colored, remembering the Jim Crowisms of the South, she doesn't know whether colored children can ride on merry-go-rounds in the North or not. And if they can, she doesn't know where. So this is what she says:

Where is the Jim Crow section on this merry-go-round,
Mister, cause I want to ride?

Down South where I come from white and colored
Can't sit side by side
Down South on the train there's a Jim Crow car
On the bus we're put in the back
But there ain't no back
To a merry-go-round:
Where's the horse for a kid that's black?

Our country is big enough and rich enough to have a horse for every kid, black or white, Catholic or Protestant, Jewish or Gentile—and someday we will. Meanwhile:

I, too, sing America
I am the darker brother
They send me to eat in the kitchen
When company comes,
But I laugh
And eat well
And grow strong.
Tomorrow,
I'll be at the table
When company comes
Nobody'll dare
Say to me,
"Eat in the kitchen,"
Then.
Besides,
They'll see how beautiful I am
And be ashamed—
I, too, am America.

–Langston Hughes Papers, James Weldon Johnson
Collection in the Yale Collection of American
Literature, Beinecke Rare Book
and Manuscript Library

* * *

*Hughes in Nigeria. In November 1960 Hughes attended the inauguration of Nnamdi Azikiwe as governor general
and commander in chief (Langston Hughes Papers, Yale Collection of American
Literature, Beinecke Rare Book and Manuscript Library).*

<u>MILES DAVIS: POET OF JAZZ</u>

by Langston Hughes

To pinpoint the qualities that make a creative artist great ~~in~~
always
~~any field~~ is not/easy. ~~To attempt~~ to isolate one single quality as
is usually
contributing espeeially to his individual greatness ~~may be~~ even more
difficult, unless that quality be distinctive indeed. In jazz, Miles
Davis is certainly an artist (in the grand sense of the word) and his
qualities of distinction are many. But sureness of technique, a great
and　　　　　　　　　　　　　　　　　　　　　　　　　　rhythmical
ear for tone, improvisational inventiveness, a complex ~~rhyt~~
sense, are all qualities shared to some degree with a number of other
famous jazz performers. There is one quality, however, that only a
few ~~or~~ of the giants of jazz have. That quality has to do with
musical poetry. Were I to coin a single phrase to describe Miles
Davis, it would be "The Poet of Jazz".

To me, poetry is the distillation of an emotion, the compression
~~ofxaxmoodxorxfeelingxxnoxsuperxinousxwordsxxwhetherxitxbexjoyxorxsorrow~~
~~intoxitsxultimatexessensexx~~

of a mood or <u>feeling</u> — whether it be joy or sorrow — into its ultimate
essence. If it concerns poetry of the printed page, no superfluous
words. If in a musical performance, no unneeded nuances, no waste,
miles
no rambling, no diffusion. There is none of these in a Davis perform-
he
ance, for ~~Miles~~ makes of each musical interpretation, a musical poem.
and
Heart, mind,/soul beat out, think out, and feel out each mood so clearly beforehand that, when his music strikes the ear, listeners cannot
help but be moved emotionally by what this music has to say.

stated
It has been ~~printed~~ on occasion that the platform manners of
Mr. Miles Davis are not always exemplary. Well, neither were those of
the late great Billie Holiday. The word poets, Dyland Thomas and
have not always
Brendan Behan ~~seldom~~ behaved in public like angels either. But each
grant it
and all produced poetry, sometimes very great poetry. ~~It~~ is the end
a
result that counts. Miles Davis is ~~the~~ great poet of jazz.

Los Angeles, March 7, 1961　　　　　　　　Langston Hughes

*Draft for Hughes's short piece on Miles Davis (Langston Hughes Papers, Yale Collection
of American Literature, Beinecke Rare Book and Manuscript Library)*

Ask Your Mama, *which Hughes biographer Arnold Rampersad considers his "most ambitious single poem," is a book-length poem of approximately eight hundred lines. Hughes wrote thirteen drafts before he was satisfied with its twelve sections, which mix jazz experimentation with a sharp critique of American history and culture. Hughes had high hopes for the book, but critics largely scorned it or dismissed it as a curiosity. Rudi Blesh, the author of an early history of jazz titled* Shining Trumpets *(1946), wrote this review. He compares Hughes's skill to the musicianship of Louis "Satchmo" Armstrong and Charlie "Yardbird" Parker.*

Jazz Is a Marching Jubilee
Review of *Ask Your Mama: Twelve Moods for Jazz*

Jazz and the blues have been with us all the years of this century; Langston Hughes not quite that long–"jazz poetry" began in 1926 with his well-remembered volume, "The Weary Blues." Now, with "Ask Your Mama," it begins to appear that perhaps we have as little understood the poet as the music. For, though jazz is "good time" music, within it has always been something else, something dark yet shining, harsh yet gentle, bitter yet jubilant–a Freedom Song sung in our midst unrecognized all these years. Just so, opening the covers of this gaily-designed book is to find poetry whose jazz rhythms hide the same fire and steel.

Langston Hughes is no mere observer of Africa's stormy, shuddering rise and the awakening of dark-skinned peoples all over the world. They are his people; he sings their marching Jubilees. But Langston Hughes is also an American: he sings to all of us, of the freedom that must go to all before it can be freedom for any.

"Go ask your Mama" is the retort–half-derisive, half-angry–to the smug, the stupid, the bigoted, the selfish, the cruel, and the blind among us, all those to whom these truths that America was built upon, are, even today, not yet self-evident.

With this great theme, a talented poet finds a universal voice. Like Satchmo's golden trumpet and

Dust jacket for Hughes's experimental book of poetry published by Knopf in 1961, which Hughes dedicated to Louis Armstrong (courtesy of Milner Library, Illinois State University)

Yardbird's blues-haunted alto, the poetry of Langston Hughes sings for–and to–all of us.

–*New York Herald Tribune Books*,
26 November 1961, p. 4

* * *

John Henrik Clarke, a founding member of the Black Academy of Arts and Sciences, wrote this review for Freedomways, *a magazine founded in 1961 to chronicle the civil rights and Black Arts movements through a blend of political commentary, poetry, and prose.*

"A Book of Social Protest"
Review of *Ask Your Mama: Twelve Moods for Jazz*

"Playing the dozens" is a part of Afro-American folklore and folkways. It is part of the black man's private humor that is sometimes used to drive its victim to anger and rage. Like poison, it has good and bad uses and if you do not understand the game, you should not play it. The sub-title of the book is "Twelve Moods for Jazz"–and this is what the book is really about. The format of playing the dozens is incidental to the contents of the book.

Like so many of Langston Hughes' books that are classified as humor, this is a book of social protest, not so thinly disguised. No denying the humor is apparent throughout most of the book. The presence of humor accentuates the social protest, making it more effective and less offensive.

Langston Hughes has used the pattern of jazz, poetry and the dozens to bring another dimension to the Afro-Americans' long and agonizing struggle to have his art and the dignity of his personality accepted in a nation that proclaimed, so long ago, that all men were created equal. The following poem from the book drives this point home:

> "They rung my bell to ask me
> Could I recommend a maid.
> I said ask your mama.
> They asked me at the P.T.A.
> Is it true that Negroes . . . ?
> I said, ask your mama.
> And they asked me right at Christmas
> If my blackness would rub off?
> I said, ask your mama."

Unlike the small group of Afro-American writers who spend so much of their time running from other members of their race, and cursing God for making them black, Langston Hughes has never "left home." For more than a quarter of a century, this steady and prolific pen has poured forth, with what seems to be an untiring consistency. Being our most versatile writer, he has the largest Afro-American reading audience, and for many years he has also been universally read and appreciated. With justification he has been called "the poet-laureate of his people."

The publication of this book, thirty-four years after he made his debut with his first volume of poems, "The Weary Blues," represents for him the reaching of a second generation of readers. If the second generation of Langston Hughes' readers want to know what the first generation of readers thought of his writing, the best answer is in the title of the present book–ASK YOUR MAMA.

–*Freedomways*, 2 (Winter 1962): 102–103

* * *

In his foreword to his book The Best of Simple (1961), *Hughes explains the origins of his most popular fictional character. Hughes selected and arranged the contents of this book from the three Simple collections he published in the 1950s.*

Foreword: Who Is Simple?

I cannot truthfully state, as some novelists do at the beginnings of their books, that these stories are about "nobody living or dead." The facts are that these tales are about a great many people–although they are stories about no specific persons as such. But it is impossible to live in Harlem and not know at least a hundred Simples, fifty Joyces, twenty-five Zaritas, a number of Boyds, and several Cousin Minnies–or reasonable facsimiles thereof.

"Simple Speaks His Mind" had hardly been published when I walked into a Harlem cafe one night and the proprietor said, "Listen, I don't know where you got that character, Jesse B. Semple, but I want you to meet one of my customers who is *just* like him." He called to a fellow at the end of the bar. "Watch how he walks," he said, "exactly like Simple. And I'll bet he won't be talking to you two minutes before he'll tell you how long he's been standing on his feet, and how much his bunions hurt–just like your book begins."

The barman was right. Even as the customer approached, he cried, "Man, my feet hurt! If you want to see me, why don't you come over here where I am? I stands on my feet all day."

"And I stand on mine all night," said the barman. Without me saying a word, a conversation began so much like the opening chapter in my book that even I was a bit amazed to see how nearly life can be like fiction–or vice versa.

Simple, as a character, originated during the war. His first words came directly out of the mouth of a young man who lived just down the block from me. One night I ran into him in a neighborhood bar and he said, "Come on back to the booth and meet my girl friend." I did and he treated me to a beer. Not knowing much about the young man, I asked where he worked. He said, "In a war plant."

I said, "What do you make?"

HILL AND WANG, INC.
141 FIFTH AVE. N.Y. 10   FOR IMMEDIATE RELEASE
ALGONQUIN 4-6975
INQUIRIES: Vasiliki Sarant

SELECTION BY LANGSTON HUGHES OF HIS BEST SIMPLE STORIES TO BE PUBLISHED OCT. 11.

THE BEST OF SIMPLE, a selection by Langston Hughes himself will be published

on October 11 by Hill and Wang in their American Century Series. In this collec-

tion, the author has picked his favorites from three previously published books,

Simple Speaks His Mind, Simple Takes a Wife, and Simple Stakes a Claim.

          Of all the fictional characters in contemporary Negro literature, Simple

is perhaps one of the most widely known; Simple has, in fact, become part of

a growing literary tradition. Some readers consider Simple the Everyman of

his people. As Hughes says in his Foreword, "...these tales are about a great

many people -- although they are stories about no specific person as such.

But it is impossible to live in Harlem and not know at least a hundred Simples,

fifty Joyces, twenty-five Zaritas, and several Cousin Minnies -- or reasonable

facsimiles thereof."

          The character of Simple - talkative, warm, cheerful -- originated in

Langston Hughes' column in the Chicago Defender. From this beginning he became

a character in books, in radio and television plays, and on the musical comedy

stage. This edition is illustrated with line drawings by Bernhard Nast.

                           ****

Langston Hughes is perhaps best known as a poet and the creator of Simple, but
he is also the author of several novels, biography, history, plays, and children's
books. He has also edited several anthologies. Dr. Hughes taught creative
writing at Atlanta University and the University of Chicago, and has lectured
extensively in the United States, Europe and the West Indies.

Bernhard Nast is a well known German artist. The illustrations in this book
appeared first in the German edition of Simple Speaks His Mind.

                           ****

245 pages; illustrated; Foreword; American Century Series, AC-39
$1.65, paper; $3.95, cloth; October 11, publication date.

Publisher's press release (Langston Hughes Papers, Yale Collection of American Literature,
Beinecke Rare Book and Manuscript Library)

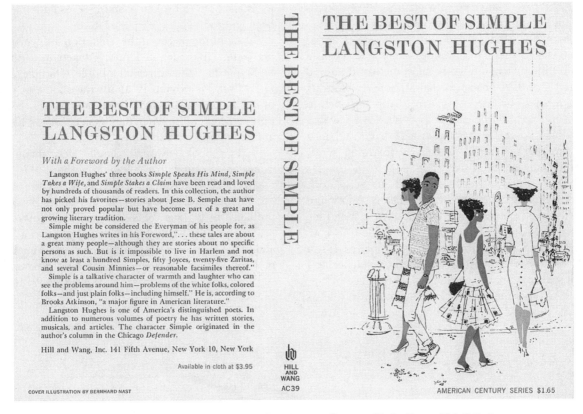

Dust jacket for Hughes's 1961 collection of Simple stories (Langston Hughes Papers, Yale Collection of American Literature, Beinecke Rare Book and Manuscript Library)

He said, "Cranks."

I said, "What kind of cranks?"

He said, "Oh, man, I don't know what kind of cranks."

I said, "Well, do they crank cars, tanks, buses, planes or what?"

He said, "I don't know what them cranks crank."

Whereupon, his girl friend, a little put out at this ignorance of his job, said, "You've been working there long enough. Looks like by now you ought to know what them cranks crank."

"Aw, woman," he said, "you know white folks don't tell colored folks what cranks crank."

That was the beginning of Simple. I have long since lost track of the fellow who uttered those words. But out of the mystery as to what the cranks of this world crank, to whom they belong and why, there evolved the character in this book, wondering and laughing at the numerous problems of white folks, colored folks, and just folks— including himself. He talks about the wife he used to have, the woman he loves today, and his one-time play-girl, Zarita. Usually over a glass of beer, he tells me his tales, mostly in high humor, but sometimes with a pain in his soul as sharp as the occasional hurt of that bunion on his right foot. Sometimes, as the old blues says, Simple might

be "laughing to keep from crying." But even then, he keeps you laughing, too. If there were not a lot of genial souls in Harlem as talkative as Simple, I would never have these tales to write down that are "just like him." He is my ace-boy, Simple. I hope you like him, too.

—*The Best of Simple* (New York: Farrar,
Straus & Giroux, 1961), pp. vii–viii

* * *

John Henrik Clarke wrote this review.

"A Later Day Aesop"
Review of *The Best of Simple*

The character Jess B. Semple, born quite by accident according to its creator, Langston Hughes, is now a permanent and very important part of Afro-American literature. Simple is an urban folk hero and philosopher whose appearance in our literature is long overdue. The author has stated that much of the material for the books on Simple is derived from actual conversations overheard in bars and on the corners of the largest urban Negro community in the world, reflecting not the Harlem of the intellectual and professional, but that of the ordinary, "man in the street," the basic Harlemite who may not always know why, but who often laughs to keep from crying.

Simple is a later day Aesop whose fables are as entertaining as they are meaningful and true. He is a man, like most men, in revolt against the world around him and those circumstances that are forever blocking the paths of ambition. In his own earthy approach to the American race problems he says more in a few sentences than some Ph.D. "authorities" have said in a small mountain of thick books. In the following quote, the problem is put in capsule:

"Now, the way I understand it," said Simple one Monday evening when the bar was nearly empty and the juke box silent, "it's been written down a long time ago that men are borned equal and everybody is entitled to life and liberty while pursuing happiness. It's in the Constitution, also Declaration of Independence, so I do not see why it has to be resolved all over again."

In this brief statement, Jess B. Simple has told us what the race and the problem of democracy in America is all about—a broken promise—a resolution that has been ignored.

All of the pieces in this collection are worth reading again. "Banquet in Honor," taken from the first book of the adventures of Simple, "Simple Speaks His Mind," is obviously about the shameful neglect of W. E. B. Du Bois by a black bourgeoisie class who only remember him when they wish to exploit his name and reputation to raise funds.

The book, through Simple, has many other things to say, and this talkative bar-hopper is now a major figure in American literature. With warmth, good humor and good sense, he has looked beyond the problems of colored folks—and just plain folks—at the problems of the world. The best thing that can be said about the character of Jess B. Simple is that he will probably outlive the circumstances of his creation.

—*Freedomways*, 2 (Winter 1962): 101–102

* * *

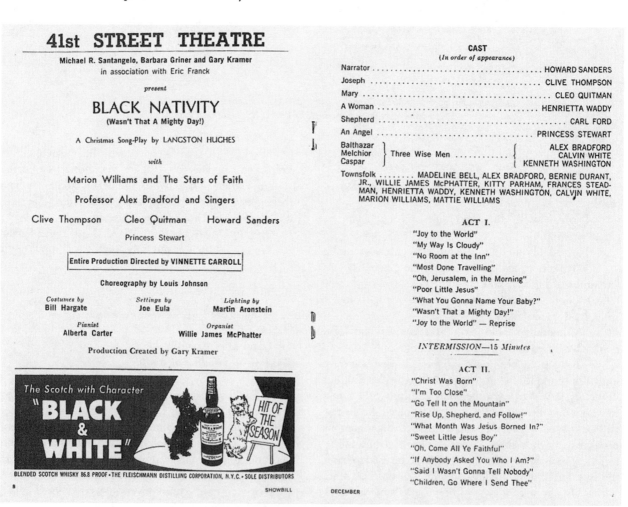

Playbill for Hughes's gospel play that premiered 11 December 1961 (Langston Hughes Collection, Schomburg Center for Research in Black Culture, New York Public Library)

Dust jacket for Hughes's history of the National Association for the Advancement of Colored People, published by Norton in 1962 (Collection of Christopher C. De Santis)

Hughes, who had first traveled to Africa in 1923, became engaged with African literature and the connections between African and African American writers during the 1950s and 1960s. He edited and wrote the foreword to Poems from Black Africa, *which included poems from fifteen countries.*

Foreword to *Poems from Black Africa*

Usually poets have their fingers on the emotional pulse of their peoples, of their homelands. Traditionally, poets are lyric historians. From the days of the bards and troubadours, the songs of the poets have been not only songs, but often *records* of the most moving events, the deepest thoughts and most profound emotional currents of their times. To understand Africa today, it is wise to listen to what its poets say–those who put their songs down on paper as well as those who only speak or sing them. Perhaps it is more profitable to know how people *feel* than it is to know what they think. Certainly the poetry of contemporary Africa indicates its emotional climate. That climate is one of

hope and of faith in a future that is coming more and more into the control of the peoples of Africa themselves.

But the best of the black poets writing today in English or French in Africa South of the Sahara are not so much propagandists for African nationalism, as they are spokesmen for variations of *négritude*–a word the French-speaking writers have coined to express a pride in and a love of the African heritage, physically, spiritually and culturally. The most interesting nonwhite poets of contemporary Africa are modernists in style, in contrast to the older writers of colonial days who were influenced by Victorian models or by the classical French poets taught in the missionary schools. Contemporary young African intellectuals, some of whom have but lately come home from Cambridge or the Sorbonne, are not unlike young writers elsewhere. They have read Auden and Spender and Eliot, Mauriac, Jacques Prevert and perhaps Brecht. Lagos, Accra or Dakar are no longer weeks away from Europe. In fact, from the heart of Africa to Paris or London by jet is now only a matter of hours. Not that all African writers have traveled abroad. But the bookshops in Africa's major cities today are fairly well stocked. Even American books make their way to the West Coast and the Union of South Africa. Then there is the BBC–the African networks of the British Broadcasting Company beaming from London cultural programs of high calibre and using much more poetry than the American airwaves ever dream of committing to the microphones. Many young African writers today augment their incomes by writing for BBC, which pays not badly for both poetry and prose.

Whatever their influences may be, local or foreign, there are sensitive and exciting poets in Black Africa now. Abioseh Nicol in Sierra Leone, Kobina Parkes in Ghana, Gabriel Okara in Nigeria, Sédar-Senghor of Senegal, Ezekiel Mphahlele of South Africa to name men who have produced more than simply an occasional magazine or newspaper verse. These poets represent their countries well on the printed page, and all of them have lately been published abroad as well as at home. The poetry of Abioseh Nicol is quietly moving and deeply personal; that of Kobina Parkes kaleidoscopically vivid and almost tribal in its imagery; while Okara's is sensitive and strange and semi-mystic to the Western reader. In the work of Dennis Osadebay and Michael Dei-Anang the poet and pamphleteer meet to cry aloud for African freedom, while in Senghor's poems of *négritude* French sophistication and the tall drums of Senegal lock arms.

In general the French African poets, and particularly Senghor, tend toward creating Whitmanesque catalogues of fruits, rivers, trees and the other physical

Fight For Freedom is much more than a collection of facts and figures. It is the dramatic and moving story of a dedicated group of men and women who have waged unceasing war against the forces of Jim Crow. Starting in 1909 on call of 60 distinguished Americans, the Association has grown in size until today it has nearly 400,000 members in 1500 units in 49 of the 50 states.

Wherever the rights of the Negro have been challenged, the NAACP has been available to take up the fight, working in the courts, in legislative halls, in public forums, on the picket line. The Association has provided leadership in the sustained struggle for equal rights.

When the Association was founded, Negroes in the United States were free in word but not in fact. Victims of mob violence and segregated in practically every aspect of life, Negroes had little hope for the future—North or South. Today, although the fight is still far from being won, the picture is quite different. Working always within the framework of the law, the NAACP has won victory after victory to attain first-class citizenship—its rights and its privileges—for colored citizens.

It has not been an easy battle; there have been setbacks and major disappointments. NAACP members have never given up hope nor stopped fighting for full citizenship rights. Here is their story, told by one of its members, a chronicle of over 50 years of the fight for liberty and justice, a drama of first importance and MUST reading for anyone who wants America to be a land with equal rights for all its citizens.

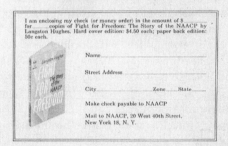

I am enclosing my check (or money order) in the amount of $_____ for _____ copies of Fight for Freedom: The Story of the NAACP by Langston Hughes. Hard cover edition: $4.50 each; paper back edition: 50c each.

Name_____

Street Address_____

City_____ Zone____ State____

Make check payable to NAACP

Mail to NAACP, 20 West 40th Street, New York 18, N. Y.

"FIGHT FOR FREEDOM"

WINS CRITICAL ACCLAIM!

Saturday Review:

"Next year will be the 100th anniversary of the promulgation of the Emancipation Proclamation . . . This stirring book by Langston Hughes will help make that historic centennial far more meaningful than it otherwise would have been. Somebody ought to put it in every library in the country!"

Chicago Tribune, Chicago, Ill.

"Any evaluation of Negro progress made during the past 100 years must be an evaluation of the NAACP; the two are inseparable. Written by a man who has received the NAACP's highest honor, the Spingarn Medal, 'Fight For Freedom' is well told. It is worth reading."

News-Call Bulletin, San Francisco, Calif.

"Without a doubt, no single organization has had a greater influence on the social struc- *ture of the United States. Such a story is not easy to research. There is nothing more powerful, in writing history, than to be accurate, objective and interesting. Author Hughes is all three."*

Springfield Republican, Springfield, Mass.

"This excellent book, which reflects new credit on its distinguished author, deserves to be widely read, and should be appreciated by all Americans who believe in democracy and fair play."

Indianapolis Times, Indianapolis, Ind.

"The work of the NAACP is not merely in behalf of the Negro. It is in behalf of American society at large. For whatever the racists may argue, the nation, to use a ringing phrase from the past, cannot exist half slave and half free. 'Fight for Freedom' is a book for everyone."

- 205 pages of easy-to-read material in handy pocket book size.

- 10 photographs of NAACP leaders and important events in Negro history.

- Complete bibliography and list of national officers and executive staff.

- Published by Berkley Publishing Corp. 50c through your local branch or the NAACP National Office, 20 West 40th Street, New York 18, N. Y.

- Also published in hard cover at $4.50 per copy.

Promotional material for the hardcover and paperback editions (Langston Hughes Papers, Yale Collection of American Literature, Beinecke Rare Book and Manuscript Library)

attributes of their land, and vie with one another in evoking the strength of black bodies, the dignity of black motherhood, the beauty of black maidens. From Senghor's *Femme Noire:*

> Naked woman, dark woman,
> Ripe fruit with firm flesh,
> Sombre ecstasy of dark red wine,
> Mouth which makes mine lyrical. . . .

The French poets of color create mosaics of blackness against the palm trees within a large and (to non-Africans) exotic framework of cultural nationalism, seldom tending toward miniatures, seldom reducing their subject matter to the framework of oneself. Black poets writing in English-speaking Africa, on the other hand, seem somewhat less concerned with color, personal or in landscape, and are more centered in self rather than race, their *I* less the *I* equivalent to *We* of the French poets. But the best poetry of both French and English expression bears the stamp of the African personality, and most of its emotional aura might be included within the term *négritude*–that "anti-racist racism," as Sartre called it, of black Africa's concentration on the rediscovery of self, a turning within for values to live by, rather than a striking outward in revenge for past wrongs. "Me fait songer à Orphée allant réclamer Eurydice à Pluton," wrote Sartre in his famous introduction to Senghor's anthology of French African poetry.

In a paper on African literature delivered at the First International Congress of Africanists at the University of Ghana, Ezekiel Mphahlele confirms that in general, "English and French writing move along different tracks, particularly in the realm of poetry. The Nigerian poet talks about things as they affect him personally and immediately. He is not protesting or trying to vindicate his blackness. The French-speaking poet, however, particularly of the *négritude* school, uses broad symbols in which immediacy of individual experience is not the important thing. These are symbols of Africa, of blackness, of what is regarded by the poet as African traits which are expected to be a unifying force–not only for the indigenous people of the continent but for the Negro world in general."

The American Negro poet, Samuel Allen (Paul Vesey) writing on *négritude* says, "It represents in one sense the Negro African poet's endeavor to recover for his race a normal self-pride, a confidence in himself shattered for centuries when the enslaver suddenly loomed in the village pathway; to recover a world in which he once again could have a sense of unashamed identity and an unsubordinate role. . . . *Négritude* includes the characteristic impulses, traits and habits

Hughes and African writer Chinua Achebe in Lagos, Nigeria, July 1962 (Langston Hughes Papers, Yale Collection of American Literature, Beinecke Rare Book and Manuscript Library)

which may be considered more markedly Negro African than white or European. It is thus something which the poet possesses in the wells of his being and simultaneously something which he is seeking to recover, to make manifest; and again it is a subjective disposition which is affirmed and which objectivizes itself in the poem."

Most of the poems of Léopold Sédar-Senghor are colored by the blackness of Africa. The titles of his various works indicate as much: *Chants d'Ombres, Masque Negre, Hosties Noires, A l'Appel de la Race de Saba,* among others. He sings of the glories of blackness, of Africa's past trials and tribulations and of its future glories. Concerning his style, really that of a chant, Senghor writes, "I insist that the poem is perfect only when it becomes a song: words and music at once. It is time to stop the decay of the modern world and especially the decay of poetry. Poetry must find its way back to its origins, to the times when it was sung and danced. As it was in

Greece, above all in the Egypt of the Pharaohs. And as it is still today in black Africa."

Certainly many indigenous poets in contemporary Africa, whether writing in the *lingua franca* of English or French, are still close enough to tribal life to know the names of the old non-Christian gods, the *orisha,* to hear in their ears the great mass chants of ancient rituals or the jolly rhymes of village feasts. Oral poetry is very much a part of daily living in tribal Africa where art and life have not yet parted company. The bulk of Africa's poetry is still that which is only spoken or sung. Most of it is not yet transcribed or translated into European tongues, and much of it is closely related to music, the rhythms of percussion and the dance, and is concerned with community rituals and the traditional gods worshipped by non-Christian or non-Moslem peoples.

Since oral poetry is highly regional, often with allusions and overtones obscure beyond tribal limits, much traditional verse is almost untranslatable. Then, too, like the Chinese, many tribal tongues utilize tone and pitch as well as mere words in communication. One example is the Yoruba of Nigeria. With them the same word pronounced in one tone may have quite a different meaning in another tone or inflection. There have been many adequate translations into English of African folk tales, the story line remaining intact. To translate folk poetry is, however, a much more formidable task. Ulli Beier of the University College at Ibadan is one of the few Europeans doing extensive work in this field. It is a privilege to include in this book some of Beier's translations from the Yoruba.

There will no doubt arise in the New Africa creative writers who will soon combine in poetry the written word and the oral traditionals of the bush as excitingly as Amos Tutuola of *The Palm Wine Drinkard* has combined English prose and tribal lore in fiction. Certainly this integration of indigenous elements can be beautifully done in poetry, as Nicolás Guillén of Cuba has proven in his poems of *ñañigo* and his use of the rhythms of *sones.* Written poetry in Africa today is moving away from the bench of the missionary school to walk abroad beneath the cocoa palms and listen for inspiration to the native songs in many tongues. Soon African poetry will capture the essence of these songs and recreate them on paper. Meanwhile, it walks with grace and already is beginning to achieve an individuality quite its own.

–"Foreword by Langston Hughes," in *Poems from Black Africa* (Bloomington: Indiana University Press, 1963), pp. 11–15

* * *

Cover for Hughes's 1963 book, his last collection of non-Simple stories (Collection of Christopher C. De Santis)

Many of the thirty-seven stories included in Hughes's Something in Common and Other Stories *(1963) were culled from previous collections and from magazines, journals, and newspapers. Journalism professor William Kirtz wrote this review.*

Mr. Hughes' Shadings
Review of *Something in Common and Other Stories*

The latest collection of short stories by Negro poet, novelist and playwright Langston Hughes is a disappointing grab-bag. It is a combination of questionable sociology and worse fiction.

The majority of the stories, written from 1933 to 1963, seem to be thinly disguised sermonettes. White spinsters lust after dark-skinned janitors. If a colored person is consistently polite to a Caucasian, that's a tip-off he'll have sold out before tale's end. And

Hughes' heroines' favorite game? Pretending they're the same hue as their white keepers.

Hughes occasionally unwinds and produces some welcome flashes of in-group humor, of raucous racial gibes. But he's in the pulpit more often than not.

Much in the way of stereotypes and ethnic platitudes can be forgiven a writer with power and style. James Baldwin, for example, can carry a disbeliever for pages with just the force of his rhetoric. Not so Mr. Hughes. He doesn't seem to put words in his characters' mouths; he wedges them there. For the Thought We Doubt Ever Got Thought department, there's this neat musing, by a "professor" invited to dinner by a wealthy white family:

"The Chandlers are a power in the Middle West, and in the South as well. Theirs is one of the great fortunes of America. In philanthropy, nobody exceeds them in well-planned generosity on a large and highly publicized scale. They are a power in Negro education, too—as long as it remains *Negro* and does not get tangled up in integration. That is why I am visiting them tonight at their invitation."

One may be convinced by Hughes' theme, but not as it is more clumsily expounded and hastily rationalized. Some perfectly natural situations are convoluted into diatribe by slick, trick endings. In "His Last Affair," for example, an actress twice dupes a pompous businessman with a paternity hoax. What is Hughes' last line? "And he never did even suspicion that I'm colored." The surprise doesn't proceed from the events, but from the author's effort to startle.

In "Why, You Reckon?" two Negroes rob and strip a wealthy white boy. Their victim is titillated by this Harlem experience. The thieves opine that if they had the lad's money, they'd always have a good time. "No, you wouldn't," the boy responds. And that sets one of his captors to thinking: "What do you suppose is the matter with rich white folks? Why you reckon they ain't happy?"

Now Negroes, as Hughes repeatedly implies, may have a premium on innocence. But he certainly doesn't go far toward proving the assumption with such hoked-up homilies.

Relaxed and antic stories like "Spanish Blood" and "Slice Him Down" are unself-conscious and successful glimpses into racial striving, fighting, making up. And "The Gun," a crisp chiller, proves that Hughes can turn out disciplined, punchy prose. It tells of an old maid who flourishes as soon as she puts a .32 under her pillow.

The 40-story collection, however, generally exudes patronizing distrust. The author continually preaches the Negro's sexual attractiveness to the white. His characters are deathly scared of any Caucasian; his whites are polite only to snare and unnerve the superior race. His heroes pity their white counterparts for their innate guilt.

But these generalizations—which are nowhere particularized, just restated—are precisely those the Southern racists chant. Both Hughes and the White Citizens Councils prate of miscegenation, of inherent antagonism, of impossible coexistence.

Is this view really the way racial affairs must be? Has there been so little progress since the 30s? Until he pinpoints it, Hughes' case must be judged unproved—for lack of evidence. And his fiction must be termed enervating, laced together by more wrath than craft.

—*Quincy* (Mass.) *Patriot-Ledger,* 17 April 1963, p. 32

Reachin' Landings

In this introduction to the collection of Hughes's plays he edited, playwright Webster Smalley provides the first extended, serious treatment of Hughes's career as a dramatist.

Introduction to *Five Plays by Langston Hughes*

Langston Hughes—poet, playwright, novelist, and short story writer—began writing during the Harlem literary renaissance of the twenties and is today, at the age of sixty, America's outstanding Negro man of letters. His poems and stories are read throughout the world. They have been translated into languages and dialects (Uzbek, for example) that many of us scarcely know exist. All of Hughes' writing has its own intrinsic merit, and his subject matter—the Negro in America—is of vital interest to Americans and, perhaps more than we are aware, to the world. No writer has better interpreted and portrayed Negro life, especially in the urban North, than Langston Hughes.

His primary interest is in the "little people." A critic from the far left might be tempted to say, "the masses," but the critic would be wrong. For Hughes, there are no "masses," there are only people. The problems and aspirations of the rapidly growing, educated Negro middle- and upper-classes concern him only peripherally. He prefers to write about those of his race who live constantly on the edge of financial disaster, who are used to living precariously, occasionally falling over the edge and crawling back up, and who have no time to be pretentious. If there are any cardinal sins in Hughes' canon, they are affectation and intolerance.

The position of the Negro in the United States is one of the facts that any Negro writer must face if he is to write at all. No one has more faith in the strength and dignity of his people than does Hughes, but only a few of his works can be called militant or didactic. Some few readers might wish that he were more belligerent, but he is an artist, not a propagandist. He writes to express those truths he feels need expressing about characters he believes need to be recognized. He has always been tolerant of human weaknesses beneath skins of all colors.

From his plays it is evident that Hughes has more and more identified with and written about the Negro community in Harlem. This crowded section of New York City, its vitality and variety, is his favorite setting, though he was born in Joplin, Missouri, and grew up in Lawrence, Kansas, Cleveland, Ohio, and Toluca, Mexico. Moreover, he has worked as a seaman on voyages to Europe and Africa, lived for some time in Paris and Italy, been a newspaper correspondent in Spain, and traveled extensively in Africa, Europe, Russia, and the Orient. To write of his life and times would be superfluous for he has done so himself in two autobiographical books, *The Big Sea* (1940) and *I Wonder as I Wander* (1956). Cosmopolitan though he is, Hughes prefers to draw most of his fictional characters from the people who live in the vicinity of 125th Street between Amsterdam and Lexington Avenues, the people he calls "just folks."

Hughes (right) with his friend Arna Bontemps (Langston Hughes Papers, Yale Collection of American Literature, Beinecke Rare Book and Manuscript Library)

Not all of his writing is about Harlem and its inhabitants, of course. His first published poem and one of his best, "The Negro Speaks of Rivers," expresses what must be a feeling universal to American Negroes and does so through the evocation of the imagery of a rich historical perspective. His strong feeling for the Negro race and for the past and present problems of the Negro in America made inevitable his concern with the lot of the Negro in the South. This concern is strongly reflected in his first full-length play, *Mulatto,* for which Hughes chose as his subject the still explosive problem of racial intermixture and based the story on the plight of the son of a Negro housekeeper and a white plantation owner. The play ran a year on Broadway in the late thirties and then toured the nation for eight months.

Perhaps because of the commercial nature of our theatre and of dramatic publishing in America, *Mulatto* has never before been printed in English, although it has been translated, performed, and published in Italy, Argentina, and Japan. It should be noted, however, that it is probably quite true that until recently the "amateur market" for Negro plays has been limited. Unfortunately, the Negro theatre in the United States, with the exception of a few vigorous groups such as the Karamu Theatre (formerly called the Gilpin Players) in Cleveland and the Howard University Players in Washington, has been short-lived, inconsequential, or both. What at one time seemed to be the most promising of all, the American Negro Theatre, is dead—perhaps killed by its one big financial success, *Anna Lucasta.*

The role of the playwright is not an easy one, at best, and a Negro playwright has all the woes of a white dramatist, with a number of others thrown in. A playwright must have at least the hope of theatrical production, but the commercial theatre shows only a sporadic interest in Negro drama. Hughes has been writing for a theatre that hardly existed. He solved the problem during the thirties by founding two dramatic groups: the Suitcase Theatre in Harlem and the Negro Art Theatre in Los Angeles. In 1941 he established a third Negro theatre, the Skyloft Players in Chicago. Few playwrights have the heart or the energy for such undertakings, and it is not surprising that the body of Negro drama in America is small. I am quite certain that Hughes' persistent desire to develop a true Negro drama is one reason he has continued to write plays. Negro drama, heralded in the twenties by such men as W. E. B. Du Bois, Alain Locke, Montgomery Gregory, and Ridgely Torrence, has been, until recently, enriched almost single-handedly by Langston Hughes. The younger Negro dramatists, from whom we are just beginning to hear, would do well to emulate his industry and to follow his ideal. If they do so, Negro drama may soon be an important segment of our literary and dramatic heritage.

Hughes has always been drawn toward the drama. Perhaps, like many of us who wish to write for the theatre, he is possessed by a kind of madness that goes beyond reason. It may have begun when, at the age of six or seven, his mother took him to see almost every play that came to Kansas City, Topeka, or Lawrence, Kansas (and this was a considerable number). In any event, his interest came early and has remained. One of his first published efforts was a children's play, written during a visit to his father who had moved to Toluca, Mexico, where he had gained a position of affluence. Hughes was only eighteen at the time, and Toluca was then a very quiet Mexican village—the great highway from the north leading to Mexico City was not yet thought of, and it would be many years before hordes of American tourists would invade the little town on its Friday market day to buy hand-woven cloth and baskets.

The play he wrote, "The Gold Piece," reflects the quiet simplicity of the Mexican village life. It is a straightforward, simply told tale of two children who make a great sacrifice in order that an old woman can help her blind son. It was published (July, 1921) in *The Brownies' Book,* a magazine for children established by W. E. B. Du Bois and the editors of *Crisis.* The editors' interest in this playlet and in two articles Hughes wrote about Mexico led to the publication of his poem, "The Negro Speaks of Rivers," in *Crisis* (June, 1921), and his professional career had begun.

During the next few years, Hughes attended Columbia University, wrote poetry, went to sea, lived in Paris, completed a degree at Lincoln University, wrote a novel, *Not Without Laughter* (1930), and spent some time with Jasper Deeter at the Hedgerow Theatre working on an early draft of *Mulatto.* It was not until 1935, however, that the play was performed on Broadway. Two years later, Hughes founded the Harlem Suitcase Theatre so that his long one-act play, *Don't you Want to be Free?,* might be presented in New York. He directed the play himself, and it ran on weekends during that year and the next for a total of 135 performances, the longest consecutive run any play has had in Harlem. He repeated this procedure in Los Angeles where the play had more than thirty performances. This play is available in the *One Act Play Magazine* (October, 1938).

Mulatto, however, was Langston Hughes' first professionally produced play and its text appears for the first time in this volume. This version is somewhat different from the play as presented on Broadway. Readers of *I Wonder as I Wander* will recall that Hughes

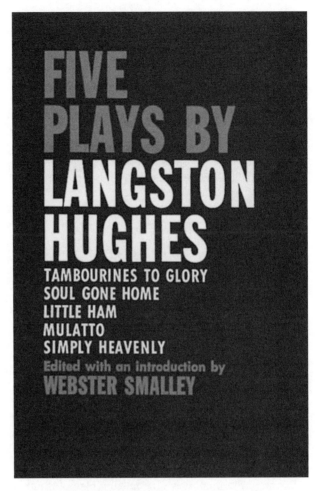

Dust jacket for Webster Smalley's 1963 collection of Hughes's plays. Mulatto, Soul Gone Home, *and* Little Ham *were first produced in the 1930s;* Simply Heavenly *premiered in 1957; and* Tambourines to Glory *was first performed in 1963 (Collection of Christopher C. De Santis).*

returned from a tour of Russia and the Orient to find, to his surprise, the play already in production. When he attended rehearsals, he discovered a number of major changes had been made without his knowledge or permission. The producer had presented *White Cargo,* a highly sensational, but very superficial, play of the twenties, with great financial success. This drama had achieved popularity by the exploitation of sex; the producer and director had therefore decided to make *Mulatto* into another *White Cargo.* When Hughes objected to sensationalism in his play, a few minor compromises were arranged, but the major changes remained. For example, since the producer thought that, for box-office reasons, there must always be a beautiful girl in a play, the Broadway production had the young Negro girl, Sallie, a minor character, miss her train to go to boarding school in the first act so that she might be raped in the last.

In the author's version of *Mulatto* printed here, Sallie remains intact, but absent after the first scene, and the focus of the dramatic action is where it should be—on Bert and Cora—if the play is to have meaning. The "germ idea" of this play was first expressed by Hughes in an early poem, "Cross," which clearly suggests the inner conflicts of the play's protagonist:

My old man's a white old man
And my old mother's black.
If I ever cursed my white old man
I take my curses back.

If I ever cursed my black old mother
And wished she were in hell,
I'm sorry for that evil wish
And now I wish her well.

My old man died in a fine big house,
My ma died in a shack.
I wonder where I'm gonna die,
Being neither white nor black.

The play, in turn, was the basis for Hughes' libretto of *The Barrier,* an opera with musical score by Jan Meyerowitz that has been often revived since its première at Columbia University's Brander Matthews Theatre.

While reading *Mulatto,* one should remember when it was written. It is very much a play of the thirties, an era when sociopolitical plays dominated American drama. The tendency was to oversimplify moral issues as in melodrama (read *Peace on Earth, Stevedore,* or even *Both Your Houses* for examples). In *Mulatto,* the injustices suffered by Bert, by Cora, and by all the Negroes in the rural South are clearly and forcefully presented. The thesis is there clearly enough. But then the characters of Bert and Cora begin to dominate the action, and the play becomes something more than mere thesis drama. Bert Lewis, the rebellious son of a white plantation owner and his Negro mistress, is placed in an unhappy, untenable situation, but it is his own stubborn, unbending pride—inherited, ironically, from his father—that brings about his downfall and death. The patient love and rich dignity of Cora and Bert's final recognition of the totality of his tragic situation raise *Mulatto* above the level of a mere problem play. One forgives Hughes the sometimes obvious exposition of the opening scenes (as one does the early O'Neill in *Beyond the Horizon*) for the tragedy and power of the play's final scenes. If the reader finds "melodramatic" elements in the play, let him look to the racial situation in the deep South as it is even today: it is melodramatic.

A Writer's Responsibility

In this statement about the social duty of black writers Hughes alludes to Warren Miller's novel The Cool World *(1959), James Baldwin's novel* Another Country *(1962), Jean Genet's play* The Blacks *(1958), LeRoi Jones's play* The Toilet *(1964), and William Hanley's play* Slow Dance on the Killing Ground *(1964). In the phrase "Crazy House of the Negro," Hughes may be referring to Adrienne Kennedy's play* The Funny House of a Negro *(1962).*

The Task of the Negro Writer as Artist

Whatever a white writer may write in this America of ours, or whatever picture he may present, nobody says derogatorily of his presentation, "That is just like white folks." But whatever a Negro writer writes today is likely to be taken as representative of us all, *"Just like Negroes."* Therefore, it behooves Negro writers in our segregated society, not necessarily to put our *best* foot forward, but to try at least to put a *balanced* foot forward, so that we do not all appear to be living in a *Cool World* in *Another Country* in the *Crazy House of the Negro* in which the majority of *The Blacks* seem to little except the graffiti of *The Toilet* or the deathly behavior of a *Slow Dance On the Killing Ground.* Pride, nobility, sacrifice, and decency are qualities strangely lacking in some of the most talented outpourings by or about Negroes these days. The Negro image deserves objective well-rounded (rather than one-sided) treatment, particularly in the decade of a tremendous freedom movement in which all of us can take pride. The last thing Negroes need now are black imitators of neurotic white writers who themselves have nothing of which to be proud. We possess within ourselves a great reservoir of physical and spiritual strength to which poetry, fiction and the stage should give voice—Cambridge, Albany, Fort Royal, Selma, Jackson, Atlanta. There is today no lack within the Negro people of beauty, strength and power—world shaking power. If I were a young writer, I would try to put some of these qualities on paper and on stage. Contemporary white writers can perhaps afford to be utterly irresponsible in their moral and social viewpoints. Negro writers cannot. Ours is a social as well as a literary responsibility.

—Negro Digest, 14 (April 1965): 65

Mulatto is the only play included here in which a white character is more than peripheral. In the other plays, where white characters do appear, they are little more than symbols—evil, good, or, as in the one-act *Soul Gone Home,* indifferent. The conception of *Soul Gone Home* is that of fantasy, and it contains some ironically comic moments, but its impulse is far removed from comedy. In a vignette-like episode, Hughes creates with great economy the kind of play Zola called for in his preface to *Thérèse Raquin*. Although a fantasy in concept and structure, its atmosphere and effects are those of naturalism. Like one of Hughes' poems, *Soul Gone Home* bristles with implications and reverberates with connotations. That which is unsaid becomes almost more important than what is put into the dialogue. The repressive dominance of the white culture is suggested only by the arrival of ambulance attendants, who are white as the mother knew they would be. The tragedy is that of a people so repressed that they can no longer love, and the ironic implications build to a shocking climax. Its impact is stark and uncomplicated, and it is a difficult play to forget.

Hughes does not always write in a serious vein, as readers of his stories and poems well know. His folk plays of urban Negro life, at once humorous and revealing, are a true contribution to American folk drama. The three included here–*Little Ham, Simply Heavenly,* and *Tambourines to Glory*–are, if one must define them, comedies. But the triple specters of poverty, ignorance, and repression can be seen not far beneath the surface of the comedy. The "numbers racket," "dream books," and the "hot goods man" in *Little Ham,* Simple's wistful sadness that no Negro has seen a flying saucer, and Laura's attitude toward the "religion business" in *Tambourines to Glory,* all indicate the near poverty, the ignorance, and the superstition that prevail in the world of which Hughes writes. Nevertheless, it is a colorful, wonderful world he presents to us, and we cannot but admire the spirit and vigor of his characters. He gives us a dynamic view of a segment of life most of us will never know and can discover nowhere else. At times he may sacrifice dramatic action for the sake of portraying nothing more than the people of Harlem absorbed in living out their lives from day to day, but if the humor of the scene and Hughes' infectious interest in his characters carry us along with him, what more can we ask?

Little Ham, "a play of the roaring twenties," is the first of Hughes' urban folk comedies. Its setting is Harlem at the time of the "Negro Renaissance," of *Shuffle Along,* and of the Cotton Club, but it is unlikely that any of its characters knew the meaning of "renaissance," had seen *Shuffle Along,* or had been inside the Cotton Club (which catered to a white clientele). Completed in 1935, *Little Ham* is a period piece, and one should remember the short skirts, tassels, brocades, and bell-shaped trousers of the era as he reads.

The play concerns the affairs (the word is intentionally ambiguous) of Hamlet Jones, a fast-talking, colorful, pint-sized Negro who shines shoes for a living. Little Ham's world is crowded, almost too crowded at times, with Harlemites of every sort except those of conventional respectability and education. It is a lively world, a society of casual morality that the white community either ignores or makes no attempt to understand. Hughes understands it, and this is the Harlem he has made into a literary land exclusively his own. One should not search too hard for profundity in *Little Ham;* it is a high-spirited revel and should be accepted as just that. Little Ham, Madam Bell, Lulu, and generously proportioned Tiny Lee are of the Harlem Hughes remembered as a young man, but are persons clearly recognizable today. If the characters in these folk comedies seem uncomplex, it is simply because these people are, in reality, direct and lacking in subtle complexity. Since they are unaware of the existence of Freud and Jung, Hughes has not hampered them with a burden of subconscious motivation.

Hughes creates his characters from life. He does not create character to fit a preconception, so he is not frightened if some of his creations do things and like things that Negroes are reputed to do and like. There is probably no group of people he dislikes more than the "passers" and pretenders of this world. He accepts, loves, and enjoys every aspect of his heritage and has the wisdom to recognize its richness. He does not write for those Negroes who have turned their backs on the spirituals and blues, nor for the people, Negro and white, who would bowdlerize *Huckleberry Finn.* He writes of what he sees, in his own way.

In *Simply Heavenly,* Hughes answered his pretentious and oversensitive critics in the only way they can be answered. When the "Character," an affected façade of a man, accuses the inhabitants of Paddy's Bar of being stereotypes, Mamie replies:

> Why, it's getting so colored folks can't do nothing no more without some other Negro calling you a stereotype. Stereotype, hah! If you like a little gin, you're a stereotype. You got to drink Scotch. If you wear a red dress, you're a stereotype. You got to wear beige or chartreuse. Lord have mercy, honey, do-don't like no blackeyed peas and rice! Then you're a down-home Negro for true–which I is–and proud of it! . . . I didn't come here to Harlem to get away from my people. I come here because there's more of 'em. I loves my race. I loves my people. Stereotype!

This speech, briefly and directly, expresses Hughes' attitude. To ask for analysis of motivation or for character study in depth in either *Little Ham* or *Simply Heavenly* is to miss the point. They should be read–or seen in the theatre–for the fun they project and for the warm understanding Hughes has of the people of Harlem.

A word should be said here about music. Aristotle long ago noted the importance of music in the drama. Fortunately, Hughes is a poet, and the rhythm of poetry and music is close to him. He is partial to the blues, jazz, and the spirituals. When he traveled to the

THE BIWEEKLY NEWSLETTER OF LOVE

VOLUME ONE, NUMBER THIRTEEN   MAY 4 , 1963 , NEW YORK

EIGHT TO TWO

by

Langston Hughes

(Mr. Hughes, Negro poet, author,
playwright, is best known for his
books <u>The Sweet Flypaper of Life</u>,
and <u>The Best of Simple</u>. He has
also written several Broadway hits,
his most recent the musical <u>Black
Nativity</u>, which was presented at
Lincoln Center and which is now
touring Europe.)

    In the popular mind all over the world, wherever I have travel-
ed, French women and black men have the reputation of being very
great lovers. As skilled and desirable companions of passion, they
are known from here to yonder. Their boudoir acclaim is international.

    In both the underworld and the upper world, amorous esteem
for the French female on the one hand and the black man on the other
holds true. In fact, in some countries--including the American South
--the sex prowess of the Negro male has become a folk legend, mag-
nified beyond the possibility of physical truth. And from Shanghai to
Cape Town the amorous charms of Gallic women are, among men,
held to be of the highest. Folk beliefs, no doubt, have made these
charms seem greater than they are.

Langston Hughes

*First page of an essay Hughes wrote on sexual stereotypes (Langston Hughes Collection,
Schomburg Center for Research in Black Culture, New York Public Library)*

far reaches of Asia in the thirties, he carried a portable phonograph and a set of Louis Armstrong records wherever he went. And he has more and more made music central to his dramatic writing. Hughes is at his best when he fuses drama and music. This he has done in the last two plays, *Simply Heavenly,* and *Tambourines to Glory.* Full appreciation of these two plays is possible only in the theatre, but to approximate their theatrical impact one must use all his imaginative faculties—the aural and visual imagination must be constantly and vigorously at play. Aural imagination is essential when the elements of poetry or music are introduced. To appreciate Hughes' most recent work for the theatre, it is essential that the reader use his musical imagination.

Langston Hughes is a most eclectic writer. In his "Simple" books and in his play, *Simply Heavenly,* he has created a hero who is almost no hero at all. Jesse Semple, or "Simple," yields to temptation so innocently but means so well, that any audience will forgive him more quickly than does his fiancée. Simple is Hughes' most memorable comic creation. He is of the same dramatic stripe as Figaro in Beaumarchais' *Figaro's Marriage*—both constantly skirt calamity and get into a good deal of trouble before they finally succeed in marrying the girls they love, and each has a unique dignity in spite of their comic weaknesses.* Like his comic compeer, Simple has more than his share of these. His power of reasoning is wonderful to follow, even when his conclusions are unanswerable. "Joyce," he tells his fiancée, "I don't want to pay for no woman's divorce I don't love. And I do not love Isabel. Also, I ain't got the money." Simple, like most of his friends in Paddy's Bar, seldom has much money. What the inhabitants of this "neighborhood club" lack in affluence, they make up for in high spirits and good humor. There are no villains in *Simply Heavenly;* indeed, the only character for whom we feel antipathy is the pretentious little man mentioned earlier. The values of this play are not built on dramatic clash and suspense, rather, they are inherent in Hughes' intimate and warmly affectionate picture of the unique inhabitants of this city within a city.

The intimacy of the writing and of David Martin's musical setting call for a special kind of theatre. I suspect that audiences who saw it in a large theatre on Broadway and who viewed the "Play of the Week" televised production missed some of its true quality and value. Though its plot is of the slenderest comic fabric, its characters and straightforward humor make *Simply Heavenly* the definitive folk comedy of life in Harlem.

Hughes' point of view and purpose in his Harlem folk plays is summed up in his description of the final play in this collection:

Tambourines to Glory is a fable, a folk ballad in stage form, told in broad and very simple terms—if you will, a comic strip, a cartoon—about problems which can only convincingly be reduced to a comic strip if presented very cleanly, clearly, sharply, precisely, and with humor.

Hughes has done just this in all three plays. Technically, each is a comedy, but, however tongue-in-cheek his approach in *Tambourines to Glory,* Hughes has made the problem of good and evil central to the action. Thus, it is at once the most serious and the most dramatic of his comedies. Neither Ham nor Simple ever comes to grips with a moral issue. Part of Ham's charm is that he is unaware that moral issues exist. Simple knows right from wrong, but there are so very many pleasant little sins lying in wait for him that we hardly blame him for straying, especially since he is such a gregarious being and his intended wife-to-be goes to bed so early.

Essie and Laura, in *Tambourines to Glory,* are presented as simply and forthrightly as are Ham and Simple, but there is no similarity of character. Essie and Laura are both strong individuals—Essie, in her goodness, and Laura, in her predilection toward chicanery. Symbolically, they represent two very real aspects of all revivalist, perhaps all religious, movements. The saint and the charlatan often live side by side, even in established religions, and sometimes exist in a single personality. Hughes chose to write a rousing musical melodrama about some aspects of Harlem religion. The result is a skillfully created, well-integrated musical play, written with humor, insight, and compassion.

It is the latter quality—Hughes' compassionate understanding of all his characters—that oftentimes minimizes dramatic action and conflict in his plays. Perhaps he likes his sinners too well, for he is inclined to justify their evil by mitigating circumstances. But it may be that he has never forgotten an early experience, gained shortly after his grandmother's death. He lived for a time in Kansas with a couple named Reed. Hughes has written that "Auntie Reed" was a devout Christian but "Uncle Reed" was a sinner, and has said, "No doubt from them I learned to like both Christians and sinners equally well." There can be no doubt that Hughes prefers the healthy sinner to the pretentious fake.

Villains are not plentiful in Hughes' Harlem plays. Big-Eyed Buddy Lomax (who informs us that he is really the Devil) is unique. Even he is a threat only through Laura's weakness for him (and all he represents). Hughes is not as interested in a conventional conflict between protagonist and antagonist as in revealing the cracks in the self-protecting façades humans erect to conceal their weaknesses. His characters are never merely subservient to plot. Thus, even within the confines of melodrama, he is able to write a moving and honest play.

Tambourines to Glory is more than musical melodrama; it is a play of redemption. It is a Faust-like tale, told with the simplicity of a medieval morality play. Hughes tells the story with great good humor, but he never asks us to laugh derisively or to smile sardonically. Behind the laughter is a touch of pity and a great quantity of warm understanding. As broadly and simply as the characters are sketched, they are utterly believable. When they show weakness, their frailties stem directly from problems that plague the average Negro in our largest metropolis. Laura's grasping drive for material things, for example, is a natural reaction to the deprivation and poverty she has suffered all her life, and Essie's honest faith is a triumph over tribulation and temptation. Both characterizations are true.

Finally, this play is in effect a "dramatic song," to use one of Hughes' descriptive terms. It has a pervasive rhythm. The integration of action, original lyrics, traditional spirituals, and the gospel music of Jobe Huntley, adds to the richness of the drama and contributes to characterization. Music is central to the lives—one might say, even to the spiritual being—of these characters. Nowhere has Hughes more skillfully interwoven and integrated music into the fabric of drama.

Since Hughes has worked and hoped for a vigorous Negro theatre movement in America, it is my wish that the publication of these five plays may help to stimulate that movement. His plays, and the plays of younger Negro playwrights such as Lorraine Hansberry, William Branch, Loften Mitchell, Alice Childress, and Ossie Davis, need to be seen and heard—projected by actors on stages before living audiences. For in the final analysis plays exist only in the theatre. Langston Hughes has long been one of the most effective literary spokesmen for the American Negro. His poetry and prose have been published both in this country and abroad. Now, thanks to Indiana University Press, these plays, representing his dramatic writing from the twenties to the sixties, are for the first time available to a wide audience. I am honored to write this introductory note. The dramatic world of Langston Hughes is a quite different world from that of any other playwright, and the discovery of that world is, in itself, an entertaining, wonderful, and enlightening experience.

–"Introduction," in *Five Plays by Langston Hughes* (Bloomington: Indiana University Press, 1963), pp. vii–xvii

—

*The Figaro in the Mozart-da Ponte opera is simplified and is more of a buffoon than in Beaumarchais' great revolutionary play.

* * *

Doris E. Abramson, a leading scholar of African American theater and the author of Negro Playwrights in the American Theatre, 1925–1959 *(1969), wrote this review article.*

"It'll Be Me": The Voice of Langston Hughes
Review of *Five Plays by Langston Hughes*

Ask anyone to name the contemporary Negro playwrights, and he will probably answer hastily and as if they were all: Lorraine Hansberry and Langston Hughes. In that order. As a playwright she is probably better known than he is, though he has been writing plays for three decades, whereas her first play is only four years old. Mr. Hughes is known first and praised highest for his poems, one of which gave Miss Hansberry the title for her play, *A Raisin in the Sun.* Both writers have been called propaganda or social protest writers. Neither seems seriously bothered by such labels, and both have had the interesting experience of receiving applause from the objects of their protest.

It is scarcely surprising that Langston Hughes is not more widely known as a playwright. Until the recent publication of his *Five Plays*[1] there was no opportunity for the American public to read his plays. Those of us who didn't see the plays when they were produced knew them only by reputation, which has always been a better way to know the critics than the plays.

Mulatto, the first play in this collection, was a Broadway success during the 1935–36 season. It ran for a year at the Vanderbilt and Ambassador, toured for eight months across the United States (though not in the South, not even in Philadelphia), and has been produced all over the world. It has been translated into Italian, Spanish, French, Portuguese and Japanese and has been published in Milan and Buenos Aires. Now we may read this remarkable play by a too long neglected American playwright.

In his introduction, editor Webster Smalley blames the commercial nature of our theatres and publishing houses for the delay in the printing of these five plays. And he points out very sensibly that "a Negro playwright has all the woes of a white dramatist, with a number of others thrown in." Commercial theatre in America (one might just as well say Broadway) shows only occasional interest in Negro drama; little is produced and, consequently, little is published. Miss Hansberry and Mr. Hughes are among a handful (about a dozen) of Negro playwrights who have had their plays produced on Broadway since 1925. Only six of these plays have been published, two of them for the first time in this book. We are indeed indebted to the University of Indiana Press.

That there have been few productions of plays by Negroes in our time is not to say that history records no

Flyer for Hughes's musical that opened on 12 January 1964 at the Greenwich Mews Theater in New York. A gospel play about the freedom movement, Jerico-Jim Crow *was Hughes's most highly praised production (Langston Hughes Collection, Schomburg Center for Research in Black Culture, New York Public Library).*

early plays of Negro authorship. They are few, but they are impressive both by their very existence and their reflection of the period out of which they came. The first play ever written by an American Negro was probably William Wells Brown's *Experience* or *How To Give a Northern Man a Backbone*. It was not staged, but the author read it during the year 1856 to numerous audiences in New York and Canada. In 1858 he wrote *The Escape* or *A Leap for Freedom*. The titles indicate the author's concerns. He was an ex-slave, also credited with writing the first novel ever written by an American Negro. Though before and after these early attempts there were plays by white playwrights *about* Negroes–such plays as *Uncle Tom's Cabin* adapted by George Aiken (1853) and *The Octoroon* by Dion Boucicault (1859)–there was not another play of Negro authorship until 1903, when Joseph S. Cotter wrote *Caleb, the Degenerate,* a play in blank verse, taking Booker T. Washington's side in the Washington-DuBois debate.

Not until the second decade of the century was there a real interest in plays about Negro life, and they were written by non-Negro playwrights (Paul Green, Eugene O'Neill, Ridgely Torrence, Marc Connelly, and others). Langston Hughes once said to a group of Negro writers:

> Sometimes I think whites are more appreciative of our uniqueness than we are ourselves. The white "black" artists dealing in Negro material have certainly been financially more successful than any of us real Negroes have ever been.[2]

These white playwrights, by their treatment of Negro themes and their attempts to destroy an earlier minstrel stereotype, did help make it possible for the Negro to come before the public in serious drama. They paved the way, no doubt inadvertently, for the "real Negroes."

Garland Anderson was the first Negro to have a play produced on Broadway; it was called *Appearances* and ran for three weeks in the 1925–26 season and for nearly five months in 1929. Though there were Negro actors in three of the seventeen roles, the Negro hero was played by a white actor. The author, who had been a bellboy in San Francisco, wrote a moralizing play that called for faith and trust in one's fellow man. He preached Washingtonian virtues in a court room melodrama.

It was not until 1929 that a Negro writer wrote a Broadway play that moved in the direction of the realistic play about Negro life. Wallace Thurman, assisted by William Rapp, wrote *Harlem,* a play about Negro New York of the twenties, complete with rent parties and racketeering. This play provided a transition from the twenties to the thirties, the period in which Negro playwrights began to speak for themselves. When they did gain access to something other than musical-comedy theatre, they were determined to write realistically, to write about Negro life as it is lived by Negroes, not as it is interpreted by white writers.

Langston Hughes made his position clear in the poem, "Notes on Commercial Theatre":

> You've done taken my blues and gone–
> Sure have! You sing 'em on Broadway,
> And you sing 'em in Hollywood Bowl.
> You mixed 'em up with symphonies,
> And you fixed 'em so they don't sound like me.
> Yep, you done taken my blues and gone!
>
> You also took my spirituals and gone.
> Now you've rocked-and-rolled 'em to death!
> You put me in *Macbeth*
> In *Carmen Jones,* and *Anna Lucasta,*
> And all kinds of *Swing Mikados.*
> And in everything but what's about me–
> But someday somebody'll
> Stand up and talk about me,
> And write about me–
> Black and beautiful–
> And sing about me,
> And put on plays about me!
> I reckon it'll be me myself!
>
> Yes, it'll be me.[3]

It has not been easy for Langston Hughes or for other Negro playwrights to get their plays produced. In a country where only a few years ago Negroes were barred even from attendance at many theatres, it has been exceedingly difficult for Negro writers to serve their necessary apprenticeship in the theatre and to get an audience for their plays. Langston Hughes has been braver (more foolhardy?) than most of his fellow Negro playwrights. He founded two dramatic groups during the thirties: the Suitcase Theatre in Harlem and the Negro Art Theatre in Los Angeles. In 1941 he established the Skyloft Players in Chicago. "Few playwrights have the heart or energy for such undertakings," Mr. Smalley observes.

On a radio symposium in 1961–in the company of Lorraine Hansberry, James Baldwin, Alfred Kazin and others–Langston Hughes said: "I am, of course, as everyone knows, primarily a–I guess you might even say a propaganda writer; my main material is the race problem. . . ." He also referred to his famous character Jesse B. Semple, or Simple, as a "kind of social protest mouthpiece." These statements contradict Webster Smalley's insistence that "he is an artist, not a propagandist." What a strange, unnecessary and impossible

Continued Controversy

Hughes continued to be hounded by right-wing protests in the 1960s, as when he visited Wichita State University in April 1965.

4 Churches Hit Poet's WSU Visit

The appearance at Wichita State University Monday of Langston Hughes, nationally-known Negro poet, has been protested by four Wichita churches.

Identical telegrams criticizing the appearance were sent Sunday to Dr. Emory Lindquist, university president; Gov. William Avery and the State Board of Regents.

"Mr. Hughes was identified before a congressional investigatory body as an active Communist," say the statements approved by the Wichita Baptist Tabernacle, 405 Cleveland, and Ark Valley Christian Church, 3851 S. Hydraulic.

Pastors of the First Bible Baptist Church, 1156 N. Oliver, and Beth Eden Baptist Church, 1600 S. Market, indicated their churches planned similar action. Members of the churches contacted Dr. Lindquist by phone Sunday.

Kenneth L. Myers, attorney, 1607 N. Hillside, Conservative party candidate for governor last year and a member of the John Birch Society, said he introduced a supporting resolution Sunday before the Twentieth Century Club, 536 N. Broadway.

Three hundred members of the club approved a supporting telegram sent to Dr. Lindquist, the Board of Regents and Gov. Avery, Myers said.

Virgil D. McNeil, evangelist at the Ark Valley church, said he "had information in the files for some time" about Hughes.

"I was shocked when I learned he was coming to Wichita," McNeil said.

The evangelist said he had never met Hughes.

McNeil listed 31 organizations which he said were subversive and to which he charged Hughes belonged.

Identical statements approved by the churches requested a public investigation.

"Academic freedom at public institutions should never be twisted to authorize a sounding board for persons with subversive records," the statement said. The churches asked that the Board of Regents authorize a "screening committee" to weed out "subversives" on school platforms.

Hughes is coming to the WSU campus as a poet, not a politician, President Lindquist said Sunday after receipt of telegrams from the protesting churches.

"The University Forum asked Mr. Hughes to speak there as a creative poet," Dr. Lindquist said.

Noting Hughes' reputation as a poet, Lindquist said the forum had been the "clearing house" for ideas from many fields.

"The university is an organism that is a part of the life of its times," the president said.

"A visiting lecturer is not instructed as to contents of his address," Lindquist said, "nor does the university have responsibility for what is said."

"The university ceases to be worthy of its calling when it yields at any point to the pressures of outside groups as to what can be said or taught on the campus," he said.

Lindquist said he would uphold the right of such persons to speak, although he and the faculty "may be in complete disagreement" with what is presented.

Dr. Walter Merrill, head of the WSU English department who arranged Hughes' visit here, said he was "very surprised to learn of the protests."

"I don't know if Hughes is a Republican or a Democrat," Merrill said.

He cited Hughes' national reputation as a poet, adding that this was the sole criterion for selection as a forum speaker.

"He is one of the leading American poets," Merrill said.

Hughes was born in Joplin, Mo., and lived for a time in Lawrence. He will speak there Wednesday before a University of Kansas audience.

His Wichita appearance will be at 8 p.m. Monday in the Duerksen Fine Arts Center with "Life Makes Poems" as the topic.

–The Wichita Eagle, 26 April 1965

---

separation. Art that has at its center a social problem must be propaganda. Mr. Smalley correctly says Mr. Hughes is not a belligerent writer, but there is propaganda in his subtle use of humor and deflating irony.

In the plays of Negro authorship written since the 1935 production of *Mulatto*–which ran longer than any other play by a Negro until *A Raisin in the Sun* broke the record in 1959–the same problems within a problem appear repeatedly. It is not surprising. Certain problems persist in the lives of American Negroes: unemployment that breeds poverty and crime; racial tensions that explode in riots, mob violence, lynching; poor housing, slums, the frustrations of too many people liv-

ing in one place; miscegenation and its real or imagined unhappy results; political and social evils and educational deprivations too numerous to mention–all the problems that grow out of the ghetto existence and general second-class citizenship forced upon most American Negroes. The plays reflect, with varying degrees of realism, life as lived by Negroes. This is true of plays written for the Negro Unit of the Federal Theatre Project as well as for commercial plays on and off Broadway.

Playwright Alice Childress commented at a writers' conference in 1959 on the possibility of Negro writers forsaking problems and just writing about people.

She sees a difficulty, because it turns out that human beings are more than just people.

> Many of us would rather be writers than Negro writers, and when I get that urge, I look about for the kind of white writer—which is what we mean when we say 'just a writer'—that I would emulate. I come up with Sean O'Casey. Immediately, I am a problem writer. O'Casey writes about the people he knows best and I must—well, there you have it![4]

Langston Hughes, too, writes about the people he knows best. The five plays in this book are *Mulatto, Soul Gone Home, Little Ham, Simply Heavenly* and *Tambourines to Glory.* With the exception of *Mulatto,* a tragedy of the Deep South, they are all comic folk plays with Harlem settings. Only in *Mulatto* is a white man more than a peripheral character.

Mulatto is a play about miscegenation, a subject that both titillated and confused nineteenth century writers and continues to fascinate in our own time. The "germ idea" was contained in an earlier short story of his called "Father and Son" and even earlier and most effectively in a poem called "Cross."

> My old man's a white old man
> And my old mother's black.
> If ever I cursed my white old man
> I take my curses back.
>
> If ever I cursed my black old mother
> And wished she were in hell,
> I'm sorry for that evil wish
> And now I wish her well.
>
> My old man died in a fine big house.
> My ma died in a shack.
> I wonder where I'm gonna die,
> Being neither white nor black.

Critics of the play have called it melodramatic. (*Mulatto,* too black and white?) The stage version must have been rather sensational, with a rape scene not even in the original text (which is what has been published) and very strong performances by the whole cast. The heroine, Cora Lewis, was played by one of the greatest actresses America has produced, Rose McClendon. This was the last role she played before her untimely death in 1936.

To read *Mulatto* with a forgiving eye, as we have to read many plays of the thirties, is a good experience both emotionally and intellectually. The exposition is obvious, and there's repetition galore. But Cora's long speeches are frighteningly beautiful. (They must have made wonderful arias in the opera, "The Barrier," which was first produced in 1950, with music by Jan

Hughes with his friend Emerson Harper in the back of 20 East 127th Street, New York, where Hughes lived with Emerson, a musician, and his wife, Ethel Dudley Brown Harper— "Aunt Toy," as Hughes knew her. Toy Harper was a friend of Carrie Hughes in their Kansas days (Langston Hughes Papers, Yale Collection of American Literature, Beinecke Rare Book and Manuscript Library).

Meyerowitz.) Here she speaks to the dead Colonel Tom who has been murdered by their mulatto child who asked to be recognized by his own father:

> He's *your* boy. His eyes is gray—like your eyes. He's tall like you's tall. He's proud like you's proud. And he's runnin'—runnin' from po' white trash that ain't worth de little finger o' nobody what's got your blood in 'em, Tom. (*Demandingly*) Why don't you get up from there and stop 'em, Colonel Tom? What's that you say? He ain't your chile? He's ma bastard chile? Ma yellow bastard chile? (*Proudly*) Yes, he's mine. . . . He's ma chile. . . . Don't you come to my bed no mo'. I calls you to help me now, and you just lays there. I calls you for to wake up, and you just lays there. Whenever you called me in de night, I woke up. When you called for me to love, I always reached out ma arms fo' you. I borned you five chilluns and now one of 'em is out yonder in de dark runnin' from yo' people. Our youngest boy out yonder in de dark runnin'. (*Accusingly*) He's runnin' from you, too. . . . You are out yonder in de dark, runnin' our child with de hounds and de gun in yo' hand. . . . Damn you, Colonel Norwood! (*Backing slowly up the stairs, staring at the rigid body below her*) Damn you, Thomas Norwood! God damn you!

This is less than half of the speech just before the curtain at the end of the last scene but one. The dialect sometimes contributes something to a mood, but often it detracts both from meaning and mood. We learn to put up with it, as we do with dialect in plays by Eugene O'Neill.

We should be grateful to be able to read this play at all. It may not be produced in the United States as often as it is abroad, but now we can read it and ponder why. It is an interesting question. Why should people in France and Spain and Japan still care about problems involving the intermingling of the races to the extent that they produce this play? Why do we not produce it? Is it that we don't care as much as they do, or has our sophistication taken us beyond this particular statement of the problem? We couldn't even begin to ask, let alone to answer, these questions before the play was published.

Soul Gone Home is one of the strangest little plays ever published anywhere. On the book jacket it is called "a fantasy of people so repressed that they can no longer afford love." That's probably true. The editor says it "bristles with implications and reverberates with connotations." Mr. Hughes told me recently that it should be played for broad comedy in order to heighten the tragedy. It gets maudlin if it is done seriously. What is this play about? A dead son comes alive long enough to berate his prostitute mother for being "a no-good mama." A strange subject for a comedy! And strangely enough it works—or one has the feeling that it could work on the stage if the director listened to Mr. Hughes and avoided any hint of sentimentality.

It is unfortunate that *Little Ham* and *Simply Heavenly* are placed side by side in this volume, inviting a comparison in which *Little Ham* is surely the loser. Both plays are urban folk plays set in Harlem. In each the hero is a little man with big ideas and a capacity for enjoyment: Hamlet Jones and Jesse B. Semple. Hamlet is a lady's man under the spell of a fat lady named Tiny.

HAM: A sweet little woman like you's got no business at a fight all alone by her little she-self.

TINY: Now you know I ain't little. *(Coyly)* Don't nobody like me 'cause I'm fat.

HAM: Well, don't nobody like me 'cause I'm so young and small.

TINY: You a cute little man. You mean don't *nobody* like you.

HAM: *(Woefully)* Nobody that amounts to nothin!

This kind of dialogue ripples along with what we take for authenticity, and *Little Ham* moves lightly through a Harlem of the "roaring twenties," introducing us to Madame Lucille Bell, Mattie Bea, racke-

teers, molls, dancers and kids and all kinds of under- and over-ground characters. The play is a pleasant experience, but it has little more depth than an old Amos 'n Andy sketch. Mr. Hughes has written better plays, one of which should have been put here in place of *Little Ham*. (My choice would have been his agitprop play, *Don't You Want To Be Free?*)

On the other hand, *Simply Heavenly* is a remarkable play about Harlem life, a comedy filled with characters who interest, instruct, transport—and please us. Only Saroyan has created a barroom to match Mr. Hughes' Paddy's Bar. It becomes as vivid a place as the Negroes who people it.

Of the hero, Jesse B. Semple, Langston Hughes has written the following:

> Simple is a Chaplinesque character, slight of build, awkwardly graceful, given to flights of fancy, and positive statements of opinion—stemming from a not so positive soul. He is dark with a likable smile, ordinarily dressed, except for rather flamboyant summer sport shirts. Simple tries hard to succeed, but the chips seldom fall just right.

Saunders Redding once spoke of "the poignant, pain-filled, pain-relieving humor of simple Jesse B." Originally a character in a play called *Simple Takes a Wife,* this little man has become a great favorite in Europe as well as in this country. He turns up in Mr. Hughes' newspaper columns ("I sit in that barber chair, thinking how God must love poor folks because he made so many of them in my image.") and in the earlier play without music as well as the current one with music. His opinions are being heard all over the world. *Simple Takes a Wife* has been done only abroad and is in the repertory at Prague, where it was originally produced in 1961. In that year, Mr. Hughes had this to say about the universality of Simple:

> . . . a regional Negro character like Simple, a character intended for the people who belong to his own race, if written about warmly enough, humanly enough, can achieve universality.[5]

The temptation for a reviewer is to quote great chunks of dialogue from *Simply Heavenly,* for this is a delightful play with a message, a play filled with the rich dialogue of Harlemites who make their lives bearable through humor and affection for one another. Kierkegaard has said somewhere that the more one suffers the more one has a sense for the comic. He speaks of people who have suffered deepest having "true authority in the use of the comic, an authority by which one word transforms as by magic the reasonable crea-

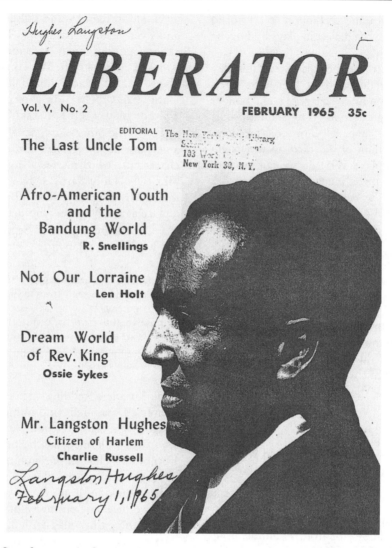

Cover for a magazine featuring a biographical article on Hughes (Langston Hughes Collection, Schomburg Center for Research in Black Culture, New York Public Library)

ture one calls man into a caricature." Langston Hughes has that authority, and in this good sense of the word Simple and his friends are caricatures.

Mamie, an unforgettable woman, has to answer the charge of being a stereotype when she feels the need to defend her tastes in the presence of a "passer," a pretender:

> Why, it's getting so colored folks can't do nothing no more without some other Negro calling you a stereotype. Stereotype, hah! If you like a little gin, you're a stereotype. You got to drink Scotch. If you wear a red dress, you're a stereotype. You got to wear beige or chartreuse. Lord have mercy, honey, do-don't like no blackeyed peas and rice! Then you're a down-home Negro for true—which I is—and proud of it! I didn't come here to Harlem to get away from my people. I come here because there's more of 'em. I loves my race. I loves my people. Stereotype!

The play is bursting with comment, sometimes a bit too obviously.

SIMPLE: This great big old white ocean—and me a colored swimmer.

BOYD: Aw, stop feeling sorry for your self just because you're colored. You can't use race as an excuse forever. All men have problems. And even if you are colored, you've got to swim beyond color, and get to that island that is you—the human you, the man you.

This kind of preaching will bother some readers. But even those who have an aversion to messages will chuckle at Simple's dream of leading white Mississippi troops into action in World War III. They will chuckle, they will wonder, and Mr. Hughes will have made his point.

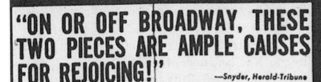

"ON OR OFF BROADWAY, THESE TWO PIECES ARE AMPLE CAUSES FOR REJOICING!"
—Snyder, Herald-Tribune

"UNCOMMONLY REWARDING EVENING"
—Taubman, Times

"YOU ARE TOUCHED BY ITS TRUTH AND HUMANITY."
—Taubman, Times

"SHEER EXUBERANT ECSTACY AND JOY...A BLAZE OF MUSIC AND DANCE."
—Watts, Post

"COMPELLING, DRAMATIC EXPERIENCE."
—Snyder, Herald-Tribune

"GENERATES EXCITEMENT WITH THE FORCE OF ITS GLORIOUS NATIVE VIGOR."
—Snyder, Herald-Tribune

"SUBSTANTIAL, DRAMATIC EVENT...TERRIFIC THEATER!"
—Gottfried, Women's Wear

"A REFRESHING SHOW ... ROUSED THE FIRST NIGHTERS THOROUGHLY."
—Jordan, CBS-TV

"A GEM OF PURE BRECHT. CYNICAL, BITTER, FUNNY."
—Probst, NBC-TV

"EXCITING THEATRE ... YOU'LL LOVE 'THE PRODIGAL SON'."—Thompson, Jrl.-Amer.

the **exception** and the **rule**
by
BERTOLT BRECHT
Adapted by
ERIC BENTLEY

LANGSTON HUGHES'
the **prodigal son**

"THERE IS SOUND AND FURY, SINGING AND DANCING, AND ABOVE ALL, STIRRING THEATER."
—Snyder, Herald-Tribune

MAIL AND PHONE ORDERS FILLED

PRICES: Mon. Evgs. at 8:40; All Seats $2.50; Tues., Wed., Thurs. Evgs. at 8:40 and Sun. at 3:00 & 8:00 P.M.: $3.90, 3.50, 2.50; Sat. at 7:00 & 10:00 P.M.: $4.90, 3.90, 2.90. Please enclose self-addressed, stamped envelope with check or money order and suggest alternate dates.

GREENWICH MEWS, 141 West 13th St. CH 3-6800

New York Herald Tribune
Friday, May 21, 1965

Brecht, Hughes And Rejoicing Off Broadway

By Louis Snyder

There was sound and fury, didacticism and lyricism, singing and dancing, and above all, stirring theater last night downtown at Greenwich Mews, where two unlikely bedfellows, Bertolt Brecht's "The Exception and the Rule" and Langston Hughes' "The Prodigal Son," made the theater's low rafters ring to very divergent tunes.

Probably it would not occur to many producers to bracket two theatrical craftsmen, so relentlessly dedicated to cynicism on the one hand and salvation on the other, as Brecht and Hughes. But the combination proved to be invigorating in both instances, even if each work, despite its contemporary qualities, was, in theatrical terms, something of a throwback to the stage of day before yesterday.

This being a season to brush up on your Brecht, "The Exception and the Rule," a product of 1930, is required seeing and hearing. Despite a pervading impression of being an impressionistic "East Lynne," this Marxist-oriented piece still comes over the footlights as a compelling dramatic experience, weighted as it is with villains in clown-white make-up and the scales of justice overloaded with obvious social connotations which are now common property.

Brecht's capitalistic Merchant, crossing a desert with a "union" Guide, whom he distrusts and discharges, is left with a Coolie to lead him. This poor man, similarly terrorised by the unfamiliarity of his surroundings, also becomes the victim of the Merchant's fears, and is killed in a misconstrued gesture of helpfulness toward his employer. At a trial, in which the chalk-faced judge bends logic many ways, the Merchant is acquitted of murder, on grounds of "self-defense."

since he could "reasonably" have expected the Coolie of wanting to do away with him, whether or not this was his real intention.

Believe it or not, as staged by Isiah Sheffer, and acted by Paul Richards (Merchant), Joseph Chaikin (Coolie), Frank Groseclose (Judge), and Richard Hamilton (Guide), this made documentary sense, not a little of which was aided by a score by Stefan Wolpe, written in the idiom of the time. Loaded dice or not, the play is offered honestly, and one may decide for himself how close to parody the passing of time has brought it.

There is no parody in Hughes' "The Prodigal Son." It is a straightforward, strong-lunged "gospel song-play," which retells the Biblical story in musical narrative, arranged by Marion Franklin, and vividly choreographed by Syvilla Fort. Restlessly staged by Vinnette Carroll, uninhibitedly sung by Dorothy Drake, Joseph Attes, Robert Pinkston and Jeannette Hodge, among others, and danced to perfection by Philip A. Stamps, in the title role, and Glory Van Scott as a devasting Jezebel, this "Prodigal" swept social significance out into West 13th Street with the force of its glorious native vigor. Mr. Hughes' words and the music by Billy Eaton, and Jobe Huntley, along with traditional songs, generated pathos and excitement, as the occasion demanded, and when, at the end, one and all were invited to "Come on in the house" to welcome the return of the Prodigal, the performers found a cheering audience ready to join the celebration.

On or off Broadway, these two pieces are ample causes for rejoicing!

Hughes clipped these notices from newspapers. The Prodigal Son *premiered 20 May 1965 (Langston Hughes Collection, Schomburg Center for Research in Black Culture, New York Public Library).*

Tambourines to Glory, the last play in this collection, is characterized by the editor as a "musical melodrama about some aspects of Harlem religion." As a play, greatly helped by the songs, it is far more effective than Mr. Hughes' novel of the same name. Perhaps the best way to sum up the author's viewpoint in the play is to quote his own description of it quoted in the Introduction to *Five Plays:*

> *Tambourines to Glory is* a fable, a folk ballad in stage form, told in broad and very simple terms–if you will, a comic strip, a cartoon–about problems which can only convincingly be reduced to a comic strip if presented very cleanly, clearly, sharply, precisely, and with humor.

There is something intriguing about a writer who knows that the form he has chosen for his work will be right if the presentation of the piece is as honest on stage as his writing was originally. Langston Hughes, like Bertolt Brecht, writes for the theatre as a knowledgeable man of the theatre. *Tambourines to Glory* comes alive on the page; you can hear it.

In this play two women, Laura and Essie, start a church. In Harlem it is quite possible to "set up shop" in an old store, a movie theatre, any little corner where the faithful poor may gather. In 1930 James Weldon Johnson noted that there were one hundred and sixty Negro churches in Harlem and that one hundred of them were "ephemeral and nomadic, belonging to no established denomination and within no classification."[6] There must be many more by now. Mr. Hughes himself has said that it is difficult to find a suitable location for a theatre in Harlem, because when the movie houses go out of business they are bought up by "churches." Laura and Essie, who start on a street corner, convert an old movie house into Tambourine Temple.

Essie is sincere. Laura is a charlatan. Good works with evil to the glory of God ultimately. The devil is in the guise, this time, of Big-Eyed Buddy Lomax, a handsome hustler in the employ of white gangsters. The plot is the least effective thing about the play and does not bear telling. What is impressive is the skillful use of songs to heighten emotional scenes and the characterizations, especially of the two leading ladies and the devil himself. Mr. Hughes shows sympathy, even pity, for all the participants in this story of hokum and holiness.

Buddy says, "This church racket's got show business beat to hell. But some churches don't have

sense enough to be crooked. They really try to be holy–and holiness don't make money." It is the good Essie, however, who wins in the end–at least of this play.

Webster Smalley's introduction is as informative as it is laudatory. He gives us a good idea of how productive Langston Hughes–poet, playwright, novelist, short story writer–has been and refers to him as "America's outstanding Negro man of letters." It would seem necessary to qualify that praise since James Baldwin has appeared on the scene. Mr. Hughes, however, is an impressive writer, and this collection of plays gives us a chance to know an important side of his work for the first time. He is still, it seems to me, a better poet than playwright, another reason why *Don't You Want To Be Free?* should appear in print soon; for in that play he uses some of his verses effectively within the framework of a play.

Negro playwrights are scarce at the moment, but they are more than promising: Lorraine Hansberry, Alice Childress, Ossie Davis, Loften Mitchell, William Branch and James Baldwin, to name most of the handful. They will, no doubt, write out of their experiences as Negroes; and they will create white characters, because the time has come for them to let us see ourselves through their art.

It is not likely that Langston Hughes will write about white men–unless they wander into Harlem. Harlem is his home, and he records for us the speech and the dreams, the agonies and the compensating joys alive in that city within a city. We are grateful for his plays and for his wise, warm sense of humor. This book should be only a beginning; his other plays and those of younger Negro playwrights should be made available to us soon.

–*Massachusetts Review,* 5 (Autumn 1963): 168–176

1. Edited with an introduction by Webster Smalley. Bloomington: Indiana University Press, 1963. $5.95.
2. "Writers: Black and White," *The American Negro Writer and His Roots.* Selected papers from The First Conference of Negro Writers, March, 1959. New York: The American Society of African Culture, 1960, p. 42.
3. *Selected Poems.* New York: Alfred A. Knopf, 1959, p. 190.
4. First Conference of Negro Writers, 1959.
5. "The Negro in American Culture," WBAI-FM, New York City.
6. *Black Manhattan* (New York: Alfred A. Knopf, 1930), p. 163.

Still Climbin'

In this article Hughes charts some of the connections between the Harlem Renaissance and the African Négritude movement, which included writers such as Léopold Sédar Senghor of Senegal and Aimé Césaire of Martinique.

The Twenties: Harlem and Its Negritude

When Ralph Ellison came from Tuskegee to Harlem in 1936 and Richard Wright left Chicago the following year, I would say that those migrations marked the tail end of the Negro Renaissance. Dr. Alain Locke, the granddaddy of the New Negro, introduced me to the recently arrived Ralph Ellison in the lobby of the Young Men's Christian Association, and Ellison almost immediately expressed a desire to meet Richard Wright, who was coming briefly to New York for a week or so to attend a writers' conference. I introduced them. They became fast friends. Wright influenced Ellison in the nineteen-forties, as I had influenced Wright in the thirties, as Claude McKay and James Weldon Johnson influenced me in the twenties. But by the time the thirties came, the voltage of the Negro Renaissance of the twenties had nearly run its course. Ellison and Wright were about the last of the young pilgrims to come to Harlem seeking its sustenance. The chain of influences that had begun in Renaissance days ended in the thirties when the Great Depression drastically cut down on migrations, literary or otherwise.

Claude McKay had come to New York from Jamaica by way of Tuskegee before the Harlem Renaissance had properly begun, and soon thereafter he went to live in Europe, leaving the influence of his poetry behind him. McKay might be termed the first of the New Negroes, of whom Dr. W. E. B. Du Bois, Alain Locke, and James Weldon Johnson were the deans. During the decade of the Renaissance, James Weldon Johnson lived at the corner of 135th Street and Seventh Avenue, in the very middle of Harlem, in a house which, I believe, belonged to his father-in-law and in which his charming wife, Grace, presided over midnight gumbo suppers following their literary soirees. James Weldon helped a number of Negro writers. We all needed help, but in sustenance and encouragement, we needed the examples of others before us who had achieved publication and who had written well and who had projected the feeling that in Harlem good writing might be done and that in downtown New York it might get published. From McKay and Johnson to Richard Wright and Ellison ran the Renaissance connections, with various plugs, switches, and cutoffs between. But the voltage in one way or another came through to all of us.

Hughes's Christmas card for 1965 (Langston Hughes Papers, Yale Collection of American Literature, Beinecke Rare Book and Manuscript Library)

I arrived in Harlem at the very beginning of this New Negro Renaissance, and I have been in Harlem off and on ever since. Richard Wright and Ralph Ellison came to Harlem several years after the Renaissance had begun to go into decline. By 1935 the Federal Writers Project of the Works Progress Administration (WPA) was in the process of taking over. It had already taken on Wright before he left Chicago, and soon it took on Ellison in New York. I believe it did them no harm. Certainly, regular checks helped them to survive gastronomically, even to loaf at times and to contemplate their souls. I was never able to enroll in the Federal Writers Project because I had had two small volumes of poems published and a novel, so the government presumed I was well off—not realizing that a writer cannot eat poems, even when handsomely bound by Alfred A. Knopf. All my relatives were registered in the WPA except me, so they looked down on me as if I did not want to work. Disillusioned and having no regular source of income, Federal or otherwise, I ceased looking for work, WPA or otherwise. I have not had a job since. On the Federal Project, Wright and Ellison worked at writing for the government and got paid. But I just wrote.

It was Harlem's Golden Era, that of the twenties. I was nineteen when I first came up out of the Lenox Avenue subway one bright September afternoon and looked around in the happy sunlight to see if I saw Duke Ellington on the corner of 135th Street, or Bessie Smith passing by, or Bojangles Bill Robinson in front of the Lincoln Theatre, or maybe Paul Robeson or Bert Williams walking down the avenue. Had I been able to recognize any of them, it would have been only because of pictures I had seen in newspapers or magazines. I had read all about them in the Middle West, where I had gone to school, and I had dreamed of maybe someday seeing them. I hoped, too, I might see in New York some of the famous colored writers and editors whose names were known around the country, like McKay and Johnson and Du Bois, or lesser knowns, like the young George S. Schuyler, Walter White of the National Association for the Advancement of Colored People, poet Jessie Fauset on the staff of *The Crisis,* or Eric Waldron from the West Indies. And I was sorry by the time I got to New York that Marcus Garvey was in prison and I could not hear him speak. But Ethel Waters was singing in Harlem night clubs, and downtown Sissle and Blake's sparkling *Shuffle Along* had just begun its long and happy run that kicked off a renaissance for the Negro in Broadway musicals.

Aaron Douglas from Kansas was beginning to paint his exotic silhouettes and Barthé from Louisiana to know the feel of clay soon to be molded into bronze. Charles Gilpin had already created *The Emperor Jones* at the Provincetown Theatre, and Paul Robeson was making his concert debut in Greenwich Village. Hall Johnson was gathering together in Harlem the first of his famous choirs. Countee Cullen was publishing his sonnets, and Zora Neale Hurston was writing her earliest stories. Jean Toomer was sending from Washington the poetic sketches that later became his book *Cane.* Mamie, Bessie, and Clara Smith were recording the blues. And Duke Ellington and his "Jungle Band" were at the Kentucky Club and later at the Cotton Club, where Negro patrons were not welcome unless they were very rich, like A'Lelia Walker, or famous, like Bojangles. Cabarets like Edmond's, Baron's, Small's, Leroy's, and the Lido were jumping. And J. P. Johnson, Dan Burley, Fats Waller, and Nappy were playing house-rent piano. All those things were happening during the years when I first lived in Harlem and wrote:

Droning a drowsy syncopated tune,
Rocking back and forth to a mellow croon,
  I heard a Negro play.
Down on Lenox Avenue the other night

By the pale dull pallor of an old gas light
  He did a lazy sway. . . .
  He did a lazy sway. . . .
To the tune of those Weary Blues . . .

That is the poem that gave the title to my first book, *The Weary Blues,* published in 1926, a year after Countee Cullen's *Color* appeared.

In 1922, Claude McKay's *Harlem Shadows* had come out. In 1923, *Cane* appeared and received accolades from the critics of the avant-garde. In 1924, Jessie Fauset's *There Is Confusion* was published, and Walter White's novel about a lynching, *The Fire In the Flint.* In 1925, Alain Locke's exciting anthology *The New Negro* appeared. The next year brought Eric Waldron's *Tropic Death* and Walter White's second novel, *Flight.* In 1927, Countee Cullen's *Ballad of the Brown Girl* and *Copper Sun* were published; also James Weldon Johnson's *God's Trombones* and my second volume of poems, *Fine Clothes to the Jew.*

A banner year for Harlem authors was 1928, the year when the Negro vogue in the arts might be said to have reached its peak. Five novels were published– *Dark Princess,* by W. E. B. Du Bois; *Plum Bun,* by Jessie Fauset; *The Walls of Jericho,* by Rudolph Fisher; *Quicksand,* by Nella Larsen; and *Home to Harlem,* by Claude McKay. In the following year, that of the Wall Street crash, came another Nella Larsen novel, *Passing,* another by Claude McKay, *Banjo,* and the advent of Wallace Thurman with *The Blacker the Berry.* I published *Not Without Laughter* in 1930, just as the Depression set in, so my first novel did not sell very well. A year later, Arna Bontemps published his first novel, *God Sends Sunday,* a little novel of great charm that had very little sale. During the remainder of that decade, nothing much exciting happened, literarily speaking, except for the debut in 1934 of the long-burgeoning talent of one of the most sparkling of Negro writers, Zora Neale Hurston, who blossomed forth in the midst of the Depression with her novel *Jonah's Gourd Vine,* followed in 1935 by an anthology of folk customs and tales, *Mules and Men,* and in 1937 by another novel, *Their Eyes Were Watching God.* Had Miss Hurston's books appeared a decade earlier, during the Renaissance, they might have been best sellers. But it was not until 1940 that a Negro writer achieved that status: Richard Wright's powerful *Native Son* burst like a bombshell on the American scene. It sold a half million copies and was translated around the world.

When Richard Wright first came to Harlem, he lived at the Douglas Hotel, near the corner of 150th Street and St. Nicholas Avenue. There, in a small paper-cluttered room, he worked at completing *Native Son,* which he had begun in Chicago. At the Douglas,

Ralph Ellison visited him, as did I and another of his friends, the playwright Theodore Ward. After the success of his novel, Wright got married and moved to Brooklyn Heights–living in the same house, I believe, in which Carson McCullers lived–and Harlemites did not see much of him any more. In 1941, Wright published his poetically written *Twelve Million Black Voices,* a folk history of the Negro in America. That same year, written in collaboration with Paul Greene, his play *Native Son,* in which Canada Lee played the role of Bigger Thomas, was presented on Broadway. And in 1945 his autobiographical *Black Boy* became a Book-of-the-Month Club selection. Then it was that Richard Wright moved to Paris, bought a farm in Normandy, and never came home any more. In ensuing years, his literary output abroad, so critics contend, was nowhere near the high quality of the books he wrote while still in America. *The Outsider* (1953), *Savage Holiday* (1954), *The Color Curtain* (1956), *Pagan Spain* (1957), and *The Long Dream* (1958) were written in Europe. Richard Wright died in Paris in 1960.

Until he came out of the Mississippi badlands, bringing with him all its mud and violence and hatred, no Negro writer in America had had so large an audience. For several years the big bad "burly nigger" of the Chicago slums, Bigger Thomas, who Wright created in *Native Son,* was a conversation piece for readers everywhere. They took sides, pro and con, on so monstrous a symbol of hate in a black skin. Should or should not Negro writers create such baleful characters? At any rate, Wright acquired a very wide audience indeed. Twelve years after the publication of *Native Son,* in 1952, Ralph Ellison, through his fantastic novel *Invisible Man,* achieved a similar public at home and abroad. But he did not move away from Harlem. Ellison still lives there.

Of the most famous of the Negro Renaissance writers, most are dead. James Weldon Johnson was killed in an automobile wreck in 1938 on the way to New York from his Massachusetts home. Claude McKay, having once been a Communist, became a Catholic and died in 1948 in Chicago. In 1960, Zora Neale Hurston died in Florida and Jessie Fauset in Philadelphia. Dr. Du Bois died in Ghana in 1964. The big names of Harlem writing deserted their old stamping grounds as the years went by. Now almost the last of the living Renaissance writers, besides myself, is Arna Bontemps, long-time librarian at Fisk University in Nashville. I still live in Harlem.

Once I was invited to a downtown party that I was especially urged to attend because my host wanted a charming white lady from Georgia who had never met a Negro socially to meet one–in this case, me. When I was introduced to the lady, she said graciously, "Oh, I am so glad to meet you! When I was at Sweet-

briar, I wrote a paper on four Negro poets, and *you* were one of them. Now, let me see! Who were the other three? Oh, yes, Claude McKay was one. What became of him?"

"He's dead," I said.

"Well now, another one–he wrote sermons in verse," she recalled.

"James Weldon Johnson," I said.

"That's right! What became of him?"

"He's dead," I said.

"Oh, my! Well now, that lyric poet with the pretty name."

"Countee Cullen?"

"Yes, where is he?"

"Dead, too," I said.

"My goodness!" cried the white woman from Georgia. "Are you the *only* Negro poet living?"

Cullen died at the age of forty-three. Among the most beautiful of his poems was "Heritage," which asked, "What is Africa to me?" Had the word *négritude* been in use in Harlem in the twenties, Cullen, as well as McKay, Johnson, Toomer, and I, might have been called poets of *négritude*–particularly Toomer of the "dusky cane-lipped throngs" with his "memories of kings and caravans, high-priests, an ostrich, and a juju man." In "Harlem Shadows," in 1922, McKay had written a poem about a Negro girl in which he presaged the images and sounds of the French-African poets a quarter of a century later:

> Her voice was like the sound of blended flutes
> Blown by black players upon a picnic day.
> She sang and danced on gracefully and calm,
> The light gauze hanging loose about her form;
> To me she seemed a proudly-swaying palm
> Grown livelier for passing through a storm.
> Upon her swarthy neck black shiny curls
> Luxuriant fell. . . .

A few years after McKay, Cullen sang:

> You have not heard my love's dark throat,
> Slow fluting like a reed. . . .

And in "Heritage" he asked:

> What is Africa to me:
> Copper sun or scarlet sea,
> Jungle star or jungle track,
> Strong bronzed men or regal black
> Women from whose loins I sprang
> When the birds of Eden sang?

In 1925, in a much translated poem, Waring Cuney wrote of the unsung loveliness of a Harlem girl:

She does not know her beauty.
She thinks her brown body has no glory.
If she could dance naked under palm trees
And see her image in the river
She would know.
But there are no palm trees on the street,
And dish water gives back no images.

This poem appeared in the first German anthology of American-Negro poetry, *Afrika Singt,* published in 1929 in Vienna and Leipzig. It also included my

I am a Negro,
Black as the night is black,
Black as the depths of my Africa . . .

and also an excellent translation of my

I've known rivers. . . .
I bathed in the Euphrates
    when dawns were young.
I built my hut near the Congo
    and it lulled me to sleep.
I looked upon the Nile
    and raised the pyramids above it.
    I've known rivers,
    Ancient dusky rivers.
My soul has grown deep like the rivers.

In France as well as Germany, before the close of the Negro Renaissance, Harlem's poets were already being translated. Léopold Sédar Senghor of Senegal and Aimé Césaire of Martinique, the great poets of *négritude,* while still students at the Sorbonne, had read the Harlem poets and felt a bond between themselves and us. In faraway South Africa, Peter Abrahams, who became one of Africa's most distinguished authors, wrote in his autobiography, *Tell Freedom,* how, as a teenager at the Bantu Men's Social Center in Johannesburg, he discovered the Harlem poets of the twenties. There for the first time he read Du Bois, McKay, Georgia Douglass Johnson, Cullen, and myself. Years later when he became a writer, he recorded:

> I read every one of the books on the shelf marked *American Negro Literature*. I became a nationalist, a color nationalist through the writings of men and women who lived in a world away from me. To them I owe a great debt for crystallizing my vague yearnings to write and for showing me that the long dream was attainable.

The Harlem poets and novelists of the twenties became an influence in faraway Africa and the West Indies—an influence reflected till today in the literature of black men and women there. To us, *négritude* was an unknown word, but certainly pride of heritage and consciousness of race was ingrained in us. But because we

Cover for a 1965 German edition of Simple Takes a Wife
*(courtesy of Kenneth Spencer Research Library,
University of Kansas Libraries)*

were Harlemites of the balling and brawling "Roaring Twenties" of midnight cabarets and bootleg gin, Wallace Thurman called us jokingly "the niggerati." In his novel *Infants of the Spring,* Thurman captured the era perfectly as it related to its black bohemians. Now in the sixties, LeRoi Jones, Welton Smith, Calvin Hernton, David Henderson, and numerous young black writers do their balling and brawling downtown in Greenwich Village—integrated. But in the twenties we had so much fun and liked Harlem so well that we did not think about taking the long subway ride to the Village, where white artists and writers gathered. We let them come uptown to us.

409 Edgecombe, then the tallest apartment house on Sugar Hill, was a sort of party-giving center and in-and-out meeting place for Harlem writers and artists. Walter White and his beautiful *café au lait* wife, Gladys, lived on the top floor there and loved giving parties. The painter Aaron Douglas and his wife, Alta, lived there, too,

and always had a bottle of ginger ale in the ice box for those who brought along refreshments. Elmer Anderson Carter, the editor of *Opportunity* who succeeded Charles S. Johnson, was on the floor above the Douglases, and actor Ivan Sharpe and Evie had a flat there, too, as did–although much later–the poet William Stanley Braithwaite, the composer Clarence Cameron White, and the Tea Cup Reader Madam Vanderbilt Smith.

Just down the hill in the Dunbar Apartments lived the famous Dr. Du Bois, the cartoonist E. Simms Campbell, and, nearby, Dan Burley, humorist, newspaperman, and boogiewoogie piano player, whose wife was a concert singer. Artists and writers were always running into each other on Sugar Hill and talking over their problems and wondering how they could get a Rosenwald Fellowship, a Guggenheim, or a grant from the Harmon Foundation. It was in the Aaron Douglas apartment, at 409 Edgecombe, that seven of us gathered one night and decided to found a magazine the better to express ourselves freely and independently–without interference from old heads, white or Negro–a magazine which we would support ourselves, although none of us had enough money on which to eat.

It was about that time that I wrote, "We younger Negro artists who create now intend to express our individual dark-skinned selves without fear or shame. If white people are pleased, we are glad. If they are not, it doesn't matter. . . . If colored people are pleased, we are glad. If they are not, their displeasure doesn't matter either." Various of my friends said, "Amen!" And we set out to publish *Fire,* a Negro quarterly of the arts to *épater le bourgeois,* to burn up a lot of the old stereotyped Uncle Tom ideas of the past, and to provide us with an outlet for publishing not existing in the hospitable but limited pages of *The Crisis* or *Opportunity.* Wallace Thurman would edit *Fire,* Aaron Douglas would be its artist and designer, and John P. Davis (who years later edited the enormous *American Negro Reference Book* for the Phelps Stokes Fund) would be the business manager. All seven of us–including artist and writer Bruce Nugent, poet Gwendolyn Bennett, novelist Zora Neale Hurston, and myself–were to be the editorial board, and each of us would put in fifty dollars to bring out the first issue. But not all of us had fifty dollars to put in, so Wallace Thurman, who had a job, assumed responsibility for the printer's bills.

He was years paying off the ensuing indebtedness. As to format, we got carried away with ourselves, and our taste proved extremely expensive. Only the best cream-white paper would do on which to print our poems and stories. And only a rich crimson jacket on de luxe stock would show off well the Aaron Douglas cover design. Beautifully laid out, *Fire's* one and only issue was handsome indeed–and the printer's bills enormous. How

Thurman was able to persuade the printer to release the entire issue to us on so small an advance payment, I do not know. But he did. The downtown newspapers and white magazines (except for *The Bookman*) paid no attention to the advent of *Fire,* and we had no money for advertising. Bruce Nugent, jobless and at leisure at the time, was in charge of distribution and collections. Being hungry, Nugent usually ate up on the spot the meager amounts he collected from *Fire's* very few sales. As we had hoped–even though it contained no four-letter words as do today's little magazines–the Negro bourgeoisie were shocked by *Fire.* The *Afro-American's* literary reviewer wrote in high indignation, "I have just tossed the first issue of *Fire* into the fire." He claimed that in his poetry Cullen tried "his best to obscure the thought in superfluous sentences" and that I displayed my "usual ability to say nothing in many words," while Aaron Douglas was "permitted to spoil three perfectly good pages and a cover with . . . the meaningless grotesqueness of his creations." When the editorial board of *Fire* met again, we did not plan a new issue, but emptied our pockets to help poor Thurman whose wages were being garnished weekly because he had signed for the printer's bills. Yet somehow we still managed to go dancing at the Savoy on Saturday nights or to Edmond's to hear Ethel Waters sing.

The Negro writers of the twenties, it seems (or perhaps it is only because I am looking back through a golden haze of memories), did not take themselves as seriously as did the writers of the thirties–the hungry era, when proletarian authors came into vogue; or as did those of the forties, who went from a depression through a great war; or those of the fifties, when integrationist tendencies of let-us-write-white developed; or of the sixties, when a vengeful James Baldwin called down upon America "the fire next time" and LeRoi Jones of the four-letter words advised all white folks, "Drop dead!" Negro literature began to acquire its share of angry young men.

Now almost nobody's writing has fun in it any more–not even *The Wig* by Charles Wright, which begins with high hilarity and ends with a red-hot steel rod jabbed into the penis of its smiling hero, who says, "I'm beginning to feel better already." But none of these contemporary Negro writers lives in Harlem, and none of them was even a gleam in their daddies' eyes when the Harlem Renaissance began, and their truculent *négritude* emblazoned in graffiti is designed to *épater* a much more blasé bourgeoisie than that which existed in the far-off days of comparative innocence when, on the printed page, not even Richard Wright's big burly Bigger Thomas dared say, "mother ———!"

–African Forum, 1 (1966): 11–20

* * *

Simple's Uncle Sam, *Hughes's last Simple book, is comprised of forty-six stories, none of which had been collected in book form before. W. Edward Farrison, an English professor at North Carolina Central University and a scholar of African American history and literature, wrote this review.*

"Too Serious to Laugh . . . Too Philosophical to Cry" Review of *Simple's Uncle Sam*

Simple's Uncle Sam is Langston Hughes's fifth book about Jesse B. Semple, better known as Simple. The first three books were *Simple Speaks His Mind* (1950), *Simple Takes a Wife* (1953), and *Simple Stakes a Claim* (1957). These three works in the form of sketches of conversations between Simple and his friend Boyd in a Harlem bar established Simple as a realistic–almost real–character in American imaginative writing. In 1961 Hughes himself selected seventy of the 143 sketches in these three books and published them in a volume entitled *The Best of Simple*. The fifth volume consists of forty-six sketches now published in a book for the first time. Most of them were written or revised within the last few years, and some in the summer of 1965. Some of them were first published in newspapers, notably in the Baltimore *Afro-American* as well as in the Chicago *Defender*.

A denizen of Harlem transplanted from Virginia, Simple continues in this new volume his reviews of personal events and comments on life in Harlem, the various phases and ramifications of the American race problem, life in the United States, and life in general. He still tells his tales and comments on people and things, as his creator said in the Foreword to *The Best of Simple*, "mostly in high humor, but sometimes with a pain in his soul" and sometimes with a resort to laughter "to keep from crying." More noticeably, perhaps, than in the preceding volumes, he is often too serious to laugh–or to do more than smile sardonically–and too philosophical to cry. Without referring to the law of compensation, he incidentally takes cognizance of its all too frequent misapplication. "Some folks think that everything in life has to balance up, turn out equal," he says in the sketch entitled "Empty Houses." "If you buy a man a drink, he has to buy you one back. If you get invited to a party, then you have to give a party, too, and invite whoever invited you. . . . But me, I am not that way." Having been "a passed-around child" because he had no home during his childhood, he learned very early to distinguish a mere house from a home, as he explains in the same sketch. Said he, "If they do not have a little love for whoever lives in the house with them, it is an empty house."

Realist that he is, Simple has no appetite for the religious provender offered by the "gospel singers" in the store-front and movie-front churches in Harlem, but he likes their singing well enough to contribute to their col-

lections just as he pays admission fees to shows. His taste for music is radically different from that of Joyce, his wife, who he says "is the most opera-listening woman I know." (P. 40.) Unsophisticated as he is, he neither pretends to tastes he does not have nor apologizes for those he has. He is no less objective about the playing of numbers, an especially popular activity in Harlem, than he is about the "gospel singers." With arresting logic he queries, "If a man can bet at the race track, or play bingo in church, why should he not play the numbers in the barbershop, in his car, or, if you are a lady, in your beauty shop or laundromat?" (P. 88.)

Simple's cousin Minnie, "an offshoot of the family," who was introduced in *Simple Stakes a Claim*, figures prominently in nine and incidentally in two of the sketches in *Simple's Uncle Sam*. Whether her creator intended for her to do so or not, she reflects a contrast between the Simple of the first book and the Simple of the most recent one. Like the former, who constantly had woman troubles, she constantly has boyfriend troubles, many of which Simple thinks that she makes for herself. On the contrary Simple has been happily married for some time and is too eager to remain so to do anything to endanger his marital bliss. Accordingly he says that "My eyes might roam, but I stay home." (P. 78) There is another notable contrast between Minnie and Simple. Like him she is a firm believer in civil rights and the freedom of which they are a part. But unlike him, who is sufficiently self-possessed to consider these things dispassionately as well as humorously, she is inclined to emotionalism concerning them. This fact is revealed in his retelling of her story that her participation in the recent Harlem riot cost her a head injury and the loss of her wig. (Pp. 139–45.)

One of the most ingenious sketches in the book is Simple's account of a coffee-break conversation between him and his white boss. The boss, Simple observes, "always says 'THE Negro,' as if there was not 50–11 different kinds of Negroes in the U. S. A." Assuming that Simple represented THE Negro, the boss inquired as to "just what does THE Negro want?" Simple replied that he neither was nor represented THE Negro, but that "I am *me*," and that "I represent my own self." Less convincingly than pharisaically, the boss avowed, "I am a liberal. I voted for Kennedy. And this time for Johnson. I believe in integration. Now that you got it, though," he asked, "what more do you want?" To which inquiry Simple replied that Negroes want "reintegration. . . . That you be integrated with *me*, not me with you." Embarrassed by Simple's insistence that true integration is a two-way process, the boss explained that white people want integration "up to a point;" whereupon Simple returned to the boss's original question and answered it succinctly. "That is what THE Negro wants," he said "to

Simple's
Uncle Sam

LANGSTON HUGHES

*Dust jacket for Hughes's 1965 collection of Simple stories
(courtesy of Spencer Research Library,
University of Kansas Libraries)*

remove that *point.*" This sketch most skillfully exposes quasi-liberalism, which is an often-concealed obstacle to improvement in race relations.

Another of the most ingenious sketches in the book is "Rude Awakening." This is Simple's account of a dream in which he found the South ruled by Negroes, and ironically enough, with its traditions, whether factual or fanciful, inverted. He found himself, "black as I can be," the occupant and owner of a white mansion in Virginia, with two white mammies at his service—"dear old Mammy Faubus what raised me" and Mammy Eastland. He just loved to hear white folks sing—but he could not understand how "some of these little blue-eyed crackerninnies" got the nerve to want to go to colored schools. Like a confirmed interpositionist, he declared that "Our great institutions like the University of Jefferson Lee belong to us, and not even with all deliberate speed do we intend to constitutionalize the institutionalization of our institutions." Indeed from such a dream world there could have been only a rude awakening into the turmoil of matters racial early in the 1960's.

The last sketch in the book is entitled "Uncle Sam," and from it the title of the work itself was derived. In this sketch there emerges again Jesse B. Semple philosopher. Simple is curious and uncertain about his relationship to Uncle Sam, "the old man in the tight pants, the swallowtail coat, and the star-spangled hat who lives in the attic above the President at the top of the White House." Boyd explains that Uncle Sam is "a symbol of the government." For Simple, however, Boyd's explanation is hardly sufficient, for he has observed that Uncle Sam is always portrayed as white—never as an Indian, a Negro, a Chinese-American, or a nisei. Therefore Simple does not find the symbol truly symbolical. Nor is he satisfied with the token representation of people like himself in other symbolical situations. As he remembers, he has never seen a Negro except Booker T. Washington portrayed on a postage stamp. In brief Simple is inclined to consider Uncle Sam a relative "on the off-side"—as his cousin Minnie is.

To this reviewer it seems inappropriate to compare Simple with Paul Bunyan and Davy Crockett, as has been attempted. Both Bunyan and Crockett were heroes of the nineteenth-century American frontier, the former being altogether legendary and the latter partly so. Their histories abound in the kind of exaggeration which belongs only to the most extravagant romances. This is not true of Simple. He is no frontiersman nor romantic creation of any kind. He is a contemporary realistic character inured to city life, especially as it is in New York City and particularly as it is in Harlem, and imbued with its spirit. He is a product, not of mere fancy, but of his creator's experience, observations, and reflections vitalized by a healthy, well-disciplined imagination.

Comparisons which have been made between Simple and Mr. Dooley are somewhat more appropriate. Both men comment, sometimes in the same ways, on affairs of their times, but there are remarkable differences between them. Simple, a product of Virginia's segregated public schools, expresses himself, withal, in a dialect more natural and indeed more convincing than Mr. Dooley's mutilated English. Moreover the simple rhymes which fall casually, naturally, and frequently from Simple's lips give his remarks such zest and individuality as are not found in Mr. Dooley's lucubrations. No matter with whom Simple is compared, he remains representative of many who see life, especially in America, as it is, contemplate much of it as it should not be, and consider much of it as it should be; and *Simple's Uncle Sam* is an excellent continuation of his reading—his criticism—of life.

—College Language Association Journal,
9 (March 1966): 296–300

* * *

In 1954 Hughes wrote to the South African writer Richard Rive to invite him to contribute a story for an anthology of African writers that he was planning to edit. Unsuccessful in finding a publisher for the volume, Hughes nevertheless maintained contact with Rive, who prepared this interview article for the South African literary journal Contrast. *Rive interweaves passages from Hughes's poems, all taken from* Selected Poems of Langston Hughes *(1959). His title alludes to Hughes's 1925 poem "A House in Taos," in which he critiqued the quest for enlightenment carried out by prominent artists and writers who used their wealth to withdraw from society and establish an artists' colony in Taos, New Mexico.*

Taos in Harlem:
An Interview with Langston Hughes

> Thunder of the Rain God:
>   And we three
>   Smitten by beauty
>
> Thunder of the Rain God
>   And we three
>   Weary, weary.
>
> Thunder of the Rain God
>   And you, he and I
>   Waiting for nothingness . . .

of a house in Taos. But Harlem is not Taos. Do you understand the stillness of a house in Taos? But Harlem is not beauty and riches and lushness. It is slum, bright, hard and brittle. The biggest, the greatest. It is not a night in Taos. Harlem is wine and dope and Lennox Avenue and the Afro-American and Leroi Jones and Langston Hughes. And Langston Hughes. It is not Taos. It is the ballad of a girl whose name is mud, madam and the number writer, the montage of a dream deferred.

Dear Richard,

Arna Bontemps will be in New York at midweek and says he would like to meet you, too . . . if you like, and can, on Thursday, February 17th, come over to my house about 5 and look at poetry . . . then about 7 or 8 we can have dinner together . . .

Langston.

> Across
>   The Harlem roof-tops
>   Moon is shining
>   Night sky is blue
>   Stars are great drops
>   Of golden dew.

But not tonight, not tonight. Tonight cold winds blow colder, making smoke of one's breath. Cold cross-town winds where one catches the bus on 125th for 5th Avenue, Harlem. And from there two blocks North then one West, ring three times and ask for Langston. Slum exterior in a slum district, up broken steps, then knock three times. Rent collector? Number man? Or a poet in search of poets? Come about 5 and look at the montage of a dream deferred.

> To fling my arms wide
> In some place of the sun
> To whirl and to dance
> Till the white day is done
> Then rest at cool evening
> Beneath a tall tree
> While night comes on gently
> Dark like me—

Langston Hughes born Joplin, Missouri in 1902, has devoted his life to writing and lecturing. His poetry, short stories, autobiographies, song lyrics, plays and books for young people have been widely read by Americans, and up-to-date he has published some thirty books. His public readings of his poetry which began after publication of his first book, *The Weary Blues,* in 1926, have continued to be warmly received. Books and doctoral dissertations have already begun to be written about him.

> Night coming tenderly,
> Black like me—

Dark like me. Franks Restaurant on 125th Street near 3rd Avenue. Corner table for Langston, Arna and me. Overawed waiter overawed by two famous Negro writers and one not-so-famous but all the way from Africa. Shrimp cocktails, oysters, scallops in shells and french fries, drowned unmercifully in ketchup.

> —Langston, how would you define the Negro Renaissance of the 1920s, and how important do you think it was towards the development of Negro literature?

Cigarett-smoking, fluttering hands toying with paper-napkin, frowning owl-eyed through horn-rimmed glasses chewing the question, then

> —The Negro Renaissance?
> —Yes. Langston, the Negro Renaissance.
> —Man, that was long before you were born. Yes, it was very important. You should read my *Big Sea.*
> —Were you on relief then? I heard the W.P.A. rescued many writers who needed help during the Great Depression. Including you?
> —Excluding me. I was never part of W.P.A.

Hughes in Dakar, Senegal, in April 1966 (Langston Hughes Papers, Yale Collection of American Literature, Beinecke Rare Book and Manuscript Library)

Puckered domed forehead of the poet carrying thoughts from Franks and the present to the thirties, the strolling twenties, with Harlem on relief and house parties on Lennox to pay the rent. What happens to a dream deferred

> Does it dry up
> Like a raisin in the sun?
> Or fester like a sore—
> And then run?
> Does it stink like rotten meat?
> Or crust and sugar over—
> Like a syrupy sweet?

Or a raisin in the sun? Browns Hotel, Mayfair, London. London and our first meeting, myself self-consciously wearing my best face to meet the greatest living Negro writer in the world.

> —What they call you, son?
> —Me? I'm Richard Rive from South Africa.
> —Richard Rive? Yes man, you wrote . . .

The reeling off of pygmy works, midget efforts, splinterings of a youth who wanted to be a writer, caught askance by the Establishment.

> —I know you, you're Dick from Africa. Come and have a drink.

Browns or Franks? London, New York or Paris? Lambeth or Harlem? Humility characterises the truly great. Sartre drinking alone at a table in the Domé, Eliot thinking of the Hollow Men in Russell Square, Langston laughing through fried chicken.

> I went to look for Joy,
> Slim, dancing Joy,
> Gay, laughing Joy,
> Bright-eyed Joy—
> And I found her
> Driving the butcher cart,
> In the arms of the butcher boy!

Langston Hughes talking to a young man from Africa who wanted to write books, then talking to a grown man from Africa who wrote books.

> —Do you think that American Negro Poetry will finally be completely integrated into American literature?
> —No.
> —And lose its ethnic quality?
> —Lord, no.

317

—And would such a state be preferable?

—No, no, no.

—And . . .

—No!

And Arna watches the word-play amused. Half a century of poetry written on his face, on his grey-sleeked hair, on the quiet of his manner. While Langston smokes and talks and talks and talks, parrying questions of the young South African who has since written.

> —And what streams or tendencies, if any, do you detect in contemporary American Negro Poetry?
> —Imitation of contemporary white 'beatnik' poetry.
> —And Leroi Jones?
> —He proves we can outdo the others.
> —Can we?

> Play the blues for me
> Play the blues for me
> No other music
> 'll ease my misery.
> Sing a soothin' song
> Say a soothin' song
> Cause the man I love's done
> Done me wrong.

Hovering waiter hovering pencil-poised, waiting to jab down instructions. Penguin-suited, evening-faced, passive.

> —Wine, Sir?
> —Yes.
> —White or red?
> —White. Dick here's from South Africa. Bring a bottle of Constantia white.
> —White an' fish.
> —Red an' meat.
> —If you're white you're all right.
> —If you're brown stick around.

But if you're black it's all right by Franks. Smell of wood and paper-napkins and clean, shiny, cardboard menus, plastic-coated. And talk of London, Paris, Dakar. Birmingham, Alabama and Martin Luther. Deep in my heart, I do believe. And Negritude and Césaire and Sedar Senghor. Ralph Ellison and Claude Brown. Manchild in the Promised Land. Should a writer preach or sing? Sing. SING.

> Night of the two moons,
> And the seventeen stars,
> Night of the day before yesterday
> And the day after tomorrow,
> Night of the four songs unsung:
> Sorrow! Sorrow!
> Sorrow! Sorrow!

Night moving slowly black like me, dark like me.

> —You know Countee Cullen, Langston?
> —Who?
> —Countee Cullen. Remember? 'Yet do I marvel at this curious thing, to make a poet black and bid him sing.' Remember?
> —Yes, I remember. I knew him, but not so well.
> —And the tragedy of his personal life?
> —I do not know.
> —Did it influence his writing?
> —I do not know. Have a cigarette, Dick.
> —Sorry, I'm not smoking.

Polite rebuff. To make a poet black. Cullen should not have been mentioned. And Richard Wright?

> —And Richard Wright, Langston?
> —He influenced Ellison. Daring and frankness in subject and treatment. Yes, he influenced Ellison.
> —And what of the African writers, Langston?

Years ago, years and years ago, when I was 17 and young, Langston wrote to Cape Town, and asked me to go on writing. And sent me autographed copies of *The Weary Blues,* and *Laughing to Keep From Crying,* and *The Big Sea,* 'to Richard with admiration and regard,' and asked me to go on writing. And to send all my stuff. And I did, nervously tying up the fledgling manuscripts and sending them over the seas. And long after a book came back, smelling sweet and fresh-paged, and there was my name on the cover, and that book was me.

> —What of the South African writers, Langston?
> —Read my anthologies on Africa, Dick, Read your own stories and read what I said about them.
> —I don't have to read Africa, I am it.
> —I also sometimes feel I am it.

> Sleepy Giant
> You've been resting awhile.
> Now I see the thunder
> And the lightning
> In your smile.
> Now I see
> The storm clouds
> In your waking eyes:
> The thunder,
> The wonder
> And the young
> Surprise.

Open the white Constantia wine, smelling of Cape Town, and the Atlantic breakers, and the mist over Table Mountain, and the green grape-lands of Harlem, Muizenberg surf washing Lennox Avenue, with the Southern Cross shining bleakly overhead, weakly over Harlem.

—And of your own contribution Langston, no one
doubts. No one doubts Arna's contribution.
Arna Bontemps sips quiet wine and listens.

—But would your poetic function have worked as
well had you not been a Negro in a white society?

—No. My dramatic subject would have been lacking but not my poetic function. Not the soul
stuff.

—Soul?

—Yes, soul. A sort of synthesis of the essence of the
Negro folk arts, particularly the old music and
its flavour, expressed in contemporary ways so
clearly and emotionally with the old that it
gives a distinctly 'Negro' flavour to today's
material in music, painting, writing or merely
in personal attitudes and conversations.

—Found in whom? what? where?

—Ray Charles; Mingus; Margaret Bond's music;
James Brown; James Meredith's autobiographies; Alvin Ailey's Negro ballet; my Simple
stories; Jacob Lawrence paintings; Nina
Simone's singing; Moms Mabley's monologues; Cassius Clay's pronouncements; the
emotional overtones of Harlem and Watts; that
whites feel but fail to understand; something to
which only 'soul-brothers' born to the tradition
can fully react in whatever form it occurs.

—And that is soul?

—That is soul.

You also took my spiritual and gone
You put me in Macbeth and Carmen Jones
And all kinds of swing Mikados
And in everything but what about me—
But someday somebody'll
Stand up and talk about me,
And write about me—
Black and beautiful—
And sing about me—
And put on plays about me!
I reckon it'll be
Me myself!
Yes, it'll be me.

Check written. Cheque signed. Overcoat-muffled
against the Harlem night, and discussion over. Langston to Harlem, Arna to Nashville, and I to Columbia
and Cape Town.

—Good night.
—Good night.
—Night.

—*Contrast*, 14 (1967): 33–39

* * *

*The last book Hughes saw through publication in his life-
time was* The Best Short Stories by Negro Writers: An
Anthology from 1899 to the Present, *which he claimed in
an "Editor's Note" was "the most comprehensive anthology of
American Negro short stories to be published anywhere." In his
introduction to the volume Hughes discussed a few of the obstacles
black writers continued to face in the United States.*

Introduction to *The Best Short Stories by Negro Writers*

Just as many Americans believe, solely from having seen *La Dolce Vita* on the screen, that Rome is one
vast seraglio teeming with orgiastic vices, so many also
think, from having seen *The Cool World,* that all Negroes
are primitive, dirty and dangerous. White persons of
the older generation add to their contemporary concepts the ancient stereotypes lazy, grinning and illiter-
ate, drawn from memories of Stepin Fetchit, Rochester
and Amos and Andy. Art (and some motion pictures
may be classified as art) molds the thoughts, opinions
and concepts of millions of people, even before the age
of reason. On one of my recent lecture tours, I was the
house guest of a charming white professorial couple on
a very advanced Midwestern campus of the caliber of
Kenyon or Antioch. At dinner my first evening there, I
was inwardly amused and not unduly surprised when
the ten-year-old daughter of the house asked me (across
the table), "Mr. Langston Hughes, can you teach me to
shoot dice?"

Her embarrassed parents blushed deeply. "Darling, why do you ask such a thing of Mr. Hughes?"

"I see colored people all the time shooting dice in
the TV movies," the child said.

I laughed. "At night they revive a lot of very old
pictures, and they show a lot of old-time colored actors
like Sunshine Sammy and Nicodemus and Mantan
Moreland. But Negroes don't *always* shoot craps in real
life and many have never even seen a pair of dice. Still,
there's no harm in your learning. So if your daddy has
a pair of dice, after dinner I can show you what I
learned when I was in the Merchant Marine. Then if
you ever go to Las Vegas—where white people shoot
dice all night—you will know. Dice is a very old game,
mentioned in the Bible—played by King Ahasuerus and
his court. And today there's a very fashionable gambling casino at Monte Carlo where high society shoots
dice."

I was talking very fast to try to keep the little girl
from becoming more embroiled with her embarrassed
parents: "Why did you ask such a question?" I knew
why. The old stereotypes of the blackface minstrels and
of Hollywood descend even unto the third and fourth
generations.

```
I dream a world where man
No other man will scorn,
Where love will bless the earth
And peace its path adorn
I dream a world where all
Will know sweet freedom's way
Where greed no longer saps the soul
Nor avarice blights our day.
A world I dream where black or white,
Whatever race you be,
Will share the bounties of the earth
And every man is free,
Where wretchedness will hant its head
And joy, like pearl,
Attends the needs of all mankind
Of such I dream —
Our world!
```

Troubled Island, an opera libretto
by Langston Hughes

Memorial Service

FOR

JAMES MERCER LANGSTON HUGHES

FEBRUARY 1, 1902 — MAY 22, 1967

†

MUSIC ....Randy Weston Trio

READINGS ....Lindsay Patterson

SOLO ....Raoul Abdul

REMARKS ....Arna Bontemps

SOLO ....Miss Marion Williams

MUSIC ....Randy Weston Trio

Program for Hughes's memorial service at the Benta Funeral Chapel in Harlem, 25 May 1967 (Langston Hughes Papers, James Weldon Johnson Collection in the Yale Collection of American Literature, Beinecke Rare Book and Manuscript Library)

Because he did not wish to be associated with similar racial stereotypes of his time, in the 1880's, the first outstanding Negro writer of fiction in the United States, Charles Waddell Chesnutt, wrote as a white man for a number of years, without revealing his ethnic identity. By hiding his color, he did not run the risk of having his material turned down by editors because of race. But after twelve years of his literary "passing," a publication called the *Critic* discovered his background and in a biographical note revealed Chesnutt as an author who "faces the problems of the race to which he in part belongs." Being very fair—about the complexion of Congressman Adam Clayton Powell—with only a small percentage of black blood in his family tree, Chesnutt was what anthropologists term a "voluntary" Negro. The same might be said of Jean Toomer. Shortly after the publication of *Cane,* he moved outside the social confines of the Negro world to live in Taos, Carmel and finally Bucks County.

Like Chesnutt, the successful contemporary novelist Frank Yerby, author of *The Foxes of Harrow* and a dozen other best-selling romances, revealed recently to a reporter, "I did tell my publishers at one time not to identify me as a Negro." Yerby's vast reading public today is on the whole quite unaware of his race. But the white people in the Georgia town

where he was born know. When the motion picture made from *The Foxes of Harrow* had its highly publicized premiere in Augusta, Yerby's relatives were relegated to the Negro section of the theater. Such are the strictures of race in America even against an author whose books are translated around the world and whose earnings from writing total well over a million dollars. For almost twenty years Yerby has lived abroad where such prejudices seldom are in evidence and racial indignities such as those revealed in his early story, "Health Card," are unheard of. "I love my country," Yerby is quoted as saying. But, "Unfortunately, my country doesn't love me enough to let me live in it."

"One of the inalienable rights is that of the pursuit of happiness," Yerby says. In this anthology the themes of many of the stories concern the search for that right and how Negroes may work out the problems of their lives in order to find a modicum of happiness in America. There are drama, comedy and tragedy to be found in this fiction—so near to fact—as put down by the best of the Negro writers since 1887, when Chesnutt published his initial story in the *Atlantic Monthly*. His "The Goophered Grapevine" marked the first fiction to be published by a Negro in that highly conservative magazine. Since that time a few Negro authors have become world famous–Richard

Wright, Ralph Ellison, James Baldwin. (Their stories are published here.) But none has become really rich, except Frank Yerby who, after "Health Card," put the race problem on the shelf in favor of more commercial themes. His historical romances have wonderful moviesque titles like *The Golden Hawk* and *The Saracen Blade,* but there are no noble black faces among their characters when brought to the screen. Black faces seldom sell in Hollywood.

Twenty years after publication, Ralph Ellison's *Invisible Man,* a major American novel, has not yet been filmed, and Hollywood would not touch Richard Wright's famous *Native Son.* In all its years of activity Hollywood has never made a major motion picture which portrayed with sympathy our foremost American dilemma–jampacked with drama–the Negro problem. So far as I know, exciting though many of these tales in this anthology are, only one has been filmed by Hollywood: Mary Elizabeth Vroman's charming "See How They Run" under the title of *Bright Road.* But this story is not concerned with racial problems and so offends nobody.

Ted Poston's Hopkinsonville tales or the stories of Zora Neale Hurston, Alice Childress or Lindsay Patterson would make delightful motion-picture, television, or radio comedies, much more human and real than *Amos and Andy.* (Alice Childress's off-Broadway comedy, *Trouble in Mind,* seemed to me as funny as *Born Yesterday.*) But Hollywood has not touched their work, nor have any other mass media to date. For screen-searing drama, John A. Williams's story, "Son in the Afternoon" (included here), could scarcely be surpassed. But unless times have changed greatly, Hollywood is not likely to buy it for screen treatment.

Since most Negro writers from Chesnutt to LeRoi Jones have found it hard to make a literary living, or to derive from other labor sufficient funds to sustain creative leisure, their individual output has of necessity often been limited in quantity, and sometimes in depth and quality as well–since Negroes seldom have time to loaf and invite their souls. When a man or woman must teach all day in a crowded school, or type in an office, or write news stories, read proofs and help edit a newspaper, creative prose does not always flow brilliantly or freely at night, or during that early morning hour torn from sleep before leaving for work. Yet some people ask, "Why aren't there more Negro writers?" Or, "Why doesn't Owen Dodson produce more books?" Or how come So-and-So takes so long to complete his second novel? I can tell you why. So-and-So hasn't got the money. Unlike most promising white writers, he has never sold a single word to motion pictures, television, or radio. He has never been asked to write a single

well-paying soap commercial. He is not in touch with the peripheral sources of literary income that enable others more fortunate to take a year off to go somewhere and write.

Fortunately, however, in recent years a foundation has occasionally rescued a talented black writer from the subway crush of his low-salaried job. And once in a while, one finds a patron. Writing is a time-taking task, and the living is not easy. I am in favor of national subsidies, as exist in Europe. State aid never seemed to impede good writing overseas. I do not believe it would hurt good writers here. It could hardly hurt black writers, who, so far, have had not anyone at all to subvert them. For the first national grant of a large and sizable sum, I nominate one of our solid and long esteemed writers, Arna Bontemps, who has been teaching all his literary life and who deserves release for the full flowering of his considerable talents–hitherto recognized by discriminating readers but unrecognized by money. Or if it must be a young talent as first choice for a subsidy, then why not the astounding Miss Alice Walker? Neither you nor I have ever read a story like "To Hell with Dying" before. At least, I do not think you have.

The stories in this book range geographically from South to North, East to West, from America's Panama Canal Zone to our Chicago Loop and, in point of time, from the Reconstruction through the Harlem Renaissance, the Depression, the Second World War, the period of James Baldwin's blues in De Gaulle's Paris, to the contemporary moment of Charles Wright's "A New Day." In fiction as in life Negroes get around. They have been covering varied grounds for a considerable time via the written word. Here they reveal their thoughts, their emotions, directions and indirections over three quarters of a century–from Chesnutt and Dunbar, Wright, Ellison and Williams, to the new young writers of the sixties, Lindsay Patterson, Robert Boles, and Alice Walker; from the fright and violence of the Deep South to the tinkle of iced drinks at an interracial party in Boston; from the twisted face of a black sharecropper to the spotlighted smile of a Harlem dancer, from tragedy to comedy, laughter to tears, these stories culled from the best of Negro writing over the years, indicate how varied, complex and exciting is the milieu in which black folk live in America.

Just as once, so the saying goes, the sun never set on the British Empire (because it extended around the world), so today the sun is always rising somewhere on books by American Negro writers whose works in English and in translations are being read around the world. Wright, Ellison, Baldwin, Himes,

LAST RITES: Immediate cremation. There shall be no display of the remains or funeral services of any sort before cremation. If afterwards a memorial is desired, it shall consist entirely of music, with no speaking whatsoever. The music should be performed in the following order, with two soloists, a man and woman, and instrumentalists; and consisting of these numbers only:

1. PRECIOUS LORD, TAKE MY HAND (Thomas A. Dorsey) sung by a soloist and/or small group of gospel singers.

2. NOTHING BUT A PLAIN BLACK BOY (Elegy) the Gwendolyn Brooks poem as set to music by Oscar Brown, Jr., sung by a soloist. If a soloist is not available, the Oscar Brown recording may be played— Columbia 4-42284.

3. THE SAINT LOUIS BLUES (W. C. Handy) played by a jazz combo of four or five pieces; instrumental only without a singer.

4. CARAVAN (Duke Ellington) played by the combo; or BLUE SANDS by Buddy Collette by the combo; or both.

5. DO NOTHING TILL YOU HEAR FROM ME (Duke Ellington) played by the combo; instrumental only without a singer.

The names of the performing artists may be printed on a card or program, as there should be no Master of Ceremonies. The artists are to be paid union scale or above. And the entire occasion should have the air of an enjoyable concert. My ashes after the memorial, may then go to the James Weldon Johnson Collection at Yale University, New Haven, Connecticut, to be catalogued with my other memorabilia, or disposed of as considered fitting and desirable by Yale. Perhaps they might be integrated with the wind.

Instructions Hughes prepared for a possible memorial service to be held after his death. This paper was not found until 26 May 1967—the day after he was cremated (Langston Hughes Papers, James Weldon Johnson Collection in the Yale Collection of American Literature, Beinecke Rare Book and Manuscript Library).

Hughes and Yerby have all been translated into at least a dozen major languages and are to be found in the libraries and bookshops of most of the earth's large cities. Today in Japanese, French, German, Italian and Polish universities, among others, students are writing theses and working toward doctorates in various phases of Negro literature. Negro authors are beginning to reap their sunrise harvest.

–"Introduction," in *The Best Short Stories by Negro Writers: An Anthology from 1899 to the Present* (Boston: Little, Brown, 1967), pp. ix–xiii

* * *

Hughes died on 22 May 1967. Joseph Mancini wrote this obituary for the New York Post, *for which Hughes had written a column since 1962.*

Langston Hughes Dies
–The Poet of Harlem

Langston Hughes, folk poet of the American Negro, died last night in Polyclinic Hospital here after a three-week illness. He was 65.

Hughes, who until his death lived in a house in Harlem with an aunt and uncle, entered the hospital for prostate surgery May 7. Complications developed after the operation, but the exact cause of death at 10:40 p.m. was not disclosed.

Poet, playwright, chef, novelist, songwriter, merchant seaman, biographer and all-around story-teller, Hughes also had been for many years a columnist for the New York Post and the Chicago Defender.

"No more Simple stories," Hughes said recently; but it was Jesse B. Semple, an outspoken, beer-drinking Harlemite drawn from real life who philosophized with gentle irony on race relations and life in general, for whom Hughes was perhaps most famous.

Race Climate Held Bitter

"I have been writing about the character for 20 years," Hughes said of the decision to turn to other things, "and I just feel it's exhausted . . . The racial climate has gotten so complicated and bitter that cheerful and ironic humor is less and less understandable to many people."

James Langston Hughes was born in Joplin, Mo., Feb. 1, 1902. In the first of two autobiographies, "The Big Sea," he described himself as a "brown" Negro of mixed parentage, including Negro, white, French and Indian ancestors.

In his writing, Hughes employed folk forms like the blues or spirituals, but his language was Anglo-Saxon English, spiced with Harlemisms or the idiom of the South or other dialects.

His first book "The Weary Blues," a collection of poetry, was published in 1926. It was received enthusiastically and the young poet rode to fame on the same vogue of the 1920's that made Paul Robeson, Countee Cullen and Josephine Baker famous and which inspired that song line about going "to Harlem in ermine and pearls."

In the course of a prolific career in which he turned out–to name but a few–volumes of poetry, four novels, countless short stories, several anthologies and four Simple books, Hughes won many honors and critical acclaim. And not the least of his critics have been other Negro writers.

But some segments of the Negro press complained that he dealt over-much with the seamy side of Negro life. He was called "Langston Hughes, the sewer-dweller," and "the poet low-rate of Harlem." James Baldwin once suggested in a review of his poems that most of them be thrown into the wastebasket.

In his column, which he stopped writing recently to devote more time to other work, Hughes once answered these critics: "I know there are many persons who prefer the formal arts, the academic arts, over the folk arts–which is their privilege. But there are also many Simples in this world–millions, in fact–from Lenox Av. n Harlem to Soho to Montmartre to the Bund in Shanghai. And they do not speak the school book languages of their lands. But they are not stupid (albeit sometimes confused) and they are human–often wonderfully warm and human–and sometimes wise."

–New York Post, 23 May 1967, p. 2

"Bright Before Us": The Legacy of Langston Hughes

In July 1967 Knopf published *The Panther and the Lash: Poems of Our Times,* which Hughes had completed before his death. Placing Hughes's most recent work in the context of the Black Power Movement of the 1960s, some critics found his words, though powerful, to be in stark contrast to the militant rhetoric of public figures such as Stokely Carmichael, H. Rap Brown, and LeRoi Jones. Poet Laurence Lieberman acknowledged that the poems had "kept pace with the times" aesthetically, but he was frustrated with Hughes's political impartiality. "The age demands intellectual commitment from its spokesmen," Lieberman contended in the August 1968 issue of *Poetry* magazine. "A poetry whose chief claim on our attention is moral, rather than aesthetic, must take sides politically." In addition to *The Panther and the Lash,* Hughes had completed work before his death on a second book co-authored with his friend Milton Meltzer; *Black Magic: A Pictorial History of the Negro in American Entertainment* was published to excellent reviews in fall 1967.

Although many of Hughes's books went out of print after his death, scholars committed to preserving his literary legacy edited important volumes that highlight his work in various genres: *Good Morning, Revolution: Uncollected Social Protest Writings,* edited by Faith Berry (1973); *Langston Hughes in the Hispanic World and Haiti,* edited by Edward J. Mullen (1977); *Arna Bontemps–Langston Hughes Letters, 1925–1967,* edited by Charles H. Nichols (1980); *Mule Bone: A Comedy of Negro Life,* edited by George Houston Bass and Henry Louis Gates Jr. (1991); *The Collected Poems of Langston Hughes,* edited by Arnold Rampersad and David Roessel (1994); *The Return of Simple,* edited by Akiba Sullivan Harper (1994); *Langston Hughes and the* Chicago Defender: *Essays on Race, Politics, and Culture, 1942–1962,* edited by Christopher C. De Santis (1995); *Short Stories of Langston Hughes,* edited by Harper (1996); *The Political Plays of Langston Hughes,* edited by Susan Duffy (2000); and *Remember Me to Harlem: The Letters of Langston Hughes and Carl Van Vechten, 1925–1964,* edited by Emily Bernard (2001). Editorial work on Hughes culminated with the University of Missouri Press's sixteen-volume *Collected Works of Langston Hughes,* which was prepared by a team of scholars and coordinated by Beverly Jarrett, director and editor in chief of the University of Missouri Press, and Rampersad, chairman of the editorial board.

We have tomorrow
Bright before us
Like a flame.

Yesterday
A night-gone thing,
A sun-down name.

–from "Poem," *The Crisis,* August 1924, p. 163

Dust jacket for Hughes's last volume of poems, published two months after his death in July 1967 (Collection of Christopher C. De Santis)

Views from the Sixties

Ted Poston, a longtime African American journalist who worked for the Pittsburgh Courier, *the* Amsterdam News, *and the* New York Post, *wrote this tribute a few days after his friend's death.*

The Legacy of Langston Hughes

He created this character and named him Jesse B. Semple and made him America's most caustic commentator on contemporary concerns. But Langston Hughes insisted to last Monday's end that only the name was fictional.

"I met him as I told you," he said once, "in a Lenox Av. ginmill during World War II. And I saw him last at the 135th IND subway station in the 1950's. He was looking for Zorita, with whom he had a big fight the night before over his plans to marry a good girl." (Zorita was his fun-loving girl friend but it was "good girl" Joyce who finally won out in "Simple Takes a Wife.")

But few doubted that Simple—as he became known in practically every Negro ginmill across the nation—was all Langston Hughes. His compassion. His angry humor. His indignation at the foibles of the human species.

Who but Simple (or Langston) could discuss everything under the sun from lynching to lexicography, from intermarriage to international relations? Ask a question.

The lack of Negro astronauts in the space program?

"This is serious, because if one of them white Southerners gets to the moon first, COLORED NOT ADMITTED signs will go up all over Heaven as sure as God made little apples, and Dixiecrats will be asking the Man on the Moon: 'Do you want your daughter to marry a Nigra?'"

Why is Simple so sure he will go to Heaven?

"Because I already been in Harlem."

And the antipathy of Negro women toward the marriage of prominent Negro males to white women— "especially *pretty* white womens." He quotes Joyce on the demotion of an African prince who had married a white typist:

"Any black king that wants to marry a white woman ain't got no business with a throne to sit on. Let him sit on a park bench."

Or the time Simple's family whipped him for lying after he'd told them, truthfully, how a kindly old white man "patted me on the head one hot day and gave me a dime, saying, 'Looks like you could stand an ice cream cone.'

"They could not understand," Simple recalled, "that there is some few people in the world who do good without being asked . . . that is why I do not hate all white folks today . . . not everybody has to be begged to do good, or subpoenaed into it."

———

The creation of Jesse B. Semple—first 20 years ago in the Chicago Defender (then a Negro weekly) and last in the New York Post—highlighted one of the many contradictions in the life of one of the most prolific contributors to American literature.

The creation became more widely known than the creator. The Negro masses recognized and loved Simple. Some Negro intellectuals hated Simple—and Hughes. So last March, Hughes told The Post's book editor, Martha MacGregor:

"No more Simple stories . . . the racial climate has gotten so complicated and bitter that cheerful and ironic humor is less understandable to many people. A plain, gentle kind of humor can so easily turn people cantankerous, and you get so many ugly letters."

Simple was all Hughes, but there was so much more to James Mercer Langston Hughes than Jesse B. Simple. Three books of poetry. Four of fiction. Four Simple volumes. Two operas. Five biography-histories. Seven anthologies. Thousands of poems. Like:

Hold fast to dreams
For if dreams die
Life is a broken-winged bird
That cannot fly.

As late as 10 days ago he told this reporter, an old friend, how amused he still was over his first newspaper story. He was 23 and unknown in 1926 when the old New York Sun told how Vachel Lindsay had discovered a small Negro busboy in Washington's Wardman Park Hotel and chanted his poems to an all-white audience. Hughes' first book of poems, "The Weary Blues," was about to be published, and that made news. The headline said: "Negro Boy Sings Some Lyrics."

The title poem began with the music of a Negro blues singer-piano player on Lenox Av., and ended with:

The calm
Cool face of the river
Asked me for a kiss.

This plump, pixyish man whose 65 fully-lived years ended on Thursday was ever amused at the contradictions of his career.

Tone-deaf ("All right. So I can't carry a tune in a basket") he left more than 40 published songs and belonged to ASCAP. "I worked with some good musicians. Kurt Weill did the music for 'Street Scene,' and William Grant Still for 'Troubled Island.'"

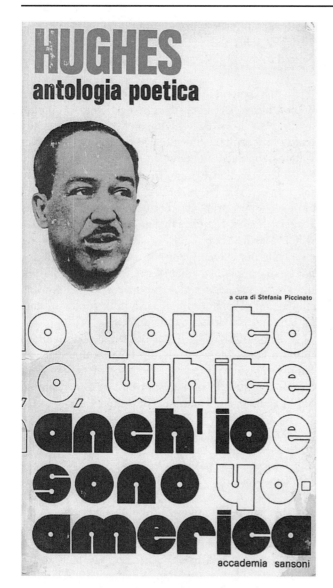

HUGHES
antologia poetica

a cura di Stefania Piccinato

io you to
o white
anch' io e
sono yo.
america

accademia sansoni

*Cover for a 1971 bilingual edition of Hughes's poems in
which the original versions face Italian translations
(Collection of Christopher C. De Santis)*

And, as one affectionate associate asked, how could a kid who had never written a poem in his life become class poet of the graduating class of the grammar school in Lincoln, Ill.?

"Simple. I was stereotyped. There were only two of us Negro kids in my class and our English teacher was always stressing the importance of rhythm in poetry. Well, everybody, (but us) knows that all Negroes got rhythm . . . so how could I let my small white classmates down?"

———

There was history behind him. His grandfather, Sheridan Leary, had been the first man killed in John Brown's raid on Harper's Ferry. His step-grandfather,

Charles Langston, had been jailed in Cleveland for operating the "Underground Railway" which spirited pre–Civil War slaves to freedom. His great-uncle, John Mercer Langston, was the first Negro Congressman from Virginia.

Yet James Mercer Langston Hughes hated his own father, James. Mainly because James Hughes hated being a Negro, and emigrated to Mexico–deserting his wife, the former Carrie Mercer Langston. He got into Mexican timber and became a very rich man, then married a very beautiful German woman while Langston's mother had a very hard time bringing him and a brother up in Cleveland, in Lincoln, Ill., or anywhere else she could find a job.

So, one of his probable last worries when he was taken to Polyclinic Hospital May 6 for the operation that failed to save him was: "If necessary, who will tell Aunt Toy?"

He needn't have worried. We live in an electronic age. Mrs. Toy Harper, his oldest and best friend, closer than any blood relative, heard it on a transistor radio while she was confined to another hospital herself.

She was probably struck with an irony that would have amused Langston. He was laid to rest Thursday, from Benta's Funeral Home at 630 St. Nicholas Av.–just two doors from the first real home that Langston had known in Harlem.

That apartment at 634 St. Nicholas Av. had been a big bone of contention between him and Aunt Toy. When he first started making a little money–never made much until the last few years–Aunt Toy discovered a house for sale over on Riverside Dr. and urged him to try to buy it.

"I know that they say the boundaries of Harlem and Bedford-Stuyvesant are exactly where the first Negro moves into an all-white neighborhood," he told her, "but that's not Harlem to me. I'll buy you the house, but I won't live there. I'm going to live and die in Harlem."

So they compromised. He bought a cute little house at 20 W. 127th St. in the middle of Harlem–just up the street from a Negro storefront church named "God's Bathtub," and both were taken from there this month to the hospitals.

It was from there that he wrote the poem which gave name to the late Lorraine Hansberry's Broadway hit: "A Raisin in the Sun." The poem began:

What happens to a dream deferred?
Does it dry up, like a raisin in the sun
Or fester like a sore—
And then run?

———

326

Langston Hughes had never lost hold of his dream. But it was deferred for years, long years, as he worked as a busboy, waiter, seaman and many other things until he was discovered in the early 20s by Lindsay, Carl Van Vechten and other whites who gave birth to the "New Negro Renaissance" during which white folks courted such Negro artists as Florence Mills, Claude McKay, Paul Robeson, Alaine Locke, Countee Cullen, Roland Hayes and Josephine Baker.

But, as a sailor and later as an internationally noted (if still struggling) poet, lyricist, short-story writer, anthologist, Broadway playwright, he traveled the world—and had been stranded on every civilized continent except South America. He had hoped to go there this fall.

His friends marveled at his seeming inability to lose his temper. But one thing could arouse his ire.

"They call me easy-going," he once exploded, "and of course, I am admittedly fun-loving. But I'm hard-working too. I start out working every night right after dinner [Simple: "Food do improve a man."] and you'll find me up here at it until 5 or 7 the next morning.

"I might go out now and then to some neighborhood ginmill, but often as not I'm working here. How do you think I met Simple?"

But money was always a problem with the open-handed Hughes. As late as 1957 when he had published three new books, with six more under contract, he said one day:

"I make a living, I guess. But it can be difficult running a major career on a minor income. I need, for instance, to get out of here, but I can't quite afford it."

He smiled shyly as his visitor scoffed. Both knew he would never leave Aunt Toy or Harlem.

But things had improved over the years—what with "Not Without Laughter," his 1930 novel; "The Ways of White Folks," 1934 short stories; "The Big Sea," his first autobiography (1940); the prodigious Simple books, along with his second autobiography, "I Wonder as I Wander." Not to mention "Mulatto," his first Broadway venture, and "Black Nativity" and other folk operas which were smash hits not only downtown but at festivals in Europe, Africa and most of the rest of the world.

———

But Simple's Boswell always seemed more at home with his creation, as when he asked in "Simple's Uncle Sam:"

"Uncle Sam, if you is really my blood uncle, prove it. Are we is or aren't we ain't related? If so, how come you are so white and I am so black?"

Or when Simple refused to be disturbed by the possible destruction of civilization in a nuclear holocaust.

"I'm perfectly willing to go myself if my enemies in Mississippi are taken along with me. Greater love hath no man than he lay down his life to get even."

His first poem was published in the NAACP periodical, "The Crisis." His last one, called "The Backlash Blues," will be published there next month. It reads:

Mister Backlash, Mr. Backlash,
Just what do you think I am?
You raise my taxes, freeze my wages
Send my son to Vietnam.
You give me second-class houses,
Second-class schools.
Do you think that colored folks
Are just second-class fools?

Langston wasn't. And Simple never was.
                    —*New York Post Magazine*, 27 May 1967, p. 5

* * *

In this review essay published some seven months after Hughes's death, Keneth Kinnamon discusses The Best Short Stories by Negro Writers *and* The Panther and the Lash *as well as contemporary scholarly works on Hughes.*

The Man Who Created 'Simple'

More than forty years ago Langston Hughes issued in these pages (June 23, 1926) a manifesto of racial affirmation entitled "The Negro Artist and the Racial Mountain." In it he spoke not only for himself but also for other young writers of the Harlem Renaissance against both the literary gentility of Negro critics like Benjamin G. Brawley and W. E. B. DuBois and the flippantly superficial assimilationism of the journalist George S. Schuyler. Hughes rejected the self-denying "urge toward whiteness" that would cause the Negro artist to abandon his most distinctive materials and his unique perspective: instead, the Negro should utilize proudly "his racial individuality, his heritage of rhythm and warmth, and his incongruous humor that so often, as in the blues, becomes ironic laughter mixed with tears."

These words may now seem dated—and indeed some would insist that they could be construed to constitute a Jim Crow aesthetic ("heritage of rhythm and warmth"!). But they specify cogently some of the durable elements in a remarkable literary career that began in 1915 when Hughes was selected as class poet in a Lincoln, Ill., grammar school and ended last May when he died in Harlem, a death that seemed oddly premature for a writer so perennially and ebulliently youthful.

Hughes wrote more than forty books, edited or translated fourteen more, and contributed hundreds of essays, poems, columns, reviews and letters to scores of anthologies, magazines and newspapers, from *Brownie's Book* to *New Masses,* from the *New York Post* to *Poetry for Women to Speak Chorally.* He also gave hundreds of lectures and readings from New York to Los Angeles and Uganda to Paris. Much of his enormous body of writing is admittedly hack work—children's books, popular history, occasional journalism—but Hughes supported himself for thirty-seven years solely by his pen and his platform appearances. No other serious Negro writer survived so long and did so much in an often unreceptive literary market place. In this respect, as in others, Hughes was a pioneer.

Aside from the value of his example, Hughes aided other Negro writers in a variety of ways. The anthology which he co-edited with Arna Bontemps, *The Poetry of the Negro, 1746–1949,* now being revised and enlarged, not only revealed an ignored literary tradition but introduced brilliant young poets like Robert Hayden and Owen Dodson to a wide audience. Hughes performed a similar function in *New Negro Poets: U.S.A.* and for the emerging African writers. Two fat anthologies offered rich samplings of Negro folklore and humor.

Hughes's last anthology, *The Best Short Stories by Negro Writers,* contains forty-seven stories from Charles Waddell Chesnutt's 1899 tale of lynching and miscegenation, "The Sheriff's Children," to stories by Robert Boles and Alice Walker, now in their early 20s. The familiar names of Negro fiction are here—Chesnutt, Dunbar, Toomer, Hughes himself, Wright, Motley, Ellison, Baldwin—but the most impressive revelation of this collection is the extraordinary variety and talent of the writers under 40, who account for almost half the stories. Perhaps the best of this group are two stories by young women about old men. Alice Walker's "To Hell With Dying" is a tender reminiscence of an ancient, guitar-playing alcoholic who maintains a tenuous hold on life through his relation to his neighbors' adoring children. The tone is movingly elegiac without becoming sentimental. Paule Marshall's "Barbados" is a brilliantly written and structured story of a Mr. Watford's repatriation to his native West Indian island after forty-five lonely but prosperous years in Boston. A sensual servant girl becomes the instrument of his devastating awakening to the waste and sterility of his life. Miss Marshall has clearly read Henry James, particularly "The Beast in the Jungle," but she has thoroughly assimilated his influence and adapted it to her own

artistic vision. No one of her literary generation writes better prose.

However valuable his services as an anthologist, it is as poet that Hughes is best known to white readers. In the posthumous *The Panther and the Lash,* his poetry is mostly that of racial protest, the snarl of the black panther under the lash—and backlash—of white oppression. Many of Hughes's recent poems catch the threatening mood of impending black retributive vengeance, but the earlier verse gathered here, going back to the *Scottsboro Limited* pamphlet of 1932, more often depicts the Negro as passive victim ("Christ in Alabama," "Jim Crow Car").

Unlike those younger writers, of whom LeRoi Jones is the most eloquent spokesman, Hughes was never quite willing to relinquish the dream of racial fraternity even in the Deep South. He affirms this again by choosing to conclude this volume with "Daybreak in Alabama." This hope, common in the thirties and surviving in Martin Luther King's address to the March on

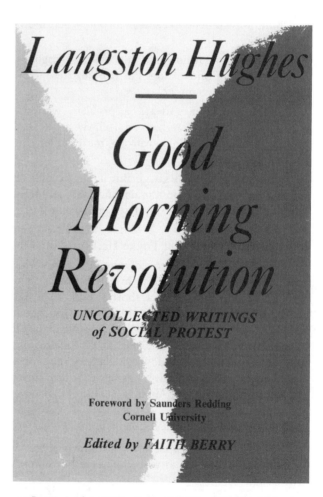

Dust jacket for a 1973 collection that editor Faith Berry claimed includes "some of the most revolutionary works by any American writer of his generation" (Richland County Public Library)

Washington in 1963, may be now all but dead among Negro writers, but otherwise *The Panther and the Lash* reminds us how accurate a poetic barometer of the Negro mood Hughes has been since his first volume, *The Weary Blues* (1926).

As a poet, he did not really improve. Of the twenty poems judged to be Hughes's best in James A. Emanuel's useful critical study, *Langston Hughes*—in which readers will find most of their favorites—all but six were written in the twenties. One could trace developments in Hughes's poetry—his movement from blues to bop rhythms, for example—but not artistic growth. Gertrude Stein's remark to Scott Fitzgerald: "One does not get better but different and older," could have been directed to Hughes as well.

Mr. Emanuel's thematic organization and cramped format do not permit him to trace this process in detail. But he does examine closely technique as well as theme in a number of representative poems and stories under such categories as "The Cult of the Negro" and "The Christ and the Killers." Occasionally one may feel that a particular Hughes piece is too slight to bear the weight of Mr. Emanuel's analysis, but generally his commentary is perceptive and sympathetic. Certainly his critical competence seems plain if his volume is compared to Donald C. Dickinson's overpriced *A Bio-Bibliography of Langston Hughes, 1920–1967.* An enormous amount of labor went into the bibliographical section of this work—though errors and omissions inevitably appear—but the compiler's efforts would have been more valuable if he had included Hughes's song lyrics and contributions to newspapers, while omitting the embarrassingly inept attempt to provide an account of his literary career.

A full-scale critical biography of Hughes is still needed. Emanuel's commentary and Dickinson's bibliography will make the task easier. When the larger study comes it will define more carefully Hughes's relationship to the proletarian literature of the thirties, arrive at a less inflated estimate of his short stories, and provide a fuller examination of the Simple sketches. It is in the four Simple books, which grew out of his *Chicago Defender* column, that Hughes created his most memorable fictional character, Jesse B. Semple, Harlemite, and realized most fully his own prescription for "racial individuality" and "ironic laughter." These and his early poetry constitute the lasting achievement of Langston Hughes.

–*The Nation*, 205 (4 December 1967): 599–601

* * *

W. Edward Farrison, author of William Wells Brown: Author & Reformer *(1969), wrote this review.*

"A Vital Contribution"
Review of *The Panther and the Lash*

This collection of poems was prepared for publication by the author himself and was in press when he died. Its title was derived from two recent outgrowths of matters racial in America–the Black Panthers and the white backlash. The work is dedicated to Mrs. Rosa Parks of Montgomery, Alabama, who refused to move to the back of a bus, "thus setting off in 1955 the boycotts, the sit-ins, the Freedom Rides, the petitions, the marches, the voter registration drives, and *I Shall Not Be Moved.*" Twenty-six of the seventy poems in the collection were selected from Hughes's previously published volumes of verse. The other forty-four are herein first published in one volume, seventeen of them having formerly appeared in periodicals, and twenty-seven now appearing in print for the first time. All of them are indeed poems of our times, for all of them pertain directly or indirectly to the Negro's continuing struggle to achieve first-class citizenship in America. The poems are written in short-line free verse or in occasional rhymes, by both of which Hughes's poetic work has long been distinguished.

The selections are grouped under seven headings, the first of these being "Words on Fire." In this group is "The Backlash Blues," one of the two title poems in the collection. Not only is this one of the new poems but also it has been said to have been the last poem that Hughes submitted for publication before he died. It is an emphatic expression of determined aggressiveness against the opponents of civil rights for Negroes. Also in the first group and new is "Black Panther," the other title poem. Avowedly militant, like Claude McKay's "If We Must Die," this poem has for its theme the determination of black men to give no further ground to oppressors but to stand and fight back desperately, like a panther when cornered.

More ironical than militant is the group called "American Heartbreak," in whose initial poem with the same title a Negro declares generically that "I am the American heartbreak– / The rock on which Freedom / Stumped its toe–" Still more ironical as a whole is the group called "The Bible Belt"–a group in which life principally in Alabama and Mississippi is portrayed at its non-Biblical worst. Singularly memorable as well as new is the poem in this group entitled "Birmingham Sunday," which consists of reflections on the deaths of four little Negro Sunday-school girls who were victims of the bombing of a church in Birmingham on September 15, 1963.

Dust jacket for a 1977 collection of Hughes's writing that includes an essay "tracing his influence and literary contacts in the Spanish-speaking world and the Caribbean" (Richland County Public Library)

Especially noteworthy at present because of prevailing international affairs is the small group entitled "The Face of War." Two provocative poems in this group are "Mother in Wartime" and "Without Benefit of Declaration," both of which deal with the common failure to understand the wherefores and the futility of war. The mother, "Believing everything she read / In the daily news," was quite unaware that both sides "Might lose." Meanwhile the draftee must go "Out there where / The rain is lead," but is told "Don't ask me why. / Just go ahead and die." What simple, convincing explanatory declaration is there to give him? Alas one is reminded of John Dewey's all but forgotten observations that "The more horrible a depersonalized scientific mass war becomes, the more necessary it is to find universal ideal motives to justify it"; and "The more prosaic the actual causes, the more necessary is it to find glowingly sublime motives."

The group puckishly entitled "Dinner Guest: Me" satirizes a variety of things. Its title poem, which is based on a personal experience, ridicules white quasi-liberalism. "Un-American Investigators" coarsely twits a Congressional committee for its arbitrary methods of dealing with persons summoned before it. "Cultural Exchange," the longest poem in the volume, envisions a radical change in Southern culture in the sociological sense—an inversion of the positions of Negroes and white people in the South with Negroes living "In white pillared mansions," white sharecroppers working on black plantations, and Negro children attended by "white mammies." The *bouleversement* imagined in this poem, which was published in *Ask Your Mama* in 1961, is more ingeniously recounted in "Rude Awakening" in *Simple's Uncle Sam,* which was published in 1965.

Finally there is the group called "Daybreak in Alabama"—a title in which there is a ray of hope for the optimistic, among whom Hughes belonged. As should now be evident, two of the poems in this group rang with prophetic tones when they were published in *One-way Ticket* in 1949. Observing that first-class citizenship would never come "Through compromise and fear," "Democracy," now entitled "Freedom," left no doubt that other means of achieving it must be employed. And admonishing America to "Beware the day" when Negroes, "Meek, humble, and kind," changed their minds, "Roland Hayes Beaten," now entitled "Warning," foreshadowed at least implicitly the various freedom movements mentioned in the dedication of *The Panther and the Lash.* From the beginning of his career as an author, Hughes was articulate in the Negro's struggle for first-class citizenship. It is indeed fitting that this volume with which his career ended is a vital contribution to that struggle as well as to American poetry.

—College Language Association Journal,
11 (March 1968): 259–261

* * *

Theodore R. Hudson, author of From LeRoi Jones to Amiri Baraka: The Literary Works *(1973), wrote this review.*

Langston Hughes' Last Volume of Verse
Review of *The Panther and the Lash*

The late Langston Hughes was never primarily a "protest" poet. Although he wrote almost exclusively of the condition of being a Negro in America, Hughes was no racist in the current sense of the word. Seemingly incapable of acrimony, he was, nevertheless, militant in his own way. Dipping his pen in ink, not acid, his method was to expose rather than excoriate, to reveal rather than revile. Indeed, in the rare instances when he approached irreconcilable bitterness, his art suffered.

The Panther and the Lash, a thematic collection of his social poems, most published for the first time, is no exception.

The poem that perhaps best expresses his attitude and his answer to America's race problem is "Motto":

> I play it cool
> And dig all jive—
> That's the reason
> I stay alive.
>
> My motto,
> As I live and learn
>   Is
> Dig and be dug
> In return.

Hate is simply not his bag. Empathy is.

A major premise of this volume is that American Negroes are disillusioned—their dream has been "deferred" indefinitely,

> And you don't
> Give a damn.

The palliatives will no longer do. For example, he says of tokenism:

> I love Ralph Bunche—
> But I can't eat him for lunch.

of promises:

> The old kicks in the back,
> The old "Be patient"
> They told us before.

of talk:

> Sweet words that take
> Their own sweet time to flower
> And then so quickly wilt
> Within the inner ear,

of Northern liberals:

> well-fed, degreed,
> not beat—elite,

of religion:

> . . . O, Lord, if you can,
> Save me from that man!
>   . . .

> But the Lord he was not quick.
> The law raised up his stick
> And beat the living hell
> Out of me!

and of gradualism:

> Go slow, they say—
>   . . .
> Don't demonstrate! Wait!—
> While they lock the gate.

America's evading and procrastinating and resultant failure to solve her race problem sorrows the innately patriotic Hughes. He does not want to be

> A Mau Mau
> And lift my hand
> Against my fellow man
> To live on my own land.

But he poses the crucial question:

> What happens to a dream deferred?
> Does it dry up
> like a raisin in the sun?
>   . . .
> Or does it explode?

And in answer he feels compelled to issue ominous warnings:

> Negroes,
> Sweet and docile,
> Meek, humble, and kind:
> Beware the day
> They change their mind!

and

> For honest dreams
> You spit in my face,
> And so my fist is clenched
> Today—
> To strike your face.

Langston Hughes believes that the Negro will survive and that his cause will prevail. In the past, troubles tried to make him

> Stop laughin', stop lovin', stop livin'—
> But I don't care!
> I'm still here!

In other words, the black man's "dream dust" is "not for sale." In the final analysis the "little" Negro alone may have to solve the problem: If the Pied Piper, Moses, Uncle Tom, Dreyfus, Jesus, Father Divine,

331

Robespierre, *et al.,* cannot "pipe our rats away," and "if nobody comes [to pipe them away], send for me," he cries.

Fortunately the humor—the whimsical, ironical, and gently satirical humor—so characteristically Langston Hughes' comes through in this book. For instance, in "Ku Klux," after being abducted by Klansmen and asked if he believes in the "great white race," a pragmatic Negro replies,

> "To tell you the truth,
> I'd believe in anything
> If you'd just turn me loose."

In another poem he muses that

> It would be too bad if Jesus
> Were to come back black.

In still another, a cynical Negro says,

> If I had a heart of gold,
> As have some folks I know,
> I'd up and sell my heart of gold
> And head North with the dough.

Technically, these poems differ from the blues [Negroes don't get the blues any more anyhow, for the blues is a passive reaction to trouble], jazz, and ballad structured verses of his early volumes. Though not nearly as artistically conceived and executed, the newer poems are more in the free-verse and "be-bop" style and mood of two of his later works, *Montage of a Dream Deferred* and *Ask Your Mama*. There are changing rhythms, oxymoron, counterpoint and counterstatement, cataloguing of names and places, and juxtaposed images. There is less of the urban folk idiom which Hughes is so adroit at using; instead, there is flat and direct statement.

Some of the best poems in this collection are those previously published, including "Merry-Go-Round," "Cultural Exchange," "Dream Deferred," "Christ in Alabama," and "Warning."

Many of Hughes' earlier poems have a spontaneous quality, a mystical effusion, a natural lilt. In *The Panther and the Lash* he seems to have tried too hard, seems to have forced his art—as if his urge to write were the result of exterior commitment rather than interior compulsion. The result is that this anthology is marred in places by the prosaic rather than the poetic, by lines that plod rather than soar. Although these poems may stimulate the reader's mind, they often do not reverberate in his heart. And, as in some of his previous protest poetry, when he is grimly earnest he occasionally loses his poetic touch and declaims rather than sings.

Overall, though, *The Panther and the Lash* is satisfying. His message is both valid and valuable. Hughes depicts with fidelity the Negro's situation and the Negro's reactions to this situation. Hughes has the discerning and accurate eye so necessary for a poet, and his poet's hand and eye are synchronized—which is another way of saying, in the jargon of the ghetto, that Langston Hughes "tells it like it is."

—College Language Association Journal,
11 (June 1968): 345–348

* * *

Arna Bontemps recalls his first meeting with Hughes in this tribute.

Langston Hughes: He Spoke of Rivers

Even a dependable memory sometimes plays tricks, and often enough I have had to call mine to task. This has never been true, I hasten to add, when the subject was the life and works of Langston Hughes. Even his adolescent poems were unforgettable. His personal history, as one picked it up from fragments in newspapers and magazines, had begun to read like a legend long before he finished college.

I seem to be the member of the Harlem literary group of the twenties elected to hold in trust a certain legacy of recollections, and the first of these is that he was our bellwether in that early dawn. The first poems by Langston that I read appeared in the *Crisis* in the summer of 1924. That magazine had been publishing articles, stories and poems by him for several years, but being away at a college that did not subscribe to such periodicals, immersed in the reading of the "Chief American Poets" and collections of British poetry of the Victorian era, I had missed the earlier Hughes works as well as most of the other American Negroana of the period. Lines like "We have tomorrow / Bright before us / Like a flame" and "I am waiting for my mother / She is Death," as they appeared in those months, struck me with such surprise, seemed so quietly disturbing, they immediately convinced me I had been missing something important, something I needed.

But I was rushing away to New York as I made the discovery, and it was not 'til I arrived in Harlem that I was able to go to the Public Library and look up back issues of the *Crisis* and *Opportunity* and other periodicals hospitable to the work of Langston Hughes and his contemporaries of that period. I did not have to be told, as I browsed, that I had been short-changed in a significant area of my basic education. So many lights began flashing all around me, I could not fail to get the message. I eagerly set about trying to correct the omissions and perhaps repair some of the damage to dreams and aspirations that should normally have flourished in school and college days.

That winter I met Langston himself. He returned to Harlem from seafaring and sojourning, and the word was passed up and down the Avenues that the Poet was back. He had been seen. I heard it first from one of the librarians in the 135th Street Branch of the New York Public Library. Then I heard it in a rather strange way in the parsonage of the Salem Methodist Church on Seventh Avenue. I had gone there by appointment to meet another young poet whose foster father was the church minister, and it was the Rev. Cullen who opened the door to me. Without even pausing to speak to me, he spun around and shouted up the steps toward the second floor, "Countee! Countee! Come here! Langston Hughes is back."

In a sense I considered this my official welcome, under mistaken identity, into the Harlem literati. I promptly explained the situation and introduced myself, but these two friends of Langston remained cordial (albeit let down) and assured me that they could not tell one of us from the other by sight, so much did we look alike in those years. A night or two later Countee and I were both included in a small group invited to the apartment shared by Regina Anderson Andrews, the librarian, and Ethel Ray Nance, an editorial secretary in the office of either the *Crisis* or *Opportunity,* welcoming the real Langston Hughes home and listening to his reading of some of the poems he had written aboard the ships on which he worked and more recently in the kitchen of the Grand Duke night club in Paris.

One of the poems he read that night won the first *Opportunity* poetry prize soon thereafter and then became the title poem for *The Weary Blues,* his first book. A few weeks later Langston sent me from Washington, D. C., manuscript copies of these and other unpublished poems in which I had expressed interest. So it becomes an enormous satisfaction to one who has watched his bibliography grow over an arch of more than forty years to see it now compiled in manuscript form and awaiting publication.

It would be much too casual to merely observe that Hughes has been prolific. He has been a minstrel and a troubadour in the classic sense. He has had no other vocation, and he lived by his writing since that winter evening we met in Harlem late in 1924 or early in 1925. Naturally, the lean years and the full years considered, this has required versatility. Hughes has

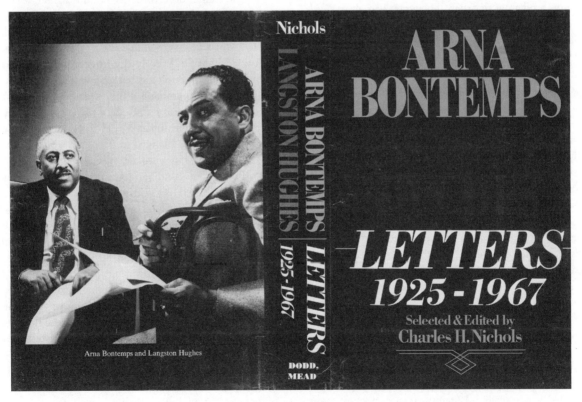

Dust jacket for a 1980 volume of a correspondence that Arna Bontemps believed provided "the fullest documentation of the Afro-American experience in the new world, artistic, intellectual, covering the mid-twentieth century, one is likely to find anywhere. The immediate response of two writers to events and conditions that touched their careers" (Richland County Public Library)

worked competently in all the literary forms. As a man of letters he has done what needed to be done: poems, song lyrics, librettos; short stories, novels, sketches, articles; plays, pageants, revues; autobiographies, books for children, and adult nonfiction. But nothing he has written has been out of tune with his first poems. Almost any biographical piece about him could appropriately be called "The Negro Who Spoke of Rivers." And his repeated use of the word *soul* in the refrain of his first widely published poem represents the first extension of this word into its current connotations, indicating a kind of "Negro" quality in certain areas of American self-expression and culture.

                    —*Freedomways*, 8 (Spring 1968): 140–143

* * *

Lindsay Patterson, a writer and editor whose work includes An Introduction to Black Literature in America *(1968), wrote this account of Hughes's generosity.*

Langston Hughes—An Inspirer of Young Writers

Maintaining privacy is an obsession with most writers. Langston Hughes was no exception until a young writer appeared at his doorstep. The writer was always welcome to leave a manuscript, ask for a recommendation or just sit and talk "having high tea" as he called it. To me and other young black writers that I know of, Mr. Hughes was indeed an inspirer, but he was a good deal more than that too, for he cared equally about a writer's welfare and his work.

It was in February 1962 that I first met Langston Hughes. I had been in New York about two months and was flush with the success of having sold the very first short story that I'd written. A friend suggested that I visit him, that he might be of help in some way, and certainly, the friend added, it wouldn't do any harm.

The same day that I left a note at his home he telephoned. I told him I was an aspiring writer and expressed the usual admiration for his work and the hope that we would meet in the future. He invited me up that night. I did not take my short story for I was not going to be "rejected" on one five-page story by someone I admired, even though a magazine had liked it well enough to buy.

I don't remember what we talked about, but it was a jovial, fun-filled evening. A week later I received a note asking to see something I'd written. I was working on a novel then that was going badly and after seventy-five pages I had abandoned it completely. I finally showed him my short story, "Patient Miz Carrie." He was very excited about it and wanted to see more, but I declined to show him any part of the novel.

About a month later, Mr. Hughes and his then secretary George Bass were in my neighborhood and dropped by. Mr. Hughes spotted my unfinished manuscript, seized it and refused to give it up. A couple of days later I received a note from him saying that he had sent it to a publisher. Meanwhile, I had completed another short story and mailed it to Mr. Hughes. I received a card from Texas where he had gone on a speaking engagement, commenting that seven more stories like "Red Bonnet" would make a book. When he returned he sent the story to an editor at *Ladies' Home Journal*. The editor liked it and tried to get the magazine to publish it, but the magazine refused by saying that the "little old ladies in Westchester would be insulted."

Spring came and my money was running out. I found a job with an advertising agency. It was grueling but exhilarating work that left little time for my own writing. In October I decided to go to Mexico and work on another novel. Mr. Hughes hailed the decision by advising me to take more clothes than books. "If you're well dressed," he said, "some one will always buy you a meal."

But Mexico turned out to be disastrous for me. I had completed only two short stories before I was stricken with a very painful and long illness. There, of course, was always a card or letter from Mr. Hughes, inquiring how I was and giving me encouragement.

After nine months, eighty pounds lighter, a lame leg and no money, I tried to get back to the States. The American Embassy was of little help at first, threatening to deport me to a small Texas town that wasn't even on the map. As luck would have it, I received a letter from the advertising agency asking if I'd come back to work. I wrote, telling them of my condition and if they wanted me under those circumstances to please send me a plane ticket. They did, and with twenty-five dollars Mr. Hughes' secretary, George Bass, had sent me, I landed in New York on a rainy July afternoon sadder but not really wiser.

I was in no condition to return to the hectic pace of advertising. I lasted two weeks.

New York can be a cruel and inhuman city. Those few friends, which included white liberals and high faluting blacks that I'd made before my departure, were suddenly not available. I looked too sad for their amusement. Mr. Hughes' house, however, was always opened to me. But I felt that I had imposed on him enough, so that when my money was almost gone, I lived on the subway and foraged in garbage cans for food. I drifted finally to the Bowery and tried to find accommodations in a flop house but couldn't, not suspecting that the Bowery was just as rigidly segregated as Park Avenue. There were only two hotels at that time which would accommodate blacks, and ironically, one of them was named the Alabama.

I had assumed that the Bowery would be one big, happy family of misery, but I came to discover how deeply embedded the white man's hate for the Negro is.

Covers for the semi-annual journal devoted to Hughes that has been published since 1982, by Brown University and then by the University of Georgia (Collection of Christopher C. De Santis)

He could be on his last leg, dying in his own excrement, barely coherent, but he could still shout "nigger!" loudly and clearly.

I got a cubicle in the Alabama which was a dollar a night. There was a notice in the "lobby" for a part-time night clerk. I applied for the position and got it. Two months after I had been on the Bowery, Mr. Hughes found out through some channel where I was, and every week for the several months that I remained on the Bowery he took me out to dinner.

I had no family that I cared to contact and his family became my family. Thanksgiving and Christmas I was always invited to share in their festivities. But I'm not the only writer he had helped as much, the list is long and the debts are quite large. I had dedicated my first book, *Anthology of the Negro in the American Theatre,* to him and was eager to present him with the first copy. But the day that it came was the day he died.

—*Freedomways,* 8 (Spring 1968): 179–181

Looking Back

In this memoir, scholar Richard K. Barksdale, the author of Langston Hughes *(1977) recalls a discussion with Hughes about the politics of black higher education, especially the cooperative relationship established by Florence Matilda Read of Spelman College and John Hope of Atlanta University.*

A Chat with Langston Hughes
Spring, 1960

I met Langston Hughes on three different occasions. Once, in 1935, on my first visit to Harlem, he and I bumped into each other, quite literally, in the doorway to the 135th Street YMCA. I was on tour with the Bowdoin College Glee Club, and we had just given a concert in New Jersey. When, however, the special kind of accommodations needed for me could not be found in Rutherford, I found my way to Harlem and its famous 135th Street "Y". Unfortunately, my meeting with the young poet was no more than a "brief encounter"; there was no time for more than a hurried "excuse me." I was on my way downtown to meet with the Glee Club for a radio concert, and Langston evidently was on his way to a "Y" meeting with friends. On the way downtown on the subway, I read an announcement in the theater section of the Sunday *Times* that Hughes' play, *Mulatto,* was still playing on Broadway. Of course, I was very unhappy that I had missed an opportunity to chat with a real, live, "colored" man of letters.

My second meeting with Langston Hughes occurred many years later when I was one of many who greeted him at the annual meeting of the College Language Association in Durham in 1959. Again, there was no opportunity for a personal chat. He greeted everyone with his characteristically warm affability, which I later found not to be characteristic of other successful writers. He attended some of our sessions that afternoon and, later, was a guest at the annual CLA Banquet. When asked to say a few words, he recalled how good Durham had looked to him one night in the early 1930's when a potential lynch mob had driven him out of Chapel Hill. He had been invited by a group of students to read from his poetry. Unfortunately, copies of his militant "Christ in Alabama" were circulated throughout the Chapel Hill area, and the poem stirred lynch talk. Before the muttering masses could form into a cohesive force, however, Langston was spirited away to Durham and to a safe haven in the city of the Spauldings and the Merritts.

My third meeting with Langston Hughes occurred in the Spring of 1960. By this time, I had become Head of the English Department at Morehouse and, in this capacity, cooperated with the Spelman College English and Humanities faculty on many projects and programs. One salient event that Spring was the presentation of Langston Hughes reading from some of his poetry. Specifically, I was asked by the College Lyceum Committee to stop by Laura Spelman Hall's guest suite, introduce myself to our distinguished visitor, and chat with him for an hour or two before lunch. In fact, I was instructed by the Committee to present myself in Laura Spelman Hall at 10:30 a.m., and, in obedience to Spelman's rule for exact punctuality, at 10:30 I was knocking on Langston's door.

We talked about many things, but the poet seemed primarily interested in Spelman College and its interesting history. He had known Miss Read, the College's formidable chief executive during the 1930's and 1940's. And, during a very exciting year as poet-in-residence at Atlanta University in 1949, he had become fully acquainted with Spelman's rules and regulations designed to shape and mold the Spelman Woman. I tried to assure him that rule enforcement was not as rigid as in days past, that the campus was much more relaxed, and

---

Langston/Blues Griot

Jazz life
like Roach, Davis, Trane;
jazz life,
laugh, erase the pain.

Angle in the blue,
so deep purple
the blue is the blues,
the spirit-chant
of history,
hungry humor,
ethereal jive
to stay alive,
to weave concrete
into stars
so brilliant
a soul-eye goes black
back to the bottom,
to roots where
hands gloved in grasslife
clap so long
so loud sound
goes black
into deep purple
spaces where
the blue is the blues.

Jazz life
like Langston,
blues griot laughing;
jazz life,
laugh, ease the spirit home.

–Jerry W. Ward Jr., *Langston Hughes Review,*
12 (Fall 1993): 27

---

that there was even some talk about changing the eight o'clock morning chapel requirement. He replied that, yes, things were changing; he remembered the chain-link fence around the campus, but now it was crested with barbed wire. Here I felt the first tiny flick of the poet's ironic wit.

We then moved on to discuss what he tactfully termed the John Hope-Florence Read "relationship." In response, I was quick to assert that, since that had happened long before my arrival in Atlanta, I knew nothing about the "relationship." I added further that if I did know anything, I was not about to discuss it within the intimidating confines of Laura Spelman Hall. He agreed that, yes, even pictures on walls have ears and eyes in certain institutions. At this point, I politely suggested that, if time would permit, we could continue our discussion about the aforesaid relationship at a small bar I knew about on Northside Drive. His eyes twinkled at the

Dust jackets for Arnold Rampersad's standard two-volume biography, published by Oxford University Press
in 1986 and 1988 (Collection of Christopher C. De Santis)

thought. Then he added, with considerable philosophic insight, that a little hand-holding in the board room could bring "hope" to any enterprise. I wanted to say at that point, "I *read* you, my man!" but I thought it best to move on to a safer topic.

At this time, we began to discuss Dr. Du Bois and his somewhat tortured relationship with Atlanta University during the 1940's. He and I agreed that the then reigning President of Atlanta University had treated the renowned scholar-author in a very shabby fashion. And I was surprised when our well traveled and highly peripatetic author related, in considerable detail, how the aforesaid chief executive purchased a new lock and, with pliers and screw driver in hand, personally changed the lock to Dr. Du Bois' suite in the dormitory in his effort to evict him from the University premises. Inevitably, the conversation then moved to a consideration of that puzzling social phenomenon, the authoritarian Black college president. After examining the whence, why, and wherefore of the subject, Langston explained that the authoritarian president did not have to be Black; there was

something about the Black college that converted congenial administrators into uncompromising authoritarians. And then he related how he had been driven off Hampton's campus in the early 1930's by that institution's then White president simply because he (Langston) wanted to organize a student meeting to protest the death of a college official who had been in an automobile accident and denied hospital care.

We were now on one of my favorite topics, and I was just about to tell him about my historic encounter with the presidential might and power of Hale of Tennessee when someone—Gladys Cooper or Millie Jordan—interrupted our very intelligent and meaningful discourse and took Langston off to lunch. Unfortunately, the day's schedule became rather complicated, and he and I were never able to slip away for a quiet drink and more dialogue on the myths and foibles of Black academia. In fact, that was the last time I saw Langston.

–*Langston Hughes Review,* 2 (Fall 1983): 25–26

* * *

Hughes respected the work of poet and critic Amiri Baraka (formerly LeRoi Jones), though he was troubled at times by Baraka's reliance on obscenities to make a point. Baraka's admiration for Hughes is evident in this 17 October 1985 interview for the New York Center for Visual History conducted by St. Clair Bourne, which was published in The Langston Hughes Review. *Baraka began the interview by reading three poems by Hughes: "Let America Be America Again," "Madrid–1937," and "Johannesburg Mines."*

Amiri Baraka on Langston Hughes

BARAKA: Yes, I think that Langston was a kind of torchbearer of black literature. And I think you can see that from his piece called, "The Negro Artist and the Racial Mountain," which I think came out about in 1926 in the *Nation* magazine, an answer to George Schuyler. George Schuyler had written a piece called, "The Negro Art Hokum," in which he said—you know, he drew the brilliant conclusion that there couldn't be really such a thing as Black Art. And for Langston laying out really the kind of basis for that kind of stance for the black artist in terms of dealing with white supremacy on one hand, the whole question of the relationship of the artist to say, culture and politics. And I think . . . I mean that's like a manifesto for the Harlem Renaissance.

BOURNE: Did he, in fact, follow it in his work in the thirties, and can you kind of give us an example of some sort of the stuff that he did?

BARAKA: Well, in the thirties Langston, I think, went further because he took the kind of "Black is beautiful" and the African history, black consciousness writing that he was doing in the twenties, and in the thirties he began to expand that to deal with the whole kind of concept of pan-Africanism, for instance. You know, showing that not only were the Afro-American people exploited by the people, first that black people were exploited all over the world, whether it was Johannesburg, you could say, or you know, Trinidad or Jamaica. And then later he, as the thirties progressed, you know, the heavy influence of socialism on American intellectuals, and black intellectuals particularly. And I think that Langston is much more profound than people realize, for the obvious reason that black literature is low-rated anyway, but Langston Hughes is not only a great poet, but a fantastic short story writer. There is no finer book of short stories written in the thirties than *The Ways of White Folk*. He's also a brilliant playwright. He still was the playwright who had, as far as a black playwright, was on Broadway longer, and with more plays, than anybody else, starting with

Mulatto. And plus Langston was a great translator. I've been thinking about trying to do a book called "the translations of Langston Hughes," because when I first read García Lorca [*LHR* Spring 1997], it was Langston Hughes' translation. Nicholás Guillén was Langston Hughes' translation. Aimé Césaire, Léopold Sédar Senghor, Léon Damas, you know, Jacques Roumain's great novel, *The Masters of the Dew*. All these are Hughes' translations, you see, and when I read García Lorca, for instance, I stopped because I saw Langston Hughes under it as the translator, you know, and such a beautiful poem. But I'm saying that it was Langston who was the kind of publicist for the whole Black Arts Movement in the twenties.

BOURNE: Well, when he did *The Weary Blues,* for example, why do you think there was such an uproar by the black press and certain critics, in using blues as a basis for his poems, and why do you think they didn't like that?

BARAKA: Langston and *The Weary Blues* (1926), why there was criticism of that. Well, it's because there were—many of the so-called—very conservative Negro critics who thought that because Langston and people like Claude McKay focussed on working people—you know what I mean, the kind of mass of black prototypes. A lot of those people thought that well, why are you, you know, talking about those kind of black folk? The black folks we want you to talk about is the kind who are like the socially mobile and aspiring to be, you know, move up in into the middle class, and so forth and so on. And interestingly enough, even somebody as progressive as Du Bois, who, you know, was going through his constant transition, made that kind of criticism, saying, you should be showing, you know, a different kind of black people. Same criticism as Claude McKay. But like Langston said in the "The Negro Artist and the Racial Mountain," he said this is the strength that the black artist can claim, to actually be able to perceive the world the way the black masses do, with the additional clarity, you know, and the additional kind of, let's say power, artistic power and political clarity that the artist can provide.

BOURNE: Okay, so there's blues, and there's that. Let's say twenty, thirty years later he dealt with be-bop in a series of poems. Now, was he also in the vanguard there, or was he taking his [cue] from somewhere else?

BARAKA: Langston has always been in the vanguard. See this is what I'm saying, see this is why people sleep on Langston. The first poet I saw in the fifties after I had come home from the service, you know, looking for the intelligentsia, you know, the modern intelligentsia. The first poet I saw reading poetry with jazz was Langston Hughes with Charlie Mingus, you see. And that was when a whole lot of people was walking around who didn't even understand what that was, who later then had to catch up with that and try to claim it. But Langston was doing that. The only other person who was doing that at the time, who could even be remotely compared to Langston Hughes was Kenneth Rexroth. But it was Langston. And Langston again in his writing, "The Negro Artist and the Racial Mountain," says, and it's very important, says that, you know, the black poet has to write, and create poetry as powerful as Bessie Smith and Duke Ellington. And that's clear. I mean that's the deal. Has to create work that is like Afro-American, that is a creation, just like you can listen to Bessie Smith and say, that is a creation of the African American people, you understand. And with that kind of high consciousness.

Dust jacket for the 1994 collection of the poet who defined poetry
as "the human soul entire, squeezed like a lemon or a lime,
drop by drop, into atomic words" (Collection of
Christopher C. De Santis)

[Baraka reads "The Negro Speaks of Rivers."]

BOURNE: Okay, Amiri, in terms of his music poems of the fifties [what is it] that Afro-American music tells [us about the] conditions? What was his poetry [telling us]?

BARAKA: Well, it depends on when you want to, you know, analyze it . . . Well, in the fifties what Langston did was try to return to some of the kind of military and intensity, I mean after the McCarthy bust, you know, after he was humiliated before, you know, [Senator John] Eastland [D, Mississippi] and H.U.A.C., when the sort of Black Arts Movement began to rise along, you know with the Civil Rights Movement and the Black Liberation Movement, Langston then began to take another fresh look, and became—and began to write poems fully as important as some of the poems he wrote in the twenties and thirties. I'm talking about the book called *The Panther and the Lash,* you know, or, *Ask Your Mama,* the jazz sequence. So I think that what Langston did took strength from the kind of rekindling of the movement after the Cold War, McCarthyism, and so forth. And his last poems showed, you know, a kind of return to the kind of intensity and grace of his earlier work.

BOURNE: Now you were on the scene then. What was your reaction to him—well you and other poets—I mean, was he sort of like, did they consider him as a guy who was past his prime, or did they consider him a tribal elder who was no longer relevant?

BARAKA: Well, I think most of the people that I knew—I guess you'd have to divide according to again who you're talking about, because if you're talking about most of the, I think, the black poets, there is a kind of, I think, a respect for Langston, but for a generation—when they're very young people, they really don't know Langston's works, you know. I remember reading his works to one young poet who said, oh wow, I always thought his works were just funny. I mean it's a complete distortion of Langston's work, but you see, Langston, like I said, was such a great publicist of poetry and such a great person and so on, when I first came to New York, when I first published a poem, he was one of the first people to actually recognize me. He sent me a letter, and he liked my poem, and you know, and we began a correspondence.

BOURNE: Did you think that—as a critic—did you think that his poems were technically that cool, or were you . . .

BARAKA: About Langston? No, see what I thought about Langston was that Langston was very glib and facile. That he could write as easily as breathing, and it's true. What I didn't understand is that the consistently high quality of all that he did write because Langston has a tremendous kind of output that I don't think people really realize. I mean he wrote books on the N.A.A.C.P., a children's book about jazz, and a children's book about Africa. I mean he wrote a book about black entertainment. You know what I mean. He's written at least about 25 songs, you know, television scripts, novels, short stories, autobiography, those kind of things—so I mean, when you really check out the enormous amount of work that Langston has done, and the high level that most of it's at, then you can begin to understand who he is.

BOURNE: Why do you think he has not been played up? Like you said people think he's just funny. Why do you think, why do you think . . .

BARAKA: Well, that's true for all Black Art. No Black Art is played up, except momentarily to be pimped off of.

BOURNE: Okay, give it full sentence. In other words, I think that . . .

BARAKA: Oh, no—I think that Langston was never really recognized at the level that he deserved to be because there are no black people recognized at that level. I mean if you have to recognize who Langston Hughes is, then what does that make you if you're part of that force that's oppressing him, and that he's talking about in his plays. If you have to admit who Duke Ellington is, what does that make American music and American culture. If you have to admit that of all the composers in the United States, there are not many that can even be spoken of in the same sentence with Duke Ellington, certainly not the ones that they think of in these, you know, these academies. But so then you say, well if that's true, if Duke Ellington is, perhaps, the greatest composer that America has produced, a man who registered two thousand pieces of music, then you have to say, well, if this country has been given to like harassing, insulting, exploiting, and oppressing black people, and in the name of white supremacy diminishing everything we do, to make it seem childish, primitive, late, backward, stupid, you know, over-emotional, corny, of no value, academically unsound, you know, whatever. Then if you have to admit that Langston—I mean, Langston Hughes is Langston Hughes or

Duke Ellington is Duke Ellington, then where does that throw the rest of your kind, you know white supremacy constructs?

BOURNE: And you're saying that's been institutionalized and therefore . . .

BARAKA: Sure. I mean, it's perfectly normal for people to admit that Duke Ellington, until the last days of his life was working one-night stands, and ditto Count Basie, who was working one-night stands in a wheelchair until the day he died. Now I was at a formal in town and the people told me the Count wanted to do that. That he really wanted to play one-night stands while he was like paralyzed until the day he died. You know, well maybe they believed that.

BOURNE: If you had to have an overview, what would you say was Langston Hughes' greatest contribution to black literature?

BARAKA: . . . I think that Langston Hughes greatest contribution to literature is that he was an author, you see, that he was principally a very skilled intellectual with a great deal of energy and optimism, and if you go to other countries and ask [other writers, you will see what I mean]. When I went to Cuba, the first person Nicolás Guillén, who is now the president of the whole Cuban Artists Association, asked me, where is Langston? If you read the signatories to the petitions in the thirties about, you know, the Spanish Civil War, you know, the anti-Fascist group, it's Langston Hughes, like I said. Any thing of value that he could find in Spanish, you know, or French, he translated. And there's an enormous amount of his translations that we have to be familiar with. But he was an unrelenting publicist for the Black Art and black people. And I think that's his greatest gift.

BOURNE: Now, this might be a separate subject, but in terms of the quality of the craft of his poetry, aside from the effects and the . . . the quality and the craft, and I know you can't talk about those outside of the effect, but in a sense you can. How do you rate him, I mean . . .

BARAKA: Well, see, Langston, and this is the problem with I think a lot of black intellectuals—we tend to be semi-literate because we go to these colleges and we study other, other, to be other, for other. You know. So the question is that when we come upon the original, like Langston Hughes, who is an original, who tells you in his essay that, what I want to do

Dust jacket for a 1994 edition of a children's book originally published in 1969. Hughes was working on this book at his death in 1967 (Richland County Public Library).

is write using the form and content of Afro-American music, that's what he's done all his life, and he's been eminently successful. And I think that you see, the whole thing about Langston–if you read *The Ways of White Folk,* there's no better book of short stories written in the twenties, and I'm talking about the period of the Harlem Renaissance as a contemporary with, you know, Anglo-American modernism. So you have to be talking about, F. Scott Fitzgerald, William Carlos Williams, the writers of short stories then, Isaac Babel, John Cheever, or whoever you want to lay out as the writers of short stories. *The Ways of White Folk* is constructed at a level equal to any of that. So I think it's important–you see because if you don't understand the whole of the movement of the twenties, it's like you're talking about Allen Ginsberg's work and leaving me out, in terms of a discussion of American poetry. Well, that might suit some chauvinist principles but it's not accurate. So it's the same thing in terms of, you know, you can talk about Stravinsky, but you must talk about Duke Ellington, since Duke Ellington influenced Ivor Stravinsky. You can talk about Gertrude Stein but you must talk about Zora Neale Hurston, whose concerns about

feminism are much more relevant than Gertrude Stein's are today, I mean in terms of the real deal, I mean in terms of studying it. In terms of the handling of literature, check out Zora Neale Hurston. The problem is that in the colleges they're only taught a very narrow kind of national chauvinist view. So you never really get to understand the kind of richness and diversity of Afro-American literature.

BOURNE: What was the kind of stuff that Langston wrote in the thirties?

BARAKA: Well, see, the kind of development that Langston went through in the twenties, his poetry was what you call, "Black is beautiful," black consciousness, you know, African history. In the thirties he began to take on more of an internationalist content. First a kind of pan-Africanist view that identified black people all over the world as being oppressed, and you know, from a common source. That is, he began to identify imperialism. And then, finally, more and more socialist ideas are incorporated into his work, and he went to the Soviet Union and so forth, and he was published a few times during the thirties by Marxist-Leninist organizations. There were a couple of books that were put out by the International Workers Order. One, of course, was *Scottsboro Limited,* which was a really avant-garde kind of revolutionary play that was never done, in fact it's never even put into the bibliography. And he wrote poems like "Good Morning Revolution," you know, "Goodbye, Christ," a poem to Lenin, a poem to the Chinese revolution. There were really some very heavy things. Plus some poems about the Spanish American war, and his continued kind of analysis, of the national oppression of the Afro-American people. Now, he paid for this in a sense, because Langston wanted to be a writer. I'm saying that he wanted to be a writer, because a lot of writers understand that they have to do something else if they want to write. Langston said he wanted to be a writer, wanted to be a professional writer, and so that's why he set out to write all kinds of things to keep himself afloat financially. What happened is, as he began to take more and more of these left positions, the state, a lot of right wing individuals, like for instance, Aimee Semple McPherson, actually they began to demonstrate against Langston. He would show up in a city to read and people would have picket lines out in front of a place. Or hotels would not let him stay because he was a Red poet. And went so far as to, when he went to Spain a newspaper published an account that the anti-Franco forces had actually killed him in Spain. And I saw that up at the Yale University Library, and there was a—his handwriting on the headlines that he'd sent to a friend said, "I'm dead." You know. So they put pressure on him leading up to the House Un-American Activities thing, when they tried to actually purge the kind of left and progressive ideas from American intelligentsia. And I mean that's whole—when Hollywood Ten—that's when Ronald Reagan rises to try to sterilize and absolutely commercialize American film. American film has never been the same after McCarthyism. All you have to do is check the films that they make today, and check out the complete works of Henry Fonda, John Garfield, Humphrey Bogart, or for that matter, Joan Crawford, Barbara Stanwick, and those people are more progressive than any women that they have playing now, even those supposed to be feminist consciousness. Those women there are much more conscious politically, you know, Stella Dallas, for instance. Barbara Stanwick is much more conscious politically than most things done even today by people who are calling themselves feminists. So that the whole culture itself is being destroyed—American popular culture—and making it serve imperialism. I mean American film was like

classically liberal, Democrat, you know, whether it was Frank Capra, you understand, it was a still liberal Democrat. That was the kind of projection that it wanted. "Good Morning Revolution," that actually "Goodbye, Christ" that wasn't his point of view, that was some unnamed person's point of view, that he just was repeating which he had license to do as an author. But I think, even though Langston said those things, it's unfortunate—still he had the sense to bounce back. And we have to understand that those were—that was a period when they attacked black intellectuals. They ran Richard Wright out of the country into exile. They indicted W. E. B. Du Bois as an agent of a foreign power. He was almost 90 years old, a little old man with round glasses and a three-piece suit. They say, this is the most dangerous man in America. Or you know, somebody like Paul Robeson, they actually destroyed. They took his passport, they would not let him perform on stage and screen. So it was an attack on black intellectuals to get rid of the whole left ideas that came out of the twenties and the thirties and the influence of the Communist Party. And Langston got beat up a little bit, but I think he came back.

BOURNE: Is there anything else?

BARAKA: No, except that I think that it's really important for people who think of themselves as intellectuals to know Langston Hughes' work.

BARAKA: In the whole culture itself. In the whole culture itself.

BOURNE: Okay, Amiri, why did he write what he wrote in the thirties—what did he write in the thirties and why did he do that?

BARAKA: Well, by the thirties Langston's poetry had moved from the early kind of "Black is beautiful," black consciousness, African consciousness phase, to a kind of pan-Africanism where he began to see that black people all over the planet were suffering from the same kinds of exploitation and oppression. And then, I think based also on the fact of the influence of socialist ideas during that period, you know, the Russian revolution had been in 1917. By 1929, the Depression came. A lot of people were disillusioned with capitalism. And the ideas coming out of the Communist Party U.S.A. had a great deal of influence on American intellectuals in general, and black intellectuals specifically. For obvious reasons. And by the fifties the leading black intellectuals were

Dust jacket for a 1994 volume including Simple stories
that had not been collected in previous books
(Richland County Public Library)

almost run out of this country by McCarthy [who chaired the Senate Sub-committee on Permanent Investigations] and company, I mean, Langston was brought down to H.U.A.C. and chastised . . .

BOURNE: *[question unclear]*

BARAKA: In the thirties? Well, Langston began to, like I said, he began to write poems that identified the exploitation, the oppression, as being a pan-Africanist kind of thing. It—everywhere black people was, there's a poem called "The Same." And it says, whether you're in Johannesburg or Harlem, whether you're in, you know, Jamaica, or you know, Trinidad, it is all the same. And really it's a kind of poem where he's seeking to internationalize his concerns. Because his concerns in the early twenties were specifically on the kind of Afro-American national oppression. By the thirties, with the intensification of Marxist ideas, the influence, then he becomes first a pan-Africanist, and

then you can see very clearly Socialist thought beginning to influence his work a great deal. I mean, poems like "Good Morning Revolution," or "Goodbye, Christ" and things like that, those are all poems that are heavily influenced by Marxist-Leninist theory and ideology.

BOURNE: At a much slower pace, tell me what was the price he paid for this sort of career. What happened—what's your analysis of what happened?

BARAKA: Well, what happened to Langston as a result of his becoming more and more progressive and clear? Because you see that Langston when he began writing was still in college. He was a young man.

BOURNE: Okay, what happened to him?

BARAKA: Well, Langston did have to pay for that, you know, his progressive ideas, because, oh, as early as the late forties then rightwing groups, the state, began to harass him about being on the left. For instance, even people like Aimee Semple McPherson, the evangelist. She picketed Langston Hughes' readings. Certain hotels refused him admittance. Certain places where he was supposed to speak, at the last minute, the hall would close up. So, since he wanted to make it as a writer this was very detrimental to him doing that. And I think essentially that's why Langston said the things he said: I'm sorry I wrote this, you know, "Good Morning Revolution," and "Goodbye, Christ," these are not my sentiments, these are somebody else's sentiments. I'm just using them in the poem. And I think he really had to pay for that, and even as late as his writing the whole "Simple" series. You see, Langston's work was not simple. What he did was focus on the masses. You know, the working class black, and draw a very profound kind of analysis out of that. But by the end of his life, you know, with that column he had in the Cleveland *Call and Post,* that to talk about black life he had to quote "make it simple," when Langston himself knew that it was not simple, but that it was very complex, and that finally a revolutionary statement had to be made. So I think by the fifties and the sixties he had sort of re-integrated himself to that stance. Because I think he was encouraged by the whole Black Arts Movement and the young writers who seemed to be taking, you know, a kind of militant stance and understanding the need for that.

BOURNE: Give me another statement about, specifically about . . .

BARAKA: Well, when he went to the H.U.A.C., you mean Langston, when he went to the H.U.A.C.? Well, first he went there, and the irony was that what's the guy's name, the great Democrat? Eastland, from Mississippi, was the one that challenged Langston on his poem, saying, you know, "Good Morning Revolution" this poem talks about the overthrow of the government . . . Yeah?

BOURNE: Mention that he came to the H.U.A.C. committee in 1953 . . . Say that.

BARAKA: In the H.U.A.C. committee, during the fifties: number one, H.U.A.C. was like harassing all the black intellectuals. And Langston had to appear before the H.U.A.C. and actually confess his crimes. They let him know that if he wanted to continue to make it as a writer, if he wanted to read, if he wanted to make these appearances, then he not only had to appear, but this kind of line had to be put out there, about how America had changed, and when he was young and wild he had written these things, but now he had changed up, and so forth and so on. You know, the same era that they took the Hollywood Ten to jail, you know, the era that they trashed American film. But I think Langston recovered marvelously from that, I think by the end of the fifties, he had gotten back that kind of militance, and that kind of broad commitment, and I think that simply that the kind of chaos and lack of organization in the fifties, particularly the C.P., was attacked so intensely and consistently and had the FBI inside the organization and all those kind of things. So I think those are things that we have to remember because all those times are back again. I mean, our boy Ronald Reagan [R, Governor of California] began his career by trashing the movie industry. That's how he got big, as president of the Screen Actor's Guild. After he killed up all the Black Panthers, I guess he showed that if he could deal with the Reds and the blacks he had dealt with the two most problematic colors in the United States. (Laughs)

BOURNE: Anything else you'd like to say?

BARAKA: No, that'll hold it until the next time. (Laughs)

New York Center for Visual History Interview
Small's Paradise, New York City

—*Langston Hughes Review,* 15 (Winter 1997): 30–38

* * *

Hughes and James Baldwin had an uneasy relationship after Hughes gave Baldwin's Notes of a Native Son *a lukewarm review in the 26 February 1956 issue of* The New York Times Book Review. *This 14 February 1986 interview, conducted by Clayton Riley for the New York Center for Visual History, was published in* The Langston Hughes Review.

James Baldwin on Langston Hughes

RILEY: James, I think many people have come to understand a certain period in Harlem's existence through your writing. Could we talk about the Harlem that you knew in the 1940s? Just kind of breeze through and tell us what that period was like and the place was like as you remember it.

BALDWIN: Harlem in the 1940s? I was born in 1924. So I was in my . . .

Taping Problem

RILEY: James, let's talk about Harlem. You not only grew up there but your writing about Harlem has introduced a lot of people to the tone and texture of the place. Tell us about it.

BALDWIN: It's a little difficult because I was born in Harlem in 1924. So the Harlem I grew up in was, you know the . . .

Taping Problem

RILEY: James, why don't we begin again (laughter) with the Harlem you remember in the thirties, forties and fifties.

BALDWIN: I began to be aware of Harlem . . . I was born during the Harlem Renaissance. But I was in a cradle. So I wasn't aware of Ethel Waters, Bill Robinson and Paul Robeson and all those people who make life very vivid in Harlem. And I became aware of Harlem in 1934–1936. There was still the Federal Works Program. There was the Lafayette Theater. There was the Apollo Theater, Harlem was a community when I was growing up—also a community which had just been uprooted from the South. So that, for example, every kid was the property of every grownup. So if you saw me doing something wrong, you would beat my behind and take me home and tell my mama and my daddy and they'd beat me again. That's how we grew up. It's a very different place.

   It happened, I suppose during the second World War. The beginning of a certain devastation was

*Dust jacket for a 1995 selection of Hughes's work in the black
newspaper to which he contributed for twenty years
(Collection of Christopher C. De Santis)*

Mayor Fiorello Henry LaGuardia (1882–1947) who after the Harlem riot in 1943–a riot brought about in part by letters written home by black soldiers in Mississippi or in Georgia and Alabama. Those letters had a lot to do with the eruption of Harlem in the summer of 1943. And Mayor LaGuardia declared Harlem off limits to white soldiers. And in effect the city began, as of that point, to create ghettos deliberately instead of more or less haphazardly. And this–which we're talking about '43, we're talking more than forty years ago–was the beginning of the devastation involving real estate, involving what we now call upward mobility. The people who could move moved, as far as Brooklyn, as far as Jamaica, Queens, maybe as far as Philadelphia. You know. They couldn't get much further than that. And now since the city and the state are recycling the land . . . I walked through Harlem about two weeks ago through the block I grew up in, 131st between Fifth and Lenox Avenue, and half the block is boarded up.

The buildings are sealed. The people are God knows where. And this is not an act of God.

RILEY: You mentioned the Harlem Renaissance a few year ago. You were born in that period. What about the Harlem Renaissance in terms of the national literature? What in your view happened during that period? What figures emerged who we should pay particular attention to?

BALDWIN: Well–again. I repeat I was too young to realize what was going on around me. But when I became aware of it, became aware of Countee Cullen, Langston Hughes, Jessie R. Fauset, Zora Neale Hurston, Wallace Thurman, it seemed to me that what happened in Harlem was a kind of–I repeat I grew up in a southern community displaced to the North, abruptly displaced! It seemed to me that what happened in Harlem was that a great many passionate people, carrying degrees of talent anyway, left the land, left the South anyway and came to what was sought as a kind of Mecca and they made it one. You know. Now how this happened is very . . .

RILEY: Do you think the effect of the arts produced during this period–is the effect on Black Art or is there an effect you feel on American art or perhaps world art?

BALDWIN: I think that's one of the aspects of what you would have to call the American dilemma is the effort to–if I may so put it–segregate art. Every artist has an effect on every other artist, you know. So on a certain level one can say that it's not so important to be a black artist. It's important to be an artist. But if you're an artist and happen to be an American black, then your experience comes from a depth and from places that the American republic does not wish to understand, does not wish to confront. These depths, these places exist in every human being. But a part of the American myth, devastating myth, is that it is a white country. And since it thinks of itself as a white country, it seals itself off from all those experiences which cannot be considered white. You see what I mean? It is not, in short, a black limitation. Or put it another way. This country does not have a black problem, it has a white problem.

RILEY: This calls to mind something in effect that by calling this the Harlem Renaissance it miniaturized the effect.

BALDWIN: There was an attempt to do that. But on the other hand the people who created it had already survived far worse labels. You see what I mean? It didn't matter what they called it. We knew what we were doing.

RILEY: You came from a family where I would have to guess writing was not considered a prior[it]y [laughter]—a future for a youngster and Langston Hughes from the same sort of family.

BALDWIN: We all did really.

RILEY: Your background has had an enormous impact on your life.

BALDWIN: Yeah that's true. I didn't . . . nobody . . . I was a kid you know. I used to write stories and rather awful pageants at Easter for the church. I wrote the school song which my brothers had to sing for years [laughter]. None of this was serious, and I never thought of becoming a writer. I didn't dare think about it. My father was very opposed to it, very frightened by it, and that frightened me. My mother was very frightened, too. But my mother was another kind of person. She didn't try to stop me. But, you know, the truth is you don't decide to be an artist. You discover that's what you are. And you don't do that, you don't do anything.

RILEY: Is there something you think in the relationship that both you and Langston had with a father not particularly disposed toward your choices personal and career choices? Is there something in that that perhaps impelled you to an art form? That pushes you even further towards being a writer? It might have been the case that your father was even more encouraging.

BALDWIN: Well, as a matter of fact as it turns out that's true. I didn't know it then. I had to fight my father very hard.

RILEY: We were talking about you and Langston sharing something. An uncomfortableness in your relationships with a father? But there could be a case made that the very nature of that relationship, perhaps created your art or your sense of it?

BALDWIN: I knew Langston much, much later. But I knew him well enough to know something about his relationship to his father—well, I understood it later. He opposed it. But he opposed the idea of my becoming a writer because he was afraid for me. And I could understand that then even. But I couldn't accept it. I fought my father so hard that in a sense I became a writer because of him. Because he was afraid I couldn't do it,

because he said I couldn't do it, and because on a level I couldn't understand then—because I loved him. And I thought if I got through, that ultimately my old man would be proud of me. I am very much like him. We're both as stubborn as both very hard-headed cats, you know. And I'll tell you this, my father frightened me so badly. I had to fight him so hard that nobody ever frightened me since. That is an inheritance.

RILEY: When we talk about the Harlem Renaissance, I think to be fair and particularly be fair to observers who hear us talk about it, it did not produce an enormous amount of great literature or great artists in other fields. It did produce a number of figures . . . we're especially concerned with Langston Hughes being one of them. If you were to just take a hard-headed look at his work and assess it for that period particularly, what are the important things that you remember?

BALDWIN: I think for me—speaking of myself as an adolescent really. But even later really there was something in the voice which I recognized. Something in "The Negro Speaks of Rivers," something in "For Me Life Ain't Been No Crystal Stair" ["Mother to Son"], which corroborated, and in that sense, began to release me from the wretchedness and the horror I saw around me every day. And that he could or that a poet could do that, you know, to reconcile you to something, not passively, to reconcile you to what it is really. And once you're reconciled to that you can begin to change it. It is not the act of poetry, if I may put it that way. It is really one of the most subversive acts possible. Because it can change you, you know. What Langston made me see helped me to grow up.

RILEY: You mentioned a voice. Is it that his work was conversational?

BALDWIN: Yeah. That's right.

RILEY: Is that the voice you heard?

BALDWIN: That's exactly what I really mean. It was as if you overheard someone talking. Like, as a kid you'd overhear the old folks talking to each other about things you only dimly know what they're talking about. Aunt Lily in the South. What happened to Duke's son in where? Virginia? And it's always you know, half heard. You don't quite know. It's something very menacing about it. Something they don't want you to really understand. You know. You begin to realize what it is. You begin to realize very quickly what it is, really.

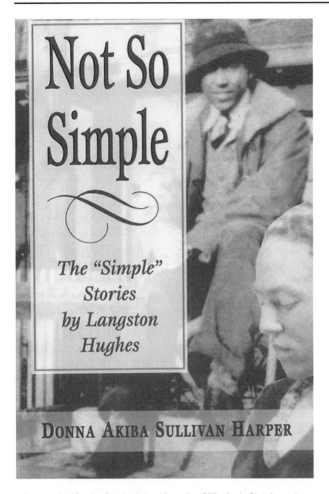

Dust jacket for the first book-length study of Hughes's Simple stories, published by the University of Missouri Press in 1995 (Collection of Christopher C. De Santis)

conscious and deliberate as it was real. He was a very sophisticated cat after all. But he affected the Jesse B. Simple manner for reasons of his own. I was a lot younger than Langston. So there was a lot I didn't understand about him.

RILEY: What does that do for him in positioning him in the Renaissance particularly? Is he in your estimation as you look back at the period, do you say this is the person who speaks most specifically for that time and that period? Or is he not representative of anything of that period?

BALDWIN: To me, the only two poets I read were Countee Cullen and Langston Hughes. And of the two when I was young, it was Countee Cullen I most wanted to emulate. Why? Because there was something in his voice, something in that voice I was talking about before which was also slightly menacing. Countee Cullen's account of a lynching in "The Black Christ" and Langston's various accounts of lynchings. I think something in Langston's account attracted me. But it scared me. In Countee Cullen's account I would have to outgrow this, but Countee Cullen's "That I may swing but not before, I sense some pale ambassador, hot footing it to hell to say the proud black man is on his way." I can deal with that for in some way the language kept the horror at a kind of arm's length. You see what I mean. In the case of Langston, you were dragged into it at once and, after all, I had never seen the South. And all I knew of the South really was my father's rages. And that frightened me.

RILEY: You raise a point that intrigues me here. Is there a power in literature? I mean when you talk about Langston Hughes, you talk about many [people from the Harlem] Renaissance. Can we say that the power of their work changed life? Would things have been different if the period had not developed with those people, had not been drawn to that particular place? Some people now are now saying that literature is just another form of entertainment.

BALDWIN: Ha. Ha. I've got news for them. No, no. Those people, this is true . . . any civilization is true of all. No. It's the role of what we call literature, for lack of a better word. But what is that role? The responsibility of the writer is to listen—right? To speech. To what people actually say, to what they actually mean as distinguished from what they think they're saying. What they are really saying, what they're really saying to each other. That's what. That's our life-blood. After all we only have each other. And the responsibility of the

RILEY: Did this seem in some instances set and apart from a lot of the other artists in the period who didn't work in that particular style and perhaps did not have the sense of the style's integrity that Hughes had? He was often criticized and I think properly criticized I think.

BALDWIN: Just for that kind of stylization. Looking back it must have been difficult for him because, I feel I was a kid, but he and Countee Cullen had very different exteriors in any case. He and Jessie R. Fauset, and I had not really known who Jessie R. Fauset really was. She was one of my teachers. And they all had a kind of polish, elegance, you see, at least from a kid's point of view, which Langston didn't have. Langston had, Langston was, I read Langston much later too. But Langston cultivated it. It seemed to me a kind of rough hue and, it was, it seemed to me, you know, at least as

writer is to give it back to the people as language. To fix it in a sense.

RILEY: So the power of Langston's work is to give a voice to introduce people to the places, people and things and times and folks.

BALDWIN: To introduce them to their own possibilities. I think that's what it's all about. Certainly I would be very different if I were here at all without that testimony.

RILEY: Could you say that again. Could you back up again and say that again because you came on the middle? I'm sorry.

BALDWIN: Oh, I'm sorry.

RILEY: Let's take it back to the part of Hughes giving a voice to people who had no voices.

BALDWIN: In the case of Langston, in the case of Langston Hughes. For me, I recognized something, well I recognized the voice. It was something . . . it was like a translation if you like. It was my father's voice, my mother's voice. I suppose it's not too much to say that meeting Langston made me to understand something about my father's rages and my mother's seeming passivity and the people on the streets, the people in the church, the deacons, sisters and brothers and when I read Langston, it was like I was reading a book and looking up and what was on the page was in a sense right before my eyes. But he helped me to see it, you know. He helped me to locate myself in it. So that I wasn't entirely lost.

RILEY: How do you think he was affected by his work in the Renaissance? The Renaissance was a very unusual period for everybody who was participating in it.

BALDWIN: Very brief too.

RILEY: Right. Brief indeed. How do you think he was affected? I mean you look at his work post the Renaissance period. How do you think the Renaissance itself affected the kind of writer he would eventually become?

BALDWIN: I don't know how to answer that. How the Renaissance would, if he was part of the Harlem Renaissance. It ended roughly around 1929. It lasted not more than five or seven years and it did accommodate a great deal in those years in terms of articulating

something which had not been articulated in that way or to that extent ever before . . .

A portion of the conversation may have been lost here, as cassettes were being switched and loaded.

RILEY: I think a case can be made of Langston perhaps surviving the Harlem Renaissance. An older writer may not have survived. Would you . . . ?

BALDWIN: I would have to agree that he did survive the Renaissance in a way, for example, that Countee Cullen did not and in a way that Zora Neale Hurston did not either or Jessie R. Fauset. But it seemed to me too that Langston, well, the Harlem Renaissance ended with the crash and all our lives were altered with the second World War. So we're talking about a span of fifteen years really. From 1940 on Harlem and the country became very, very different. And I think that one of the things that may have happened to Langston is that one of the things that matters to every black artist in this country anyway is a certain . . . One runs the risk perpetually of being divided from one's sustenance. That is to say one's interaction with other black people. One's interaction with one's inheritance is the only way I can put it at the moment. It's a very peculiar society, this one and in which you can be a success or a failure, black or white, up or down. So that what matters on the one hand as obscurity even more matters by . . . In either case you risk losing your voice. Cause you risk losing the contact with whatever it is you come from. I think that is part of what happened to Langston really. In a sense, he no longer created the blues, he began to recite the blues. Do you see what I mean? And the blues is a form which is quicksilver. It is not a quotation. If it becomes a quotation then it becomes irrelevant. And in a sense [that's what happened to Langston].

I once reviewed a book of his [*Selected Poems* (1959)]. And since I had grown up with Langston, his poetry, it didn't occur to me . . . I simply, you know, remembered what I had read. So it never occurred to me that I would have altered . . . but, of course, when I picked up the book and read it, that was so long ago being the boy I was, I was still moved by it. But I could see that, or perhaps I simply feared, perhaps I was thinking about myself, it seemed that Langston had not moved from who he had been that he was becoming an echo of himself. And that's not meant to be . . . that's not a judgment exactly. It's an observation. An observation grounded properly in terror. Cause it is probably of one of the, it is the great danger.

RILEY: Of course, he also had what I gather have been a traumatic experience in the breaking from his patron. I guess you'd call him.

BALDWIN: Oh yeah. I heard about that.

RILEY: I think that was probably a process that went on for a number of years. I mean freeing oneself from the dependency . . .

BALDWIN: Yes. That was another aspect of the Harlem Renaissance–the Harlem Renaissance was a kind of tourist trap. You know. What people were discovering that niggas could not only sing and dance, but they could sculpt. They could paint and, my God, they could write. So here the white world came bearing gifts. But you had to be very, very, very, very careful of people bearing gifts.

RILEY: I'm intrigued also by where he went from there. If he did in fact make the break with that particular kind of relationship. Where did he go beyond that? I mean what happened to Langston?

A Pictorial History of
AFRICAN AMERICANS

FROM 1619 TO THE PRESENT

Langston Hughes, Milton Meltzer, C. Eric Lincoln, Jon Michael Spencer

More Than 1,300 Illustrations – 6th Edition

Dust jacket for the 1995 updated edition of A Pictorial History
of the Negro in America, *which Hughes and Milton Meltzer
first published in 1956 (Richland County Public Library)*

BALDWIN: That is a hard question. I hear you very well. What did happen to him? Well the first, the second World Wars, after all we're talking about a phenomenon between two World Wars, 1919 to 1940. 1940, everything changed. The menace of reality changed, Harlem changed. And a man like Langston would have found himself, I suspect, in a kind of limbo. No longer the atmosphere of the Renaissance being gone and the white folks being gone and no young poets coming up. You know. No one in the horizon. Not until Richard Wright. You know, 1938–1940. But there was a tremendous vacuum created by, created by poverty and created probably most importantly by a loss of compassion. You know, like what are we doing here in this strange land? How are you gonna sing the Lord's song in a strange land?

RILEY: Very disoriented.

BALDWIN: Yes, that what I'm trying to say.

RILEY: I wonder if you'd comment . . . I tend to believe, I hope, I believe you . . . I think perhaps it was out of that confusion, out of that disorientation that you mentioned before about that removal from one's roots and sources that might have driven Langston Hughes into testifying to the House Un-American Activities Committee. Not being certain where he was between the government and where he'd.

BALDWIN: Yeah.

RILEY: . . . been as an artist.

BALDWIN: Yes, well I'd think that Langston's testimony before the House Un-American Activities Committee was a part of the vacuum we're trying to discuss. Who was he gonna talk to? You know. Really? I would think it was that and I also think it was Langston's flirtation with the left was in the first place very brief. And to be fair, this country has such a short memory. But there was a moment when the Russian Revolution did look like the hope of the world. There's no point in pretending otherwise. And a great many very valuable people, very honest people tried to understand what was happening in Russia. You see what I mean? And Langston was one of them. Now what he made as unfair, unjust to penalize him for doing what a poet or what a person should be able to do. To look at something. The House Un-American Activities Committee which condemned so many people is really a terrible judgment on the morality of this country. [It] doesn't say anything about Communism or anything about that. It says something about an American paranoia that I don't want to get into that, you know [laughter]. But Langston's testimony before the House Un-American Activities Committee . . . Frankly, I often wonder what I would have said. What I would have done? But I wasn't there.

RILEY: But you must remember that a lot of people testified. Jack Robinson testifies. Robert Rossen testifies [on 1 May 1953].

BALDWIN: Yes they did. Indeed they did.

RILEY: I say that to say that out of all this energy, I think there was a lot of confusion.

BALDWIN: Oh yes, there was. A vast amount of confusion. A vast amount of immoralization. At least Langston did not name names. I knew people later in my life who had gone through that crucible. And I repeat, I don't know what I would have done if I'd been there. But a great many people I'm thinking about did not really survive that moment in their lives.

RILEY: Elia Kazan; crushed by it.

BALDWIN: Elia Kazan is one of them, yes.

RILEY: You mentioned you had reviewed Langston's work. During a period of time, during the fifties roughly, you said quite honestly, quite sincerely, that you thought Langston's work was still unfulfilled, that he was unfulfilled as yet as an artist. Would you talk about that?

BALDWIN: Yes, I came to that, I can't say conclusion really, that Langston's work had not grown the way perhaps I thought it would, could hoped. And, of course, when a black poet is talking about another poet he's in a way discussing, whether or not he knows it, it's better to know it, he's also discussing what may be happening to him. Because all black poets in this society operate under very particular stresses and strains and very particular habits. So it's by no means easy. It is not to be taken for granted that you will move from one place to another, especially if as in Langston's case and not only in his case, but in Langston's case, through what is in small way divorced from and it's not something you can really do anything about, it is not your will, divided, something divorced from the people who are your subjects is an awful way to put it. Langston lived in Harlem, up on the hill. Countee Cullen lived on the hill. Sugarhill, we called it. Langston actually lived on 130th Street not far from where I was growing up. I didn't know that then. Later on I thought to myself that he should have moved. There

may have been something a little too willed in remaining in the middle of the ghetto.

RILEY: Almost drown.

BALDWIN: Yes, because you are surrounded, you no longer see it. Do you know what I mean?
A portion of the conversation might have been lost here, as cassettes were being switched and loaded.

RILEY: We're talking about Langston's decision to live in Harlem when, of course, a number of artists including yourself chose to live elsewhere. What are the particulars of that? What are the pros and cons of that?

BALDWIN: Of living in Harlem, for example?

RILEY: Yes, saying you're a black artist and you're gonna live in the community with the people and . . .

BALDWIN: I think, you know. First of all, the last thing that any black artist has to prove is that he's a black artist. And living in the ghetto doesn't necessarily prove anything. It's very strenuous and there's also something strangely patronizing about it. It's a mistake to underestimate people. People are not so easily fooled and in my own experience, people–are not really the people you hoped to serve–are grateful in a sense for a certain distance between yourself and them. It does not help them to watch you share their misery. They don't want you there. They want you somewhere else.

RILEY: Similar to our people being very proud of the fact that Adam Powell ate at "21" [Manhattan's Club "21"] and not Singleton's [in Harlem].

BALDWIN: Something like that, yes. It may be ridiculous. But it's part of reality in any case. In order to get your work done, you know. No one asked me to become an artist. It's my responsibility. So I'm under the obligation to find and create the terms under which I can work. To find the tape, the room and the paper and sit down.

RILEY: James, can you remember the conscious decision to leave Harlem? Cause obviously, I shouldn't say obviously because you left very clearly in a very definitive way. You said, "I am going." Do you remember making that decision, consciously?

BALDWIN: Yes, I remember that decision. I remember the day that I decided to leave home. I was in a funny position because I was in the pulpit. I had been a boy preacher for three years and those three years in a

Dust jacket for a 1998 children's book that illustrates five Hughes Christmas poems (Richland County Public Library)

RILEY: I meant to ask you about that period. Had you come to the conclusion that you couldn't write where you were living?

BALDWIN: Oh yes, I came to that conclusion. I started writing when I was very, very young. I started being published when I was about 22. But in the two years between when I started being published and when I left in effect . . . well, I was a book reviewer and wrote some of the early, early essays in that time. But I had written myself into a wall. I was expected to write about one subject only. So for two years I reviewed all those post war "be kind to colored people, be kind to Jews" books. All 47,000 of them came across my desk! And I simply had to go and try and figure out what in the world was happening to me. It was very significant. The first thing I wrote in Paris once I caught my breath was "Everybody's Protest Novel" to get that behind me and to find out what I could really do, if I really was a writer and not a pamphleteer.

RILEY: Does the term expatriate have any meaning to you?

BALDWIN: Not to me. For me it's a very romantic term. Once I got to Paris, I was very lucky. Once I got to Paris, I realized that you don't ever leave home. You take your home with you. You better, you know. Otherwise you're homeless and the people who thought of themselves as expatriates were dreamers, you know. And when the reality closed in on them they either collapsed in Paris or took the first boat home.

RILEY: Someone once said to me that leaving your country is like trying to get out of [. . .] You can't do it.

BALDWIN: Once I left here I began to see it. I began to see how helplessly American I was myself.

RILEY: You have said recently in your writing that you do in fact see this in a very deep and personal way, your country.

BALDWIN: It is.

RILEY: And you're not gonna be driven out of it.

BALDWIN: Certainly not.

RILEY: Talk about that a little more.

BALDWIN: Well, from my point of view, not only from my point of view, my father's father's father, your father's father's father, they paid too much for it, you

sense, you know, those three years in the pulpit, I didn't know it then. That's what turned me into a writer really. Dealing with all that anguish and despair and that beauty for those three years. I left because I didn't want to cheat my congregation. I knew that I didn't know anything at all. And I had to leave . . . I knew I left the pulpit I had to leave home. So I left the pulpit and I left home the same day [laughter]. That was quite a day and it was a conscious decision and once I was out of Harlem, I began to see some things. Of course, they were not like coming into another situation in the army, in the white world really. Nearly got my brains beat out. And when I began to hate my people, which was another danger. That drove me finally out of the country. I left in 1948 when I was 24, with forty dollars, and a one way ticket. I was moving, you know. But at that time that is how, you know, what saved my life. I got out. I could look at it and I could forget it and I could begin to use it. I had only been out of the country four years, long enough to finish my first novel. Long enough in a sense, if you ever do, grow up and to understand my relationship to my country and to my past. And after that my life was not simple certainly, but it was never after that as horrible as it was before.

know. And romantic. It seems from my absolutely personal point of view, my media speaking for Jimmy only, Jimmy. Unless, I were driven, absolutely had no choice, I would never, no, I would never leave here. It's a great deal, there's too much happening here. There's a tremendous potential here. A potential I don't sense in the world happening in the same way. God knows the handicaps and hazards are very, very real and tremendous. But if we can get beyond the place where we are now, something very important might happen in the world. I believe that. And now I'm past sixty, so I guess I'll not change very much. I can't prove it, you know. But I've seen some remarkable things. I know some remarkable people who could only have been produced here. You know. And I can't bear witness to any other place, any other history. You know. I would become a part of it transcendentally. But I have to produce here. I'm the grandson of a slave and my responsibility, to use that grandiose term is my sustenance. In any case is, you know, lies from whence I came. And I can't pretend I came from anyplace else.

RILEY: James, considering all that and looking at the experiences you had here and other parts of the world, what does literature really mean? We talked about that. But what does writing and reading and being in touch with language and words and I mean particularly talk about that from your own perspective. But let's include Langston in that. Does his work now come to have a larger meaning? Or perhaps a lesser meaning? But what does literature really come down to mean given the pressures put on all of us which may mean that we don't even feel safe reading books anymore? But you've lived personally as a witness to fifty-five to sixty years of American literature and you're the inheritor of hundreds of years of literature. What does it all come to mean?

BALDWIN: I don't know. It seems to me that what we call literature, what is it after all? It is one of the ways we have of confronting reality with the intention of changing it. Someone once told me years and years ago when I was in terrible trouble. He said, "describe it." It didn't make sense to me at first. He said, "describe it. If you can describe it, you can get past it." I think literature in short is that. If I can describe it and you recognize it, you can get past it. You can alter reality. It's one of the ways human beings have of confronting and altering reality.

RILEY: Let's apply that specifically to Langston. Are we saying perhaps, I'm searching here, are we saying perhaps that by Langston putting people in touch in some instances with their own voices, as you suggested,

that he described a time and a place and helped people get beyond that?

Tape change here.

RILEY: We're talking about Langston and I'd like to relate here to the story you told about someone told you if you're in trouble, describe it. You're grieving, describe it, if you're hurt describe it. Do you think Langston was able to do it?

BALDWIN: In a sense, as less and less time went on, it says at least as much about one as it says about Langston. I think that in some of the Simple stories, he, from my own evidence watching the people I knew, people I know in barber shops, watching people I knew and knew very well with whom I'd grown up with, Jesse B. Simple meant something to those people. Meant something to me as well. His kinds of observations. Langston was really a very sophisticated person. So that, I was always a little uneasy about Jesse B. Simple, homespun, homespun from this really sophisticated cat, you know. But somehow it worked. I must admit that I had the feeling, too, that Langston had sort of settled for Jesse B. Simple, because he didn't, I had the feeling that he didn't have, didn't trust himself to go further than that—didn't trust his powers to take him further than that. I didn't know him very well but I liked him very much, cared a lot about him. He was always very nice to me and I thought, I always had an uneasy feeling that he should have tried, he should have trusted it more, his gift.

RILEY: Isn't it people [who] say that if things are as they are, Richard Wright will take us part of the way, Langston Hughes will take us part of the way, James Baldwin will take us further along? Maybe that's the real terror of being an artist. You have to confront the real fear of going that next half step and finding out that maybe you should've stood where you were.

BALDWIN: It's a risk that you have to take, you know. I know it. I think every artist knows it, especially as time goes on. But the whole thing is a leap in the dark, an act of faith and it's better . . . I'd like to go . . . I want to die in the middle of a sentence. I don't want to . . . I'm scared. Of course, I'm scared that I don't want to be scared to death. I don't want to be paralyzed by fear. You see what I mean? You don't know what you're doing next. You don't . . . what is it? Actually it's a matter of life and death. You know people die. This endeavor is enough to kill a human being. You know. But it is also . . . there's something very beautiful about it. I will tell you this that . . . it does prevent you for having many delusions about yourself. It's one of the ways you may learn humility. That blank piece of paper and you.

RILEY: What would you say to somebody who had never met or heard of Hughes or read any of his work. How would you sum his life up?

BALDWIN: I always thought of him as a very gentle, very gallant, really gallant, a beautiful man. A weary, weary, weary, weary man too. He's seen a lot. It was in his eyes. And it was in his gentleness. To be that gentle and to be that strong, you had to suffer a lot. He knew a lot about suffering. And he knew a lot about people and I think in a sense the loneliness overtook him. And you know, it can overtake any one of us any minute, any hour and, I think, it overtook him. And that is what makes you weary and that's when you close your eyes. Marvelous I really enjoyed that.

New York Center for Visual History Interview
Lombardy Hotel, New York City
—*Langston Hughes Review*, 15 (Winter 1997): 125–137

* * *

Maurice A. Lubin, a scholar of African and Caribbean literatures whose books include L'Afrique dans la Poésie Haïtienne *(1965), wrote this essay, which was translated from the French by Faith Berry.*

Langston Hughes and Haiti

I became acquainted with the literature of Langston Hughes through Dr. Mercer Cook. Around 1943–45, under the auspices of the Ministry of Public Education in Haiti, Dr. Cook was Supervisor of English responsible for training future instructors who intended to teach English in the national secondary schools, lycées, and colleges. He introduced us not only to American literature in general, but also to the spirituals, jazz and Harlem Renaissance writers, such as Langston Hughes, Sterling Brown* and Zora Neale Hurston, who had lived in Haiti and devoted a book, *Tell My Horse* (1938), to the island. Dr. Cook's initiative greatly enlarged our cultural horizons.

In 1948, I came to the United States on a scholarship from the Bureau of the Census in Washington, D.C. One evening, in 1949, Dr. Cook, who was then teaching at Howard University, invited me to a book autographing party for the anthology, *Poetry of the Negro,*

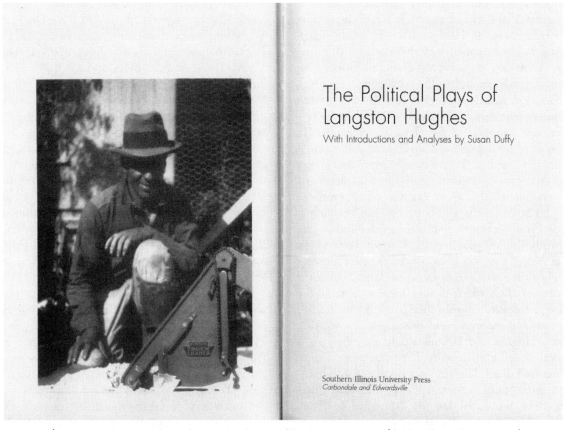

Title page and frontispiece for the first book-length study of Hughes as a dramatist (Richland County Public Library)

edited by Langston Hughes and Arna Bontemps. On that occasion, I had the pleasure of meeting Hughes face to face, and he wrote a friendly inscription in the copy of the anthology I had then just obtained. His anthology accorded favorable attention to fourteen Haitian poets: Oswald Durand, Isaac Toussaint-l'Ouverture, Louis Morpeau, Ignace Nau, Luc Grimard, Philippe Thoby-Marcellin, Christian Werleigh, Normil Sylvain, Duracine Vaval, Émile Roumer, Charles F. Pressoir, Jacques Roumain, Roussan Camille, and Jean F. Brierre.

I can assure you, in all candor, that the Hughes-Bontemps anthology made me decide, in 1950, to publish *Panorama de la Poèsie Haitienne,* in collaboration with the late Carlos Saint-Louis, for the occasion of the bicentennial founding of the city of Port-au-Prince. It was a literary survey which produced poetry representing the intellectual élite of Haiti.

Langston Hughes was not a stranger to the Haitian landscape. He was not content to know Haiti from a distance, as is the case with many others whose concern or compassion for this nation of blacks is often not real. A great traveler at a time when air travel was not common, Hughes pursued his quest and left his footsteps across the planet. He did not miss the opportunity to see Haiti, above all that continuing constitutional challenge of our Founder Jean Jacques Dessalines to every member of the black race to make Haiti a homeland. Hughes went to Haiti in 1931, at a time when "the American occupation was sprawled out in all its beauty," according to the expression of one former Haitian minister[1] who supported the occupation.

First and foremost, Hughes was shocked by the misfortune of the masses and the vast difference he saw between two segments of the Haitian population. He spent most of his sojourn at Cap-Haitien and its environs where he had the leisure time to examine Haitian realities in depth. As a writer, he deplored the misery of the "va-nu-pieds"—that is to say the people without shoes who carried the weight of the country's economic burdens. From previously published articles and books, it is already generally known that Hughes wrote about Haiti in *New Masses, The Crisis,* as well as in a children's book, *Popo and Fifina,* and in *Drums of Haiti,* also known as *Emperor of Haiti,* which in turn became material for his three-act opera, *Troubled Island.* We know from *I Wonder as I Wander: An Autobiographical Journey* that Langston Hughes and Jacques Roumain cultivated a reciprocal, fraternal friendship. They exchanged letters and discussed ideas. Hughes later circulated an appeal in the United States and abroad when a Haitian tribunal in 1934 sentenced Jacques Roumain to three years in prison on a charge of conspiratorial writing. Moreover, Hughes translated some of his Haitian col-

league's poems[2] into English for the aforementioned *Poetry of the Negro* anthology. He shared with Mercer Cook the task of translating into English Jacques Roumain's posthumously-published novel, *Gouverneurs de la Rosée,* which became known as *Masters of the Dew* to the American public and the English-speaking world in 1947.

I call attention to the fact that the first public tribute to the talent of Hughes, in the form of a biography, came from Haiti, in 1940, through the work of Dr. René Piquion. He had then just completed a master's degree in social science at Howard University and was enthusiastic about the militant emphasis in Hughes's poetry. Initially he translated some of Hughes's poems for publication in Haitian newspapers and, above all, for the journal *La Relève.*[3] The Haitian public was overwhelmed by those verses. At that time, more than once, you could hear people on the streets reciting by heart the poetry texts of Langston Hughes. We still have as one witness Félix Morrisseau-Leroy.[4] The warm welcome toward the verse in French of the American poet was a determining factor for René Piquion to publish in French the first book to focus on Hughes—*Langston Hughes: Un Chant Nouveau* (1940). Since that date, works too numerous to mention concerning Hughes or his works have appeared in foreign languages.

Many writers of varying perspectives, including Frederick Douglass, W. E. B. Du Bois, Dr. Carter G. Woodson, Richard Wright, James Baldwin, Hannibal Price, Anténor Firmin, Louis Joseph Janvier, Duracine Vaval, Dr. Jean Price-Mars and Dr. J. C. Dorsainvil have written illuminating works which uphold the black race or demonstrate its capacities and contributions to civilization. Langston Hughes can be credited with the distinction of taking advantage of the emotional side, and calling attention to the spirit and the heart as a means of accenting the moral and intellectual worth of blacks. His poetry is social and racial at the same time. I do not insist on the similarity of Langston Hughes and Jacques Roumain. It is important to stress that in literature, and even in scientific matters, often the same tide of ideas may arise at the same period and inspire writers and scientists separated by geography or the barrier of different languages.

The poetry of Langston Hughes has not been ineffectual in Haiti. Jean F. Brierre, who knew Hughes in New York (in 1943–44), was influenced by the tonality and the quality of the poetical work of our confrère Hughes. But at the beginning of his own literary career, Brierre was undisguisedly a poet in the Romantic tradition, making use of classical or Alexandrine verse, in the manner of a Lamartine or an Oswald Durand. Later, patriotic fever appeared in his work. As with Hughes and Jacques Roumain, the racial sentiment of

Dust jacket for a 2001 collection of letters that document one of Hughes's most important and longest-lasting friendships (Richland County Public Library)

the Haitian people was a stimulant which marked Brierre's new style. For a long time a dedicated poet, Brierre took his inspiration from Hughes. In 1945 he released a long free-verse poem, "Black Soul," from a slogan which owed its good fortune to the United States and was a tribute to black people.

After the American occupation ended in 1934, "Langstonienne" zeal could be found in Haitian poets. For example, we can see that Carlos Saint-Louis was inspired by Hughes and that he used nearly the same terms as the black American poet:

> I am black
> And as such
> my heart is love.
>
> —Carlos Saint-Louis, "Je Suis Nègre"

or again:

> I love the black
> For whatever is black
> Is a portion of myself
>
> —Carlos Saint-Louis, "J'aime le Nègre"

From the beginning of his career, Hughes was classified in the poetry domain by his poem which had as a theme the flow of rivers. Roussan Camille mentions different rivers in his verse "Notre Chanson" ("Our Song") to achieve the effect of continents uniting by way of water:

> All along the Niger
> A song had the slow rhythm
> Of untroubled passions
>
> . . . .

From the islands of the southern hemisphere
As far as the Nile
My melody extended
Like a river of crystal

. . . .

Muddy the course of the river
Which flows from now on
Nostalgic and wandering
From the Atlantic islands
To the Mississippi
And all the way to
Endless sorrows.

–Roussan Camille, "Notre Chanson"

Other poets of less talent have trailed in the steps of Langston Hughes. We need a study in this sense to isolate the influence of Hughes on Haitian poetry.

Hughes had the ability to be the interpreter of an ideology which was both social and racial, in allying himself with the compassionate cause of the oppressed–the people without shoes. He was a fighter on behalf of his race, whether in the Americas, in Africa, or the Caribbean. That is where he is in agreement with the Négritude movement, whose main thrust is to give authenticity to blacks. Thanks to his cultural influence, Hughes contributed to shaping a new humanism in which our race from now on has its place as a pillar of civilization.

–*Langston Hughes Review*, 6 (Spring 1987): 4–7

*Sterling Brown, though frequently identified as a Harlem Renaissance writer, has himself disclaimed that identification, stating that he neither lived in Harlem nor considered it the only cultural citadel of a Negro Renaissance of the 1920s. (Source: interviews by Faith Berry with Sterling Brown, including radio broadcast, "A Tribute to Langston Hughes: Let Us Remember," WPEW Pacifica Radio, Washington, D.C., May 17, 1979, in observance of D.C. City Council Resolution for Langston Hughes Day in the District of Columbia.) –F.B.

1. Constanton Mayard, Interior Minister under President Sudre Dartiguenave, whose "Pro-Conventionniste" government did not openly challenge the American military occupation. Dartiguenave was president of Haiti from 1915–1922.
2. "When the Tom-Tom Beats," "Langston Hughes," and "Guinea."
3. *La Relève*, a literary journal edited in Haiti from 1932–1938 by its founder, Jacques Antoine, published the following ten Hughes poems translated into French by René Piquion: "Proem" ("Negro"), "Nuit D'Éte" ("Summer Night"), 1 June 1933, pp. 17–18; "Danse Africaine" (original title), "Poème" ("Poem: For the Portrait of an African boy after the manner of Gauguin"), "Poème" ("Poem–'My People'"), 1 Sept. 1933, p. 15; "Nôtre Pays" ("Our Land"), 1 March, 1934, p. 15; "Les Histoires de Tante Sue" ("Aunt Sue's Stories"), Sept.–Oct.,

1934, p. 21; "Un Chant Nouveau" ("A New Song"), Nov. 1935, pp. 18–20; "Voix de l'Éthiopie" ("Call of Ethiopia"), "Poème" (emended translation of "Negro"), Feb. 1936, pp. 25–26.
The first three issues of *La Relève* included an article entitled "La Renaissance nègre aux états-unis" by Dr. Jean Price-Mars, who acknowledged the importance of Hughes and other Afro-American authors. (The latter article is cited in Mercer Cook, "Some Literary Contacts: African, West Indian, Afro-American," *The Black Writer in Africa and the Americas,* ed., Lloyd W. Brown. Los Angeles: Hennessy & Ingalls, 1973, p. 130.)
La Relève, similar in purpose to a literary predecessor, *La Revue Indigène* (1927–28), published some of the most active Haitian writers of the period and directed renewed attention to Haitian literature and culture following the American occupation. Many of these were of Hughes's generation, including the editor, Jacques Antoine (1906–1985).
4. Félix Morriseau-Leroy (b. 1912–) Haitian poet, scholar, novelist, whose own works include: *Récolte; Natif-natal. Un conte en vers; Diacoute;* and *Antigone en créole.* He was a contributor to *La Relève,* and later met Hughes in the United States.

* * *

Scholar Michel Fabre wrote this essay.

Hughes's Literary Reputation in France

The early infatuation of Langston Hughes with France, his shock in finding himself almost penniless in the cold City of Light in February 1924, as well as his gradual reconciliation with what quickly became "a place dear to his heart," have been somewhat romantically recounted by the poet in his first autobiography, *The Big Sea.* The details and importance of his initial stay in France, and his attendance later at two international writers' congresses in 1937 and 1938 in Paris, have also been carefully documented in Faith Berry's *Langston Hughes: Before and Beyond Harlem* (1983), and in volume one of Arnold Rampersad's biography, *The Life of Langston Hughes: I, Too, Sing America* (1986). I have also devoted a part of a chapter to Hughes's French experience during the 1920s and 1930s in *La Rive Noire* (1985). As a consequence, I intend to focus here on Hughes's French experience and the growth of his reputation in France from World War II until the poet's death in 1967.

In France, his reputation already had been made by the 1930s, not so much as a poet of the Harlem Renaissance–although he had been translated and anthologized as such–but mostly as a left-wing writer naturally taking sides with the Scottsboro boys but also supporting Communist poets Jacques Roumain and Louis Aragon and the proletariat. By the time he met Pierre Seghers, who was to become his friend and

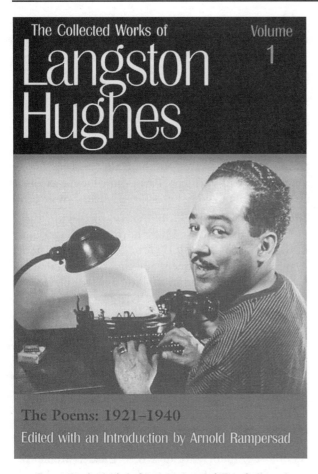

The Collected Works of   Volume
Langston
Hughes   1

The Poems: 1921–1940
Edited with an Introduction by Arnold Rampersad

Dust jacket for the first of sixteen volumes of The Collected
Works of Langston Hughes, *published by the University
of Missouri Press (Collection of Christopher C. De Santis)*

major French publisher, Hughes had been published in most progressive Paris reviews, including the prestigious *Europe* magazine, and Éditions Rieder had issued *Sandy,* a translation of *Not Without Laughter* in 1934.

During World War II, the Nazi occupation understandably marked a break in transatlantic contacts, although Hughes's poems appeared in a special issue of the underground, Algiers-based publication, *Revue Fontaine,* dedicated to American poets in 1944. At the same time, Mercer Cook, the teacher of romance languages and specialist of black Francophone writing–with whom Hughes and Guyanese poet Léon Damas had spent much time in August 1937–was making every effort, with Claire Goll, to alleviate the plight of their mutual friend René Maran, the black author and Goncourt prize-winner who was being harassed by the Germans for his staunch patriotism and refusal to participate in their propaganda program in Paris. Hughes's support was forthcoming.

Shortly after the liberation of France, the French National Radio broadcast a selection of Hughes's

poems adapted by Raymond Deprez in early 1945. His collection of short stories, *Histoires de blancs* (*The Ways of White Folks*), published by Éditions de Minuit in 1946, had gone largely unnoticed among the general public, although reviews had been fine. More important was the 1947 publication by Seghers of a translation by Georges Adam of *The Big Sea;* the book benefited from excellent reviews and contributed to establishing the image of Hughes as a writer with many interests: aesthetic, cultural, and humanitarian–and not only as political or racial. Meanwhile, Hughes himself was involved in disseminating black literary achievements, including those of French-speaking writers.

At nearly the same time, in Paris, Richard Wright was helping to found the review, *Présence Africaine.*[1] He suggested to its editor, Alioune Diop, that he approach Hughes for possible contributions. By 1950, *Présence Africaine* was planning a volume on Hughes, and Diop requested some of his unpublished poetry. Hughes had only a few Simple stories available. The project was not completed, but when they considered organizing the First Congress of Black Writers and Artists, the members of the planning committees, both in Paris and London, invited Hughes as a delegate, requesting a paper on "Poetry and Racism." Apparently, the invitation was misdirected, then forwarded to Fisk University, and Hughes received it on August 16, 1956–only too late, he declared, to be able to attend the Congress[2] in Paris on September 20; too late even to send an article. [Following the success of the Congress, however, Alioune Diop in late 1956 created the Société Africaine de Culture (S.A.C.), and Hughes was chosen a member of the *Conseil exécutif* (Executive Council).].

Later, when the American branch of the Society of African Culture (AMSAC) was formed, shortly after the Congress, Hughes's participation was again sought. And when Alioune Diop visited the United States for the first time in 1957, he expressed the wish to see the poet. Hughes never wrote the essay "Culture and Colonialism" *Présence Africaine* requested of him, but he did attend several cultural events and meetings sponsored by The American Society of African Culture in the late 1950s and early 1960s. He significantly collaborated with the poet Samuel Allen and the novelist John Oliver Killens, among others, to make the concept of Négritude better known among Afro-American intellectuals.[3]

In 1955, Pierre Seghers had published a bilingual edition of a selection of Hughes's poetry.[4] Again, the reviews had been good but the sales rather low. In the fifties, therefore, Hughes's reputation in France did not grow much. From Brussels, Raymond Quinot wrote him as early as 1954, sending him *Ciel Bleu*–a collection of blues and choruses–and requesting new poems for publication in the *Journal des Poètes.* However, Quinot's volume-length study of Hughes's poetry, *Langston Hughes ou l'étoile noire,* did not appear in print until 1964. Likewise, François Dodat, one of Hughes's translators, initiated a correspondence with him in 1955, but his slim bilingual volume in the prestigious "Autour du Monde" series remained somewhat confidential. The major Paris event concerning Hughes during the fifties decade probably was a very successful broadcast of his drama *Mulatto* by the French National Network on March 2, 1957. It was produced by Eleanor Kramer, with actors Charles Vanel, Jean Toulot, Morena, and Georges Aminel, who was "especially good in the role of the son," wrote Jimmy "Lover Man" Davis, a black American expatriate singer, who had befriended Hughes in 1947.

In October 1958, Hughes received the visit of Jean Wagner, at work on a Ph.D. on the religious theme in Afro-American poetry of the Harlem Renaissance. Hughes was struck by the knowledge and thoroughness of the French academic who asked him to clarify a number of points in his own works and career. By that time, Hughes, who had been held in suspicion by official American channels because of his left-wing leanings, had apparently been cleared after his 1953 appearance before McCarthy's Senate Permanent Subcommittee on Investigations. Government-sponsored agencies abroad, such as the United States Information Services (USIS), which was in charge of cultural activities, were not unfavorable to giving him more exposure. In 1960, Jean Wagner was asked to write an essay on Hughes's poetry for the USIS French-language publication, *Informations et Documents.*[5] However, after holding the piece for over a year, the USIS left out the last line of two of Hughes's poems (the important "punch" which provided the anti-racist message). In response to an indignant letter from Wagner, they replied only in a subsequent issue that the verses printed were only "excerpts." Hughes good-humoredly wrote Wagner that he was amazed, not that his lines should have been cut, but that the USIS should want to publish him at all!

In 1960, when Hughes was invited to Nigeria for the inauguration of its President, his old acquaintance Benjamin N. Azikiwe, he made a point of stopping in Paris on his way back, after a wonderful week in Lagos and Kano. It was his first trip to France in more than twenty years. However, he had remained in touch with French cultural life, especially with the works of French-speaking black writers, while his own works were being translated, performed and warmly welcomed in Paris. During his 1960 trip, he stayed at Hotel Logos, in the Latin Quarter, where he met a Sengalese, Diallo Alpha, with whom he spent, he acknowledged, "trois beaux jours, à Paris." A number of old friends

were around, such as [Louis] Aragon, [Pierre] Seghers, and the [Henri] Cartier-Bressons, but Langston mostly visited Jimmy Davis and Richard Wright. In his new apartment on rue Régis, Wright was very sick with amoebic dysentery. When Hughes called upon him, he was about to leave for a check-up at the Clinique Eugène Gibez. He died there unexpectedly in November; Hughes was, as he put it in his *Ebony* magazine obituary piece, "Richard Wright's Last Guest at Home." Upon his return to the United States, Hughes wrote Carl Van Vechten: "Paris seemed to me as lovely as ever. I want to go right back. "[6] He had to wait, however, for more propitious times.

On January 25, 1962, he confessed to Jimmy Davis: "I miss Paris."[7] He had told everyone about Davis's pleasant apartment and the delicious dinner at his place, and he asked him to keep an eye open for the reception of his *Black Nativity.* The play was produced, beginning January 3, 1962, at the Théâtre des Champs-Elysées and continued for four weeks. The reviews were excellent. *Paris Presse* even carried a front-page article with a photograph and the heading "A Dozen Black Angels Invade Paris." In *Arts,* another reviewer called Marion Williams "A mystical Josephine Baker . . . probably one of the most extraordinary personalities seen on the stage."[8] The performance was so successful that it was resumed for several weeks in June 1962. The South African writer Ezekiel Mphahlele, who was then working for the Congrès pour la Liberté de la Culture in Paris, wrote Hughes: "We saw *Black Nativity* there. Very good singing, boy. It rocks you and leaves you quivering: Audience participation was most gratifying."[9]

In 1963, on his way back from Israel, Hughes traveled through parts of Italy and the South of France, stopping in Nice at the Hôtel Negresco in early July and reaching Paris again in August. The weather was grey, rainy and cold, but Hughes was in the mood to enjoy the city, thinking of good old memories after revisiting Bricktop in Rome.[10]

In 1962, Jean Wagner's *Les Poètes Nègres des États-Unis*[11] had been published, and Hughes read it with great interest. He had been impressed by Wagner's thorough research, by his honesty when dealing with the USIS, and he had allowed him to print unpublished verse, such as "Poem for Rich Churches," in the appendix to his French dissertation. Hughes wrote Bontemps [about the book] on April 13, 1963:

> . . . Wagner seems not to grasp Negro humor too well, anyhow—which I think weakens his discussion of the blues in my chapter. He's also a bit off the track relative to religion and myself—which I indicated to him in my note congratulating him on his 'monumental work'

The Department of English & Philosophy at Missouri Southern State College
invites you to attend

THE
LANGSTON HUGHES
CENTENNIAL CONFERENCE

A conference to celebrate
the life
and work of
the
Dean of the
Harlem Renassaince
in his birthplace
January 31-February 2, 2002
Missouri Southern State College
Joplin, Missouri

KEYNOTE SPEAKERS

ARNOLD RAMPERSAD, STANFORD UNIVERSITY
Hughes biographer
DOLAN HUBBARD, MORGAN STATE UNIVERSITY
President, Langston Hughes Society
AKIBA SULLIVAN HARPER, SPELMAN COLLEGE
Past President, Langston Hughes Society

Topics for panels will include, but will not be limited to, the following:

Multiculturalism/the canon	America
Jazz and the blues	Modernism
The Harlem Renaissance	Expatriation/exile
Oral traditions	Communism
McCarthyism	Children's literature
Africa	Contemporary literature
The New Negro	Teaching

For more information, or to submit an abstract or proposal, contact:

Bryan Vescio
Department of English and Philosophy
Missouri Southern State College
3950 E. Newman Road
Joplin, MO 64801
(417) 625-9640
vescio-b@mail.mssc.edu

Conference updates can be viewed at www.mssc.edu/english/langhughes/

Poster for a centennial conference held in the city of Hughes's birth (Bruccoli Clark Layman Archives)

and thanking him for the first really comprehensive critique of my poetry as yet in print, done with great sympathy and over-all understanding on the whole. But I wish I had had (for the sake of his book, not mine) a chance to clarify him a bit more on the two areas mentioned above. Re humor, he takes as dead serious some of the things that we would take as jive. And sometimes confuses the universal or racial 'I' as personal . . .[12]

When Wagner was appointed full professor at the University of Grenoble, he tried to have Hughes come as an exchange teacher and also to have the University award him an *honoris causa* doctorate, but the plans did not materialize.

In 1964, Hughes was invited to the Berlin Poetry Festival, whose theme was "Poetry in a Changing World." The initiative was taken by the French poet Pierre Emmanuel, a member of the Festival committee, and seconded by Mauritius-born poet and playwright Edouard Maunick, a great admirer of Hughes. Emmanuel wished to establish a double confrontation: Africa vs. the West, and French-speaking poets vs. English-speaking ones, and he counted on Hughes as moderator and chairman. After the festival, which was held on September 22–27, Hughes again spent a few weeks in Paris, staying at the Hôtel California on the rue des Écoles. François Dodat had been entrusted by Seghers to prepare a selection of Hughes's poetry and prose, with a long introduction on his career and writings, for the by then prestigious collection, "Poètes d'Aujourd'hui." Hughes was the fourth writer chosen, after Whitman, Poe and Emily Dickinson. This was important proof of the high literary reputation of Hughes among the French. On that occasion, Seghers gave a party in Hughes's honor, with Louis Aragon, Elsa Triolet, and many progressive intellectuals in attendance. This was followed by a reception hosted by the Comité National des Écrivains at Hôtel Lutétia on October 29. The following day, Hughes gave a reading at the American Cultural Center, where he was introduced by Sim Copans, who had done much to supply French enthusiasm for jazz on French radio during the 1940s. Decidedly, Hughes was becoming more and more an official ambassador for Afro-American letters at large.

He returned to the U.S. with yet another contract from Seghers, who this time wanted him to prepare an *Anthologie Négro-Africaine,* all in French, in time for publication prior to the First World Festival of Negro Arts [Dakar, Senegal, April 1–24, 1966]. By December 8, 1964, Hughes could write Carl Van Vechten: "I had a wonderful eight weeks in Europe and came loaded with medals and books . . . things publishers in Berlin, Paris and London gave me."[13] On that trip, he also met a young African, Blanchard Kekeh, who lived in a settle-

ment house for immigrants at Chevilly-Larue, in the southern suburbs of Paris. Langston tried to help him for several years, sending him money and books. In December 1964, he wrote Kekeh that he had been invited to Europe in January [1965] and, should he come, he would try to see him. In fact, his gospel play, *Prodigal Son* had been performed with great success in Brussels in September 1964, and it was taken to the Théâtre des Champs-Elysées in December. But the play's Paris success did not equal that of *Simply Heavenly,* and Hughes did not make the trip.

Meanwhile, plans were developing for the First World Festival of Negro Arts. As early as June 2, 1963, Senegalese President Léopold Sedar Senghor had written Hughes: "No festival claiming to represent Negro arts would be complete without your presence." In July of that year, Hughes therefore became a member of the American Committee of Friends of the Festival of Negro Arts. That same year, his anthology *Poems from Black Africa, Ethiopia and Other Countries* was published, but Senghor regretted that so few French-speaking black poets were included. He praised Hughes's "admirable, though brief" introduction: "It poses the problem very well and accurately defines the differences that exist between African poetry in French and African poetry in English," he wrote on September 19, 1963. "I am particularly thankful to you for defending the concept of Négritude which is, in the last analysis, nothing but the sum total of the values of the black world."[14] Shortly afterwards, Hughes was organizing events in New York in conjunction with the visit of Alioune Diop to discuss preparation of the festival.

With Aimé Césaire, Hughes had fewer contacts. In June 1961, to Diop's request that he prepare an English translation of *Cahier d' un retour au pays natal,* he replied that he could do no better than Yvan Goll's already completed rendering. In 1964, however, he drafted a statement "Politics and the Poet," which shows he recognized Césaire's major importance among the Négritude poets:

What is poetry? It is the human soul entire, squeezed like a lemon or a lime, drop by drop, into atomic words. The ethnic image does not matter. Ask Aimé Césaire. He knows. Perhaps not consciously—but in the soul of his writings, he knows. The Négritudinous Senghor, the Caribbeanesque Guillén, the American me are regional poets of genuine realities and authentic values. Césaire's 'Cahier' takes all we have—Senghor, Guillén, Hughes—and flings it to the moon, to make it a space-ship of the dreams of all the dreamers of the world. As a footnote I must add that, concerning Césaire, all I have said I deeply feel is for me true. Concerning politics, nothing I have said is true. A poet is a human being. Each human being must live within his time, with and for his people, and within the bound-

Dust jacket for Alice Walker's 2002 biography for children (Collection of Christopher C. De Santis)

aries of his country. Therefore how can a poet keep out of politics?

Hang yourself, poet, in your own words. Otherwise you are dead.[15]

In May 1965, Hughes returned to Paris on a USIS-sponsored trip. The new political developments of the Civil Rights struggles and the incipient Black Power movement were giving Afro-Americans greater visibility in the media. The cultural office of the U.S. embassy in French accepted Jean Wagner's suggestion that, for the benefit of French and African teachers and advanced students, a three-day seminar be held at Royaumont, an abbey turned into a cultural center. The general theme was Afro-American writing, and the participants along with Hughes were novelists Paule Marshall and William Melving Kelley. Prior to the gathering, a spirited round-table was held at the Centre d'Études Américaines in Paris, where racial and political issues were discussed vigorously by the participants. At Royaumont, Hughes read his poetry, spoke abundantly of his early career and of recent literary developments in America and Africa.

I had briefly corresponded with him the year before, concerning my research on Richard Wright; in Paris, he talked with me for hours, late into the first night, about the spiritual excitement and the sense of

breaking new ground he had experienced during his early Harlem Renaissance days, comparing that period to the present rebirth of black pride. But he was visibly tired, trying to keep up with the new developments and encompassing them in a perspective spanning several decades; he also felt that he was one of the few survivors of his generation with Arna Bontemps and Sterling Brown. Yet he attempted to capture the new mood in embattled poems later to appear in *The Panther and the Lash*. On that trip, Hughes was invited to attend a celebration of Gertrude Stein, with a performance by Nancy Cole, which he found "delightfully right." He also visited with Kekeh and his fiancée, Marie-Noelle, with great pleasure and consideration for these African friends.

A year later, in Dakar at the First Festival of Negro Arts, Hughes was feted like no other black American, being considered the embodiment of the glorious generation of forerunners of the Négritude movement. He stressed the links between the different groups of the black diaspora, often resorting to the erudition of his good friend, the American ambassador to Senegal, Mercer Cook, in order to prove points in private conversations. After the festival, he gave a series of lectures on a USIS-sponsored tour in African countries. He had covered much of the continent when he traveled to Paris again in late June.

During that sojourn, he gave a well-attended reading at the Shakespeare and Company bookstore, in front of Notre-Dame, persuading his unconditional admirer Ted Jones to play the trumpet while he recited jazz poetry from *Ask Your Mama*. It was a triumph. By then, Hughes seriously considered taking up residence in Paris, at least part of the year, like James Baldwin. He had alluded to it repeatedly in letters to Kekeh and Jimmy Davis. He even asked several American friends to find a small, inexpensive place for him. They located one on Boulevard Raspail near Denfert-Rochereau in 1966, and he apparently paid the rent for a few months but gave up the flat in early 1967, for financial reasons. To his plans to settle in France, Arna Bontemps had responded with enthusiasm:

If you go to Paris for always, as you say, we will visit you now and then. Suddenly I feel footloose. Maybe we're approaching that age. In any case, I think one whose career has reached the point of warm reflection and the reading of biographies of himself has earned residence in Paris, prior to residence in glory. It would be the ideal place to write volume III of your *autobiography,* for instance. Moreover, Harlem's problems appear to have reached a certain plateau and can probably be viewed just as well from a certain distance . . .[16]

In May 1967, death prevented Hughes from fulfilling his dream. By that time, his reputation in the French-speaking world had reached unheard of proportions. Not only was he the living embodiment of a black folk poet, concerned with popular literature and the man in the streets but also a full-size American poet treated as such in the *Poètes d'Aujourd'hui* series. Furthermore, his physical presence on the African continent and his persistent struggle to make certain that black American writers would be present on the shelves of USIS libraries abroad had made him the most popular of black American writers in French-speaking Africa and the Antilles. To gauge the scope of his literary reputation in Paris, one need only go through the varied, but unanimously laudatory remarks of French critics—of every ideological affiliation—when *L'Ingénue de Harlem,* a collection of selected Simple stories, was published the Spring of 1967. In *La Quinzaine Littéraire,* a highbrow magazine, pro-establishment Marc Saporta located Jesse B. Semple's humor somewhere between Jacques Prévert and Art Buchwald. In the Communist *L'Humanité Dimanche,* Martine Monod recalled Hughes's militant career and emphasized the authenticity of the Simple stories. Emmanuel Buenzod placed his long review in the *Gazette de Lausanne* under the caption *castigare ridendo,* making Hughes a real moralist: "If it happens that laughter makes you drop your weapons, it also happens that it incites you to act," he concluded in his May 20, 1967 piece.

After that date, all reviews became obituaries for the dead writer. In *France Nouvelle,* Serge Gilles spoke of the mourning of black Americans and the "great loss to American letters" ["*L'Ingénue de Harlem* de Langston Hughes," 7 Juin 1967]. In the militant daily newspaper, *Combat,* Pierre Kyria stated that "Negro American literature had lost one of its best representatives and Harlem its poet ["Langston Hughes: Candide à Harlem," 1 Juin 1967]. In *Afrique Actuelle,* the Dahomean author and journalist Olympe Bhély-Quénum declared that *The Best of Simple* was also the best fiction by Hughes, although he doubted that humor could solve society's problems; he ended with a reminiscent note:

> For me, as for many others, there is only . . . one Langston Hughes, the one who took your arm affectionately because he had read a book, or simply a short story of yours, and started to speak about it . . . full of admiration and surprise at finding him so close, you would have liked to speak with him about his poetry. ["*L'Ingénu de Harlem,*" par Langston Hughes, *Afrique Actuelle,* no. 21, 1967.]

Even in distant Addis-Ababa, one found a Daniel Joski, who wrote in French:

> Had he not been a writer, Langston Hughes would have belonged, just like Simple, to the still lingering race of the great authors of oral tradition, those who are still to be found in Arab countries, in Ireland, and in Brittany, and even here in Ethiopia. . . . ["La Semaine Littéraire," *Addis Soir,* 29 July, 1967.]

Obviously, by that time Langston Hughes had earned residence in glory—in literary glory—in the French-speaking world, as well as in the rest of the globe.
—*Langston Hughes Review,* 6 (Spring 1987): 20–27

1. The first issue of *Présence Africaine–Revue Culturelle du Monde Noir* appeared simultaneously in Paris and Dakar in November–December 1947.

2. Premier Congrès des Écrivains et Artistes Noirs–Paris, September 19–22, 1956.

3. See also Langston Hughes, "The Twenties: Harlem and Its Negritude," *African Forum,* vol. 1, No. 4/Spring 1966, pp. 11–20. (*African Forum: A Quarterly Journal of Contemporary Affairs* was published by The American Society of African Culture.)

4. *Poèmes,* translated by François Dodat. Paris Seghers, 1955, p. 89.

5. Jean Wagner, "Langston Hughes," *Informations et Documents,* 15 January 1961, pp. 30–35.

6. Langston Hughes to Carl Van Vechten, Dec. 12, 1960, Beinecke Rare Book and Manuscript Library, Yale University.

7. Michel Fabre interview with Jimmy Davis, June 1984.

8. Langston Hughes to Arna Bontemps, Jan. 14, 1963. See *Arna Bontemps Langston Hughes Letters, 1925–1967,* ed., Charles H. Nichols. New York: Dodd, Mead & Company, 1980, pp. 453–454.

9. Ezekiel Mphalele to Langston Hughes, Apr. 23, 1963, Beinecke Rare Book and Manuscript Library, Yale University.

10. For Hughes reminiscences of this stay in Paris, see *Arna Bontemps-Langston Hughes Letters,* pp. 464–65.

11. Jean Wagner, *Les Poètes Nègres des États-Unis.* Paris Librarie Istra, 1962. See American edition, *Black Poets of the United States–From Paul Laurence Dunbar to Langston Hughes,* trans., Kenneth Douglas. Urbana: University of Illinois Press, 1973.

12. See *Arna Bontemps-Langston Hughes Letters,* p. 459.

13. Beinecke Rare Book and Manuscript Library, Yale University.

14. Letters here quoted from L.S. Senghor to Langston Hughes are from the Langston Hughes Papers in the James Weldon Johnson Collection, Beinecke Rare Book and Manuscript Library, Yale University, with translations supplied by Michel Fabre.
Editor's note: In the context of Hughes's efforts to anthologize African writers, his *Anthologie Africaine et Malgache* (1962), included a selection of African literature written in French—one year before publication of *Poems from Black Africa, Ethiopia and Other Countries* (1963).

15. Langston Hughes, "Politics and the Poet," December 3, 1964. The Langston Hughes Papers, James Weldon Johnson Collection, Beinecke Rare Book and Manuscript Library, Yale University.

16. May 1, 1967. See *Arna Bontemps-Langston Hughes Letters,* p. 487.

* * *

Postcard for a centennial celebration held in the city where Hughes spent most of his childhood (Collection of Christopher C. De Santis)

Jo Thomas wrote this article on The Collected Works of Langston Hughes *(2001–2004) for* The New York Times.

Gathering Up Every Word of the Prolific Langston Hughes

Langston Hughes was born in Joplin, Mo., but he did not stay there long. He was already living with his grandmother in Lawrence, Kan., when a year later a white lynch mob burned the black neighborhood of his birthplace. Rural Kansas, not Missouri, was home to

his earliest memories, his first novel and some of his best poetry.

Now the University of Missouri Press is placing a claim on its native son by publishing for the first time the complete "Collected Works of Langston Hughes" in 18 volumes. The first three volumes were published in June. The entire set will be available in time for the centenary of his birth, Feb. 1, 2002.

Mr. Hughes's reputation rests largely on his poetry, essays, short stories, novels, plays and news-

Alice Walker with the postage stamp honoring Hughes, at the University of Kansas, 31 January 2002 (photograph by Aaron Paden/KU University Relations, University of Kansas; Collection of Christopher C. De Santis)

paper articles, but he also gained stature as a leading voice in the Harlem Renaissance of the 1920's. He published more than 35 books before his death in 1967, but most of his work is not available today.

"Hughes has been only half there in our culture," said Cary R. Nelson, editor of the "Anthology of Modern American Poetry," recently published by Oxford University Press. "For many decades, he has been at the top of the pantheon of 20th-century poets by any reasonable standard. He deserves to have every word he wrote be in print."

The first three volumes in the new Hughes collection contain poetry edited by Arnold Rampersad, author of the two-volume biography "The Life of Langston Hughes" (Oxford University Press, 1986 and 1988). The poems are grouped together as they were originally published so "we are able to see Hughes's hand, as it were, shaping each volume," Mr. Rampersad said. The previously unpublished poems are grouped chronologically.

The fourth book, issued on July 7, contains "Not Without Laughter," the story of an African-American boy growing to manhood in a small Kansas town, a novel first published in 1930, and "Tambourines to Glory," a comic novel set in Harlem and published in 1958. This volume is edited by Dolan Hubbard, who also edited "The Sermon and the African

American Literary Imagination" (University of Missouri Press, 1996).

Beverly Jarrett, director and editor in chief at the University of Missouri Press, has been working for 12 years with the executors of the Hughes estate to get the rights to reproduce his work. Harold Ober Associates, which was Hughes's literary agency, helped her negotiate with his commercial publishers.

"We hoped to publish in hardback in reasonably priced editions," Ms. Jarrett said, adding that the current price of a volume is $29.95. "Our goal is to hold this within the reach of people Hughes was writing for. We want these books in the libraries. It's hard for them to buy a $50 book."

The editorial board for the collection decided to draw its texts from first editions, but when Jane Lago, managing editor of the publishing house, began collecting them, price was a huge barrier. "I started looking at eBay and at used-book stores," she said. "I quickly discovered we could not afford to buy them. First editions were selling for $500 to $5,000 each. Our library had some, and we tried inter-library loans." The Beinecke Rare Book and Manuscript Library at Yale, which has the Hughes papers, allowed her staff to photocopy four books.

The unpublished material will include two volumes of plays, cantatas, operatic librettos and gospel plays. "For a lot of these plays, it's not clear what the performance text is," Leslie Sanders, the editor, said. "But plays are like that. There isn't necessarily a clean text." When possible, she said, she is using the texts of first performances, although not in the case of "Mulatto," which ran on Broadway. "It was not a production he had any control over," Ms. Sanders said. "The producer inserted a rape in it and made other alterations that displeased Hughes."

The author revised constantly, Ms. Sanders said. She is respecting his wishes in some cases but not in others. "Hughes became uneasy, starting toward the end of the 1930's, with the ways in which dialect was being written and used," she said. "He moved away from extremely derogatory language, even when it may have been 'realistic.' I have respected his choices in that." But in some of his comedies, like "Little Ham," he took a particular dislike to "dese" and "dose," Ms. Sanders said. "Sho" in "Sho, you kin be de boss" became "Certainly." "Is you?" became "Are you?" and "I makes money" became "I make money."

"I'm going back to the 1930's version where the language is a little saltier, a little looser," Ms. Sanders said.

James V. Hatch, the co-author with Errol G. Hill of "The History of African-American Theater From Its Beginnings to 2000," to be published next year by Cambridge University Press, said the new collection "should increase Hughes's recognition as a playwright.

"Some of the unknown plays are of historical value," he said. "People have not been aware of how political many of his plays were or of his humanistic approach to labor, lynching, racism and his attempts to erase stereotypes."

Mr. Hatch continued: "Every year, almost all the major black theaters produce his Christmas play, 'Black Nativity.' It always sells out — like the 'Nutcracker.' People love it."

Editors and scholars agree that politics took its toll on the quality of Hughes's published work. Mr. Nelson said: "When Hughes revised his poems, he revised them to make them less good. The revisions took place in the late 1940's through the 1950's, when he was under so much pressure from the right wing. He revised his poems on the left to blunt their force somewhat. More surprisingly and more troublingly, some of his most searing poems about race he made less tough when he revised them."

Mr. Nelson added: "For decades, the version of Langston Hughes you could buy was a version of Hughes with his hands and feet chopped off, completely truncated. He left many of his strongest poems out and bowdlerized others. It will make a difference when you read the real man."

Christopher DeSantis, editor of the Hughes essays, which have never been collected in their entirety, said he does not plan to include all of Hughes's articles, but he will include the Hughes newspaper coverage of the Spanish Civil War for The Afro-American in Baltimore as well as other essays.

"The essays give a sense of a different Langston Hughes," Mr. DeSantis said. "It's still the Langston Hughes of the democratic voice, conversational voice, voice of working masses that everyone loves in his poetry. I think this book will give scholars and general readers more of a sense of Langston Hughes as an intellectual. People, wrongly, haven't thought of him in that way."

–The New York Times, 31 July 2001, pp. B1–B2

For Further Reading

BIBLIOGRAPHIES:

Bloom, Harold. *Langston Hughes: Comprehensive Research and Study Guide*. Broomall, Pa.: Chelsea House, 1998.

Dickinson, Donald C. *A Bio-Bibliography of Langston Hughes, 1902–1967*. Hamden, Conn.: Archon Books, 1972.

Mikolyzk, Thomas A. *Langston Hughes: A Bio-Bibliography*. New York: Greenwood Press, 1990.

Miller, R. Baxter. *Langston Hughes and Gwendolyn Brooks: A Reference Guide*. Boston: G. K. Hall, 1979.

Ostrom, Hans A. *A Langston Hughes Encyclopedia*. Westport, Conn.: Greenwood Press, 2002.

BIOGRAPHIES:

Berry, Faith. *Langston Hughes: Before and Beyond Harlem*. Westport, Conn.: Lawrence Hill, 1983.

Rampersad, Arnold. *The Life of Langston Hughes, Volume 1: 1902–1940: I, Too, Sing America*. New York: Oxford University Press, 1986.

Rampersad. *The Life of Langston Hughes, Volume 2: 1941–1967: I Dream a World*. New York: Oxford University Press, 1988.

BIOGRAPHIES (JUVENILE):

Berry, S. L. *Langston Hughes*. Mankato, Minn.: Creative Education, 1994.

Cooper, Floyd. *Coming Home: From the Life of Langston Hughes*. New York: Philomel Books, 1994.

Dunham, Montrew. *Langston Hughes: Young Black Poet*. New York: Aladdin Paperbacks, 1995.

Hill, Christine M. *Langston Hughes: Poet of the Harlem Renaissance*. Springfield, N.J.: Enslow, 1997.

McKissack, Pat, and Frederick McKissack. *Langston Hughes: Great American Poet*. Hillside, N.J.: Enslow, 1992.

Meltzer, Milton. *Langston Hughes: A Biography*. New York: Crowell, 1968.

Myers, Elisabeth P. *Langston Hughes: Poet of His People*. New York: Dell, 1970.

Osofsky, Audrey. *Free to Dream: The Making of A Poet*. New York: Lothrop, Lee & Shepard, 1996.

Raatma, Lucia. *Langston Hughes: African-American Poet*. Chanhassen, Minn.: Child's World, 2003.

Rhynes, Martha E. *I, Too, Sing America: The Story of Langston Hughes*. Greensboro, N.C.: Morgan Reynolds, 2002.

Walker, Alice. *Langston Hughes, American Poet*. New York: HarperCollins, 1998.

CRITICAL STUDIES:

Barksdale, Richard. *Langston Hughes*. Chicago: American Library Association, 1977.

Bloom, Harold, ed. *Langston Hughes*. New York: Chelsea House, 1989.

Bonner, Pat E. *Sassy Jazz and Slo' Draggin' Blues: Music in the Poetry of Langston Hughes*. New York: Peter Lang, 1996.

Cobb, Martha. *Harlem, Haiti, and Havana: A Comparative Critical Study of Langston Hughes, Jacques Roumain, Nicolás Guillén*. Washington, D.C.: Three Continents Press, 1979.

Dace, Tish, ed. *Langston Hughes: The Contemporary Reviews*. New York: Cambridge University Press, 1997.

Dodat, François. *Langston Hughes*. Paris: Seghers, 1964.

Emmanuel, James A. *Langston Hughes*. New York: Twayne, 1967.

Gates, Henry Louis, Jr. and K. A. Appiah. *Langston Hughes: Critical Perspectives Past and Present*. New York: Amistad, 1993.

Gibson, Donald B., ed. *Five Black Writers: Essays on Wright, Ellison, Baldwin, Hughes and LeRoi Jones*. New York: New York University Press, 1970.

Harper, Donna Akiba Sullivan. *Not So Simple: The "Simple" Stories by Langston Hughes*. Columbia: University of Missouri Press, 1995.

Jemie, Onwuchekwa. *Langston Hughes: An Introduction to the Poetry*. New York: Columbia University Press, 1976.

Mandelik, Peter, and Stanley Schatt, eds. *A Concordance to the Poetry of Langston Hughes*. Detroit: Gale Research, 1974.

McLaren, Joseph. *Langston Hughes: Folk Dramatist in the Protest Tradition, 1921–1943*. Westport, Conn.: Greenwood Press, 1997.

Miller, R. Baxter. *The Art and Imagination of Langston Hughes*. Lexington: University Press of Kentucky, 1989.

Mullen, Edward J. *Critical Essays on Langston Hughes*. Boston: G. K. Hall, 1986.

O'Daniel, Therman B., ed. *Langston Hughes, Black Genius: A Critical Evaluation*. New York: Morrow, 1971.

Ostrom, Hans. *Langston Hughes: A Study of the Short Fiction*. New York: Twayne, 1993.

Tracy, Steven C. *Langston Hughes and the Blues*. Urbana: University of Illinois Press, 1988.

Trotman, C. James, ed. *Langston Hughes: The Man, His Art, and His Continuing Influence*. New York: Garland, 1995.

SPECIAL JOURNAL:

The Langston Hughes Review (1982–   ).

PAPERS:

Langston Hughes's papers are in the James Weldon Johnson Collection, part of the Yale Collection of American Literature, Beinecke Rare Book and Manuscript Library, Yale University, New Haven, Connecticut. Other major collections of Hughes material are at the Schomburg Center for Research in Black Culture, New York, and the Kenneth Spencer Research Library, University of Kansas.

Cumulative Index

Dictionary of Literary Biography, Volumes 1-315
Dictionary of Literary Biography Yearbook, 1980-2002
Dictionary of Literary Biography Documentary Series, Volumes 1-19
Concise Dictionary of American Literary Biography, Volumes 1-7
Concise Dictionary of British Literary Biography, Volumes 1-8
Concise Dictionary of World Literary Biography, Volumes 1-4

Cumulative Index

DLB before number: *Dictionary of Literary Biography,* Volumes 1-315
Y before number: *Dictionary of Literary Biography Yearbook,* 1980-2002
DS before number: *Dictionary of Literary Biography Documentary Series,* Volumes 1-19
CDALB before number: *Concise Dictionary of American Literary Biography,* Volumes 1-7
CDBLB before number: *Concise Dictionary of British Literary Biography,* Volumes 1-8
CDWLB before number: *Concise Dictionary of World Literary Biography,* Volumes 1-4

Cumulative Index

Cumulative Index

Radishchev, Aleksandr Nikolaevich
1749-1802 . . . . .DLB-150

Radnóti, Miklós
1909-1944 . . . . .DLB-215; CDWLB-4

Radrigán, Juan 1937- DLB-305

Radványi, Netty Reiling (see Seghers, Anna)

Rahv, Philip 1908-1973 . . . . .DLB-137

Raich, Semen Egorovich 1792-1855 . . . . . .DLB-205

Raičković, Stevan 1928- DLB-181

Raiderman (see Parshchikov, Aleksei Maksimovich)

Raimund, Ferdinand Jakob 1790-1836 . . . . .DLB-90

Raine, Craig 1944- DLB-40

Raine, Kathleen 1908- DLB-20

Rainis, Jānis 1865-1929 . . . . .DLB-220; CDWLB-4

Rainolde, Richard
circa 1530-1606 . . . . .DLB-136, 236

Rainolds, John 1549-1607 . . . . .DLB-281

Rakić, Milan 1876-1938 . . . . .DLB-147; CDWLB-4

Rakosi, Carl 1903- DLB-193

Ralegh, Sir Walter
1554?-1618 . . . . .DLB-172; CDBLB-1

Raleigh, Walter
Style (1897) [excerpt] DLB-57

Ralin, Radoy 1923- DLB-181

Ralph, Julian 1853-1903 . . . . .DLB-23

Ramat, Silvio 1939- DLB-128

Ramée, Marie Louise de la (see Ouida)

Ramírez, Sergío 1942- DLB-145

Ramke, Bin 1947- DLB-120

Ramler, Karl Wilhelm 1725-1798 . . . . .DLB-97

Ramon Ribeyro, Julio 1929-1994 . . . . .DLB-145

Ramos, Graciliano 1892-1953 . . . . .DLB-307

Ramos, Manuel 1948- DLB-209

Ramos Sucre, José Antonio 1890-1930 . . .DLB-290

Ramous, Mario 1924- DLB-128

Rampersad, Arnold 1941- DLB-111

Ramsay, Allan 1684 or 1685-1758 . . . . . . .DLB-95

Ramsay, David 1749-1815 . . . . .DLB-30

Ramsay, Martha Laurens 1759-1811 . . . . .DLB-200

Ramsey, Frank P. 1903-1930 . . . . .DLB-262

Ranch, Hieronimus Justesen
1539-1607 . . . . .DLB-300

Ranck, Katherine Quintana 1942- DLB-122

Rand, Avery and Company DLB-49

Rand, Ayn 1905-1982 . . . DLB-227, 279; CDALB-7

Rand McNally and Company DLB-49

Randall, David Anton 1905-1975 . . . . . . .DLB-140

Randall, Dudley 1914- DLB-41

Randall, Henry S. 1811-1876 . . . . .DLB-30

Randall, James G. 1881-1953 . . . . .DLB-17

The Randall Jarrell Symposium: A Small
Collection of Randall Jarrells Y-86

Excerpts From Papers Delivered at the
Randall Jarrel Symposium Y-86

Randall, John Herman, Jr. 1899-1980 . . . .DLB-279

Randolph, A. Philip 1889-1979 . . . . .DLB-91

Anson D. F. Randolph
[publishing house] DLB-49

Randolph, Thomas 1605-1635 . . . . . .DLB-58, 126

Random House DLB-46

Rankin, Ian (Jack Harvey) 1960- DLB-267

Henry Ranlet [publishing house] DLB-49

Ransom, Harry 1908-1976 . . . . .DLB-187

Ransom, John Crowe
1888-1974 . . . . .DLB-45, 63; CDALB-7

Ransome, Arthur 1884-1967 . . . . .DLB-160

Raphael, Frederic 1931- DLB-14

Raphaelson, Samson 1896-1983 . . . . .DLB-44

Rare Book Dealers
Bertram Rota and His Bookshop Y-91

An Interview with Glenn Horowitz Y-90

An Interview with Otto Penzler Y-96

An Interview with Ralph Sipper Y-94

New York City Bookshops in the
1930s and 1940s: The Recollections
of Walter Goldwater Y-93

Rare Books
Research in the American Antiquarian
Book Trade Y-97

Two Hundred Years of Rare Books and
Literary Collections at the
University of South Carolina Y-00

Rascón Banda, Víctor Hugo 1948- DLB-305

Rashi circa 1040-1105 . . . . .DLB-208

Raskin, Ellen 1928-1984 . . . . .DLB-52

Rasputin, Valentin Grigor'evich
1937- DLB-302

Rastell, John 1475?-1536 . . . . DLB-136, 170

Rattigan, Terence
1911-1977 . . . . .DLB-13; CDBLB-7

Raven, Simon 1927-2001 . . . . .DLB-271

Ravenhill, Mark 1966- DLB-310

Ravnkilde, Adda 1862-1883 . . . . .DLB-300

Rawicz, Piotr 1919-1982 . . . . .DLB-299

Rawlings, Marjorie Kinnan 1896-1953
. . . . .DLB-9, 22, 102; DS-17; CDALB-7

Rawlinson, Richard 1690-1755 . . . . .DLB-213

Rawlinson, Thomas 1681-1725 . . . . .DLB-213

Rawls, John 1921-2002 . . . . .DLB-279

Raworth, Tom 1938- DLB-40

Ray, David 1932- DLB-5

Ray, Gordon Norton 1915-1986 . . . .DLB-103, 140

Ray, Henrietta Cordelia 1849-1916 . . . . . .DLB-50

Raymond, Ernest 1888-1974 . . . . .DLB-191

Raymond, Henry J. 1820-1869 . . . . . .DLB-43, 79

Raymond, René (see Chase, James Hadley)

Razaf, Andy 1895-1973 . . . . .DLB-265

al-Razi 865?-925? DLB-311

Rea, Michael 1927-1996 . . . . .Y-97

Michael M. Rea and the Rea Award for
the Short Story Y-97

Reach, Angus 1821-1856 . . . . .DLB-70

Read, Herbert 1893-1968 . . . . .DLB-20, 149

Read, Martha Meredith DLB-200

Read, Opie 1852-1939 . . . . .DLB-23

Read, Piers Paul 1941- DLB-14

Reade, Charles 1814-1884 . . . . .DLB-21

Reader's Digest Condensed Books DLB-46

Readers Ulysses Symposium Y-97

Reading, Peter 1946- DLB-40

Reading Series in New York City Y-96

Reaney, James 1926- DLB-68

Rebhun, Paul 1500?-1546 . . . . .DLB-179

Rèbora, Clemente 1885-1957 . . . . .DLB-114

Rebreanu, Liviu 1885-1944 . . . . .DLB-220

Rechy, John 1931- DLB-122, 278; Y-82

Redding, J. Saunders 1906-1988 . . . . . .DLB-63, 76

J. S. Redfield [publishing house] DLB-49

Redgrove, Peter 1932- DLB-40

Redmon, Anne 1943- Y-86

Redmond, Eugene B. 1937- DLB-41

Redol, Alves 1911-1969 . . . . .DLB-287

James Redpath [publishing house] DLB-49

Reed, Henry 1808-1854 . . . . .DLB-59

Reed, Henry 1914-1986 . . . . .DLB-27

Reed, Ishmael
1938- DLB-2, 5, 33, 169, 227; DS-8

Reed, Rex 1938- DLB-185

Reed, Sampson 1800-1880 . . . . .DLB-1, 235

Reed, Talbot Baines 1852-1893 . . . . .DLB-141

Reedy, William Marion 1862-1920 . . . . . .DLB-91

Reese, Lizette Woodworth 1856-1935 . . . . .DLB-54

Reese, Thomas 1742-1796 . . . . .DLB-37

Reeve, Clara 1729-1807 . . . . .DLB-39

Preface to *The Old English Baron*
(1778) DLB-39

The Progress of Romance (1785)
[excerpt] DLB-39

Reeves, James 1909-1978 . . . . .DLB-161

Reeves, John 1926- DLB-88

Reeves-Stevens, Garfield 1953- DLB-251

Régio, José (José Maria dos Reis Pereira)
1901-1969 . . . . .DLB-287

Henry Regnery Company DLB-46

Rêgo, José Lins do 1901-1957 . . . . .DLB-307

Rehberg, Hans 1901-1963 . . . . .DLB-124

Rehfisch, Hans José 1891-1960 . . . . .DLB-124

Reich, Ebbe Kløvedal 1940- DLB-214

Reid, Alastair 1926- DLB-27

Reid, B. L. 1918-1990 . . . . .DLB-111

Reid, Christopher 1949- DLB-40

Reid, Forrest 1875-1947 . . . . .DLB-153

Reid, Helen Rogers 1882-1970 . . . . .DLB-29

Reid, James ?-? DLB-31

Reid, Mayne 1818-1883 . . . . .DLB-21, 163

Reid, Thomas 1710-1796 . . . . .DLB-31, 252

Reid, V. S. (Vic) 1913-1987 . . . . .DLB-125

Reid, Whitelaw 1837-1912 . . . . .DLB-23

Reilly and Lee Publishing Company DLB-46